D1238675

As If the Land Owned Us

As If the Land Owned Us

An Ethnohistory of the White Mesa Utes

Robert S. McPherson

THE UNIVERSITY OF UTAH PRESS
Salt Lake City

Copyright © 2011 by The University of Utah Press. All rights reserved.

 The Defiance House Man colophon is a registered trademark
of the University of Utah Press. It is based upon a four-foot-tall,
Ancient Puebloan pictograph (late PIII) near Glen Canyon, Utah.

15 14 13 12 11   1 2 3 4 5

LIBRARY OF CONGRESS CATALOGING-IN-PUBLICATION DATA

McPherson, Robert S., 1947–
　　As if the land owned us : an ethnohistory of the White Mesa Utes / Robert S. McPherson.
　　　p. cm.
　　Includes bibliographical references and index.
　　ISBN 978-1-60781-145-9 (pbk. : alk. paper)
　　1. Ute Indians—Utah—White Mesa—History. 2. Ute Indians—Land tenure—Utah—
White Mesa. 3. Ute Indians—Utah—White Mesa—Social conditions. 4. Ethnohistory—
Utah—White Mesa. 5. White Mesa (Utah)—History. 6. White Mesa (Utah)—Social
conditions. I. Title.
　　E99.U8M4 2011
　　979.004'974576—dc23
　　　　　　　　　　　　　　　　　　　　　　　　　　　　　　2011018202

Printed and bound by Sheridan Books, Inc., Ann Arbor, Michigan.

To the people of White Mesa —
For their love of the land
and the history that they share

Contents

Maps

Acknowledgments

In the geographical center of the White Mesa community sits a library, a part of the Education Building. The facility is unpretentious but busy with its growing collection of books, ever-glowing computers, and cramped study areas. Residents file in and out in search of answers to questions or to complete homework assignments. Many of them find what they are looking for. But when it comes to their history and traditional culture, the answers are not readily available. The limited Ute book section, despite tattered bindings suggesting frequent use, offers little about the community and its people. Indeed, the young are limited in the knowledge of their history, while the elders who lived part of it are frail and in the last stages of this life's journey. Not many are left. As with the close of day, what used to be in sharp relief now fades.

So it was with a sense of excitement spurred by urgency that I accepted the invitation of the White Mesa Ute Council to write an ethnohistory of this people. Executive director Cleal Bradford, the driving force behind much of this, worked with council members Elliot Eyetoo, Aldean Ketchum, Loretta Posey, and chair Mary Jane Yazzie. They all became involved by arranging appointments with elders, translating interviews, clarifying information, and working with linguist Brian Stubbs to produce a 250-page White Mesa dictionary and proper Ute spelling for this book. Their support of the history project was just as invaluable as we spent days in Allen Canyon recording memories of times long past, the land serving as a mnemonic device. Their review of many of the manuscript's chapters verified concepts that Stella Eyetoo, Annie Cantsee, Adoline Eyetoo, Bonnie Mike Lehi, and others provided. Stella, the oldest of the group, was particularly helpful since she remembered a number of historical personalities, including their nicknames and interesting anecdotes.

There were three individuals who were absolutely invaluable in providing crucial information. The first two, Edward and Patty (Mills) Dutchie, consented to be interviewed in 1996, twelve years before the project was fully underway. For hours this couple patiently sat, answering questions, sharing place-names, talking about personal experiences, and opening up the world of the White Mesa Utes. I have read many interviews with Ute people, and theirs are among the best, furnishing local information while explaining a way of life. Both have since passed away, but their legacy to children, grandchildren, and future generations remains. The third individual, Jack Cantsee Sr., was particularly helpful with his understanding of the Bear Dance and Worship Dance, both of which he still conducts. Drawing upon the teachings of his grandfather, Anson Cantsee, Jack provided information that connected the Worship Dance to earlier Ute religious rites. He and his wife, Mary Jane, opened up their home (and their back porch) to interesting discussions and, later, a review of part of the manuscript.

There were also those from the Blanding community who were of tremendous help. Archaeologist Winston Hurst, my trusted friend and advisor, was excited, supportive, and involved in the project. No one knows the land better, can take notes while driving slowly over back roads, use a GPS from his car window, or come up with his own transcription of the Ute language like he does. Whether wandering over forgotten battle sites or trails, mapping the ruins of the agency and irrigation system in Allen Canyon, or using Google Earth, he always has insightful comments. Others who put flesh on the bones of bare history are Rusty Salmon, who shared her research of the 1881 conflict; Steve Baker, with his understanding of Colorado prehistory/history; Zelma Acton, Ardelle Ostergaard, and Thell D. Black, all now deceased, who lived in Allen Canyon in the 1930s; and ninety-two-year-old R. Stewart Hatch, who with his brother, Joe, ran the trading post in Allen Canyon in the 1930s. His incredible memory has been extremely helpful in re-creating the life of the people and a functioning of the facility that is all but forgotten.

There were those who over the years amassed information that also tells part of the story. At the top of this list are Floyd O'Neil and Gregory Thompson, who in the 1980s completed extensive research in local, state, and federal archives, then placed their materials in the White Mesa Ute Collection of the American West Center at the University of Utah, Salt Lake City. The Center, now under the direction of Matthew Basso, was kind enough to make these voluminous materials available. Gary Shumway, southeastern Utah oral historian extraordinaire, spent years interviewing people whose lives are now recorded and on file in the library of California State University, Fullerton. I also benefited from collections located at the National Archives, Washington, DC; the Federal Records Center, Denver, Colorado; the Utah State Historical Society, Utah State Archives, and the Marriott Library, University of Utah, all in Salt Lake City; the Harold B. Lee Library, Brigham Young University, Provo, Utah; and, with Gregory J. Kocken's expert assistance, the holdings of the American Heritage Center, University of Wyoming, Laramie.

There are one hundred photographs in this book. Many of them came from institutional holdings, including the Utah State Historical Society, Colorado Historical Society, Montana Historical Society Research Center, San Juan County Historical Commission, Utah Fine Arts Council, Denver Public Library, Dolores Anasazi Center, White Mesa Ute Council, Marriott Library, Southern Utah University Library, University of Nevada—Reno, University of Wyoming, and Northern Arizona University Library. There were also individuals who assisted in finding or providing personal photographs: Jack Cantsee, Cletis Hatch, R. Stewart Hatch, Nada Black, Rebecca Stoneman, Jill Bayles, Steve Lovell, Peggy Palmer, LaVerne Tate, Ron McDonald, Gary Shumway, Heather Young, and Winston Hurst, who also created a number of maps for the book. To all who assisted—thank you for sharing.

The College of Eastern Utah—San Juan Campus, under the leadership of Guy Denton, allowed me to have partial released time paid for by the White Mesa Ute Council. This was absolutely critical in completing the manuscript. The Utah Humanities Council, one of the finest organizations I have ever worked with, provided financial assistance in the form of oral history grants and fellowships over the years in exchange for public programming. They are responsible for capturing a good piece of that disappearing history.

On a more personal note, I thank my wife, Betsy, for her patience in allowing me to escape on Saturday afternoons to "Walden" instead of working on "honey-do's." She has the unerring wisdom to know that I am hopeless, the foresight to believe in what I do, and the patience to let me do it. To Betsy and our children, thanks for helping "dear old Dad." But above all—both personal and professional—I give thanks to the people of White Mesa who have shared their history and insight. The world is a richer place for their experience.

Introduction

Places possess a marked capacity for triggering acts of self-reflection, inspiring thoughts about who one presently is, or memories of who one used to be, or musings on who one might become.

Keith H. Basso, Wisdom Sits in Places

The pickup truck turned off the pavement into a graveled parking area outside of Stella Eyetoo's gray ranch house. The home appeared vacant, but as I walked to the backyard, I found the eighty-six-year-old woman, kerchief pulled loosely over her silver braids, staring at me with expressive brown eyes and a quizzical look. Her smile, framed by wrinkles earned from years of being outdoors, welcomed me. Born in nearby Cottonwood Canyon at Anasazi Spring (Muugianiip), Stella has spent her life within a one-hundred-mile radius and now holds the title of the oldest local Ute still inhabiting this area. Spotting me, she gave a hearty laugh and waved hello, then continued watering a withered sapling. She dipped an aluminum pan into a heavy steel cylinder that had once been part of a plumbing system, but not much water was getting to the plant. Stella made a futile attempt to move the tank, but it was too heavy. I offered to assist; she declined, saying she would wait for her son Elliot.

Now it was her turn to help. Would she be available this next Saturday to do some field-work near Allen Canyon, where we could talk of the past and let the land jog her memory? She was not sure what her schedule held, so we drove to see Shirley Denetsosie, the bus driver for senior citizens living in the community. It was not as if Stella lacked desire

to go; she had been thinking about returning to her old homestead for some time. Luckily, the fates were with us. Shirley told her that it would be Monday, not Saturday, that they would go on a trip to Towaoc. Stella thought this just fine. As I drove her back to her house, she mentioned that another person named Larry had taken her to Allen Canyon a couple years before. "He was a terrible cook—mixed everything together—it was terrible." I asked what she wanted for a sandwich and she said, "Spam or corn beef." That was what she was comfortable with.

On July 11, 2009, archaeologist Winston Hurst, translator Loretta Posey, and I went to Stella's home. Attired in a dark blue and purple floral design dress reaching well below her knees, she had encircled her thin waist with a dark brown, two-inch-wide leather belt serving no apparent function other than being a part of traditional Ute dress. Midcalf boots encased tan socks pulled up to her knees. Modified crescent-shaped abalone shell earrings completed the ensemble. When I asked how tall she was, she replied, "Five feet," but she looked closer to four foot ten. She carried a green bag and a gallon jug of water—ready for the day.

During the trip Stella pointed out more than a dozen places where her family had lived, ranging from Cottonwood Canyon and Whiskers Draw to the Forest Service boundary line at the north end of the Ute allotments. When I asked why they had moved so many places, she explained that caring for livestock meant traveling to find feed and water for them. All of the Ute camps were associated with at least one of the dozens of springs that dot the Cottonwood Basin; the closer one approaches Elk Ridge and Blue Mountain, the more plentiful the water.

Stella mentioned numerous times how the canyon system today has so much more sagebrush than in the past, when it was sparsely vegetated with trees and relatively sagebrush free. Now the old Ute campsites are overgrown, and little evidence remains of the brush shelters, tents, and hogans that once dotted Allen Canyon. Few recall where Mancos George, Jack Fly, Pochief Mike, and dozens of other families once called home. But Stella remembers. Just past the barbwire gate to her forty-acre allotment at the mouth of Allen Canyon, we parked the SUV under a gnarly old cottonwood tree, four feet in diameter, whose limbs stretched above a nearby sandstone wall. While eating lunch beneath this monarch, Stella sat perched on a large, weathered wooden table, the gray boards an inch and a half thick. Although it was not that high, she used a cut log to step up and get settled. As we sat there, she turned and pointed to the far side of the tree, to a flat spot where her family had set up a tent so that she could deliver her first baby, a boy, in the traditional Ute way. She also talked of people buried in the surrounding canyons, of the irrigation ditch that ran through her property, and how the mosquitoes used to bother her. I kidded about burning cow manure, a technique she said the people used in the past to keep the pests away, but she only giggled.

Throughout the day, as we traveled to different sites, Stella identified plants used for food, medicine, and crafts. At one point she spotted a small group of shoots poking two or three inches out of the red, sandy soil. She announced that they were food and asked me

to pick some. After brushing off the dirt, she ate with relish the long stem and elongated bulbous end, which we later learned was called broomrape (*Orobanche* sp.), a parasite plant that by definition does not produce its own chlorophyll. I picked one for each of us. It was bitter, but Stella explained that these were usually eaten earlier in the year. "Everything in the spring is sweet." Later we found a bush heavy with sumac berries and plucked some of the little reddish-orange fruit to munch. Stella showed how to roll the ripe berries in the palm to make it easier to remove the pulp. Loaded with vitamin C, the berries puckered the lips, confirming Stella's observation that "They make good lemonade."

At the end of the day I returned to White Mesa with forms and money to pay Stella and Loretta for their time. Stella had changed into a white, patterned ankle-length dress and removed her leather belt, replacing it with a two-inch-wide beaded belt whose white background accentuated its geometric designs. She looked "freshened." A late afternoon rain shower was also freshening the land, hitting within the reservation boundaries as a brief, driving deluge. She thanked me several times for the day, for the chokecherries and sumac berries we had picked, for memories shared, and then shook hands. Before I left, she smiled and pointed to a sign mounted on a Styrofoam backing which read, "Stella Eyetoo — White Mesa Ute Basket Maker." She had every right to be proud, not only of her work as an artisan, but also that she represents the last of a fading generation familiar with the old ways. As I left the community, the slanting rays of the sun shone through the dispersed clouds, playing across the Bears Ears and into distant Allen Canyon. A long day was over, but I was thankful for the opportunity to have spent it with Stella recalling her experiences from the past. A slice of history had been preserved.

There were other times with other people who shared their memories, each experience distinct. Bonnie Mike Lehi sat in the

SUV overlooking the vast canyon system of Brushy Basin and Elk Ridge, saying that she would like to sing a song from the Worship Dance. Beginning low, increasing in pitch, she shared the mournful tune that had no specific words, only vocables. Her father had taught this song to her; after singing it, she wiped her eyes with a handkerchief, declaring she felt "at peace, like when you are in church," and that the song was holy. Annie Cantsee, who herded sheep as a teenager, spoke of friction over rangeland between the Utes and white ranchers in Blanding. Store owners and other people there were more accepted, receiving names such as "Skinny Neck" (Kent Redd), "Hairy Chest" (Gordon Redd), "Cripple Hand" (Thell D. Black), "Talks too Much" or "By His Lips" (Parley Redd), "Hollow Eye" (Parley Hurst), and "Blue Eyes" (E. Z. Black). Friction also arose with Utes from Towaoc, who called the people of White Mesa "Paiutes" and were in turn referred to as "Lizards." Neither group appreciated their labels.

Adoline Eyetoo is a deeply religious person who views events as a series of interactions with the Creator. Her garrulous, friendly disposition framed her discussion of how health and sickness, right and wrong, happiness and sadness, blessing and cursing are all part of God's intervention in her life. When we stopped for lunch in a grove of cottonwoods, she said, "Whenever I go with white men, they always pray. Do either of you pray?" I told her that I did and asked if she would like me to offer one; she did not hesitate to assert that she would, so I did. Then I asked her to sing a song, and she immediately sang a Worship Song. We thanked her for sharing it.

Aldean Ketchum was young enough to hike over the land, free from the walkers, bad knees, and other ailments of the elders. As we investigated parts of Allen Canyon, he pointed to an alcove where his family had kept their sheep, an old swimming hole in a wash, camping spots where he had lived as a child, and types of plants that his family

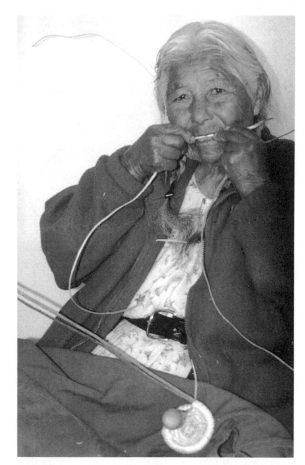

Stella Eyetoo — born at the foot of White Mesa, raised with traditional teachings, and knowledgeable about the past — shares her skill as a basket maker during a Ute culture reception at Edge of the Cedars Museum, 2008. (Courtesy of Rebecca Stoneman)

used. In one clearing where an old box spring lay rusting on the ground, a rattlesnake slithered away, prompting him to later tell a story he had received from his grandfather Billy Mike. The old man had spoken of a serpent that lived long ago and terrorized the people by preying on the weak and the young. It roamed the canyons in search of victims and feared nothing. Eventually a Ute warrior, "the One Who Watches Over Us," decided to use his supernatural powers to put an end to the carnage. The man located the serpent in one of the canyons and with his powerful bow slew it, freeing his people from future loss. After killing other harmful creatures, he told the Utes to call on him if they ever needed help and then departed. The snakes we see today hold the big snake's power and are avoided. Aldean mused that near Bluff a large

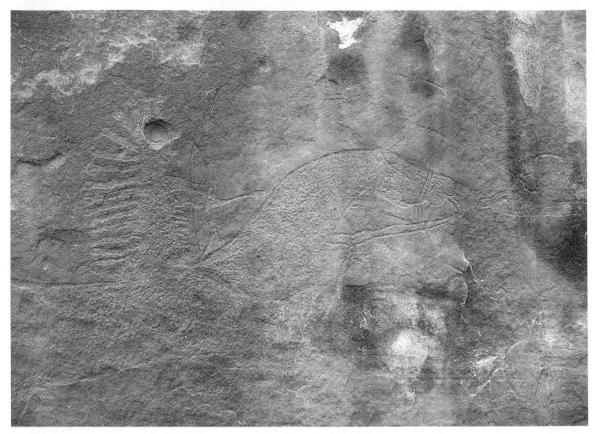

This Ute petroglyph, located in Cottonwood Wash, is of a mounted warrior confronting a serpent, recalling the story told by Billy Mike to his grandson. Armed with a bow and arrow and wearing a headdress, the man charges on his heavily breathing horse toward the snake, which has a plume on its head. A bullet hole has marred the warrior's face. (Courtesy of Winston Hurst)

petroglyph depicts a mounted warrior with full warbonnet facing a huge serpent. The man appears to be charging the reptile, and the image very well could represent the event in this tale. Aldean cautioned that snakes should be left alone, and noted that this rock art serves as a bridge from yesterday's teachings to today's generation.

In a sense, that is what these trips with elders and this book is about: a bridge to contemporary generations. In 2007 the White Mesa Ute Council asked me to write an ethnohistory of their people. I was more than eager to do so. While much of my previous writing has told the story of the Navajos in Utah, I have also produced articles, collected information, and socialized with the Utes of southeastern Utah for years. I was very aware that they are a mostly forgotten people in the historical and anthropological literature of

the Four Corners region. With the exception of the 1923 Posey incident, badly distorted by limited perspective, little is known about these fascinating Native Americans who roamed through the Colorado Plateau, Rocky Mountains, and parts of the Southwest. Often subsumed with larger groups of Utes and Paiutes, the people of White Mesa and related bands have not been clearly defined, studied, or given their due.

Why has it taken until now to have their history told? The White Mesa Utes represent a relatively small group of Native Americans affiliated with the Ute Mountain Utes, who also have not been studied extensively. As will be discussed later, the White Mesa (Weenuche) Utes have intermarried with Paiute and Navajo people as all three groups have shared the land and forged a common history. In some respects, this diversity has created a situation in which none of these tribes solidly claim this relationship. Starting in the 1870s, the historic record often refers to these tribes as separate entities, so even other Weenuche Utes view them as detached. A quick glance of the tribal roles at Towaoc today, however, shows that there has been a strong interchange of people from both communities. Still there remains an undertone. The conflict over land that characterized white–Indian interaction between the mid-1870s to early 1920s did not help either. The people of White Mesa successfully remained on their land, but they paid a price in relationships that the white community often characterized as hostile. Bad press can lead to either notoriety or oblivion; for the White Mesa Utes it was the latter.

A review of the literature shows how misunderstood and neglected this group has been. The first person to provide an overview of the White Mesa Utes beyond specific reports of soldiers, agents, and other government officials was Albert R. Lyman, a local historian who lived in San Juan County from 1880 to 1973. A prolific writer, keen observer, and avid interviewer, Lyman interacted on a daily basis with Ute and Navajo people at a time when conflict over land, enforced changes in lifestyle, and cultural misunderstandings resulted in a seething bitterness that occasionally erupted into warfare. A man of his times, Lyman recorded this strife, and, thankfully for later historians, he included personalities and incidents that would otherwise have been lost. For a short time he served as editor of the local newspaper, the San Juan Blade (1917–1918), capturing on a weekly basis the events around Blanding; later he acted as editor and contributor to the San Juan Record. His columns were published for years, the most notable being "The Old Settler," which told of his experiences and evolving relationship with the Utes. Perhaps his best factual work is found in "History of San Juan County, 1879–1917," an unpublished manuscript that gives a yearly

account of Mormon settlers living in Bluff and later Monticello and Blanding.[1] Much of that history made its way into his newspaper columns and articles, as well as publications of the Mormon Church (formally known as the Church of Jesus Christ of Latter-day Saints, or LDS).

Lyman also published two books that have long colored perceptions of the Ute people. His Indians and Outlaws: Settling of the San Juan Frontier and The Outlaw of Navaho Mountain are both based on oral history and personal observation, but mixed with fiction, which gives them a particularly Wild West flare.[2] The first is a potpourri of events that, as the title suggests, centers on conflict, whether with outlaws, cowboys, or Indians. The second book is about the life, from start to finish, of William Posey, usually just called "Posey." Concentrating on the dramatic, but reading like a historical novel, it is difficult to separate reality from fancy. Although Lyman was the man on the scene and knew many of the characters, he also loved to tell a good story, often casting people into uncomplicated roles of good and evil. Ute characters usually become the "bad guys" and are presented with little reflection as to why they were acting as they did. As conflict subsided, the "Posey incident" became just a story in the past, the Utes lived on their allotments in Allen Canyon, and Lyman returned from serving in the Southwest Indian Mission of the Mormon Church. Over time he became increasingly sympathetic to and understanding of the Native American experience. It is interesting to note that Ute elders today remember him with fondness as a person who helped them in time of need. When asked how they felt about "White Whiskers" (Samačögwat), Adoline said that Lyman and his wife, Gladys, were "good people. The Utes cried when they died."[3]

Two other authors have written specifically about the people of White Mesa. The first, Forbes Parkhill, a Denver newspaperman-turned-researcher, wrote The Last of *the Indian Wars*, concerning the Tse-ne-gat (Činigatt) incident and trial in 1915.[4] Unlike Lyman, Parkhill had access to a wide variety of government documents, including Indian agent reports, as well as newspaper articles. He did not cite specific sources with footnotes, so it is difficult to evaluate the reliability of some of the information he shares, but he is generally accurate and offers considerable insight into the events and attitudes of the times. Not as much can be said for *Posey: The Last Indian War*, by Steve Lacy and Pearl Baker.[5] A combination of warmed-over Lyman and Parkhill, the book presents little original research and is riddled with errors. Emphasizing the negative and showing insensitivity to the people, Lacy and Baker perpetuate the tired Wild West theme, and although the title declares the book to be about Posey, it is equally concerned with the settling of Bluff and general incidents in San Juan County.

The story of the White Mesa Utes cannot be told without including the larger band of Weenuche Utes now living on the Ute Mountain Ute Reservation in southwestern Colorado. The two histories are tightly intertwined. Those books that do mention White Mesa Utes vary in the amount and quality of information offered. The best general overview is provided by Virginia McConnell Simmons, who discusses all of the Northern and Southern Ute bands. This is a daunting task considering the different historical experiences of each group. Well researched and documented, *The Ute Indians of Utah, Colorado, and New Mexico* provides a valuable context with a fair smattering of information, given the breadth of her topic, on the Utes in southeastern Utah.[6] The same is true of Robert W. Delaney's *The Ute Mountain Utes*. This slim volume leans heavily on government sources to paint a contextual picture of Weenuche history, but the author bypassed the culture and lives of the people.[7]

Far more information about the White Mesa Utes is found in Richard K. Young's *The Ute Indians of Colorado in the Twentieth Century*.[8] As the title implies, the author focuses on developments within the last century among both the Ute Mountain and Southern Utes. Since the White Mesa community is governed by the Ute Mountain Ute Agency in Towaoc, it is also included in part of the discussion. Young has done a good job of describing and evaluating the many changes that these groups have faced over the past hundred years, and while the experience of White Mesa Utes may be somewhat peripheral to events on the larger reservations, many of the trends hold true for them as well. Two other books — *When Buffalo Free the Mountains* and *West of the Divide* — also provide more contemporary accounts of life on the Ute Mountain Ute Reservation, with an occasional nod to the people of White Mesa or to general tendencies affecting the Weenuche in the Four Corners region.[9]

In 1980 the American West Center of the University of Utah completed a project funded by Energy Fuels Nuclear to collect written and oral information about the history of the White Mesa Utes. Under the direction of Floyd A. O'Neil and Gregory C. Thompson, the effort included research at the National Archives in Washington, DC, and regional repositories throughout the Intermountain West; a review of oral histories from the Utah State Historical Society and the Doris Duke Indian Oral History Collection at the University of Utah; and twenty-two interviews with White Mesa residents. The end result was a significant compilation of information. A follow-on project ensued when the National Endowment for the Humanities and the tribe at Towaoc published a series of books and booklets for grade school and middle school children.[10] So it was surprising that in the American West Center's *Utah Indian Curriculum Guide* (2009) — which was designed to correct the oversight of historically ignoring the tribes in the state — the White Mesa Utes are mentioned in only two paragraphs, continuing to remain largely forgotten.[11] Fortunately, an associated website (www.utahindians.org) has more information and is updated regularly. With the growing use of technology by teachers in the classroom, this website will help to facilitate the sharing of the White Mesa people's history and culture.

What, then, can one expect to encounter in the following pages? The White Mesa Ute Council insisted that this book be not only a history but also a cultural expression, rich with the people's own voices. That meant ethnohistory defined as "a kind of historical ethnography that studies culture of the recent past through oral histories; through the accounts of explorers, missionaries, and traders; and through analysis of such data as land titles, birth and death records, and other archival materials."[12] I have interviewed most of the elders, spending time with them visiting places important in their memory. While all were helpful, three individuals proved to be exceptional: Edward and Patty Dutchie, and Jack Cantsee Sr.

Interviewing the people from White Mesa is often difficult. When O'Neil, who compiled materials on the community in the 1970s, learned that I was working on the project, he reminisced about his experiences in taping oral histories there. Recalling that he had performed similar work with dozens of tribes in the Intermountain West and Southwest, O'Neil firmly believed that the White Mesa interviews were the most difficult he had conducted. People's hesitancy to share information, perhaps because of their historical experience, meant that even the broadest, most open-ended questions were met with the briefest of answers. Having read the transcripts, I agree that much more could have, and should have, been said. Most of those whom O'Neil interviewed are now gone, and what could have been an opportunity to tell their story was lost. The Dutchies and Jack Cantsee, however, were open to sharing information and have played an important part in telling the Weenuche story.

Another difficulty arose in providing accurate spellings of Ute names and terms.

In writing this book, as the endnotes attest, I culled through thousands of documents ranging from oral histories and censuses to government correspondence and official reports. Written by white men who were not linguistically adept in the Ute language, these documents contain spellings that are usually far from being phonetically correct. Add to this the dialectical differences between Ute and Paiute, Northern and Southern Ute, and Weenuche and Capote/Muache—not to mention historical language shifts—and one begins to realize how difficult it is to resurrect a fading language. To get as close as possible, linguist Brian Stubbs met with translator Mary Jane Yazzie and elder Stella Eyetoo to record the pronunciation and spelling of many Ute words and names. They had partial success, but as Stella noted, "Those old people had hard words…they used to know those things but I am not aware of it… [and] that sounds more like Paiute."[13] The result: some confirmation and clarification, but also some dead ends. In this book, whenever possible, correct Ute spelling and interpretation will be given. If this is not possible, then the original spelling is maintained.

From bits and pieces pulled from a variety of sources comes an explanation of the White Mesa Utes' culture and history. In order to tell it accurately, I have provided detailed information and citations whenever possible. To those unfamiliar with the geography of the Four Corners area, it may seem excessive. Personalities appear, then disappear, events are tied to specific locations, and issues evaporate as time moves on. Coursing through the pages, however, is the consistent theme that the Weenuche love their land and are bonded to it. Billy Mike once recalled, "It was as if the land owned us," and one sees that concept played out through the history and movements of "the People." To this day that is a shared belief—one that explains the conflicts that arose and the determination of the Ute people. They would not budge.

Companion to this theme is the second, equally important one of cultural pride. In writing about the Utes, who have had a difficult history at best, it may appear that trouble surfaced around every corner and was quickly beckoned. Certainly much of the early literature leads readers to believe that. Yet while every culture has those who revel in conflict, there was not an overabundance of those seeking it among the White Mesa Utes. Despite their constantly being cast as "renegades," "outlaws," and aggressive troublemakers, they were only trying to hold their own at a time of tremendous loss. True, they reacted to some situations violently and did not hesitate to notify their white neighbors of their unhappiness with each turn of events, but when one considers the magnitude of the disruption of their lifestyle, it is easy to understand their feelings.

This may be contrary to the prevalent view of the White Mesa Utes' history, but it was certainly recognized by agents, settlers, and others who took the time to stand back and understand what was transpiring before their eyes. That is why in writing this history I have chosen to extensively document my sources of information and to use exact quotations—the people's voices—so that the information will not be credited to the author's wishful thinking. I have tried to present a balanced picture of what happened, to avoid sugar-coating issues, and to place into perspective what contending sides felt at the time. Errors in fact or interpretation are unintentional and, I hope, few and far between so as not to detract from the story of the White Mesa Utes.

The final proof of the product, however, is in how the Utes themselves feel about it. In December of 2008 I brought the first third of the draft manuscript to some of the elders to listen to what had been written thus far and to receive any corrective direction they wished to give. A cold, blustery wind swept across the parking lot in front of the White Mesa Education Building. Small pockets of snow crowded into the corners of the curb, lay beneath the sagebrush, and filtered be-

tween clumps of cheatgrass, hiding from the early morning sun. As I walked through the double glass doors and into a large, tiled white room, I looked at the metal and plastic chairs and tables. White like the walls, the furniture seemed cold and out of place for the elders who would soon be sitting there. When all four of them — Stella Eyetoo (eighty-five), Lola Mike (eighty-four), Chris Lehi (seventy-nine), and Adoline Eyetoo (seventy-two) — arrived, they seemed comfortable with the surroundings as Loretta Posey translated for them. Some of these people had lived through the last days of the old ways, when tepees, tents, and traditional practices were part of daily life. White plastic and shiny steel seemed to be as cold and indifferent as those who had intruded upon their land. I could not help but wish that Edward and Patty Dutchie were there. Both of their fathers had been healers who raised their children with knowledge and insight. Now Patty and Edward were gone, their spirits residing in the West with their forefathers, taking with them their understanding.

For the next two and a half hours the six of us sat around the table and reviewed parts of the manuscript. By the end it appeared that they were satisfied with both content and accuracy. Stella was the first to express appreciation, saying, "Oh thank you, thank you for doing this," followed by Adoline, who said she had enjoyed the morning and felt that what she had heard was good. The others agreed, I promised to make suggested additions, and the group dispersed.

As I sat in the car, enjoying the warmth from the midday sun, I remembered what one Southern Ute had said concerning their history: "Everything moves on and is lost. That is why the Utes say: 'It is bad luck to plan ahead.' For nothing can stop. Nothing is left of those [old] days but my story and your words. Nothing remains behind."[14] I was determined that at this point, whatever could be preserved would be available for those in the future.

CHAPTER 1

White Mesa Ute Origins and Puwá-v

Creating the World, Empowering the Universe

Utes don't tell lies to the spirits. They don't tell lies about their sacred places. They don't tell lies about hearing God talk....They talk to their Creator.... They talk about the future.

Edward Dutchie Sr., 1996

He was alone. Sináwav, the Creator, sat in his world of sky, sunshine, clouds, and rain, ruling over all.[1] But he was lonesome. Wanting something new, he fashioned a stone drill and bore a hole through the bottom of the heavens, pushing aside rocks and dirt until he could see below. Once the hole was large, he poured snow and rain, boulders and soil, through it, filling the void yet wondering what was happening in that space. Finally he looked and beheld a large mountain with other mountains nearby and to the east a great plain. Delighted with his work, he widened the hole and stepped upon the great mountain, but then noticed that all of the stones, dirt, and water were bare and ugly. Sináwav touched the earth with his fingers and forests grew; his hand swept over the plains where grass and plants sprang up; the sun shone through the hole in the sky, and the rivers flowed to the oceans, or Sky Blue Waters, having taken their color from the heavens; and the rains brought forth blossoms upon the earth.

Sináwav loved his creation, but still something was missing. As he roamed the earth, he realized there were no animals or people. Taking his magic cane, he broke off its tip and made fish of all sizes. He breathed on them and they came alive; he stroked them, placed them in water, and they swam away. Next, he went to the woods and collected many different kinds of leaves of various colors from which he fashioned birds. When he blew on them, wings sprouted and feathers appeared. Eagles, hawks, and ravens came from oak leaves, the red bird from sumac, and the blue jay from aspen. Each had their own song. From the middle of Sináwav's cane came antelope, buffalo, rabbits, squirrels, Coyote, and all the other animals. He believed that he had done well, but as he watched the strong prey upon the weak, Sináwav decided to create one more creature—Bear—from the large end of his staff. To this animal fell the responsibility to maintain peace, interpret, and teach the rules of harmony to the other animals.[2] Later, following the creation of the Utes, Bear told them that he was going to the Bears Ears country because that is where he would find "bull-grass, strawberries, and good eating."[3]

Other animals also chose where they wished to live. Hawk picked his home high in the rocks. As told by Ute elder Fred Conetah, "Eagle loved the crags and peaks and mountain summits, the fierce wind and roaring storm. He said, 'My home will be in the cliffs.' Badger said, 'I will make a warm burrow in the ground.' Wolf said, 'I will roam over the plains.' And Bear said, 'I will live in caves.' Duck liked the marshes of the lakes and streams, Deer the forests, and Buffalo the grassy plains."[4] They went their way to inhabit their homes and have remained there ever since.

Fire was next. The Creator gave Indians fire by placing it in every visible form. When a tree or grass burns, it is the fire coming out, and when sparks fly from a rock, it is releasing the power trapped long ago.[5] Another story tells of when the Sun became embroiled in a fight against Sináwav. The two battled on the ground and in the air; Sináwav's lightning arrow shafts turned into petrified wood, while the missiles hurled by the Sun are cobblestones. Since the rainbow was one of the weapons used against the Sun, it now remains on the other side of the sky, away from the fiery orb. Realizing that he was losing the battle, Sináwav dove into a hole to escape the pelting rocks. His movements caused water to bubble to the surface in the form of the warm waters of Pagosa Springs near the head of the San Juan River in Colorado.[6]

Peace reigned until Coyote, the trickster, began to cause trouble among the animals, turning one against the other, encouraging conflict.[7] Death and bloodshed became a part of this world where the strong triumphed over the weak, much to the disgust of the Creator. A powerful leader with wisdom and strength had to be selected to rule in Sináwav's absence, and so the Grizzly Bear became his representative. Bear, growling his commands, warned the other animals that the fighting must stop and peace prevail or he would punish them. All but Coyote listened; he is still mischievous today. Sináwav returned to the heavens, leaving Bear as his ruler on earth.

There was still the question of seasons. Patty Dutchie, from White Mesa, shared how this annual cycle of change came about.[8] All of the animals, birds, and insects met in a cave one winter day as the snow fell outside. Some of the creatures complained that the season was too long, while those that hunted liked it because their prey became easy to catch. The council continued into the night, so the animals built a fire of pine bark to warm the room. At the back of the cave sat a beautiful bird with snow white feathers tipped with yellow. By dawn, its feathers were sooty, and the bird had become ugly and dark. That is why the crow is black. Another bird sitting in the back remained silent until someone told a funny story. He opened his mouth and started to laugh, but his breath was so bad the others cleared a space about him. Even today other birds will not associate with *kučiget*, the buzzard.

Some of the animals sitting away from the fire were cold and thought that three months was plenty of time for winter, but they were afraid to speak up. One suggested, "You shout out 'three months' then run away." A dog said to the council members, "Winter should be as long as the number of hairs which I shed, counted one by one." The crow argued, "That is too long. Will we even live that long? You, too, may die before that much time has passed." Two quiet ones decided to take a chance and yelled, "Three months! Winter should last for three months," and then ran off. The others gave chase as the two ran down washes, over hills, and through the brush. Qui-doo-wichi (*kwiyú-tukú-č* [bobwhite?]) met the two, leading them into the bushes and tossing out his eyes as he ran. One eyeball returned to its socket, but the other became stuck in some branches. All of the plants started to turn green, blossom, and ripen. The pursuers caught up to the two animals but were amazed. "It is already spring, summer, and fall!" they cried. "Everything is ripened, even the chokecherries." Then they sat down and began to eat. With mouths full of cherries, they spoke of how good it was to have only three months of winter and three months full of chokecherries. The animals had decided.[9]

Following the earth's creation by Sináwav, Bear decided to go to the Bears Ears country because that is where he would find "bull-grass, strawberries, and good eating." Shown here on a visit to his former home, Aldean Ketchum (*right*) shares memories of his life in Allen Canyon, located near this prominent rock formation. The day the photo was taken, in July 2009, bear tracks traversed the canyon bottom. (Courtesy of Winston Hurst)

Dividing time was another concern. The Sun became the standard measure, with three parts to the day—"Sun climbing up time" (morning), "Sun overhead" (noon), and "Sun going down time" (afternoon)—and night lasting from sunset to sunrise. The Sun was the father and the Moon the mother in the sky, but the only time they got together was during an eclipse; otherwise each had their own work and responsibilities. A month's time is measured from new moon to new moon. If a season lasts longer than usual, it is because the Sun is loitering along the path he travels. If winter stays longer one year than another, Sun is just taking more time on his journey north.[10]

But this cooperation eventually changed. In the beginning all of the animals spoke a common language and ate vegetation. During a time of hunger, however, Coyote and Fox decided it would be easier to catch birds and small animals. They gathered them around and were friendly until they pounced on them, killing many. The other animals became afraid, the birds staying in the sky and the small animals hiding in holes, under rocks, and in the woods. Each type was frightened and invented their own language so that other animals could not understand, and they refused to talk to them. Eventually they forgot their common tongue, and so today animals cannot communicate with each other.[11]

Sináwav now looked for a place to put his people. The earth was ready to be settled, but there was no plan as to where to place its many different human inhabitants. Sináwav would do it in his own time and way but wished to ask his brother, Coyote, for help. Southern Ute storyteller Ralph Cloud tells what happened.

Sináwav, the one who created everything, lived with his younger brother Coyote. The two of them roamed the earth, when no one else yet lived on it. Sináwav told his younger brother, "Go cut some brush, all kinds that grow on this earth. Cut them into really small pieces, about this size, and put them in this bag." Coyote did as he was asked. He walked through the hills and over the land, gathering and cutting as he had been told. Finally, the bag was full.

"Now, my little brother, go that way, over the open country and dump the sticks over there," Sináwav said.

As Coyote started his journey, he began to wonder, "What is this that I am carrying? What is this all about? Perhaps I should open it and take a look." Once out of sight of Sináwav, he undid the knot at the top of the bag. As soon as the tie was loosened, out rushed people of all kinds, whooping, hollering, and speaking many different tongues. Most of them escaped, Coyote being able to catch only a few of them and stuff them back into the bag. Later he dumped out the remaining ones and went back home.

Sináwav realized what had happened. "You did it didn't you? Why don't you ever listen to me? Now they will start making arrows and soon they will be fighting you and me."

So Coyote made arrows, and later they all fought each other on the Plains, the Comanche and others as well—all kinds of Indians. The last ones to leave the bag were the Utes. Sináwav said, "Those few ones, no one will surpass them in fighting. Even though the Ute tribe is small, they will keep slaughtering all the others."

That is the way it turned out. Long ago nobody could beat the Utes. They used to fight the Comanche and everybody else, just as Sináwav had predicted; that's the way it was; I have spoken.[12]

A somewhat different version of this story tells of Sináwav living in a large home on the great mountain. Dressed in white buckskins beautifully decorated with beads, he dwelled alone. Desiring company, he created a brother, Sunawiga, who soon disobeyed him and opened some buckskin bags that had voices calling from within.[13] Inside were men of many different sizes, colors, and languages—all of whom were not ready, or "ripe," to be released, but too late, the open bag allowed them to scurry out. Sináwav learned of his brother's disobedience and warned that the people were loose, without having been placed where they would not bother each other; war was imminent. Sunawiga begged for Sináwav's help, urging that the Sioux would soon be after them. Sunawiga made many arrows, Sináwav only one. Wherever this one arrow touched, a crack in the earth formed. Sináwav cautioned that the two could jump back and forth over the crack, but that his brother should not turn and look at him as he fought.

Soon the Sioux attacked.[14] The fight went well until Sunawiga glanced between his legs to see how his brother could kill so many enemies—one hundred at a time—with only one arrow. The indestructible power of protection disappeared. A Sioux arrow pierced Sináwav's knee so he could no longer jump over the crack. The enemy swarmed him, tore the god to pieces, and carried him off in all directions. Sunawiga had the ants gather the remains and put them back together, then wept and danced for his brother's return to life. For a long time he pled to the sky, asking for Sináwav's revival. Finally the Creator's voice called, "I will not come back. You have disobeyed me again and you have spoiled everything." At last he relented and returned to earth, but told his brother that he would be changed into Coyote so that he could always call to the sky, asking for his brother's return. "If I am to be Coyote, all the animals must be like me. They must not speak anymore, but always hunt and kill each other. They should not be able to dance and sing."

Sináwav opened the bag to let the rest of the people out. On the bottom were the best, the ones he had saved for last—the Nũche (the People), or Utes.[15] He told them that they were his people and that "when bad things happened in the world, they must not be afraid, for they would be all right." There were only four things on this earth that they needed to fear: fire, flood, wind, and war. He commanded:

You will carry with you always a little piece of rabbit brush and when fire comes, you will crouch down behind it. It will grow big, so that the fire burns over the top of it and does not hurt you. You will carry with you always some little feathers from certain birds, and when the floods come, these feathers will grow to become a boat to carry you over the water. Against wind you will carry with you always a little stone and your women may cover these with beads to look pretty. When wind comes, these stones will become heavy and hold you down. But against war, I can give you no protection, only what is in your hearts.[16]

As with most oral traditions, there are other variations to these basic narratives told by storytellers in different regions. The people of today's White Mesa community are predominantly a blend of Southern Ute and Paiute people, each group having their own version of how the sack was opened in their particular territory, creating a "homeland."[17] The last people taken from the sack and given the Four Corners region adapted well to the desert and mountains of this land.[18]

From these various versions comes insight into the personality and role of the Creator and his interaction with his people. Although powerful and living in the sky, this man (or wolf) is also mortal: he can be physically injured and killed, tricked and become angry, and appealed to before relenting. The main thrust of these narratives tells how the land became inhabited and the Utes received their territory, formed their special relationship to Sináwav, became a small tribe, and gained their traditional enemies. These are also historical concerns. But historical and anthropological sources also paint a different picture than traditional teachings. Current research suggests that Numic-speaking peoples entered the Four Corners area close to the time of its abandonment by the Ancestral Puebloan (Anasazi), or Mokwič (Muukwitsi), roughly between AD 1200 and 1300. Exactly when and where these Native Americans came from is still open to debate.

Both Ute and Navajo creation stories tell of Ute origins associated with mountain plants. Bonnie Lehi, photographed in June 2007 cutting sumac for basketry, understands her people's dependence on and use of nature to support their existence. (Courtesy of Rebecca Stoneman)

Ute dialects belong to the Southern Numic sub-branch of the Uto-Aztecan (UA) language family. Thirty UA languages are spread from Idaho to Mexico City, with about half in the American Southwest and half in western Mexico. Previous linguistic opinions assumed this language family's homeland to be in the Southwest, based on the general belief that Amerindian language families entered from the north and then spread southward. However, three leading Uto-Aztecan linguists—Alexis Manaster Ramer, Jane Hill, and Brian Stubbs—have more recently presented evidence that a homeland in western Mexico for the entire language family existed before a northward migration of half the language speakers took place. Whether the migration originated in the north or the south, southern California appears to be the homeland for the Northern Uto-Aztecan (NUA) half of the language family. NUA consists of four branches: Takic

(all still in southern California), Tubatulabal (in southern California), Hopi (in Arizona), and Numic.[19]

Numic is further subdivided into three branches: Western Numic (Mono, Northern Paiute), Central Numic (Tumpisha Shoshone, Shoshone, Comanche), and Southern Numic (Kawaiisu, Chemehuevi, Southern Paiute, Uintah Ute, White Mesa Ute, and Colorado Ute). Glottochronology word counts (degree of agreement of one hundred basic words between each pair of languages) show the Southern Numic languages have a high correlation within each branch (76–88 percent) and lesser correlations with the Numic languages of the other branches (49–62 percent). Data show the innermost language of each branch to be more closely related to the outermost languages of the same branch than to the closer, neighboring Numic languages of different branches. This pattern displays considerable diversity in southern California between languages of differing branches only a few miles away, as opposed to closer ties to those of the same branch perhaps a thousand miles away. For example, Tumpisha Shoshone in southern California is linguistically much closer to Shoshone (87 percent) in Wyoming and Comanche (79 percent) on the Plains, all three of which are Central Numic languages. When the Tumpisha Shoshone are compared to either the nearby Mono (59 percent), Western Numic speakers, or the nearby Kawaiisu (54 percent), Southern Numic speakers (both in southern California), one sees a greater diversity.[20]

Some scholars feel that the initial starting point of Uto-Aztecan speakers within the United States was in the region of Death Valley, in southern California.[21] Approximately three to five thousand years ago the Numic branch started to diversify into the three sub-branches just mentioned. Fanning out from a central location, what would become today's Utes and Paiutes moved easterly, remaining on the edge of the Great Basin until about a thousand years ago, when they moved rapidly into the basin and eventually onto the neighboring Colorado Plateau. Their language became increasingly diversified as splits in groups occurred. One anthropologist has suggested that the Utes separated from the Southern Paiutes four hundred years ago as they settled in the Four Corners region.[22]

Today the two languages remain mutually intelligible. The Utes refer to themselves as Nūche and think of themselves as mountain people, while the Paiutes are Pa-Nūche, or Water Utes, in each case denoting one of the group's main resources in different ecological niches.[23] Southern Utes and Southern Paiutes recognize dialectical differences in speech. One Ute informant says that the Paiutes' language is more "clipped" or abbreviated, while the Paiutes accuse the Utes of "talking fancy." This goes along with the Southern Paiutes' general view of the Utes as "fancy" cousins who went off to the Plains and learned "everything."[24]

The archaeological and ethnographic records of the Utes' and Paiutes' entrance into the Four Corners are vague. Campsites and material remains are difficult to find and differentiate from those left by earlier peoples because of the small amount of pottery, nondescript dwellings, and limited technology necessitated by a hunting and gathering lifestyle. Archaeologists estimate that a Ute wickiup built of piñon and juniper branches, a standard dwelling still in use long after first contact with Euro-American culture, will last no more than three hundred years. Later dwellings, such as the tepee, did not have rock circles to hold the bottom down, as is characteristic among the Plains tribes. There is no significant archaeological data in southern Colorado even for the most intense contact phase (1860–1881), when the Southern Utes ranged throughout this area.[25] Analysis is made even more difficult by the Utes' practice of using other people's camps and adopting elements of their material culture.[26]

Robert Euler, a noted Paiute historian, suggests there were two migrations of Numic speakers into Nevada and Utah. The first took place around the beginning of the Christian era, and the second more than a thousand years later, around AD 1150; this last movement possibly caused the resident Mokwič to withdraw into larger, more defensible sites. At the same time, Paiute culture became quite stable, with few changes in lifestyle and technology until well into the late nineteenth century. Other archaeologists place the date of entry later, during the 1300s.[27]

Some scholars argue that the Utes and Paiutes were not even in the region at this time. One explanation of migratory trends places Numic speakers in southwestern Utah some 430 years ago (about 1560), in southeastern Utah and southwestern Colorado 370 years ago, moving along the Rio Grande 330 years ago, and out onto the Great Plains — their easternmost expansion — some 300 years ago.[28] Still others argue that they arrived in their present location 10,000 years ago and have remained there since.[29] All of these dates are speculative, but most agree that the Utes and Paiutes were in San Juan County and their general historic setting by the 1500s.

Spanish reports from the early 1600s indicate that Utes were then living in northwestern Arizona, north of the Colorado and San Juan Rivers, and in eastern Colorado.[30] Early accounts do not provide exact distinctions between different Numic speakers — the Utes, Paiutes, and Chemehuevi all being designated by the Spanish as "Yutas." Today, however, a clearer understanding provides knowledge of the three bands that comprise the Southern Utes. Starting from the east, the Muache (Maġwáčí, meaning "Cedar Bark People"), lived in the Denver area; the Capote (said by some to mean "Blanket People") lived in the Sangre de Cristo Mountains of Colorado and as far south as Taos, New Mexico; and the Weenuche (meaning "Long-time

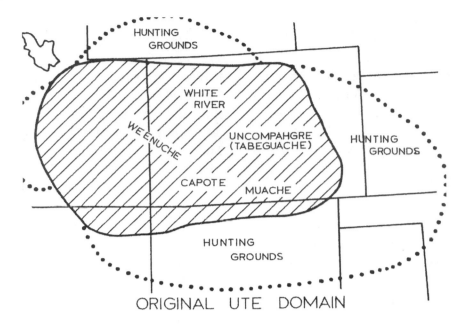

Map 1. Southern Ute bands' territory. (Courtesy of the White Mesa Ute Project, American West Center, University of Utah)

Ago [Ancient] People") ranged from the Dolores River in the east to the Green River in the north, the Colorado River to the west, and the San Juan River in the south.[31] William Wroth suggests that the names *Capote* and *Ute*, or *Yuta*, are related, both coming from the Jemez Puebloan word *guaputu*, meaning "shelters covered with straw," referring to the conical brush or dome-shaped lodges these people lived in. The Spaniard Zárate Salmeron first transcribed the word in 1620, and it was later shortened to *Yuta*, while *Caputa* (how the band refers to itself now) later became anglicized to *Capote*.[32] Whatever the derivation of the names *Ute* and *Capote*, the people themselves were highly mobile and ranged far into the Great Basin, throughout the Colorado Plateau, and onto the Great Plains during the post-contact period.

Some confusion concerning names still exists in the historical record. Anthropologists and historians have collectively lumped the three aforementioned bands together under the title of "Southern Utes." To the Ute people in southeastern Utah and southwestern Colorado today, however, this title prop-

erly refers only to those living on the Southern Ute Reservation (primarily Muache and Capote) headquartered in Ignacio, Colorado. The Weenuche band's name also has been misrepresented. The literature concerning this group refers to them as "Weeminuche," with a variety of spellings — Wimonuntci, Weminutc, Guibisnuches, Wamenuches, and others — that have evolved over time since white contact. It likely was introduced as an inside or interband joke that plays on a word associated with sexual activity (*wiį'mi-nuu-č*, meaning "to copulate," as opposed to *Wii-nuu-č*, meaning "Old [Ancient] Utes"). For whatever reason, use of the word has become entrenched among scholars but is not accepted by many Ute people today. Thus, the term *Weenuche* is used in this volume to describe the band of Southern Utes who inhabit southeastern Utah.[33]

The second group of Numic speakers in this area is the San Juan band of Paiutes. Historically, they have been the least understood of an already amorphous group. Southern Paiute territory was centered in southwestern Utah and Nevada, with its most eastward extension pushing into the Monument Valley region of the Utah-Arizona border. Sixteen identifiable bands comprise the Paiute tribe, with the San Juan band being the only group to occupy lands south and east of the Colorado River. Perhaps this is why their name has been translated as "Being Over on the Opposite Side," or as the "San Juan River People."[34] Historic interface with the Navajos caused the Paiutes to either shift or become immersed within the larger, more expansive culture. Anthropologist Isabel Kelly points out: "Although the San Juan [band] claimed the territory from Monument Valley to the Little Colorado, and from the San Juan to Moenkopi Plateau and Black Mesa, they seem to have kept pretty much to the westerly half of the region, at least after the start of Navajo aggression.… Wholesale displacement of the Paiute took place in the 1860's."[35]

William R. Palmer, during his interviews with Paiutes around Cedar City in 1928, found they had only a slight knowledge of groups in southeastern Utah. His informants indicated that these people were called "'Nau-wana-tats,' which to the Pahutes [*sic*] means fighters or wrestlers. If there is a tribe of this name, the Indians interviewed think they are in the San Juan Country."[36] This vagueness underscores the fact that there was little cohesiveness between certain bands and that the area of southeastern Utah was peripheral to major Paiute activity. The San Juan band may be subdivided into the Tatsiwinunts, who ranged over the area between Tuba City and Navajo Creek, and the Kai-boka-dot-tawip-nunts in the Navajo Mountain — Monument Valley region.[37]

By 1935, Palmer's interest in this elusive group was peaking. Accompanied by a Paiute translator, he visited Allen Canyon, home of the allotted Ute/Paiute faction in southeastern Utah, to determine exactly how "Paiute" and how "Ute" these people were. He reported that he was "surprised, almost amazed, to find this long isolated band speaking more nearly Pahute than some of the clans that attend the tribal saparovan

[council] every year and do much visiting back and forth every summer."[38] The sacred stories told by an esteemed raconteur (*narra-guinip* or *pisǽri'nianápügat*) were also identical to those of other Paiute bands.

Later anthropologists concur. Anne M. Smith, who worked extensively with Ute oral tradition, saw the lore of these two groups, as well as other Numic speakers, "unmistakably similar." Pamela A. Bunte and Robert J. Franklin believed the San Juan Band "closely related to other Southern Paiute groups, and somewhat more distantly related to the Southern Utes, such as those of the Ute Mountain and Southern Ute Tribes in southern Colorado." More recently, anthropologist/historian Joseph G. Jorgensen agreed with others that the differences between mythological narratives of the Utes and Southern Paiutes, as well as other Numic speakers, were minor, and for the most part were "as similar as peas in a pod."[39]

Today, family groups such as the Dutchies, Mikes, Cantsees, Lehis, and Poseys have Paiute roots that extend back to the Douglas Mesa–Monument Valley–Navajo Mountain area, while other families, such as the Ketchums, Whytes, Hatches, and Eyetoos, are more closely related to the Weenuche, or Ute Mountain Utes living at Towaoc. Until the mid-1920s, the three main permanent camps of Numic speakers in southeastern Utah were at Navajo Mountain (Paiute), Allen Canyon (predominantly Paiute, but with a significant mix of Ute), and Montezuma Canyon (predominantly Weenuche Ute).[40] This point should not be stressed too heavily, since a great deal of intermarriage, trade, and social interaction characterized all three groups, while many of these families have descendants living on the Ute Mountain Ute Reservation today.

Indeed, the major distinction between the Utes and Paiutes in southeastern Utah was cultural, not linguistic, affected by the environment and resulting technology. There was no clear line of demarcation. Paiutes

The brush wickiups of these Paiute women, photographed by John K. Hillers in the 1870s, served as their summer homes. Easy to construct with local materials, these shelters provided shade from the sun and protection from the wind, and were quickly assembled—important qualities for a hunter-gatherer lifestyle. (Used by permission, Utah State Historical Society, all rights reserved.)

operated in family groups, and, when resources allowed, came together as bands. They hunted and gathered in an austere desert land, had no centralized local chieftain, few collective religious practices, and no common goal or practice (other than survival) that united the different groups. The Utes arose from the same cultural roots, but with the introduction of the horse in the late 1600s and full adoption by the mid-1700s, those farthest to the east, with access to buffalo, began to adopt parts of Plains Indian culture. The Weenuche, farthest west, were the last to do so. Historically this is important because the "larger bands of Utes could mobilize a greater number of adult fighting men than could the smaller pedestrian camp groups [such as the Paiute]."[41]

Several anthropologists have used the triumvirate of a common language for both Utes and Paiutes, horse nomadism for the Ute, and agriculture for the Paiute with a separation date into defined groups of about 1700–1750, but in southeastern Utah the record cannot be read with this type of clarity.[42] There is frequent mention of Utes planting small gardens, of Paiutes having horses, and of members of other Ute bands, as well as Navajos and Jicarilla Apaches, being added to the mix. Even historical reports written during the last quarter of the nineteenth century and first half of the twentieth had trouble separating the two. For reasons of simplicity, this amalgamation of Ute/Paiute groups will be referred to here generally as "Utes."

In the traditional teachings of these people, one finds deep cultural beliefs that tie them to their land. Unlike the neighboring Navajos, the Utes did not have an extensive pantheon of gods, an intricate ceremonial cycle, an elaborate understanding of sickness and cures, or a deeply unified explanation of life. They turned to the physical world—a place filled with power—for answers and cures, frequently on an individual basis. The world was much more than just a natural realm to sustain life. It was a gift from the "Creator of All Life," Sináwav, imbued with spiritual powers.

The boundaries of the earth replicate those of the Ute and Paiute territory. John Wesley Powell, who spent time with groups from both tribes in the last quarter of the nineteenth century, recorded beliefs concerning the cliffs and canyons that dissect their country, most notably those along the western boundary. He wrote:

> The earth they believe to be bounded on the West by such a line of cliffs. That is, by going beyond the sea in this direction, you climb to a summit of a mesa and then look off from the brink of the cliffs where the world ends. They believe too that these cliffs are very treacherous, that there are projecting rocks at the summit that are delicately balanced and that too inquisitive people in looking over the brink have fallen over and gone—ah! they know not where....
>
> The eastern edge of the world is a line of cliffs like that on the west. It may seem strange, but in talking with them I have never been able to obtain from them any idea of what they supposed might be the northern or southern boundaries—in fact they do not seem to understand what I mean or to appreciate that it is possible for there to be more than two boundaries, those already mentioned. Their usual reply is, "The ancients never told us about a northern and southern end to the ground."[43]

Differences in elevation also divide Ute territory into cosmological zones. For instance, the "upper earth" is comprised of ridges, mountains, and other high elevations; the "middle earth" includes slopes, alluvial fans, and foothills; and the "lower earth" is made up of valleys, canyon bottoms, and low elevations. "Each 'earth' has its animal spirits, ones peculiar to that area and Ute families adopt these spirits for their 'clan' symbols."[44] There are five different colors tied to these various vertical levels. The sky

is associated with white and is the domain of Eagle; mountaintops are yellow and home to the Mountain Lion; mountain slopes have a combination of blue/green/gray as their color and are represented by Wolf; basins and lower elevations are the lower earth, colored red and occupied by Weasel; and the underworld, a reflection of the earth above and the place where the planets and sun pass through during the day and night, is black and inhabited by Rattlesnake.[45] The four cardinal directions divide the horizon.

Within the boundaries of Ute lands are special sites, or "power points," where sacred forces reside. Spiritual leaders, or medicine men, understand how to use the supernatural powers (*puwá-v*) associated with this sacred space. Such a person goes to a place of power during the season of use and on behalf of his group prays, leaves an offering, and asks for help. Other band members practice individual prayer, but not at the "power point" used by a medicine man.[46] Different types of spirits live in caves, rocks, springs, rivers, mountains, and other places, and they may provide help or cause harm depending upon how they are treated. These same powers— as well as those associated with animals, plants, and natural phenomena such as whirlwinds, the moon, and lightning—may also "transmit the high voltage of supernatural power to humble practitioners or doctors."[47] Utes believe that the locations of specific power sites, which are not general knowledge, should be discussed only with those who have a need to know.

An example of the operating principle behind a power point is found in the Escalante Desert in southern Utah. Palmer noted that a shaman's dream revealed that a certain rock held healing powers. To appeal to this force, a person brings a stone from a streambed near their home and leaves it on top of the healing rock. The ill person names the afflicted part and asks for the power of the site to effect a cure. Stones lie deep about the rock, brought by numerous sick people

Sleeping Ute Mountain, on the horizon, has a general north-south orientation. Said to be a resting warrior waiting for his time to awaken, this formation looks like a man reclining with his head to the north, arms folded across his chest. At the southern end is his large toe (*left of tepee*), where special powers are believed to reside. (Denver Public Library, Western History Collection, H. S. Poley, P-79, 1908)

from a hundred-mile radius.[48] Power points are also associated with things other than sickness and specific natural objects, and offerings of some type are made at all of them, accompanied by prayer. It is important that individuals asking for assistance understand what the spirit force desires.

Connor Chapoose felt that everything — trees, rocks, and other natural elements — received their qualities during the creation, whether good or bad. They obtained their very nature at this time, so if, for example, a rock fell off a cliff and hit someone, it was a treacherous rock fulfilling the measure of its creation. Thus everything has a character, and whatever qualities comprise that character can be appealed to. Pursuing this thought in relation to creation, Chapoose said, "We believe that these formations [such] as rocks and trees and this shrubbery has a meaning…. At one time they [newly

created animals and elements] were showing their powers and how all creatures had different powers to do this and that and what gifts they had in competing with one another. That is why I say a rock has some meaning [qualities] at this time."[49] Clearly an animate universe continues to be a standard Ute belief.

Utes believe that Sleeping Ute Mountain, near Cortez, Colorado, is one of seven giants who fought against other tribes' gods during the time of myths. As these forces struggled, their feet and bodies pushed the land, forming mountains and valleys. The Great Warrior grew tired from the battle, fell into a deep sleep, and there he will remain until needed again. Blood poured from his wounds, creating streams of water. Sticks and leaves covered his body as he slept, with his head to the north, face toward the sky, arms across his chest, and his legs to the south. During the four seasons he changes his blankets—light green in the spring, dark green in the summer, yellow and red in the fall, and white in the winter. Before slumbering, he collected rain clouds and put them in his pocket. When a storm arises, it is only the clouds issuing forth. Some people say that the Sleeping Ute will one day awake to fight his people's enemies.[50] This mountain is also believed to be inhabited by small supernatural beings who are appealed to through prayer and offerings.

The origin of the Four Corners area's large canyons also has its place in Ute lore. During the time when animals and gods talked together, Hawk and Sináwav went hunting. Sináwav obtained many more rabbits, making Hawk jealous, and conflict ensued. Hawk let out a piercing scream that shook the earth, cracked its crust, and fragmented it into the canyon system that exists today.[51] A second version of this story tells of Hawk and Sináwav practicing with their bows and arrows and deciding to use Hawk's quiver as a target. Sináwav shot, the arrow glanced off, ricocheting across the land. The point created deep canyons and ravines, plowing up mountains and hills, and digging the course of rivers and streams. Large boulders flew everywhere, all of which added to today's landscape.[52]

Another narrative hearkens back to this creative period, when the chief of all the Utes lost his wife and did not know where to look for her. Tavwoats, Sináwav's older brother, answered his prayers by taking him to the land of the dead to locate her. The god rolled a great magical ball of fire before them, cutting the earth and its mountains, creating a path upon which the two could walk. The husband arrived in the land of the dead, saw how happy his wife was, and returned to the living after being cautioned that he should not walk upon this trail again. Tavwoats ensured that humans kept this law by forming an enormous river canyon to block the trail—the Grand Canyon of the Colorado.[53]

One of the most interesting phenomena in Ute mythology that ties directly to the San Juan, Colorado, and other rivers is belief in Paá'apači, or "Water Boy," sometimes called "Water Baby" or "Roams Along in the River."[54] There are varying descriptions of what this creature looks like. Some people say it resembles a fish with long black hair and a flowing mustache. Others tell of it having legs like a man. Accounts exist of both male and female water babies, one version suggesting what happens when a young man falls asleep by a river and awakes to find a beautiful woman in a green dress lying next to him. After he sleeps with her, she may lure him into the water to remain with her people.[55]

There are other stories of this creature's activity in the rivers and lakes of Utah. One is about a woman who left her baby strapped in a cradleboard by the river and then went off to do her work. While she was gone, a water baby removed the infant and climbed into the cradle. The mother did not realize what had happened, nursed the water baby, and was swallowed by the creature. Another story tells of how two female water babies pulled a man into the river and took him to their home beneath the water. They wanted to marry him, but he thought they were ugly and eventually escaped. Water babies cry like humans and are often heard near the river. Whirlpools are an indicator of a water baby's presence. They accept tobacco for smoking, can affect a person's dreams when mistreated, but can also be playful, especially with older people. They have the power to temporarily raise the level of the water.[56]

Because of these beliefs, Utes say a baby should never be left by the river or it may be lost. People who camp by the water say they hear the water baby crying, but when someone goes to investigate, it slips away undetected. And it's generally agreed that people should avoid going down to the river at night. Stella Eyetoo recalls what the old people of White Mesa say. It seems a woman left a baby in a cradleboard by the river as she picked willows [sumac] for a basket. A water baby crept on shore, swallowed the infant, assumed its form, and then waited for the mother to return to nurse. The creature swallowed the mother and dove into the water, but could be detected by the whirlpool eddies and a crying sound.[57] Belief in these creatures also explains why Utes took baths only in the shallows. Even though they considered themselves good swimmers, they often crossed deep rivers by holding on to the manes or tails of their horses. Swimming unassisted in deep water was dangerous because a water baby could pull people down in a whirling funnel and drown them.[58]

Northern Utes have stories of their own. They tell of people who get too close to these yellow-bodied creatures and hear them call, "Wal-la-loo," drawing them into the water. One woman fishing on the Green River near Ouray heard this call but mustered all the willpower she could, broke away to her village, and alerted some warriors. They went to the river, saw the swirling water, broke camp, and never returned to that spot.[59] Connor Chapoose knew a man who frequented a large pool of clear water on the Green River, where fishing for trout was good. As he made his way through the bushes to the river's edge, he saw a creature that resembled a child, two feet high, with long hair. After the water baby jumped into the pool, the would-be fisherman looked into the clear, blue water to see where it went and heard a noise. "It sounded like there were several in there. He said they sounded pretty much like babies when they are three months old."[60]

In 1986 two travelers sighted a water baby near the Colorado River. Some Utes returning to White Mesa from a Bear Dance spent the night in Moab. There was the usual mix of cars, trailers, tourists, and general hubbub. After things settled, they went to sleep in their vehicle, but during the night they heard an infant crying. When they sat up to see where the noise came from, they saw it,

"standing under the security light; [it] was crying and his body was naked and his skin still wet. They got scared. Somehow that thing noticed that somebody was watching and he ran back to the water. That is when they left."[61]

Utes also describe other supernatural beings, Turúúkčičin, "Little Dark People," small but powerful men and women with the ability to change into different forms. According to Åke Hultkrantz, an anthropologist who has specialized in the religion of Numic-speaking people, "The beliefs in the dwarf spirits were very uniform over the Numic area and, to judge from reminiscences and legends, attracted more attention than any other religious belief."[62] These beings stand two feet tall and are usually dressed in green but sometimes red. The Utes believe them to be one of the strongest sources of power for healing the sick, able to cure any illness, including those caused by ghosts. They are also able to inflict sickness, their little arrows giving an individual pneumonia. If horses graze too close to their homes, they may be killed.[63] But usually these little people are pleasant until they get "grouchy" and harm people.

Edward and Patty Dutchie were familiar with them, saying that their tracks are the size of a man's hand and the area around their home's entrance is about the size of a gopher hole and often packed hard by their comings and goings. This is where offerings of cloth or food may be left to obtain their assistance, although rings and beads are often preferred. A person might lie there for a moment and explain what kind of help is required. When one returns to the site, the piece of cloth is gone, taken by that "little medicine man."[64] These beings are found wherever there is a place that holds power, so not surprisingly, "they live along Comb Ridge in the side of the hills, and early in the morning you can see their smoke fires, but no one sees them because they have medicine."[65] Jim Mike watched some Little People play in a side canyon of Comb Ridge. One of them spotted him, let out a scream like a wildcat, and then they all scattered.[66]

On the valley floor just below the southern end of White Mesa sits a short hill mass where these beings used to reside. Ute people left cloth near their holes, the interior of which have purple, blue, or red dirt. Usually, "Little People are found in areas with red rock and red sand."[67] People used to see smoke coming from their homes in this hill, but now they have moved away because they did not like the Ute people moving so close. The table mesa on the east side of Towaoc, south of Mesa Verde, is another location where they have been spotted. In other canyons and mesas the Little People either hide or show deer and elk to hunters who have prepared themselves through ritual. If these Little People are seen, the individual must leave a blanket, food, or some other useful object and then depart. They prefer things that are Ute. By saying nothing about the incident, the person is guaranteed good fortune in the future.[68]

Exactly who these Little People are is unsure. Lola Mike suggested there could be a connection between these beings and the Mokwič (Ancestral Puebloan), or perhaps their children.[69] To Connor Chapoose they were "dwarfs" who lived in isolated places where humans and animals seldom venture. The tell-tale smoke coming from the ground is an indicator of their presence, and often there is some prominent terrain feature in the vicinity. If a person has something bothering him, like "soreness or isn't feeling good…headache or hiccups," he can dust himself with dirt from around the hole and leave an offering for assistance.[70] Ute elder Harriet Johnson believed that these beings were dangerous and could kill a person. The local people called them "the Keith Brothers," with little explanation given. Harriet offered a few specific details, suggesting that the tell-tale smoke appears about 3:30 or 4:30 in the morning, the beings may appear in different colors, their moccasin tracks are about three

inches long, and there are little doors to their homes.[71] They have the ability to know if you really need assistance and are sincere in your efforts when asking for help or just going through the motions and not really caring. The Little People watch and know one's heart.[72]

John Wesley Powell learned that these "little beings or pygmies" were everywhere and received credit for many things that happened in daily Ute life. When one of them gets angry, a whirlwind may form; they are responsible for strange noises among the rocks or in the woods; if something is missing, it may well have been stolen by one of them; headaches, stomachaches, rheumatic pain, and other health issues are brought on by not treating them with respect; children are cautioned against whistling at night because one might fly into their mouth; and even when "gas from a burning stick of wood bursts out in a little stream of flame, they say an u-nu'-pits [Little Person] is lighting a brand."[73]

Near Chimney Rock, not far from Towaoc, lies Mancos Canyon. A road traverses the valley and eventually ascends to the top of the mesa to a place called Ute Pasture. According to Jack Cantsee of White Mesa, twenty years ago a construction crew with bulldozers was operating there. When the men returned in the morning, none of their equipment started because the Little People had been offended by their presence. There was a Ute man, however, who understood how to talk to them, and he rolled a tobacco offering and set off alone to pray to the Little People. He explained why the workers were there and asked permission to continue the construction. After he returned, all the vehicles started and the project was completed.[74]

The Dutchies felt that places where the Little People lived have been unintentionally destroyed. Edward knew of some sites where they still exist but was rightfully reluctant to say where, stating that these beings communicate in a spiritual way and do other things hard to believe. "Some white guys don't know; they say it's just a story. Those kinds [Little People] can get to you if you tell lies about them or talk against them." Patty connected their disappearance with the end of the world, something that the elders have warned about. Nature itself is turning against humans because they are not doing what they should. She went on:

> The Creator said, "When you don't believe, when you destroy things or when you don't follow the way you were created, this is what's going to happen someday. The rain is going to come—the flood. Someday the wind is going to come with heavy rains that will destroy your home. Someday a big drought will come and will destroy everything. It will destroy you in any way because all of the sacred is gone." He is going to do that to us. That is what the old people said when they danced.... That is our belief and we will have to hang on to what is left.[75]

There are other types of supernatural beings inhabiting the land. The *ku'-ni-shuv* is pure white, lives on the tops of mountains, and comes out when the peaks are shrouded in clouds. Both Utes and Southern Paiutes believe that these beings control mountain animals—deer, bear, elk, mountain sheep—making them available to hunters, who leave part of the animal where it was killed as an offering.[76] These creatures can also transform themselves into ravens. They are generally kind and can teach a person important things.

Tu-mu-ur'-ru-gwai'tsi-gaip, in contrast, are said to be old, wrinkled, ugly, and vindictive. They inhabit large, rocky areas and "take great delight in catching unwary, foolish people and then scamper to the brink of some cliff and throw them over to be dashed to pieces against the rocks below."[77] All of these beings have human forms.

Jack Cantsee is also aware of another type of being. This one is two feet tall but black. He tells of a time when some relatives were in a sweat lodge purifying themselves. Others

had advised them to be done with the bath before night, but they disregarded the warning. One of the little black men got inside the lodge, which was pitch dark, and began putting water on the heated rocks, creating so much steam that the bathers could not tolerate it, became frightened, and immediately quit the area. Jack is sure that at least one of them still lives in the area of White Mesa.[78]

Even sites created by people hold power that requires respect. The Utes were very aware of the Ancestral Puebloan ruins dotting their hunting territories, but they avoided them, referring to the people who built them as "Mokwič" or "Muukwitsi," meaning "the dead." They believe that these people's spirits are related to spiders, explaining why arachnids haunt the ruins. The same name is used to refer to the Hopi: "Moqüi (pronounced "Mawkwi," which has been anglicized into "Moki,")—a term applied only to that Puebloan group. The word appears to have entered general usage following the Domínguez-Escalante expedition of 1776, which depended heavily on Numic speakers for guides.

According to some Ute informants, there never was conflict between their people and the Mokwič; among other things, they shared a language that was almost intelligible. The Utes tell how they would sporadically catch a glimpse of their neighbors because the Mokwič appeared "like phantoms and would be seen at a distance or be heard to scream, but would disappear into the piñon when a Ute approached."[79] According to one Northern Ute, "The [Mokwič] went back down south a long time ago when they found there were a lot of other Indians coming in."[80] A study of Southern Paiute beliefs corroborates this point: the Mokwič are said to have come from the south, were short people like the Hopi, mean at times, and when they left the area, they returned south.[81] Another Utah Paiute story tells of how they were enslaved by these Puebloans until "the Indians from the north waged war upon them and drove them across the Colorado River, the Moquis agreeing never to re-cross the river."[82] Utes believe that visits to their abandoned dwellings can cause sickness, and if children enter, they can be bitten by snakes.

Edward Dutchie was born at Sand Island, which is close to Butler Wash and its extensive ruins. He and his wife, Patty, offered their understanding of traditions concerning the Mokwič.[83] When asked what Utes say about them, Edward promptly replied, "They don't say anything. They are scared of them." Henry McCabe, a cowboy who spent much of his time on the range in southwestern Colorado and southeastern Utah at the turn of the twentieth century, agrees. He tells of how the Utes did not like talking about the Mokwič and would not enter a site "beyond the point where the water from the overhanging cliff fell."[84] Acowitz, a Southern Ute, warned Richard Wetherill about the Mesa Verde ruins and the danger lurking there. Acowitz advised, "I could tell you [about the ruins], but I warn you not to go there. When you disturb the spirits of the dead, then you die too."[85]

The Ancestral Puebloan people are often associated with conflict. Lola Mike believes that some sites around Comb Ridge have strong spiritual energy, but there are also places where something bad has happened — "that was in Comb Wash."[86] Exactly what and where she did not say. Pioneer photographer William H. Jackson, however, received specific information as he rode through McElmo Canyon in 1874. He wrote that the Utes he encountered "have no knowledge whatever of their [cliff dwellings'] former occupants. Not even traditions," just that the sites were Mokwič dwellings. But with the next breath Jackson pointed to "Fortified Rock" (today known as Battle Rock) and said, "There our guide informed us, these [Mokwič] aborigines made their last stand before being dispossessed and driven out of the country by the northern bands, the American Aztecs [other prehistoric (non-Aztec) Indians].

Moqui tradition has it that here 10,000 warriors were engaged upon either side, that 2,000 were slain, that blood ran in rivers on the rocks, staining them with unalterable dye. From here they went to their present habitations in New Mexico."[87]

McCabe shares a similar story, this time about the Dolores River. Unlike many other streams in the vicinity, this one was believed to have Mokwič spirits living in it. Some Utes would not eat fish they caught in its waters, but would trade them off to other people because a spirit was in the fish. This idea may be connected with a site two miles below the town of Dolores, where "the Ute Indians and the Mokis had their battle," and where farmers often surfaced human remains.[88] Buckskin Charlie supported this observation, saying, "We have fish in the streams now, but we don't eat them because some wicked people threw dead bodies in the water and they became fish. We don't know now which are the real fish and which are dead people."[89]

Going into a cliff ruin held different challenges. Once one passed beyond the drip line, he or she was in the Mokwič's "home." In order to avoid angering the spirits of the prior occupants, a prayer is offered in which one "talks to the person." Their presence can be felt and their voices heard blowing in the wind. The spirits are very aware of what goes on in their abode, so if something is needed or an object taken, an offering is left behind so that the spirit will not follow the person home.[90] Sunshine Cloud-Smith, a Southern Ute, suggests that before entering a ruin, people announce that they have come "in a good way" to visit the home, see how things are going, and that nothing will be taken or disturbed. Food may be placed outside or tobacco sprinkled about to ensure that the spirits are happy and resting peacefully.[91] Patty Dutchie, who was raised in the Mesa Verde area, tells of how her mother and grandmother said, "They have seen the last of the Mokis up there. Not just one or two or three, but a family.... Others were

A Ute encampment in Mancos Creek Canyon, above the Mancos trading post, 1950. This is a good example of the alcoves favored by the Mokwič (Ancestral Puebloans) and, later, the Ute people seeking protection for their homes. Both cultures left pictographs on the rock walls. (Northern Arizona University, Cline Library, NAU.PH.98.20.5.69)

wiped out by some kind of sickness, that's what they say. Those who were left were so lonely they had to move away from there."[92] Edward chimed in that the Utes did not "mess" around with bones or pottery because "it is still alive.… It is still alive yet.… They say you can hear them move around in the museums where the remains are. They make noise like they are moving around. You might hear something if you sit in there all night." The old people used to know the prayers said before entering a site, but this generation of grandmothers and grandfathers knows little about it.

One of Edward's daughters brought home a Mokwič pot full of seeds. Prayers made it safe. The only thing that can be picked up and kept without concern are surface-find arrowheads, but even these should be prayed over with an offering to determine what it was originally made for.[93] If it was for killing people, then the power must be appeased before using it for protection against ghosts and evil. When hung above the head at night, the point keeps bad dreams away.

Ghosts and spirits, in general, are abroad in the dark and should be avoided. The elders used to teach, "'They'll take you' when you are a little kid. 'You'll be lost. They have a *big* basket water jug they will take you in and carry you on their back to that place.' That's what they used to tell us.… Now it seems like the ghosts are already here with us. The kids wander around and everything. They do unusual things like breaking windows or taking things away. The kids are with the ghosts."[94]

Failure to keep a Mokwič object in "a precious way—a religious way" may result in disorientation, accident, or loss. Prayers ascend to the "Great Spirit" (Sináwav) because he was the one who taught them how to make the pottery and their homes. Patty said, "The Mokis were more intelligent than we are. We Indians have wandered all over and never put up that kind of house. We never made jugs that we could cook in." But Edward felt more kinship. As he talked about the burial of Ute bodies in Mokwič caves, he offered a number of explanations as to why it was acceptable. The first was pragmatic.

In the winter, if a death occurred, alcoves offered sheltered soil that was soft for digging, so "some Utes are buried there too, just like Mokis." By leaving the Puebloan bones undisturbed, they will not come looking for the person. Ute and Mokwič bones are compatible—"everything is the same. They're the same color.... If you buried a white man in there, I don't know about that. White men were brought up differently from the beginning of time."[95]

Today, construction on or near ruins is an ever-present concern for Utes following traditional practices. Terry Knight, a tribal religious leader at Towaoc, had the responsibility of "quieting" a site of potential problems before construction of new homes could begin. Observer James Carrier wrote:

> This week [Terry Knight] performed special prayers prior to ground-breaking for units being built near an Anasazi ruin. Dressed in jeans and cowboy shirt, Terry built a fire and burned cedar and herbs near the old kiva wall, a round ceremonial chamber used about ad 1000. "I talked to the old Anasazi spirits and told them we're going to be building new homes, and not to let the machinery and people disrupt them. I told them families would be living there. I asked them to be more like a guardian force."[96]

Even with this compatibility, the dwellings, objects, and remains of the Mokwič are dangerous. Anthropologist Greg Johnson has written the only formal study of Ute beliefs associated with these people, and he found that central to their teachings is an underlying fear that is a part of their culture.[97] His research suggests that Ute people have great respect for the dead, classifying Mokwič remains as dangerous. Those who disturb them will be afflicted with illness because spirits or ghosts inhabit the area in which the remains are located. And in the canyons and ruins where Mokwič bones lie, their evil persists, "for it is in the geographical, metaphysical, and mythical canyons of the Ute

that diseases, ghosts, echoes, the spirit of the Anasazi, and other dangerous things dwell. It makes sense to the Ute to avoid such places. Health and society—individual life and collective existence—are at stake. To keep Anasazi things in place is to keep balance."[98]

Palmer offers another example of the power contained within human remains. Interpreter Woots Parashont shared with him the following story about Brig George, a Paiute acquaintance. Brig found an Indian bone, ground it, and placed the material in a medicine bag. The spirit of that bone came in search of it, and after finding it, talked to the Paiute just like a man and said, "You have my bone. I want to kill someone. Who shall I kill? You tell me or I will kill you."[99] Brig pointed to a man and said that the spirit could kill him in fifteen days, which it did. "The spirit came many times that way." Three medicine men eventually determined what was going on and were going to kill Brig, but he lost his pouch, and another person found and destroyed it, so they allowed him to live. There is no doubt that objects associated with the dead hold great power in both the spiritual and physical world.

In summarizing Ute beliefs about the creation of the land, its animals, and the supernatural powers that invest them, one recognizes three main points. The first is that it is a foreordained and powerful environment. The things that comprise it, whether classified as animate or inanimate in Western thought, are animate in their beliefs. In other words, a rock or tree or animal are sentient beings that hold power that can be petitioned for help. While the creation stories involving Sináwav are not philosophically complex, they explain the Utes' understanding of how the world operates. The Creator fulfilled his role, left an empowered environment, and then withdrew to allow his people to make their way on a relatively individual basis. As Hultkrantz suggests, "There was no unitary religious system and no worldview that provided a dogma of supernatural sanctions.

Religious ideas and practices were diffused through the culture but did not constitute a set of defined beliefs, values, and rites."[100]

The second point is that the world is dangerous. Inhabited by Little People and water babies, Mokwič ruins and spirits, and supernatural beings on mountain tops or rocky slopes, the lands of the Utes held elements that needed to be appeased. Sickness and death were all too prevalent to be left to chance by not enlisting prayer and offerings for protection. Some people refer to these beliefs as superstition. Hardly. Superstition is always the other man's religion. Tough-fisted reality suggests that the Utes faced a difficult environment, and that inviting powers beyond human ability was a very real means, prevalent in their worldview, to survive. People living on today's Colorado Plateau have insulated themselves from potential starvation and warfare and limited their dependence on the supernatural. The historic Utes enjoyed no such luxury.

Finally, for the Utes, all was local. This is not to suggest that they did not travel long distances or that they were so isolated from other groups that there were no outside influences. Indeed, Utes were great travelers who both adopted and had forced on them things from other cultures. But their beliefs are centered on their homeland, defined by where they hunted and gathered. Power points connected the tangible to the intangible; knowledge of them was critical. The Utes were created for the land and placed there by Sináwav for protection and survival. Though relatively small in number compared to some of the Plains tribes, the Utes earned respect as tough fighters and capable hunters in an environment that at times was stingy. As the next chapter shows, they were well adapted to a lifestyle that maximized use of the land's resources. The Nūche were equipped and knowledgeable for their journey in the Four Corners region.

CHAPTER 2

"It Was as If the Land Owned Us"

Ties to the Land, Resources for the People

Older Utes would say that all of San Juan County was special. That is why they never left this area. A lot of Ute families roamed the whole county. No one really owned the land. It was as if it owned us—the Ute people.

Billy Mike

Billy Mike (Čičíč), the oldest resident of the White Mesa community in 1993, sat comfortably as he slowly ran his fingers through his gray hair. The thick glasses perched upon his nose served more as a token of past vision than as an aid to see today's world. Blind in one eye, with failing sight in the other, he moved about hesitantly with the assistance of a cane. His life of ninety-some-odd years had spanned a period of transition for the Ute people. At times his mind wandered clearly over events from the past, but at others it became clouded. Still, he clearly remembered his people's association with the land before white men had divided and taken control of it. He recalled, "No one really owned the land. It was as if it owned us—the Ute people."[1] The relationship of which he spoke—of land and people—goes back, according to the Utes' oral tradition, to the beginning of time.

This and the next chapter describe the life of the Ute people in southeastern Utah during the mid to late 1800s, before they were forced to abandon their traditional hunting and gathering lifestyle. Ties to the land and resulting cultural practices and beliefs testify to the close relationship that grew from dependence on the environment. The

adoption of new technology, such as guns, as well as horses and other livestock, had a tremendous impact on certain cultural traits, diminishing some, but many Ute practices remained intact. Not until the dominant culture severed the tribe's traditional ties to the land did many of the Ute ways shift. Stella Eyetoo recalled, "There were a lot of different areas along the mountain ranges that the Ute people roamed freely. There was a lot of rain and the grass was tall. I do not understand how we lost all the land."[2] What follows is a brief look at how the Ute people once lived—and what they lost.

The Utes bestowed the land with a multiplicity of names, sometimes more than one for the same place. The most prominent terrain features—the mountains—have tremendous significance to them for a variety of reasons. Most names are descriptive. For instance, Sleeping Ute Mountain is called Yucca, Bitter Root, or "Bread Fruit" Mountain. Blue Mountain (also known as the Abajos) is known as Blue (when seen from a distance), Water, Water Soaked or Spring Mountain, and in 1855 it was referred to as Moccasin Track Mountain.[3] The hunched and rounded Shay Mountain, its neighbor to the north, received the title of Mountain

Billy Mike was one of the last traditional flute makers on White Mesa. He carved them from a cedar branch three inches in circumference, split the eighteen-inch piece of wood in half, drilled six holes, fashioned the mouthpiece, and then channeled the center of both halves for airflow. He next inserted a flattened piece of lead to serve as a reed, glued the two halves together with pine pitch, and bound them with buckskin. (Courtesy of the San Juan County Historical Commission)

Sheep Back. The La Sal Mountains are called Snow-Capped or Elk Mountain, and are associated with rain. A person, merely by saying its name in Ute, can invite a storm to the area.[4] One of its peaks is Mount Tukunikivats (Tuġúttu níkyet — "Where the Sun Sets Last" or "High Place Where the Sun Still Shines"). Navajo Mountain, known to the Utes as "Black" or "Round Mountain," or "Standing Alone Mountain," was "like a stronghold for many Ute families" and was "famous for meat…before beef came."[5] The Henry Mountains are called the "Hot Mountains" and also sit alone. Blue Mountain, Navajo Mountain, and the La Sals were Ute places of worship. Horse Mountain, near Beef Basin, is where the Utes grazed many of their horses, as they did on North Elk Ridge and in the Gooseberry area. Edward Dutchie explained the importance of all of these mountains to the people who "called themselves the mountain people or mountain Utes. The

highest peaks were where they would go to out-run any tribe during the fighting days — head for the peaks and fight down from there. That's why the peaks are very important. On foot, white men could not run to the peaks like the Utes could."[6]

Other important terrain features include the San Juan River, called Water Canyon, Big River, or "River Flowing from the Sunrise." Both Stella Eyetoo and Chester Cantsee spoke of this body of water being the southern boundary of White Mesa Ute territory: "It is what kept the Navajos on the other side. They did not dare come across. The northern boundary was the Green River, and the western one the Colorado River ("Water Down Deep in the Earth"). Lizzie Jacket, from Towaoc, affirms, "The land was ours. The different bands of Utes traveled and visited one another. The land was divided by the San Juan River and the Green River."[7] The eastern boundary was somewhat ambiguous, but the Dolores and Animas Rivers are strong candidates.

The Utes were drawn to this region by its rich resources, chief among them the mountains and rivers of the Colorado Plateau. The connecting links between the two were the major canyon systems that descended from the mountains, draining to the waters below. Sagebrush Canyon, or Crows Canyon, or Oak Canyon Wash, or Much Greasewood Canyon (all names for Montezuma Canyon) was like a Ute "homeland," offering many campsites near springs. Medicine men such as Brooks and leaders such as Johnny Benow (Green Ute), Narraguinip ("Storyteller"), and Poco (or Polk) Narraguinip ("Slow Storyteller") all had camps there.[8]

Comb Wash ("Mountain Sheep Testicles," named after a rock formation) and Butler Wash ("Slick Rock Wash" or "Yellow Knoll"), separated by Comb Ridge, were other important sites. Comb Ridge — called "Slick Rock Mound" or "Backbone of the Earth" — was a favorite place to camp in the winter.[9] The San Juan River cuts through the ridge at a

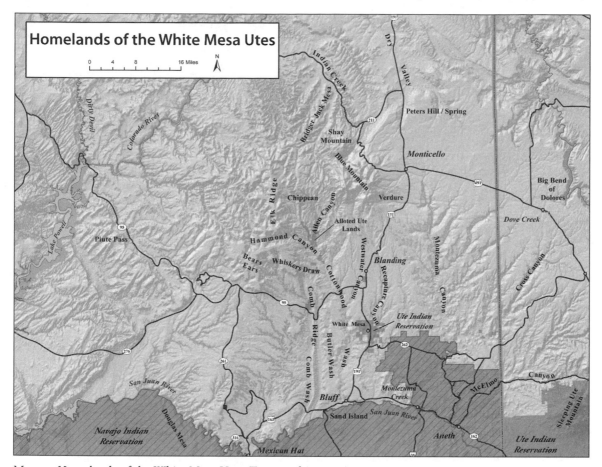

Map 2a. Homelands of the White Mesa Utes, Topographic.

place called "Coming Together," where "all nations will come together, much like what is happening today."[10] It was also a favorite camping place because of its lower elevation, river access, springs, and canyon walls that reflect the sun's heat.[11] In other seasons, Comb Wash, on the west side of the ridge, was favored for gathering Indian ricegrass and herbs for tea, while Butler Wash, on the east side, was an excellent source of willows and sumac for making baskets. Lola Mike, an eighty-year-old weaver, claimed that the pictorial elements of the traditional "Navajo wedding basket" (manufactured by both Navajos and Utes) was inspired by the broken skyline of Comb Ridge, which she believes was the birthplace of the basket. She also considers Comb Ridge's springs "the lifeblood of many living things which rely on that water."[12]

Other drainages include "Two Rocks" or "White Man's Cave" (Cow Canyon), "Cedar Ridge Wash" (Westwater Canyon), "Rock Wash" (Arch Canyon), "Streambed/Cobble Stones" (Dry Wash), "Honey Canyon" (Hammond), "Dark/Dusky Canyon" (because of the high walls limiting light), Cottonwood Wash (called "Red Wash" because of the silt that flowed when it rained), and "Water Runs Through Every Day" (Recapture Canyon). This last site was known as a hiding place during times of conflict. In speaking of this and the South Fork of Montezuma Creek, Edward Dutchie recalled, "During the time when the tribes fought each other, women would hide there [Recapture]. There are [also] several places clear up to the foot of Verdure [South Montezuma Creek] where women hid. When Mormons and Utes were about to fight, they hid their women in Verdure. Before that, this [Recapture Canyon] was their hiding place; nobody can get in

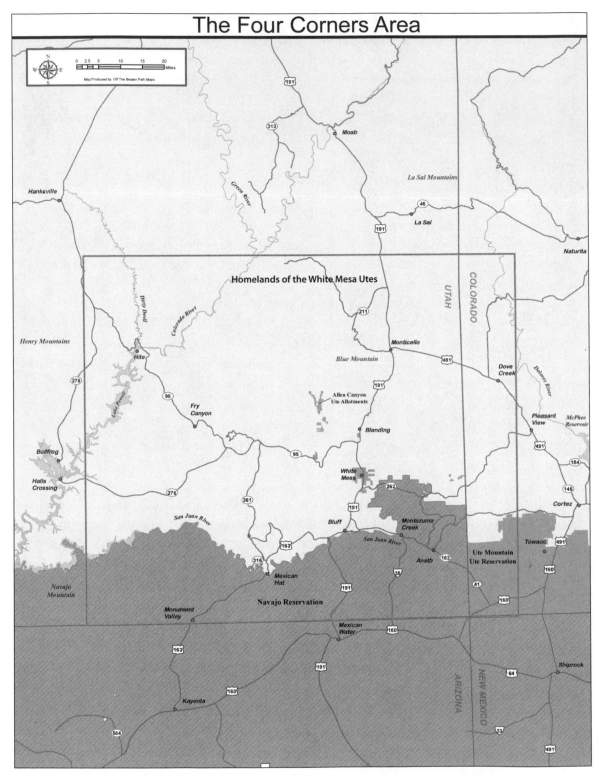

Map 2b. Homelands of the White Mesa Utes, Regional.

there to look for people…. The Utes during the winter would follow that river and camp along its side."[13]

But of all of the thousands of canyons spreading across the hundreds and hundreds of square miles that made up White Mesa Ute territory, none seemed to resonate as strongly as Allen Canyon, known to the Utes as Avi Kan, or "Mountain Canyon," or "Where the Big Red Rock Sits." To Stella "it is the homeland," a place, along with Montezuma Canyon, where the Bear Dance and Worship Dance were held. Many prominent leaders and family members are buried in this canyon, which has been occupied by Ute people since well before the 1850s. Not only is it important because of the stream, springs, and alcoves, but also for its abundant plant resources, access to higher ecozones, and sheltered environment. When asked what it meant to the White Mesa people, Edward Dutchie replied:

> Well, Allen Canyon is like their headquarters. They would go someplace and come back, because they had their leader, Mancos George, living right there. Before he left, I heard him talking to his tribe, just west of Westwater, the east side of Slickrock. He said, "There is something here that you people should never forget that I am going to tell you. You remember this as long as you live — that Dry Wash, Allen Canyon, Cottonwood, Hammond Canyon, and Comb Wash — whenever a white man says something about them, tell them it's yours, that all canyons with running water are yours."[14]

Besides the mountains, canyons, and washes there were other sites important to the Utes. The area where Moab is today was called "The One That Bites," after the mosquitoes and horseflies that frequent marshy places there. Blanding was known as "Cedar Ridge" or "Thick Cedars"; White Mesa as "Land Lying Down from the Mountain," "Edge of the Cedars," "Place with No Trees," and also "White Mesa," because of clay deposits at its southern end. On the northern end of today's community, west of the water towers, is "Mourning Dove Spring," while in Westwater Canyon are "Coyote Nose" and "Moqui (Anasazi) Springs."[15] Bluff City, before the Mormons settled there, was "Down by the River," while neighboring Cow Canyon was called "Two Rocks." The rest area nestled in the bend of Highway 95 just below Comb Ridge was a favored camping area known as "Tall Cottonwoods." When the wind blows hard there, the Utes believe it tells of things that are going to happen.[16]

Hundreds of trails also crisscrossed the land. Billy Mike recalls that the most traveled trails led to the Towaoc area and southward to Navajo Mountain. Stella remembers that a main trail went from the San Juan River to Blue Mountain, and another took travelers from the east side of Blue Mountain to White Rocks, near the San Juan River, so that they could trade. Still another went from the La Sals to Sleeping Ute, most likely down Montezuma Canyon, with a network of other trails branching off.[17] In general, trail systems followed drainages or ridgelines when flat terrain was not available, with campsites appearing in a linear fashion along them.

Natural formations also had their names. The Bears Ears and Soldier Spring were direct translations. The former is said to be the first place that bears come out of hibernation in the spring, and where the Ute people held their first Bear Dance. Just north of the Bears Ears is a spring called "Flirting Around" (Na-gwitti-paači — "Look for Girl Friend") because while men hunted in its vicinity and the accompanying Elk Ridge, other would-be hunters would return to flirt with the women remaining in camp.[18] Elk Ridge was called "Big Bridge of Land"; Chippean (Čihppí) Ridge, near Blue Mountain, is Ute for "Water Bubbling Out." Valley of the Gods was called "Standing Rocks," and Monument Valley, "Rocks Jump Up." Deadhorse Point received its name when Ute leader Johnny Benow had his horses stranded there in deep snow and they starved to death.[19] Both Mancos

The Ute people consider themselves "mountain Indians," dependent upon higher-elevation resources for food, clothing, and protection. Following the movement of the deer they hunted, the Weenuche spent much of the summer in the cooler mountains. (Used by permission, Utah State Historical Society, all rights reserved.)

(Jim) Mesa and the Mossback Mesas ("Green Back Mesa") were said to have been "fortified strongholds" for the Utes, who in times of trouble barricaded themselves above the steep, rocky slopes and walls of these mesas.[20]

In 1908, while conducting a survey of rock formations in Natural Bridges National Monument, William B. Douglass asked the "Paiutes" he encountered if any of the arches and bridges had individual names. Old Mike, father of Jim Mike, told him no and then illustrated their collective title. "Bending over until his hands touched the ground, he explained the word meant 'Under a horse's belly between his fore and hind legs.' In other words, an arch or bridge."[21] Jim Mike, born in 1872, told his great-grandson Aldean Ketchum that arches served as portals to the spirit world and were the place of origin and end for whirlwinds. The wind itself is a form of spirit, so if a person wishes to communicate with the deceased, he should take an object belonging to that spirit and go to an arch such as Rainbow Bridge or Red Top Ridge in Allen Canyon and pray.[22]

The life of a nineteenth-century Ute, before intense white contact forced drastic changes, was tied closely to the rhythms of nature. The challenge was to be in the right place and time given the season, the land, and available resources. Organized in small family groups varying from one to ten families in size, these mobile bands hunted and gathered throughout their territory. Each of them had a leader, a man who was selected for making wise decisions about where to obtain food and how to keep the group out of trouble. As times changed and white settlers and cattlemen encroached on more and more land, these groups became bigger as pressure forced them into larger concentrations, primarily in Montezuma and Allen Canyons. Even after this time, however, the Ute people tried to follow an ancient seasonal pattern bound to the harvesting of plants and animals.

The Utes incorporated this natural cycle into their descriptive names for the seasons. Fall is "leaves turning yellow" or "leaves get dry—go hunting then"; winter is "heavy snow" or "hard times month"; spring, "snow melting" or "snow on one side of the trail" or "bear rolls over at this time"; and summer, "leaves coming out" or "much warmer for growing things." Three months had specific names: March, "warm days beginning"; April, "green grass appearing" or "bear goes out"; and May, "mother of the two preceding months." The Utes started their move back to the mountains at the time "when the doves sound soft," around June.[23] These views parallel the five colors that denote different ecological levels and their associated animals.

The spring is red, this is red weasel's domain. The summer is yellow, this is mountain lion's domain. It matches in with the mountains; it's appropriate for the folks to be up in the mountains, where the light of the sunrise hits first.... The autumn is characterized as white. Things are beginning to drop their leaves, beginning to lose their colors. Then the winter is characterized as black. Sort of lose all colors in the winter time when everything is black or white if there is snow.[24]

Not surprisingly, water and grass played a prominent role in this seasonal cycle. The people selected campsites based on the availability of springs, streams, and rivers for drinking water, grass for livestock, firewood and trees for shelter, and lower elevations to avoid the deep snows of winter. Just as the deer moved down from higher ranges in the late fall, the Utes followed the same pattern, descending to valley and canyon floors where shelter and more abundant food were available. Lola Mike recalls, "The Ute people lived all over the place. They traveled to different parts of the area like in the mountains where they would harvest chokecherries and pick piñon nuts, and just move around the area."[25] John Wesley Powell's observations support this assessment, pointing out that rarely

was a specific site occupied a second time, though the stream or grove or other natural resource that drew the Indians there the first time was used again; only the actual campsite changed. When the people departed, they did not destroy the bivouac site, but because they returned to the general area, it might give the impression that many more had been present than actually were.[26]

The Utes established winter camps in locations such as Montezuma Canyon, with its neighboring Cross, Squaw, and Benow Canyons; Dry Valley, Harts Draw; Beef Basin; Westwater and Cottonwood Canyons; Allen Canyon and Butler Wash; White and Douglas Mesas; and along the San Juan River—especially in the vicinity of Bluff, Sand Island, and McElmo Canyon. The east side of Comb Ridge, where the winter sun warms the rocks, was a favorite camping area that extended down Butler Wash all the way to the San Juan. Mariano Spring, near the southern end of Sleeping Ute, was known as "Salt Water" and was another winter camp where the snow did not last.[27] As the weather warmed and grasses appeared, streams such as La Sal, Deer, Coyote, Two Mile, Hop, Geyser, Taylor, and Beaver in the La Sal Mountains and Spring, North and South Montezuma, Cottonwood, Dark Canyon, Recapture, and Indian Creek on Blue Mountain poured off into the canyons. Numerous springs including Dodge, Paiute, Soldier, Chippean, and one at the top of Peters Hill also invited the Utes to scatter and camp as they searched for food.[28]

The historic record is clear that the Ute people also planted small gardens watered by seeps, springs, and creeks. Favorite places to cultivate small plots of corn, beans, squash, and melons were in Montezuma, McElmo, Paiute, and Allen Canyons, Indian Creek, and Paiute Farms. At the bases of Blue and La Sal Mountains, small check dams caught the runoff from snow and rain, holding it until needed. No doubt there were many other sites. While some plots were planted along the San Juan River, such as at Sand

Island, there were no large gardens like those achieved by the Navajos with their more sedentary lifestyle.

James T. Gardner, before sending survey parties into southeastern Utah in 1875, talked to Ouray, a Tabeguache Ute who was not from this area but was familiar with its people. Ouray explained that some of the "Sierra La Sal Indians" "farmed in the valleys on the east and west side of the mountains alternate years, and that this year [1875] they ought to be on the east side of the range," indicating how predictable this practice had become.[29] Later in the season, William H. Jackson and his photographic group accidentally allowed their mules to wander into Ute corn fields in Montezuma Canyon, raising the ire of the Indians who had recently fed these white men a meal of fresh corn. The survey parties later recorded: "Certain it is that we found Utes and Navajos settled by some little uncertain alkali springs, cultivating their patches of corn and melons with but small returns, while the broad, rich bottom-lands of the San Juan were entirely deserted."[30]

Animals played a crucial role in daily life. The Utes believed that at the time of creation men and animals talked to each other openly, but that as humans became increasingly insensitive and tarnished, they had been punished by not being able to communicate with other types of creatures. They no longer understood animals, although the animals understood them. There were some people who had the right attitude and could still communicate and control animals, but they were few in number.[31] Ultimately, the hunting process lay in the hands of the gods for "Tavwoats (or Tovwoats) made the legs for the country the animals must run in."[32]

Deer and elk were crucial in the Ute economy. As spring arrived, the Indians frequently moved their camps, ascending to higher elevations as the snow melted and the deer moved upward. During this time the deer "bunched," aggregating in groups as

large as 130 in a herd as they ate the sprouting green grass.[33] By the beginning of June they were in their summer range, munching forbs and grasses, while the Utes camped at nearby springs for long periods. With the advent of cold weather and approaching snow, the Utes left the summer ranges a month before weather pushed the deer down. Frank Silvey recorded a standard Ute phrase: "No wano snow; me go Montezuma Creek, Ute Mountain, me go."[34] But even the cold weather camps were not immune to snow. Bridger Jack once recalled, "When my grandfather was a boy, his people wintered in Dry Valley with snow so high," and he reached with his hand above his head to indicate a depth of more than six feet. The ponies all died, as did some Indians, before the weather let up.[35]

Deer were essential to traditional Weenuche lifestyle, comparable in many respects to the buffalo used by the Plains Indian tribes farther east. Food, shelter, clothing, and tools came from these animals found throughout the Four Corners area. Favorite hunting places for deer and other large game were Elk Ridge and the La Sal, Blue, Navajo, and Sleeping Ute Mountains, while pronghorn were hunted in the Dry Valley area. Men took deer and antelope in a variety of ways, including individual stalking, ambush, driving them over cliffs, running them down on foot or horseback, and using a call with a cottonwood leaf to imitate a fawn and attract a doe.[36] Hunters often went in pursuit of game individually, but in some cases a formal hunt chief might be called to organize and direct the activity.

Both before and after the hunt men showed proper respect for the game they pursued. Abstinence from sex before departure, a sweat bath before and after the hunt, and prayer encouraged success. A menstruating woman could not eat deer meat or she would contaminate the hunter, and for a long time he would not be successful in providing for his family. In order to reverse this problem, deer fat was rendered into oil and poured down the barrel of his rifle. The Little People might also hide deer from hunters. If they are believed to be in the area, one should not look at them but leave something useful that they will be happy to receive. Failure to leave food, a blanket, or a tool may result in paralysis from the neck down or death. If one does give a gift, good luck will follow long after the hunt is over.[37] Adoline Eyetoo believes that sometimes a deer may not want to die and so leads the hunter to a very dangerous place; however, if the hunter prays sincerely, it will allow itself to be taken.[38]

Once a hunter killed a deer, he butchered it in a prescribed manner, showing respect. The Weenuche way was to cut the animal from the chin down the abdomen to the anus. From there, the hunter made cuts to the inside of each leg, and from the nose to each antler and around it. The hunter skinned the head first, removing the skull but leaving the fur attached, and then completed the rest of the skinning.[39] He butchered the game where it was killed, placed a piece of the meat on a tree in thanksgiving, offered a prayer to the Creator that there might be continued good fortune, and kept the hide and spinal cord as part of his reward before dividing the meat with others. Hunters who did not plan to eat the meat immediately cut it into thin slices that were dried in the sun or over a slow fire. The women, after drying it, pounded and mixed the meat with grease and berries before packing it in parfleches, or rawhide bags, to be taken on trips or stored in alcoves.[40]

Edward Dutchie shared just how important this relationship with the deer still is. Before a hunter leaves home, he prays to the Creator and explains how he will treat the deer and use the meat. A specific prayer, one that has been passed down from previous generations, is used. "You can't put in a new word. There is no renewal in that. You will always use the same [prayer] that they told you to use." As he continued to explain traditional practices, his voice cracked, and tears

Edward Dutchie Sr.—veteran, councilman, and traditionalist—was extremely knowledgeable about the history and culture of the White Mesa people and a major contributor in preserving it. His relationship to the animals he hunted, and nature in general, exemplified the close bond the Weenuche Utes felt with Sináwav's creation. (Courtesy of Cletis Hatch)

welled up and trickled down his cheeks. He made no excuse for his feelings.

You're asking what we do, how we go about getting deer. Our [actions are passed] from generation to generation to our time. It is already [specified] how we are going to handle that deer, how we are going to do it…. You have the four directions to complete with the meat. Feed to the four directions [first south, north, east then west]. That is how my corners are set. That is how my corners are set. That is what I do with the meat. Cut four pieces, feed everybody—the universe—then I eat the meat…. It has got to be with prayers. You said that the deer is very important. That's how important it is to me. I shed tears when I talk about that deer, when I pray for that deer, that meat. It is going to be here in my home. Anybody that wants deer meat can come.... I grew up with those people who used to do that—grandpas and grandmas.... That is how they taught me about all the things that have been passed down to them from generations.[41]

Besides providing food, deer supplied hides that the Utes made into something useful or traded with other tribes, especially the Navajos. Everything but the eyes, which were removed following the kill, was used — the hide for clothing or shelter, bones and antlers for implements, and the hoofs for glue. The people prepared a deerskin by first soaking it in water and then stretching it over an inclined post so the hair could be scraped off. A serrated bone scraper fashioned from a deer leg was used to remove any flesh or fat, and then the worker rubbed deer brains into the hide, rinsed it in water, restretched it, and, if desired, rubbed it with either a yellow root or white clay obtained near Moab, or smoked it over a fire to soften and color it.[42] The woman tanning the hide chose wood that would give the color she wanted. Cedar chips turned the hide light yellow; cedar bark or greasewood, dark yellow; cottonwood, brown; and willow, black.[43] For a half hour the hide, stretched on a frame, rested in the smoke. Next, if it was for clothing, the hide could be fashioned into a shirt, pants, or dress and decorated with dyed porcupine quills or, later, trade beads.[44] Before cloth was available, deer and other animal skins provided clothing, moccasins, tepee covers, ropes, and sinew for cordage or to strengthen bows. Pressure flaking with an antler tip chipped razor-sharp arrowheads, knife blades, and spear points. Deer were the staff of life.

In addition to deerskin, the Utes made robes from mountain sheep, antelope, and twined sagebrush bark or yucca cordage with rabbit fur. Yucca sandals and soft-sole or hard-sole (buffalo skin bottom) deerskin moccasins covered feet in the summer, and skins with the hair left on inside with sagebrush bark leggings and padding provided warmth in the winter. Buffalo skins traded in from the Plains also created warm robes and sturdier material for clothing. Breechcloths of hide, fur, or bark, as well as dresses, skirts, and shirts also fashioned from hides or bark, were decorated with dewclaws, elk teeth, and trade shells. Men wore necklaces of bear, wildcat, and eagle claws, while bear teeth, juniper berries, bone tubes, fringed leather, and braided buckskin served as decoration on apparel. Trade beads eventually replaced dyed porcupine quills on shirts and dresses used for formal occasions.[45]

Before whites introduced cloth, beads, and other trade items, all Ute clothing and bodily ornaments came from nature. A description given in 1893 illustrates the Utes' dependence on animal skins as well as trade items for daily clothing during this period of transition.

The male costume consists of an undershirt of cotton, a long-sleeved overshirt falling to the knees, leggings of cloth or buckskin, a gee-string and moccasins. The overshirt is usually fringed at the neck, cuffs, and bottom, and generally the breast piece is made of double thickness. Should the overshirt be of buckskin, it is almost invariably painted, yellow being a favorite color. The leggings fit the limbs very close; they reach from the ankle upward to the beginning of the hips and are fastened to a belt that encircles the body.... [The gee string] is a strip of cloth or buckskin about eight inches wide, and from three to five feet long, that passes between the hips and hangs down in front and behind.... As an outer garment there is the invariable blanket which is worn almost constantly, winter and summer. The top of the blanket is passed over one shoulder and under the other, and is fastened around the waist by a belt; over this is worn the invariable cartridge belt and six-shooter, as all the Utes go armed....

The costume of the women consists of a dress that reaches from the neck to below the knees, leggings that reach from the knees to the ankles, and moccasins. They all wear very wide belts to which they hang their purses, awls and tools, and as outer garments they wear shawls or blankets. Some of their dresses are made of buckskin or tanned skin of wild mountain sheep. These skin dresses are almost always painted, and small bells and rattles are attached to them....

The men wear a great many ornaments, consisting of ear rings, finger rings, bracelets, armlets, breast plates, and hair ornaments.... [They] take good care of their hair, parting it in the middle and braiding it in two long queues... often wrapped in beaver or otter skin, and bear teeth and claws are sometimes tied to them. The women also part their hair in the middle but do not braid it, cutting it off so that it falls only to the neck.... Both men and women pluck out their eyebrows, and nearly all the men pluck out their scant beards, although an occasional one will indulge in a small mustache. The men paint their faces almost constantly, the women more rarely. On ordinary occasions a man will have his face painted in but one color, but for a dance, a council meeting or a ceremonial occasion of any kind, he will use many different colors and designs.... The women paint their clothing but little, and their face painting does not often go beyond round spots on the forehead.[46]

Animals that contributed to the Utes' diet included elk, desert bighorn and mountain sheep, wild turkey, rabbits, badger, porcupine, wildcat, beaver, and bear. Each was taken in their own ways. Hunters might surround mountain sheep, drive them to a peak, or stalk them wearing a disguise of skin, head, and horns. Rabbits were taken in communal drives or scared from hiding by burning brush. A stick could be thrust down a hole and twisted to catch the rabbit's fur and pull the creature from its refuge. Silvey recalls Indian neighbors drowning prairie dogs in their holes and then taking them to camp, where "they would roast them overnight — hide, entrails, and all — in hot ashes and coals, then strip off the hide with their long thumb nails, and eagerly eat them."[47] Birds such as doves and bluebirds, and insects such as cicadas, crickets, and grass-

hoppers added to the larder. The latter had their legs plucked before being cooked in a campfire and turned into a rich paste.[48]

Patty Dutchie's father, James Mills, served as a medicine man and used plants and feathers in his practice. She remembers his extensive knowledge of birds and how he used to trap them by placing some fat on a branch, putting a fine-twined string around it, and then waiting under cover. When the bird landed on the branch and began eating, he pulled the string, tightening it around the bird, which fell to the ground. He never killed his prey, but only plucked the feathers he needed and then released it.[49]

Bears were shown particular respect before being killed. Addressed as "Grandfather" or "Grandmother," they were smoked out of their caves or hunted in the open. When Utes encountered bears while picking berries, they talked to them and told them to depart; the bears seldom bothered them. These animals were believed to have their own furnished home, secured by a door, in which they stored roots and berries. Since Ute teachings explained that bears held the responsibility of presiding over all of the animals, they figured prominently in the hunting cycle. The Bear Dance, in addition to being a social activity held on the vernal equinox, also "authorized" the Weenuche to move from the lower areas into the mountains to begin hunting and gathering activities there. "You have to make sure you have a good treaty established with the bear. You see you are working cooperatively with the bear — sharing resources with the bear people. So the tradition is that the Bear Dance should be done on the first day of spring when bears are coming out of hibernation."[50] The dance, by following the movements given to the Utes by the bears, shows respect for what they have been taught and the human-animal relationship. There is also a belief that the first spring thunderstorm is the growling of the bear as it rolls over, arises from its bed of hibernation, and begins its quest for food.

Other animals also had special status, whether they were perceived as good or bad. Coyotes were "God's Dogs" and left alone.[51] After killing a deer, a hunter would plug its nostrils and lay its carcass on the hide. He could then drink the warm blood and roast milk-filled udders, elements not eaten from other animals.[52] Snakes demanded particular respect. As inhabitants of the underworld, they are dangerous, with powers that go back to the time of creation. One story tells of snakes meeting together with different colored ants in a contest to see who could hit a flat rock target. Yet there was danger from large animals such as deer and antelope protecting their territory. One antelope stood guard above the rest as a sentry. A small snake received the task of getting rid of this "enemy" and so went underground. Edward Dutchie, as he told this story, sang the snake's song as the reptile made its way towards its prey, popping up a number of times to see how close he was. The last time, he emerged by the sentry's hoof and struck between the cleavage. The antelope died instantly. "That's how powerful that little thing [snake] is and that is why we are careful of them. He's that way—we have to watch out for snakes."[53]

The conversation continued, Edward saying that when a snake crossed ahead on a person's path, it had to be moved or pushed aside, and the traveler would have to detour away from the initial direction. Before killing a snake, the person talked to it. "My Grandpa used to kill [snakes]. He said, 'I'm going to show you one thing. If you ever kill this kind, don't just jump over him. Take one step then jump over him. Then you won't see anymore snakes again.' So there's something about those snakes." The following conversation ensued between Edward and a snake he found in his yard. It was evening and his black dog kept barking, then hopping back. Edward approached, found a small rattlesnake "trying to get to my dog," so put it in a coffee can, brought it to a hill, tossed the can, and then went over and opened it, warning the snake not to return. He said:

"Next time, I know you now," I said. "I looked at you; your name is on me," I said, "and if I see you again, I'm going to kill you. It's going to be too bad for you. Go your way. There's plenty of country for you. You might have some food or water over there. Go over there. Go over there I said.… There's lots of food for you over there in the rocks [where] you can keep warm. Maybe there's some water down there. There are plenty of things out there for you. But you don't want it up there at my place. If somebody else was doing this, they might kill you. Let's be good friends.[54]

No more came around.

Utes also believe that one should not play with snakes or hit them because a "bad curse" will result. Although Patty Dutchie told of a cure her father had that was made into a tea and a poultice that "healed right away," this knowledge has been forgotten, and snakes are to be left alone.

The Utes in southeastern Utah ate fish, but information on their fishing techniques is sketchy. Accounts indicate that it was a male activity, but fish were part of the general diet, with certain restrictions. Southern Utes used weirs of willow screens to direct fish into shallow waters to be speared or shot with unfeathered barbed arrows. Fishing lines of braided horsehair with a bone, wood, or later a metal hook, as well as sumac nets, provided the angler with other tools for capturing his prey. If not eaten immediately, the catch was dried, placed in deer or elk skin sacks, and stored underground in a dry place for future use.[55]

While fish were not a mainstay in the Southern Ute diet like deer and other animals, they were important enough to be incorporated into some taboos. For example, for thirty days following childbirth, a mother could not eat meat or fish without spoiling her husband's chances of obtaining game. Likewise, if a woman ate fish during menstruation, she permanently damaged her male relatives' hunting ability.[56]

The Weenuche, until the reservation era put a stop to nomadic ways, had only a few types of domesticated animals. Dogs were important as pets, camp scavengers, and limited beasts of burden. Vicente de Zaldivar reported as early as 1598 how the Utes used dogs to move camp equipment.

> It is a sight worth seeing and very laughable to see them traveling, the ends of the poles dragging on the ground, nearly all of [the dogs] snarling in their encounters; to load them the Indian women seize their heads between their knees and thus load them or adjust the load, which is seldom required, because they travel at a steady gait as if they had been trained by means of a rein.[57]

By far, the most important beast of burden was the horse, which greatly enhanced mobility. Future chapters will discuss travel out onto the Plains, forays into what is now New Mexico and Arizona, jaunts to the Wasatch Front and Great Basin, and trips to southwestern Utah. Suffice it to say that mobility changed the Utes' way of life dramatically in terms of social, economic, military/political, and tribal relations. The Spanish introduced the horse to the Americas in the early 1500s, but the Utes did not have a real opportunity to adopt them until much later, the first documented instance being 1692.[58]

When the Weenuche were fully mounted on horses is open for debate. Some archaeologists believe that since they were the farthest Ute band to the west, this did not occur until the mid to latter part of the eighteenth century.[59] Until that time dogs continued to pull small travois or carry loads. The shift to an equestrian lifestyle carried the Utes into the twentieth century. This is not to suggest they became a part of the full-blown Plains Indian complex. As Ann Smith points out, "The true picture is that of one people with a basically Basin culture, with a veneer of Plains culture in Colorado, which becomes thinner (and more recent) as you move from the Southern Ute bands to the White River and on over into Utah."[60] Still, horses allowed larger factions to come together temporarily for seasonal economic and military purposes.

On the other hand, forage for horses limited the time groups could remain together, especially as herds expanded later in the nineteenth century.

Men and women both rode horses but had different kinds of saddles, the women's saddle having a higher cantle and pommel. The frame of the saddle was wood covered with hide and a stuffed pad for comfort. A rope around the horse's chin and in its mouth served as a bridle, leather hobbles restricted horses' movement at camp, and panniers were used for packing supplies. Utes used a fifty-foot, four-strand braided rope made of rawhide, buckskin, or goatskin with a knotted loop at one end for roping. They loved their horses, through which they gained status and wealth. Owners braided horses' manes and tails, shamans might decorate them with paint, and the animal's color provided a name. Colts were gelded at the age of two unless their outstanding qualities made them desirable as studs. Selective breeding by some, including Mariano of the Weenuche near Ute Mountain, ensured that desirable traits were passed on, with the owner receiving personal recognition. Others were not as careful and had smaller, inferior mounts. Still, Ute racetracks at Babylon Pasture, Chippean Ridge, the Bears Ears, and Allen Canyon attest to a tribal-wide interest in horse flesh. Women, however, often rode mares that were "lazy [and] sore-backed…with a large wide pack on tepee poles…the poor pony grunting along under the heavy load."[61] These were horses that had ended up being "slow pacers" but were suitable for pulling the family possessions packed on a travois.

The training of horses is done in two ways. The first is with an individual astride the "bucking bronco" until the rider obtains mastery. Silvey, from Monticello, describes a second technique that he observed around 1886.

> The Utes and Paiutes often break their horses when young (one or two years old) in the following manner: With a stout lariat around the colt's neck, they would select a springy sapling and

This Ute woman's saddle with the sheepskin beneath, photographed in Allen Canyon in 1935, shows the lingering influence of the Spanish. The high cantle and pommel are reminiscent of earlier saddles, hearkening back to the conquistadors and later Hispanic riders; men's saddles had a less pronounced cantle. (Special Collections, Sherratt Library, Southern Utah University)

about six feet from the ground, they would tie the other end of the lariat, thus giving the colt forty to eighty feet freedom before reaching the end of the rope secured to the sapling. Now two or three Indians would swing their lariats in a circle above their heads. This would frighten the colt and he would make a dash to get away from the whizzing, circling lariats. Coming to the end of the lariat at full speed, the colt would be thrown violently to the ground, again and again. This swinging of ropes by the Indians would be repeated until the colt would give up and stand with his head up ready to be bridled.[62]

Conditioned behavior to keep the head upright and to not run created a horse that could be easily caught by someone afoot.

Another domesticated animal, in addition to the dog and horse, was the goat. Unlike the Navajos, who depended heavily on sheep for food and wool but were relatively sedentary compared to hunters and gatherers, the Weenuche preferred goats when traveling long distances. Mobile enough to keep up with horses and tough enough to survive on a meager desert diet, these animals were at times the Utes' food storage on the hoof. Some warriors took them along on military expeditions. The Utes made little use of the hair, but goatskins provided leather. Later sheep came into the fold as reservation life became routine.

Women provided much of the food by gathering plants. Among the many edible plants harvested in southeastern Utah were pine nuts, chokecherries, yucca fruit, Indian ricegrass, wild onions and potatoes, sunflower seeds, bulrushes, serviceberries, and raspberries.[63] Herbs and plants grew along the rivers, in the canyons, and on the mountains, each ecozone providing its own variety of flora. Today Ute informants bemoan the loss of knowledge of plant use for both food and medicine.[64] Comb Wash was a favorite place for harvesting Indian ricegrass; the Bears Ears supplied pine nuts; and serviceberries in the washes along the San Juan River made a tart condiment for mush. Plants such as wild garlic, onions, carrots, potatoes, and sego lily provided variety to the diet. Roots baked in a pit lined with heated rocks and covered with grass made this food tender and easy to grind for making cakes to store. "More than a dozen kinds of wild berries—blackberries, blueberries, raspberries, strawberries, chokecherries, currants, gooseberries, juniper berries, buffalo berries, service berries, wintergreen, and squawberries—grew in Ute lands."[65]

One gets the impression that all the world was once a pharmacopoeia and storehouse. When sickness struck, Ute patients drank a tea brewed from sagebrush leaves, used boiled juniper berries to make a broth to fight colds, drank the liquid remains from boiling rabbitbrush to settle stomachaches, treated a sore throat by applying piñon sap boiled with grease to the neck or by chewing sweet anise roots, ate spearmint leaves and the roots and flowers of sandpuff to remedy stomach and bowel problems, and used the gum plant as cough syrup.[66] Nursing mothers who wanted to wean their children rubbed masticated sagebrush leaves on their nipples.

Men and women who understood the use of plants as medicine knew the proper way to treat herbs to maintain their healing properties. One important quality is that the plant be able to listen to the person picking it. Instead of just finding the herb and cutting what was needed, a healer observes a group of them growing nearby and selects a certain one to address. Patty Dutchie, whose father had this knowledge, remembers him naming the plant before breaking it off. "He used to go there to talk to that weed or plant. He used to pray. He said that the Great Spirit might be with you, that I'm gonna cut you and take you home, and then that Great Spirit might be with it, when I give this medicine to that certain person. That's how his prayers were. So he never used to break anything for fun. He used to have respect for all the plants because he was that kind of man."[67]

Stella Eyetoo, when asked to name specific geographic sites replied, "I don't know what they call it, because mostly they would name a place by the plant that grew near the spot. For instance, that area is known for its different herbal plants or yucca or green tea or rabbitbrush. These plants thrive when there is good moisture."[68] Ricegrass (*Oryzopsis*) rested at the top of the shopping list. This plant prefers dry, sandy soil, intense summer heat, and intermittent moisture. Found in the vast piñon and juniper zone throughout San Juan County, Indian ricegrass was easy to collect and to separate the seed from its chaff. By beating the seeds with a stick into a basket and then cracking the outer husk with a mano, the kernel was freed from the refuse, which blew away when winnowed. Since the plant could be

harvested by mid-June, before most wild plants bore fruit and corn had not yet matured, it was a welcome addition to the diet. Plant specialists who have studied Ancestral Puebloan dietary habits in this same geographic area conclude, "Indian ricegrass was probably the most valuable wild cereal harvested in our study area during prehistoric times."[69] No doubt the Utes also took full advantage of this plant's nutritional value.

Some wild plants offered a lifeline to survival. Prickly pear cactus (*Opuntia phaeacantha*) was one of the "starvation foods" that thrived during extremely dry periods and whose sweet fruit could be picked and eaten well into the winter. The stems were roasted in ashes, and the needles on the buds burned off. The seed pod, or banana, of the yucca (*Yucca baccata*) contains high-energy nutrition, while the plant itself can be used to fashion baskets and cordage. Its roots, when crushed and swished in water, provide a powerful soap and shampoo, and the tips of its leaves served as a comb. Indians ate chokecherries (*Prunus virginiana*) fresh, or dried them to concentrate their sugar before adding them to soups and mush or eating them plain. The Bears Ears was a favorite place to gather these berries, while Zeke's Hole Point was well-known for pine nuts.[70] Juniper berries (*Juniperus scopulorum*) were another persistent crop that grew regardless of weather. Harvesters picked them while young and ate them fresh, put them in stews, brewed them to make a diuretic tea, or cached them for later use.[71] Women and children also harvested currants, gooseberries, and rose hips, which they ate fresh or dried for storage in rock shelters, overhangs, or pits for the "starving time," around February, when preserved food supplies had diminished and game and plants were scarce.[72]

Ponderosa pine (*Pinus ponderosa*) also served as a food, particularly in times of emergency. Between the outer bark and the dense wood lies a thin layer of soft cell material called phloem that conducts water and nutrients to the living parts of the tree. In the spring the phloem is especially rich in nutritional material and easily scraped from the outer bark once it has been removed. A pound of this substance provides 595 calories containing 5 grams of protein, 139 grams of carbohydrates, 3 grams of fat, and 56 grams of crude fiber. High in calcium—equivalent to nine glasses of milk (2,740 milligrams, or 342 percent of the recommended daily dietary allowance)—as well as phosphorus, magnesium, and ten other trace elements, this food substance was used in time of plenty as well as famine.[73]

Three sites in Colorado with forty different trees harvested in this manner indicate that most of these ponderosas yielded their bark between 1815 and 1875, during which there were several droughts and the Utes were being pushed from their land.[74] Often the peeled or "culturally modified" trees (as the Forest Service calls them) are found in groves of thirty to forty now old-age ponderosa stands, most of which date back to the 1800s. Archaeologist Leann Hunt believes that "Almost every major area that has had large stands of ponderosa has stripped trees found in groves within it."[75] The problem with identifying these sites now is that many of the old-growth trees that bore these scars were logged during accelerated harvests in the 1950s and 1960s or they were burned in forest fires. Still, documented local sites include the La Sals in the vicinity of Ray Mesa and Buckeye Reservoir, and in the Abajos near Little Dry Mesa, Chippean Ridge, Dark Canyon, and Glade Pond north of Elk Ridge. Joes Valley, near Ferron, an area thirty miles southeast of Gunnison, and the Uncompahgre Plateau have similar stands, while the Ashley National Forest contains trees peeled between the 1920s and 1930s.[76]

When gathering this food, a woman would cut a slice at the top and bottom of the desired strip and with a pointed stick pry the outer bark away from the tree. With a split mountain sheep horn, a knife, or can lid, the worker scraped the phloem from the bark in strips, rolled them in balls or tied them in knots for storage, and wrapped them in green leaves to prevent immediate drying. To prepare it for consumption, a person would pound it thoroughly to break down the fiber and then boil, bake, or smoke it. An added benefit to removing the bark was the sugary sap that was immediately exposed. Edward Dutchie was very familiar with the process, recommending cottonwood trees and aspen over pine. "All you have to do is strip the bark off a branch, peel it away, and you will see a really thin layer. That is nothing but sweet. You just lick it if you want to. They used to have some kind of spoon or knife which they used to put it in with something to catch it [sap] in a bucket.... We used to use ponderosa pine too, but it tastes more of pine than cottonwood."[77]

A variety of other products also came from ponderosa pine. Resin and pitch served as adhesives and for waterproofing baskets. The inner bark and sap were turned into a poultice and also used as a tea to cure tuberculosis, stomach ailments, infections, rheumatism, heart problems, gonorrhea, and colds. It also "cleaned out" a person and could be added to soups as an extender, and to ground corn to make "pitch corn."[78] Northern Ute Clifford Duncan, in an interview with Forest Service personnel, recalled that his people peeled the pines for a ceremony related to "something that the women did" which was performed for his grandmother, but he could not recall specifics. He felt that these old scarred trees, as well as the young ones that grow beneath the "mother tree," should not be removed because of their sacred nature associated with ceremony.[79]

Other trees bore useful nuts and seeds. The most important one for food was the piñon (*Pinus edulis*). Thought of as a sister to the juniper (*pa-wáp*, or cedar) tree because it grows at the same elevation and in the same type of soil, the piñon (*wa'áp*) is viewed as part of a supportive family network.[80] The importance of this crop is underscored by the Pine Nut Dance, held at the autumnal equinox and serving as a counterpart to the spring Bear Dance.[81] "When there was a good yield of piñon nuts, only about once every six years, food value from the harvest of this plant would probably have exceeded that from all other wild species combined."[82] If the nuts were ripe, the Utes knocked them out of cones with a stick and then gathered and ate them raw, baked, or added to mush and stews. They were also stored in leather sacks. If the cones holding the nuts were green, they were burned open and then pounded with a rock on a flat stone. Women also ground the nuts and molded them into balls. Piñon gum, mixed with grease, fought infection by drawing out the poison from a festering wound. Acorns from the Gambel oak (*Quercus gambelii*) had to be leached several times to remove the tannic acid before being ground and added to cakes and mush. The Dutchies remember roasting the nuts after removing the shell, but they did not use the tannic acid that came from leaching the acorns for tanning hides as some Native American groups did.[83]

The Utes used different plants to manufacture various items. Weavers fashioned willow and sumac (also called squaw brush) into "Navajo" wedding baskets, winnowing and berry baskets, pitch-covered water jugs, bowls, and cradleboards. Sumac was preferred over willow because it was not hollow and so lasted longer. Its bark served as medicine for diarrhea, while "shoes like tennis shoes" were also fashioned from it.[84] Twined vertical rods formed the cradleboard with a basketry hood, all of which was covered with buckskin and decorated. Women either carried the cradle in their arms or used a strap across their forehead or on their chest. Blankets of fawn skin or rabbit enfolded the baby, whose shredded bark diaper was made from cliffrose or shredded juniper bark. The inside of juniper bark was woven into fabric to make stockings, leggings, and baby clothes if animal skins were not available, and it was

durable enough to wash. Bows made from oak, juniper, chokecherry, or serviceberry were smoothed by rubbing with a rock and then bound with sinew to give them a stronger cast. Arrow shafts, spears, axe handles, shelters, digging sticks, drills for fire making, tinder, cottonwood and oak bowls, as well as stirring sticks and spoons also came from plants.[85]

The storage of food, medicine, and other plant and animal products was another concern. The White Mesa Utes selected a spot that could be paced off from a specific object such as a rock or tree; they used a hand-fashioned grubbing hoe for digging. The pit was narrow at the neck but wide at the base and deep enough for a person to climb into. The digger hardened the sides with fire, making it rock solid, removed any debris, and lined it with juniper bark. Rawhide bags or gunnysacks of dried food were then lowered into the hole, and peeled oak logs or rocks were placed in recessed slots above the top of the opening. These were covered over with bark and dirt to make it flush with the ground and airtight. Livestock walking over the cache site quickly erased any trace of its presence. In February or March, when food stores were depleted, the owner of the stored goods returned, paced off the correct distance, and dug up the food, which was "just as good as the day you put it in there."[86] Patty Dutchie recalls Ancestral Puebloan ruins and cists also being used for storage after they were refurbished with mud to keep out bugs and rodents.

Shelter was another important concern for those living in this austere environment. Initially, the Utes built brush enclosures, often referred to as wickiups. The Weenuche continued to use them extensively even after they adopted the tepee. Length of occupation determined the amount of effort put into construction. One to be used for two to three days was usually small and not very carefully put together, whereas those built for winter were larger and tighter, and shed rain

A Ute wickiup, 1873. These shelters could be free-standing (as seen here) or set up against a tree or protruding limb. The side with the prevailing wind, or facing the direction of an approaching storm, was covered with waterproof material for additional protection. Note the woven basket and slim-necked water jar, as well as the corn and meat drying in the sun. (Used by permission, Utah State Historical Society, all rights reserved.)

or snow. A domed, circular summer shelter made of willows might be eight feet high and fifteen feet in diameter, covered with brush, with a door facing east. The conical house used in the winter had a four-pole construction, as did the later tepees. These structures were ten to fifteen feet in height, with a similar diameter, and covered with cedar bark or brush. The six-foot-high doorway usually faced east and was covered with a hide. Inside, beneath a smoke hole in the roof, was a foot-deep fire pit. Later a waterproof covering of cloth was occasionally added to the roof. The conical sweat lodge followed the same construction pattern, with the floor six feet in diameter and covered with bark, which also concealed the doorway. Hot

rocks placed in a central pit provided intense heat when sprinkled with water carried in a wooden bowl.[87] The structure remained in use as long as people occupied the camp.

Archaeologically, traces of wickiups are the central focus in determining Ute settlement patterns. These nuclear family household dwellings were large enough to sleep ten to twelve people, and were constructed of materials that can be found and dated, unlike the tepee. Since home was the woman's domain, it is interesting to note that "although Ute women are nearly invisible in the historical record, the archaeological record is written almost entirely from their presence."[88] Standing or downed collections of wickiups provide the oldest identifiable Ute camping sites, but their presence is hard to detect. Even in the Blanding area, where a study of Navajo and Ute campsites incorporated oral testimony about Utes who had lived along Westwater Canyon, no definite Ute sites were recorded. Tentative wickiup sites, as well as Ute-adopted hogans, were known to be in the area prior to 1920, but because of the ephemeral nature of the construction materials and the presence of Navajos, the task of finding Ute dwellings there proved impossible.[89]

The tepee followed a blueprint similar to that of the conical shelter but was transportable, more waterproof, and better suited to a mobile lifestyle. Adoption of horses made it possible. A Spanish account written in 1720 provides the earliest reference to Southern Ute tepees. "According to what is said, the Utes are to the north of Santa Fe about one hundred leagues distant more or less, and that they are like republics of itinerant nations who today dwell in one place and tomorrow in another, and carry with them tents of bison hide to camp when it occurs to them."[90] While the Weenuche adopted the tepee somewhat later and did not use buffalo hides for construction, they nevertheless had most of the Plains Indian technology associated with this type of home. Lizzie Jacket and Stella Eyetoo remember them being made out of elk skin, while Edward Dutchie recalled that elk skin was used for the bottom, "about a foot or a foot and a half high to keep the warm air in," with deerskin being used for the upper portion.[91] "On top it is deer hide. It's light to take down and put up." Women worked together to sew a ten-hide cover in two or three days, using sinew from the back of a deer or elk because it provided the longest thread. Canvas eventually replaced skin structures.

Women wrapped the cover around a ten- to twelve-pole frame, fastened the two edges with wooden skewers, and covered the entrance with a blanket or hide. Some people hung deer or antelope dewclaws on the door to notify the occupants that a visitor was entering.[92] The "ears" at the top could be adjusted to control the size and direction of the smoke hole, preventing winds from forcing smoke back into the structure. Pegs or logs secured the tepee's bottom skirt. The sides could be raised six inches to help draw the smoke through the hole at the top, and in the summer they could be raised three or four feet to let the air circulate under the cover while the breeze cooled those in its shade.[93] Edward remembers that the top parts of tepees, where smoke had darkened and burned into the hide, were used for moccasins because "when it gets wet, it doesn't get stiff when you use the smoked hides."[94]

Inside the tepee, the dirt floor would be covered with skins or bark, or left bare and swept with a brush broom. Beds of shredded bark or grass covered with deerskin lay around the periphery of the tent, with a fire pit three feet in diameter dug in the middle of the floor. The fire drew well as long as the door flap remained closed. Before retiring, the occupants put a big log in the pit and covered it with ashes so that the embers in the morning could be used to start the next day's cooking fire.[95]

Stella remembered her people also using dew cloths, or a liner, that extended from the ground to a height of five or six feet around the inside of the tepee. She noted that for the winter, the women sewed together flour bags and hung the liner to retain heat. Hides were used before cloth was available, and the liner was often decorated. The person setting up the tent ran a rope around the poles at the desired height and tied the top of the dew cloth to it, creating a dead airspace of three to six inches between the inner and outer material. This insulation kept the tepee warmer in the winter and cooler in the summer. Drips from rain, snow, and condensation ran down the outside of the dew cloth, the fire drew more effectively, sending smoke out of the hole at the top, and drafts were minimized. The dew cloth also prevented the casting of shadows at night, the thicker layer

The Utes in southeastern Utah adopted the Plains Indian tepees, which met their need for mobility. Originally made of deerskin or elk hide, these structures used dew cloths in the winter for warmth and had sides that could be raised for ventilation in the summer. The poles were used to adjust the "ears" so that smoke exited the dwelling properly. The parfleche, or leather envelope, in the foreground was used to carry things. (Used by permission, Utah State Historical Society, all rights reserved.)

screening observation from people outside. When a camp was on the move, the occupants often dispensed with it because of the extra effort required to tie it up. But any prolonged stay made it worth the time spent.[96] In later post-hunting and gathering years, as sedentary life became part of reservation experience, the Utes adopted Navajo hogans and sweat lodges, as well as frame houses, but they also continued to use tepees and conical brush shelters.

This generalized picture of Weenuche material culture in the nineteenth century was constantly changing. At the same time that Anglo goods were replacing traditional items obtained from nature, there was a commensurate loss of land and resources. Smaller hunting groups joined together in decreasing territory, which in turn forced them to try to survive on what white society willingly provided or take what they needed by force. A brief snapshot of the Utes in 1895, as reservation lands were proving inadequate, shows what occurred during the beginning of the reservation era, a decade and a half after some of the Southern Utes had given up their hunting and gathering ways, but when the White Mesa Utes remained free.

On January 5, 1895, Utah governor Caleb W. West sent two National Guard army officers, Captains John Q. Cannon and George W. Gibbs, to San Juan County to ascertain how many Southern Utes and "renegade" White Mesa Utes, who had never gone to the reservation, were present. This came in the aftermath of Indian agent Dave Day's invitation to the Utes to settle in southeastern Utah with the idea that the entire county would be turned into a Ute reservation. The governor, local cattlemen and settlers, and the federal government put a stop to this plan, but not before the Southern Utes from the Colorado reservations had already arrived. Cannon and Gibbs received orders in January to see if the Southern Utes had returned to Colorado and to "ascertain the number and location of the Indians therein and of their flocks, herds and horses and to what extent, if any they have depredated or are depredating upon the settlers; also further to ascertain the number of Southern Utes off their reservation found in said counties [Grand and San Juan], and the number of so-called renegade or Piute Indians."[97] What this provides now is very specific information as to winter camp locations, size, and composition, as well as herds of livestock and the integration of the local Indians with the Southern Utes. This report is one of the few instances where this type of information—especially about winter camps—is available.

Cannon and Gibbs traveled over nine hundred miles, splitting into two groups with local white guides for each. Word of mouth, travois tracks, chance encounters, and traditional camping spots provided the direction for each officer as they encountered bitterly cold temperatures, drifted snow as high as the horses' chests, and winter camping. But they did a thorough job. What they found was an extensive mix of "renegade," or White Mesa, people with the Utes from Colorado. The camps were small, ranging between a high of seventeen tepees and a low

of one, with most sites having four to seven. The area around Hart's Draw had three different camps, and there were other encampments twelve miles below Moab and in Dry Valley, Big Indian Wash, Church Draw, Church Rock, Photograph Gap, Monticello, Cottonwood Wash near Bluff, McCracken Mesa, McElmo Canyon, Beef Basin, Bug Park, Cajon Mesa, and Ruin Canyon. A total of 238 Southern Ute men, women, and children were recorded, and 125 White Mesa Utes. The former owned 1,779 "ponies" (as the Utes referred to their horses) and 1,225 sheep and goats, while the latter had just 132 ponies and 40 sheep. Leaders in the various camps included Ignacio, Mariano, Colorow, and Johnny Benow of the Colorado Utes, and Bridger Jack of the White Mesa group.

Resources and weather determined how the Indians eked out their existence. A few groups were pushed into sheltered areas to avoid the snow and to provide enough forage for the relatively large horse herd: one camp in Hart's Draw had 536, and another at the head of Ruin Canyon 400, with sheep and goats numbering 650. This latter group "intended to move up and down Cajon Mesa and further westward as their stock might demand, but their ponies will hardly need much moving, for scores of them are surely about to die of starvation." Food was just as scarce, and Agent Day hauled supplies to McElmo Canyon in Colorado to assuage the reservation Indians' hunger before they returned. As for the White Mesa Utes,

The renegades of the two counties named are a poverty stricken band and their condition generally is deplorable. There is absolutely no game to be had and any depredations they or the Southern Utes may make upon the cattlemen's and settlers' herds are easy to be accounted for. The Colorado Indians look fat and hearty and, in comparison with the other, are comfortably clothed; but their ponies are pitifully poor and hardly half of them will survive.

How the so-called renegades became this way is discussed later. For now it is enough to recognize that when the land was lost, in many ways so were the people.

In summarizing the hunting and gathering lifestyle of the Weenuche Ute before the extensive and permanent invasion of white people, one can see the importance of every aspect of the land in determining where and how the people lived. Even without the intruders, life was hard, the environment unforgiving. Plants, animals, topography, and weather were interrelated to an extent that demanded careful attention and a compatible belief system that taught the Indians where to go and what to do with what was available. When Billy Mike said, "It was as if the land owned us," he spoke as a witness born from experience. Nature was a tough taskmaster, but the Utes had learned its lessons well.

CHAPTER 3

Daily Life in an Austere Environment

Weenuche Beliefs and Life Cycle, 1880s

Nature held the deepest beliefs they had. From nature they knew what to do, how to act, how to have their mind set straight so they can think well and think better towards their people. Nowadays, it seems like they don't care for each other, but at that time, people used to care for each other a lot.

Patty Dutchie

The Weenuche people living in the last half of the nineteenth century had already undergone extensive change since the first white contact, introduction of the horse, and losses of land to both white and Native American groups. New traditions and beliefs lay on the horizon as the twentieth century loomed, yet many of the old ways were still practiced. What follows is a reconstruction of daily life, or the life cycle, of the White Mesa and Ute Mountain Ute people. Some Northern Ute sources are used for additional information since only "slight differences exist between the groups in social and political organization whereas almost no differences exist in ceremonial organization, and in measures of shamanism they are virtually identical."[1] From birth to death, these people remained dependent on the land and its resources while carving out a distinctive lifestyle that strengthened families, provided for social and economic needs, and fostered a belief system adapted to the Four Corners region. From the first cry to the last breath there was no question as to the value of Ute heritage. "Nūche" was a distinctive title that set them apart from all other Native American groups.

Beginning with conception, a Weenuche life assumed a characteristically Ute approach. Once a woman became pregnant, she and her husband followed a number of regimens that bonded the two in a parental relationship called the couvade. Both practiced certain restrictions even before the birth. Animals such as mountain lions, badgers, bobcats, and foxes believed to have strong supernatural powers were not eaten by her or hunted by the husband lest the baby die. Eating beaver might cause a blockage in the woman so that her water would not break. Intercourse during pregnancy with a second man could create twins, a portent of bad luck and a disgrace. Fattening foods caused a baby to grow too large so were avoided. Other taboos associated with pregnancy included sitting any place on or near a gopher hole, laughing at strange animals or jokes, playing cat's cradle, and viewing blood from a violent incident. Knowledgeable people could determine a baby's sex before birth by viewing the mother's abdomen: a flat one foretold of a girl, a round one a boy.[2]

Birth, according to traditional practices, took place inside a non-dwelling tepee or conical-shaped, cedar bark birthing hut. Women served as midwives, although the husband or a medicine man could assist in the case of a difficult delivery. The helpers drove a stake or pole into the ground and then swept the area around it clean, covering the floor with grass or bark. The expectant mother squatted or kneeled, grasped the pole, and pushed with the contractions. If problems arose, a woman behind her encircled the mother's midsection and squeezed when necessary. The fire in the tepee kept the temperature uncomfortably hot as women boiled water and assisted in the process. The baby's arrival called for the cutting of the umbilical cord—a part of its previous life—with a flint or obsidian knife or arrowhead; the midwife then coaxed the placenta out with the palm of her hand, took it outside, and either buried it or placed it in a tree so that the person would be like the tree, sturdy and strong.[3] She might also place the cord in a small pouch beaded or painted with protective designs that were repeated on the infant's cradleboard. Part of the cord could later be brought to an anthill and left there after the person offering it had prayed and talked to the ants. This encouraged the baby to be industrious in the future.

Following the initial washing of the newborn, one of the women covered it with red earth paint made from powdered rock mixed with grease. The midwife next "shaped" the infant's head and "stretched" its limbs before wrapping it in a rabbit fur blanket. The first cradleboard was small and plain, and might not have a wood backing, but when the child required a larger one, the sex determined the color: a girl received a yellow cradleboard, and a boy a white one. An aunt or grandmother would make the board, "putting a lot of work into it, beadwork, and a lot of thoughts and prayers."[4] Cattails and cedar bark served for diapers. In some instances a hole in the exterior cover allowed boys to urinate, while a girl was given extra padding for her needs. A special prayer was offered,

presenting the child to the four directions, by an older woman for a girl, and an older man for a boy.

> He [the elder] had to hold it up and present it to the creation, that here was a new spirit, a new being that came into the world for the creation, for the four directions. It is the grandfathers and grandmothers you know like that and spirits of mother earth, grandmother and the mountains, we call them, they're all part of this world. And they offer that child to them and say here's the [one] to be recognized as an introduction to the creation.[5]

The mother and father continued to follow their prescribed activities after the delivery. The mother rested on a bed built over a pit with hot coals or stones covered with sand, boughs, and blankets. Each day for a week the father renewed the warm bed and slept separate from his wife, though nearby.[6] Several women from White Mesa recall hearing of this practice. Stella Eyetoo remembers hearing of "Alice May's mother, Henry May's wife," lying on a bed of heated ashes covered with dirt following the delivery. She slept too long on the bed, the heat roasted her buttocks, infection set in, and she died. This happened before Stella was born.[7]

The new parents drank only warm water so that all of the excess blood associated with the delivery drained from the mother. For thirty days they did not eat meat, fat, or salt, or scratch their head with the hand, using only a twig lest their hair fall out. Shortly after the birth the husband was free to be out and about completing his usual tasks, but the mother remained confined for a month. She did not touch her hand directly to her face, even during pregnancy; to do so caused white splotches or liver spots. If they appeared, rubbing some of the baby's excrement on them made them vanish. An expectant mother also could not sew or do beadwork because the movement of the needle or awl could cause the umbilical cord to tangle around the baby; however, a woman did a lot of handwork after the baby was born so that she would not become lazy.[8]

The father, with the mother in confinement, did many of her chores of hauling firewood and water, and other tasks. He did not gamble, smoke, or ride horses, but remained around the birthing hut with his wife for ten days, until the remainder of the child's umbilical cord fell off.[9] Once this time of special activity ended, a grandfather would come to the father's dwelling, cook a meal of meat for him, and say, "After you eat, you can be like me and live long to an old age and be strong. You can be a good hunter. Take care of this wife and child. Shoot plenty of game. Let us teach this child the right way to do everything and bring him up the right way.... But your wife is not out yet. When she comes out, we will return and tell her the right ways. My wife will tell her."[10] While many of these practices depended on individual beliefs and were not followed by all, they do emphasize the importance of bringing new life into the community.

A day after the child entered the world it began to nurse, a practice that continued for two or three years. If the mother could not produce enough milk, a "wet nurse" might help, and in extreme cases an animal could substitute. Patty Dutchie learned of her grandmother's rearing when still an infant.

Patty Mills Dutchie was born at Navajo Springs, Colorado, and later married Edward Dutchie from White Mesa. Raised in a traditional home, she once told an interviewer, "Deep inside of me, I'm still with my old ways.... I always dream about my old times of wandering, roaming, walking, horseback riding, and all the free time I had at home." (Courtesy of the Utah Arts Council)

She [Patty's grandmother] believed the Great Spirit gave her the [holy] songs because he had pity for her because she was raised as an orphan. Her mother died when she was about four or five months old. At that time there were no white men, no milk, nothing. They didn't know what to do with her. They knew babies needed lots of milk. So Grandma said her aunt had a horse that was raising a colt. They had to wash the nipple of that horse and then feed the baby. The horse raised her. They had to have the horse there all the time with them in order to raise that baby. So that is how she was raised. "It is really pitiful that I grew up this way," she said. "I don't know my mother. I don't know my father. So I am glad today I'm living. The Great Spirit pitied me. This is the way I am. I never throw away my faith in nature," she said. So that is how she was raised and that is how she got her songs and her beliefs. She deeply believed in the Great Spirit.[11]

The child received a name after a month, when the mother left the birthing hut. The parents bestowed the name for an action, a characteristic, or an animal, bird, or plant, and then added a diminutive such as "little," "small," "young," etc. Adult names dropped the diminutive, so "Little Rabbit" became "Rabbit" when the boy or girl became a man or woman. Often a male received an animal name, and a female one associated with a flower or plant. The name would be kept for life unless a shaman changed it during a ceremony to cure an illness. As a person moved through childhood into maturity, he or she might have several nicknames given by friends or relatives because of a deed or characteristic.[12] Bertha Groves, a Southern Ute mother, recalled that if a person had a dream or vision or something unusual happened to her, that might also bring forth a name. "Maybe a hawk flew over head or a butterfly or something like that came into where they had it [baby] in the tepee, a bird or something the people noticed. That was the guardian spirit of the child."[13]

While many of these names have been forgotten, tribal censuses between 1915 and 1931 recorded some in phonetic Ute, providing an illustration of how people of White Mesa and Montezuma Creek were named. Those named for notable physical characteristics include: "A Long Time Before He Learned to Walk" (Joe Bishop's little boy), "Cross-eyed" (Arthur Dutchie), "White Stick Lady" (Olive Maxwell), "Slanted Eye" (Anson Cantsee, also known as Scotty [pronounced "Sketty"]), "White Eyebrows" (George Eyetoo), "Left Handed" (William May), "Goatee" (Jesse Posey), and "White Stomach" (John Dutchie). Others had names that required more imagination or knowledge of the individual: "Jack Rabbit" (Francis Posey, because he was tall), "Tumbleweed" (Joe Bishop), "Big Spoon" (Edward Dutchie Sr.), "Two Guns" (Harry Dutchie, because of what he wore as a tribal policeman), "Beaver" (Harry Lang, since he worked with E. Z. Black on developing irrigation ditches), "Metal Buttocks" (Jack Sanup), "Star" (Pochief Mike), "Gnats" (Tahzhuni or Taahšuni ["Pretty' in Navajo], Baby Deer's wife), and "He Has Tail Feathers" (Jack Ketchum). The family name Cantsee came from a translation of the Ute word kmaái'wą, which means "blind"; "ketchum" was a common English word used by the Utes to mean "go and get"; "Mike" came from maiq, which is a greeting comparable to "hello" or "how are you doing," while "Dutchie," because of

partial Navajo ancestry, probably originated from that language's word táchééh, meaning "sweat lodge."[14]

The community, not just its immediate family, accepted and raised the baby, but "it was Sináwav who first showed the Ute people how to raise their children."[15] Many felt a commitment to watch and train the child during its life. The Ute language captures the different developmental stages of childhood with terms for "new-born infants, small baby, little child, child before puberty, pubescence and maturity. Parents and the entire extended family trained and guided the children, cherishing them as they grew."[16] Family members followed a permissive approach, allowing children to explore and learn for themselves what the world held. Grandparents played a major role in teaching children, since mothers and fathers were intimately involved in the daily tasks of survival. Grandparents often received these children as their own to help with the chores and to train. Unless danger threatened, learning through observation and trial and error taught children the importance of studying a situation before jumping into something new. A comforting hand or a gentle word came from parents and siblings, but once old enough to understand, sarcasm often directed children in appropriate behavior. Toilet training was relaxed, respect for elders was taught, and different skills learned. Older children were warned to behave or they might be kidnapped by a witch and carried off in a large burden basket.[17]

Boys and girls wore their hair parted down the middle and left hanging straight or in braids. Beaver or otter skin wrapped around each braid was later replaced by red cloth after Anglo trade items entered the economy. Children after the age of four had their earlobes pierced with a metal awl, the hole held open with a piece of greased wood. Boys and girls played together until around the age of six or eight, when the girls gave up their clay dolls and miniature horses to

These two women are dressed in clothing typical of the 1870s and 1880s. The one on the left has dentalium shells sewn as a yoke, and her beaded belt and moccasins are decorated with customary Ute designs. The fringed buckskin dress worn by the woman on the right, with beaded shoulder and arm strips, is a good example of the finished, tanned hide work for which the Utes were famous. (Special Collections, J. Willard Marriott Library, University of Utah)

prepare for future roles, learning different skills from their mothers while assisting with chores and child care. Young boys began to sharpen their skills in horseback riding, hunting, target practice, and feats of daring in anticipation of becoming warriors and providers.[18]

A normal day started with prayer. As the sun rose, individuals faced east, motioning with their arms in the four directions without turning around. They prayed as they received the first light, for it was "the beginning of our life. When we get up, it is the beginning of our first step, first word, first look, first breath. We stretch ourselves and get ready to do good work. It is all coming in with that daylight."[19] In the evening similar motions

were made and similar prayers offered as the people addressed the Creator of All Things. "The light, sun, moon, stars, and earth we walk—with all of nature and nice things growing. He is the one that turns the earth, changes the seasons, and puts different coats on it. That is what they used to pray to, those old people, before the white man brought this paper over—the Bible."[20]

John Wesley Powell noted that at dawn, the leader of a Ute group would call upon his people to listen to his words. They did not cluster about but sat by their fires and absorbed his instructions. If there had been quarreling in the camp, those involved were to become friends; a special activity for the day, such as hunting and gathering, would require hard work and cooperation; and future travel would be outlined. The elders would agree, telling the youth to listen, that "the talk is good."[21]

Activities such as berry picking, collecting piñon nuts, or harvesting other crops from nature's bounty brought young and old together for a common good. Cowboy Henry McCabe watched Utes living around the east fork of the Dolores River as they gathered berries and cut tepee poles in the 1880s. Upon arriving at the best spot, the men set to work chopping tall lodgepole pines, stripping the bark, and tying them together upright against a living tree. This ensured they would season and remain straight. Poles cut the previous year, now lighter and ready for use, were taken down, secured to the horses' backs with the butt end dragging in the dirt, and hauled home, wearing several inches off in the transport. McCabe noted the Utes liked a tepee to stand tall but were not concerned about any length worn off the pole. Often a collection of poles was left at a favorite camping spot, ready for use the next time the people returned. In the meantime, women and children set about gathering berries.

The papoose would get into the berries that were drying while they thought their mothers were too

A Ute tepee. Before canvas became available, a dozen elk or deer hides were sewn together, placed around the pole frame, and then smoked inside to waterproof the material. Once the tepee was no longer serviceable, hide near the smoke hole was cut into moccasin soles because of its water-repellant qualities. (Special Collections, J. Willard Marriott Library, University of Utah)

busy to watch them. It was so much easier for the papooses than picking their own berries would have been. They were caught in the act of eating the berries quite often and from the sounds that they made, I'm sure they felt real sorry that they had been so lazy and were sure that they wouldn't be guilty of stealing berries again. The Indians had picked and dried berries in that location for a long time. They had come every year for as long as the oldest ones could remember. They said that we were welcome and I have often wondered if it had been white people there picking the berries, just how welcome we would have been. The Indians were far better neighbors than some white people. They gave me buckskins that were as soft as a cloth. They had tanned the buckskins themselves.[22]

Just as there was division of labor in tasks, there was also division of space in the home.

Bertha Groves explained that living in a tepee followed specific rules. As a young girl her place was on the south side, the men's area was to the west, and the women were on the north, with a fire in the middle and beds on the outer circumference. The women's area held the food since that was their responsibility, while wood and water was stored in the south since the children hauled that. A child understood that play inside the tepee was forbidden and that each person's space was honored by staying in their own part. A person entering the tepee lifted and pushed the flap to the south and then moved in a clockwise circuit around the interior; when exiting, the individual pushed the flap to the north, keeping the "traffic from bumping into each other. That was the rule; that is the way it was made."[23] In later years, when hides were no longer available and canvas could not be obtained, the women made tepees out of muslin—often from one-hundred-pound flour sacks—creating a double wall of material with a dew cloth for added insulation.

A primary means for teaching and maintaining cultural values came from stories. Raconteurs told certain narratives only in the winter so as not to offend the animals mentioned. Tales about witches and their evil deeds or trickster stories instructed the children in appropriate behavior and of consequences for misbehaving. Edward Dutchie, after telling the story of Sináwav letting the people out of the sack, said that it was one saved for winter, that it was a "man's story," and that women were not supposed to listen. He then advised that when it is being told, the men are not supposed to have their legs out in front of them, but turned to the side. By doing this, when one gets old, they will not have trouble with their legs. To Edward, who had been raised with these teachings, there was real power in them.

> This is a man's story. I don't know how the women tell the story, but it gets down deep in men. Women and men love like that and there are a lot of songs that go along with it. You talk about Rabbit or Bear or any kind of animal—there's a song that goes with that. You have to sing those songs while you tell that story. When you get to Coyote, he also has a song that you have to sing. Birds too—about the time that the birds talked—there are stories about them too. They sing words about what is taking place. Just like the Utes, they have spiritual songs. Songs about the end [of the world].… All the songs are connected to those kinds of things. Today she [Patty] and I see all those things happening, along the coast and all over the world. We heard about it through the songs of the old people, like rabbits, all the small animals and snakes. Some Indians could tell a story like a comic book.[24]

Each camp had a number of storytellers who shared their knowledge. They passed their legacy down to the next generation on winter nights, when most of the stories were told. Edward suggested that this process usually started after the first snow, the same time that hand games of chance began. In spring both activities stopped. One narrative may take an entire evening with a lot of people listening. "You can't go around and tell several stories in one night. One man will tell a story. The next night another man will tell a story, and so it goes on like that.… But now they play that hand game [and tell stories] all twelve months of the year. Maybe that is why the rain does not come to us. We are misusing one of our religious ceremonies."[25]

Because many of these legends are about animals, some outsiders believe them to be cute children's stories without much cultural significance. Linguist James Goss believes it is just the opposite.[26] One finds a rich system of beliefs in the following paraphrase of a lengthy tale Goss tells. In it are four main characters—Sináwav ("Older Coyote"), Yugupits (Yogópiči—"Younger Coyote"), Tugupits (Tukupiči—"Mountain Lion"), and Unupits (a cannibal spirit).

In the story, Older and Younger Coyote leave camp and hike up a long mountain ridge hunting deer. Four times Older Coyote is ready to shoot, but Younger Coyote speaks and scares the game away. Finally Older Coyote shoots a deer, but by now it is late in the day, so they secure the game in a tree without eating any of it and build a brush shelter so they can stay until dawn. In the middle of the night Younger Coyote awakens his brother, complaining of his hunger, but after being warned not to go outside, he does anyway. Older Coyote hears a terrible fracas in the dark but waits until morning to view the blood-spattered ground and to search for Younger Coyote. He returns to camp, tells his father, Mountain Lion, what happened, and then accompanies him back to the scene of carnage, where they had spent the night. A noise outside arouses Mountain Lion, who springs to action and kills the cannibal spirit that had eaten Younger Coyote. The next morning he cuts the monster open, removes all the bits and pieces of his dead son, urinates on them, and brings him back to life. The three then return to camp.

What this story illustrates is, first, a family system with a hierarchy established by age. One learns that the older the person (animal), the greater the respect; the younger a person, the more foolish and less prone to follow traditional practices. When a question arises that cannot be solved, one should go to the elders, in this case the father, for a solution. Older brothers hold the responsibility to teach, and the younger ones to listen, a point Younger Coyote struggled with. Another teaching derives from the two brothers being too far up in the mountain to return to their camp, and since one does not wander around in the mountains at night, they had to stay where they killed the deer. They did not cook any of the meat because that was a woman's duty. Thus, one should not overextend and get caught in a situation where it is difficult to return to camp. Goss, commenting on this, says, "The pattern was to go up a ridge until noon, and if you didn't get your game, you should cross over to the next ridge and come back down that ridge and hunt that ridge on your way back down. So that is the standard hunting pattern that the Utes still practice."[27] Stories like this established proper behavior and traditional teachings for all ages.

As a child entered teenage years, societal roles became more clearly defined. Traditional beliefs recognized the importance of four as a sacred number. There are four seasons, four directions, four parts of a day, four elements (air, water, fire, and earth), and four divisions of life. For a girl this meant moving from a time of limited responsibility to the teenage years and potential parenting, thus leaving the first stage. The second stage is brief, preparing her for the third, adulthood, before reaching the fourth and final stage of old age. Menstruation, or her first "moon," was an unmistakable change of status. Philo-

sophically, blood is life, and women are given the power to create it. The "moon" becomes a cleansing process within the cycle. "Blood is life and it is really powerful and precious, so how you deal with it is [important].... The girl left her childhood behind and is ready for the woman part now."[28]

Menstruating women would stay for three or four days in a brush hut located a short distance from the camp. After a girl had her first menses, she no longer had to remain alone but could join other women in similar circumstances. The hut was large enough to stand in, roughly eight to ten feet in diameter, and made of willows in the summer and interlaced cedar (juniper) in the winter that repelled the cold.[29] The Utes called this structure a "separate home" and built a new one each month as needed. Since most nuclear families would use one, some archaeologists suggest that in an era when family brush shelters and tepees were prevalent, these menstrual huts might be dependable diagnostic structures to determine if an abandoned site was used by the Utes or some other Native American group; others, like the Navajos, did not require isolation.[30] Adoline Eyetoo recalls these huts in use in Allen Canyon and how the women used yucca root soap to cleanse themselves after separation.[31]

Greater significance is attributed to a female's first "moon" than subsequent ones. The girl is secluded for four days in a separate menstrual hut while her mother, grandmother, and aunts attend to her needs and protect her from unwanted suitors, afterward receiving a gift from the girl. During this time they also teach her about womanly tasks, care for her hair, and bring her food—a special diet that excludes meat. Other practices highlighted eating cooked yucca fruit, drinking limited water (which must be warm), and not sleeping during the day. Menstruating women must use a wooden stick for scratching; cleanse her face with sagebrush leaves; avoid gazing at departing warriors; shun hunters, fishermen, and gamblers; and steer clear of cohabiting with a man or else illness or death might follow. During her first "moon," a girl would run early in the morning toward the east for four days and also take long walks with an old woman. Work was also a necessity. The young girl would carry wood, fetch water, gather plants, prepare plant food, grind corn, weave baskets, and process hides.

At the end of the four-day period, an old woman would give her a warm sponge bath, fix her hair, change her clothes, and rub her with a sagebrush bough. The first meat that the girl ate following her seclusion was chewed with sage or juniper leaves; she would give some of this meal to the woman who bathed her. The young woman, as part of a rite of passage, was also allowed to go alone to pick berries or dig roots, signifying that she had become a provider, was independent, and was ready to assume adult tasks. She returned with the fruits of her labor, was bathed and blessed by a relative, and gave away the plants she had found. As the young woman continued to mature, subsequent moons followed a modified list of prohibitions that included seclusion, food taboos, and avoiding hunters, gamblers, and the sick.[32] There are some indications that men took this opportunity to visit women who were in seclusion. There is also a hint that if things were not going well for a married woman in her home, this separation provided a respite.[33]

A boy's rite of passage in adolescence was much simpler, with a grandfather or uncle or his father taking him hunting big game for the first time. After killing a large animal, but before eating its meat, the young man had deer intestines placed on him, the deer's diaphragm slipped over him, and then his mother or an old man or woman bathed him. The boy obtained the qualities of the animal killed: "if a deer, he became a tireless hunter; if a coyote, he was henceforth crafty and clever; if a mountain lion, powerful and stout, a cunning stalker of game."[34]

The young man would give the meat to the old man to ensure his own long life, and the mentor would paint the young man red. He was then ready to assume the role of a hunter, following a prescribed procedure for killing and butchering animals, and also to begin courtship.[35]

A successful Ute hunter would keep part of the animal he had killed but distribute the rest to the members in his party. The person butchering the deer or animal cut it in such a way that it could be a balanced load on a horse. There were two different practices associated with the unused remains. One was to clean all of the meat off the bones, place the entrails and bones in a neat pile, and leave them for animals to use. Another taught that any meat that could not be eaten, as well as the animal's entrails, should be thrown high in a tree or bush so that meat-eating animals could not get it. "If an animal that makes its living by killing other animals could get these remains and eat them, the hunter would have a hard time finding any more game in the future. [Also], if a hunter came into contact with a woman's blood or if a woman had eaten meat during her menstrual period, the animals would be able to smell the hunter or know that he was coming and he wouldn't be able to kill them."[36] Jack Cantsee suggests that if women and children come in contact with the residue from the deer, its power could affect them by making them wild, "running around out there when the deer start running."[37]

Both men and women purified themselves in sweat lodges but did it separately. The structure could seat four or five people comfortably. Once the participants heated the stones, they pushed them into a foot-deep pit, entered, and pulled the hide or blanket door covering closed. The bathers might loosely stuff their nostrils with soft cedar bark, and men would tie their penises with some type of string for protection from the intense heat created by water poured on the hot rocks. Songs and prayers followed. The purpose of the sweat was to physically cleanse, to share a social occasion with friends, and in some cases to heal the sick. In this instance, sagebrush would be placed on the hot rocks for a pungent odor. The sick person might be accompanied by an assistant or a healer as part of the process. The Utes believe that sweats can cure ailments such as rheumatism, fever, and venereal disease, as well as provide a sense of general well-being.[38] Adoline Eyetoo suggests that prayers said in a sweat lodge are more powerful than normal ones.[39] Another purpose of a sweat was to offer instruction. Edward Dutchie paints a vivid picture of a sweat with his father.

> My first understanding came around my teenage time. My grandpa was talking about sweats; I didn't answer him but he said, "Let's go." [Edward describes the hut like a "little hogan" that was airtight once they covered the doorway with blankets.] He had a stick with three branches that were cut up like a shovel to haul the rocks into place. When we got in, that thing was hot. It was hot. He had his own way of talking; he was a medicine man. He had different types of grasses and some kind of roots. He put them on that thing [heated rocks] and it would smell. He didn't use water on it like this generation.... He had several songs to sing and a long prayer with them. It affected me and he didn't mind, but I wanted to go out. He had these long songs and long talks too. Finally he said he wanted to go out. I was weak by the time I got to leave.... He had been singing some kind of medicine songs. He knew eight songs completely, long songs, and in between places he had to talk, too. That was his way of doing it. That was passed down to him by his grandpa or father because he was Ute.[40]

Following the sweat, when everything had cooled, a plunge in a cold stream or lake — or, if there was no water, a rub with sand — concluded the event.

Social contact between potential marriage partners became formalized during the Bear Dance, a distinctively Ute occasion that

The Bear Dance, specific to Ute culture, is a continuing source of pride and entertainment, and open to all who wish to participate. Held each fall at White Mesa, the dance draws community members and travelers from near and far to join in the celebration. (Courtesy of White Mesa Ute Council, 1993)

lasted three or four days and nights. Characterized today as a purely social event, this dance once held significant cultural meaning. The dance's origin is based in a story about a hunter who remained in the mountains too long, after the fall hunt ended and the people had left the mountains for their winter camps below. A female grizzly bear found the hunter tramping about in the snow, captured him, and then forced him to hibernate with her all winter. She taught her captive many things before the vernal equinox arrived, heralding the first day of spring. Before releasing him, she warned that he should tell the people to stay out of the mountains in the winter, but on the first day of spring they should pay homage to Bear, who watches over and controls the high country and its resources. The dance she taught, the Bear Dance, was to remind the Utes of their relationship with Bear, keeper of game, and to signal the time that they could return to the mountains for hunting and gathering.[41] In the spring, when bears came out of hibernation, the Utes killed one. Its spirit was an honored guest at the ceremony/dance, where they ate its flesh as a sacrament.

The circular brush enclosure, or corral, used for the Bear Dance represents a microcosm of the Ute world, as well as a bear's den (*ivikwi'yakat*, or "cave of sticks") whose entrance faces east, where the sun and new life appear. The west symbolizes the earth and change and is associated with thunder, lightning, rain, and the growl of a bear. Inside the corral the men form their dance line along the northern quadrant of the circle; the women form a facing line on the south side, with both extending along an east-west axis. During the dance the women's line of the south meets the men's line from the north, depicting "the balance of forces [and] emphasizing the feminine principle of life-giving nurture and fertility."[42] Participants' health and the recognition of young women now capable of bearing children are other reasons for holding the dance.[43] The singers providing the music sit on the west side, where, in older days, a pit with a resonator amplified with a notched rasp called a morache (*muurači*), meaning "metate," or grinding stone. This instrument, used only for the Bear Dance, makes a distinctive rumbling noise that sounds like thunder (a sign of spring) or a growling bear.

Known to the Utes as "woman-step dance" (*mamákwa-nhká-pu*), the Bear Dance is performed at the spring equinox under the direction of the women, who select with whom they wish to dance or consider potential suitors. Arising from courtship relations were interfamily alliances as groups united. This was also the time for a person to prove their ability to withstand weakness and error. Bertha Groves tells of how in the old days, when a girl reached the age of twelve or thirteen, her grandparents took her to a Bear Dance dressed in traditional clothing of moccasins, beadwork, and shawl to have her

dance. There were a variety of songs, but the last one was a lengthy compilation of many to test endurance. A female friend can tag a woman to take her place, as can a man for one of his friends, but the dance continues. If a person falls, there is laughter, and the couple must be prayed over before resuming. This was considered a bad sign, a breaking of unity between males and females, and in the past, the person who fell could no longer participate; they had "lost." Bertha's grandfather told everyone to leave her and the man she had selected alone, to let them dance to the end. Her partner did not have the necessary stamina; she outperformed him and at the end of the dance received an eagle plume. To her, the experience "was kind of like a ceremony, but today it is social and they don't have things like that for their kids."[44]

Marriage was the next step into maturity. An enamored couple primarily made the choice to become husband and wife, although some parents might get involved in the selection. Marriage outside of a person's immediate group or camp was preferred. Most Weenuche had only one wife at a time, but marital bonds were fragile, a chance of change ever-present, and polygamy possible. A proposal to wed could be as simple as a mutual attraction following which the man kills a deer, puts it on a horse that is tied outside of the woman's dwelling, and goes in to visit with the family. He may ignore her presence, but if she is interested, she will go out, care for the horse, butcher and cook some of the deer meat, and offer it to the husband-to-be. This signifies that the marriage partner is accepted.[45]

One practice undertaken by Southern Utes to test marriage compatibility was "smoking out." The future bride and groom would enter a tepee with no ventilation and filled with acrid, burning smoke from a fire built with green wood, and remain there for hours. "If they both did not run out, it meant that they would be together for a long time

The collection caption of this photo, taken at the Wetherill ranch in Mancos, Colorado, around 1891, suggests that this Ute couple are newlyweds. Al Wetherill is standing behind the husband and wife, and Indian Jim, wearing a bone breastplate, is to the right. While divorce was uncomplicated in traditional Ute culture, many marriages lasted until death. (BLM — Anasazi Heritage Center)

and they would not get angry or upset too much."[46] Failure to meet the test meant the person was quick-tempered and irritable.

A man's ability to provide as a hunter and protect as a warrior were primary responsibilities, while a woman's skill at tanning hides, making a comfortable home, and being industrious were important; however, physical attraction was often the reason a couple considered marriage.[47] The future husband and wife would consult their parents about the union, but if the elders were not in favor of it, the two might elope. Connor Chapoose mentions that at public dances a member of the girl's family would cover the potential husband with a blanket while the young man's family did likewise to her, symbolizing both households were in agreement.[48] A bride-price of some horses or meat for the future wife's family was sometimes

given for the loss of the daughter, but it was not a standard requirement.

Patty Dutchie tells a story that illustrates the principles of attraction, elopement, and bride-price (reversed) mixed with a tinge of supernatural. It seems that there was an old Ute woman who lived with her beautiful daughter far from any camp. One day a young man arrived at their tepee and proposed to the daughter while her mother was away gathering wood. The young woman accepted, mounted the young man's horse, and fled. They rode over hills, through arroyos, into a lightning-struck smoking forest, and by way of a friendly village, but they could not evade the old woman. She was astride her superhorse, Pike-soo-wahats, who had the uncanny ability to follow the tracks of the fleeing couple. Finally the chase ended, the young man making camp and preparing to meet his new mother-in-law. The old woman reined in her powerful steed to confront the two lovers, asking why they had eloped. The daughter replied that she was in love with the man and that they wanted to live with people, not with the old woman, who insisted on being alone. The elder relented and gave the couple Pike-soo-wahats as a wedding gift so that they could visit her often.[49] Cultural traits referred to in this story include the couple deciding to marry based on physical attraction, eloping when they thought they would not have social approval, owning an animal with the supernatural ability to understand its owner's intentions and to tirelessly pursue, and acknowledging the importance of living with other tribal members, not alone.

To the Ute people, once a couple had slept together at the girl's camp, the marriage was consummated and official. The woman's female relatives had the responsibility of providing a tepee for the newlyweds. During at least the first year the couple remained in the village of her family. Divorce became acceptable if sterility, infidelity, or incompatibility interfered with the couple's relationship. If another man became involved, the husband took or killed a horse belonging to the interloper, which left the woman free to go with her new love. If another woman became involved with a husband, it was not uncommon for there to be a fight between the two before the three reached a settlement. If the couple separated, a blanket might be cut in half, signifying the end of the relationship. Usually, the children went with the mother.[50]

Friction from divorce not only challenged the family but could disrupt the group. While men were free to become involved with paramours, a wife was expected to be faithful. Punishment for infidelity in the 1880s included killing the favorite horse of the man who trespassed with the married woman; whipping and then leaving the adulterous wife; slitting an adulterous woman's nose and killing her suitor; or killing both. "Usually, however, if the wife consorts with

another Indian her punishment consists of being beaten or divorced; but if her crime is committed with a negro, a white man, or a Mexican, the punishment is death."[51]

The nuclear family—father, mother, sons, and daughters—comprised the basic unit of Ute social organization. This group was best able to provide food, shelter, and clothing, so grandparents and others less capable of taking care of themselves "attached" to those who could provide, forming a loose extended family. Ute teachings emphasized respect for elders as they lived through their last stage, the fourth, of life. All members of the family used kinship terms as well as personal names, which strengthened familial bonds. Different paired kin positions required respect. For example, relationships between mothers- and fathers-in-law with daughters- and sons-in-law were respectfully reserved; brothers and sisters, as well as fathers- and daughters-in-law, avoided inappropriate joking and obscenities, whereas brothers-in-law and cousins often played jokes on each other. Some types of labor were shared but others divided. For instance, both males and females collected piñon nuts by knocking them off branches and preparing them at the fire. But cooking was a woman's task, so she was the one who made them into a meal. Both males and females hauled water, but it was the man's job to make a new fire, while the woman was the one who tended it. Hunting and fishing were men's domain, while preparing the skins and making the clothing fell to women, as did setting up the tepee.[52]

Social and political control within the camp was fairly unstructured and based primarily in individual rights. Camps varied in size depending on the season and its accompanying activities, but year-round residence groups varied from fifty to a hundred people.[53] Until American intervention, with its treaty making and reservation system, changed the pattern, the largest social unit with central authority was the camp. The leader, or "chief," required community

The Utes were known for being well-armed, and fighting on horseback made light, rapid-firing rifles like these Winchesters particularly desirable. While they lacked the range of some weapons, maneuverability and ease of reloading fit the close-in fighting that the Utes preferred. (Used by permission, Utah State Historical Society, all rights reserved.)

approval based on his making good decisions, especially those associated with food gathering and defense. Failure to meet these requirements could lead to his removal from that position. Once a person became a chief, however, this responsibility could be passed down in the family. Edward Dutchie commented that the chief "passes it on to his son. The chieftainship never dies out.... The chieftainship is passed on through generations."[54] Weenuche leaders sometimes had a couple of assistants, but the real decision-making on significant issues was done by the council, comprised of the men of the camp. Each one had an equal voice, but good orators and respected individuals enjoyed greater influence.

Proven leadership also attracted followers interested in war. For the Weenuche, war was much more of a practical business of obtaining horses or women than achieving glory.

A successful warrior might lead a handful of men interested in revenge or capturing goods, but large-scale, united efforts involving multiple bands were rarely undertaken. War parties avoided a standing fight whenever possible; often enemy encounters arose from chance meetings. Traditional enemies considered worth raiding were the Comanches, Navajos, and white settlers. The war party either rode horses or went on foot, and might be accompanied by a shaman who could dress wounds. Dreams and omens foretold the outcome of the raid and warned of impending disaster. Other than this, there were few beliefs involving supernatural aspects with war.

Before departing camp, participants held a war dance, which also signaled the end of all social dances until the men returned. Scouts wearing eagle feathers led the way, communicating with the group through bird calls, smoke signals, or waved blankets, depending on the proximity of the enemy. All members of the party wore one or two feathers in their hair and war paint. Once they encountered their opponents, their tactics included ambush, circling to the rear to capture enemy horses, and small group delaying actions. Participants recognized the brave deeds of combatants, taking scalps from the fallen and mutilating the dead. Captive men were killed instantly, while women and children had a better chance of surviving, the former being married to their Ute captors and the latter being sold as slaves. When the victorious party returned to camp, they entered triumphantly, with enemy scalps hung on a pole, followed by a dance that evening. Victors then displayed the scalps outside their dwellings.[55]

Due to their mobile lifestyle, the Utes owned little individual property. Except for their homes, clothing, weapons, horses, and some household equipment, they had little to call their own. Slain animals, gathered plant materials, and cleared agricultural lands could belong to a family, while larger areas used by the camp or the band belonged to the group. The Weenuche Utes recognized ownership through use-rights as opposed to actual possession of the land. John Wesley Powell observed that "The greater part of the Indians' property is held in common.... They own but little property at best, and the Indian has no word signifying rich or poor in its ordinary sense — that is having much or little property, but when an Indian says, 'I am rich,' he means, 'I have many friends,' or 'I am poor: I have but few.'"[56] Thus human relations were of high import, while wrongs against an individual were the usual point of friction, defining the closest thing to a "crime." Public opinion proved to be a strong motivator in conflict resolution, and since there was no "police" force, as found in some Plains tribes, there was no other means of enforcing a decision. Harold Amoss, in his study on the Weenuche Utes, comments: "The bald facts state the case more precisely:

there were infrequent murders, some stealing, and nothing was done about it."[57]

Another form of social disruption came from sickness. Healing took two directions: one that dealt with natural remedies and sweats, and the other with exorcising something evil that had entered the body. Both men and women used herbs to cure the sick. The physician soaked green yarrow leaves in water and then put them on a cut or sore as a poultice. The Utes used sage more than any other plant to cure sinus problems, hay fever, hemorrhoids (as a poultice), morning sickness, and when inhaled, to remove drowsiness. Moss from rocks was good for hives and hiccups, squaw berry for dysentery, bitterroot for headaches, spearmint for upset stomachs and bee stings, and cedar leaves for colds.[58] The list goes on. What is important to realize is that Ute physicians drew upon nature and understood cause-and-effect relationships in the physical world.

Edward Dutchie recalls being in a sheep camp in Allen Canyon near where the national forest boundary is today. A black spider bit him, and with the poison spreading through his body, he walked a long distance, bent and cramped with pain, until he reached his grandfather's home. The elder directed Edward's nephew to go to a certain place and obtain a plant that looked "almost like rabbit-brush," pick and peel the bark, gather some leaves from another plant (no names given), and return to him. After the elder pounded the leaves and bark, he boiled them in water, allowed the medicine to cool, and then had Edward drink the bitter concoction. "In about two hours [the swelling] was gone.... Water was coming out just like sweat out of my skin from the swelling. He laughed at me and said, 'Now you go down and look for that [plant] and keep it with you. You are up there close to that mountain with all those spiders up there.'"[59]

More complex was the role of the *póo-gat*, or Indian doctor, referred to in the literature as a shaman, medicine man, or healer. Often male but sometimes female, these people operated in the world of spirits. It was the spirits who selected the person in childhood or later in life. Dreams were essential to much of Ute religion, specifying things from the past as well as the future. They were the connecting link between the unseen and the physical world by which a person received supernatural power and direction. When bad dreams arose, crushed red rock or plants mixed with grease were painted on the forehead to remove the evil influence.[60] Dreams as a medium of communication, though at times unsought, came to the future *póo-gat*, usually more than once. In them an animal or bird taught of the power it held and what was needed to cure an illness. Bears and mountain lions were particularly strong, but badgers and eagles as well as wind, cyclones, lightning, the moon, and stars also were powerful.[61] A novice might refuse to accept the proffered power, but this could cause illness.

The beginning *póo-gat* might be assisted by another who divines a dream's or omen's meaning. From the dreams came sacred songs, specified equipment—such as an eagle wing or down, pollen, bull roarer, tobacco, and painted designs—as well as information about how these powers were to be used. Patty Dutchie remembers her father, Jimmy Mills, "who knew the rocks," selecting sandstone-covered rocks "that were pretty rocks inside," cracking them open, and then carving them into animals. "He knew these rocks had power, that's what he used to say. This power brought good memory or health to a person. As he was working, that is when he used to pray for it that way.... Use it in a sacred way. Talk to it; it can help you, he used to say."[62] Loss of any of this paraphernalia was dangerous for its owner. A specialist might call upon "woodpecker power which could both cause and cure hemorrhage, badger power to cure foot troubles, and kingfisher power for venereal disease."[63] For instance, a *póo-gat* who heals the effects of a rattlesnake bite would dream about the

snake and the cure, suck out the poison, and bind the wound.[64] However, curing information based on the teachings of the "little dark people" was believed to be the most potent.

Just as this type of information cures, it could also curse, bringing sickness to an individual. A *póo-gat* might receive threats or be put to death if people thought he was involved in witchcraft or that he had intentionally not tried to heal a person. On the other hand, he could also identify those practicing against others, which in turn led to revenge. Given the small nature of Ute hunting groups, conflict could be devastating.[65] The people also recognized that malevolent power was wielded by other tribes. The Utes referred to Navajos as "Pagáwič," associating them with "holding a knife," and feared their supernatural ability. The Hopis were "Mokwič," or "dangerous ghosts," who practiced evil medicine. Yet the world of spirits held potential for many different kinds of sickness and mishaps. What was intangible was uncontrollable. "Though the Utes do not specify that particular sorcerers (Ute, Navajo, or Pueblo) cause much sickness, death, or generally disastrous happenings, they do attribute the causes of some phenomena to unspecified evil spirits. The belief is widespread that ghosts, dwarfs, and even shamans can be, and often are, mischievous (as opposed to being malicious or evil)."[66]

Various techniques to bring problems under control included singing, smoking, appealing to a personal power, removing a foreign object by sucking it out of a body, brushing the patient with feathers, and laying hands on the sick. A *póo-gat* might specialize in rattlesnake and insect bites, attracting or stopping rain and wind, or controlling witchcraft.[67] He or she might use more than one form of power. A curing ceremony usually took place at night in a lodge. The *póo-gat* would sing, accompanied by those present, and was the first to smoke a pipe and pray to the four directions before passing it in a clockwise manner to those attending.

He next prayed to his personal power while his assistant interpreted; the *póo-gat* then removed from the person's head or afflicted part the offending object, showing it to the people and then rubbing it between his hands and blowing it away. Eagle feathers were used to brush the patient's body and water would be sprinkled before the *póo-gat* laid his hands on the patient. Placing his hands in fire and picking up coals, putting them in his mouth, or walking in them attested to the *póo-gat*'s power to heal and work with the extraordinary. He then retrieved the sick person's soul while in a trance. To do this he would at times be held down by his assistant. After the shaman returned to normal, the patient was healed.[68] Others believed that it was not the trancelike state but rather the assistance of the cooperating spirit that actually performed the healing.[69]

Edward Dutchie witnessed these events, and when asked what a medicine man did, he described it as a "spiritual way," "creation way," and a "miracle way of doctoring." The pain "makes some kind of noise…if it is just liquid, he spits it out, if it is the appendix, then maybe he sucks out the rocks—the no good part—and spits it out." The process is as much a diagnosis as it is a cure; the *póo-gat* first sings the song to the part that hurts, which in turn tells him what the problem is and how to remove it. He informs the patient how it entered the body and asks if that was not what happened. "You have to tell him the truth about it. He already knows, [but] he is just asking to see if you are going to tell him the truth…. The only thing he is going to do is suck out that bad thing, clean it all out, and then show it to you [by] putting it in his hand." Once the patient has seen the object, the healer does not throw it away but eats it. "Spiritual things in him need something to eat; they will eat it—something in that medicine man needs those things."[70] The small manikin within, known as a *pöwa'a*, should not be angered or mistreated. If this happens, it can kill a patient and transform the *póo-gat* into an evil sorcerer who causes illness and death through witchcraft. An evil *pöwa'a* can also turn on the shaman's family and afflict them.[71]

After treatment a patient is placed in a wickiup or tepee for healing and is attended by the shaman. Men may visit, but women do not because of the power present. If a cure is not obtained, the healer may be suspected of evil and be killed. There is no penalty for killing a medicine man for misusing his powers, and it is often done with the consent of the band leader.[72] Speaking of Southern Paiute practices, Martha Knack points out that antisocial behavior may be an indicator of a *póo-gat*'s disposition and his desire to use witchcraft. If he successfully heals a person, he becomes suspect because he has shown that he has extraordinary powers, while if he fails to heal the patient, he is believed to have killed him with his power.[73] Being a shaman is thus a risky occupation.

Smoke was an important part of sacred rituals. Edward and Patty Dutchie mentioned two different ways that it served as a spiritual medium. The first is with tobacco. While today's store-bought tobacco is acceptable, the Utes in the past used cane, elderberry, and kinnikinnik mixed with other dried plants. A person seeking a *póo-gat*'s help sits down with him, rolls a smoke, and lights it.

> Take about four puffs and then give it to the medicine man. Right then, he knows what you want. The smoke communicates to him and he says, "I'll be there." The man does not have to tell him why he came. The smoke talks for itself. The man leaves and later the medicine man follows him to his place, the place that he wanted him—maybe for a sick person, to help him or her—that's the only communication to the medicine man. That is why he wants that smoke passed to him—it tells him what is needed…. This has been passed down from the beginning of time for the Indian. The smoke travels up to the Creator, who knows the words and thoughts.[74]

The interior of a Sun Dance lodge, White Rocks, 1911. Inside the lodge is a sacred space where those who have pledged to dance (five here) renew themselves and their people spiritually. Adopted at the end of the nineteenth century, the dance has never been performed at White Mesa, but men from the community have participated in dances elsewhere. (Used by permission, Utah State Historical Society, all rights reserved.)

The "Indian smoke," or tobacco, used to grow in this area but is no longer available. "The white man killed it, I think, so that they could get our money from our pockets."

Patty mentioned the second use of smoke in ceremonies: purification. The people used to put cedar bark and sweet grass on coals to send messages "like smoke signals." A person would motion the smoke over them to purify him or herself or to have the smoke carry prayers to the Creator. Patty mentioned that she was burning cedar the day I visited. Edward picked up the conversation.

> When the smoke goes out of the house, it goes to that person who is not feeling well or who needs help. The prayer with that cedar is going to be carried wherever that smoke goes. It is carried to that person or the doctor's hands. If you go into that sick person that hand might go with that cedar and the doctor's eyes might find that and do a good job on the operation. Let the cedar go to that white man's hands so he might do a good job.

When asked if the Creator had designed cedar and sweetgrass for this purpose, Edward responded, "I can't tell a lie to you because one time, Jesus, as you call him, was on Mother Earth. He turned the Indians out to be on their own and put the word into that cedar. He picked the cedar, that main cedar tree."[75]

Another means of healing is the Sun Dance, which the Ute Mountain Utes obtained (around 1900) from the Northern Utes (1890s) and then passed on to the Southern Utes at Ignacio in 1904.[76] The ceremony originated with Plains tribes to the east. While the White Mesa Utes did not sponsor this dance in southeastern Utah, there were those who attended and participated in the ceremony at Towaoc, and so a brief explanation is given here. Unlike many of the Plains Indian practices, there was no piercing of the body, and the ceremony was not associated with successful hunting of the buffalo. Rather, it focused on curing the sick and alleviating problems and poverty.

The Sun Dance chief, who had received instructions in a dream and pledged to direct the dance, announced the time for the ceremony during the spring Bear Dance. When the time arrived, he selected a center pole of willow, aspen, or cottonwood and with the help of others cut it down, trimmed it, and painted it red. The pole represented the medium through which supernatural power was channeled from the sun as well as having its own inherent power. At the top was a willow nest, which also represented power. The participants replanted the pole in an enclosure made of twelve outer posts with brush and branches forming the wall. This corral, known as the "Thirst House" or "Place Where One Thirsts," stood for God's house, while the east entrance was "God's mouth." Many different interpretations followed.[77]

The spirits first told a dancer in a dream that he should participate; failure to do so would cause him to wither and die. Young men might have these dreams interpreted by a *póo-gat*, but it was not a prerequisite before starting the initiation process. Men were advised not to dance too hard during the first day so that they could gradually build endurance, as each dance became progressively more difficult. They were also instructed to be kind to family members, meet their needs, be wise in their behavior, and stay close to traditional ways. It was in the last dance that participants received visions for future direction. This was described as being "jolted by power" that lifted him in the air and knocked him to the ground, at which time his spirit left his body to be instructed. The dancer had to be committed to remaining in the ceremony all four days without eating or drinking. He also had to pledge to maintain good health, share the supernatural power he received with relatives and those he danced for, and to become a shaman if his dreams directed him to do so.[78] Accepting these responsibilities, Sun Dance participants entered the corral for four days of focused prayer, song, and dance.

The final part of the life cycle is old age

and death. Owls, crows, and coyotes may forewarn of the impending loss. The Weenuche Utes believe that each person has a spirit located in the heart. When a person dies, the heart leaves the body and ascends to the Creator's house, located in the sky to the west. There it joins others in living in a world very similar to the one the departed has just left. Unlike Coyote, who was banned from joining his family in the afterlife because he had disrupted the life of human beings in this world and so plaintively howls at night, people move on to a spirit world very similar to this physical one.[79] Some spirits or ghosts wish to take loved ones with them, so there is a fear of spirits being evil. Mourners talk to the deceased, telling them that they are going to a better place and so to be happy, to not return, and to not bother them or make them sick. Dreaming of them, as well as being near places where the dead had lived or died or been buried, can cause a person to get sick and possibly die. To cure this problem, one takes a cold bath, prays, and paints his face.[80] Edward tells of Ute elders traveling to Glenwood Springs, Colorado, where they obtained material for three types of paint: yellow, pink, and dark red. "If a person is not sleeping well, they put paint on their forehead or anywhere to take the bad dreams away. That's what they say. The one [paint] they talk about is red."[81]

When a person died in the old days, they were either cremated in their dwelling or buried in a rock crevice, alcove, or the earth. Relatives washed and painted the deceased's face, dressed the body in its best clothes, wrapped it in a blanket, and buried it extended, with the head toward the east. Relatives stepped over the corpse, acknowledging the death, and placed grave goods with the corpse before shooting a favorite horse to accompany the spirit in the afterlife. Adoline Eyetoo said that when a person dies, "the animals know that you are gone and they cry too, because that person is lost."[82] For four days family members wore old clothes, remained quiet, and avoided singing and laughter so as not to offend or entice visiting dead relatives who had come to accompany the recently deceased.[83] The family destroyed most of the remaining property, except for a few choice items such as horses or a particularly significant object. Washing or standing in smoke cleansed those who had prepared the body, while those intensely involved in mourning cut their hair and burned the clippings, cropped their horses' manes and tails, and "cried every day for about a year."[84]

Once the spirit leaves the body, it travels to "a fair land in the sky where there is no death, where there are towering mountains, broad forests, grassy plains, and rivers of sweet water that flow undiminished forever.... Each tribe of Indians has its own land, and when an Indian dies, he dwells with his own people."[85] This spirit is accompanied to the next world by a friend or family member. There the person lives in an idyllic state, hunting and feasting and dancing; everyone is youthful and beautiful, and all is happy. Another belief suggests a person's spirit stands above him, and that when he dies, the spirit departs. The dead only change camps — from a physical to a spiritual one — but remain nearby, even though they cannot be seen. This is not true for those who commit suicide. "When one kills himself on purpose, no one comes to get him and he goes out alone. Then after a while he gets scared and begins to run around and shout and call and cry. He would like to come back, but he can't, and the Indians do not want him back. They are afraid of his spirit."[86]

Excerpts from Dr. A. J. McDonald's eyewitness account of a Ute burial conducted near the Los Pinos Agency sometime between 1868 and 1875 give a feeling for the flow of events surrounding a death.

As soon as death takes place, the event is at once announced by the medicine man, and without loss of time the squaws are busily engaged in preparing the corpse for the grave.... At the same time that the body is being fitted for interment, the squaws

having immediate care of it, together with all the other squaws in the neighborhood, keep up a continued chant or dirge, the dismal cadence of which may, when the congregation of women is large, be heard quite a long distance. The death song is not a mere inarticulate howl of distress; it embraces expressions eulogistic in character....

The men during this time have not been idle, though they have in no way participated in the preparation of the body, have not joined the squaws in chanting praises to the memory of the dead, and have not even as mere spectators attended the funeral, yet they have had their duties to perform. In conformity with a long-established custom, all the personal belongings of the deceased are immediately destroyed. His horses and his cattle are shot, and his wigwam furniture burned.

The widow goes into mourning by smearing her face with a substance composed of pitch and charcoal. The application is made but once, and is allowed to remain on until it wears off. This is the only mourning observance of which I have knowledge.[87]

Thus ended the life of a Ute person. Whether male or female, adult or child, the practice of mourning was similar. From birth to death, the Weenuche Utes lived a life without elaboration. Simple, direct, and rational, the people met the world with a set of spiritual beliefs that taught its members what it meant to be Ute.

The life cycle of the nineteenth-century Weenuche Utes carried the people through a time of traumatic change, which by the first quarter of the twentieth century made their traditional lifestyle increasingly impossible to pursue. Loss of land curtailed their mobility, Christianity tore at their belief system, food and clothing increasingly came from the government, and education occurred in boarding schools. Persisting under these difficult conditions, the people faced the reality of change and compliance with the dominant society's mandates. How this process of cultural change started is discussed in the following chapter.

CHAPTER 4

The Invasion Begins

Hispanic Entradas, American Trade,
and the Mormon Mission, 1600–1855

The Coyote is always making trouble, making wars, telling lies.
The White Man is like that....That's the same thing that Coyote
was doing to the ants, taking everything. He was the first one to
do that. He was the first one out of the sack, leading the White Man.

Edward Dutchie Sr.

Edward Dutchie sat outside his home mending a rawhide rope he needed for his bull. The May sun, close to completing its journey for the day, still felt warm; the trees in full bloom nodded slightly with the breeze. Edward, dressed in blue jeans, a dark plaid shirt, and ever-present thick glasses perched on his nose, felt content. I pulled up a nearby log next to his seat and began some pleasantries before realizing that all was not well. Ants were on the attack. Swatting and brushing, I removed as many as I could as we both laughed at my little dance before pushing the log back to where it had been. Those "bad boys," as Edward called them, were minding their own business until I ruined their afternoon. Living peacefully, unconcerned with impending events, the ants suddenly encountered a foreigner who threw their world into chaos. All the ants wanted were to be left alone. One could argue the same was true of the Ute people when whites invaded their homeland. Unprecedented change to their world followed. The first meetings called for no alarm, but as the "ants" began to swarm, the combatants became locked in conflict

that disrupted both worlds. Unlike the insects I disturbed that day, these "ants" were not easily brushed off.

This chapter covers the first 250 of the 400 years in which the Weenuche endured and adapted to change.[1] Not all of it was harmful, but much of it was. Much did not happen quickly, but some of it did. But all of it moved the Ute people from the slower pace of life associated with a hunting and gathering lifestyle to one that pushed them toward the Euro-American culture and eventual assimilation. Conflict with even the earliest agents of change took various forms—noncompliance, subtle resistance, and open hostility—but no tactics were effective enough to stem the tide that moved the Weenuche ever closer to white society. Whites, on the other hand, eagerly sought to make the Indians their allies, and later, remodel them in their own image. In the earliest stages of contact, the Utes, as a whole, held the upper hand. They forced the Spanish, then the Mexicans, and then the Mormons to acknowledge their power and seek their assistance. Their control of the land, mobility with horses, and effective raiding techniques persuaded adversaries that the Utes were a power to be reckoned with.

Precisely what role the Weenuche played in these early years is difficult to separate from the other Southern Ute bands. Certainly they tied in to the activities of the Muache, Capote, and Northern Utes, but to what extent is vague. Indeed, the Spanish record did not begin to identify separate bands of "Yutas" until 1745, well over a hundred years after first contact.[2] Yet there is also proof that "the Weeminuche ranged over southeastern Utah, northeastern Arizona, and northern New Mexico, while all three [Southern Ute bands] followed a southeasterly path to Texas and Oklahoma to strike at the settlements of Plains Indians."[3] Enough of a picture of these early years is drawn here for the reader to sense the general ebb and flow of their activity in the larger pattern of history. Whenever possible, circumstances or events tied to southeastern Utah and its people are highlighted, but the historical record is indistinct compared to what follows in the later half of the nineteenth century.

On a regional level the Weenuche, as part of the Southern Ute complex, encountered similar events and trends. A quick glance at what occurred on a broader basis places more specific incidents in context. When the Spanish conquistador Juan de Oñate captured the pueblo of Acoma in 1598, he set in motion a series of incidents that reverberated throughout the Native American Southwest for the next two hundred years.[4] In addition to occupying various pueblo towns and enslaving "wild" Indians, the Spanish induced a power struggle between tribes for goods that provided an advantage. Primary among these were horses. Exactly when horses began to diffuse through trade or capture to the Southern Utes is not known; the first recorded instance of their having them was in 1692, when Don Diego de Vargas was embarking on a reconquest of the Pueblo people following the revolt of 1680. Some

Utes, serving as allies to the Hopis, were mounted. Still other groups of Utes were not, indicating a period of transition. The farther one traveled from the Spanish settlements, the less likely the possibility of encountering Utes on horses, with some "still apparently walking well into the latter eighteenth century."[5] Friendly trade relations with the Spanish came to a close in the early eighteenth century, in part because of the Utes' intense desire for horses, if for no other reason than self-preservation.[6]

Instead of having, as in the past, relatively stable hunting and gathering territorial boundaries for small groups of people, the Utes began to gather in larger, more mobile bands that ranged farther and faster than ever before. These circumstances called for more powerful leaders in an expanding system of relations that either promoted cooperation or intensified war. Patterns of warfare shifted from fighting in static line defense or small brushfire engagements to faster paced events and rapidly changing alliances, creating greater vulnerability for all concerned. Horses, even more than guns and other metal goods, were paramount in this energized environment. Increased mobility also fostered larger camps, larger dwellings, larger needs, and a more complex economy.

Spanish towns such as Santa Fe, Taos, and Abiquiu had been established on the southern end of the Southern Ute winter hunting and gathering range, and in the midst of the Rio Grande pueblos, where Utes had bartered for centuries. Occupied now by the Spanish, who controlled new and desirable trade items, these towns served as a nexus for many of the "wild" (non-Pueblo or settled) tribes to visit and obtain what were becoming necessities. Horses, at the top of the list, became the edge of power between rivals. Since the Utes did not adopt a large-scale practice of breeding horses to increase their herds, trade or raid became the primary means to maintain this edge. Meat and hides, staples of exchange with Pueblos and other

Capote warriors in northern New Mexico, 1874. Trade was critical to Ute hegemony in their homeland. In the early years of white contact, the horse became paramount. Metal products, especially weapons, helped maintain a fighting edge. Items of trade obtained for personal adornment included conchos sewed on a cloth blanket (*left*), beads, and buffalo skins. (Used by permission, Utah State Historical Society, all rights reserved.)

Indian groups, did not fetch a big price from the Spanish. One horse required a huge amount for payment. This left two options. The first was to maintain friendly relations with the Spanish and find something that was of high value to trade. The second was to ally with the Spanish and steal horses from other Indian groups. The Utes did both.[7]

The general tenor of Spanish interaction with the Utes began in friendship and ended in hostility.[8] One prime reason for the constantly changing relations was the shifting and breaking of alliances with other Indian groups surrounding the Spanish. The Byzantine complexity of this period is beyond the scope of this chapter, but briefly, the Comanches, Apaches, and Navajos are of main concern. In 1675 the Utes entered into their first treaty, which committed them to fight alongside the Spanish against the Apaches.[9] They also helped to quell Pueblo unrest. By 1700 the Apaches had pushed from the Plains into the area north of Taos. Between 1700 and 1748 the Utes and Comanches formed a brittle alliance that allowed them to force most of the Apaches to the south and west. The Utes also waged war, starting in 1720, against their traditional enemy, the Navajos. Intermittent warfare between the Utes and Spanish began in 1706 as the Indians became increasingly upset with settlements creeping into their southern hunting territories. They attacked Abiquiu, which in the 1730s was the third largest town in New Mexico. These efforts forced abandonment in 1747 and again around 1750. It was not reoccupied until 1754. The Spanish continued to play warring factions against each other through a series of alliances. From 1749 to 1786 the Utes turned against the Comanches, waging a bitter conflict of raiding for captives and horses. Eventually, Governor Juan Bautista de Anza forged an alliance between the two warring tribes in which "The Indians, after various charges and satisfactions on both sides, exchanged clothing before Anza, according to their custom to renew friendship."[10] The same conflict/alliance scenario played out between the Navajos and the Utes.

In 1821 Spain abandoned its holdings in the southern United States and Mexico, and Central and South America. From this time until the end of the Mexican War in 1848, the Mexican government assumed control of the western third of what is today the United States. What this meant in Ute and Hispanic relations is that much of the power and control that Spain had brought to the New World, though tenuous, was now gone. The Mexican government had even fewer resources to work with on its northern frontier, causing Ute relations to deteriorate. While there were times of peace, the general tenor of this period was one of conflict. The Utes and Navajos allied to drive settlers out of their lands, traders made illegal expeditions into Ute territories, American fur trappers based out of Taos headed into the interior, and the establishment of a vibrant slave trade along the Old Spanish Trail (actually Mexican Trail) added more turmoil.[11]

At the bottom of much of the conflict during both Spanish and Mexican rule was the necessity of obtaining horses for military advantage. In addition to those already mentioned, there was a growing list of enemies such as the Kiowas (allies of the Comanches), the Cheyennes, and the Arapahos. Horse raiding, not war honors, was a primary motivation, giving rise to new tactics. If pursued, a raiding party scattered into ever smaller groups. By pealing off at various points in their flight, the Utes created less vulnerable targets. To protect villages on the move, they formed columns, with warriors on the outer edge for defense. "The men went in files at the front and along the sides of each squadron, carrying shields made of three thickness buffalo hide stretched over a frame.... Close by the women, in files, went the men with their weapons in hand ready for use."[12] While this was most likely practiced by larger bands of Southern Utes venturing onto the Plains, the Weenuche applied similar but modified strategies in canyon country, as noted in later conflicts.

The second means of obtaining horses was to provide something that Spaniards and Mexicans desired; during an era when production was based on manual labor, slaves became that object. Early accounts of slave trafficking make clear that Utes preyed upon Paiutes and Navajos as major sources of women and children to be sold in Abiquiu and Taos. What is not as clear is how much of a role the Weenuche of southeastern Utah played. The Utes had traditionally used the mountains as a refuge. With the increase of internecine warfare among all of the tribes, a safe haven attracted some groups into more protected areas, from which defending parties sallied forth. At the same time, bands with large horse herds were forced to change traditional secluded campgrounds for places with sufficient water and open space for grazing.[13] Because of the mixed Ute and Paiute ancestry and the unclear distinctions drawn between Numic-speaking peoples at this time, no definitive response for those living in southeastern Utah is available. For instance, in 1750, Governor Tomás Vélez de Cachupín advised his successor that for stability in northern New Mexico, "It is necessary that the zeal of your grace be completely applied to maintain with these four nations of Utes, Chaguaguas, and Payuchis the best friendship and good relations, treating them with generosity…be very humane in your contacts with them."[14] Cachupín considered the "Payuchis" one of the four Ute bands and a force to be reckoned with, suggesting that they were not the same type of Paiutes found farther west. Very plausibly, they were Weenuche in southeastern Utah and southwestern Colorado.

Twenty-five years later Father Escalante again named the four groups — "Yutas Muachis, the Yutas Payuchis, the Tabehuachis and Sabuaganas." Southern Paiutes received the designation of Yutas Cobardes. S. Lyman Tyler, who has worked extensively with Spanish records, affirms that there was no indication of the Yutas Cobardes using tepees, and he believes "The Yuta Payuchis, who seem to have been more like the eastern Yutas than the more sedentary Yuta that Escalante called the Yutas Cobardes or Timid Yutas, inhabited the area from the fork of the Colorado and San Juan Rivers, east, apparently both north and south of the San Juan, to the area inhabited by the Yutas Muhachis."[15] Tyler further believes it was primarily the Timpanogos Utes living around the Utah Lake area that were the aggressors in selling Paiutes to Spaniards and Mexicans. "Among the eastern Yutas, including the Payuchis, this practice was not common. These brought captives to trade in New Mexico, it is true, but they were usually taken in raids on other tribes and did not come from their own people."[16]

Whether as captors or captives, the Weenuche and San Juan Band Paiutes were involved in the slave trade. Starting in 1750 and continuing for the next hundred years, northern towns in New Mexico, including Abiquiu, served as the southern terminus for a system of exchange that ranged as far north as the Great Basin, as far west as California, and as far east as the Great Plains. Ever searching for a vulnerable target, the Utes "enslaved semi- and non-equestrian Great Basin peoples in the arid and mountainous terrain of southern Utah, Nevada, and eastern California."[17] Anthropologist Marvin Opler cited a Southern Ute informant telling of Yoa, a Capote, who knew of Mexicans sometime between 1821 and 1848 leaving Santa Fe to buy Indian children to assist with herding sheep. "First they went to the Paiute at Monticello. There they captured some children. When the old Paiutes found this out, they followed the Mexicans…. The Capote were around Tierra Amarilla then, and their chief at that time was Yoa. The Paiutes came to Yoa and asked him to help them get their children back."[18]

White Mesa resident Billy Mike recalls his grandmother talking of those days of slave raiding.

> Long ago the Spanish came into this area. They would take our women and children as slaves. They always went south. My grandmother told stories about these men who wore metal on their head and chest. She was taken prisoner by six Spaniards. They were traveling down by what is called today Mexican Water, Arizona. This is where my grandmother and others escaped. When the Spaniards fell fast asleep, the women stepped between their snoring captors and ran as far as they could. By the time the Spaniards woke up, the women had gained some distance from them. Seeing that the Ute women were gone, they shot their guns into the air in anger.[19]

Family stories of this nature and time are rare, but the details of the slave trade during this period have been covered elsewhere.[20] Suffice it to say that it disrupted peaceful relations, tore families apart, and fostered inhumanity. Slaving expeditions by Hispanic and Native American groups moved into more isolated regions in search of captives while pushing the unprotected into even less accessible areas. Mountainous terrain and canyon country became favored spots for those trying to evade capture. Yet southeastern Utah, while less known and more inaccessible, was still within reach.

Some Spanish and Mexican leaders officially sought more peaceful relations and a settled frontier. As early as 1712 the governor of New Mexico, Juan Ignacio Flores Mogollón, forbade traders from venturing into Ute lands, which lay generally in northern New Mexico and southern Colorado and Utah.[21] Not until June 1765 did Governor Cachupín grant special permission for Juan María Antonio Rivera to travel into Indian country. The hidden tide of traders was never totally stopped, and the devastating incursion of slave raiders continued to foment economic and political turmoil. How many unofficial expeditions preceded the officially sanctioned Rivera entrada is unknown.

The primary reason to bend official policy in a move to the north sprang from Governor Cachupín's wish to find a crossing of the Colorado River, to identify the local Indian groups en route, and to determine their attitude toward the Spanish. A less publicized reason was to verify the truth of a rumor of silver deposits in the Four Corners area. The tale seemed probable, based on a Ute named Wolfskin who appeared in Abiquiu from this region carrying a small silver ingot. More precious metals might be found, and so Rivera, in the guise of a trader with a small expedition of eight men, set out in late June to find mineral wealth, confirm the existence of a large river (the Colorado [known then as the "Grand"] or Río del Tizón [Firebrand]) believed to go to the Pacific Ocean, and establish an overland route through this area.

There are two interpretations as to how far west into Weenuche country the Rivera expedition actually traveled. Ethnohistorian Steven Baker provides the most convincing explanation.[22] Examining the topography of the Four Corners area, he argues that there were three major "gateways," or choke points,

in southwestern Colorado and southeastern Utah located on a well-worn system of prehistoric and historic trails used by the Anasazi and, later, the Utes. These sites—on the Colorado River at Moab, the confluence of the Colorado and Dolores Rivers, and the Gunnison River at Delta, Colorado—were crucial in Indian trade networks and overland travel. Otherwise, a five-hundred-mile barrier of mountains, canyons, and rivers would either slow or stop movement coming from the east or south. Baker explains that "the Dolores [River] was the first place west of the Continental Divide where Mother Nature would allow the great wall to be breached without great effort, particularly by horsemen"; it thus played a prominent part in both the Rivera and Escalante expeditions, the establishment of the later Spanish Trail, and the use of the Navajo-Uncompahgre Trail that headed north.[23]

Rivera eventually took this last trail to reach the Gunnison River. Before traveling on it, however, he went in search of Wolfskin, and according to Baker's calculation, arrived at the Animas River near Durango and then went as far west as the Dolores River, which was in the "land of the Payuchis," in search of his guide. The Spaniards located their man on the La Plata River, prospected for a short while, and then went back to Santa Fe. They returned in the fall and pushed to the Gunnison before turning back. During these expeditions Rivera noted the extensive exchange of deer and elk hides as well as salt from the Paradox Basin. Each band of Utes was protective in maintaining control of the trade within their territory. Friction between some Weenuche and Muache over this point resulted in a "physical altercation."[24]

A second interpretation of Rivera's expedition has his party crossing a "very lovely and fast flowing [river], which we called San Juan." This is the first appearance of the name in Spanish documents, the river serving as a boundary between the Navajos and Utes. Four days later Rivera arrived at the Animas

River in Colorado, where he found an adobe retort used to reduce the impurities of gold. The explorer took some of the bricks with him as proof of Indian metallurgy and sent four Spaniards and a Ute guide to locate Wolfskin. Learning that he had gone to the land of the "Payuchis" to see his mother-in-law, the party traveled from the Dolores River to Cross Canyon, then down an old Ute trail to Montezuma Canyon and the San Juan River.[25]

On July 14 the smaller group of explorers encountered some "Cimarron-Paiutes" camped along the San Juan River in today's Montezuma Creek–Aneth area. Rivera wrote, "[The Spanish explorers] saw about three Cimarron ["dark" or "slave"] Paiute encampments on the other side. After they saw our group, one of them dove into the [San Juan] river to see who our people were. At the same time one of ours dove in and they met in the middle of the river and after having spoken by signs, ours persuaded him to cross to our side and converse with the Ute interpreter."[26] The Spanish next refer to the "Payuchi" leader, Capitan Chino (glossed as Chief with Dark Skin [Chinese]), and his people as Utes-Paiutes. They received presents, formalized peaceful relations, and two days later accompanied the Spaniards back to the main camp on the Dolores River.[27] Chino said that Wolfskin had recently left for his home on the La Plata River, and cautioned that the heat and lack of water and grass would make the trip to the Colorado River in July dangerous. However, if they returned in the fall, he would guide them to their destination.

Captain Chino also tried to discourage the travelers by describing the people they would meet as they crossed a desolate wasteland.

Among those people encountered before arriving at the [Colorado] river, there is one which has pierced ears, and they lie all the time to the Cosninas, who are people who wear buckskins all the time and are very likeable. The Paiutes say, and we also have been told by Chief Asigare, that there is among those tribes one which kills people with only a vapor; that they do it but it is not known how it is made; that those vapors are strong, that after inhaling one dies rapidly; and before arriving there, there is in the route a large underground cavern, guarded by a man and in it are a great variety of animals among which is one, especially, which cuts up in pieces anyone who comes or goes without giving a skin. With a contribution, when crossing there, one leaves freely. Also, they say that in the other part of the river there is a huge ditch, that when those of this side go there they accomplish their trade without crossing, those of this side hurling the bridles and knives and those things which the Spaniards trade to the Utes, and each tribe goes to the Rio del Tison and those of that [side] hurl over to this [side] the chamois [skins].

That there is such a variety of languages that many do not understand one another. That the method of crossing the river by those on the other side is in baskets in which only two people fit, the one facing the departure [point] and the other facing the arrival and those on this side cannot cross until the river is clear. That it is so wide that one cannot see across it, and on the other side there are barbarian white men dressed in iron suits; that their helmets are of iron and their women have on their arms iron rings, which is to say they are bracelets. These wear two tresses, they appear to be Spaniards, and among them there is one called El Castira, which is to say Castilla. That is all they know about the said river.[28]

Considered tall tales by the Spaniards, this information gives insight into some of the Utes' beliefs and is one of the first ethnographic accounts of the White Mesa/Weenuche people. Armed with this information, Rivera headed back to Santa Fe with a request for Governor Cachupín to allow his second expedition.

Rivera received permission to outfit a second entrada but was told to do nothing to upset the Indians, only to find a ford of the Río del Tizón. He returned by a more direct route to the Dolores River, where he again stayed at the camp of Asigare, a "Payuchi" who Rivera interchangeably identified as a Ute-Paiute. A Muache Ute and another person from Asigare's camp came to blows over whether the Spaniards should go any farther, the Muache fearing that the Spanish were reconnoitering the land for occupation. The other Ute argued that the foreigners had already been given permission and so should be assisted. Finally Asigare appointed Chino's grandson, a "Paiute," to lead the group, settling the difference. From the Dolores, the party moved north, where they met Chief Chino "with five families because most of his people were hunting mule deer in the mountains…and he did not have a large territory."[29] The explorers saw other "Cimarron Paiutes" on the way, many of whom fled from the Spaniards until they learned of their peaceful intentions.

Rivera traveled north in western Colorado, reaching the Gunnison and Colorado Rivers east of Grand Junction.[30] His account specifies that he met other Utes belonging to the Muache and Tabeguache bands, the latter "engaged in dancing for Comanche horses, which they had acquired in battle a few days before."[31] They stayed with their Indian hosts, feasting on mule deer and sharing tobacco, presents, and information. The Tabeguache warned that farther north there were more hostile Indians, that their guide did not know the way, and that Comanches were prevalent. Sabuagana Utes arrived in camp on October 17 and confirmed reports of danger if the party crossed the Colorado River. They heard of Indians who ate their own children, others with "pearl-colored hair," and of a place where there were "people more numerous than stones."[32] If these reports were intended to discourage Rivera from going beyond the Colorado River, they worked. Once he had found a suitable ford, planted a cross, and inscribed "Viva Jesus" in a cottonwood tree, the group returned to Santa Fe in two weeks' time. He had asserted Spanish rights to the territory while his entradas set the stage for

the next act in the drama, the Domínguez–Escalante expedition, which would play out eleven years later.[33]

There were undoubtedly unofficial expeditions to this area, such as the one of Pedro Mora, Gregorio Sandoval, and Andrés Muñiz, who reported seeing Rivera's cross in 1775, but these excursions are lost to history. Muñiz, however, served as a guide the next year for Fray Francisco Atanasio Domínguez, Fray Silvestre Vélez de Escalante, and seven other men as they wound their way through western Colorado in search of a feasible trail from Santa Fe to Monterey, California. The padres' account of the Indians living near southeastern Utah is informative. They encountered Utes who warned them about running into a Comanche war party and being killed, but the priests replied that God would protect them. They also obtained guides by paying each a blanket, knife, and beads to lead them to the north. One of the Utes overindulged and became so sick from eating that he accused the Spaniards of poisoning him, until he eased his discomfort through vomiting. Other Utes willingly sold food and listened to the Catholics' preaching, but often they tried to impede the journey to the north. Later the explorers learned that some of their companions were telling the Indians to do this because they did not want to continue. This was to no avail, as the expedition moved on as far north as Utah Valley.[34]

As Domínguez and Escalante journeyed up the western side of Colorado, near southeastern Utah, they gave a description of the Indians encountered. They noticed how reticent the Indians were to approach them, no doubt in part because of the slave raiding and intertribal warfare that dominated relations with other Indian groups. The Utes were happy to learn through an interpreter that since their enemies—the Navajos, Comanches, and Apaches—had not been baptized, they could not enter heaven and would "burn forever like wood in the fire."[35] They also mentioned that the La Sal Mountains were "so called for there being salt beds next to it from which, as they [Utes] informed us, the Yutas hereabouts provided themselves."[36]

On the return trip down the southwestern side of Utah, Domíngez and Escalante traveled near Navajo Mountain, which the Paiutes called "Tucane, meaning Black Mountain."[37] They made special note of a group of Numic-speaking people east of the Colorado River whom they called "Payuchi Yutas," who spoke the same language as neighboring Paiute groups. The padres used some of the Paiute trails in the Navajo Mountain area, reporting that they were built up with loose stones and sticks.[38] Domínguez and Escalante returned to Santa Fe on January 2, 1777, having traveled via the Hopi villages. They provided a treasure trove of accurate ethnographic information of many of the Indian groups they had encountered, among them the Weenuche.

The peaceful intentions of Domínguez and Escalante meant little to those interested in economic gain. For instance, Muñiz, who initially guided the group, smuggled trade goods with him, acting expressly against the fathers' wishes. He and his brother had spent time — three to four months in some instances — trading among the Indians of the Four Corners region.[39] Such expeditions, exchanging furs, horses, guns, and slaves, caused consternation for the government, which was trying to regulate Indian relations. In 1778 officials issued an edict to stem the flow of unlicensed trading activity in the borderlands. Ten men and two Indians stood trial in Abiquiu in 1783; two years later several others were in similar circumstances for trading "in the interior of the country of the Utes in violation of repeated edicts."[40] Again, in 1812, officials passed a law to prohibit buying slaves from the Utes, and, not surprisingly, a year later seven men under Mauricio Arze and Largos García stood before the judge for slave trading in Utah Valley.[41] No doubt many of these expeditions — either coming or going — passed through southeastern Utah.

Utes and Spaniards continued their tenuous relations right up to the Spanish withdrawal from the American Southwest in 1821. Generally, these relations were characterized by the Spanish currying favor with the Utes in order to use them against the Navajos and Comanches. However, by the time the Mexican government faced the problem of controlling the Indians in the territory, the Navajos had formed a friendly alliance with the Utes, much to the dismay of the settlers of New Mexico. Reports filtered in to Santa Fe of Navajos and Utes working together to steal horses, uniting for slave raiding, and living together in the La Plata and Sleeping Ute (also known as the Datil or Le Late) Mountains. Later, however, animosity again erupted between the two tribes.[42]

Traffic into the region, built upon prior exploration, created by 1829 a 1,200-mile route between Santa Fe and Los Angeles known as the Old Spanish Trail. Thanks, in part, to the efforts of Rivera, Domínguez and Escalante, and other less-publicized explorers, this horse and pack mule trail connected the interior of New Mexico with the Pacific Ocean while bypassing a section of Arizona noted for hostile Indians. Much of the trail crossed Ute territory belonging to the Capote, Weenuche, Tumpanawach, Sheberetch, and Pah Vant.[43] Southeastern Utah held part of the route. From the 1820s to the early 1840s, a portion of the Spanish Trail saw use from fur trappers as well as traders. This section was part of the "Old Trappers' Trail," serving mountain men as they moved from the Southwest into the Great Basin.[44] William Wolfskill and George C. Yount are credited with being the first trappers and traders to travel the entire length of the trail from Santa Fe to Los Angeles, which they did in 1830.[45] Other trappers, such as Kit Carson, Antoine Robidoux, and Denis Julien, also used the trail and trapped in the wilds of southeastern Utah. No doubt these luminaries of the fur trade had extensive contact with the

Ute warriors. Horses allowed Ute warriors to travel long distances—east as far as Kansas, south into New Mexico and Arizona, west to California, and north throughout the Great Basin and into Idaho. The warrior's headdress and coup stick show a strong Plains influence. (Used by permission, Utah State Historical Society, all rights reserved.)

Weenuche Utes, but no record remains of these dealings.

The Old Spanish Trail crossed present-day state boundaries at Ucolo near Piute Spring, dropped into Dry Valley, then generally followed the path of today's Highway 191 through La Sal Junction, past Kane Springs, down Spanish Valley, and into Moab. The ford across the Colorado River at this point had the name of "Ute Crossing on the Old Trail" and was well-known to travelers. From there the road went to Green River, near the future town of that name, then headed generally west through Salina Canyon, out to the Sevier River, south to Richfield and Circleville, and then dipped into extreme northwestern Arizona and southern Nevada.[46]

A second spur of the trail in southeastern Utah traversed different territory and was known as the Bears Ears Trail. Although piecing the route together from cursory mention by travelers who followed parts of it after the Mexican period is difficult, the suggested route crossed the San Juan River, perhaps at Chinle Wash or farther to the east, and then traveled up Comb Wash to the Bears Ears. It is interesting to note that a petroglyph of what appears to be a Hispanic lancer is carved into a rock part way up Comb Wash before the trail passed near or between the Bears Ears. From there it followed Elk Ridge heading generally northwest, ending below the junction of the Colorado and Green Rivers at a place known today as Spanish Bottoms. From there travelers could either join the main route of the Old Spanish Trail near the town of Green River or go to the Henry Mountains, rumored to be opened to mining.[47]

A number of caravans set out from Santa Fe and Abiquiu each year, usually in September or October to avoid intense summer heat and early winter snow. Two and a half months later, they arrived in Los Angeles having traded their woolen products carried on mules, and also having acquired slaves along the way. In April the pack trains started their return journey, driving large herds of horses and mules, before melting winter snows had swelled the rivers.[48] While the trail held its dangers for travelers, for Paiute women and children it held sheer terror. Some were traded by men who wanted to obtain horses and firearms, but many were taken by force, and all dreaded being ripped from their homes and pushed into servility.

David Brugge's work on Navajo and "nomadic Indian" slavery as reflected in Catholic Church baptismal records gives a quantitative look at what went on with "Yuta" captives during a one-hundred-year period in northern New Mexico. Realizing that this is only an indicator from official records and not all-inclusive, the trend is still unmistakable. Between 1700 and 1775, there were 48 "Ute" baptisms; between 1776 and 1800, 45; from 1801 to 1850, 640, with 412 of this last number representing 65 percent of baptisms categorized as "North of Santa Fe," primarily in Abiquiu, the jumping-off point for Mexican slave trade expeditions. Of the 626 total number of captives baptized between 1830 and 1860, 271, or 43 percent, were "Utes," most likely Paiutes.[49] There is little doubt that the Weenuche were aware of this expanding enterprise.

One of the major functions of the Spanish Trail was to expedite this trade, the northerly route into central Utah being the most practical. Indeed, slave and horse trading boomed during the Mexican period. Exchange of human captives and other commodities along the trail by Utes, Navajos, and Paiutes reached an apex during the 1830s and 1840s, then declined in the 1850s. While American fur trappers played a part in establishing the trail, Mexican traders were the foundation upon which wool and slaves moved to California and horses, mules, and slaves flowed back to New Mexico. Entering the San Juan region in caravans with as many as three hundred men "dressed in every variety of costume, from the embroidered jacket of the wealthy Californian…to the scanty habili-

ments of the skin-clad Indians," the traders sought out women and children to sell in New Mexico and to exchange for horses and blankets along the trail or in California. As much as $200 might be paid for a young girl who could be trained as a domestic, while boys were worth only half that much.[50] According to Martha Knack, "This trade became so entrenched that by 1850 there were standard values for Paiute slaves, from $50 to $200 depending on their sex, age, and state of health."[51]

Of all the colorful personalities that used the trail, Chief Wakara (translated as "Yellow"), a Timpanogos Ute, was among the most prominent and consistent in using it for his business.[52] Although he was born in the Great Basin along the Wasatch Front, he was extremely well traveled, ranging into California as well as New Mexico and Arizona. There is no doubt that he had extensive dealings with the Utes and Navajos of southeastern Utah. His presence along the Old Spanish Trail is well-documented. T. J. Farnum tells of his friend Doctor Lyman, who during a stint on the trail traveled with Wakara. After writing that the Timpanogos Utes he was with were very friendly with the Americans but felt real contempt for the Mexicans, he said, "I traveled through their country with one of their head chiefs, named Wah-cah-rah, who was on his return from an unsuccessful expedition across the St. John's [San Juan] river in pursuit of his faithless wife who had left him and fled over the border with her paramour. He was quite sad during the early part of the journey, and was constantly muttering something of which I frequently distinguished the expression…'very bad girl.'"[53] While this description is the opposite of how Wakara is usually described—as a truculent warrior who showed little mercy when it came to business—the passage does illustrate that he was very familiar with the Four Corners region.

More in keeping with how travelers on the Spanish Trail viewed Wakara are the notes of John C. Frémont taken as he mapped part of Utah during his 1844 expedition. The two met along the Sevier River on May 20. Fremont paints a picture not only of the chief, but the Utes traveling with him as they plied their trade. He wrote:

> We met a band of Utah Indians, headed by a chief who had obtained the American or English name of Walker, by which he is quoted and well known. They were all mounted, armed with rifles, and use their rifles well. The chief had a fusee, which he carried slung, in addition to his rifle. They were journeying slowly toward the Spanish Trail, to levy their usual tribute upon the great California caravans. They were robbers of a higher order than those of the desert. They conducted their depredations with form, and under the color of trade and toll for passing through their country. Instead of attacking and killing, they affect to purchase—taking the horses they like, and giving something nominal in return. The chief was quite civil to me. He was personally acquainted with his namesake, our guide, who made my name known to him. He knew of my expedition of 1842; and as tokens of friendship and proof that we had met, proposed an interchange of presents. We had no great store to choose out of; so he gave me a Mexican blanket, and I gave him a very fine one which I had obtained at Vancouver.[54]

Wakara's heavy involvement in slave trading—often in Paiutes—is symptomatic of the type of trafficking that went on in southern Utah.

In 1848, with the signing of the Treaty of Guadalupe Hidalgo at the end of the Mexican War, the United States officially became responsible for protecting northern New Mexico and controlling the Utes. During this time, much of southwestern Colorado and southeastern Utah became even better known as different government survey groups passed through the area. The development of white domination in neighboring regions—northeastern New Mexico (1846), Salt Lake City (1847), Denver (1859)—created bases for an even greater influx of travelers and settlers into Indian territory. Although the Utes had not noticed a significant difference during shifts in leadership between the Spanish and Mexican governments, there was a noticeable increase in power when the United States assumed control.

Indian agent James S. Calhoun arranged for the first treaty with the Southern Utes, signed by twenty-eight leaders. They agreed to maintain the peace and allow military posts and agencies to be established on their land. Their first agency, started in 1850, was in Taos, with subsequent ones established in Abiquiu, as well as Maxwell's Ranch and Conejos in Colorado. These agencies served primarily the Muache and Capote, while the Weenuche remained comparatively isolated and uninvolved. From 1853 to 1859 Kit Carson served as a Ute agent, a point to be emphasized given the future war against the Navajos. By 1855 the Capotes began challenging the whites looking to settle on their land, leading to conflict and a treaty; in 1859 a gold rush in the Colorado Rockies again sent shock waves through the Capote and Muache bands, but the Weenuche Utes were generally unaffected.[55]

By the 1850s use of the Spanish Trail had dropped off as other routes opened. Some were developed as expeditions moved through the Southwest during the Mexican War; others, like the California-Oregon Trail to the north, were established by miners and settlers heading to the coast. A few groups continued to use the Spanish Trail when convenient. One such group, composed of twenty-eight New Mexicans under Pedro León, received a license to trade with the Utes in southeastern Utah in 1851.[56] That September the group exchanged horses and mules with the Utes for Indian children and then camped at Green River for a short while. They sent some of their people to the Salt Lake Valley to see if the Mormons, who had arrived five years previously (1847), were interested in buying human chattel. Brigham Young was not. He refused to deal with them, told them to leave, and the eight that did not were arrested, stood trial, fined, and then released.

The horrors of this trade are described in the preamble to a bill passed by the Utah legislature in 1852 in an attempt to stop slave trafficking by New Mexicans in the Great Basin. Beginning with the practice of purchasing women and children of the "Utah Tribe of Indians," it tells of how they were obtained through gambling, war, or theft, and then "carried from place to place packed upon horses or mules; larietted out to subsist upon grass, roots or starve; and are frequently bound with thongs made of rawhide, until their hands and feet become swollen, mutilated, inflamed with pain and wounded, and, when with suffering, cold, hunger, and abuse they fall sick so as to become troublesome, are frequently slain by their masters to get rid of them."[57] The fact that some of this was internecine in nature made the crime all the worse. Because of the destructive nature of the conflict, Brigham Young put a stop to the sale of slaves in Utah. A year later the Walker War started, and although there were a number of other incidents that triggered the conflict, part of the souring of relations between the Mormons and the Utes living along the Wasatch Front was due to this cessation of slave traffic. Slaves, however, continued to be traded between Utes and New Mexicans into the mid to late 1860s.

Other travelers keeping journals along the trail also provide accounts of Indian activity. Two examples follow. The first comes from Lieutenant E. G. Beckwith, who was journeying with Captain John W. Gunnison, in charge of surveying a possible railroad route in 1853. This party was the first to officially map a good portion of the Spanish Trail. In writing of the mountains laying before him, Beckwith mentions, "The [La Sal — Salt] is directly upon the noted Spanish trail leading from California to Abiquiu, New Mexico, and is a favorite resort for the Utah and Navajo Indians for trade; while the Abajo [Span-

ish for "Lower" or "Below"; also known as Blue Mountain] is near the junction of the Grand [Colorado] and Green rivers, considerably below the fords of this trail…hence its name."[58] The travelers, with wagons in tow, made their way to Green River, where they crossed three miles below the present town site on October 1. Beckwith says of the Utes he met:

> We crossed the river by an excellent ford, which we had observed the Indians crossing a few yards below our camp (on the Spanish Trail) to an island opposite, and from its upper end to the shore…. Indians thronged our camp for several hours. They are the merriest of their race I have ever seen, except the Yumas—constantly laughing and talking, and appearing grateful for the trifling presents they receive. A wrinkled, hard-faced savage, with whom I shared my luncheon of bread and bacon, quite laughed aloud with joy at his good fortune.[59]

A month prior to this encounter another group of travelers had also crossed the Green River but faced a different experience. Lieutenant E. F. Beale, en route to California to assume the position of superintendent of Indian Affairs, had also followed the Spanish Trail. With him was Gwinn H. Heap, who was keeping a journal of events when they arrived at the river. He recorded that after the party had crossed, they gave the Indians their boats, which they "ripped to pieces to make moccasin soles of the hides."[60] Twenty-five Utes joined them in their camp a mile upstream and remained there for the night. The two groups were friendly, ate supper together, and spent time talking about recent events. The following morning, however, the Utes became insolent. Most were armed with rifles, and "all had bows and quivers full of arrows with obsidian heads."[61] The Indians traveled with Beale's contingent for several miles, asking for presents, and then left in a bad mood.

Ever since the Mormons, members of the Church of Jesus Christ of Latter-day Saints, had arrived on the Wasatch Front and established Salt Lake City, they had had an ever-increasing impact on the Utes in their area. In 1848 there were five thousand Mormons in Utah; by 1850 there were eleven thousand.[62] Church president Brigham Young, who was also the governor, believed expansion would be key to holding territory for the Mormons, so during the next thirty years he established more than 250 settlements throughout the Intermountain West, primarily in Utah, Idaho, and Nevada.[63] Despite having his hands full fighting with local Timpanogos and other Utes in 1849–50, the Walker (Wakara) War in 1853, and with Shoshones to the north, he continued to push settlement into Indian lands throughout Utah. In 1855 Wakara died of natural causes, passing the leadership of the Timpanogos Utes to his brother Arapene. Young desired to establish a foothold in southeastern Utah along the Spanish Trail, pounding a stake for Mormon holdings in well-known terrain that held potential. His followers set forth into Weenuche lands.

A prominent topographic feature in the area, Elk Mountain, also known as the La Sals, offered water from melting snow, lumber for construction and heating homes, and game to hunt, and the fertile bottom lands beside the Colorado River could be irrigated and farmed. Partial access to previously established routes made communication easier, while controlling entrance into the Great Basin. Trade with the neighboring Utes and Navajos was another possibility. Weighing these factors, at the April Church Conference of 1855, Young directed forty-one men under the leadership of Alfred N. Billings to settle the area.

The La Sals were then the home of a band of Utes identified in the historical record as the Sheberetch. Although other clearly identifiable Ute groups also used this area, historical documents written in the 1850s and early 1860s primarily link this group with the area, calling them Elk Mountain Utes.[64]

Anthropologist Isabel Kelly, when speaking of the Sheberetch as well as the San Pete, Yampa, and Fish Utes in the early years, believed they were "unmounted and indistinguishable from Southern Paiute."[65] By 1862, reports said they were well mounted, well armed, and well traveled. In the spring they began extensive hunting and gathering trips that took them to the Colorado and Bear Rivers, the Laramie Plains, Shoshone country, and the Green River. In September, after hunting buffalo and fishing, they returned to Elk Mountain. These Indians also traded with the Navajos and, at this time, were under the leadership of "Saviot" and "Enthorof."[66]

Anthropologist Julian H. Steward wrestled with identifying exactly who these people were but found it a "particularly difficult problem as they have been located in Colorado, Utah, and Arizona by different sources."[67] He cites other reports that claim these Utes were from Arizona and Colorado, had attacked southern settlements (unspecified), were responsible for closing the Elk Mountain Mission, and participated heavily in Black Hawk's war in the 1860s. While some scholars suggest these Indians had ties with the Yampa, Tabeguache, or Uinta bands, "whoever they were they had completely lost identity after 1873."[68] Given that Steward never mentions the Weenuche band of Utes, there is a real possibility that he placed them primarily in Colorado, and that the Elk Mountain Utes were most likely part of this group. According to the Ute Mountain Utes, "some of the White Mesa Utes are Weeminuche. Others are descendants of the Sheberetch band and other bands of Utes who did not move to the Uintah Reservation in Utah. These Utes intermarried with Southern Paiutes."[69] If the Elk Mountain Utes are not totally Weenuche, there is no doubt they had extensive dealings with them.

Returning to the issue of their disappearance, explorer and ethnographer John Wesley Powell gives the most satisfactory answer. In his 1873 report on Utes, Paiutes, and re-

Site of the fort built by forty-one Elk Mountain missionaries under the direction of Alfred N. Billings in 1855. Nothing remains of the sixty-four-square-foot stone structure, which was located approximately a half mile north of modern downtown Moab. The Mormons abandoned their enterprise after less than a year due to hostile action. (Courtesy of San Juan County Historical Commission)

lated tribes, he mentions that previously the Sheberetch were in continuous alliance with "Navajos and Utes who inhabit the country to the east of the Colorado River" as they preyed upon Mormon settlements. This included the Weenuche of San Juan County.[70] With the end of Black Hawk's war, the Sheberetch eventually settled down, but generally steered clear of reservation life; however, "early in the last summer [1872] a terrible scourge swept off great numbers of this tribe, until but 144 remain, and these, terrified and humble, sue for peace and promise to work."[71] At least some of them settled on the Uintah Reservation and became integrated with that Ute population. For years to come, Navajo and Weenuche trading expeditions traveled to the Uintah Reservation, perhaps to maintain contact with relatives and trade partners carried over from this era.

On May 21, 1855, a contingent of Mormons departed Manti, heading east for the Grand (Colorado) River. Twelve days later they reached the "Green River Road," camped on the river at Gunnison's old camp site, and told the Utes living there that their "business was to learn them the principles of the Gospel and to raise grain."[72] The In-

dians were "well pleased." Eight days later the settlers reached the Grand, and by June 15 they, their livestock, and fifteen wagons had made it across the river. Following initial land clearing nearby, the group decided to move farther from the river, to a spring off the floodplain. Elk Mountain (Mill) Creek proved essential for diverting water for irrigation, the river being less easily controlled. The men formed four work companies and set to building shelters, a 130-foot corral, and a 64-square-foot rock fort, as well as burning wood for charcoal, building a dam and ditch, clearing additional acres, and planting crops. That Sunday they rebaptized each other to renew their commitment to their mission and to strengthen group harmony.[73]

A few Utes were camped in the general vicinity, but most were "off fighting the Spaniards [Mexicans] and whites."[74] Eventually, a band of fourteen warriors appeared on the north side of the river, asking to be ferried across in the pioneers' boat because the Shoshones were in pursuit. They spent the next four days on the south side of the river with the settlers, committing to be "friendly and quit stealing." Others arrived, a group of twenty men, ten women, and children, who had the "hand of God resting upon [them] because they felt friendly toward us." In mid-July, by which time the Indian corn had tasseled and the Mormons' corn was knee high, Arapene passed by the settlement on his way to trade Piede children to the Navajos.[75] Many of the local Ute leaders had already been to the settlement and established relations. Before Arapene departed, he told these men, first in Ute, then Navajo, that the Mormons were here to help them and that they should deal fairly and not steal from them or the white men would return to the northern settlements.[76]

The most important visitor on a local level was "Quit-Sub-Socketts" (or "Quilsos-sockett"), designated as "the Elk Mountain chief." He soon received the new name of Saint John. On June 30 he arrived with a handful of men to learn the cause of all the smoke swirling through the sky from burning sagebrush. He claimed that the land being settled was his and that he liked it, so wanted something for it. A blanket and two shirts made him "well satisfied." According to a Mormon interpreter, Saint John said

> that we were the first white men or red that he
> ever gave any privileges to stop on his premises
> any longer than they had time to get away. But,
> said he, "I had a dream the other night and I saw
> the Mormons coming here to live on my land. I
> went and got my men to get them and was go-
> ing to drive them off, but the Great Spirit told me
> to let the Mormons alone, that we must be good
> friends, and not fight any more." From that he
> said he knew it was good for us to be there; that
> he wanted us to learn his wild boys how to plow,
> raise grain, and work like we did.[77]

The next day four men visited him at his "farm"—ten acres planted in corn, melons, squash, and pumpkins—located on "Pack Saddle" (Pack) Creek, twelve miles south of the Mormon settlement. The settlers helped irrigate his crop, which pleased the Elk Mountain Utes.[78]

Good relations prevailed. On July 22 the Mormons baptized and confirmed fifteen men and women, gave them all English names, ordained four of them as Elders, and sent them with a charge to preach to their tribe. Among these were Saint John's brother and family and two of his sons. Later word came that the Navajos were anxious to fight the Utes, who were afraid that Brigham Young would call the settlers back. Many of the other tribes were at war, but they did not want to fight since the Mormons were perceived as "the only friends they had." The threat proved to be a false alarm, Arapene sending word that his trading with the Navajos had gone well and that he would soon be arriving with four of their chiefs to make peace with the Elk Mountain Utes and meet the Mormons. Two days later the party arrived. The Ute groups represented were "very independent" but agreed to give back all of the horses they had stolen. The Navajos desired peace with everyone, "but if they [Utes] would not make peace, they would come upon them and kill them all off." The warring factions formed a truce, with the Navajos also receiving permission to travel through Ute land to get to the Mormon settlements for trade.[79] Following the council Arapene left for his country, the Navajos returned to theirs, and the Elk Mountain Utes started for the Tabeguaches' land. Everything seemed peaceful on August 21, when sixteen settlers left for Salt Lake City.

Nine days later, making good the agreement, Billings and five other men set off with a Ute guide, Shinobby, and five other Utes to trade with the Navajos. The six Mormons brought almost fifty pounds of powder, twenty-six pounds of lead, and three thousand caps for Indian firearms, as well as sixty-four deer hides and an assortment of knives, fishhooks, and needles. Billings and Ethan Pettit recorded the same information with apparent detail in distance and direction traveled, but when charted on a map, their route becomes much more hard to determine than one would expect. Definite landmarks after leaving Spanish Valley include Church Rock in Dry Valley and Peters Spring.

The men camped in the vicinity of the eventual town site of Monticello and then started their journey over hills and through canyons. The best "fit" to their description—which could actually play out into three different routes—was down Mustang Mesa, north of the Bluff Bench, to the end of Tank Mesa, and then to Butler Wash, the San Juan River, and over Nokaito Bench to a Navajo village forty miles south of the river. Before crossing, the Utes and Navajos held a trade fair. Once the party arrived at the Navajo camp, the exchanging commenced, and the whites were impressed with the Navajos' livestock and blankets. On September 12 the expedition arrived back at the mission to find that eighteen more Utes had been baptized, three of whom were ordained as Elders and two as priests.[80]

Relations, however, were souring. There had always been the question of why the settlers had built a fort if there were to be peace between the two groups, and the way some of the resources had been appropriated by the whites also did not seem right.[81] But even more telling was an incident involving Arrapene's brother Spoods, who lost a breast pin; in the hands of the wrong person, this object could be used to direct evil against its owner. He and ten other men accompanied Saint John to question the Mormons about their intent. "They thought that we had fixed something to kill them all off, such is their superstition. Four of them are strangers from beyond Elk Mountain."[82] Obviously associated with witchcraft, this incident suggests underlying mistrust. In mid-September, with the Mormon's corn ripe, the Indians appropriated it for their own use. Potatoes, turnips, beets, melons, and squash met a similar fate. The settlers reacted, getting as much of their crops as they could back to the fort. At this crucial time five more men returned to Salt Lake City, reducing the settlement to

less than half its strength.[83] Weakness bred contempt.

September 23, 1855, was a fateful day for the Elk Mountain Mission. Although there had been rumors that many of the Utes had left for their fall hunt, the settlers moved their livestock closer to the fort. Shortly thereafter a large number of Indians crossed the river, acting "saucy and impudent" and wanting to know why the cattle had been moved to a different pasture. Billings gives a detailed account of what happened next.[84] Charles, a Ute warrior who had recently been eager to trade for a gun, accompanied James Hunt from the fort to get his horses. A mile from safety, Charles shot Hunt in the back, encouraged an Indian nearby to collect some of the horses, joined up with some other warriors and recrossed the river. With war whoops, they charged for the herds. The alerted settlers retrieved Hunt's body, fought a delaying action back to the fort, corralled the animals the Indians had not gotten, and exchanged fire until dark. The Utes torched the harvested corn and hay and set the corral on fire while seven Indians left for the mountain to kill two unsuspecting Mormon hunters. The report of seven rifles told the end of that story.

As events unfolded a few Indians came to the fort to parley. Admitting that two or three had died, with as many wounded, the Utes swore to avenge the deaths by killing more Mormons, while denying having shot the two hunters. Nevertheless, they requested bread to eat, which they received. "The Indians engaged in this sad affair were all baptized.... They do not belong to our particular band or chief. Some are Green River Utes, some of White Eye's band, and a band of thieves and murderers."[85] The next day a second dialogue opened, the Utes telling the Mormons that they had sent to the mountains for more warriors to come and help, and so the settlers had better leave the country now. After a short deliberation, the white men turned the final decision over to

Billings. He chose to leave. Horses, cattle, and equipment that could not be easily taken remained at the fort. Before noon they had abandoned the Elk Mountain Mission.

Once the settlers had crossed the Grand, a brother of Saint John, described as "an old chief," and his two sons caught up to them and inquired what had happened.[86] He told them he felt bad about what had occurred and that he would attempt to get the cattle, but it was "only one against so many." He went to the fort and talked to the Indians, explaining that he intended to return the livestock to its owners. As he began to drive them out of the corral, other Utes started to shoot them. One made the mistake of trying to shoot the old chief; an arrow through the assailant's neck stopped him. Another Ute said that he would follow the Mormons and kill one of them. Saint John's brother "caught him by the hair of the head, pulled him off his horse, and hit him severely on the back part of the head and ear with his bow, and

left him." He drove fifteen cattle to the settlers before they had started on their long trip to Manti. Seven animals were too badly wounded to make the trip and so were either killed for food or left with the old man. On September 30 the beleaguered group reached their destination.

While having pushed the white man out of their territory was a victory for some Utes, more turbulent times lay ahead. Hostilities with the Navajos would fill the next decade, and they would face a concerted effort against them supported by the U.S. military—a campaign that extended throughout the Southwest. In the Great Basin Black Hawk's war consumed much of the Northern Utes' energy. Both of these major events had an impact on the Weenuche in southeastern Utah, involving patterns of exchange, travel, and relations established during the years of the Old Spanish Trail. It would be a long time before lasting peace reached the land of the Weenuche.

CHAPTER 5

"Enemies Like a Road Covered with Ice"

Expanding Weenuche Dominance, 1855–1870

Don't be sorry when we get enemies like a road covered with ice —
starvation, poverty, and cold. You will suffer; then you will understand.

Hascon Benally, Navajo

By the end of the 1850s, the Utes had established a pattern of dominance in the Four Corners area. Over the next decade the Weenuche in southeastern Utah monitored the comings and goings of Navajos and the U.S. military, while reaching down into Arizona and New Mexico to wage war against the Navajos. At the same time they assisted the Ute leader Black Hawk in a war against the Mormons in central Utah. Like a distant rider crossing the great sage plain beneath Blue Mountain, the role of the White Mesa Utes was at first indistinct, its general outline visible but not yet differentiated from that of other Ute bands. As time progressed, an ever clearer view of what they were doing emerged. Earlier correspondence occasionally referenced the Weenuche, but the interactions between all three southern bands remained muddled. Increased development of Ute agencies clarified their roles. Still, there is enough specific information from the earlier years to indicate that the ancestors of the White Mesa Utes played a part in both fighting and protecting the Navajos during this confusing and turbulent time.

Interestingly, some of the most complete accounts of Ute activities come from Navajo oral history. Although Utes rarely mention their role in this conflict, the Navajos, who were on the receiving end, provide a detailed description of what they encountered. From their voices comes this story. Other Native American groups, as well as New Mexican volunteers, also played a part, but in the northern part of Navajo lands the Utes held sway. As will be seen, prior relations between the two groups at times caused a role reversal, with the Utes actually protecting the Navajos, but in general, their interactions were characterized by intense warfare.

Beginning in 1855, incidents edged their way toward the major conflicts of the 1860s.[1] The historic record is clear that the Capote, Muache, and Tabeguache Utes prosecuted much of the war. There is no mention of the Weenuche per se. Problems first erupted to the east, in Colorado and New Mexico. Friction between settlers and Utes in the San Luis Valley, coupled with the death of fifteen white men in Pueblo, Colorado, opened the door for military intervention. The army defeated the Southern Utes twice, bringing them to the conference table at Abiquiu, where they signed a treaty never ratified by Congress. The 1855 agreement placed the Utes on a one-thousand-square-mile reservation, extending through much of western Colorado, and promised $66,000, which was never paid.[2]

The Utes remained peaceful, yet suspicious of white intent. And rightly so. Two years later, with brushfire incidents popping up in the general Four Corners area, the commissioner of Indian Affairs warned the New Mexico superintendent, James L. Collins, that if every effort to establish peace failed, he should "array them [Utes] against such other Indians as may be found on the side of the enemies of the government and to spare no pain to prevent them from attacking the whites."[3] Friction between the military and Navajos in New Mexico was increasing, so why not play those two Indian groups, as well as others, against each other? The Ute-Navajo conflict had been growing from a series of isolated incidents and, in the eyes of military strategists, was ready to be exploited. In 1856 a Navajo war party had raided the Utes, killing three principal chiefs—Surdo, Cumabo, and Sobeta—near Abiquiu and stealing livestock. Other Navajos heard of the attack and went to the Capotes with horses to pay for the wrongdoing, but were killed despite their peaceful intentions. A month later reports trickled in that the Utes had killed eight Navajos near the northern part of the Tunicha range; the Navajos retaliated by killing five Utes. Pressure increased on the Capotes, forcing them to move closer to the agency to protect their dwindling horse herds from raiders.[4]

In February 1858 some principal Navajo chiefs arrived in Santa Fe for a peace conference with the Utes. Before the meeting began, nine or ten Navajos stole two thousand sheep from Abiquiu. Utes and Mexicans pursued the thieves, killed five, and took three prisoners, none of whom had been involved in the robbery. Little wonder that when six Ute and five Navajo leaders met on March 11, 1858, they accomplished little. The Utes believed the Navajos could not be trusted and pointed to recent thefts as an example. Instead, they swore vengeance as soon as the weather cleared, promising to join other groups to chastise these inveterate thieves. They also denied growing rumors that they were accepting support from the

Mormons and insisted on their allegiance to Washington.

Kit Carson, the Ute agent, and military officials also believed there was no foundation to the rumors of Mormon intervention in Ute affairs.[5] There was, however, some basis. During the mid to late 1850s, Mormons in southwestern Utah were feeling the effects of Colonel Albert Sydney Johnston's attempted invasion of Salt Lake City and the general animosity of the federal government. They reacted by encouraging Navajos, Utes, and Paiutes to serve as auxiliaries in the Nauvoo Legion and to act as allies. Some Utes attended meetings with Brigham Young in Salt Lake City, sending emissaries to the Navajos to invite them to a peace conference held in the Navajo Mountain area. There the settlers reportedly handed out guns and ammunition to solidify a cooperative agreement.[6] Whispers about a massacre involving Paiutes at Mountain Meadows, in southwestern Utah, fueled greater concerns. The effects of these rumors were twofold. First, the Utes received increased annuities from the government as bribes to keep them peacefully tied to their agency. Second, the agents and military authorities were alerted to new concerns in the tangled web of conflict between the Navajos, Utes, Pueblos, and Mexicans.

While there was a fair amount of military and governmental correspondence concerning the involvement of Mormons with the Indians, of primary interest is the "go-between" who brought the four different entities to the conference table. Since the term "Weenuche" is absent from the military record, and assuming that part of their activity is conflated with that of the Capote, their neighbors, it appears that their involvement was attributed to the "Pah-Utah." On September 13, 1859, Captain John G. Walker led a reconnaissance force through Tsegi Canyon, near today's Kayenta, Arizona. He noted that this was the "home of a band of Pah-Utahs" and later remarked that "no part of this region is inhabited...as we saw many abandoned

Ute warriors tracking a trail in southwestern Colorado, 1899. Few scholars have examined in detail the role that the Utes played in defeating the Navajos in the northern part of their territory. The success of the campaign is often attributed to Kit Carson and the American military, but its sustained pressure and ultimate effectiveness should be attributed to the Utes. Familiar with the land, excellent trackers, and implacable foes, they brought the fight to the heart of Navajo land. (Denver Public Library, Western History Collection, H. S. Poley, P-54)

Navajo huts. Our guide says the reason is the Navajos are afraid of the Pah-Utahs upon whose country it borders."[7] A week later a group of "Pah-Utahs," or Weenuche, visited Walker's camp, eighty miles west of Canyon de Chelly. One of them spoke Navajo and related to the expedition's guide that the Mormons had sent them and others to meet with the Navajos, make peace, and invite them to Sierra Panoche[a] (Ear of Indian Corn — Navajo Mountain) for a council in mid-October. They then displayed their gifts of shirts, beads, and powder.[8] Later another Pah-Utah messenger presented a signed letter of introduction from an LDS bishop stating that the bearer was a baptized member in good standing. It's possible that these men had been previously involved in the Elk Mountain Mission before its abandonment.

Carson, at this point, was serving as a positive force on behalf of the Utes. From 1853 to 1860 he worked as their agent at the main agency in Taos and became a trusted counselor to them, the military, and the white communities he was charged to protect. His facility with the Ute language and understanding of their culture built confidence in his judgment. He estimated in 1857 that the Capote band was comprised of eight to nine hundred members, and the Muache six hundred, but he gave no figure for the Weenuche. He estimated that the Navajos numbered around twelve thousand.[9] Carson and the next Ute agent, Albert H. Pfeiffer, promoted the use of their wards as "spies and guides," and as soldiers against their traditional enemy, the Navajos. Their effectiveness on the northern Navajo frontier later proved instrumental in destroying the offensive capability of these people, who bestowed upon them the Navajo title "The Enemies You Continually Fight With."

By the summer of 1858, there were numerous reports of Utes operating in large numbers in the heart of Navajo territory. In one incident "a large force of Utahs attacked the band of Cavilliard Mucho on the San Juan opposite (north) of the Carizzo mountains, killing ten Navajos, capturing six women and children and the whole herd of (500) horses," and in another, "a party of Utahs, forty in number, crossed the Rio Colorado below the mouth of the San Juan into this country (Arizona) and came as far as the Canyon de Chelly and there killed Pelon, a chief of considerable property."[10] The government encouraged these forays, saying that the Utes "appear to have inspired the Navajos with a dread not to be gotten over."[11] In the words of General Dixon Miles, "Let loose on these [Navajo] Indians all the surrounding tribes and inhabitants, particularly the Utahs and Mexicans, the two they seem to dread the most."[12] The number of operations against the Navajos grew, netting large herds of livestock and captives for sale.

By the beginning of 1860 the Utes' fluid frontier had also changed. In 1859 miners discovered gold in the San Juan Mountains of Colorado. Occasional skirmishes with trespassers and increasing strain on a hunting and gathering lifestyle tied to a shrinking land base created greater dependency on the agencies. The shadow of the Civil War loomed more ominously across the nation as the North tussled with the South before the onslaught of hostilities, while local friction and poor crops created general unrest throughout the Four Corners region. Stretched to the limit financially and lacking manpower, the government posed an important question to the military commanders and agents of the region: What was to be done with the Utes?

The obvious solution, and one that the Utes heartily agreed with, was for them to be hired by the military as auxiliaries to the regular forces. Colonel Thomas T. Fauntleroy, working with Carson, suggested that a band of three to four hundred Utes could augment the six to eight companies of Mexican volunteers and spearhead the thrust against the Navajos. Nothing would be more effective than to have them ferret out the enemy from the deep recesses of the Chuska/Tunicha Mountains, Canyon de Chelly, and areas as far west as the Little Colorado River. Indeed, field reports had already indicated that camps in the Navajo Mountain region and the Carrizos were abandoned, the Navajos having pushed their large herds of livestock into the region south of the Tunicha Mountains.

Fauntleroy insisted that Carson guarantee the eagerness of the Utes, "the best riflemen in the world," to wage war. He continued,

> I desire that I may be allowed to employ them, as they do not require pay as soldiers, but only to be supplied for a short time with provisions, until they can get well into the Indian country. I cannot but recommend this plan as it will at once have the effect to get the cooperation of a most valuable force, and at the same time employ these restless people, who otherwise must foray upon our own settlements.[13]

This proved to be the perfect solution—let the Utes provide for their welfare at the expense of the Navajos, while rendering a service that was difficult, at best, for the conventional military. With Collins's acquiescence to this plan, Colonel Edward R. Canby appeared at Abiquiu to work out details with Agent Pfeiffer. Eighty Utes serving as his guides and spies then marched into the area of Canyon de Chelly, while Pfeiffer took another three hundred Indians and headed in the same general direction. Much of this fighting broke down into small unit actions as the Utes forged ahead of the main body. The cumulative impression is that their primary goal was to obtain horses and captives as much as to defeat the Navajos.

Canby's summary of his October–November 1860 campaign illustrates the Utes' effectiveness. He claimed his troops killed 28 Navajos and captured 360 horses and 2,000 sheep, while his Utes killed 6 Navajos and captured 600 horses and 5,000 sheep, almost double the soldiers' take.[14] Pfeiffer reported the same trend, saying that in a month's time he had killed 6 Navajos, taken 19 prisoners, and obtained 5,000 sheep and about 500 horses, the latter captured by the Utes. The agent complained that once the Indians obtained the horses, they left him with 20 Mexicans to herd, with great difficulty, the prisoners and sheep to Abiquiu. Both white leaders resented the Utes for leaving after getting what they wanted.[15] For the next five years the war and this pattern of seizure of animals and captives continued.[16]

The effect of this raiding soon became apparent. Navajo leaders straggled in to various forts to escape harassment and seek mercy. The Navajos agreed to return to their country, persuade others to stop fighting, and live peacefully as long as "the Utahs might be hindered from making any campaigns against them."[17] Despite these overtures, the Utes continued the war for captives and booty. As Civil War battles over slavery raged between the North and South, the slave trade was booming in Río Arriba, Abiquiu, and Taos. By January 1862 a minimum of 600 women and children were being held captive in New Mexico through a system described as "worse than African slavery." The number of unreported slaves can only be guessed, but by 1865 General Carleton estimated that at least 3,000 were living in Mexican households.[18]

Navajos in southeastern Utah give clear testimony of what they experienced at the hands of the Utes during and after the "Fearing Time," lasting from 1858 to 1868. Navajo and Ute relations, which had previously vacillated between uneasy friendship to overt hostility, now reached their zenith in a full-scale war. But part of the blame for this friction can be placed on the traditional form of Navajo government. Agents at this time

pointed out that fragmented band leadership had "no power to punish the bad men of the nation or prevent them from committing depredations when they are disposed to do so."[19] Often these leaders were wealthy and paid an indemnity from their own herds. These rich men, or *ricos*, had the most to lose when total war occurred and so wanted to maintain a peaceful status quo. This was not true of the young men interested in building their herds and acquiring status.

Navajo oral tradition confirms this view. Approximately half of the forty or so stories told by Navajo elders blame the start of hostilities on their people. A few examples follow. "The reason for being taken to Fort Sumner was that the Diné were stealing from other tribes…and they were caught sometimes in stealing livestock." "It was because of the fighting between the Navajos and other Indians that our ancestors were taken to Fort Sumner." "They [our ancestors] said it was our own fault that we were rounded up and taken to Fort Sumner. They said we used to kill Ute Indians, Pueblo Indians and Mexicans and bring their sheep back and that those actions caused the wars between us, the army, and other Indian tribes." "Our late forefathers, those that were wise, begged their fellow Diné to stop going around stealing horses, sheep and cattle from the Mexicans; but the stealing went on. One of the men who was begging the Diné to quit stealing said, 'Don't be sorry when we get enemies like a road covered with ice — starvation, poverty, and cold. You will suffer; then you will understand."[20] Martha Nez, living near Mexican Water, attributed the problem locally to Navajo men harassing Ute women picking sumac berries. The men killed some of the women, starting the conflict. "The uprising did not begin with the white people. It started with the Utes first."[21]

Yellow Horse, who became a Navajo leader, tells of traveling with friends to Mancos Creek, the "traditional boundary between Utes and Navajos."[22] There they encountered an encampment of Utes, mostly women and children, whose husbands were hunting in the Gallina Mountains. Seizing the opportunity, the Navajos killed some of the men and women, and stole the horses in retaliation for past wrongs. A Ute runner alerted the hunters, who chased the offending party toward the San Francisco Mountains before giving up and returning home. Many Navajos living along the San Juan River feared retaliation and left the area, heading for the Lukachukai Mountains and other secluded spots away from the enemies' domain. "Eventually the Utes won the battle because the refugees lost many people to starvation before spring arrived."[23] As for those who initiated the raid, they fled to the Fort Defiance area until taken to Fort Sumner. By then Yellow Horse and his friends were starving and nearly naked.

George Littlesalt remembers some Navajos who heard the piñon crop was plentiful in the La Sal Mountains and so "moved up there; and they picked the little nuts and lived with some Utes that they used to know before they went to the La Sals."[24] While harvesting the crop, other Utes appeared and chased the people, who escaped and fled to Oljato. Eventually they moved to Navajo Mountain and joined a growing number of Navajos collecting in that area. There were frequent skirmishes against their enemy as each vied for advantage. Littlesalt's grandfather, Old Whiskers, a powerful medicine man who spoke Paiute, befriended some of these people, who joined his group. It is interesting to note that although these Navajos fought some of the Utes, they also had both Ute and Paiute friends in this area.

Some Navajos initially knew little about the raids and fighting. Wolfkiller, living in the Monument Valley–Kayenta area, recalled that he and his brother were herding sheep one day when they spied four successive columns of white smoke. Unsure what this meant, they asked their grandfather that evening, who after a second day of signaling, knew that it called for a council. After

attending, he returned with confirmation of his suspicions. War with the Utes was upon them, caused by the theft of sheep and women by young warriors. The grandfather explained,

> My children, it is as we feared. The spirit of war is trying to walk into our land, but we must try to stop it.… We have done nothing to cause this thing, but some of the people have made another raid, and our chief, at what they call Washington, has sent us word that we must leave our land and go with the soldiers to a place far to the east.… Now I think the people who have brought this on themselves should be taken, but we who do not want to have trouble should not be taken away from a land we know and are contented to live in.[25]

As the Utes invaded Navajo camps, the Diné retreated to nearly inaccessible canyons to avoid capture. Compare the life of Wolfkiller with that of Hashkéninii, two men from different family groups who started out in the same Monument Valley–Kayenta area. Wolfkiller and his family, determined to stay in their country, did all they could to avoid detection. He left a chilling account of what it was like to live during this time. The feeling of helpless uncertainty, being ever vigilant, maintaining sentinels and scouts, moving constantly, surviving in winter weather without permanent shelter, building fires near large rocks that acted like a chimney to dissipate smoke, and continuously worrying about food took its toll on the family's morale. Winter ended, and spring brought a new onslaught of enemy forays. Wolfkiller remembers a scout coming into camp and announcing, "We are lost. The enemy has brought Utes to help them track us down, and they are coming nearer. They are cutting down the cornfields and killing the old people who cannot travel. They have taken many of the people out."[26]

The family moved farther into the canyons, but to no avail. As the soldiers approached, signal fires were set to indicate

Left Handed Manygoats's camp in Monument Valley. Many Navajos sought refuge from death or capture in the rugged periphery of their territory, but isolated camps such as this were easy targets for roaming Ute warriors. (Used by permission, Utah State Historical Society, all rights reserved.)

that the group was surrounded and resistance was futile. The grandfather determined that surrender needed to be accomplished at night because "The Utes would welcome the chance to kill as many of our people as they could if our people came while it was light."[27] He and two elders left the others behind and made their way to the soldiers' camp. Mounted Utes rode about maintaining vigilance until long after dark. The Navajos were mainly concerned with avoiding any contact with them before reaching the soldiers, whom they considered their source of safety. After a close call the men infiltrated past the sentinels and made contact with a white man who spoke their language. They explained, "We would have come in to the soldiers' camp before, but we were afraid of the Utes. They have always been our enemies, and we knew that they would welcome the chance to kill as many of us as they could.… I asked him not to take any Utes to our camp. He

said he knew he could trust us and would not send any Utes to our camp."[28] The party returned, gathered their belongings, and began their "long walk."

Hashkéninii, like Wolfkiller, was surprised one day when a rider came to his hogan and announced that the dust on the horizon belonged to the soldiers, and that "there were some Ute scouts among the white soldiers and we were more afraid of them than the whites, as we had always been at war with them."[29] Scattering about the desert floor and nearby canyons to avoid detection, seventeen people reassembled at night and, with a few possessions, headed north. Hashkéninii, mounted and armed with an old rifle, led the party and scouted for enemies. Next he turned west, traveling through a maze of canyons until he reached the south end of Navajo Mountain. His wife, her two sisters, and the rest of the group were exhausted, hungry, and footsore. His wife sat down and refused

Hashkéninii, shown here at John Wetherill's trading post in Oljato around 1909, fled to Navajo Mountain during "the Fearing Time." He successfully evaded capture and was there to greet the Navajos returning from Fort Sumner, where they had been incarcerated for four years. (Used by permission, Utah State Historical Society, all rights reserved.)

to go any farther. The group selected a campsite, located a permanent source of water, began collecting seeds and nuts, killed an occasional rabbit, and prepared for winter. No sheep from their flock of twenty were to be eaten, so that they would increase. Hashkéninii was a taskmaster, pushing his people to constantly work to do whatever was needed to survive. His son recalled, "He drove everyone all day long and would never let us rest, knowing that we might starve." From this he received his name, which translates as "Giving Out Anger" or "the Angry One."[30]

Hashkéninii and his group remained at Navajo Mountain for six years, during which only one Ute ever found them, and all he did was trade. Hashkéninii Biye' [Begay] (Giving Out Anger's Son) did not realize until later that this person was Grayhair (a.k.a. Cabeza Blanca, or "White Haired Ute"), a scourge to Navajos in hiding. He is described as a bad man

who pretended to be our friend only in order to spy on us. When our flocks began to increase, he organized a group of young warriors and started for Navajo Mountain to kill us and also to get revenge on the people [Utes] who had thrown him out. At the south end of [Sleeping] Ute Mountain, he stopped to visit with some Utes, but he was so bad they killed him and his nephew. After that all the Utes moved away from Navajo Mountain and we had no more trouble.[31]

By the time the government released the Navajos from Fort Sumner, Hashkéninii and his family were wealthy, with large herds of sheep and silver jewelry made from a vein of ore he had discovered.

Other Navajo groups collected in the Comb Ridge–Bears Ears area. Old Man Bob recalled, "There were no permanent homes because there were Utes raiding in this country in those days so we were afraid to stay in one place too long."[32] His mother told him that her family used to inhabit the area between the Dolores River (in Colorado) and the Bears Ears long before the conflict began. After the Ute attacks began, they stayed more in the Bears Ears area, living in fear of Cabeza Blanca. Old Ruins, born in 1871, shared a family story of his mother, Woman Who Walked Like She Was Crippled (Asdzáán Jidii), and his father, also called Old Ruins (Kit'siili), living north of the Bears Ears. Crippled Woman's mother remained west of the Bears Ears and north of the San Juan River. A raid by the Utes pushed her group across the river, but they doubled back to the Bears Ears and joined a noted headman named K'aa Yélii.[33]

Not all Navajos were as fortunate. "Woman Who Had Her House Burned" (Asdzáán Kin Díílid) was born near the Bears Ears, but after hostilities broke out, she ended up on Black Mesa, in Arizona. The enemy, under the leadership of Cabeza Blanca, raided her camp, captured her, and sold her as a slave to a Mexican; she did not return home for two years, until the soldiers released the Navajos from Fort Sumner. "It was told by the Navajos that this leader [Cabeza Blanca] looked for Navajos who had sheep, horses, or young girls that he could capture and sell to other people such as the Mexicans."[34] Her great-grandfather, "Man Who Regained and Lost Horses" (Hastiin Bilį́į' Nádláhí), received his name after Utes and Mexicans stole his large horse herd. After he obtained more livestock, the Utes again took a sizeable portion of them. Finally, his camp, comprised of many hogans located on Long Point, near the Bears Ears, came under attack. Utes from the Dolores River area raided the settlement, killing him and others.[35]

As previously noted, there were exceptions. In a few instances, some Navajo groups actually fled to the Utes during times of trouble. Take Cayetano, for instance. As early as 1805 this wealthy Navajo living in the Four Corners area had become an influential leader. His three sons were intimately involved with southeastern Utah and, no doubt, the Weenuche living there. Manuelito, born five miles south of the Bears Ears around 1820, grew to be one of the most prominent Navajo war leaders and was one of the last to surrender at Fort Sumner, in 1865. K'aa Yélii ("One With Arrow Quiver") was born for the "Within His Cover People" (Bit'ahnii) clan near Shonto, Arizona. During the Long Walk period, when he was thirty, he lived at the Bears Ears. A third brother, Cayetanito (or K'aak'eh—"Wounded"), lived near Beautiful Mountain but also frequented the Montezuma Creek area.[36]

Cayetano had close ties with some of the Utes living north of the San Juan even though the river was said to serve as a boundary between the two tribes. During the 1850s he planted crops in the vicinity of the San Juan River under the protection of the Capotes. Indeed, at one point a Ute named Yeusache pursued a Navajo who had stolen some of Cayetano's livestock. This incident may be one referred to in a report given by Charles H. Dimmock, who was with the Captain John N. Macomb survey trip through southeastern Utah in 1859. He mentioned how a group of

Ute warriors—among whom was Tamuche, a Capote, and Souvetah (or "Sowictte," whose "Northern Utes spent so many winters near the Elk Mountains that Colorado whites often referred to them as Elk Mountain Ute")—and the Navajo Manuelito visited in his camp.[37] Five days later Tamuche returned, saying that a Ute named Nutria, assisted by some fellow tribesmen, had run off all of Cayetano's horses. A month later some of Cayetano's Navajos stole two horses from Macomb's group "in retaliation for those taken from him by the Utes with us."[38]

Yet when the Capotes had eight horses stolen from them by Navajo raiders, two of Cayetano's sons-in-law, along with other Navajos, killed three Mexican herders and stole ten thousand sheep in revenge. A report of the incident stated, "The Navajos that committed this depredation are rich and influential men,…they live with the Capote Utahs… have procured the return of the horses stolen from the Utahs who they say have promised to aid and assist them in defending themselves against all enemies."[39] Four months later Cayetano appeared with Tamuche in Abiquiu to let the agent know that "on the branches of the Chama River some eighty miles from Abiquiu, all the Capote, Tabeguauche, and Mouache Ute Indians and the Navajos that are congregated within his agency are united."[40] Until some Mexicans killed him in January 1860, Cayetano spent much of his time camped on the Animas and La Plata Rivers—Ute country—during a time when most Navajos fled south and west away from their vengeful enemy. Cayetanito (Little Cayetano) met a similar fate as his father in 1863, also at the hands of the Mexicans.

Manuelito, one of the last *ricos* to surrender, by this time lived near the Little Colorado River. His success as a war leader had made him a symbol of Navajo resistance—and thus a military target. In February 1865 he received a visit from a Navajo he trusted, but ended the talk by insisting that "he intended to die where he was, that he was not stealing, that he could always be found…and did not intend to run away."[41] At that point Manuelito's band of six *ricos* had approximately six hundred horses, three thousand sheep, thirty warriors, and a hundred old and young followers. Less than a month later, following a Ute raid, another visitor found less than half the people, and only fifty horses and forty sheep. Manuelito said, "Here is all I have in the world. See what a trifling amount. You see how poor they are. My children are eating roots."[42]

Ten months later a captive Navajo told the military that the Utes had dispersed Manuelito's group and that the war chief was living with his brother, surviving by hunting and eating buried corn he had gotten from the Hopis. Two months previous, Utes had attacked his band while he was absent. Cabeza Blanca killed most of the men, "the Ute chief taking survivors and a large number of women and children with him to his own country.... A number were killed by the Utes on their way thither...[but] a treaty was made by the remnant of the band with the Utes, who told them...that we [military] intended to keep them in confinement, and that it was better for them to live in amity with them and in freedom."[43] In spite of this peace, Manuelito turned himself in to the army. In September 1866 he surrendered at Fort Wingate along with twenty-three followers.

K'aa Yélii, the third brother, faired somewhat better. He remained in the vicinity of Elk Ridge and the Bears Ears during this era and became the most powerful Navajo headman in southeastern Utah. Five or six hogans comprised his settlement near a spring at what is today the Kigalia ranger station, named after him.[44] The people accepted him as their leader, adopting his policy of avoiding conflict by not provoking the enemy. At the same time he had an uncanny ability to escape raids and ambushes.

K'aa Yélii's sister, Asdzáán Kin Díílid ("Woman Who Had Her House Burned"), lived in his camp behind the Bears Ears with other Navajos at Naznidzoodii ("Place to Escape from the Enemy"), a canyon that facilitated disguised movement off Elk Ridge.[45] Her husband, Naakai Diné ("Mexican Man"), was born near the Bears Ears, where the couple stayed during the Fearing Time. Her maternal grandmother (no name) was not as fortunate. The Utes captured and sold her to Mexicans, who guarded her in a log cabin. She found a ladder inside and escaped, making her way to the mountains, where snow covered her tracks. She eventually reached the San Juan River, recognized Shiprock, followed the south side of the river to Douglas Mesa, and then wended her way back to Naznidzoodii and K'aa Yélii's band.[46]

Cayetano and his three sons illustrate the complexity of Ute and Navajo relations at this time. From Cayetano's fleeing to and living with the Utes, to the decimation of Manuelito's band, to the studied avoidance of K'aa Yélii, there was a range of responses, for two interrelated reasons. The first is the porous border created by Ute, Paiute, and Navajo expansion into the Four Corners region. As all three groups mingled at a distance from their tribal centers, each established their own use areas. Relations in trade, friendship, and marriage resulted. Items traded by the Utes included buckskins, buckskin clothing, elk hides and elk storage sacks, buffalo robes, saddlebags, horses, bandoleers, beaded bags, beaver skins, buffalo tail rattles, pitch for ceremonial whistles, and baskets. The Navajos traded woven blankets, silver, and agricultural products.[47] Navajo Mountain provided red earth paint sold by Paiutes to the Utes.[48]

Paiutes also worked for wealthier Navajo families with large herds of livestock that required tending. Navajo informants tell of using Paiutes to provide early warning of danger. George Martin says that his father first met the Paiutes in the Bears Ears country, and they became his "watchers."[49] K'aa Yélii "had men posted to watch for the approach of enemy tribes," so that his group could flee.[50] Hashkéninii practiced the same technique at his camp near Navajo Mountain. Others mention Paiutes hiding Navajos from Ute raiders, of intermarriage, and of sharing resources.[51]

These practices led to the second reason for the wide range of Navajo responses to the Utes: ties of kinship and inherent familial responsibilities. Several times during these years of conflict Navajos lived with Utes, a fact that can only be explained by family bonds that offered protection. Oral history suggests that there were fairly peaceful relations between some Utes and Navajos living in southeastern Utah, and that it was the Utes living farther east who actually hunted for those in hiding.[52] At least in the Bears Ears and Navajo Mountain areas there were strong ties among some of the San Juan Band Paiutes, local Weenuche, and Navajos. Hashkéninii, an "outstanding" trader, visited many Utes and Paiutes living around the Bears Ears. He also had several Ute and Paiute wives.[53]

Surprisingly, the most dramatic proof of Ute, Paiute, and Navajo cooperation and protection involves one of the Navajos' worst enemies, Cabeza Blanca, a Weenuche who the Navajos describe as "a bad one, diseased, and very mean to his women," famous for ferreting out hidden Navajos, stealing the women, and killing the men. Many of his attacks occurred at night during a full moon or in bad weather, while the Navajos were at home. He would rope the top of a forked-stick hogan, pull it over with his horse, and shoot the occupants as they fled. The military is said to have agreed to his keeping anything he took, including horses, women, and children, giving him strong motivation.[54] Not only did he track, capture, and kill many Navajos, but he was said to have weakened the effectiveness of Navajo prayers by taking a baby's heart, placing it in a crow's heart, and then shooting it up a canyon cliff, where besieged Navajos were eventually defeated.[55]

One story tells of how the Navajos outsmarted Cabeza Blanca and his band.[56] Four Navajo warriors saw his war party entering a canyon and decided to prevent it from going any farther, even though they were heavily outnumbered. They built several large piles of wood for bonfires some distance apart. One man rode down and told the Utes that they could not proceed because there were many warriors with bows and arrows and rifles waiting for them. The Utes did not believe him, so he gave the signal to the other men to light the bonfires. Suddenly a great cloud of smoke went up, and he restated that there were many warriors ahead. The Utes decided not to take any chances and retreated.

There are mixed accounts of how Cabeza Blanca died. One asserts that the Navajos killed him through witchcraft chants, while another says that his own people killed him over woman troubles.[57] Hashkéninii's previously cited account is a third version. The military recorded its own version, linking Cabeza Blanca's death directly to southeastern Utah and friendships with Navajos living in this area. In September 1866 a group of "Pah Wymin," Capote, and Mexicans planned to go to the San Juan River to entice a band of Navajos to join them through pledges of friendship. Once they had lured the unsuspecting prey, the group would kill the men and capture the rest. "It appears that Cabeza Blanca, a chief among the Wymin Utes, had some friends among the Navajos whom he wished to except from being killed to which the Capote Utes objected."[58] A fight ensued, the Capotes killed Cabeza Blanca, and they then fled to Tierra Amarilla with two of Cabeza Blanca's sons in hot pursuit. The Weenuche arrived at the settlement, killed three Mexican herders, wounded a woman, and captured some livestock before fleeing. "The Indians then left, joining as is supposed the Wymin and Pah Utes who had made friends with the Navajos in the meantime. The whole party of Wymin, Pah Utes, and Navajos then left that region and went to the neighborhood of Rio Dolores, Sierra del Latir (Mountain of the Throbbing, Beating—Ute Mountain), and Sierra Orejas (Bears Ears) about one hundred miles from the settlements." Agent Pfeiffer, author of the letter, wished the "Wymin, Pah, and Capote Utes to bury the hatchet and be friends"; he then noted that "the Wymin numbered some 1200 or more, the Pah Utes some 1500, and the Navajos with them about 800 more, numbering in all 3500 [and] have been joined by the Green River Utes — driven from Utah by the troops or Mormons." As late as 1889, settlers in Aneth reported the presence of Cabeza Blanca's sons, who were acting as "mean and saucy as they can be."[59]

Returning to 1861, the Abiquiu Agency became increasingly important to the "Pah Utes" and Weenuche as the place to obtain their annuities, while the Muache, who had been at Taos, reoriented toward Lucien B. Maxwell's ranch in New Mexico and away from the settlements. Collins reported that "All, except the Pa-uches, Capotes, and Mouaches, fall within the limits of Colorado Territory."[60] A year later the "Womenuche (also known as the Pa-Uches)" received a new special agent, Henry Mercure, and an agency at Tierra Amarilla, sixty miles northwest of Abiquiu. There were two reasons for the move. The first was to separate the Indians from the settlements to avoid conflict and incidents. Ute horses grazing in farmers' fields and crops annoyed the citizens, while unscrupulous whiskey venders fueled volatile relations. The move also reduced round-trip travel time to the agency by four days. The second reason was to avoid infectious diseases that ravaged Indian populations. Collins observed at the distribution of presents to the two bands that many of the Weenuche were absent due to their "great fear of the smallpox. Quite a number had died during the summer from that disease and they are now afraid to approach the settlement.... They stand in great dread of the disease and when one of their people is taken down with it they run from him and leave him to die unattended."[61]

Even with these problems, the Capote and Weenuche Utes had "conducted themselves with more propriety than any wild tribe in the Territory."[62] At the same time, they refused to settle on a reservation, wanted nothing to do with agriculture, and lived by hunting and gathering and fighting Navajos. "The Capote band of Utah and the Womenuches, known as the Payuches band of Utahs exert great influence in the western part of the Territory. They stand between the unfriendly Indians and the whites, and but for them there would be no security for life or property, except at a heavy expense to the government in military protection."[63] One agent estimated that these two bands roamed over forty thousand square miles of territory, but even with that, game was becoming scarce, and there was an increased dependency on the agencies.[64] He believed it would be just a matter of time before the reservation system became a necessity.

Continued white expansion from the east and south solidified in the government's mind that the Utes needed to relinquish part of their holdings and move to a reservation. Primarily concerned with Ute lands to the east and north, Tabeguache country, the government still invited the Southern Utes to attend a meeting to accept agriculture and the trappings of reservation life. The one representative from the Muaches refused to sign, and the Capotes in attendance did likewise, while the Weenuches were absent. They had no desire to live on a reservation held common by all bands, and they would give up neither their lands nor their free-roaming way of life. The Tabeguache, however, signed and relinquished one-fourth of the Ute lands, all in the eastern section of the Colorado mountains. President Abraham Lincoln signed the agreement on December 14, 1864.[65] One result was to push Northern Ute hunting and gathering activities farther to the west and south, onto Southern Ute territory.

By 1865 the main efforts against the Navajos had ceased, although the Weenuche agent reported that many of his charges continued to fight with Navajos still on the loose. But to the north, a new conflict attracted the Utes of southeastern Utah. Over the previous years Mormon settlers had encroached upon large tracts of land belonging to Ute tribes in the area along the Wasatch Front and to its south. While these events and the ensuing conflict were peripheral to the Southern Utes, they maintained their long-standing contact between the two tribal regions. In 1861 Ute agent Harvey M. Vaile reported three thousand Indians in eight hundred lodges under White Eye (or Antero), from the Colorado–Green River area, camped in Provo. In Salt Lake City there were a thousand well-armed, well-mounted Elk Mountain, or Sheberetch, Utes.[66] Thus, when relations between the whites and Indians ruptured in northern Utah, it is not surprising that the Utes to the south became involved.

Black Hawk's war began in 1865 after insult and injury between the Mormons and Utes had reached a breaking point. For two years each side had waged a brushfire war that had consumed lives, livestock, and property as the settlers abandoned towns, attacked both peaceful and warring factions, and ensured that their enemies learned that resistance was futile.[67] Although many of these events are beyond the scope of this book, the involvement of the Elk Mountain Utes became central to the war. As in Wakara's conflict with the Mormons, Black Hawk depended on the Sheberetch, with their mixed ancestry of Ute, Paiute, Navajo, and Hopi, to encourage other groups to participate. Correspondence sent to Brigham Young at the beginning of hostilities notified him that "Black Hawk is at their head and is joined by the Shiveretts."[68] The Timpanogos Utes encouraged other bands, including the Tabaguache, Weenuche, and Muache, to participate.

As early as 1863 Black Hawk had held councils with Southern Ute leaders to enlist their aid in resisting the Mormons. When the fighting began on April 9, 1865, the Shebe-

retch comprised the majority of his warriors. Familiar with the ground they traversed due to their involvement along the Old Spanish Trail, these warriors effectively used the land to their advantage, attacking and escaping easily. In the winter of 1866, as fighting slowed, Black Hawk camped near the La Sals, "having gone there to endeavor to procure recruits from among the Elk Mountain Utes, the most powerful tribe in the territory… [and successfully] swelled his force to three hundred warriors."[69] A year later Utah agent Franklin H. Head described the Elk Mountain and Sheberetch Ute bands as having four thousand members (a large overestimation), occupying the area in southeastern Utah that is south of the San Rafael River and east of the Wasatch Mountains. "Their country supplies them with game sufficient for their maintenance, and they are rarely seen in the settlements of this Territory. They are much visited by Spanish traders from New Mexico, and, whenever they leave their country for the purposes of trade, usually travel in that direction."[70]

Among these Elk Mountain warriors were leaders such as Jake Arapene, Mountain, Augavorum (Öögwarüm — "Thin One"), and Tamaritz. The latter did not stop fighting, even after the war had ended, until Black Hawk persuaded him to.[71] At one point Tamaritz's horse was killed in combat and so changed his name to Shenavegan, meaning "Saved by Almighty Power." Yet one agent estimated that half of the warriors that came from this region were Navajos from New Mexico. He asserted: "How these combinations among them can be easily conceived, and how dangerous these combinations might become can easily be understood by those who have the least knowledge of the Indian character," primarily because they were "so mixed up by marriage."[72]

New Mexico's newspapers even reported some of the comings and goings of this group, saying that the Weenuche and Elk Mountain Utes were camped on the Dolores

River, having just returned from the Mormon settlements with large herds of stolen stock. They were later reported wintering near where the Green and Colorado Rivers meet. The reason for this interest was plain: what was not consumed by the Indians was bought by New Mexicans, delivered to them via the Old Spanish Trail. Other Indian groups—Navajos, Jicarilla Apaches, Hopis, and Yampa, Tabeguache, Capote, Muache, and Uintah Utes, as well as Hispanic traders—joined the winter camps near today's town of Green River, buying, selling, and trading goods.[73] Their involvement encouraged continued conflict by providing an outlet for the stolen stock.

On August 12, 1867, Black Hawk met with Agent Head to conclude a peace agreement. During the discussions he reported that he had twenty-eight lodges of his own band but there were three Elk Mountain chiefs—Tamaritz, Augavorum, and Sowah-point—who each had ten to twelve families under their control. Black Hawk could not speak for these leaders, only for his own people, when it came to formulating a final peace. He promised to try to have them cooperate, but it was another year before they agreed to cease hostilities. Until then, the raids continued.[74] Their independence, band composition, knowledge of the terrain, and effectiveness, all rooted in past activities, also established a pattern for the future. Anxious to assert their independence, this band of people, as they coalesced into today's White Mesa Utes, were able to avoid moving to a reservation for another fifty-five years.

In New Mexico and Colorado, events pushed the Southern Utes toward greater government control. While the military employed some Utes and Jicarilla Apaches in a campaign against the Comanches, Kiowas, and other Plains tribes in 1864–1865, it also began insisting that Navajos no longer be pursued. The problem of survival loomed large upon the horizon. In January 1866, Agent Henry Mercure and 112 people of Tierra Amarilla signed a petition asking that a military post be established nearby because of the growing unrest among the Indians for food. Travel outside of the settlements had become dangerous, but of greater concern was "that some of these Utes and Paiuches are in large numbers united with the Navajos near [Ute Mountain] and we do not know at what moment they may come here and destroy us."[75] Six months later the same people faced 1,200 "hungry and naked" Utes begging food, taking livestock, and feeding their horses on settlers' crops. The superintendent of Indian Affairs ordered the Abiquiu agent to purchase 200 sheep at three dollars a head, 75 pounds of powder, 200 pounds of lead, 10,000 caps, and 100 pounds of tobacco, which he issued to the Indians. He gave them this ammunition with the understanding that they would leave the settlements and hunt for at least two months.[76] This, however, proved to be only a temporary solution to Ute encroachment on white communities.

A more permanent fix was in the offing. As Civil War veterans poured into the West, mining strikes became more prevalent, and agricultural settlements were established. The whites demanded that Indians be kept on reservations far from civilization. The Utes refused. They wanted nothing to do with wholesale agriculture, enjoyed their freedom, and insisted that they had performed a good service for the Americans and so should remain unmolested. Western Colorado had always been theirs, and so the people of New Mexico urged that they be expelled to this territory and the Abiquiu Agency closed to the Capote and Weenuche Utes. The Muaches at Maxwell's Ranch, "with a little management," could also be persuaded to leave. Underlying the Utes' hesitance, among other things, were religious beliefs. Diego Archuleta, an unsympathetic agent who was later relieved of his responsibilities, explained, "These savages are possessed of the most heathenish superstitions against abandoning those places where the remains of their ancestors lie…[and] they consider their reduction to reservations as a species of slavery."[77]

Ute agent W. F. M. Arny contributed to the loss of Indian lands by stating in his annual report of 1867 that several thousand white families could homestead in the area north and east of the Animas River. By establishing a reservation, the mining and agricultural resources of the region would be opened for development, and it could be "done at comparatively small expense, for it is cheaper to dispose of these Indians in this way than to fight and exterminate them."[78] By establishing a military post between the reservation and the settlements, the Utes could be controlled, the settlers protected, and resources developed. He felt he could move the Capote and Weenuche Utes onto a reservation on the San Juan River for $49,500. Within a year he had completed the paperwork.

On November 6, 1868, President Andrew Johnson signed a treaty that placed the Northern and Southern Utes on two reservations, decreasing their combined territory by one-third. Again, the land came primarily from Tabeguache holdings.[79] All of the bands had representatives sign the treaty; from the Weenuche came "Claw" (Persechopa—Sučupi), "Broad Brow" (Panoar), "White Eyes" (Tesagarapou, a.k.a. Antero, of the Elk Mountain Utes), "Big Belly" (Sapoeuawa), and "Bear" (Querata).[80] Rather than go to Washington, these leaders met at Pagosa Springs on August 19, 1868. They wished to maintain access to their territory, which reached from "the Green and Grand rivers on the north, the [headwaters of the] San Juan River on the east, the Colorado River on the West, and the Navajo country on the south (40,000 square miles)...which embraces some of the most fertile and richest mineral lands of Colorado and New Mexico."[81] The Capote and Weenuche Utes expressed a desire to be "separate and distinct from all other bands and tribes."

One reservation headquarters, at White River, served the Northern Utes, while the Southern Ute agency was headquartered at Los Pinos. Ten years elapsed before the Abiquiu and Maxwell, or Cimarron, Agencies closed and the Los Pinos Agency opened its doors. In 1873 the Utes signed another treaty, the Brunot Agreement, that removed massive chunks of land from their reservation, so that by 1880, and one more treaty, comparatively little remained of their holdings. Ironically, on June 1, 1868, the Navajos also signed a treaty, giving them approximately one-fourth of the territory they used to roam. Unlike the Utes, the Navajos consistently obtained additional reservation lands.

It took a while for old Navajo and Ute wounds to heal. As early as 1866, Navajos told the soldiers at Fort Sumner that "without protection from the Utahs who are our enemies, we would not care to go back."[82] Once returning became a reality, the Navajos indicated that they wanted to make a peace agreement similar to the one they had in the past, so that they could trade and become "one people with them." On May 28, 1868, just before the treaty signing, General William Tecumseh Sherman warned the Navajos "that if you go to your own country, the Utes will be the nearest Indians to you; you must not trouble the Utes and the Utes must not trouble you.... You must not permit any of your young men to go to the Ute or Apache country to steal."[83] This advice was hardly necessary. Agent reports indicate that for the next few years, large Navajo populations avoided spreading close to the San Juan region. The friction of the previous war had burned an indelible scar into their memory—a scar remembered to this day through their oral tradition, which recounts how the Utes earned their reputation among the Navajos as "the Enemies You Continually Fight With."

The Utes were more pacific in the early reservation era, but there were a few sporadic raids for women and livestock. The most notable was conducted by a Capote named Chaves, who with a dozen warriors captured seven women (five of whom escaped), several horses, and a Navajo man. The other Capotes and Weenuche disagreed with this action

Ute warriors crossing the Pinos River, 1908. With the cessation of hostilities, an uneasy peace was established between the Utes and Navajos, but both sides continued to lodge complaints with the government for wrongs perpetrated by the other. Conflicts over boundaries and traditional rivalry persisted well into the twentieth century. (Denver Public Library, Western History Collection, H. S. Poley, P-57)

and promised to remain at peace as long as the Navajos did not come to their lands seeking revenge.[84] It was this same Chaves who two months earlier had gone to Santa Fe with a small group of Capotes and a Weenuche named Chino. While there they obtained whiskey, became drunk, and killed Chino and his sister before returning to the village and killing his wife to prevent her from marrying "any other Indian." Agent Arny approached Persechopa, leader of the Weenuche Utes, and Sobatar, leader of the Capotes, and exacted a promise that they would try to peacefully work through the issue. He then went to Chaves, Coronea, Washington, Timpiatche, and Cutchimpiache, who controlled a group of over sixty men, women, and children, issued supplies, and told them to head north to the mountains.

Instead they went west into Weenuche lands, where four Capotes were wounded and many of their horses stolen. Persechopa sent word that the Weenuche had decided to kill Chaves's entire band for their own protection since these Utes were "murderers

and thieves that steal and kill stock from the people and that honest Indians are charged with it."[85] Arny felt his only hope was to not issue powder and lead, keep the bands separate, and provide more domestic animals to eat since hunting would be curtailed. In true Arny fashion, he requested more money in his agency account.

With a signed treaty and the start of a new year, the Southern Utes began to feel increasing pressure to move to their reservation. They resisted. Part of the problem lay in an unsurveyed boundary between Colorado and New Mexico. Part of it was the presence of Animas City, located thirty miles inside the new reservation boundaries. Part of it was the number of people scheduled to move onto the Los Pinos Reservation—all members of the Capote, Weenuche, Tabeguache, and Muache bands. And part of it was general resistance to leaving the Abiquiu Agency and their familiar haunts in New Mexico. The government sought to appease. A resident agent would live with the Utes, annuity goods were to be distributed regularly, and all of the rivers that drain into the San Juan, as well as Pagosa Springs, a sacred spot, would be within their boundaries.

What had supposedly been agreed upon in previous talks was tossed to the wind as white encroachment continued. Sobatar, spokesman for the Weenuche and Capotes, was adamant, saying,

> they did not want any one in their country. They are not too lazy to come here to their agency at Abiquiu and they want it here. We like Tata [Father] Arny, and always have liked him, but we do not like him to bring papers here running lines through our country. What we said in Santa Fe is what we want and nothing more. And we do not want Tata Arny to write any more. We want him to go to Washington with his papers and let us alone. We wish you to say to Washington what we said at Santa Fe. We are not children. What we said once, we say again. Ever since we saw Governor Hunt [Colorado], we said we did not want any person, soldier, American, or Mexican in our country to live.[86]

Arny urged that the Weenuche and Capotes be allowed to remain where they were until they could be broken into small bands and gradually moved onto a reservation. Otherwise, there would be an expensive, ineffective war with all of the tribes, including the Jicarilla Apaches, if the military tried to root them out of lands that only they knew.

To add to the furor, Major Albert Pfeiffer, a previous Ute agent, was now, as a civilian, leading a group of prospectors onto the Chama River in search of gold. The Indians went to their agents, Arny and John Ayers, demanding to know if this was legal, and if it was not, would they stop them. Pfeiffer and company sent a reply stating that the white men were free to travel through the mountains and they intended to do so.[87] Arny feared that if they confronted the Utes, all of the bands would join the fray, leading the agent to conclude that "Indian relations in New Mexico never were in as dangerous a position as at present."

War with the Navajos also raised its ugly head. Some of their young men entered into Ute country in search of horses, sneaked into a camp of Capote and Weenuche hunters, and stole four animals. The Utes tracked them to their settlement, and one was approaching a hogan to discuss the matter when the Navajos opened fire and killed him. The fight commenced, the Navajos fled, and the Utes took six horses and one hundred sheep and goats. When they reported the incident to their agent, the Weenuche Sebo explained the events, and Persechopa, "the best Indian in the territory," vouched for him.[88]

That was one side. The Navajos told an entirely different story, claiming that the Utes had stolen eight horses from some Mexicans, and that the Navajos had been peacefully eating lunch at "Benito's" camp when they were brutally attacked, with a man and woman being killed, and that 250 head of livestock had been stolen. Coronea, a Capote, corroborated this story, saying these Utes were from four lodges that wanted the war to persist and desired nothing to do with the Americans. Leading Navajo chiefs, including Manuelito, came in and vouched for the veracity of the speaker and his story. To the Navajo agent, this is where truth resided. He demanded that the horses, sheep, and goats be returned, and the guilty party punished.[89]

The Utes also wanted to have the situation corrected. Persechopa traveled with some of his Weenuche warriors to Fort Defiance, Arizona, to see the agent. Navajo headmen agreed to return the horses, but it never happened. Worse, as Persechopa rode back to his land, he sickened and died of dropsy. The Utes believed that the Navajos had poisoned him, adding more reason for renewed hostilities. Arny's familiar view — that "it is cheaper to feed than to fight," that a "war that will cost millions of dollars" was about to start, and that the "frontier settlers had a fear and apprehension of the total destruction of the border settlements" — now became his incessant cry.[90] More soldiers and more money

was the answer. Agent Bennett smoothed relations by paying the Utes for all their claims
against the Navajos, with the understanding
that the Utes relinquish all stolen livestock.
Happy with the payment but uninterested in
returning their booty, the Utes refused.[91]

Navajos also launched raids into Utah's
"Mormon country," as well as stealing eighty
horses from settlers around Abiquiu. Agent
Captain Frank T. Bennett, with written statements in hand, called in many of the principal Navajo chiefs and demanded that all such
activity stop. After a night of discussion the
Navajo leaders agreed to make every effort
to control the young men and to deliver any
transgressors to the government.[92] From this
point on, incidents of this nature between the
two tribes became increasingly rare.

The Weenuche Utes at this time had an
estimated 400 to 500 men, with 1,500 people
total, and were divided into bands led by
Ignacio, Cabeza Blanca's sons Tobats and
Sewormichaca, and others. They did not
have as many firearms as the Capotes, but
they did have more horses. Some practiced
limited agriculture, all hunted and gathered,
and many mixed with the "Pi-Utes" of Utah.
Also, "they steal less than the Capotes, are
more independent and energetic, and better
provided than that tribe."[93] Because of their
ability to sustain themselves, many of the
Weenuche did not travel to Abiquiu to receive annuities. Some of this independence,
however, soon changed.

Surveying the turbulent decade of
the 1860s from a distance, it appears that
each entity played its own aggressive role.
Whether looking at the raiding between Navajos and Utes, the intraband conflict among
the Southern Utes, the role of the military,
and the issues between agents and citizens,
the Mormons and the federal government,
and a number of other combinations, it
seems that no group knew peace. The Utes
played a part in all of the turmoil. So it may
be surprising to read the end-of-the-decade

memorial sent by New Mexico governor
William A. Pile, with state legislative backing, to the U.S. Senate, House of Representatives, and president of the United States.
In short, the governor explained that there
were breeches in the treaty agreements of
1868 on the part of the federal government
and that the Utes wanted them changed. The
governor insisted that the government mend
the wrongs and avoid a costly war with the
Weenuche and Capotes, the "most powerful
and important bands of the Utah nation." Pile
went on:

> Considering that these two bands of the great
> Utah tribe have always lived on our frontier and
> have been a most powerful ally of our border
> population, obstructing the hostile invasion of the
> barbarous savages, we therefore ask, and trust that
> some steps will be taken, to prevent these bands
> from being exiled from their present abodes and
> hunting grounds.... Now they are at peace and
> commit no depredations whatever upon the lives
> or property of our people, but on the contrary,
> are regarded by the whites as a wall of protec-
> tion against the forays of the Navajos and other
> barbarous Indians, so that of all the frontier of our
> territory, there is no part that is so secure as that
> adjoining the Utahs.[94]

Agent Ayers concurred, feeling that "they
form a better protection for the people of the
territory than a line of forts could, as these
marauding bands can always outwit our
troops but they cannot the Utes."[95]

The welcoming arms that now embraced
the Weenuche people soon began to close.
As the Navajos became established on their
reservation and Ute lands were targeted for
their resources, conflict between Indians and
whites grew. Alliances fell apart, and a new
set of controversies developed. For now the
lands of southeastern Utah lay firmly within
the Utes' grasp, but it would not be long before white fingers began prying loose, bit by
bit, their territory.

CHAPTER 6

Decade of Decision, 1870–1880

Losing Land, Gaining Restrictions

The whites did not keep their word. They give us land and a home,
where we have always lived.... They eat the bread and give us the crust.

Ignacio, 1870[1]

Special Agent W. F. M. Arny was anxious to be on his way for a tour of the Indian country that stretched across Southern Ute, Hopi, Navajo, Zuñi, and Apache lands. It was May 1870, and first on his itinerary began with a trip north to visit the Utes. Rumblings of war with the Utes at the Cimarron Agency appeared unfounded, but to ascertain the state of affairs with the Capote and Weenuche bands, Arny would have to go into the heart of their territory. He knew that issues existed. Although the treaty of 1868 had set these lands aside exclusively for the Utes, the tired story of white invasion of Indian holdings had begun. Arny needed to ensure that outbreaks of violence remained at a minimum.

In the Numic language, the English sparrow is called "E-ink-agunt," which loosely translates as "Thieving Stranger." It is said that the bird does not belong here but came with the white man. "He doesn't go off in the winter like other birds because he is a stranger and does not know about the warm south lands."[2] Instead he stays in one place and robs what is there. Like this bird, miners led the vanguard of interlopers who, over the next forty years, trampled treaty rights and came to stay. In 1869 Sheldon Shafer and Joe Fearheiler made their way up the Dolores River to the vicinity of today's Rico, Colorado, and established a claim they called

the "Pioneer."[3] The next year more miners joined them, while other groups prospected along the Animas. Although the real rush to the Dolores for silver would not occur for another eight years, the miners remained at their sites during the summer; the tap of their hammers on stone made the Utes uneasy. They understood that although these men were few, their numbers could increase dramatically overnight, as the Utes around Denver had found in 1859. Perhaps the Indians were also aware that Colorado governor Edward M. McCook, also serving as superintendent of Indian Affairs for his state, believed "Mines that will pay $100 per day, with soil richer and more fruitful than any other territory, is included in the Ute Reservation."[4] Recent events did not bode well for the Indians.

Two days out from Tierra Amarilla, Arny met a party of twenty-two miners who complained that Southern Utes had forced them to leave the mining region and get off their reservation. Three days later he met the Capote Sobatar, who told Arny in short order that "They wanted their country solo, that they intended to drive out all the miners from the country, and that I must return, as they did not see any necessity of my going farther."[5] By now it was apparent that the more white men knew about their lands, the greater the possibility of losing them. Arny persisted, continuing his journey to the north. The next day he encountered sixteen Weenuche camped on the Piedra River; they also objected to his going any farther.

On May 24 Arny found three lodges of Capotes with eighteen Indians. Although he enjoyed the beaver tail, green corn, trout, and pancakes they had for dinner, the Indians warned him to suspend his travels. If he did not, he would probably lose his horses and might be harmed. The Utes assured him that they "'talked straight. But the Indians west on the Rio La Plata and Rio Dolores were talking crooked.' (The Indians they spoke of are the Indians who have not been to Abiquiu Agency for two years, and who killed several persons at Tierra Amarilla.)"[6]

Because the Animas River was at flood stage, and Arny did not want to chance crossing it, he moved south, retracing his steps, to find a better fording site. The Weenuche who were camped to the west, including Cabeza Blanca's sons, were aware of his intent. They sent "Josepha," one of their members, with a message that their people were on the La Plata, Dolores, and Mancos Rivers and were of the same mind as the Capotes. They wanted peace but would fight if their country was threatened. They also insisted that the miners who had left the Dolores should not settle in their territory. They did not have a problem with them taking the gold or silver, but they should not remain in Ute lands. Arny penned a quick note to the retreating white men to that effect and then continued on his way.

On the Chama River he met Ignacio and Cutchumpiache with twenty-one lodges of Capote and Weenuche. At noon the agent counseled with the leaders and recorded what they said.

> The whites did not keep their word. They give us land and a home, where we always lived. They find gold and silver and take our land from us. They send us to Colorado and then say is not the land ours. They promise much but do little. The great Chief, our Father in Washington, will do right. Tata Arny and Tata [Agent J.B.] Hanson will do right, but [miner Adnah] French gave us a paper which said no white men must go into our country, then he comes and says he wanted to take our land for miners, and McCook and [previous governor Alexander C.] Hunt put us in a cold country. They eat the bread and give us the crust. They do not give us the cattle and sheep the Great Father sent, but we are contented without, if we are left in our own country where we have always lived.[7]

Arny countered with the fact that they had not gone to the agency to get their annuities, to which they replied the new agency was in the wrong place; they preferred Abiquiu, and the proposed agency on the Los Pinos had not yet been built. The agent pointed out that Abiquiu was not on the reservation, and since they were driving white people off their lands, they were not to trespass on white territory. Finally, they should submit to the will of the government.

Arny departed the next day determined to reach the most western Ute camps. He continued to meet miners returning from their claims along the Dolores. On June 17, after traveling forty-five miles in one day, he arrived at the junction of the Dolores and San Juan Rivers, where he encountered "Cabezon," "Powarie" (Powárvi — "Gaining Power"), and the sons of Cabeza Blanca, "who with nearly three thousand Weemenuches are on the Rio [La] Plata."[8] While this number is highly questionable, certainly the encampment with its large herds of horses, goats, and sheep was impressive. The leaders, being more distant from the other groups, took a modified approach to what the others had said. They agreed to the agency being at Los Pinos because it was not as far as Abiquiu, and they were willing to sell mining lands in the Dolores Mountains on which thirty rich lodes had been discovered. Their reason: they could go to Sheberetch lands to live. Arny, who championed economic development, recognized the land's wealth. He also recognized the interband friction between the Capotes and Weenuche, saying that although the Weenuche west of the Animas were friendly and did not oppose the presence of miners at this point, they were "afraid of the Capotes who roam between Pagosa Springs and the Animas and who are double their number."[9] Arny left early the next morning for other tribal lands, with no doubt in his mind that the region held great potential for whoever claimed it.

Correspondence continued between agents and superiors trying to maintain peaceful relations with their charges while still getting the Utes to move to the reservation in Colorado. For many bands, game was scarce, the agents could not provide sufficient food, and whites were invading their territory. A cold December with heavy snows in the San Juan country led Agent J. B. Hanson to write that his people had been poorly provided for by the government, and "that if it was not for the bear and deer skins that these Indians have been successful in obtaining by their skill as hunters, many of the children must have perished."[10] The Weenuche, in their own territory, obtained sufficient deer and turkey that winter so that Ignacio could come to the agency and trade for sugar, coffee, and other provisions. The Capotes, on the other hand, were heavily dependent on the agents' largess.[11]

It became increasingly difficult to get the Southern Ute bands to accept the reservation and stay away from the settlements. Friction between the Weenuche and Capotes was replicated between the Weenuche and Muaches when Ignacio killed Savillo, brother to Kaneache (Kaníæč — "Little Village"), a primary leader of the Muache. Savillo, a healer, had prepared some medicine for a member in Ignacio's band. Shortly after the man took it, he died. Ignacio believed the victim had been poisoned but waited six months before entering Savillo's tepee with three other men — each firing one shot, with Ignacio

providing the coup de grace with his knife.[12] The Muache were incensed, decreasing even further the chance of getting all three bands on one reservation.

In September, shortly before his transfer, Abiquiu agent Hanson submitted his annual report to Colonel Nathaniel Pope, New Mexico superintendent of Indian Affairs.[13] Hanson was observant, providing excellent ethnographic detail. He extolled the praiseworthy virtues of the Weenuche, describing them as "well disposed toward the government…peaceable…and with few complaints against them," placing their numbers at nine hundred. Hanson also lauded their self-sufficiency, estimating they had trapped or hunted $1,400 worth of furs and skins — primarily bear, deer, and beaver taken during the fall and winter months — some of which they had traded for horses, rifles, mantas, sugar, and coffee. The rest they made into clothing. Nearly all of the men owned muzzle-loading rifles and Colt revolvers.

Livestock played an important role for the Weenuche. Hanson noted that "The greater part of these Indians own Mexican ponies and many of them are very fine and pretty. These they seldom take into the agency for fear they will get stolen. Some Weeminuche chiefs own fifteen and twenty ponies each. All of the Utes are very choosey and proud of a good horse and they will not sell one for money, but they will often trade off an Indian pony for a rifle or a nice Navajo blanket." Goats were another important item. They provided not only meat but milk, which was put on ground roasted corn or wheat as a mush. "This food is very nutritious and the children especially thrive on it."

The Weenuche did not come to the agency often, perhaps once every three months, and when they did, they came in groups of twenty-five to fifty or as families. The agent handed out powder, lead, percussion caps, and tobacco liberally, while to the chiefs he gave additional lead and tobacco "to take to their friends and relations that do not come in." They remained for only a day and a night before returning to their hunting grounds west of the San Juan River. Compare this to the Capotes, the majority of whom remained around the agency and were dependent on government handouts. They also had far more conflict with people in the local settlements. Thus, while the government had solved part of its Indian problem by establishing them on a smaller land base, it had also created a financial drain and a whole new set of issues necessitating further solutions.

Agent reports began mentioning southeastern Utah more frequently. In late March Sobatar's Capotes stole thirty horses for a trip to the Green River country. They needed these mounts for a general meeting with other Utes and because they "had heard that God was in the vicinity of Green River and that he [Sobatar] and his band went to see him, [but] they had learned nothing important on their trip."[14] Most likely this refers to a Ghost Dance held at a sacred spot in the Sanpete Valley, where Northern Utes hosted the occasion. Elk Mountain Utes, Sheberetch, and Navajos, as well as others from the Four Corners area, attended to "dance, sing, and pray and offer ceremonies to Shenob or the Great Spirit."[15] This initial development of the Ghost Dance, which became more pronounced in the late 1880s and early 1890s, aligned well with traditional Ute beliefs of the afterlife. Before Kit Carson passed away in the mid-1860s, Kaneache had told him that in the future the Utes would become immortal in another world,

> [where] all the game which the Indians had killed from the earliest periods of time would reappear; the Indians who had died natural deaths would wear the same appearance they formerly did on earth but the warriors who had fallen in battle would be pale and bloody. And after a while, when all Indians had been gathered into that other country, they would then come again to this world and dwell here supreme forever.[16]

To Sobatar's Capotes, this could be the time heralded and should be investigated.

God or no God, whites protested the theft of the horses, which the Capotes were reluctant to return. A meeting between the Indians and Agent Armstrong, backed by a military detachment, resulted in a firefight that left one Ute dead and men wounded on both sides. Following attempts to calm the situation, regain the horses, and turn over the thieves, Sobatar explained that the Weenuche under Ignacio had the balance of the stock and were in southern Utah. No one was anxious to identify the men who took the animals.[17] The citizens near the agency responded by asking the agent and his superiors to establish another place for the Indians in the northwest corner of New Mexico, away from their settlements. By June the agency at Abiquiu had closed, with Tierra Amarilla serving as the new headquarters. Still, the government entertained thoughts of establishing something farther north because of the San Juan River and its potential for agriculture (which the Utes emphatically rejected), good grasslands for livestock, the potential for an industrial school to teach trades, and the increased distance from white communities.

Those concerned with the Utes' welfare were not the only ones eyeing this country. Ever since the Navajos had departed from Fort Sumner, they had fostered a desire to return to their old territory along the San Juan River. One thing stood in their way: "their dread of war parties from the Utes, who also claim this territory."[18] Navajo agent James H. Miller set off from Fort Defiance with agency farmer B. M. Thomas, trader John Ayers, and interpreter Jesus Arviso to select a site for a subagency. On the morning of June 11, 1872, as the men slept, two Weenuche warriors rode into camp, fired at the drowsy men, and stole their horses and mules. Miller died instantly. The warriors fled to the "Pi-Utes" in Utah, becoming almost impossible to ferret out. The grapevine soon identified the culprits, but the use of traditional means to bring them to justice never succeeded. Tabeguache leader Ouray, however, who was now looked upon by the federal government as "principal chief of the [Ute] nation," vowed "that the murderers shall be delivered up to the proper authorities."[19] He hunted them all summer and, when found, reported that the two men were starving, having eaten both of the captured mules. Ouray killed one of the men, but the other fled to the Hopi pueblos in Arizona.[20]

In 1872 southeastern Utah also served as a refuge for the sick. Agent John S. Littlefield reported an epidemic of lung diseases afflicting more than two hundred White River Utes. Under the leadership of Douglass, sixty lodges packed and left because "'White River no bueno; all die if we stay here;' they were going to the Navajo country to get well; should return in three moons."[21] For two months Littlefield knew nothing of their whereabouts. Not until the Indian agent in Salt Lake City contacted him did he learn that they were in southern Utah; he left immediately and visited them as well as camps of "Capotes, Sheberetch, and Elk Mountain Utes from New Mexico." Littlefield urged them to return to Colorado, but many people were too sick to be moved. Douglass assured the agent that by the time the annuities were ready for distribution, all would be back on the reservation. True to his word, Douglass was, but not before losing eleven killed by disease at the agency and ten men and fourteen women and children on the trip to and from southern Utah. There was, however, an even greater threat than disease to the Utes' way of life—miners.

The years 1871 and 1872 laid the foundation for the loss of four million acres of land, affecting seven bands of Utes. The process started slowly, with trickles of miners coming to the mountains in the summer and leaving in the fall. The Las Animas Mining District around Silverton, for instance, had scores of claims filed in 1871 on more than two hun-

dred silver lodes in just the one district.[22] This was clearly in violation of the 1868 treaty. Agents notified the commissioner of Indian Affairs, the government directed the miners to depart, mining lobbyists went to work in Washington, and the military remained ready to remove the miners but were never sent. The result: more miners, camps that grew in size and sophistication, and angrier Utes.

1872 was no better. Colorado governor Edward M. McCook went on record saying that the relatively small number of Utes did not require as large a reservation as they had received by treaty. Surely some of that land could be relinquished for mining and general economic development. There was, however, the problem of the treaty, and so on April 23, 1872, Congress authorized the secretary of the Interior to hold negotiations with the Utes to see if they were interested in giving up the southern portion of their land where miners were entrenched. On August 26, a five-day council commenced at the Los Pinos Agency. Present were McCook; Felix R. Brunot, chairman of the Board of Indian Commissioners; Colonel Price, commander of the Eighth Cavalry, stationed at Pagosa Springs; and an assortment of Indian agents and other government officials. Ouray served as spokesman for the Utes, who also had representatives from the Tabeguache, Muache, Capote, and Uncompahgre Utes, and the Jicarilla Apache. Fifteen hundred Indians, in all, gathered for the occasion. The Weenuche were conspicuously absent.

Following preliminaries, the council got down to business. Throughout the meeting both sides maintained a "most kind and friendly feeling."[23] For five days the testimony did not change. The government's position was simple:

> There is no desire to force you to do that which you may not wish to do.... This action on your part must be voluntary and be concurred on by the chiefs and by the people of the nation.... We want

Following the signing in 1873 of the Brunot Agreement, which gave miners access to the San Juan Mountains in Colorado, some of the participants in negotiations went to Washington, DC, where this photo was taken: *front row, left to right*, Guero, Chipeta (Ouray's wife), Ouray, and Piah (Ouray's brother); *second row*, Uriah M. Curtis, Major J. B. Thompson, General Charles Adams, and Otto Mears; *back row*, Washington, Susan (Ouray's sister), Johnson, Jack, and John. No Weenuche accompanied these White River and Uncompahgre Utes. (Denver Public Library, Western History Collection, photographer unknown, X-30679)

you to be happy and enjoy life as long as you live.... We have come here to talk with you and see if we can help you.[24]

At the same time the commissioners realized, "The miners are already present in such numbers that their expulsion by legal measures would be almost impracticable." Duplicity characterized the government's attempts to wrest the land from the Indians.

There was no missing the Ute position. Ouray was direct: "The Ute Nation does not wish to sell one span of its lands. We have all we want and the government is bound to protect us.... We are not satisfied with these trespassers. We do not wish to sell any of this land." Others were even more

pointed. Kaneache, looking at McCook, said, "There are so many people who cannot keep their mouths shut, that many have told me that Governor McCook has been trying to buy these lands," which the good governor refuted. Cutchumpiache of the Capotes introduced himself as a "quiet man." He continued: "I have been around at Tierra Amarilla where the miners are moving in, and they have always told me that they were there by permission of the Government.... In that land, in the southern country I was born, and for that reason I cannot sell my land. All of the country where the miners are is what we consider as the Capote country.... The soldiers at Pagosa Springs ought to be taken away. I do not like to have the soldiers in there, running about my country, for I am afraid of them."[25] The Utes felt their position clearly understood and that both sides agreed that there would be no loss of land.

The evening before the commission departed, Ouray visited and assured them that the miners and others did not have anything to fear. The Indians were "unanimously determined upon peace" and believed that the Great Father was ready to enforce the agreements made in the treaty of 1868. The commissioners understood this, later writing, "we became satisfied that at least for the present it would be impossible to conclude any satisfactory negotiations with them."[26] Case closed, or so it seemed. In a year's time, almost to the day, Commissioner Brunot was back, this time singing a different tune. The hue and cry from the mining community and other interested parties had been heard, loud and clear. Now the commission was there to take land.

Supposedly, the Indians in the 1872 meeting had been prejudiced by "outside parties" but had now changed to a more "favorable disposition." The three reasons given for the negotiations had not changed: too much land for the reservation, too few Indians, and the real reason — "The people of Colorado are anxious to have that portion of the reserve not needed for Indian purposes thrown open to entry and settlement…in order that the agricultural and mineral resources thereof may be more thoroughly and rapidly developed."[27] Brunot led the discussions, and this time the Weenuche participated with seven representatives. Talks started on September 6, 1873, but there seemed "little to encourage us [Brunot] in hoping for a successful termination," refuting the premise that the Indians had changed their mind. Little wonder when one considers Ferdinand V. Hayden and a group of his men had been surveying the reservation "which excited the suspicions of the Indians"; that "parties of miners had repeatedly endeavored to pass by the agency and enter the reservation at places where the Indians were not willing they should go"; and that these miners had told the Indians that the government was in the East, could not protect them, and that "whether they sold the mines or not, they were going to stay."[28] The fact that the government had done nothing to remove the miners from reservation lands earlier only encouraged the white men and frustrated the Indians. Ironically, the commission felt that the only advantage it had in negotiating with the Utes was an "oft-tested friendship" and their earnest desire to keep the peace and build a positive relationship.

The first round of discussion began with the Utes realizing there had to be some give. They offered to sell only the tops of the mountains that now held mines, but none of the valleys. The miners could not build structures, had to leave in the fall, and could build only one road in to each site. The commission, however, wanted a whole piece of land on the southern end of the reservation. One Weenuche delegate took issue. He pointed out that forty Utes were currently living there, engaged in farming. Others chimed in that soon agriculture and livestock would be the way they would be forced to support themselves, so to give up prime land now could cause problems later. The only place suitable for farming was on the southern end of the reservation, and even the Los Pinos Agency was so high that it had frost every month of the year. Stockmen claimed that it generally took five acres of land to raise one sheep and fifty acres for a horse or cow, which meant ranchers needed access to five to ten thousand acres of public land. The Utes, with their estimated six thousand horses and many cattle and goats, did not want to see their holdings diminished.[29]

As part of the deliberations, members of the commission and Ute leaders visited some of the six hundred lodes and three hundred miners actively working claims. The Utes were impressed, but more importantly reassured that the good agricultural land they

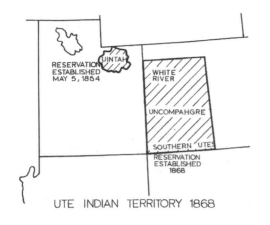

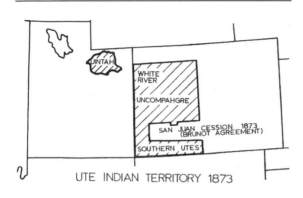

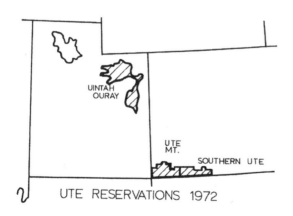

Map 3. Loss of Ute lands, 1868–1972. (Courtesy of the White Mesa Ute Project, American West Center, University of Utah)

desired had now been taken off the table. Those prime southern lands were to remain part of the reservation for the Weenuche, Capotes, and Muaches. Four days of discussion resulted in the Utes signing over four million acres of land in what is now called the Brunot Agreement. They also scheduled a trip to Washington, D.C., for those leaders

who desired to go, Ignacio being one of them. Ouray summarized his view of the government's process by saying,

> All Utes understand the line, and it is as we say. The lines in regard to the mines do not amount to anything; it is changing them all the time—taking a little now and a little again—that makes trouble.... The miners care very little about the government and do not obey the laws.... With you it is different; you talk in the name of the Great Spirit; we understand that, and think it right and ought to have great weight.[30]

More than two hundred Indians signed the agreement, relinquishing territory they could never regain. Congress ratified the agreement on April 29, 1874.

For the Utes living in southeastern Utah, the reverberations from this act would take longer to reach than those living to the east, where the loss was immediate. But the Weenuche were well aware of what had happened. It was just a matter of time before they felt the impact. George W. Manypenny, a former commissioner of Indian Affairs and contemporary advocate for the Utes, put it this way:

> With the surrender of the portion of the Ute reservation obtained by the Brunot agreement, the Indians had a right to, and did expect that, they would be relieved from any further inroads; that having given up the mining territory, they would be protected in what was termed the agricultural lands. But this was a delusion. The grazing country was just as much coveted as the mineral, and the "ranchmen" intruded to prospect for good locations....[31]

This soon proved so true for the White Mesa Utes.

Little wonder that when members of the 1875 Ferdinand V. Hayden survey party appeared in southeastern Utah, they were unwelcome. As part of a national effort to survey unmapped territory, they had spent the two previous years in Colorado. Now

W. H. Holmes, commander of the southwestern division of the Ferdinand V. Hayden Survey, penned the following caption to this picture: "My own party with parts of the Gardner party which had just reached my camp [on the La Plata] after having been attacked by the Paiutes and had lost everything but their riding animals. They arrived a sad and hungry lot, 1875." *Left to right*, Frank Pearson, E. A. Barber, G. B. Chittenden, A. C. Peale, William H. Holmes, Henry Gannett, Charles Aldrich, W. R. Atkinson, T. S. Brandegee, and Harry Lee (the guide?). Pearson, Peale, Gannett, and Atkinson were involved in the fight with the Paiutes. (Hayden Party Photo File, Folder 3, American Heritage Center, University of Wyoming)

they needed to complete the unfinished portion of southwestern Colorado, a small adjoining strip in northern New Mexico, and part of southeastern Utah. Hayden divided his team into seven groups—four assigned to work in specific geographical areas, a fifth to handle general triangulations, a sixth to collect photographs of the landscape and Ancestral Puebloan ruins, and the seventh to transport supplies. The southwestern division, under geologist W. H. Holmes, covered an area of 6,500 square miles that included part of the San Juan River, the La Plata, Mancos, Dolores Rivers, and McElmo and Montezuma Creeks, all of which were part of Weenuche/White Mesa Ute terri-

tory. Smaller teams, one led by topographer Henry Gannett, another by James T. Gardner, in charge of triangulation, and a third, the photographic team under the direction of William H. Jackson, also explored and recorded parts of the same area.[32]

Holmes was aware of the Indians' sensitivity to what the white men were doing. The year before the Utes had denied access to one survey party, believing they were working on reservation boundaries. Holmes hoped to gain their cooperation by assuring them that they were not charged with that responsibility and that he wished to maintain their goodwill. To do this he hired Captain John Moss of the La Plata Mining District, who spoke their language and knew many of the local Indians. With the exception of a small party of miners under his direction and a single farmer on the Mancos River who provided food for the camp on the La Plata, there were no other white settlers in the area. Moss sent word to a large Ute encampment thirty miles below his mines that the survey team should not be molested, and they were not.

By June 22, 1875, Holmes was in the southwest corner of Colorado, heading for Utah. He visited Sleeping Ute Mountain and then worked his way over to the area drained by McElmo, Hovenweep, and Montezuma Creeks. At that point Jackson departed with Moss, E. A. Barber from the *New York Herald*, two packers, and a cook. The night of July 28, Indians stole all of Holmes's livestock, but chief packer Thomas Cooper had the animals back in camp by morning. The party spent time around the Carrizo Mountains and then headed north, where they learned the fate of two of the other groups.[33]

On August 4, Gannett's party joined forces with Gardner's since both were heading for the La Sal Mountains. Prior to their departure, Ouray had warned "that the Indians in the Sierra La Sal Mountains…were likely to steal stock if they got a good chance. He said that a group of seven men would be safe in the region, but they must watch their animals carefully, and if one man was caught out alone he might not be safe. In short, these Sierra La Sal Indians were represented to me as sneak thieves, who would bear much watching."[34] When the combined party left their base camp on the Dolores River, there were thirteen men — seven armed with rifles, the rest with revolvers. They saw no signs of Indians until they reached the base of the mountains, estimating that nine lodges were camped on the Utah-Colorado line. Six more joined them two days later. By that time the geographers had climbed the highest peak twice, completed their topographic sketches and triangulations, and set off for Blue Mountain.

Ben Northington, one of the packers, encountered two Indians while hunting. They shouted, "Amigos, amigos!" and then spent a short time conversing with him in Spanish before departing in the opposite direction of a small camp of nine lodges located two thousand feet below and eight miles east of the surveyors' concealed encampment.[35] None of this raised much concern, although everyone except the cook pulled a nightshift to guard the livestock. By the time they left, another six lodges had joined the Utes below.

On August 15 the men broke camp, having christened the highest peak in the range Mount Peale (12,721 feet) after a member of the party, and departed for the Abajo range (known locally as Blue Mountain) approximately forty miles due south. An interim destination was "Cold Spring" at the top of Peters Hill, marked on a map produced by a previous survey party led by Captain John N. Macomb in 1859.[36] They traveled over Indian trails much of the time, reaching the southern drainage running off the La Sals, where they surprised an Indian boy and old man irrigating several small patches of corn. Both fled, but their presence encouraged party members to believe other Indians might be nearby. Concerned that there might be an unfriendly encounter, the white men left the area.

Late afternoon found the party in the hot, sagebrush-covered Dry Valley, with Gannett taking topographical notes a half mile behind the main group, and Gardner ahead searching for water. Some Utes approached Gannett making signs of peace, shook his hand, and then accompanied him to the larger group, where a second party reined in whooping amidst a cloud of dust. Members of Gardner's group recognized three of the warriors as men they had encountered hunting twenty miles east of the Dolores; the Indians had similar recollections. The Utes produced a paper showing that they were from the White River Agency and declared themselves to be Yampa. They urged the survey party to camp with them at a muddy watering hole and not proceed to the spring at the top of what is today known as Peters Hill, even though the water from the runoff was not potable, and the terrain open to attack. Next they wished to trade for powder and tobacco, but there was none to spare. All this time, the white men noted how the Indians were evaluating their weapons and generally eyeing the group. With a friendly "adios" the groups shook hands and parted.[37]

As soon as the surveyors' rear guard cleared the brow of a nearby hill, the Utes reached the top and opened fire. At first the surveyors thought it was not aimed at them, but when other shots followed, the men flew into action. Some raced to the rear of the pack train and wanted to charge, but Gardner declined. Given the tired mules, the Indians' fresh mounts, and the protective hill they were firing from, the white men decided to break contact but dispatched a small group to a nearby knoll to cover the main party's southern advance across Dry Valley. The warriors maintained a running engagement, directing fire from a number of hills while keeping about five hundred yards' distance. As evening approached, the animals were exhausted, the men tired and hungry, and there was no chance of reaching water before dark. Finding a spot in the flat sea of sage out of range from firing points on surrounding hills and the South Point plateau, the party formed a defensive perimeter of packs and *aparejos* (pack saddles) and "corralled" or tethered the livestock on both sides of the defense. Gardner and two other men moved three hundred yards from this position to a ravine that prevented the Indians from infiltrating to a place from which they could put effective fire on the defenders. Part of this strategy was based on men carrying "needle rifles" with a maximum effective range of 650 yards.[38] The Utes were armed with muzzle-loaders and a sprinkling of Winchester rifles, neither of which had an effective distance of three hundred yards. Thus the night defense and the following day's movement were based on maintaining a large gap between the two forces, keeping Indian fire from the distant hills ineffective.

As the defense took shape, the Utes maintained a steady volume of fire which either fell fifty yards short of the target or whizzed wildly overhead. At one point a shot hit the bell mare, Polly, and was close enough to send Gannett, Ben Northington, and Peale diving for the enclosure. Peale got his foot entangled on the way, pitching him in an inglorious sprawl behind the barricade.[39] Their weapons — "seven breech-loading rifles, more or less good, and four large revolvers, which it was quite obvious were no use against those long range-loving cowards" — were supplied with "ammunition [which] was neither very abundant nor very good."[40] Two canteens of muddy water and some crusts of bread left over from breakfast provided a hasty supper. A schedule to replace the picket at midnight and a watch within the barricade freed some to sleep before their turn to guard arrived.

A full moon rose, making the landscape as "bright and light as day."[41] The Utes began infiltrating through the sagebrush, while each of the opposing sides fired at muzzle flashes. Those who returned fire would shoot and then roll three times to avoid being pinpointed. By concealing themselves effectively in the sagebrush and crawling closer, the Utes reduced the disparity in firepower, making their weapons more effective. For five hours the sporadic exchange continued. Lack of water, food, and sleep took its toll; Gardner, who at midnight was relieved of picket duty, realized something had to be done. Knowing that he had a slow-moving, eighteen-mule pack train and tired mounts, that he was open to ambush from surrounding hills as soon as the party left its barricade, and that the Indians held part of the ridge that led up the valley and canyon to the top of Peters Hill and the spring, he decided to find an alternate route onto the plateau to their south.

Gardner ordered the animals saddled, packed, and formed into a column protected by four riflemen skirmishing in pairs to the front and three to the rear to deny any high ground before the party passed out of rifle range. At first light the group abandoned their position amidst war whoops. Besides seeking a slope that allowed them to gain the plateau, they desperately needed water. For five hours the men rode "around the whole of the open [Dry] Valley," exchanging fire while trying but failing to beat the Indians to commanding terrain.[42] Wishing to avoid the trail that headed up the canyon to Peters Hill for fear of ambush, the party sought tentative breaks in the escarpment that allowed them to reach high ground. An old warrior positioned on a high rock to the rear signaled the party's every move with a red cloth, directing the reaction of the Utes below. Whenever a rifleman from the survey group dismounted to take a shot, the targets dispersed, maintaining a healthy distance. Cuthbert Mills of the *New York Times* paints a vivid picture of what this fighting was like:

> And now commenced a game of long shots, which if we had not been so anxious about getting out of this natural trap, would have been quite amusing. Some of the Indians rode to our rear, a fellow on a powerful gray horse kept to our right, and [Clarence] Kelsey, Ben Northington, and I fell back as rear guard. The enemy commenced banging away at us, and the gray horseman was especially active in wasting his ammunition. This was endured for some time, and then Ben, losing patience exclaimed: "Dash me but I'll try a shot at that fellow, though I am short of ammunition," and dismounting he did so then shook his head. The shot was a wide one.... At this time they were paying their attention to us from the left. There were three there—two close together, the third a little way behind. I aimed at him, and, as the gun cracked, our fellows gave a shout of derisive laughter. The bullet struck up dust just at the horse's heels, and the rider gave the animal such a sudden stroke with his whip that it jumped

> and fell headlong over the sagebrush. When it scrambled up the Indian was still in his seat. He had never lost it.[43]

The exhausted mules walked slowly, spurning the spur as the sun parched man and beast. The valor of the survey party was not enough to carry the plan, which seemed checkmated at every attempt. Some members of the group were showing signs of faltering. After explaining their options, Gardner took a straw vote. Did the men want to go back the way they had come, proceed up the canyon fighting all the way, or continue to search for another route? Most agreed to do whatever the majority wanted, which was to press forward to Peters Spring. Gardner agreed, and although he might lose some men in the effort, it appeared to be their best chance.

Following a feint to the west, his party headed for the eastern side of Peters Canyon, where piñon and juniper trees provided cover and concealment over the foothills leading to a small plateau, then talus slope, and finally rimrock at the top of South Canyon Point. It was the only practical choice, as the Utes, mounted on fast horses, raced to the west side and assumed positions in the rocks, approximately three to four hundred yards from where the party would begin its ascent. Gardner and another man provided initial covering fire from a hill on the east side of the canyon, and then Gardner moved higher to provide continued support while his companion returned to guide the train. Those Indians not ensconced in the rocks traveled up the canyon and then skirted down the east side below the rimrock. The white men urged the heavily laden pack mules and tired mounts over the slope, using the terrain and vegetation for concealment. Effectively hidden, the Indians provided "nothing but whiz-bang, whiz, bang, whiz bang" as their targets labored uphill.[44] At this point Gardner wondered if there might be some type of break in the rock formation

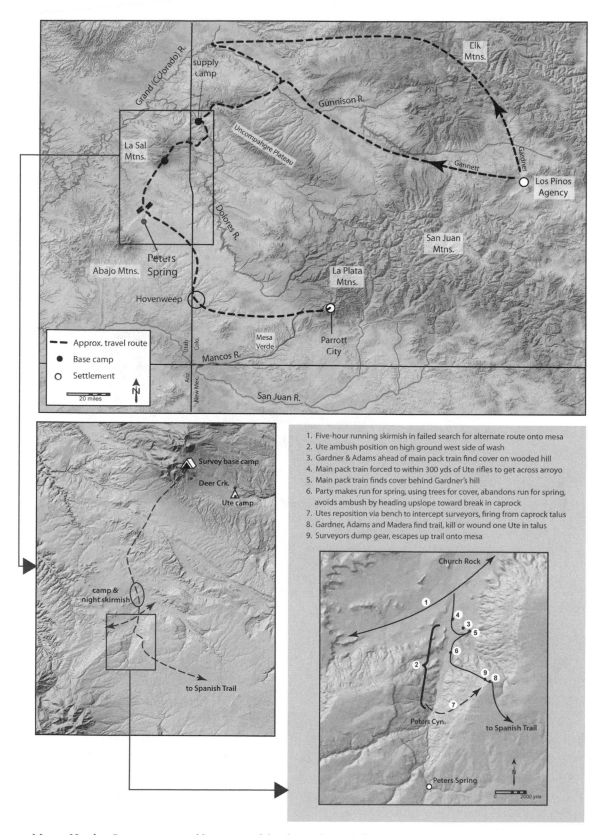

1. Five-hour running skirmish in failed search for alternate route onto mesa
2. Ute ambush position on high ground west side of wash
3. Gardner & Adams ahead of main pack train find cover on wooded hill
4. Main pack train forced to within 300 yds of Ute rifles to get across arroyo
5. Main pack train finds cover behind Gardner's hill
6. Party makes run for spring, using trees for cover, abandons run for spring, avoids ambush by heading upslope toward break in caprock
7. Utes reposition via bench to intercept surveyors, firing from caprock talus
8. Gardner, Adams and Madera find trail, kill or wound one Ute in talus
9. Surveyors dump gear, escapes up trail onto mesa

Map 4. Hayden Survey route and locations of the skirmish in southeastern Utah. (Courtesy of Winston Hurst)

This steep talus slope of loose sandstone and boulders, covered with trees and capped with a tall rimrock, made the ascent for Gardner's party difficult even after finding this hidden deer trail. (Hayden Party Photo File, Folder 3, American Heritage Center, University of Wyoming)

that would grant access to the plateau above — "one chance among a million, but the odds were better than going through the canyon."[45]

As man and animal plodded up the slope and onto the narrow flat, they found a pool of alkaline clay water, almost the consistency of paste, that they drank to slake their thirst. Aware that the Indians were intending to head them off, Gardner pushed the party forward, traveling on the plateau at the base of the talus slope. Five packs fell off or had to be readjusted due to the difficult travel, giving more time for the Indians to assume new vantage points in preventing escape. Suddenly the Utes opened fire from the high ground, perhaps sixty yards away, just below

the rimrock. "Jim," the white mule, made an easy target and was the first to be killed. Two others eventually suffered a similar fate, with another lost in the trees and three more being wounded. The fire grew intense. Each member of the party took up a position behind a tree or rock, reporting that the Indians' fire was accurate, with clipped branches and chips of rock falling close about. As for the Utes, they were perfectly concealed.

Gardner, in the meantime, had been able to get around an angle of the slope, where he spied a narrow deer path leading upward and possibly through an indentation in the rimrock. He and packer Shep Madera traversed the steep incline to see if there might be a trail. Their first thought was to relieve

Below the slope, in the shelter of some boulders, Hayden's survey crew jettisoned unessential gear such as cooking equipment, pannier, tripods, and extra food, and led their animals up the trail. In August 1964 P. K. Hurlbut located the site and equipment. (Hayden Party Photo File, Folder 3, American Heritage Center, University of Wyoming)

the pressure on the men below, but a ledge masked their view of the enemy. However, one unlucky Ute fifty yards away fired and then exposed himself to see his effect, only to have Madera bring him down. Cheers from below reported the result. Robert Adams next joined the pair as they traversed part of the slope, locating the exact route of the barely visible deer trail, which took them to the edge of the plateau.

Elated at this stroke of luck, the three rejoined the party to report the good news. There was no doubt that the mules could never make the ascent under fire while loaded with all of the equipment. After a few minutes' deliberation, Gardner "order[ed] to 'cut loose' with feelings which actually brought out tears. Had there been time,

everything would have been piled up and burned; as it was they went to work with knives and cut everything from the backs of the mules in such a way that scarcely a whole rope, an unbroken package, an unsmashed can or box, or anything cutable or breakable was left."[46] Ammunition, four days' rations, a frying pan and pot, and their field notes and scientific work was all the group equipment taken, while each man secured a coat for warmth and a sleeping blanket. The rest they destroyed. Then up the slope, herding or leading the livestock. "A miracle, almost, now occurred"—an unopposed ascent.[47]

Men and animals clambered to the top, left the protection of the small piñon-juniper forest rimming the canyon, and began their flight over a sagebrush-covered plateau. Their destination was the Mancos River, thence the La Plata River and the supply camp. It was 1:30 p.m. on August 16 and the heat was intense. Water remained uppermost on everyone's mind, second only to the Indians' signal shot notifying their comrades that they were aware that the whites had given them the slip. The Utes' efforts a couple hours later to head off the whites and keep them from water failed. Gardner believed that the Utes would guess that the surveyors were heading to the Dolores River and so rode ahead, but the white men took a trail that snaked its way to the southeast in the general direction of the Mancos River. Five hours later the party found a spring, rested, watered, ate a supper of bread, ham, and tea, and then plunged on. Two hours later they stumbled upon a Ute encampment, the Indians pursuing them to a hill ki-yi-yiing, but then moving forward saying "amigo" and asking who these travelers were and where they were going. The groups parted as friends, the surveyors continuing for another two hours before camping.[48]

Two more days of constant travel brought them to springs at Hovenweep, where they rested. The next day they arrived at McElmo Canyon, and then traveled near Sleeping Ute Mountain, the Mancos River, and finally, just before dark, arrived at Merritt's ranch, where they made pea soup from the produce of his garden. They also learned that Holmes's party had camped five miles ahead as they wended their way to the supply base at Parrott City. The next day, August 20, both groups arrived. Gardner's men were bedraggled, Peale writing, "A more haggard-looking party could scarcely be found. Out of about sixty consecutive hours we had been in the saddle forty-eight, with about five hours sleep and nothing to eat save a few scraps of bread and ham."[49] Gardner added: "The fight was incessant from 5 o'clock p.m. on the 15th, till the afternoon of the 16th, except three hours in the night. Out of thirty-two animals we brought off twenty-eight. Three of these are wounded, but not badly. Not a man was

wounded and none are sick. The work is not much interfered with, for the western part of the topography, in the dangerous country, was about complete."[50] The leader went on to praise his entire group. Other participants gave additional reasons for success: (1) "our men were armed with long-range needle guns;" (2) Gardner's cool courage in leading and his topographical knowledge of the area; and (3) lack of boldness of the Indians.[51]

For some of the surveyors the next few days were ones of rest, but not so for Gardner. There was still the question of the supply base on the Dolores, close to the territory of the fractious Utes. Holman and Dallas were situated approximately forty miles from where the fight had occurred and close to a large network of Indian trails. They were actually on one of the main thoroughfares leading south to Navajo country. Gardner and others feared their demise. Selecting six volunteers to accompany him—all armed with breech-loading rifles except the hunter-cook Jacque Charpiot, who preferred a double barrel shotgun—Gardner had them mount their mules at noon on August 22 and depart. They did not return until August 30, having traveled a round-trip distance of 310 miles, during which "two nights we had been nearly washed out of our blankets by heavy rains, one night had been almost frozen, two days had been long drives across a dry country under scorching sun, and every day had been in the saddle almost from sunrise to sunset."[52]

Little of note occurred until the third day, when Gardner spied Holman's horse grazing alone about twenty miles from the supply base. The party suspected foul play, assumed Indians had taken it, and so dismounted and prepared to charge. Believing the culprits were in the trees across a creek, Gardner "intended [that] if Indians were there, to surround them in camp, cut them off from their ponies, and kill them among their lodges. Each man strove to be foremost in the charge, but much to our disappointment no camp was there."[53] After a good laugh, they continued their journey. The next day the men arose at 3 a.m., had breakfast, and reached the supply base later in the morning. Two miles outside, there were numerous Indian pony tracks and so as the men approached with caution, they readied themselves for the worst. Outside a large grove of cottonwoods, where the camp had initially been pitched, they saw nothing but moccasin prints. One of the men, however, spotted a boot print, and upon further investigation found Holman, Dallas, and their tents within the brush-enclosed grove of trees.

The quartermaster explained that the previous week twenty or more White River Utes had visited the camp. Holman, having worked at the agency, knew several by name and read carefully their agent's pass authorizing absence from the reservation to trade with the Navajos to the south. "The Indians were extremely angry at finding white men apparently established in this remote section, and exhibited much insolence of demeanor. They threatened that if he did not leave by tomorrow's sun they would 'heap kill'; demanded food, which he refused; tobacco, which was also refused; and finally a drink of water which was given."[54] Before leaving the next day the disgruntled Indians hinted that other Utes might visit them and "heap scalp" then fired the grass and brush to burn out the camp. Holman and Dallas extinguished the blaze and settled down to wait.

Gardner directed that anything of high value be loaded on a supply mule brought for the purpose, and that everything else be destroyed. Charles McCreary set-to with an axe, declaring it was the best thing since Sherman's raid, but all the time cursing the Indians with each stroke. In two hours anything that was not packed was inoperable or burning in a central fire. With the salute of a final rifle volley echoing through the canyon, the men turned their mounts toward Parrott City.

There was still one group unaccounted for: Jackson's, returning from the Hopi mesas. Nothing had been heard from him, so two men familiar with the terrain left to divert the photographic team away from the "Sierra La Sal Utes." Jackson had departed the Hopi villages on August 15 and headed north. After crossing the San Juan River five days later, the group explored some ruins and then proceeded up Comb Wash toward Blue Mountain.[55] When they reached a place where three towers stood, "quite a batch of Ute, who first made themselves known from away up on the bluff by loud shouts," descended to talk with the party. They wished to trade deerskins and camp with the white men, but there was little to exchange and maintaining a distance seemed wise. Three of the Indians accompanied the explorers to Arch Canyon and then over Comb Ridge to Cottonwood Creek to camp for the night. After feeding their new companions supper, the explorers settled down for the evening, only to have the Utes stampede their stock and "raise a rumpus generally." The event soon ended, with the livestock retrieved.[56] Jackson continued his travels to Blue Mountain and eventually into Montezuma Canyon, oblivious of the fight that Gardner's group had experienced.

To enter Montezuma the party found a "practicable" way into the canyon through a narrow valley that widened as the men reached the bottom. Jackson recalled that "The ruins were so numerous now that frequently one or more were in view as we rode along. Arrow points were so plentiful that there was an active rivalry as to which one of us found the greatest number. Broken pottery of all kinds and beads and other trinkets were also collected."[57] The next morning as the men broke camp, they discovered their horses had gotten into some Indian cornfields, but since the owners were not around, the group continued on its way. Eventually a large canyon from the east entered at a right angle to the main course. One man emerged from the site and greeted them, soon joined by fifteen to twenty warriors.

Shouting their shrill "hi, hi" and swinging their guns over their heads, they did not stop until they had run right into us and, turning about, surrounded us completely.... Crowding around us, all the Indians joined in a noisy chorus of greetings and shaking of hands.... They appeared to be friendly, however, and finally insisted upon our going to their camp. In a spirit of pure mischief or deviltry, they got behind us, and with quirt and lariat, lashed our horses and mules into a breakneck race, never letting up until we dashed among their wickiups. It was a regular stampede all the way.[58] As Jackson put it, "All of us were having the time of our lives—but in different ways."[59]

The party was quick to explain that they were not surveyors, the tripod legs protruding from a mule's pack were for a camera, they were good friends of John Moss, and the party was just passing through. The men were now amidst "a score of wickiups, the characteristic rounded wicker-and-canvas shelters of nomadic tribes in the Southwest, and from one of them the Pah Ute chief stepped forth." Poco Narraguinip (Pogonobogwint), who was "an old man, twisted and gnarled like a wind-swept tree," presided over them.[60] He offered a lunch of boiled green corn and insisted his guests stay overnight. The white men declined the offer, left the camp as hastily as possible, and searched for a way out of the canyon. Two Indians followed the party but were soon lost by a sharp turn up a brushy side canyon. Although Jackson tried to climb out of this defile, they lost a mule to a fall and then wandered about for a couple of days without finding a safe route. They returned to the Indian camp for water and a better course of travel. The Utes greeted them again in a peaceful manner before Jackson returned to his men at a nearby campsite. The next day before the party left, the Indians confronted them about the newly discovered damage done to their cornfields by the white men's livestock. Jackson recounts, "We had nothing to give them, and when they got ugly about it, I had the packers

rush the train ahead, while Harry [Lee—a guide who replaced Moss] and I remained behind to stand them off until we could make a get-away." From there the party went to Hovenweep and on to the La Plata.

A number of points can be drawn from the seemingly insignificant Gardner and Jackson incidents. First is the Utes' hatred for survey crews and what they portended for their land. Jackson said, "All times we avoided any mention of the Geological Survey; for even the word 'survey' was anathema to all Utes."[61] Second is to understand how relatively unexplored and unsettled this area was in 1875. With the exception of Parrott City, the mining camp on the La Plata, and a small support farm on the Mancos, there were no white habitations in a very large geographical area. In five years that picture changed dramatically. Perhaps most important is the identification of the Ute/Paiute/Navajo faction living in southeastern Utah and southwestern Colorado as a group of "outlaws," "renegades," and a "robber band," epithets used for the next fifty years. Even though the Utes who had attacked Gardner were definitely identified as Yampas from White River, blame shifted immediately to the Sierra La Sal Utes and thence to the "Pah Utes" inhabiting the area. Ouray, who appeared to be no friend of these people, suggested that these same Indians had been killing white miners coming down from Salt Lake City, were well supplied with arms and ammunition, which they traded with the Utes, and did not recognize the government's wishes to move to a reservation. To Gardner, "severe punishment [should] be meted out to them."[62] Holmes went so far as to say that this conglomeration of "Utes, Pai-Utes, and Navajos, who were under the lead of Pah-ghe-nob-i-gant, infest the canyons of southeast Utah, and acknowledge no tribal or other authority."[63] Colorado papers were quick to chime in that the government therefore had the responsibility to "root out at once the nest of freebooters and murderers.... [and that] the people of Colorado...know the character of the red devils."[64] While white theft of Ute lands did not make them thieves, the Indians of southeastern Utah were summarily, though inaccurately, branded as such after the Hayden incident.

On several occasions Ouray butted heads with Ignacio, who accused him of taking payments that belonged to the Weenuche, favoring his own band over theirs, and following a course of self-aggrandizement. Ouray had no love for the Weenuche, particularly those in Utah, telling members of the Hayden expedition that they were "likely to steal stock, if they had a good chance… [and] were sneak thieves that bear watching."[65] The surveyors believed that "being on the boundary lines of the ranges of three tribes, the Utes, the Paiutes, and the Navajos, the most desperate rascals from each congregate there for mutual protection and plunder when they dare not openly appear anywhere else. They acknowledge no authority but that of their own chiefs — murderers and robbers every one."[66] Fed this type of information by other Utes about Indians living around the La Sal Mountains, there is little wonder the survey parties expected the worst.

Following the incident, these Utah Utes continued to serve as convenient tinder, feeding the flames of antagonism. Ouray identified the leader of the attack as Big Head, half Weenuche half Navajo, an outcast of the agency Utes whose following of twenty warriors was comprised of "renegade Paiutes, Jicarilla Apaches, and Navajos, there being no Utes among them."[67] While there may very well have been some of these mixed Weenuche Utes living in southeastern Utah who participated in the fight, the only Indians identified beforehand were Yampas. Holman definitely identified those who confronted him at the supply camp as a trading party from the White River Agency, home of the Yampa and Parusanuch bands, both Northern Utes. Jackson's encounter with Narraguinip in Montezuma Canyon, however, introduced the photographer to local

Weenuche Utes, previously characterized as brigands and troublemakers. These Indians openly welcomed the surveyors to their camp and fed them. Still, the label persisted.

The white men, or "Americats," were not the only ones fiddling with labels. To the Utes of this time there were two types: the "Washington Americat" hailed from any place east of the Rocky Mountains, while the "California Americat" lived to the west. "As a rule, they are most friendly to the latter, for the reason that they have generally received the fairest and most friendly treatment from them.… The way they [Utes] deport themselves on being informed is a sufficient inducement for everybody to hail for the time being from the Pacific States."[68] One reason for this classification can be laid upon Captain John Moss, whose reputation for taking care of Indians, understanding their point of view, and treating them fairly gave him a voice that was listened to. Although California investments paid for much of the mining that wrested lands from the Utes, the Indians still appreciated Moss's even hand in his dealings with them. People from Washington, on the other hand, did nothing but take from them and fail to keep promises. More miners, more farmers, more cattlemen, more land loss, fewer resources danced in the wake of the mapmakers. Add to this no promised payments, one agent's inactivity except for profiteering, and insufficient game, and it is little wonder some Utes declared that "they will fight before they will starve to death." They also turned to raiding herds of sheep and cattle of Colorado and New Mexico ranchmen, creating even more friction.[69]

1876 saw rapid expansion onto Capote and Weenuche lands. The San Juan mining area was "filling up with surprising rapidity; the roads are filled with trains of emigrants, and that whole region bids fair to be soon well-peopled."[70] New mines opened, towns constructed, three public roads and a toll road graded on the southern part of the reservation, the Denver and Rio Grande

Chief Ignacio, 1898. Old enough to have fought the Navajos in the 1860s and to have enjoyed total freedom, Ignacio saw massive changes take place in the lives of the Ute people. He was involved in all of the major treaty negotiations for land, assisted the Weenuche during the initial occupation of their reservation, and taught by example how to adjust to white society. When he died in 1913, the Utes lost a great leader. (Denver Public Library, Western History Collection, Rose and Hopkins, H-471)

Railroad were pushing toward southwestern Colorado, where plans for an agency were evolving, and citizens sent petitions for military protection. Settlers gobbled agricultural land and pasturage at a rapid rate, unauthorized roads created an expanding network to ingress onto Ute territory, and the Weenuche felt that Ouray was a thief and liar for allowing it. They also believed the Jicarilla Apaches had pulled a similar trick — relinquishing lands that did not belong to them.[71] The pioneer juggernaut paid no attention, moving each day closer to southeastern Utah.

The Weenuche were angry. Although their agent viewed them as being a naturally quiet and peaceable people who did not make trouble, he also knew that they felt

"to have been greatly deceived in making the treaty [of 1873]."[72] Ignacio threatened to drive the settlers out of the lower Animas Valley. Three years had passed since the commission had signed the agreement, and there had been no payment for the lands that he now saw inundated with whites. The chief "could not live on promises.... Ignacio does not want to be a bad Indian if he can get his rights by being a good one. He is a very intelligent man, bold and determined and of great influence with his people."[73] When Ouray had "given away" much of the Weenuche farming land, they had not understood or agreed to it. If accepting the annuities clinched the loss, they did not want them. Just stop the development and remove the settlers.

There was another reason that the Utes did not receive their first annuity of $25,000, which was to be used to purchase horses, sheep, and guns. True, the funds were slow in coming due to bureaucratic and transportation issues, but more important was the concern over weapons. The commissioner of Indian Affairs would not grant permission to purchase them until the attack on the Gardner party had been explained. The answer pinned the blame on "a little patriarchal band of outlaws, called by the head-chief Ouray, Pi-Utes, but admitted by many others to be Weeminuche Utes. Up to within a few months, they acknowledged allegiance to no one.... According to their story, which can hardly be credited, all the shooting was done by one man, and he a Pi-Ute from Nevada."[74] They had now visited the agency, received some goods, and promised that there would be no more trouble.

The next three years, 1877–1879, witnessed a mounting flow of traffic that surged around, nibbled, and then chomped at Ute lands. The area of Farmington, New Mexico, on the San Juan River saw rapid settlement after it was officially opened to homesteading in 1875. In 1874 the Mancos Valley sported a small ranch and farm, but by 1876–1877, large numbers of settlers had claimed Ute property. Ranches established at this same time on the Dolores River took advantage of a huge open range that spread cattle across southwestern Colorado and into southeastern Utah. These ranches also served as a springboard for settlements along the Utah portion of the San Juan River; by 1879 there were eighteen families living in the vicinity of McElmo Creek and Riverside, today's Aneth. Two years earlier a small handful of people had begun building in the Moab region, while Tom Ray, his wife, and eight children settled in the Coyote/La Sal area south of the La Sal Mountains. Paradox Valley, at the southeastern base of the La Sals, was first settled in 1877. Mining interests kept pace, so that by 1879 the entire San Juan region was filled with prospectors working claims.[75] The government announced a new Ute agency for Los Pinos in 1877 in an attempt to keep Southern Ute activities under control, as the Indians watched their treasured lands disappear. What the treaty agreements were doing was abundantly clear.

Settlers and miners next demanded protection. The citizens of Parrott City sent a petition to General William Tecumseh Sherman, commander-in-chief of the army, asking for a military post in their proximity. After stating that the undersigned had settled the valleys of the Pinos, Florida, Animas, La Plata, and Mancos Rivers, as well as their tributaries, they now felt it was time for the military to defend their lives and interests. They were all about progress — agriculture, mining, and livestock — but now the Indians were taking their possessions, killing their cattle, and threatening their families. The petitioners had "so far patiently borne their insults and divided with them our last mouthful of flour, when we did not know where the next was to come from nor how soon our children would be crying for bread."[76] They believed that the Indians had become bolder because they had met little resistance. Three months later a second peti-

tion followed. According to it, settlers on the lower Animas and Grand (Colorado) Rivers had been driven out, traffic to the San Juan stymied, and settlements on the Mancos and Dolores Rivers threatened. Now that an agency was going to be built on the Los Pinos River, the citizenry had a suggestion — appoint a local, Henry R. Crosby, as agent. He knew both sides of the Indian-white fence and was recognized by a number of influential people.[77] If someone else had already been appointed, then transfer him, because Crosby was the man they wanted. Thankfully, it did not happen.

Ossipawiz, a medicine man in Ignacio's band, was tired of the immigrant flow. He was ready to enlist all of the young warriors to push the whites out of the "lower country," but wanted either Ouray's help or at least his young chiefs to assist. His visit to the Tabeguache camp was not only unsuccessful in enlisting aid, but Ouray killed him for attempting it.

There were other problems. The three southern bands reiterated that they had not been consulted about losing the San Juan country, with its prime hunting grounds and camp sites, plus their expected payments had still not come. "The Great Father talks to Ouray only [who] discards their rights and they all say that he has a giant pocket in which everything goes."[78] Ouray was a great friend of the whites, who valued his ability to restrain the young warriors. That is why he received an annual salary of $1,000, which had only recently been reduced because of bureaucratic entanglements.

Ignacio had implored Ouray on a number of occasions for the Weenuche Utes' share of the treaty money but never received it. In July 1877 the two chiefs met in a grand council on neutral ground. They agreed to maintain friendly relations, and Ouray had a letter written to persuade the government to put the permanent Southern Ute agency not on the Los Pinos but rather on the Navajo River, and Ignacio vowed to go to Washington to get his people's money. The Weenuche, on the other hand, had not traveled to the agency at Tierra Amarilla for a year because of an epidemic of smallpox, "of which they stand in mortal fear." The disease, however, killed one-fifth of the local Mexican population. The Utes wisely avoided contact and lost only two people to the scourge, one of whom was a man who had come in to find out if it had abated.[79]

Many of Ignacio's Weenuche were then camped at Sleeping Ute Mountain, from which "they keep up a constant lookout—all our [military] movements having been signaled whilst in sight for two days." Some of the ranchers had lost cattle to the Indians, but in the same respect, they had animals running loose and grazing on Indian lands. The cattlemen knew this could be a problem, so they had agreed with Ute leaders that if cows were nearby and the Indians needed food, they could go to the ranches and receive what they needed. As for theft, Ignacio blamed it on "a few bad Indian renegades and some Pi-Utes of Utah…roaming through the western strip and the country east thereof, shooting or stealing cattle…. at best they are a rascally looking set." Once again, the Utes and Paiutes of southeastern Utah became the "fall guy" in absentia.

The spring and summer of 1878 held more upheaval. The first incident was the removal of the Utes and Apaches living at the Cimarron and Abiquiu agencies. In March the commissioner of Indian Affairs, responding to settler complaints, decided to close the two agencies and send the Jicarilla Apaches south to the Mescalero Reservation near Fort Stanton, while the Muaches and remaining Capotes and Weenuche would go to southwestern Colorado. The cost of operating the two agencies had been $40,000 per year; their closing would save an estimated $10,000. The government contracted for wagons to carry the children and old people and made preparations for military escorts. General John Pope, commander of

the Department of the Missouri, had issues. His forces were stretched thin, covering part of an area that extended from Missouri and Kansas to Colorado and New Mexico. There were already troops committed in Colorado and elsewhere, which would force him to transfer mounted infantry from a long distance. The Indians had left the Cimarron Agency and were out on the Plains, which could then entail a long and fruitless search. Why not wait until they came in to the agency in the fall for rations, thus saving time, expense, and saddle sores?[80]

General Philip H. Sheridan, commander of the Division of the Missouri and Pope's supervisor, did not agree, feeling Pope was "making more fuss than is warranted."[81] He set June 5 as the date of movement for the two groups and directed three troops of cavalry, with fifty men in each, be there to assist. Reports that the Southern Utes already in Colorado were becoming insubordinate added urgency that a large armed force not only assist with the move but help other elements in the region quell any disturbance. There were delays. No rations and annuities were to be distributed after July 18, forcing the Indians to receive them at their new locations. As an addendum, the secretary of the Interior requested that at the same time, sufficient force be used "to compel Indians in Utah to go upon reservations."[82] On July 19 the Apaches and Utes were on their way under their own power, without military assistance.[83] The first group of Muaches reached their destination on August 15, with the women and children soon following.[84]

Meanwhile, things were not going smoothly in southwestern Colorado for Agent F. H. Weaver. He had requested that the Weenuche and Capotes under his care be exempted from a directive sent to reservations that in order to receive supplies the Indians had to work. The Utes felt that their loss of land was enough to justify payment, which they perceived had been agreed upon when some had gone to Washington. Even then there were problems. The first supplies arrived in January, the annuities in February, and the Indians on the first day of March. Unusually heavy snow and cold forced them to leave their tepees and equipment behind, stay at the agency for only five days, and then return to their camps. Even so, 358 Utes and 44 Navajos showed up for distribution. To add to the ill will, Lieutenant Valois, with a detachment of fifteen men of the Ninth Cavalry, an Afro-American unit referred to by the Indians as "buffalo soldiers" because of their curly hair, arrived.[85]

The Utes were surly, realizing that such a small group could not enforce any demands. Weaver wanted to have them either receive ration checks or provide their names so that he could get an accurate count of the supplies he issued. They refused. He asked that the men dismount and people cluster according to their lodge group. They declined and stayed on their horses. When the agent attempted a simple headcount, they milled around, some leaving for a fair distance, so that it could not be accomplished. Next it was the Utes turn to make demands: Issue a fifty pound sack of flour to every woman there and do likewise with all of the other goods. "There was to be no more talk about it, that when the supply was exhausted, the Great Father would send more, and all that I [Weaver] had to do was to give it to them."[86]

The April issue of rations was just as bad. When Weaver began to build a fence around the agency building, Ignacio forbid it. When he tried to fence the agency garden, Ignacio halted him until Weaver agreed to build it as the Ute instructed. The work stopped, the agent convinced the whole event was a ploy to start a confrontation.[87] He opined that even though the "government has lavished upon them annuities, which have been most bountifully bestowed," the rumors of Ute and Navajo cooperation in a war seemed to fit the surly condition of his charges.[88] A large military force would be the only way to humble them.

In May that large force arrived in the form of five troops from the Ninth Cavalry under Major A. P. Morrow.[89] They were there to investigate rumors of Navajos disturbing settlers along the San Juan River, Utes burning cabins, and the belief that the two may be joining forces. The major sent for Cabezon, the Ute leader in this area, to pay a visit. Cabezon arrived the next day with ten warriors, one of whom was "Blind Dick," Ignacio's brother, named for his missing eye. Cabezon, an eighty-year-old man who had been a renowned warrior, also had his son with him. He admitted to farming a plot of land that he knew was not on the reservation, but one that he and his father before him had used. He had in his hire Navajos who raised corn and other produce for the Utes, who in turn allowed them to keep part of their vegetables and live under their protection. The chief attested that the two groups had been "living together on that spot since his boyhood and had there a site sacred to their annual corn feast."[90] More reports of Navajos and Utes joining forces to drive settlers out came in.

Colonel Edward Hatch, who had accompanied the party, said that unless the Navajo women were married to Ute men, all Navajos had to return to their reservation. They were employed to grow the gardens, tend the flocks, saddle Cabezon's horse, and perform other tasks, and the Utes did not want to see them leave. Blind Dick, blowing smoke from his cigarette, replied, "Who knows. I am very deaf today. I don't hear you." Hatch countered that in a few days he would not be so deaf. The Indians made it clear that Ignacio would be glad to talk to the white men, that the Utes did not want trouble, "but damn the settlers." Hatch said that he would return to Cabezon and his fifteen lodges in three days after traveling to the Mancos River and the Big Bend of the Dolores. If Ignacio wanted to talk, that would be the time.

The Weenuche leader was there waiting for them. He professed his love for Weaver, Hatch, and others in the party but was adamant that the Ute rations were inadequate, the meat poor, and that his land loss was overwhelming. He did not know where the boundary lines were because there were no natural terrain features to go by, settlers came and "fenced up my land and eat up all my grass," he had sold only the "tops of my mountains and now they come and make roads all over it." In addition, the reservation he was on was only 15 miles wide and 110 miles long, and there were white invaders with their livestock even on that. In the winter he had always gone into New Mexico, where it was warmer, but now he had been told he could not do that. Whites were taking over the Utes' favorite camping spots and their sacred Pagosa Springs, and he did not want the military around. Although there was no change in the situation, the Utes visited the agency following this meeting on friendlier terms.

Yet another storm brewed. Lack of knowledge of intratribal politics, and the Ute situation in general, led government officials to toy with the idea of consolidating all of the agencies into one at White River. The Indians would forfeit the southern part of Ute lands totally. Some whites cried foul and offered the possibility of at least allowing the Southern Utes to move to the headwaters of the Navajo, Chama, Piedra, and San Juan Rivers. On May 3, Congress empowered a commission to hold talks with all of the bands at Los Pinos; Weaver received instructions to have all three Southern Ute groups present. On November 9, the Ute leaders reached an agreement. No doubt the $2,000 worth of gifts helped, although the Indians feared deceit and would not at first accept them. Eventually, all consented to giving up their holdings on the Consolidated Ute Reservation in southwestern Colorado and moving by the summer of 1879 to the headwaters mentioned. They also accepted that traffic on either already existing or newly constructed roads across their land would not be molested. One hundred Muaches, eighty-seven

Capotes, and thirty-seven Weenuche signed the agreement. By doing so they gave up a reservation of 1.1 million acres for one of 700,000 acres.[91] To add final injury, in October, Company I of the Fifteenth Infantry established a cantonment at Pagosa Springs, fifty-two miles from the Los Pinos Agency. The structure soon received the name of Fort Lewis, the first of two to have this title.[92]

The year 1879 promised to be more of the same. Henry Page, the new agent at the Southern Ute Agency, issued his annual report in August. At first he felt his charges were arrogant and sullen, but won many over by providing medical attention from a physician from the Ninth Cavalry. Others appreciated the agent, who in accompaniment with Ignacio, removed squatters on Ute lands who had prematurely anticipated the Indians leaving for their new reservation. President Rutherford B. Hayes had withdrawn these lands from settlement, but Congress had taken no action, so the Indians remained at Los Pinos. The Utes still had no interest in assuming the trappings of civilization—speaking English, going to school, farming land, or accepting Christianity. The old ways were tried and proven, and intertwined in the fabric of their culture.[93]

Daily friction continued. For example, during the annual cattle roundup held just off the reservation, a drunken cowboy, Hank Sharp, shot and killed a Ute warrior without provocation. The Indians moved out of range of the cowboys' revolvers and then forced them to take cover in a corral with their rifle fire. Prompt action by Page and Ignacio brought the offender to justice, the Utes placing their desire for revenge aside.[94] Another issue rested between the Weenuche and Muaches. The latter returned to their old haunt around Cimarron in mid-September. Aguila, their spokesman, told Captain Charles Parker that they were not welcome among the Weenuche and Capotes. "When we were on the Los Pinos last year, Ignacio came to me and said what are you doing here? You had better go back to the Cimarron where you belong. He refused to let my people hunt in the mountains and was very angry with me for coming there and wished to kill me. We like this [Cimarron] country very much."[95] Parker offered assistance, and Aguila relented and agreed to return to Los Pinos, but not before the Muaches complained that on the reservation, "the white people were thick and that the white men's cattle had grazed the grass off the hills."

But these problems dwarfed in comparison to those between the White River Utes and their agent, Nathan C. Meeker, which played out in what is often referred to as "the Meeker massacre." Events leading up to this, involving a number of bloody incidents, have been aptly described elsewhere.[96] Briefly, a new, zealous, reforming agent, Nathan Meeker, insensitive to Indian wishes and cultural protocol, alienated many of the White River Utes. Events escalated both on and off the reservation to the point that Major Thomas T. Thornburgh crossed the reservation boundaries and was summarily attacked. On September 29, Thornburgh and ten of his men died. His four troops of the Fourth Cavalry remained pinned down for six days, even with other units joining the fray, unable to break through to the agency. The same day that Thornburgh and his troops were attacked, the Utes killed Meeker and ten civilians, and kidnapped Meeker's wife and daughter, along with another woman and her two young children. Eventually, the Indians saw the futility of resisting the mounting odds, freed the captives, and surrendered.

Of interest here is the role of the Southern Utes, and the Weenuche in particular. Three days after the killings, uncertainty reined. There was no doubt that the Southern Utes were unhappy about constantly moving onto new but dwindling reservation lands, but would they assist the White River Utes? Soldiers poured in from Texas, Oklahoma, New Mexico, and Colorado, all targeted for Ute country. Ouray ordered all of the South-

ern Utes to remain on their reservation and to not participate in any of the war talk. Still, six White River Utes rode 250 miles, appearing at the agency to hold a victory dance over Thornburgh's losses and to attract more men for the fight. The temptation proved too great, and "many young warriors left with them."[97] Chiefs Savan (Capote) and Aguila (Muache) arrived at the agency the next day to say that they were doing all they could to control their young men, but it was proving to be impossible. As for Ignacio, he did not attend the meeting, wishing his warriors' absence to remain quiet, but all three chiefs pledged to stay out of the fray.

Ute leaders and warriors attended a second meeting on October 13, again promising to be quiet. Among the one hundred participants were Ignacio, Aguila, Poco Narraguinip—"chief of the renegades," Red Jacket, Cabezon, and "old chief Kaneache."[98] The Indians reported that "Ignacio's band is, with few exceptions, on the reservation near the agency; Pi-Utes on the Mancos and Dolores."[99] These same leaders went with Agent Page to visit General Hatch to ensure their peaceful motives were understood. It is important to recognize that Poco Narraguinip was among them and was considered influential enough to represent the "renegade Utes" (not Pi-Utes) at this time.[100]

It was also important for the Utes to realize how quickly military forces could travel and be massed at any sign of insurrection.[101] A year-end report to General Sherman outlined the troop disposition: on the Animas River, three companies of the Fifteenth Infantry, one mounted company of the Nineteenth Infantry, and two troops of the Ninth Cavalry—a total of 234 men; four companies of the Twenty-second Infantry had just been sent to Texas; at Fort Garland, five troops of the Fourth Cavalry, five companies of the Nineteenth Infantry, and two companies of the Sixteenth Infantry—in all 542 men; expected shortly were five infantry companies from the Department of the Platte, and five more from the Twenty-third Infantry from Oklahoma—a grand total of 942 men.[102] This figure eventually shrank, but not before the cantonment at Pagosa Springs, serving as a temporary camp, awaited construction of a second Fort Lewis on the La Plata River near Durango in 1880.

Thus ended a decade of decision in which the Utes saw sweeping changes. Between the 1869 petition to the president of United States from Colorado citizenry asking that the Utes remain in their territory to the shrill cry of 1879 that "the Utes must go," there occurred monumental shifts. Their lands had shrunk from roughly the western third of the state of Colorado and two agencies in New Mexico to, by 1882, the total expulsion of the northern bands to Utah, with the Southern Utes tucked into a corner of southwestern Colorado. Hunting and gathering for most became impossible following these land losses. The government gained stewardship and general control over most of the Indians, while towns, railroads, and road networks sliced through their territory. Miners and ranchers rejoiced at the vast potential of the lands now opening to expansion. Presiding over much of this were local, state, and federal governments that encouraged and protected these efforts during the Gilded Age of the late 1800s.

To the Weenuche and Paiutes living in southeastern Utah, these events were well-known and carried a startling message. Although they had felt the vibrations from incidents at a distance, they still held much of their hunting and gathering territory. Other Weenuche groups had used their lands, but this had been on a temporary basis. Others may have relinquished their sovereignty to the agents and the federal government, but these people, characterized by both Indians and whites as "renegades" and "outlaws," were known by all for paying allegiance to no other government. Thus far, they had been able to retreat into the canyon country and mountains in their territory and continue to live free. The next decade, however, would see an end to their isolation as whites continued to advance. A bitter struggle was about to ensue.

CHAPTER 7

Stemming the Flood, 1880–1882

Miners, Cowboys, and Settlers

Agreements the Indian makes with the government are like the
agreement a buffalo makes after it has been pierced by many arrows.
All it can do is lie down and give in.

Ouray, 1879

Events of the 1870s were but prologue to
the clashes of the 1880s. What had been a
trickle of miners and a few small cattle outfits into southeastern Utah during the late
1870s now became a flood. Coloradoans
from the east, Mormons from the west and
north, and the expanding Navajo reservation
in the south placed pressure on traditional
Weenuche hunting, gathering, and camping sites while devouring resources. Individual holdings burgeoned into settlements
and extensive ranches, which soon became
towns and villages catering to mining, livestock, or agricultural interests: Dolores and
Big Bend on the Dolores River (1877),[1] Rico
(1879), Durango (1880), Mancos (late 1870s,
incorporated 1894), and Cortez (early 1880s,
incorporated 1886) were all in southwestern
Colorado; in southeastern Utah, along the
San Juan River, Montezuma Creek and Riverview (today's Aneth) arose with Colorado
(1878–1879) and Mormon (1879–1880) settlers, while Bluff (1880) and Monticello (1887)
were primarily Mormon settlements; large
non-Mormon cattle outfits included those of
Bill McCarty (1877), Joshua B. "Spud" Hudson (1879), Lacy Cattle (or L.C.) Company
(1880), the Kansas and New Mexico Land
and Livestock Company (operated by Harold
and Edmund Carlisle — starting 1883), and

the Pittsburgh Cattle Company (1885), all of
whom ranged their herds around the Blue
and La Sal Mountains and across the open
sage plains of Utah and Colorado.[2] Little
wonder the Utes in the area were angered
over their shrinking land base.

To fuel this growing economy, the Denver and Rio Grande Railroad spread its steel
tentacles through Colorado, and by 1881 into
a railhead at Durango in support of the San
Juan mine fields. Two years later the railroad
extended from Colorado to Salt Lake City,
with part of the route running north of Moab
with a station at Thompson. The Meeker
massacre, fresh in the minds of Coloradoans,
had more and more people calling for the
removal of the Northern Utes and the movement of the Southern Utes onto a reservation.
The general unrest in the area and changing Indian policy required the military to
reassess its posture; the main force shifted
from its previously established cantonment
at Pagosa Springs nearer to the rail line and
the reservation. What had been called Fort
Lewis, after Lieutenant Colonel William
N. Lewis, killed by Cheyennes in 1878, now
became Cantonment Pagosa Springs, a sub-
post of the new Fort Lewis near Durango.[3]
On July 9, 1880, Lieutenant General Philip
Sheridan directed through Special Order 78

that companies A, B, C, D, and E, Thirteenth Infantry, under the leadership of Lieutenant Colonel Robert E. A. Crofton from Fort Stanton, District of New Mexico, establish the new post.[4] By October construction was well under way, and the command settled in for a relatively uneventful winter, but for the next ten years Fort Lewis played a prominent role in maintaining peace in the Four Corners region.[5]

Southeastern Utah, which had been hinterland to the white population and refuge for the increasingly pressured Utes, now became a heavily traversed and contested region. The spotlight shone brightly in one of the darkest, least known corners of the Four Corners, illuminating a land for future development. There were three primary economic forces eyeing the possibilities. They were concurrent but came in waves, the first being mining, then agriculture, and finally livestock. The story of violence that erupted between the warring factions often overpowers the fact that the struggling Ute bands were trying to maintain their lands. The vitriolic prose found in newspapers as well as the letters of desperation penned by settlers, ranchers, and miners illustrate too well the feelings they held, but also generally underscore a disregard and lack of understanding of why the Indians acted as they did. What follows is a sampling from each element of the white triad as they took control of these lands.

Miners entered the scene in groups as small as two and as large as thirty people. The Weenuche had just witnessed a decade of land loss that had begun with small mining efforts and then escalated; they were not interested in seeing the scenario repeated. Regardless, mining parties went into the La Sal, Blue, and Navajo Mountains to determine what wealth they held. Now that mining towns like Rico, Parrott City, and Animas were well-established, there was a large, sympathetic, and interested body of miners to support any move into these areas if gold or silver were found. Not surprisingly, if a conflict arose, these towns raised many of the anxious recruits ready to fight Indians. The *Denver Republican* reported "a powerful secret organization to clean out the [Ute] reservation" for mining interests and general principle. The group boasted 150 members who had signed a "covenant" to wage war against their foes, to "arm and equip themselves ready for military service," and then "explore and develop the Ute Reservation."[6] The article urged this move as a part of God's plan to go forth and subdue the earth, as cited in the Bible and as part of the best tradition of nineteenth-century "progression."

The Mitchell-Merrick incident illustrates the problems with this attitude.[7] In late 1878, Henry L. Mitchell, a cantankerous man from Missouri, settled at Riverview on the San Juan River near the mouth of McElmo Creek. For seven years he created, fabricated, and fueled more incidents concerning Indian issues in this area than anyone else during this time.[8] His son, Ernest, appears to have been of a similar nature, but was more interested in prospecting than farming or operating a trading post with his dad. On December 29, 1879, Ernest Mitchell and his partner, James Merrick, met an advance party of Mormon settlers heading to Montezuma Creek. The two men invited one of the Mormons, George Hobbs, to join them in a search for silver mines in the Monument Valley area, but he declined.[9] The miners moved on to meet their fate.

Two months passed, and Mitchell had not heard from his son or Merrick. The first indication that there had been trouble came when a Navajo, "Boy with Many Horses," visited a Paiute camp sixty miles above Lee's Ferry. There he saw four mules taken by Paiutes after they had killed the owners. Since the Navajos were often blamed for deeds they did not commit, they were anxious to have the affair investigated.[10] At the same time, Mitchell wrote to Navajo agent Galen Eastman, saying that both the Utes and Navajos were acting "sassy" and that if fighting occurred, most of the settlers would be in trouble because the men were out looking for Merrick and Mitchell. However, if nothing happened in the next couple of weeks, there would be two hundred men present to hold out against Indian attacks until soldiers arrived.[11]

As February drew to a close, Mitchell's fiery rhetoric grew more urgent. After a search party discovered the missing miners' bodies in Monument Valley, Mitchell went to retrieve them. Although it was a Navajo guide who led him to the corpses, no single group claimed responsibility; the Navajos were blaming the Utes, the Utes were blaming the Navajos, and the Paiutes were serving as a third scapegoat.[12] Following the burial, Mitchell launched into another tirade, claiming that five other men had been killed (although no bodies had been found), that the Utes were in league with the Navajos, and that both were equally bad. Eastman sent out representatives to investigate the murders. They returned with word that the guilty party was a group of renegades who were not attached to any agency. A second inquiry by a Navajo and a Mexican named Jesus Arviso confirmed that three or four Indians of Ute-Paiute ancestry, living north of the San Juan, had killed the two miners.[13]

In November of the same year, the *Dolores News* reported of "Trouble near Home, and War in the Blue Mountains," claiming that a series of incidents gave proof "that the Indians have resolved to wage war upon the isolated miners and ranchmen. It is evidently their intention to steer clear of towns and large settlements, but to kill single families who are separated by miles from their nearest neighbors."[14] The paper published that a group of prospectors had left Parrott City that week and been massacred in the Carrizo Mountains on their way to northeastern Arizona. It went on to say that the country was "overrun with renegade Pi-Utes and Navajos," and although the fight was just a rumor, the prospectors had lost all of their horses and

so were doomed. "The chances are that they are all slaughtered long before this time." The paper next called for the extermination of the Utes. "History will tell us that explosive bullets have more influence with savages than folios of vigorous editorials. We cannot appeal to an Indian's sense of justice or cause him to feel the pangs of remorse. Let us substitute Winchester rifles for brains and note the results."

A year later another mining party, twenty-five men from Rico and Durango, converged at Mitchell's and then set off to search the Navajo Mountain area for the lost silver mines that Mitchell's son and partner were supposed to have found. The party met "Pah Utes" and were treated well, but the terrain and lack of water were more than they could handle, and they returned. The paper noted the formula for success with Indians. "Hitherto the savage Pah Ute has kept all out save a few adventurous souls, but this party went in well-armed and equipped."[15] Miners operating in small groups continued to comb the countryside for wealth. Not until the early 1890s would there be a gold rush along the San Juan River, so although they were a threat to the Utes, until they found enough ore to generate interest on a large scale, there was no reenactment of what had occurred in the San Juan Mountains.

At the same time that Mitchell's and Merrick's bodies lay in the sands of Monument Valley, a large party of Mormons were standing on the precipice known as the Hole-in-the-Rock on the Colorado River. After building a road down the steep incline, they toiled their way across the river, over the slickrock, and through the canyons of San Juan to Bluff, where they arrived on April 6, 1880. All 250 men, women, and children, with 83 wagons and over a thousand head of livestock, descended upon the river and Ute territory to make their home—an instant settlement—overnight. Albert R. Lyman, a Bluff native and historian, tells of when an older Ute man rode up to the advancing

Corrals on Elk Ridge, 1890s, two of many that held cattle grazing on range that the Utes considered theirs. Livestock were the greatest source of conflict between the Indians and whites. A hunting and gathering lifestyle quickly became impossible to sustain. (Courtesy of San Juan County Historical Commission)

wagon train and asked where it had come from. "He dropped his jaw and raised his hands in surprise" when the settlers pointed in the direction of the Hole-in-the-Rock Trail.[16] "'No!' he grunted in disgusted unbelief, they couldn't cross there; they might have crossed farther up, but there was no place to cross at the Hole-in-the-Rock. 'And the old man was perfectly right,' affirmed one of the company, there never was and never will be a place for crossing at the Hole-in-the-Rock.'" The clash between cultures commenced soon after the establishment of Bluff, not only with the Mormons, but with everyone who depended upon the land to survive. Lyman later noted with hindsight that the settlers' impact on the Utes, which was about to commence, would be tremendous. "If I had been a Paiute or Navajo, I'd have helped myself to everything the invader had."[17]

As new groups came to southeastern Utah, they challenged the carrying capacity of this high desert environment. The Utes, as hunters and gatherers, had depended on a

wide-ranging cycle of travel to summer and winter areas to obtain different resources. The livestock industry of the Mormons, non-Mormons, and Navajos depended on good summer and winter ranges, and called for keeping competitors off of them. The Navajos' cultural agenda, while not unified like that of the livestock companies, encouraged expanding herds of sheep, goats, cattle, and horses. The Utes reacted against this rising pressure and competition over rangeland; for more than fifty years the jousting persisted, fostering animosity among all four groups. The areas west and north of Bluff were favored grazing sites for the Mormons. Relatively close to town, making them within reach of assistance, the Bluff herds grazed under the watchful eyes of young men. Their numbers were relatively small compared to future herds, but these cattle and sheep were the start of an ever-growing problem. For example, like many men who came through the Hole-in-the-Rock, Hanson Bayles arrived with only a handful of what he had started out with. His holdings had shrunk from twenty-one cows to six by the time he settled in Bluff.[18] But it did not take long for Mormon herds to grow. Seven years later there were three thousand head of cattle grazing the summer range on Elk Ridge.[19]

Reaction against this encroachment and that of non-Mormons' herds spawned intense retribution from the Utes. In 1881 a posse of Mormons traveled beyond the head of Butler Wash in pursuit of cattle taken by the Indians and viewed for the first time the lush pastures in the valleys below Elk Ridge. Shortly after, the white men intercepted a group of Utes at the head of Butler Wash, coming from the Pinhook Draw fight (discussed later) on their way to Elk Ridge. The Indians had helped themselves to part of the Mormon herd but allowed the settlers to peacefully retrieve their stolen horses. As they returned to Bluff, however, the white men found many of their cattle dead or mutilated. Later, a similar incident repeated itself, with the Navajos returning stolen horses obtained from the Utes. In another instance, when the Bluff settlers retrieved eleven stolen horses at gunpoint, one of the Ute men identified them as Mormons; the animals immediately went to their rightful owners, but on the return trip to Bluff they found more dead cattle.[20] Events of this nature became common.

One way the Mormons maintained more peaceful relations with the Utes than other groups is their appointing of men like Thales Haskel and Kumen Jones to serve as Indian missionaries. Both gained facility with the language, had calm personalities, and were genuinely interested in working with Native Americans. Haskel obtained experience with Jacob Hamblin in southwestern Utah and Arizona, this expertise becoming particularly important for the newly established settlement of Bluff. One incident illustrates the cool nerve he displayed in trying circumstances. A group of Utes encountered him with two other men on the range. Not knowing any of the settlers spoke their language,

the Indians decided which white man each would kill. Haskel waited until the discussion was over and then revealed their plans to them in their own language, calling them "brave men" to hatch such a plot. The Utes quickly changed their minds, offered their guns and knives as tokens of friendship, and then went on their way. Until the Mormon Church released him from his responsibility in 1893, Haskel served as an effective, popular translator and peacemaker with the Navajo and Ute people.[21]

First Valley, or what is today known as Whiskers Draw and vicinity, enticed the settlers to greener pastures. Moving closer to Elk Ridge, with its summer range, cattle ranchers ran into four Navajo families living in the area with their flocks of sheep. The settlers worked at persuading them to remain south of the river, but the Utes were not ready to relinquish their homeland. Mancos Jim and others killed more cattle, stole more horses, and refused to accept the loss of prime hunting lands. Moencopi Mike, however, softened his angry attitude when fed and encouraged by the explorers to grant permission to use Elk Ridge.[22] Again, the Utes were angry with this loss of land. The Bluff community, with church approval, appointed Haskel and Jones to defuse the situation. While they generated goodwill, the problem of land loss was just too serious. The response:

> The Utes looked with ugly disfavor on the efforts of the colony to stock the range…they had emphasized their feelings, after every unpleasant contact, by shooting cattle and leaving them to rot on the hills. In answer to the Bluff men's efforts to build in Little Valleys, the Utes stole more horses, and when Haskel, by his magic personality, took these horses back to their owners, more cows were found dead on the hills.[23]

Feelings about land grabbing only got worse. But as the Utes in southeastern Utah were challenging the influx of settlers, the ones in Colorado were being forced into submission. In May, the Ute Commission—comprised of Colorado entrepreneur Otto Mears, chairman George Manypenny, and three others—informed Agent Berry that they wished to meet with the Uncompahgre and White River Utes at the Los Pinos Agency. Beginning on July 21, a series of "open councils" addressed the issue of the Indians' removal to Utah. By July 26, "a pressing invitation was given to the Indians present to come forward and execute the instrument ratifying the agreement.... Ouray, in response, said that he did not know an Uncompahgre Ute who was prepared to do so."[24] Two days later all present signed.

The reservation, located on the Green, White, and Duchesne Rivers in Utah, concerned the Utes for a number of reasons: it was not their traditional area, there did not seem to be sufficient grass to graze their livestock, they had received no money for the improvements made at the Los Pinos Agency, and the Uintah Utes were already settled in that general area. Their refusal prompted Agent Berry to have the chiefs hold a meeting with Colonel R. S. Mackenzie, Fourth Cavalry, at his headquarters at the cantonment. "After learning they were under his charge, and hearing from him good and friendly advice as to their peaceable compliance with their agreement, they concluded at once to remove."[25] The next day Berry issued three weeks of rations, and two weeks later he penned that he was "happy to say [it] has been accomplished successfully," and that the people forced into exile from their homeland were "all apparently cheerful and happy."

The Southern Utes were next. The commission arrived at their agency on August 15, accompanied by Ouray. Ignacio suggested that the conference be postponed for a few days since other leaders were en route. On August 18, Ignacio, representing the Weenuche, Aguila of the Muaches, and Toopauche (Tuupawíč—"Black Beaver") of the Capotes, as head chiefs started the delib-

erations with 123 other men of their bands present. Alejandro (Weenuche) arose at once and "made a very vigorous speech against the ratification of the agreement."[26] To add to the confusion, Ouray, who had been ill ever since he arrived, died shortly before the discussion got under way. As news spread, the Utes struck their tepees and fled "as from a pestilence." A few days later lightning struck and killed Kaneache. A week elapsed before the council reconvened. Ignacio said he "thought the Utes had done all that could be asked of them; that they had already given up the mountains in which the minerals were, and wished to retain the remainder of their country." The next day he and seventy others capitulated and signed, but it took another month to obtain the required number of signatures for a binding agreement.

While there is no clear explanation for the reversal, the agreement was undoubtedly spurred by the Utes' desire to at least partially control their destiny. There was no telling what would be forced on them once the commission departed. Even to the commission, it was

painfully evident that it was a fearful struggle for them to give up their country where from infancy and their fathers before them had roamed at will over the mountains and through the valleys of western Colorado...and they had fears as to the fidelity with which the government would fulfill its part of the agreement. With a sad expression of countenance and with a voice which impressed everyone present, Sapavanari, when about to touch the pen, said, "It was the best they could do, though not just what they wanted." And Ignacio, when in the act of signing the instrument of ratification, remarked to us in a very impressive manner that it was the desire and hope of all the Indians that the commissioners would be careful to see that the government faithfully fulfilled and carried out its part of the agreement.[27]

No doubt part of the reason for this capitulation was that Mackenzie gave them one day to decide and in the meantime, "posted his troops, so as to be ready for refusal."[28] Even at this late date, specific reservation lands had not been selected, emphasizing the goodwill and trust that the Utes had shown without knowing exactly what their boundaries would be.

As this transpired in Colorado, the Utah Utes were showing no willingness to give up their lands or limit their autonomy. Forces from various directions may have been descending, but they refused to give up their right to live where they always had. At this point, Colorado cowboys were by far the greatest challenge. The first in a series of annual incidents surfaced on the border between the two states. Colonel Crofton received on May 2, 1881, concrete glimmerings of what would evolve into a long-standing feud between livestock owners and Utah Indians.[29] D. D. Williams, a rancher living near the Dolores River, opened with a complaint. Southern Utes had stolen three horses, torn down his fences, allowed livestock to destroy his crops "beyond redemption," killed or mutilated thirty-five of his cattle without taking any meat, threatened him to the point of abandoning his home, and treated his neighbors in the same fashion. John Thurman, who lived near the Utah territorial line, reportedly had his home burned, while Indians stripped another neighbor named Reese of six horses and then sent him packing on foot. Williams feared war was imminent with the "one hundred and fifty bucks with their squaws and families" who were heavily armed. "Within the last 24 hours [other] bands of Narraguinip and Mariano and a band of Paiutes—about 150 lodges—had been crossing the Dolores River at the Big Bend," heading north to the Uncompahgre.[30] Agent Henry Page had previously described the Southern Utes as having 2,500 horses that are "always with them," with "all adult males" being armed "with firearms of the best quality usually of the Winchester pattern…[with] a liberal

supply of fixed ammunition." They were a formidable force.[31]

A week later Williams reported to Crofton that he had returned with the remains of his neighbor Richard May and had buried Thurman at his cabin, but he could not find the body of a third man, Byron Smith, alleged to have been killed by the Utes during the same fight. Events leading to this incident began in 1877, when three brothers—Dick, George, and Billy May—settled as cattlemen in the Big Bend country of Colorado. They prospered, utilizing the open range between Mancos, Colorado, and the Blue and La Sal Mountains in Utah. The mining camps of Rico, Telluride, and Silverton welcomed their beef and encouraged expansion of the business.[32] Two years later, businessmen John Thurman and J. H. Alderson went into partnership on a large herd of high-quality horses and pastured them on the Utah-Colorado border near present-day Dove Creek, where they built a cabin. The men opened for business, selling their stock to local buyers.[33]

Among these buyers were Dick May and his friend Smith, who appeared at Thurman's cabin on May 1, 1881, to purchase horses, presumably for the spring cattle roundup, just starting. On their way they met some cowboys who warned of a group of Utes "on the prod," and told May and Smith to turn back. What they did not realize is that a few days before Thurman had discovered these same Indians trying to catch some of his prize stock. He beat them soundly and sent them angrily on their way.

How events unfolded next and who discovered the results are left to conjecture.[34] There is, however, no doubt as to the outcome. The Utes killed Dick May at the cabin following a hard fight. Around his body lay a quantity of expended cartridges, outside were two dead horses, and the cabin was burned.[35] The Indians also killed Thurman, approximately a half mile away from his home, and stole an estimated $1,000 from the bodies, a hundred horses, nine hundred pounds of flour, five rifles, three pistols, a shotgun, seventy-five pounds of ammunition, and assorted other goods.[36] According to an Indian account received during an interrogation after the Pinhook fight, four Utes met May at the cabin. He came to the door, grabbed one Indian and threw him down on the ground, and then walked over and shot two of their horses. The Utes became angry, killed the two men, and left.[37]

The record is unclear as to who first uncovered what had taken place. Different versions suggest a wandering prospector, neighboring cowboys, or a friendly Navajo Indian named Little Captain.[38] Whoever made the discovery rode to the settlement at Big Bend, approximately forty-five miles away, and notified the residents that at least one man had been killed. Dick May's brothers, George and Billy, along with several other men, left on May 3 to determine what had happened and to retrieve the bodies. After a thorough search of the area and the discovery of Thurman's corpse on Cedar Point in Colorado, the group buried him where he fell, but they took May's remains back to Dolores. Byron Smith was never found.[39]

Meanwhile, the Utes left for Dodge Springs, located ten miles southeast of present-day Monticello, where they met with others camped there.[40] They did not stay long; the Mormons in Bluff reported them stealing horses on May 5. Platte D. Lyman recorded in his journal that the Indians had fired on one of the settlers, Joseph Nielson, and that eight or nine of the "boys" rode to Butler Wash to investigate. "They found about 30 Indians with about 60 or more squaws and papooses," as well as sheep, goats, and 150 horses. Some of the latter belonged to owners in Bluff, and two of these animals had been taken from there some time before. The next day Lyman went to the Ute camp as they prepared to leave. He wrote:

> They seemed very friendly but a few of them were very mad when another stolen horse was taken away from them. As they moved off [still] another stolen horse was taken from them. We traveled with them for several miles and as we returned found that they had been shooting down our cows and destroying the calves.... They had about 40 horses branded B, some of them fine large horses of good stock. They also had plenty of greenbacks to which they attached very little value. It is evident they have raided somebody's ranch as in addition to the horses and paper money, they have harness lines and blind bridles and halters.[41]

Not until May 15 did the Mormons in Bluff learn about the deaths of May and Thurman.[42]

The Utes left Butler Wash, traveling north to Blue Mountain and stealing horses from Joshua B. "Spud" Hudson and other ranchers along the way. "Spud," a Colorado cattleman hailing from the Purgatoire (universally called "Picketwire") River country of southeastern Colorado, was angry. His camp, called the Double Cabins, about six miles north of present-day Monticello, became an important landmark in the events that followed. But not only Hudson's stock was lost; others in the vicinity were missing animals and had their cabins raided. On May 14 several ranchers again encountered Indians taking stock, and after some shooting during which perhaps one Indian died, they returned to their towns to form a posse.[43] They soon joined forces and went in search of the culprits; the Utes by this time had procured a herd estimated at 350 stolen horses plus their own animals. They had also "wantonly killed hundreds of cattle belonging to the stockmen of this vicinity."[44]

Hudson formed an initial posse of twelve men, but after finding the Indians' deserted camp at Dodge Spring and realizing their numbers, the Blue Mountain posse spent a few more days recruiting help, doubling their force to twenty-five. They then followed the Utes' trail to the southern end of Blue Mountain.[45] Along the way the cowboys

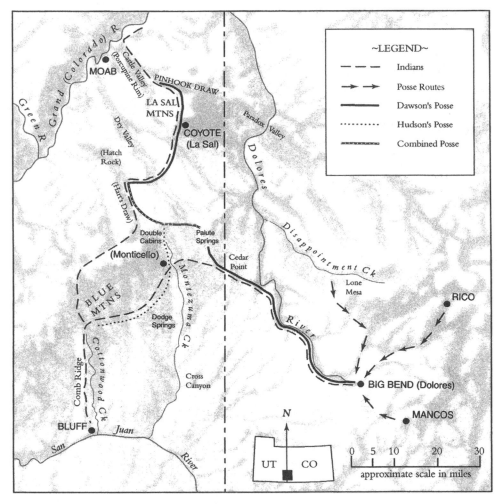

Map 5. Pinhook Draw fight. (Courtesy of the Utah State Historical Society)

found tired ponies and an occasional goat from the Indians' herd, but feared pressing the chase because of possible ambush in the canyons.[46]

At the same time another small army, this one from Colorado, was under way. While some of these volunteers came from the livestock communities of Mancos and Dolores, most hailed from the mining town of Rico, population 1,500. Their stated intention was to protect the cattlemen and recover stolen animals as the spring roundup played across the ranges of southeastern Utah. Their real intent was to fight Indians. They had formed at Dolores on May 31 and selected their leaders: Bill Dawson as captain, with Billy May second-in-command.[47] The papers reported that "a company of about sixty-five

men, well-armed, left Big Bend (Dolores) for the Blue Mountains to try and gather up stock.... And should the Ute Indians molest them, they are determined to fight for their rights."[48] On June 1 they set out for what they hoped would be a quick victory.

Colonel Henry Page, agent for the Southern Utes, commented about the wisdom of any group undertaking such a mission. He may or may not have been aware that Dawson's men were en route to Utah when the *Dolores News* printed his remarks on June 4, but he certainly was accurate. Page pointed out that this particular group of Indians, "who make their home in the Sierra La Sal and Blue Mountains are a fearless and wayward set."[49] More importantly, he identified who comprised this group of Indians.

The Pah-Utes, as they are termed, are a powerful party of renegades from the four Ute tribes — the Uintahs, White Rivers, Uncompahgres, and Southern or Ignacio Utes. They are comprised mainly of the younger bucks of these tribes and number about 100 families. They make their home in the Sierra La Sal and Blue Mountains, and are a fearless and wayward set. No organization exists among them. They are practically free lancers, although in cases of emergency, where some leadership is essential, they recognize that power in two of their members. If war should be opened on these renegades, the Government would find their conquest difficult…. [Their] country is rough and inaccessible to troops throughout…. Hence it will be seen that a small and moderate band of Indians could keep at bay an immense army.[50]

Dawson's force was neither an immense army nor trained as soldiers, and they did not know the terrain. Future events proved Page's wisdom correct.

The posse traveled over the rolling sagebrush country along the Colorado-Utah border, arriving at Hudson's Double Cabins on June 3. There they met yet another group, members of Company C, Thirteenth Infantry, under the command of Captain Benjamin H. Rogers from Fort Lewis, Colorado. The soldiers had arrived four days before with orders to scout the region for Indians while protecting any whites collecting cattle. They reconnoitered the area along the eastern edge of Blue Mountain and reported the Hudson and O'Donnell cabins deserted, indicating the Blue Mountain posse had already left. As soon as Dawson's men arrived, they sent out scouts to determine the Indians' location, the soldiers apparently unaware that they were attempting to find the Indian camp for a future attack. However, by the time the soldiers were out of food and ready to return to Big Bend and eventually Fort Lewis, they realized that this band of men was doing much more than just looking for cattle. There is some suggestion that the soldiers and the cowboys were at odds with each other, the

former feeling the latter should stay out of the Indian fighting business.[51]

It is reasonable to assume that shortly after the military left, Hudson's Blue Mountain posse and Dawson's men from Colorado joined forces. For seven more days the entire group remained in the saddle. The Utes separated into small bands, taking different routes and then rendezvousing at predetermined sites, making tracking even more difficult in this terrain.[52] The posse scoured the area of Comb Wash, Blue Mountain, Indian Creek, and parts of Dry Valley, all favorite Ute camping sites.[53] The men traveled through Hart's Draw to Hatch Rock, where Hudson had his winter camp. Horses belonging to members of the Blue Mountain group were fatigued, having been out for more than three weeks. One man described them as "leg-weary and foot-sore."[54] Consequently, once scouts cut into the Indians' trail crossing Dry Valley and headed toward the La Sals, the Colorado cowboys left in pursuit, but Hudson's group remained behind, arriving after the fight had ended. The land had exacted a toll on his force as it traveled through the canyons and over the mountains. Dawson's group was also dwindling for various reasons. Billy May and seven others had returned to Colorado because they did not agree with the existing leadership, while another eight men went on a separate scouting expedition and ended up at the Double Cabins. By the time the fight started, there were only thirty-eight in the field.[55]

As the Colorado cowboys continued on the trail, they encountered tired stock, waterholes used by the Indians, and increasingly fresher sign. A full lunar eclipse on the evening of June 12 was an auspicious occasion in both camps. According to A. (Albert) M. Rogers, whose account is the only one to mention this, two of the cowboys spotted the Utes' camp, reported its location, and urged forming a plan of attack. There were those who argued that the eclipse should be used as a powerful sign for the Indians

Cowboys from the W. J. Carpenter outfit, Telluride, Colorado, 1887. Several men in the photo participated in both the 1881 and 1884 fights in southeastern Utah. Most Utes and cowboys felt strong animosity toward each other, which often erupted in warfare. (Courtesy of San Juan County Historical Commission)

to give up the murderers of May and Thurman as well as the captured livestock. Most of the men, however, wanted a fight. The disagreement was strong enough that when Dawson, speaking to those not in favor of a fight, said, "Boys! Strike for your country and your homes," twenty-two of them left the next morning.[56] This could be referring to Billy May and his group, although the time sequence, numbers, and events seem somewhat askew and embellished.

The remaining cowboys followed the Indians undetected the next day. That night an exceptionally bright comet was visible in the evening sky, presenting another opportunity to play upon Ute beliefs. It was again voted down. Rogers said that he had been told "by Indians who were in the fight, that they had no heart to fight the white men after the Great Spirit had darkened the full moon

and burned up a star, and that if we had demanded the surrender of the guilty Indians and the return of the stolen stock, they would have given them up without resistance; but we wanted an Indian fight and we got it."[57]

The morning of June 15, Dawson's men struck. They found the Indians' horse herd, said to have numbered 1,500, as well as 800 goats. The Utes, resting in the area of today's Wilcox Flat/Warner Lake on the La Sal Mountains, were just breaking camp. Some of them spotted the cowboys on a mesa approximately three-quarters of a mile away and sounded the alarm. The men prepared to fight while the women hastily packed what they could and started toward the north end of the La Sals.[58]

According to Rogers, the cowboys swept down one long hill and up another to the Indians' camp, capturing a sizeable portion of the Utes' livestock as well as nine women guarding them. Dawson decided to leave thirteen men behind to retain the prize before giving chase to the fleeing enemy. Those who stayed settled in and eventually began playing "seven up" and "coon can," two card games, with some of the younger women. Other cowboys slept while some guarded. The older Ute women, however, quietly and peacefully prepared an escape. On signal, all of the women fled to their horses and drove the Indians' herd before them, along with the mounts of the cowboys. "The discomfited heroes [cowboys] sadly shouldered their saddles and wended their way to Moab, eighteen miles distant."[59] In reality, this group probably attempted to rejoin Dawson's pursuing force and became disoriented by the terrain.

Exactly how much credence can be given this story, told only by Rogers, a member of a later rescue party, can be argued. That there was an eclipse and bright comet can be proven. Nothing has ever been said about this group of cowboys straggling into Moab. And for Dawson to deplete his fighting force by half on the verge of battle seems unwise. Eyewitness accounts vary as to the number of men involved in the ensuing fracas, but there were probably between fifteen and eighteen who actually participated in the major firefight of the first day. The other half became separated and ineffective, but little has ever been offered as explanation for their not going with the attacking force. It seems highly probable that these were the men who had remained with the Ute livestock and only later attempted to take part in the battle. They failed because of lack of communication and knowledge of the land.

The pursuing cowboys estimated that the Indian band numbered about 100, with some 65 men and 35 women, children, and old people; these figures are the reverse (30 men, 60 others) of what Platte Lyman reported near Bluff.[60] Whatever the group's composition, the white men gave chase through the Indian camp, with its assorted unpacked goods scattered about the clearing. They continued the pursuit, moving across Bald Mesa and hoping to intercept the Utes before they got away. Dawson needed to develop the situation before committing the entire force to an ambush and so moved down the trail, leaving the rest behind and ending any coordination and planning between the two groups.

The Ute men fought a rearguard action, slowing the advance of the cowboys while the women and others herded the remaining stock ahead. The posse pursued them for several miles, fighting cat-and-mouse through the trees, rocks, and brush along a well-established Ute trail. The group halted when it reached Mason Spring at the head of Little Castle Valley, which descends to the north end of the mountains and the Colorado River beyond. Dawson selected six men, one of whom was Jordan Bean, and sent them forward to fix the enemy. According to Bean, their instructions were to "overtake the Indians and make a stand on them, and he [Dawson] would bring the rest as fast as possible."[61] Risky business for sure, but the leader was slow to commit his entire force to an ambush.

The point element traveled warily down the trail, passing over Bald Mesa and toward Pinhook Draw and Harpole Mesa. It was ideal terrain for a defender. From Mason Spring and Draw there are two possible routes into Little Castle Valley. The first is the steep, V-sided Porcupine Draw, a straight canyon approximately a mile and a half long but less than a fifth of a mile wide, opening directly into Castle Valley. Its southwestern wall is the twelve-mile-long Porcupine Rim; the northeastern side is a sharp-spine ridge covered with huge boulders and large rocks. The far side of this ridge descends into the larger, U-shaped canyon known as Pinhook Draw. This valley forms a wide, sloping bowl, approximately a half mile across and three miles long. With almost vertical walls to the east and northeast, and with Harpole Mesa to the north, these features pinch into a "hook" that narrows to a quarter mile before opening into Castle Valley. Both Pinhook and Porcupine Draws are cut by intermittent streambeds thick with scrub oak and slopes covered with oaks, piñons, and junipers.

The six men moved cautiously down the trail, detecting the flash of a red blanket and an Indian pony in the oak and rocks on the slopes to their side. As they descended, the Utes opened fire, and as planned, Dawson moved the rest of his force forward to develop the situation. The Indians held the high ground on both sides and poured murderous shots from the hillsides onto the valley floor below. Command and control of the cowboys fell apart. Most sought shelter in the brush or in the streambed and hillocks in the valley before returning fire. All accounts agree that Dave Willis was the first killed as he stood in the open and blasted at targets in the scrub oak.

The men in the lead rode for the protection of an arroyo. Thinking they were safe from the bullets sweeping the battlefield, they discovered too late that the Indians had enfilading fire from various angles down into the winding ditch. Mancos Jim, a Ute participant, later recalled the bravery on both sides. He said:

> Dave Willis never took shelter but stood out in bold relief and fought till he fell dead. The other boys tried to protect themselves by getting into a shallow arroyo or washout, but they were surrounded and when the Indians charged from one side, hanging onto the ponies, yelling and shooting, the white boys would raise to fire. The Indians in ambush in another direction [would] shoot them down.
>
> The white boys were extravagant with their ammunition, which they exhausted about dusk after fighting all day, and the Indians then rode around the washout in a circle, shooting into the living and lifeless bodies till there was no sign of life in the bloody pit.[62]

With the main force an estimated 100 to 150 yards distant from those in the arroyo,

Dawson knew that he could not provide effective supporting fire. Tim Jenkins, a slightly built member of the posse, rode to the men in the ditch and urged them to retreat from almost certain death. Indian marksmen maintained a steady fire until Jenkins regained the main body, but none of the trapped men followed, paralyzed by fear.[63] Six eventually died in this general area, some of them being wounded before they were killed, suggested by the bandages found on their bodies.

The Utes, "armed with Winchester rifles," maintained pressure on the beleaguered cowboys.[64] This point is made by a number of the participants. The cowboys felt that their enemy was far better armed—supposedly with .44 caliber Winchesters and plenty of ammunition. Probably some of this weaponry was booty from the Thurman cabin. The white men, on the other hand, had a "'duke's mixture' of old buffalo guns, Sharps rifles, and a few Winchesters, old fashioned black powder guns with a short range and a slow velocity of bullets [that] made distance shooting a guess."[65] This last statement is only partly accurate. The Sharps rifle had approximately three times the range (six hundred yards versus two hundred yards) and a heavier bullet (five hundred grain versus two hundred grain) compared to the Winchester. But the single-shot Sharps could not compare to the fourteen-shot lever-action Winchester, especially appreciated by the Utes for in-close fighting. On the Pinhook battlefield, most of the Indians' positions were well within range of their weapons.

One story from the battle tells of a large warrior who climbed on top of a boulder and directed the fire of his men to critical points of the battlefield. Many of the cowboys shot at him but were ineffective.[66] Perhaps this was the same person who the newspapers falsely reported was a "Mexican seen with the Indians, apparently commanding different squads of Indians. On the second day, the Mexican rode to the summit of a knoll, patted his Winchester and six shooters and cried aloud, 'Shoot you cowardly sons-of-bitches,' and the boys fired but failed to get him."[67]

There were other frustrations in the fight. Jordan Bean tells of how he and Harden Tarter entered the fray, and then

> it was every man for himself…. We soon found some big rocks, lay down there and were shooting at some Indians above us on the mountainside. We were doing fine until one Injun seemed to be a pretty good shot for he got me in the left temple. I had my head thrown back so far — the hill was steep — the bullet didn't go in very far but grazed my skull and knocked me out.[68]

Later that afternoon Bean regained consciousness, unaware of what else had transpired. None of his companions were in sight; he learned later that his friend Tarter was dead. As he looked about, he spotted a large Indian standing on a rock. Fearing that the Ute had seen him, Bean dropped down and crawled into a thicket of scrub oak and remained silent. A horse standing nearby attracted the Indians' attention, and two warriors walked over. They talked about the blood on the ground, and one man started toward the brush that concealed Bean and made a low whistling noise but didn't find him.

Under cover of darkness the wounded cowboy made his way back to a spring he had used that morning. His overwhelming thirst drove him to drink too much, which made him even sicker, but after some rest and more-controlled drinking, he began to feel better. In the morning, with the resumption of activities, Bean spotted members of the posse moving out to the battlefield. Believing he was dead, they were surprised to see him, but moved him back to camp and rendered aid.[69]

Once the cowboys had extricated themselves from the battlefield and returned to Mason Spring, they counted their numbers.

At that point, before Jordan Bean arrived, but after the trapped survivors had left the intermittent streambed and hillocks, there were nine men missing. Depending upon whether or not Dawson had actually detailed thirteen of his men to guard the Ute herd, this figure could represent as much as half of the force engaged in the fight. As the sun set, a cloud of dust approaching up Porcupine Rim provided another answer. The missing group of cowboys appeared with a new appreciation of the terrain they had encountered. They had heard the firing in Castle Valley starting around noon. Hoping to come in behind the Utes, they traveled a good distance along the rim, searching for a route down the 1,400-foot escarpment to the valley floor below. They found none. Realizing their mistake, they had returned to the head of the draw, but were ineffective for the entire battle. In Dawson's words: "We have had hell here all day and we don't know how many men have been killed. It's just too bad you were not here with us. More than likely we could have routed the Indians out of their trap."[70]

There were also the wounded to take care of. Harden Eskridge received a bullet below the ankle that shattered many of the small bones in his foot. During the fight he wore, "a large, gaudy Chihuahua hat…that was riddled with bullets so that it cannot be worn and his hair was nearly all cut off with scalp wounds from grazing bullets."[71] James Hall received a shoulder wound, injured ribs, and a leg wound that began above the knee and exited through his calf. Miraculously, he healed without any permanent damage. In the morning Jordan Bean arrived with a wound in the temple, most likely caused by a ricochet.[72] After receiving immediate first aid, these men remained with the posse for the next two days.

In the meantime, Dawson spent the first night hoping to continue the battle in the morning and at least determine the location of his missing men. With the second half of his group present, he would reenter Pinhook

Draw with around twenty-five of the original Colorado posse. The combined force of Moab and Colorado men headed down to the battlefield to learn about the fate of those missing. The fighting of the previous day had ranged around Pinhook Draw and Harpole Mesa. The searchers found the first body out in an open area near an old trail that passed over Harpole Mesa. As they gathered around the body, most likely Dave Willis, the Indians on the side of the mesa opened fire and commenced the second day of fighting. The white men retreated uphill towards Bald Mesa, taking cover in an aspen grove on its side. An old Ute woman came through the brush, apparently unaware of the disposition of the cowboys, and was killed.

Dawson took stock of his situation and realized how desperately he needed additional help. He did not believe sufficient assistance could be garnered from Moab, eighteen miles away, so he turned to the next closest source, Rico. Midmorning of June 16, the second day, D. G. Taylor began the 150-mile ride. According to Bean, sixteen settlers from Moab, on their way to investigate the Indians' activity on the mountain, saw the rider and fired shots, but missed.[73] Taylor completed the journey in five days, arriving on the afternoon of June 21. The next day a portion of the rescue party left Rico, camped at Dolores that night, and was joined by the remainder of volunteers in the morning. The group elected Worden Grigsby as its leader and set out for Utah. On June 24 they arrived in the vicinity of the La Sal Mountains, but by this time their initial group of forty had dwindled to twenty-four.[74] They also were far too late to help against the Utes.

The Colorado cowboys had other concerns. Dawson worried about the three wounded men and their small detachment of two guards left to protect them in camp. A group started back but received fire from the Utes, who now were between them and their destination. The cowboys again retreated to the aspen grove, and after a few more hours of fighting the Indians broke contact and began moving toward Dolores and the Ute reservation. The Colorado and Moab men returned to their camp, ending the second day of fighting.[75]

That evening the cowboys decided they had had enough. The contingent traveled to the lower end of Pack Creek, near the settlement of Moab, to rest and obtain assistance for the wounded. The three injured men descended the mountains on horseback to a point where a spring-cushioned wagon could be used for the rest of the trip.[76] Four days after the fight a group of men returned to the battlefield to bury the dead. The land lay silent, the Indians and the sounds of battle long since faded. By then the corpses were badly decomposed, and some accounts tell of how the heads had been smashed, as if with a rock. Another version states that all the bodies were riddled with arrows and rifle shots.[77] No other mutilation had occurred. The burial detail interred the dead, but the body of T. C. Taylor remained missing, bringing the final count to ten men killed.[78] The following day the entire group started for Colorado.

In the meantime, Worden Grigsby and the twenty-four men of the rescue party completed the trip from Rico in two-and-a-half days, arriving at Coyote, southwest of the La Sals, on June 24. Although they did not encounter the main body of the returning posse, they did meet two of the participants, who related recent events. They spent the next day at Coyote and then traveled to the site, noting how much of the terrain lent itself to ambush. Unsure of exactly how the fight had unfolded, they pieced together events from the equipment and dead animals encountered along the way.

That night they camped on a mesa overlooking the battlefield. It was a somber occasion. In the distance, the setting sun played across sandstone ridges, changing their color from a "grayish blue to a lurid red, and many a heart felt weary as we thought that beneath that gory pall, lay the forms of our friends.…"

Mancos Jim, or "Winchester," 1890s. He defended his lands against white invaders and participated in the Pinhook Draw and Soldier Crossing fights. He was well-known by both sides for his bravery and leadership. (Denver Public Library, Western History Collection, Unknown Photographer, X-32489)

An Indian dog slunk into camp and as we drove him off, added his dismal howls to a weird and ghostly picture which already held the soul in a thraldom of solemnity."[79] The following morning, after a hurried breakfast, the searchers found the freshly dug graves, the gulch where a number of men had died, the old Indian woman murdered by the cowboys, the body of a Ute warrior, and other telltale remnants of the fight. The men left that day intimately aware of the price paid on both sides.

Grigsby's group met the returning posse camped at Hudson's Double Cabins and four troops of Buffalo Soldiers of the Ninth Cavalry. Their commander, Captain Henry Carroll, had elements from three different posts — Fort Bayard, Fort Cummings, and Fort Seldon — all in southern New Mexico. The next morning the two groups parted company. The Colorado men returned by way of Paiute Springs, Cross Canyon, and the

Big Bend of the Dolores, then splintered off to Rico, Mancos, and Durango. The soldiers continued on their way in search of the Utes but found the trail cold. Many of the Indians had traveled to Dolores and the safety of the Ute reservation. The soldiers reported that their pace must have been slow, estimating six to seven miles a day based on the location of the Indians' campsites. At each of these the pursuers found bloody rags used to care for the wounded.[80] The military returned to Fort Lewis on July 24 empty-handed after their two-hundred-mile jaunt.[81] Observers were convinced that the Indians were hiding behind the sanctity of the reservation and government control (read "interference"), to the detriment of the settlers.

The Ute side of the Pinhook Draw battle is available in only fragmentary pieces. One definite participant was Mancos Jim, who not only discussed the incident, but was in possession of Dave Willis's rifle. In conversation with a local trader in 1886, Jim said that he lost "eighteen of his best and four average Indians in that fight."[82] This figure is in complete agreement with the estimates made by white participants, although only three bodies were actually found near the battlefield. Still, the number seems far too high, given estimates of male participants, the reported dead, and the fact that the Indians deemed the battle a victory. Various accounts suggest that among those killed was one of the sons of Cabeza Blanca and "Oco-co-mo-want, the chief or principal man of the renegade band," which could possibly be the same person.[83]

Polk took pride in telling white men about his part in the fracas. He claimed three individual kills, and according to Albert R. Lyman, "his years of insolent safety since that time have no doubt convinced him that it was a good business."[84] During a skirmish on Blue Mountain before the Pinhook fight, some civilians captured Polk's horse with things on it from the O'Donnell cabin, identifying him with the group that had passed through and ransacked it and the Hudson cabin. His father, Narraguinip, boasted to a number of white men at Dolores that the Utes would attack Fort Lewis and "'clean it up.' That the Utes knew the killing of Thurman and May was to take place is shown by their telling several men the day before the massacre 'not to go beyond the Great Bend, as somebody would heap kill white people out there pretty soon.'"[85]

Peaceful bands of Utes living on the reservation made forays onto public lands to hunt, which was totally in keeping with treaty rights; some Indians involved in the fight melted into these friendly groups. Family and band relations demanded a certain level of loyalty, while other Indians felt no such allegiance. The Ute/Paiute/Navajo renegades flowed among their own tribal elements easily. In the mind of at least one officer, the answer was simple: "When west of the Rio Mancos, all Southern Utes become Piutes [troublemakers]. The above statement can be corroborated by every citizen living on the Rio Mancos and Rio Dolores."[86]

On July 18, Southern Ute agent W. H. Berry at the Los Pinos Agency wrote to the commissioner of Indian Affairs about two "Pah Ute" Indians of the "Tah-kun-ni-ca-vatz band" he had arrested and interrogated about the fighting around the La Sal Mountains.[87] Uncompahgre Utes had captured them and turned them over to the befuddled agent. The two men, Ca-cah-par-a-mata and Pah-gie, were slow to admit any knowledge of what had transpired. Their information was, of course, only secondhand, but they were aware of some of the details concerning May's and Thurman's deaths. The single Ute responsible for this had been wounded in the Pinhook fight, "started out on the trail and has not been heard from since."[88] The military sent the two Utes to Fort Leavenworth.[89] One interesting question that arose early on was what to do with military prisoners. For at least two Utah Indians, a bizarre odyssey ensued.

Having come from the "Sierra La Sal" region, the captives were branded as part of the band of Indians who had been committing depredations for a long time, and these two "have been bad men for years."[90] The recent Pinhook fight did not help. The guardhouse door slammed behind them. A month later the commissioner of Indian Affairs, Hiram Price, wrote to the secretary of the interior wanting to know what to do. While there was no proof to support specific charges, he repeated that "these two Indians have been bad men for years and should be sent to prison in the East" until enough evidence can be found to bring them to trial.[91]

In mid-September the military sent the captives to Fort Leavenworth; a month later the two men had become even more evil. Characterized as "great rascals" with "as bad a character as words could set forth," the prison did not want to be "saddled permanently" with these Indians and claimed that the Interior Department should take care of them.[92] The new year brought little change. The commanding general of the Department of the Missouri, John Pope, wrote that for the past four months the presence of the "Pah-Utes" had been "a source of great annoyance and trouble and involves also, of course, the expense of their subsistence and other necessaries."[93] Commissioner Price responded that since these Indians were "renegades" and belonged to no agency, there were no funds to pay for their food, no place to incarcerate them, and not enough evidence to bring them to trial. After presenting a litany of historic crimes by the renegades of Utah, some going back to 1875, the commissioner determined that these two could not be released but should remain in army custody.[94]

At one point Commissioner Price suggested that the prisoners be returned to their native lands when the proper time arose during scheduled troop movements. He saw no point in maintaining their "close confinement" and felt the humane thing to do was to put the past behind. Sometime in the spring of 1883, the military shipped the two prisoners to Fort Riley, Kansas. There they joined three Mescalero Apaches who had participated in a raid in 1879 and were also in custody. The two Utes learned that they would not stand trial in Colorado for any past wrongs and could be freed in the future. Mysteriously, on July 11, 1883, the two Paiutes "escaped," and though "the most vigorous measures were taken to pursue and recapture the fugitives, [this was] without success."[95] Just as miraculous was the "escape" three weeks later of the three Apaches, who were also going to be returned to their agency. They, too, were never found.

By the fall of tumultuous 1881, the Southern Utes were settled on their official reservation, 110 miles long and 15 miles wide in the extreme southwestern corner of Colorado. Hemmed in by settlers on three sides and the Navajo Reservation on the fourth, all of whom trespassed onto Ute lands for one reason or another, the stage remained set for continuing conflict. Considering the large land base they had already relinquished, the Utes received little mercy from the white community. Settlers controlled on either end the rivers — Animas, Florida, Los Pinos, and Piedra — that flowed through Ute lands. Boundaries were geographically indistinct, grazing lands appropriated, roads traversed certain parts of the reservation, and the Den-

ver and Rio Grande Railroad crossed part of their territory. "The prevailing and only sentiment among the [white] people is that the Utes should not be permanently settled on the lands selected for them.... In such a condition of things, to assume that the Utes will not be disturbed, but permitted to dwell in peace, would be to nurture a delusion of the gravest kind."[96]

Agent Page, who worked with them on a daily basis, felt that the Southern Utes were the "purest type of the American Indian now existing."[97] There were no "half-breeds" or "squaw-men" among them, and their worst vices were horse racing and gambling. They had a propensity for taking care of livestock, hated farming, did not want to send their children to school, and spoke little English, but most spoke some Spanish. All were concerned about what had happened in the past and what they saw going on around them at the present. This "contented and seemingly well-disposed" people had seen too much recently to be at ease. As for their relatives in Utah, those "renegades" were still in their own lands and as aggressive as ever. Their whole fate was yet undecided, but there was little doubt that more conflict lay in the future. Either they would have to capitulate and move to the Southern Ute Reservation or fight. They chose the latter.

CHAPTER 8

Winning the Battles, Losing the War

Military Operations and Cowboy Incursions, 1882–1885

I'm a cowboy from the Mancos
Hear my gun—
Click—bang!
...
And I'd like to sight a Ute,
And cut his throat to boot;
I'm a holy, howling terror
Of the hills. Ki-yi.

Dolores News, July 25, 1885

By the fall of 1881 the Utes in southeastern Utah were rejoicing over the recent events that had culminated in their victory at the battle of Pinhook Draw. The fight sent a sharp message to local cattle outfits that encroachment on Ute lands would come at a bloody price. The white survivors of the fracas had received stinging lessons on the problems of pursuing Indians in their own territory, the danger of riding into a well laid ambush, and the importance of clearly developed tactical and logistical plans. For the military troops who arrived after the battle, there were other lessons: the difficulty of pursuing a victorious foe who melted into the landscape and then claimed ignorance of events; the fleeing Indians' use of reservations' protected status; the conflict over operational control between civilian and military groups; and the necessity of a well-defined policy in areas bordering Indian lands.

What lay in the future was anyone's guess, but as the Utes celebrated their victory, the cattlemen simmered over the drubbing.

One of the Indian leaders, Mancos Jim, had played a prominent role in the recent fight and openly boasted about it to the Mormon settlers in Bluff, who had not been directly involved in the incident. The Utes used the battle to discourage any thought of further white expansion and forcefully prove their ability to hold onto their lands. Albert R. Lyman recalls how they "looked with ugly disfavor" at any efforts by whites to use the San Juan grasslands to graze their horses and cattle. Any animal found doing so was fair game for theft, mutilation, or appropriation as a quick meal.

Since their larder was becoming increasingly thin due to competition for resources, the Utes felt justified in replacing what had been lost to the whites. Lyman tells of a group of stockmen inspecting possible rangelands and how "in the Little Valleys [located near Elk Ridge] they met a band of Utes headed by Mancos Jim, who registered his sullen objection to any white man entering this last splendid hunting ground where the Ute reigned supreme."[1] The Utes' economic and religious ties to the land were unquestionable and not to be trifled with, and Mancos Jim's determination to remain is summarized in his simple phrases: "Me no go; my father die here, my father's father die here, me die here too."[2]

To cattlemen searching for free and easy resources, these sentiments held little weight. This was the era of the open range and when land was not being used according to Anglo-American standards, then it was free for the taking. No doubt the animosity felt towards the Utes, a less than equal group of humans in nineteenth-century Anglo eyes, justified even further the "right" to appropriate the land. Thousands of cattle roved the mountains and canyons of southern Utah and Colorado, with more appearing every year, increasing the animosity on both sides. Those cowboys who had lost friends and relatives and had felt the sting of defeat at Pinhook were among those waiting for the right time and place to settle a heavy score. It was only a question of when that opportunity would arise.

Many of the twelve or so relatively small cattle outfits would also feel the pressure of change. Their market for beef lay in the mining camps and towns of southwestern Colorado, but with the railroad now available, markets back East offered their own lure. Profit increased, giving rise to bigger outfits with more money and staff, who sniffed at regional possibilities. One of the most prominent, and the single most important located at the foot of Blue Mountain, was the Kansas and New Mexico Land and Cattle Company. Backed by British and Scottish investors and operated by brothers Harold and Edmund Carlisle from England, this company entered southeastern Utah in 1883. Harold Carlisle purchased 7,000 cattle at $210,000 from four of the smaller local outfits and obtained grazing rights from them on Blue Mountain and adjoining lands.[3] By 1896 the herd had quadrupled, with 30,000 head being sold

that year.[4] The Carlisle outfit had reached its zenith as the largest of a number of cattle operations competing for grass in the region.

The Utes appreciated none of this growth and development. Direct confrontation appeared to be the only way to stem these forces interrupting their traditional way of life. The settlers in the Mancos and Dolores Valleys of southwestern Colorado, who grazed their cattle there and in the vicinity of Blue Mountain, also felt the Utes' resentment. The *Dolores News* complained of events surrounding the Pinhook fight, and then went on to tell of "Indians kill[ing] hundreds of cattle belonging to the stockmen of this vicinity, permitting them to lie where they fell, not making any use of them."[5] The editorial argued that what was needed to stop these depredations was a new military post at Cross Canyon, on the Utah–Colorado border. The recently established Fort Lewis had already proven ineffective in deterring Indian activity because of distance and mountain snows that cut off travel.[6] The citizens demanded that the government establish an outpost to prevent a massacre, "with all of its attendant horrors." The 252 signatures affixed to this petition were published in the newspaper and sent to the secretary of the Interior and the secretary of War.

That was in October 1881. The newspapers in December and January continued the tone, first complaining about the soldiers at Fort Lewis being withdrawn to Fort Leavenworth for their winter quarters, then stating that Colorado had no permanent military forts to call upon for protection. At this point even a garrison in Denver would be better than nothing. Henry Mitchell, on the other hand, had figured out how to get his own "private" garrison. He was in constant conflict with Navajos and Utes in the area and so received the protection he wanted.[7] In 1882 the military sent a "detachment of infantry of not less than 25 men to the Lower San Juan River to remain for a month to six weeks to give temporary protection and endeavor to restore

Twenty-second Infantry soldiers at Fort Lewis, Colorado, 1880s. Soldiers from the fort served in southeastern Utah between 1880 and 1890. The military on the frontier spent as much time protecting the Indians as they did fighting them, and many were sympathetic to the Utes' plight. (PAC 95-68B307, "Soldiers at Fort Lewis," photograph by Christian Barthelmess, Montana Historical Society Research Center Archives)

confidence to the settlers."[8] Given Mitchell's penchant for requesting assistance, fostering controversy, and ferreting out an opportunity to sell goods from his trading post shelves to troops stationed nearby, it is not surprising that he had the military at his settlement for five years in a row, until he moved away in 1885.

Soldier involvement increased in the spring, with the newspapers in March advertising that "rich specimens of gold and silver ore" had been discovered on the northern part of the Southern Ute Reservation, and that "as soon as the season is open there will be a rush of miners and prospectors to the new fields."[9] With the removal of the Northern Utes to Utah and the settlement of Southern Ute bands along the La Plata River, the miners hoped to have free access to an extensive source of minerals.[10] As the *Dolores News* put it: "The section now occupied by them [Southern Utes] may be opened up to settlement by the busy, pushing white popu-

lation which is flocking to us and spreading all over the Southwest. The Southern Utes should have gone to Uintah when the rest of the tribe transferred."[11] A bill introduced to do just that never passed, even though one justification given was that the Denver and Rio Grande Railroad, although trespassing on fifty miles of reservation land, was "in no degree safe from depredation." Unfortunately for these white entrepreneurs, the Southern Utes were there to stay and would serve as a thorn in the paw of the land-hungry animal of western settlement in times to come.

The miners, not to be discouraged, launched surveying expeditions into the heart of Indian territory in 1882 and 1883. Cass Hite led an expedition to the Monument Valley—Navajo Mountain region in search of the "lost" Merrick-Mitchell mine. A second group entered the La Sal District looking for copper, but because of the amount of snow in the mountains, they were not able to prospect. They did, however, note that there were twenty mines in the vicinity, none of which made the Indians very happy.[12] Between the cowboys and the miners, the Utes had their hands full protecting their lands.

Farmers also were a challenge. Peter Tracy, who lived a mile below Mitchell's ranch at Riverview, displayed the same temperament as his neighbor: violent and quick to offend. On the evening of August 28, 1883, a group of Utes visited his homestead, found that he was not around, and helped themselves to corn and melons. The next night a band of seventy Utes returned, and Tracy demanded pay. A fight ensued, and a Ute named "the Sore Leg" shot Tracy through the neck, killing him instantly. As members of Narraguinip's band, the Sore Leg and others in the group had most likely been involved in the Pinhook fight and were not averse to shedding white blood. The Indians fled to the mouth of the Mancos River, where they threatened to kill or drive away all of the inhabitants along the lower San Juan, but five days later a detachment of twenty-four soldiers under Lieutenant Guilfoyle from Fort Lewis arrived and found everything tranquil, and the Utes avoiding confrontation.[13]

The fall and winter passed quietly as the Indians moved to their winter camps, but the spring of 1884 saw renewed activity. The military and Indian agents received complaints from almost every white community or settlement within a hundred-mile radius of the Four Corners. The people of Colorado demanded that soldiers be stationed at Navajo Springs and on the Dolores River to protect the growing population. Settlers in McElmo Canyon and on the lower San Juan River grumbled about Ute travelers begging at the door; tearing down fences; destroying crops; running off, mutilating, or killing livestock; and threatening white men who did not comply. Navajos joined the fray, though they were not quite as militant, pushing livestock across the San Juan River, appropriating vegetables and fruits, and generally adding to the chaos.[14] The Utes hit the large cattle com-

panies the hardest. Why there was so much friction can be found in a newspaper article published in 1887, giving a few facts and figures that provide a telling picture of what was happening to the land over the years. W. J. Forham, an entrepreneur in Salt Lake City, noted that in San Juan County alone there were 11,000 sheep and 32,000 cattle belonging to white stockmen on the range all year long, and another 100,000 cattle that came in from Colorado for winter grazing.[15] As a people dependent on hunting and gathering, the Utes ground their teeth as they watched livestock destroy their livelihood — plants not eaten were trampled, and game not shot scared away. Something had to give.

As usual, the action started in the spring. According to citizen reports from Mancos, Navajos and Utes were threatening their livestock, herders, and the mail carrier who traveled from there to Bluff. He would no longer ride the route without armed escort. A telegram from the District of New Mexico's commanding officer in Santa Fe notified Fort Lewis that the people in Mancos were capable of protecting themselves. Agent Warren Patten assured the local commander that the Southern Utes were moving onto the reservation to avoid any type of conflict. Cattlemen at Navajo Springs made a similar request for assistance, but the military told them that they could not protect them since they were trespassing on Ute lands.[16]

On April 15 opening shots of conflict rang out at Mitchell's store. Some transient white men visiting the post killed a Navajo and wounded two others over a misunderstanding. The Navajos took advantage of the incident to run off Mitchell's horses, which he took as an opportunity to claim the loss of fifty mounts, recruit twenty-three Colorado cowboys to stay at his establishment, and have a military force stationed there, too. A group of Utes who had pitched camp nearby also joined in, riding four miles upriver to another post to tell two hired hands that a fight had broken out. The men fled the store, providing a wonderful opportunity for the Indians to appropriate an estimated $2,400 worth of supplies.[17] Another fourteen miles upriver, Edgar Oen Noland closed his post's doors and windows in preparation for a Ute attack after having been ordered to leave.

Six days after the confrontation Lieutenant J. F. Kreps arrived with a detachment; one week later Captain Hiram Ketchum from Fort Lewis descended on Mitchell's ranch with one company and a month's rations, as did Captain Allan Smith from Fort Wingate, New Mexico, with three weeks' rations. Once upon the scene, all agreed that there was no need for this size force and that much of what had happened had been caused by Mitchell and greatly exaggerated. In the meantime Kreps learned that the Indians wanted to "kill the white gentile [non-Mormon] settlers," and that the Utes wanted plunder, while the Navajos wanted plunder and revenge for the previous shootings.[18] By mid-May, Sergeant Christian Soffke, a corporal, with ten privates from B Company, Twenty-second Infantry, received instructions to remain at Mitchell's, create a defensive position from which to "make a stubborn fight" if necessary, and prevent Indians from having access to his position.[19]

Other reports of discontent filtered in. Two cattlemen told of how Navajos and Utes had killed no fewer than a hundred cows that spring, "actuated by pure deviltry, as the carcasses are usually untouched, save to cut out the tongue."[20] The newspaper rendering this report by "Messrs. Adams and Ptolemy" continued:

> They saw two or three Indians of Narraguinip's band who were shot by the Rico boys in the fight at La Sal. One of them, an old buck, is minus two or three inches of one of his legs, which shortened as it healed [possibly the Sore Leg]. They have very little use for Rico. Oscar Carter, of the West Dolores, told them he came from Rico, and every one of his Indian visitors left the camp instantly. The Narraguinip band is composed of renegades from the Uncompahgre, Paiutes, Navajos, and other tribes and are not recognized at any agency.[21]

Still, Agent Patten had the responsibility of keeping track of this group and took the jabs of discontent when things went wrong. He must have just shrugged his shoulders when E. L. Stevens, acting commissioner of Indian Affairs, directed him to "take the necessary steps to have your Indians return to their reservation at once and remain there."[22]

Within three weeks of the writing of this directive, these Indians were embroiled in the turmoil of the Soldier Crossing incident. Sources of information about this conflict are fairly abundant, including accounts from Harold Carlisle, the military, and the *Dolores News*. But the most complete rendering of events comes from a Colorado cowboy named Sam Todd.[23] Although he wrote about this fight in 1925, roughly forty years after the dust had settled, his account seems accurate and meshes well with contemporary reports, estimates of mileage, and internal details.

The affair started simply enough. On July 3, 1884, a substantial group of cowboys had assembled for an early summer roundup at the foot of Blue Mountain.[24] Three combined outfits belonging to William "Billy" H. Wilson, Charles "Race Horse" Johnson, and the Carlisles were camped on the South Fork of Montezuma Creek (known today as Verdure Creek).[25] The one-armed Texan, Billy Wilson, had lost his appendage in a fight with Comanches. He and Johnson now owned ranches in the Dolores area and grazed their herds on Blue Mountain.[26] The Carlisles also controlled part of this range, and all shared the roundup efforts, separating stock for the respective owners.

A group of Utes, some of whom had off-reservation passes signed by Patten, were in the area to hunt. They camped below the cowboys and, surprisingly enough given past events, were invited to visit and eat with their white neighbors. During the interchange the cowboys noticed the Indians had three horses belonging to Johnson, and another to cowboy "Spud" Hudson, whose involvement in the Pinhook incident was well known. Four men went to the Indian camp to reclaim the livestock but met resistance. As the cowboys attempted to cut out the horses from the Indian herd, a medicine man named Brook drove the animals back. According to white accounts, when Hank Sharp attempted to get a rope on one of the horses, Brook drew his knife and stabbed him two or three times, leaving a slight slice on Sharp's neck. Whether it was more of an attempt to cut the rope than to kill the cowboy, no one will ever know, but there was enough provocation in the cowboy's mind to shoot the Ute in the mouth, with the bullet passing through his neck.[27] Brook lived, but he was not the only person to be wounded that day.

The Utes took up positions near their camp and started firing while the women and children fled. The four cowboys retreated to their camp, sounded the alarm, and joined the others in gathering horses in the corral, hitching four large mules to a wagon to haul gear, and preparing for a hasty retreat. By this time the Indians had surrounded them and were firing at the hustling men. Joseph H. Nielson, a Mormon from Bluff who was working with the cowboys, grabbed Billy Wilson's two sons, ages eight and ten, and headed for a nearby gully. There they lay until the fighting ended. "Only a heavy hand on the neck of each curious lad kept his head from popping up each time a shot was fired."[28] These boys later rode twenty-nine hours, without food or rest, back to Durango with the surviving cowboys. Nielson took a separate route that night, fleeing down Montezuma Canyon to the San Juan River and back to Bluff, fearing his involvement might antagonize the Utes against the settlers there.[29]

In the meantime the cowboys started up the hill from Verdure on what was then called the Bluff Road. Apparently they abandoned two wagons and some equipment at their camp, while the third wagon made it

only as far as a place known as the "Salt Lick" (later named the Roundup Ground), about three miles southwest of Verdure, before it too was lost. Hidden in clumps of oak brush, the Utes allowed the slow-moving vehicle, surrounded by the men and many of their horses, to get within range before opening fire. Four mules died, the Utes captured the horse herd (estimated at 100 to 150 animals), and two men—a cook called "Cook" and Adolf Lusk, who was in charge of the herd—were wounded in the foot and thigh, respectively. Some of the cowboys lost their horses and had to ride double.

The situation was desperate. With only seven rifles and the rest six-shooters, "most of them out of cartridges, having shot them away at deer for fun," the cowboys were in no position to resist.[30] The Utes, on the other hand, "wore new shirts and had new Winchesters and revolvers, bought in Durango with the money paid them as an annuity at Ignacio, the Southern Ute Agency, by Agent Patten."[31] It was time for the white men to withdraw. They made their way to the towns of southwestern Colorado, exhausted and chagrined that they had once again been bested. The Utes picked through their booty, gathered their newly acquired horse herd, and began a leisurely move to the rough country west of Blue Mountain, a proven refuge during times of conflict. They left behind the remains of the burned wagon, "the old iron from which was scattered in the Roundup Ground for years after."[32]

Word spread quickly, with varying reactions. The Mormons in Bluff were concerned about the possibility of escalating violence. Platte D. Lyman wrote in his diary: "During the past week a difficulty occurred between cowmen and Indians on the South Montezuma during which 2 Indians were killed and 2 white men wounded. This may yet lead to considerable trouble."[33] To the people of Colorado this incident was one more example of Indian depredation and a threat to their financial investments. Their estimated 17,000 cattle were part of a $2 million investment in the livestock industry, which was now "at the mercy of the Indians."[34] Circumstances were ripe for another showdown. This time, however, the military took charge.

Captain Henry P. Perrine with F Troop, Sixth Cavalry, left Fort Lewis with forty-nine men on July 6, 1884, the day after receiving the news. On the way he stopped at Dolores and asked for volunteers to help get the horses back. According to the *Dolores News*, "eighty cowboys armed to the teeth and swearing vengeance against the Utes," departed for the battle.[35] Military accounts are more modest and say only forty-five joined the expedition, while Sam Todd estimated ninety.[36] At least part of the cowboy force rendezvoused with the main body at Cross Canyon, where they selected Rube Lockett from Dolores as their leader.[37]

On July 7 Second Lieutenant B. K. West left Fort Lewis with a detachment of 35 men of B Troop, Sixth Cavalry, to assist Captain Perrine. The latter reached the scene of the earlier fight on July 10, with West joining him three days later, bringing the final count of white participants to no fewer than 130, with perhaps as many as 175.[38] The Utes were probably at not even half that strength, and many of these were noncombatants. A contemporary estimated their force at "from 75 to 100 strong under Narraguinip and Mariano."[39] Being encumbered with women, children, and all their belongings, the Indians were at a distinct military disadvantage.

On the other hand, Perrine created a logistical problem with such a large force. Not only did he have to bring supplies for his own men, but according to Todd, he told the civilian volunteers not to bring any food because his sixteen pack mules would carry plenty for everyone. While no one knew how long this expedition would take, the two weeks that it required strained the supply resources of such a large group. Water, an even more precious commodity than food in this high desert environment, proved most critical.

Paddy Soldiercoat, 1890s. Paddy probably obtained his namesake cavalryman's jacket from the Soldier Crossing fight of 1884. As a participant in the battle, he served under Mancos Jim's leadership. (Denver Public Library, Western History Collection, photographer unknown, X-33079)

The same day that Perrine's force arrived at the battlefield, Sergeant Soffke and his soldiers from B Company, Twenty-second Infantry, on an unrelated mission to Mitchell's post, arrested five Utes who had been involved in the Verdure fight. He took their arms and horses and placed them in custody because "several settlers on this river threaten to kill them on sight," and he felt he could protect them until they returned to the Southern Ute Reservation.[40] Two days later Red Jacket, leading forty men, threatened an attack if the sergeant did not release the prisoners, promising to bring them to Agent Patten within five days. Red Jacket, Topine (Tahpuni'—"Drowsy"), Johnny Benow, and Narraguinip, who was supposedly leading the main group, were among those demanding the prisoners' freedom. All four of these men were notorious for their parts in previous conflicts. Once the sergeant learned that Captain Perrine's force was headed in another direction and there was no hope of assistance, he freed the prisoners.[41]

Patten, in the meantime, had sent Ignacio and other Southern Ute leaders to the western end of the reservation to ascertain if any of their people were involved in these conflicts or if it was just the band of renegade "Paiutes." The agent wrote with satisfaction that he was convinced that his charges were innocent, and as far as they were concerned, if these "Paiutes…all got killed, it will be a good thing."[42] Patten's desire to exonerate "his" Indians reflects more his desire to remain clean of accusation than total reality. No doubt there were many Southern/Ute Mountain Utes who claimed no affiliation with the fleeing Indians, but there is also no doubt that others had strong links to or were members of the Utah group. Still, many Utes professed innocence. Perhaps part of their denial sprang from a letter supposedly received in Durango by government officials stating that the Interior Department had "authoriz[ed] settlers to shoot any Indian seen attempting to join the renegades from the reservation."[43]

When Captain Perrine arrived at the scene of the fight, he found nine dead horses, eight others wounded beyond use, and Billy Wilson's dead mules. The Utes' trail was easy to follow as it skirted around the southern edge of Blue Mountain. Bloody bark poultices used to dress wounds were left at various campsites. Harold Carlisle, who apparently was not accompanying the military but was intimately connected to the events, described what the soldiers found: "the band had traveled slowly, making about ten miles a day, camping in more than one place for two days, playing cards, barking trees, and even making race tracks on the heads of Cottonwood and Indian Creeks, to test the metal [sic] of the stolen stock, and tending their wounded, as was shown by the rags littered about in their camping places."[44] Finally, the sheer number of horses—stolen or

otherwise—as well as the goats being herded along as a mobile source of food, left an indelible, easily followed trail.

Today this path is not as readily discerned. According to Albert R. Lyman, it was called the "Big Trail" or "Old Trail" and was a well-known thoroughfare that led westward into a maze of canyons, slickrock, and widely separated sources of water and campsites.[45] Based on Todd's description of where the Utes went, a best-guess mapping of the trail would start in Verdure, cross upper Recapture Wash and Johnson Creek, and then proceed to the Round Mountain—Mormon Pasture area on the divide between the San Juan River and Indian Creek drainages via a trail across what is now known as Bayles Ranch. From the Round Mountain area they traveled south along Elk Ridge through the Big and Little Notches to the Bears Ears area on south Elk Ridge. At the springs, or ponds, near the northern end of the Bears Ears the Utes rested. They then moved northwest about ten miles to the vicinity of a small land formation now called the Pushout, thence off Elk Ridge to the north bench of Cheesebox Canyon and on to White Canyon, where the next fight occurred. Once the military expedition left the springs at the base of the Bears Ears and the aspens and ponderosa pines of Elk Ridge for the piñon and juniper canyon country below, they were in terra incognita. Todd states that if the men were unable to find water near the trail, they would look for birds to find it, a risky proposition at best.

As the pursuers sat astride their horses on the western rim of Elk Ridge, they spied two pillars of smoke about a half mile below and two Indians riding their ponies down the steep slope to the valley. Todd believed these were signal fires to warn the main group. Harold Carlisle goes even further, suggesting that these two Indians were actually Southern Utes sent by Agent Patten to bring in any of his charges involved in the incident. Now they were serving as a rear guard and had ridden seventy-five miles at a rapid pace

The probable route of pursuit off the Pushout looking south: (1) the Pushout rim; (2) the trail, which descends a hogback ridge crest to saddle, traverses the lower north slope of the ridge, and then breaks out southwest onto the Cheesebox Canyon bench; (3) charred juniper stumps next to trail, possibly the trees burned by the Ute rear guard. (Courtesy of Winston Hurst)

to warn the renegades. Patten and Ignacio denied any knowledge of these two men supposedly working in their employ. While Carlisle's suggestion appears to be mere conjecture, it does portray the feelings of distrust toward the Indian Service in general, and Agent Patten in particular.

A large cloud of dust ten miles away revealed the Indians' encampment, and through binoculars the military could see them preparing to move. The steep, rough, mile-long descent off Elk Ridge took much longer than the cowboys and cavalry had anticipated.[46] By the time they reached the Indians' camp, their prey was long gone, as was the water they had hoped to find. The Utes had availed themselves of rainwater trapped in a sandstone basin and, before departing, had watered all of their stock. Todd wrote that "From the tracks the goat herd had been watered last, and they had taken it all. (The goat herd they always took with them on the war trail, as they could out-travel a horse and they had them to eat while they were too busy to hunt.)"[47]

The lack of water proved crucial. It was one o'clock on a hot July afternoon, when temperatures in that country easily rise to well over 100 degrees. The soldiers had filled their canteens that morning but were now out of water. The cowboys had even less but, according to Todd, complained less, even though the soldiers did not share what they had. The horses suffered from lack of water

even more, being described as "wet with sweat after the first ten miles."[48] Although the heavy, six-foot Todd had brought a second mount and changed horses every five miles, the rough canyon country had taken its toll on his mounts. To compound the problem, there was no breeze to disperse the dust. As the gap between the pursuers and pursued closed, the soldiers and cowboys rode in suspended dust clouds "like ashes" left by the fleeing Indians.

As the chase wore on, the Utes separated into three bands. Closest to the advancing white men was a rear guard of six or seven warriors prepared to fight a delaying action; two miles ahead rode the main body of warriors, and another four miles ahead of them were the women and children, and some men, driving livestock and hauling equipment. Occasionally a tired Indian pony stood in the trail, so played out that it would not step aside until whipped with a quirt, an indication of fatigue that encouraged the pursuers. Captain Perrine felt that his prey was close at hand, and at any moment he would close with the enemy. He followed relentlessly. Todd recalled, "We thought we could surely catch them before sundown and kept at a hard gallop.... While we couldn't see them, we thought we were right at them and would catch them in a few minutes. So it kept up all that afternoon."[49] One account tells of how an occasional shot or two from the Utes' trail element also slowed the soldiers down.[50]

Even after sunset the pursuit continued. Not until total darkness made tracking impossible over slickrock did the exhausted pursuers get to rest. "We tumbled off, layed [sic] down with the bridle reins in our hands, and lay there until the moon came up. [We then] took the trail again, a tired, thirsty, hungry outfit, our horses suffering for water more than we were."[51]

The cowboys pursued the Utes across the inner gulch of White Canyon at the location named on modern maps as "Soldier Crossing." From there the chase turned northwest, following the southwest bench of White Canyon along what Carlisle identified as the trail leading from Bluff City to the Colorado River, traversed today by Utah State Route 95. The road passes along the bench between the inner gorge of White Canyon on the right and the massive, 1,500-foot, cliff-capped escarpment of Wingate Mesa on the left. Daylight found the pursuers between these geographical features, hot on the Indians' path.

The trail soon left the White Canyon bench and climbed westward to the high, narrow mesa dividing White Canyon from Red Canyon. There the Utes positioned themselves for an ambush at what has since been called "Piute Pass," a narrow declivity through the caprock overlooking a steep, exposed talus slope. According to Todd,

> When full daylight came we were at the foot of this wall and the trail led to a narrow break in it, barely wide enough for one horse to go into. We halted, of course, to investigate. We knew we were close to them because for the last three miles we had found a number of give-out horses wet with sweat, and some of the last ones were still panting. And while we were talking, we heard a goat bleat just on top, and it was plain to us boys that we were in a trap. The Captain, however, said no, there was no trap and we must climb that mesa, but considering the necessity for water, we would halt and send a detail to hunt for a rain water tank.[52]

The command was now unsure what action to take. Joe Wormington, a civilian packer and scout for the military, volunteered to climb to the gap and see if he could determine the Indians' location. A young cowboy named James "Rowdy" Higgins offered to join him. Higgins's mother and father had been killed by Indians in Nevada when he was a child, and he often expressed his eagerness for revenge. Although party members warned them of a trap, every indication being that the Utes were waiting on top, the two men disregarded the cautions and started up the hill. When they approached within seventy-five feet of the gap, the Utes opened fire. Higgins fell wounded but had enough strength to crawl into the protection of a large boulder. Wormington, also wounded, picked himself up and tried running straight down the slope. Struck by a second volley, he tumbled head over heels before coming to rest with his feet and legs propped against a large rock and his head and shoulders downslope. His face was not visible to those below, but they heard him moan and say something inaudible. He never moved again.[53]

Below was pandemonium. The Utes' attention now focused on the swirling tangle of men and horses. They fired round after round, tearing up the ground but hitting only Todd's horse. Bunched together in the confusion, the mass of men made an easy target. Todd, in retrospect, found it difficult to explain how so many shots could miss so many people, unless the Indians were just shooting at the clump of men without picking out specific targets.[54] Some of the cowboys and soldiers were in such a panic that they fled without their horses, "the crowd tearing down the hill to a bunch of cedars for shelter."[55] They left seven saddled mounts behind, a dangerous move given their situation. Others were more determined and took the time to lead their animals over the rough, rocky terrain to protective cover. Extra

View to the south from the Piute Pass battle site: (1) the Ute position at pass; (2) probable U.S. position in the talus slope and grassy bench area; (3) the probable location of Wormington's and Higgins's bodies; (4) cached .50-70 caliber unfired rounds; (5) modern bladed road; (6) the trail route from the Pushout via Cheesebox/White Canyon bench. Dotted lines indicate inferred trail routes. (Courtesy of Winston Hurst)

horses, the pack train, and now the soldiers' mounts were safeguarded in the rear, while the cowboys and cavalry maintained fire on the gap and its surrounding area. The Indians still had the upper hand. Lying flat on the rocks above, they were invisible to those below. The steadiness of aim that they seemed to lack at the beginning of the fight was now replaced with more accurate shots and a freedom to "[shoot] close at whatever they could see, so that a hat held up on a stick was sure to get a hole in it."[56]

Captain Perrine now faced three major problems. The first was the two wounded men on the hill. According to a later newspaper account, he tried without success to find volunteers who would follow him up the exposed slope to retrieve the wounded.[57] Around nine that morning, with the sun baking the landscape, Wormington stopped groaning and breathed his last. The soldiers turned their binoculars on Higgins, who was gasping for air. By noon he was dead, too. Mancos Jim took advantage of the situation to amuse his followers and taunt the soldiers below. He would jump up on the rock face, dance around, and holler, "Oh my God boys, come and help me" or "Oh my God boys, a drink of water," mimicking the cries of the wounded that the Indians could hear so

clearly because of their close proximity.[58] No doubt this was met with a shower of lead, but without effect. A short while later Mancos Jim repeated his performance. Thus the day wore on.

Perrine's second problem was water. After a day and a half of heavy exertion and fear in blistering heat, the situation had turned desperate. No one in the party knew the country well enough to locate any of the several small springs that lay hidden within a few miles of their position, and there were no birds in the area to lead them to water. The nearest sure source was the one behind them at the foot of the Bears Ears, and that was twenty miles straight-line distance in a land where nothing is straight-line, and most of that was uphill. All the men could talk about was water.

As the shadows lengthened in the canyon, Captain Perrine faced his third concern. He knew the Indians had an intimate knowledge of the land, and he did not. If his troops were to be flanked and perhaps driven from the rocks and trees at the foot of the trail, the situation could degenerate into a chaotic rout, especially if it took place at night. To prevent this from happening, and with the idea of retrieving their fallen comrades, the soldiers agreed to sight their rifles in on the gap during the day so that at night they could maintain a steady fire that would deny the Utes' use of the pass. Under this covering fire and protected by darkness, four of the cowboys, including Todd, would move up the slope and retrieve the two bodies. Following that, they would retreat.

As the four cowboy volunteers quietly crawled along the trail on the rock-strewn hill, Todd heard a noise. He turned to his companions to find they were gone and seven Indians were coming up behind him along the path, each leading one of the saddled horses left behind earlier that day. He dropped off the side of the trail and lay flat, the Utes clearly silhouetted against the night sky. Alone, he slithered toward Higgins's body, only to see the Indians stripping it. Moving to Wormington's location, he found more Utes going through the same process. There was also a dog sniffing around that started to growl. Todd knew that he could "do no good" and, if detected, could fire only a few shots before the muzzle flash gave away his position and all was over. He slowly picked his way back down the hill.

When he returned to the perimeter, he learned that his companions had heard the horses coming, feared calling ahead (thus giving away their position), so moved off the trail and lay low. Oblivious to the danger, Todd had continued blithely up the trail. His companions had returned to safety, assuming that he would also recognize the danger and come back down. All during this time the force had maintained a steady volume of fire on Piute Pass. How the Indians had managed to get through it was a mystery.

To the captain this was bad news. The Utes had apparently descended by another route to collect the horses, thus signaling the very high risk of a flanking attack. If they gained control of the trail to his rear and stood between him and water, all could perish. He ordered everything hastily packed and prepared for movement, and by 10 p.m. the column, frazzled and parched from two days of stress, got under way. Fear was still a factor. Four hours into the retreat a man named Joe McGrew became deathly sick, most likely from dehydration and exhaustion. As Todd called for assistance, McGrew fell from his horse and had to be carried to the side of the trail. The sergeant of the troop asked what was wrong and then told the men to tie the sick cowboy onto his saddle and continue, explaining, "[We] can't delay the whole command or a part of it here in a hostile country," to which Todd replied, "Sergeant, we have quit and are no longer under command."[59] An hour's rest put McGrew and his companions back on their horses, and by eight the next morning they had caught up to the retreating column as it climbed back up on Elk Ridge.

The Utes, at this point, were headed in the opposite direction. According to Albert R. Lyman, Bluff cattlemen reported that at least some of the Indians followed the Old Trail across Red Canyon, thence across North Gulch (now Moki Canyon) via a large sand slide[60] to the Pagahrit, a natural body of water in Lake Canyon.[61] There they camped for a time, celebrating their victory. When they moved on, they left behind their wickiups and a scatter of dead and wounded cattle belonging to the Bluff Mormons before eventually making their way southward across the San Juan River to the isolation of Navajo Mountain.[62]

Three hours after the military topped out on Elk Ridge, they reached the spring at the base of the Bears Ears, where they "drank and drank. As soon as the men had drunk all they wanted, they began to tumble over and go to sleep."[63] A lone sentry, who was himself groggy, had the responsibility of keeping watch. Around two in the morning Todd awakened him by telling him that Mancos Jim was coming. The half asleep man quickly sprang to life and had to be reassured that it was a false alarm. The men now discovered that the packs containing all of the provisions had somehow been lost. All that was available were two jars of pickles donated by

Captain Perrine. His willingness to share was admirable, but given the fact that no one had eaten in two or three days, his offer did not go far. As for Todd, he was not "pickle hungry."

The cavalcade next moved to Johnson Creek at the foot of Blue Mountain, where they located five stray cattle belonging to "Race Horse" Johnson. The men killed two steers, skinned them, and cut the meat off in slabs, "every fellow having a stick with a chunk of meat roasting on it.… in less than an hour after the animal was dead, it was eaten up."[64] The party camped there that evening, and then some moved on toward Colorado while Perrine's cavalry headed south to Mitchell's trading post to assist in peacekeeping efforts there. The captain dispatched Lieutenant West's B Troop back to Fort Lewis, while he and F Troop established a summer encampment on the San Juan.[65]

At least some of the civilian participants blamed Captain Perrine and the army for the Piute Pass debacle. Although some of the following statements would later be retracted, the initial report in the *Dolores News* reveals the feelings that many Colorado settlers felt toward their supposed protectors. The newspaper portrayed the soldiers as afraid to fight, staying "in camp a mile and a half back until after dark," and not rendering any assistance to the cowboys. The Colorado men, on the other hand, "all day long…had kept the red devils from the bodies and hoped under cover of darkness to get them." Following the fight,

> the cowboys left for home [and] were joined by the gentlemen in brass buttons and the little pleasure trip was over.… With the soldiers, who did not care to be left alone and unprotected in Indian country, they turned their faces from the field and their heels to the foe and are now rounding up cattle on their respective ranges. The soldiers returned to Fort Lewis, where they will continue to play penny ante while the bones of their scout lie bleaching under the hot rays of the Utah sun and his slayers go unpunished and unpursued.[66]

A week later, however, the *Dolores News* had changed its pitch. One article noted that part of the force involved in the fight had just returned to Fort Lewis (Lieutenant West's unit), while another part was camped in the Mancos Canyon area (Perrine's F Troop) to prevent further depredations. It went on to say that Mitchell and others living along the San Juan River had been advised to leave because of the Indians' attitude toward past events that went sour. The Utes had "sworn vengeance on these families."[67]

A second article was apologetic to the military. George West, a well-known cattleman and participant in the fight, provided his views. He spoke to the issue of "the bravery of an army officer who was blamed by many for seeming cowardice."[68] West felt that the terrain had dictated the outcome of the battle, and that Perrine had acted prudently and led by example. Amid the "[deafening] war whoops and 'ki-yi-ing' of the Indians which they kept up for a long time," the commander had done what he could. When he saw that his scout was shot, he "repeatedly exposed himself in his efforts to induce his men to do some execution and finally called for volunteers to follow him to the point where Wormington was dying. Not a man stepped out and it would have been certain death to every man who went up the hill. Perrine said he would ask no man to go where he himself would not go and that he would lead in person." Certainly, nothing more could have been asked of him as a leader.

The article closed by noting that two companies from Fort Wingate, two from "the new cantonment on the San Juan," and another one from Fort Lewis were heading after the Utes. Armed with Gatling guns, these five well-equipped companies were supposed to punish the miscreants. If true, they met with no success. West was correct when he said he believed it ineffective to chase the Indians in their own territory. He felt it was better "to kill every Indian on the range or else give up the country."[69] Some cowboys took this idea to heart. Two weeks later they killed three Indians they encountered in their travels— or, as the paper said, "turned their [the Utes'] mud-hooks to the primroses."[70] More was yet to come.

In the same article, the editor discussed how reports were surfacing of large numbers of Indians collecting at Navajo Mountain in preparation for a raid. Navajo agent John H. Bowman had gone to that area to arrest a Navajo man but found he had taken refuge with a band of Utes who were not only defiant, but prevented the Navajo's arrest. Most likely these were some of the same group that had participated in the Soldier Crossing incident. At the same time, Billy Wilson was in the midst of rounding up cattle around Blue Mountain under the protection of a cavalry escort. From his perspective, the Utes had learned that "their agent is powerless to restrain them; that the government takes but little notice apparently of their movements; that in every fight with the whites they have so far come off victorious and they have therefore resolved to do on the frontier about as they have a mind."[71]

As for Agent Patten, his concerns were almost over. On September 8 he tendered his resignation, two weeks after submitting his annual report, a forthright assessment of conditions on the Southern Ute Reservation. Under different categories he drew a compelling portrait of why there was so much conflict. Patten reported that of the 4,800 ewes issued the previous year for a stock-raising venture, there were now only 1,500. Although the Utes had expressed a real interest in animal husbandry, "owing to the limited supply of provisions furnished them, they were compelled to subsist on the sheep or starve. They preferred the former."[72] There were only four farms open with fifty acres in wheat, forty in oats, and eight in potatoes. Of the twenty-seven Ute children sent to Albuquerque Indian School the previous year, three had died from disease. There were an estimated 400 "renegades" living in Utah

over whom he had little control; the Utes on the reservation left often to hunt, something the local white people wanted stopped immediately; and many of the cattle grazing on Indian land belonged to white settlers living near the boundaries. Most troubling, however, was lack of adequate rations.

> The fact is simply this: It is impossible to keep starving Indians on a reservation when they can go into the mountains but a few miles and get plenty of game to subsist on. They will either do that or kill cattle, which graze on the reservation by the thousands, and the Indians receive no benefit for the same…. I consider the present action on the part of the government a reward for depredations. Why? Because as soon as an Indian shows a disposition to become civilized, the government cuts off his rations and he must either steal or starve.[73]

In September the Southern Utes received an interim agent, William H. Clark, former special agent of the Interior Department, quickly followed by Christian F. Stollsteimer. The latter certainly could not have any false hopes about success in keeping the Indians on their reservation after reading Secretary of the Interior H. M. Teller's response to the petition sent by the residents of southwestern Colorado. Briefly, Teller said that there was little that he, his agent, or the military could really do to ensure that the Utes would remain on their lands. He complained that he had predicted the current problems back in 1880, had therefore encouraged removal, and that now his prophetic advice was being realized. He was not authorized to reimburse for losses, and the best thing to do to address these problems would be for citizens to contact their elected congressional representatives. In the interim, the military at Fort Lewis would remain in the field, and he would appoint a local citizen to work at the agency "to keep the Indians on their reservation," but he also understood the enormity of the task.[74]

Spring 1885, while quieter in Utah, was not without its issues. Underlying much of the conflict remained the lack of food. The Southern Utes were starving. In June a group of fifty "quiet and peaceable" men, women, and children camped at Mitchell's ranch before going to Blue Mountain to hunt. This was earlier than usual, and there was little doubt that they would help themselves to the "immense [cattle] herds as they say they will and always do [have] nothing else to eat."[75] The Ute agent noted that he issued only one pound of beef and three-and-a-half pounds of flour each week for every man, woman, and child.[76] A few months later Colonel Peter T. Swaine, commander of the Twenty-second Infantry, Fort Lewis, did his own math and calculated there were 983 Southern Utes on the reservation, who for the past year had received a per capita daily allowance of less than a half pound of beef and about a quarter of a pound of flour.[77] Little wonder that the Indians left their reservation in search of food.

On June 19 one such party, with at least six men, four women, and a child, were camped at Beaver Creek near the Dolores River. According to the Ute version told by Chief Jack House in 1940 and a statement given by Ignacio six months after the incident, there were twenty-five to thirty people in this hunting party. They had traveled from Sleeping Ute Mountain and were camped on the west side of Beaver Creek approximately twenty-two miles north of Dolores.[78] Both cowboy and Indian accounts agree that there were several tepees set up on a grassy flat, which the white men surrounded at night to await the dawn. There is also mention of a "sentinel tepee" located on a prominence overlooking the camp to provide early warning.

At sunrise thirteen cowboys "at last carried out their threats to shoot Utes on sight."[79] Holding the high ground and hidden by boulders, the cowboys waited for the sentinel to come out of his tepee. When he did, they killed him, and then poured shots downslope where the awakened Indians sought cover

and returned fire. One woman came out holding an infant over her head to show that it was a peaceful hunting camp with women and children present. By the time the cowboys finished, they reported one woman standing in the open, screaming hysterically, while others had escaped down the canyon. Four men, two women, and a child lay dead (in some accounts only three men died).[80]

Following the cowboys' departure, the woman went through the remains and found a young man shot through the legs, an old woman wounded in the leg, and a baby unharmed. The party started back to Ute Mountain, but the travel was too painful for both the man and woman. He found shelter in an oak grove and camouflaged himself with leaves to await help. When the baby started whimpering, the terror-stricken women, fearing that they were being pursued, covered its mouth and accidentally smothered it. They hid the infant's body a short distance downcanyon for future burial, traveled a bit farther, and then concealed the old woman in the oak brush. The younger woman traveled by night for three days before returning to Ute Mountain and her people.

Once news of the unprovoked attack arrived, reaction was instant. Utes set fire to rancher John Genther's home in Montezuma Valley and then killed him and wounded his wife as they fled the burning building. Not one of their five children was injured. One of the three infantry companies (thirty men) already deployed in Mancos Valley went immediately to the scene, where they joined two troops (sixty men) of cavalry. With the distinct possibility that the Indians who committed the outrage had already fled to the reservation, Major David Perry of the Sixth Cavalry proceeded to Blue Mountain to "protect cattle interests" so that "the spark of war may not have an opportunity to kindle the hearts of the young bucks," while at the same time giving "confidence to citizens."[81] Ignacio, other Ute leaders, Agent Stollsteimer, and two cavalry companies went to the massacre site, where the position of the unburied bodies indicated that they had been attacked while asleep.[82]

Word of the massacre spread throughout the Four Corners. Navajo agent John H. Bowman complained of Utes trespassing in the Carrizo Mountains and other Navajo lands. He reported ten tepees occupied by old men, women, and children who were "Utes and Piutes" from Utah. The younger men and women had left them there for protection while they avenged the death of the six killed in Colorado, having already killed three white people. They "were prepared to fight and would send their women and children across the [San Juan] River on the mountain as soon as trouble commences."[83] He requested that the Ute agent control these "renegade cut throats and thieves" because they were in Navajo territory "for no good purpose and their influence is bad upon our people."

The planned disposition of troops worked. Colonel Swaine wrote with surprised relief that he had prevented the Indians from wiping out all of the scattered settlers and rampaging on the "warpath." As for the cowboys who openly boasted that they would kill any Indians encountered, and who welcomed "a disastrous and bloody war," the colonel believed they had "little regard for the fate of the innocent settler" or the "lives of inoffensive Indians whom they so cowardly assassinate."[84] With so many men already in the field providing protection and taking preventive measures, Swaine had to balance his operational arm with the possibility of a Ute uprising that could besiege both the agency and the fort. He also feared that units traveling about could become so splintered by different tasks that they could be "whipped by detail." Still, elements received missions to remain on the Mancos and go to the Big Bend of the Dolores River, reconnoiter in the area of Blue Mountain, provide escort duty to Navajo Springs, investigate general rumors, man an outpost at Mitchell's ranch, and maintain a general presence.

All of this was not good enough. Coloradoans sent reports to state authorities saying that the regular troops were not providing sufficient protection, the situation becoming so bad that some settlers had abandoned their homes to live in the brush for safety. They insisted that the state militia be mustered for duty since the regular soldiers were more interested in protecting Indians than whites.[85] Just how wise this scenario would have been is evident in a poem published that summer in the *Dolores News*. While not much on rhyme scheme, it certainly communicates its message.

> I'm a cowboy from the Mancos
> Hear my gun —
> Click — bang!
> I'm a leather-legged herder —
> Fiving high.
> And I'd like to sight a Ute,
> And cut his throat to boot;
> I'm a holy, howling terror
> Of the hills. Ki-yi.
>
> And I'm a state militia man,
> Fight I can —
> Never ran.
> And I'd laugh to meet the Injun
> In his lair.
> On parade I'm not so slow,
> And no slouch at war with Lo.[86]
> Send up a Ute for breakfast —
> Red hot — done Rare.[87]

Mercifully, the state never called up the militia and both sides cooled.

From the field came word that "the situation was never more quiet."[88] Even Mancos Jim, who had been one of the "Paiute" leaders in the Soldier Crossing fight the year before, and who lived around Blue Mountain, said he wanted to avoid conflict, would stay away from the cowboys, and just wished to hunt. Mancos Jim's desire was apparently not delivered from a position of weakness. According to Swaine, "If we went to war with [these Paiutes/Utes], it is believed from the nature of the country they could successfully defy a much larger force of cavalry than we have here."[89] F. A. Hammond agreed, citing "Winchester [Mancos] Jim's" name as sufficient provocation for cowboys to be terror-struck and fleeing "helter-skelter." He noted, "There have been many brushes between the cowboys and the Indians but the latter have always come out on top and Winchester Jim has a habit of taunting them of the fact whenever he gets an opportunity. If the Indians are never obliterated from the face of the earth until it is done by the cowboys, their existence is good for all time."[90] The previous year underscores his point. Troops remained in the vicinity of Blue Mountain at least through mid-September.

As these soldiers returned to Fort Lewis, two officers from Fort Douglas in Salt Lake City, charged with determining conditions in southeastern Utah and the role that their troops might play in the area, visited San Juan County. On September 25, Lieutenant Colonel N. W. Osborne and First Lieutenant R. R. Stevens of the Sixth Infantry boarded the Denver and Rio Grande and traveled to Blake (now Green River), then Moab, Blue Mountain, Bluff, and Montezuma Creek, Utah; from there they went to Mancos, Fort Lewis, Silverton, and Montrose, Colorado, before returning to Fort Douglas. The entire trip took twenty-eight days.

Their findings were objective but with a few surprises. Based on many interviews throughout the white settlements, Osborne felt that the "Mormons are disposed to speak well of the Utes," whereas Navajos were more involved in petty theft; the Utes had "a more predatory inclination of a more damaging character" when it came to outfits ranging cattle; people who farmed or ranched and did not share with the Indians received most of the trouble, the Indians claiming that "the ground is not the white man's but their own"; non-Mormon cattlemen believed that the Mormons were encouraging the Utes to work against them, but "such stories may be received with a grain of allowance"; many of the Colorado settlers wanted the "extinction of the Southern Ute Agency," removing the Indians to "anyplace whatever"; and the land the Indians held was desirable for expanding white cattle ranches.[91] As for the Utes' numbers and leadership, Osborne reported that the band had a nucleus of about forty men, with others from the Southern Ute Reservation joining them from time to time. Mancos Jim was considered their main leader, with Little Captain second in command. Only the principal men visited the reservation; the rest stayed away.

As the bloody events of 1884 and 1885 receded into the past, there appeared no respite from the turmoil. Swaine wrote to Stollsteimer at the end of November asking him to respond to charges in a letter that also summarized the challenges that lay ahead in the next year.[92] For instance, Narraguinip seldom came to the agency, but when he did, he attracted young warriors eager to steal horses and kill cows. The agent knew who had killed the Indians at Beaver Creek but refused to prosecute them because of community pressure to sweep the deed under the carpet and forget it. As a result, an Indian war lurked on the horizon that next spring. The grave of "Old Chief Cabezon" had been robbed, and the Indians were demanding retribution. Many of the Utes were off the reservation burning grass and timber, killing cattle, and threatening difficulty. Red Jacket, Mariano, and Sanáp were "constantly flitting between the Piutes and young bucks at the agency [and] are represented as very bad Indians." These men had enough of a following to overpower Ignacio's efforts for peace. But why should there be peace when the Indians were constantly hungry, the government did not feed them, white men's cows were consuming their grass, and they dared not hunt—even though they had treaty rights guaranteeing this privilege. They would be killed by settlers if they left the reservation.

Thus, Stollsteimer, as a relatively new agent, was just as boxed in by contention as the Indians he supervised.

Within the blood, gore, and friction of this tumultuous period lay the reason that the Utes in southeastern Utah did not surrender to agency control. They were well aware of the impoverished conditions on the reservation, had no desire to give up their homelands, and wanted to stay away from the Colorado cowboys as well as the government in general. Their experience with the Mormons, while not stellar, was at least tolerable. As the next decade showed, they had friends as well as enemies securely lodged in their own territory. Yet there was nowhere else to turn.

CHAPTER 9

Agony with Little Ecstasy

Hunting, Travel, and Subsistence Curtailment, 1885–1895

If I had been a Paiute or Navajo, I'd have helped myself
to everything the invader had.

    Albert R. Lyman, Bluff historian

Inadequate rations on the reservation, discouragement with farming and livestock results, encroaching stockmen, and coercion into a foreign lifestyle drove the Utes to solve problems in their own way. As pressures encouraged them to move off the reservation, lands to the west held the fewest settlements and offered the least resistance. Not only did the Utah Utes remain where they were, but soon large groups of Colorado Utes joined them to hunt and share the freedom they enjoyed. Settlers on the border of southwestern Colorado and southeastern Utah were anything but happy. Ute hunting rights became an issue, travel more restricted, and survival both on and off the reservation more difficult. This triad of problems pushed the government to present its own solution, discussed in the next chapter.

The free-roving days of seasonal hunts in the mountains and canyons were fast coming to a close. Not only were the Utes actively pursuing the deer herds, but so were the Navajos, while white stockmen saw the animals as a nuisance to be gotten rid of. Bands of Navajos and Utes left their reservations to hunt and quickly encountered cattlemen grazing herds in the same places and at the same time of year as the deer. Grass, forbs, brush, and water were most plentiful in the mountains, and so it was not long before

Indian agents received blistering correspondence spelling out Indian activities. As early as 1883 the *Dolores News* complained of Southern Utes hunting in the Lone Cone area. They had a pass from Patten and reportedly killed three hundred deer and four elk, all of which was out of season according to state hunting laws.[1] Edmund Carlisle, owner of the huge Kansas and New Mexico Land and Cattle Company, informed the Southern Ute agent in 1884 that a group of Indians had left the reservation with written permission from a local trader. According to Carlisle, they had been setting fire to the timberlands on the south side of Blue Mountain in San Juan County, causing severe damage, and had not only killed deer but also cattle.[2] The livestock owners wanted soldiers sent to control the Utes and "other Indians." More letters followed, indicating that this hunting group, composed of forty Southern Utes and the same number of Navajos, were heading west to continue the chase.[3] Cowboys and citizens alike threatened to form groups to attack the Indians, and though no organized posse moved against them, anger and frustration continued to mount.[4]

The mention of setting fires was very likely part of what settler Frank Silvey called "the great deer roundup" during that year. He had enjoyed frequent contact with many of the San Juan Paiutes and Utes, including Bridger Jack. According to Silvey, many of the Southern Utes saw that they had lost everything and viewed the remaining deer as their last opportunity to return to the old days. They came into San Juan County around the La Sal area and either killed or drove many of the deer to southwestern Colorado, leaving the area "stinking with dead carcasses of deer. Our cattle and horses were so frightened that they would not stay on the fine grass on the mountain but would string out for the low country."[5]

The Weenuche living in the San Juan area joined the Southern Utes this first year, collectively forming a group estimated at three hundred men. With guns firing and red blankets waving, they drove thousands of deer south and into Colorado. This happened again in 1885 and 1886, by which time the Utes living in southeastern Utah were totally opposed to outsiders taking deer; friction resulted. According to Silvey, "The many fights they had with the Southern Utes for many years were based on this disagreement."[6]

The next years showed little improvement. In 1885 one man complained that half of the Southern Utes were off the reservation, burning grass and killing cattle because the Indians were suffering from hunger, and that he dared not hunt for fear of being killed. The following year the people of Moab recounted how they had been bullied when the Utes passed through on a hunting expedition that had netted "several thousand deer [killed] simply for their hides."[7] The townspeople swore that if the Utes and their friends did not leave, the whites would handle the situation in their own way. Reports in 1887 read much the same: an estimated two hundred Southern Utes "armed to the teeth and hunting" were in the La Sals and Blue Mountain area; at the same time, eighty Utes went north and killed more than two hundred deer. Many of these were fawns, whose skins sold for twenty-five cents each. Only a tenth of the meat was taken. White

settlers again complained bitterly about this wanton destruction.[8] Another party of forty Utes with seventy-five to one hundred horses was killing deer, while "Mariano and Red Jacket [had] returned from their hunt and had lots of buckskins." A petition signed by sixty-four men from McElmo Canyon, located west of the Ute reservation, complained that the Indians would not allow the whites to kill game.[9] The settlers felt it would not take much to start a large conflict.[10]

By 1889 the new Ute agent, Charles A. Bartholomew, was in a quandary. Based on the 1874 treaty provisions, the Southern Utes had the right to hunt off their reservation "so long as the game lasts and the Indians are at peace with white people." As far as the agent was concerned, the problem was not a matter of the Indians being at peace with the white people, but vice versa. When Ignacio and others approached him for permission to leave on a hunt, Bartholomew sent a letter to the commissioner of Indian Affairs in Washington, Thomas J. Morgan, asking what he should do. Morgan waffled. Citing what he considered a "lawless class of white people in Colorado" who looked for opportunities to create conflict, he was not anxious to grant permission for the Indians to leave their reservation. Yet, they were promised by treaty that they could. His response: "I will not consent to their going, nor prohibit them from exercising their lawful right. If they choose to go, they must take the responsibility."[11] The question rested again on Bartholomew's shoulders; the Southern Utes went hunting.

White men, however, were not the only ones concerned about the herds. Southern Utes again ventured into Utah to either kill or drive more deer, which the Weenuche in San Juan County wished to put a stop to. Hatch and a small group of "Paiutes" were camped at Peters (Hill) Spring with a group of Southern Utes led by Cowboy. During what had been to that point a friendly card game, Hatch verbally attacked the Southern Utes for their useless slaughter of the deer herds. Cowboy went on the defense, became angered, and shot Hatch, forcing the groups to separate. Hatch's friends immediately killed both Cowboy and his brother. Before leaving, Hatch's family placed his body under a small ledge, burned the remains, and killed three horses for his afterlife journey. Later, a vicious fight between two women from the different factions ensued in Monticello, while the men dismounted and prepared for a shootout amidst the settlers' cabins and stores. Cooler heads prevailed, and both groups went their way, but not without leaving a vivid reminder of the importance of the deer herds to all Indian peoples.[12]

Local newspapers cried foul. One article, titled "Send the Soldiers," told of how Navajos and Utes were "killing game and alarming the people." Edmund Carlisle wrote to the governor of Utah, who wrote to Morgan, who wrote to Bartholomew, telling the agent to recall all Indians to their agencies. The Ute agent sent runners to the principal chiefs asking about their kinsmen. He was told that most were at home, that they had not been and were not now involved in hunting for skins only, and that the cattlemen had fabricated these reports in an effort to control the range.[13] Bartholomew agreed with the chiefs' point of view, sent a notice to the newspapers explaining the Indians' position, and said he was making every effort to recall any stray groups.[14] The military concurred with the agent, stating that the Indians had as much or more right to the public domain than the cattlemen, they were not receiving enough food on the reservation, they had been behaving themselves, and that "it would be extremely cruel to drive them back."[15]

To investigate the conflicting reports, the military sent Second Lieutenant George Williams to Blue Mountain in December 1889. Although he saw no hunters, he estimated that two to three hundred Navajos and Utes had been hunting there, but had returned to their reservations. The Indians had "killed a good many deer as is shown by the number of hides they have sold to the trader."[16] The twelve families living in Monticello, at the base of the mountain, reported that the Utes were after hides and meat, the Navajos primarily hides. The trader, Mons Peterson, believed that the latter sold more green hides than the Utes because of superior horses and hunting techniques. Many of the cowmen complained that with all of the Indians chasing through the woods, the livestock had grown wild and harder to herd. Williams also reported a problem with too many Indian hunting parties in the same territory. Navajos and Utes did not traditionally get along with each other, and rubbing shoulders while armed in the isolation of the mountains could lead to an explosive situation.

Williams noted that camped outside of Monticello was a group of "ten to fifteen Renegade Indians commonly called Pi-Utes. The principal Indian and leader among them, although not recognized as a chief, is Mancos Jim." This band had Uintah, Los Pinos, "and some few from other tribes" who spent the winter near Bluff. The settlers got along well with them, which was not true of people from the cattle companies. According to Williams, "It is not likely that the Indians are guilty of doing nearly all that they are accused of."[17] Incidentally, the Southern Utes had returned to the reservation from hunting on Blue Mountain as soon as they received word from their agent, whereas the Navajos lingered for several additional weeks.

In the 1890s decreased access to resources for the Utes and an expanding Navajo population intensified competition for what remained. Dozens of individuals from Grand and San Juan Counties signed more petitions complaining about Indian hunting practices and depredations on livestock. They still mentioned Ute activities, but the Navajos now stood center stage in the drama of pursuing the herds.[18] Bartholomew took the opportunity to show that despite the fact that his charges were on the reservation and much of the hunting was being done by Navajos, the blame was still being placed on the Utes. He even sent a letter to the Navajo agent saying that the Utes and their white neighbors were complaining about Navajos killing game both on and north of the Ute reservation. He commanded them to leave with all of their livestock and no longer make the Utes' land their headquarters for preying on cattle and deer.[19] Others also expressed concerns about the Navajos living outside their reservation. Citizens of Spar City, Colorado, complained that a party of twelve Navajos had killed seven elk and thirty deer, leaving the carcasses to "rot and fester in the sun." The settlers blamed the Navajo agent for allowing the "red pests" to be away from their lands. In 1893 the governor of Colorado wrote to President Grover Cleveland griping about groups of 100 to 150 Navajos and Utes who had left their reservations because of lack of rations and then proceeded to destroy bucks, does, and fawns. When the deer "congregated at certain times of the year…[they were] attacked in full force," leaving the game wardens helpless when confronted with such large numbers of Indians.[20]

Bartholomew again denied it. He pointed out that he rarely gave passes to Utes for off-reservation hunting, that the Utes at his agency were all present and accounted for, that he knew of large Navajo foraging parties operating in the area, and that his charges were faithful to the United States, kept the game laws, and were ready to serve as a force for good against the "Navajo menace."[21] He went on, "I can safely say that the 250 young warriors with their own chiefs to lead them would be of greater service to the government than the entire state militia could possibly be as every warrior is a veteran, fully armed and equipped and always ready and could be thrown to the front while the militia is getting ready." Bartholomew also did not believe that the Weenuche hunted for hides only. All the meat, even the intestines, was used and was "dried as fast as killed and sent to camp."[22] From Ignacio's perspective, "When [we] gave up the mountains and the mines [we] did not give up the game, and [we are] only going after that which belongs to us…. The whites pass through the reservation every day; they camp and lie down and sleep; no one hurts them. When we go it is the same. We are friends."[23] The agent concluded by saying that the Indians were going about their lawful business and that if there were to be issues, they would be raised by the white people.

While there are few quantitative tallies of how many deer were killed by Indians, and certainly some of the white accounts were exaggerated for effect, a couple of accounts give a glimpse of this period. In the fall of 1890 Old Mexican, a Navajo from the Montezuma Creek/Aneth area, told of hunting with a group of relatives on Blue Mountain for thirty-three days, killing a total of seventy bucks and does. Less than a week after his return home, he left again with a party of three. They hunted only for skins and killed sixty-seven more animals. He personally had twenty-two hides, twelve of which he sold to a trader at fifty cents apiece. Ten years later he could have sold two hides at the Aneth post for $7, but chose to sell them in Crystal, New Mexico, farther inside the reservation, for $30.75.[24] Supply and demand economics operated across the counters of the trading posts.

This decimation of game was not confined to the Southwest.[25] By 1894 the Shoshones and Bannocks, as well as white hunters, were also whittling away at deer and elk populations. Reports came from Idaho, Wyoming, Montana, northern Utah, and the Dakotas, but were especially prevalent around Yellowstone Park, where visitors complained of some gruesome sights. A Supreme Court decision pertaining to the Wyoming-Bannock case stated that the Indians were now subject to the game laws of the state or territory in which they hunted, and that agents could issue passes for travel off of the reservation, but that the Indians could not hunt while en route. According to the government, "The slaughter of wild animals in vast numbers for hides only and the abandonment of carcasses…is as much a violation of the treaty as an absolute prohibition on the part of the United States against the exercise of such privilege."[26] All Indians now fell under this stricture and were responsible for abiding by state laws.

In the spring of 1886, a season when trouble usually arose between cowboys and Indians on the open range, there was none. Indeed, once the Weenuche in southeastern Utah felt the government was going to leave them alone, they went to the trading posts and exchanged rifle ammunition for other needed supplies. Equally important for the military, the cowboys were quiet. "There will be no trouble this summer unless a fight is started by the whites. This is the usual manner in which trouble begins, and the cattlemen have been warned both by Captain Thomas and myself [Second Lieutenant C. G. Morton, Sixth Infantry] against such proceedings in the future."[27] By early fall the cattlemen had completed their roundup, and the Utes were still hunting. Companies from Fort Lewis continued to provide security for cattlemen to prevent a low-grade fever of discontent from erupting into something larger.

That same year, however, issues with settlers flared into prominence. McElmo Canyon, a prime agricultural spot as well as major thoroughfare for Indian and white travelers moving from the San Juan River to Sleeping Ute Mountain, turned into an arena of conflict. Mariano and Red Jacket's people camped near its mouth and intimidated the settlers living in its confines by demanding food, tearing down fences, visiting ranches when the men were away, grazing livestock on white ranges, stealing tools and horses, and killing cattle. The whites demanded that soldiers be permanently stationed there to maintain peace, while the Utes accused the settlers of building on reservation lands. Captain J. B. Irvine, Twenty-second Infantry, spent Christmas week sorting out the matter.[28]

Irvine visited the Utes in their camps and found them friendly and desiring peace, but he was also aware that when he left, problems would arise. They spoke freely of their frustration. McElmo Canyon was narrow, so the settlers built brush fences spanning the canyon width about every mile to control their livestock. When the Indians passed through, they made a gap in the fence and did not repair it, or took down the gate bars and did not replace them. The trading post at Mitchell Springs served as a constant draw. The settlers, on the other hand, were tired of chasing strayed stock, fixing fence, and being forced to cook for "squads" of Indians who ranged in number from four to twelve and demanded food. When the men were gone, the Indians intimidated their families to the point that husbands had to remain home and could not conduct business.

Consider, for example, the situation of A. L. Smaed, who lived near Fortress Rock, midway in the canyon. One night a Ute known as "Billy the Kid" and six others arrived at his ranch. They invited him to their camp nearby. When he refused, Billy grabbed his ear and tried to yank him out of the cabin. The settler retreated inside, returned fire that chased them off, hid his valuables, and traveled upcanyon under cover of darkness to another settler's homestead. The Utes arrived there soon after, demanding to see Smaed, but with several well-armed men in the vicinity, they did not push the point and left. The end result was a petition signed by sixty-four local settlers, which brought Captain Irvine to their door. After hearing this and more, the captain contacted Stollsteimer, urging him to have all of the Utes return to the reservation without delay; if the agent did not do this, a party of soldiers would have to be stationed there to keep the peace. Apparently Stollsteimer succeeded, because Irvine returned to his post later in January. The

The conflicting forces of acculturation on the Ute Mountain Ute Reservation at the turn of the century are represented here. Agent Joe Smith (*back left*), while sympathetic to the Weenuche situation, insisted that they abandon traditional practices. Ignacio (*center*), as tribal chief and head of Indian police, had to enforce the government's plans but did not always agree. Mariano (*seated right*) represented the old ways and resisted change, coming in conflict with both the agent and Ignacio. (Denver Public Library, Western History Collection, photographer unknown, X-30732)

agent suggested that the troops remain at McElmo throughout the spring and summer.

But if the Indians were guilty of perpetrating wrongs, so was the white community. To their credit, some citizens called foul on their neighbors on behalf of the Utes. Postmaster J. F. Daugherty in McElmo complained of white men grazing herds of sheep on reservation land, which in turn forced the Utes to leave in search of other pasture. This gave rise to complaints from men like Harold Carlisle, who demanded that the Utes return to their own lands with their flocks and stay away from the winter range, with its springs on the public domain near the western boundary of the reservation.[29] Another settler living in the Cortez area said that not only were "hundreds of cattle" grazing on Ute lands, and that horses had been stolen and cabins burned by white men who then blamed the Indians, but that it was white entrepreneurs who were encouraging the Indians to steal horses and sell them to white buyers. Ironically, some cattlemen wanted the Indians to remain where they were be-

cause reservation lands were easier to access when under the control of the Utes, whereas farmers wanted them removed in order to open the land for settlement.[30]

The whole business of horse stealing infuriated both sides. Alonzo P. Edmonson, who lived in McElmo, had horses stolen from him and driven to Mariano's camp. When confronted, "Mariano acted very ugly and gave Mr. Edmonson to understand that it is his intention to clean out the settlements on the lower San Juan...and he [Mariano] had a great deal to say about the loss of [his] horse," which he had bought from John R. Pond. The animal had been previously repossessed by its true owner. This incident was "still rankling in the breast of Mariano."[31] A week later a letter warned that Mariano had moved his camp above Edmonson's ranch and that he had driven some of the settler's hired hands out of Yellow Jacket Canyon. Many of the women left alone on the ranches in McElmo were at the mercy of these "red devils." The agent quickly replied that there would be no problems since Mariano was now on the reservation, lying sick in Ignacio's camp. As for the issue of Mariano's replevied horse, Bartholomew investigated the incident, exonerated the Ute of misdeed, and charged Pond to either return Mariano's payment or face a trial in court against the U.S. government.[32] No doubt Mariano appreciated Bartholomew's stand.

During this course of events the situation on the Ute reservation unfolded in an equally irritating manner. Cattlemen were grazing their herds at Navajo Springs. Ignacio demanded their removal. Colonel Peter T. Swaine insisted that the cowboys "do so without the use of a military force to eject them."[33] While the commander appeared willing to use troops if the cowboys did not comply, his superior was not as eager. With Ignacio's desire to camp at Navajo Springs, the unrest in McElmo Canyon, and the encroachment of livestock on Ute lands, Swaine's commander suggested establishing a subagency in that general vicinity. This would enable them to monitor problems on the western end of the reservation, decrease the use of troops, and provide an authoritative presence.[34] While the development of this site was another eight years away, the seed had been planted, and the Navajo Springs Agency (later moved a short distance to today's Towaoc) eventually established government control in this troubled area.

This was not true for Bluff, another hot spot. By 1884 the Utes, who had historically used this area as a winter camp, were confronted with dramatic changes. The Mormons had obtained a large flock of sheep from New Mexicans, adding to their burgeoning cattle herds; non-Mormon livestock companies controlled much of the grazing land to the north; and Navajo herds were pushing from the south. All of this placed environmental strain on the ranges and put grazing land at a premium. Kumen Jones, a Mormon missionary to both Utes and Navajos, hoped to deal with the land issue by holding open discussions with them.

There was a big powwow held with all of the Utes and Paiutes that were come-at-able at that time and a treaty or contract was entered into with them, by which on our part were to pay the Indians two or three hundred dollars in flour, merchandise, and ponies. And with the exception of Posey and one or two others, the Indians lived up to their part of the contract very satisfactorily.... The way that mountain was eaten up by cattle and sheep from the day of that treaty to the coming of the Forest Service, probably made the old Indian's [Mancos Jim] head swim.[35]

Even with the urging of Mariano, who visited the Utah Utes, to remain at peace and not accept payment for the use of Elk Mountain, there was still discontent.[36]

The Utes' situation became increasingly untenable. Starvation stood at their doorstep, a major change from ten years before. Hammond easily identified why, on November 28, 1887, when he wrote: "A few Utes and Paiutes are camped near our house, just down in the bottom. They are constantly begging, poor creatures. They have a hard time since the white man has come with his immense herds of stock. The game which was formally plentiful is now very scarce and the poor Indian is hard pushed to obtain a living."[37] Hammond assigned Thales Haskell, interpreter and ambassador to the Navajos and Utes, to establish an Indian farm at the southeast base of Elk Mountain. The potential of raising fruits and vegetables was good except for the fact that agricultural undertakings were anathema to the Utes, who for the most part did not get along with the Navajos. Few came, and those that did complained of a "heap sore back." But Haskell had won their respect through perseverance, with Henry, a friendly young Ute, declaring, "Haskell all the time one talk." Mancos Jim echoed these sentiments with "me heap like um."[38]

In spite of the goodwill toward some Mormons, for those grazing cattle on Elk Ridge the "Pahutes and renegade Utes" were "feeling quite ugly and mean." They remained on their land, killing cattle and grazing large bands of horses in direct competition with white livestock herds.[39] In July there were also large Ute camps on Montezuma, Recapture, and Indian Creeks. So when a Ute reported finding Henry Hopkins, a young cook for George Brooks's cowboy outfit, shot twice in the back at the head of Devils Canyon, suspicion immediately fell on the Indians. The young man's pistol and rifle were missing, but nothing else in the camp had been touched. An evening thundershower had erased all tracks. There had been two Navajos in the area who had argued with Hopkins a few days previous. In spite of the investigation, the crime was never solved.[40] Mariano, however, went with a group of twenty or thirty Southern Utes to Brooks's camp and explained that they knew nothing about the killing and wanted to live in peace. They then returned to the reservation. The investigating officer linked this event to the Beaver Creek massacre, two years before, since the Indians "still spoke of that dastardly affair in the most bitter terms and with violent hatred towards the cowboys in all their talks with white people."[41] Potential for increased violence was enough to keep the soldiers in the area for months, not only to watch the Indians, who had been urged three times to return to the reservation, but also "the white men in the locality [who] are contemplating to secretly organize a strong force and attack and massacre not only the [Pahutes] but all Southern Utes they would be able to get at."[42]

Although friction continued, there were also friendly relations with many Ute people living in southeastern Utah. Two astute Anglo observers—Albert R. Lyman and Frank Silvey—recorded personal observations and experiences of people who would otherwise have been lost to history. What they wrote may be tinged with a slanted view of the time that might be criticized from a twenty-first-century perspective. Yet their observation gives a somewhat sympathetic

impression of daily life on the frontier of the 1880s and '90s.

Take, for instance, Silvey's experience with Bridger Jack.[43] The two met around 1882, when Bridger Jack was about eighteen, three years older than Silvey. He spoke a little English, and so after he and a group of Utes had been fed by the Silveys on two different occasions, the family selected him as their representative. They pointed out that they had to haul supplies 135 miles from Durango and so they could not continually be feeding large groups of guests. The Indians understood and came alone or with a single companion. Bridger Jack often brought buckskins to trade for potatoes or money, and gave the family a piece of deer meat as a present. Silvey's sister, Clara, made gloves and shirts from the hides, which were "always good ones."

Bridger and Frank became personal friends. The young cowboy had bought a horse from two men who found the stray on the range. They warned that it very well could be an Indian pony and so buyer beware, but Frank had worked enough with the horse to know it was a first-rate cowpony and tireless worker. Man and animal forged an inseparable bond. One day a dozen Indians, including Bridger, Hatch (recently back from a year in a federal penitentiary), and Wash, appeared at the cabin door, described the horse in detail, and demanded its return. Frank was irate, his mother and father scared, and the Indians insistent that the horse belonged to a member of their party named Jim Crow. Frank, in his youthful inexperience, strapped on his six-shooter, ready to fight for what he wanted, but also realized the Indians were probably justified. After thinking it over, he went with two of them to the pasture to get the animal, but upon his return, learned that Bridger and Clara had worked out a deal that satisfied all. The young cowboy kept his horse and strengthened a friendship. "I could have shouted for joy, but remained stolid and Indian-like and did not express my feelings."[44]

Bridger, who lived with his band around La Sal, was a handsome man and dressed well, but he had one weakness—living a life on luck. Mons Peterson ran a store in Monticello from 1889 to 1891. During his travels he encountered Bridger with a group of ponies. He inquired where the Ute had gotten them and received the reply, "My grandmudder she die at Uintah, leave me pony." With that he was on his way. A month later Mons met him in Dry Valley with more horses and was told, "My brother at Uintah, he die and leave me more ponies and me swap with Navajos." A few weeks later Mons saw a large dust cloud approaching, with Bridger herding horses as fast as he could. He dismounted, got on a fresh animal, and stopped only long enough to reply to the query of "Your grandmother die again?" "Maybe so," he said. "Me no time to talk, heap go." Four Uintah Utes rode in hot pursuit but never caught him. Silvey concluded his recounting of this episode with, "It is said that Bridger soon gambled them off to the Navajos at 'Monte.'"[45]

Gambling turned out to be his undoing. In 1894 Bridger was camped with his band at Peters Spring with some other Utes, among them one of his friends, Wash. Their gambling turned into a dispute that ended with the two men each taking twenty paces before turning and firing at each other. Bridger whirled and shot in the air; Wash shot him through the heart. Years later Silvey saw Wash at the Navajo Springs Agency, looking old, depressed, and acting a little crazy. Those days he brooded a lot about having killed his friend.[46]

Farther south, at Bluff, Albert R. Lyman was recording his life with the Mormons. While their experience was far more settled than that of the Colorado cowboys, there was still friction over lost land. The story told by Willard Butt, through Lyman, serves as an anecdote of the love-hate relationship that grew over the years between two struggling cultures.[47] Around 1885 Butt was in the

Albert R. Lyman, "One With a Beard," late 1950s. As a local historian, Lyman did more to record otherwise irretrievable information about the Ute people in southeastern Utah than any other person of his time. Although he was occasionally in conflict with them, he grew increasingly sympathetic toward their plight as he aged. White Mesa elders today remember him for his kindness and educational efforts. (Courtesy of San Juan County Historical Commission)

Little Valleys east of Elk Mountain. In a cave known as Milk Ranch, he was preparing to fix a lunch when Whiskers, a Ute so named because of a short, bristly beard that curved under his chin, stepped out from the brush. Leveling his rifle at the Mormon cowboy and squinting down the barrel, he demanded, "Me heap hungry! Biscuits you pixum. Meat you pixum, coffee, peogament (sugar). Hurry up, you. Maybe so me killum you." Butt was not the type to trifle with, but the constant bead on his chest convinced him to comply. Amidst demands of "Mo biscuits you now pixum; heap big eat me likeum," "Mo meat," and "Hurry up, whatsa matta you," the cowboy set to work under the Ute's furtive gaze. When the meal was ready, Whiskers ate his fill and then backed into the bushes and disappeared. Butt fumed and swore revenge, but it would be years before he saw the old man again, this time in Montezuma Canyon. It was around noon, and Butt was following the tracks of a horse ridden by an unknown Paiute. When he came abreast, he recognized Whiskers, who "seemed passively friendly now and had no recollection of their meeting before. He was old and alone; the once ebony braids were streaked with gray, his face pinched and withered, looking forsaken and forlorn. Even his pony was jaded and poor, and fortune seemed to have frowned on him from every side." The two rode together until Butt needed to take a different fork in the trail. Although he had always thought of the day he would exact revenge, the cowboy asked the Indian if he was hungry, as if he needed confirmation of what he saw. Reaching behind his saddle, he took his "special" lunch and gave it all to the old man before spurring his horse up the diverging path. Behind him he heard, "Adios, my heap perty good prien."

Poverty had also exacted its toll on the marginalized Utes living around Bluff. Lyman shares short vignettes that portray the lives of a struggling people who were becoming increasingly dependent on the community because of lost self-sufficiency.[48] Mike Moancopy (Moenkopi) visited the San Juan Co-op Store to exchange wool for his "necessities of life." The storekeeper, realizing that the same amount of wool was missing from his supply as Mike was selling, placed a wolf trap by a loose chink in the storeroom wall and checked his bait the next morning. He found Mike waiting for him. Corporal punishment put an end to the Paiute's theft and threats.

Paddy Soldiercoat, so named for the cavalry jacket he obtained at the Soldier Crossing fight, took punishment one step further. A Ute called Grasshopper made the mistake of stealing some of Paddy's horses. A lengthy chase eventually led Paddy, in warpaint with drawn rifle, through the town of Bluff, in pursuit of Grasshopper, dressed in a red shirt. The two disappeared, and for days no one

knew what had happened until a boy herding sheep near the mouth of Recapture Wash investigated a pile of stones and found a body dressed in a red shirt with a hole in the center of the forehead. Another time a Navajo named Mustache ran into Paddy in the store after stealing some of his horses. Before the town, "Paddy hopped like a cat onto him, bore him to the ground and dragged him around in the street to his heart's content, jerking his long black locks left and right. He stomped, kicked, and slapped him and called him 'skane spirit' and other terrible names in perfect Navajo eloquence."[49] Lyman closes this tale by commenting, "It is not known that Paddy received any reward for this good work, though he deserved to be mentioned."

The historian also identified relationships and favorite family campsites of some of the better-known Utes.[50] Narraguinip, for instance, had four sons—Hatch, Bishop, Polk, and Teegre—all of whom followed in their father's footsteps in resisting white encroachment. Polk Narraguinip became particularly well known during the late nineteenth and early twentieth century, not only for his warlike posture, but also as the brother-in-law of a Paiute named Green Hair, also known as Posey, who married Polk's younger sister, Toorah. Posey received his name from a cowboy he admired, Bill Posey, while his brother Scotty received his from a wrangler named John Scott. Both Paiutes were born at Navajo Mountain and had a subservient relationship to Polk, with his Ute ancestry. Posey camped at favorite spots like Elk Mountain, Long Point, Peavine Canyon, Cottonwood Wash, Woodenshoe, and the area below Bluff. Mancos Jim, on the other hand, considered Allen Canyon his primary home, saying that "his fathers were sleeping in Allen Canyon…his own bones should rest there with them."[51]

There were other Utes and Paiutes who evoked gentle memories. Peeage (Piágaki— "Itch"), Paddy's grandmother, always said, "Mucho tired," and so endeared herself to the people of Bluff that when she died, the settlers laid her body to rest in their cemetery. There was Broken Arm, who raised her motherless granddaughter by chewing food in her worn teeth before giving it to the young girl to eat. Chee-poots, Posey's father, had warts all over his hands; Frank was stooped and slow, but had a reputation for killing bad medicine men; and George Ute, who told one of the settlers where five stray cows were grazing but failed to tell about a sixth one he had butchered, received chastisement for his partial truth. Despite their shortcomings, for Lyman, "To be in their camps in the hills and mountains, to nibble their dry hunks of unsalted venison, to hear them sing and see them dance, to watch them milk their goats and trail the wild buckskin among tangles of oak and quaking-asp, was somehow to cherish for them a strong sympathy akin to love."[52]

While the Bluff historian, in reflecting upon the past, may have felt "strong sympathy akin to love," very little of that was experienced on the Southern Ute Reservation at this time. A rapid glance at what transpired between 1887 and 1893 shows a group of people in painful transition. Population numbers remained fairly constant—approximately 260 Muaches, 180 Capotes, and 535 Weenuche Utes—but everything else was in flux.[53] Attempts to grow crops met with mediocre success. There were few irrigation ditches, without which agriculture became impracticable "in order to bring crops out of the ground [upon which] the white farmer often fails."[54] Between early snows, heavy rains, drought, market conditions, and related expenses, little profit came from the fourteen farms growing oats, wheat, and barley.[55] All of these were on the eastern, or Muache/Capote, end of the reservation and not under cultivation by the Weenuche Utes, who struggled with their own efforts with animal husbandry. Unfortunately, the boundaries of Ute lands were so porous that white thieves regularly stole their livestock, while white ranchers continued to avail themselves of Ute grasslands. Winter-kill of cattle unable to paw through the snow to find feed forced the Weenuche Utes to divert part of their effort to growing and storing hay.

But of all of the problems that the Utes faced, education received the most attention. Stollsteimer, in 1886, faced strong resistance from the mothers, who pointed to the experience of some of their children who two years before had gone to school in Albuquerque. Half never returned because of disease. That is why of the 267 children between the ages of six to sixteen who were eligible to attend, only twelve to fourteen entered the classroom.[56] Power politics came into play when the commissioner of Indian Affairs suggested that "rations be withheld and a sufficient military force be stationed at the agency for protection in case the Indians should resist the measure."[57] The next year Stollsteimer achieved the same results, with 1888 being even worse due to a measles epidemic that lasted all winter and killed several people. The fact that the boarding school was located two miles from agency headquarters at Ignacio, in the eastern part of the reservation, did not encourage the Weenuche Utes to think about sending their children such a long distance to join the fourteen enrolled. Plus, the dormitory was unsafe, constructed of rotting logs and a heavy dirt roof that could collapse. The fact that water had to be hauled from the river, bathroom facilities were lacking, and accommodations for the children were inadequate were also disincentives to enroll. Even the parents of those attending noticed how "the structure [dormitory/mess hall] had become a veritable death trap and was liable to cause a catastrophe."[58] The school soon closed, and the buildings were demolished.

The commissioner, however, was upset. He demanded to know from the agent why the school, which had the capacity for 25 students, had only an average attendance of 13, even though there was a potential of 354. "With the authority placed in your hands, I see no excuse for the very meager attendance at the school."[59] Stollsteimer again reported the poor condition of the building and the necessity of its destruction, the fact that an influenza epidemic on the reservation had sent students home, and above all, that there was significant distrust of the government. Congress had not ratified past agreements, there was no apparent resolution of issues, and previous agents had raised hopes over false expectations. Commissioner Morgan returned again to hard-ball politics, saying that for an Indian to receive any money from a gratuity fund tied to the 1880 treaty agreement, one of the principal qualifications was for "his willingness to send and keep his children in school."[60] The money was now a reward attached to education.

Even more abrasive were events surrounding the Utes' leader, Ignacio. In 1889 he had received praise and over $250 from the gratuity account for "being the most influential man in the tribe who uses his influence to a good advantage in advising his people to settle down permanently and be quiet and peaceable…. [He was currently] farming and very reliable."[61] In 1892 Morgan again complimented him and others, offering to do whatever he could for their prosperity and happiness as well as to personally meet with them. He did, however, wish that they would send forty boys and twenty-five girls to school immediately. It did not happen, so two months later Morgan wrote another letter to Ignacio, then chief of police of the Southern Utes, castigating him for opposing Ute children going to school. Morgan discharged him from his position, chastised Bartholomew for not doing it himself, and directed that a new leader be put in place. The agent fired off a response saying that Ignacio was chief of the Southern Utes, that both the Navajos and whites recognized him as such and shared mutual respect, that he was a strong influence for peace, and that his advice was excellent. At one point he had encouraged students to go to school, but when an epidemic of "sore eye" broke out,

he ceased all efforts and became immoveable in resisting any efforts to put children in that setting.[62] Petitions and congressional support followed, backing Bartholomew's position and demanding that Ignacio be promptly reinstated. A week later Morgan revoked the dismissal and Ignacio returned to his influential positions.

In 1892 Fort Lewis became a regional school for Native American children.[63] Boasting about the ability to convert the barracks and administrative building into dining, boarding, and classroom facilities to accommodate "a very large number of students," the government increased pressure to enroll more students. Morgan directed Bartholomew to "use such compulsion as may seem wise…that the largest possible number of Ute children should have the advantages of the school," which meant he should "secure at least 100 children from the Utes."[64] The commissioner also made clear that Bartholomew's failure to comply would confirm rumors that the agent was working from his own agenda — "if you fail to procure Ute children for this school, the fault will be yours." That year sixteen children attended; two of them died, and three went blind. The next year the Southern Utes had a new agent.[65] There was also a new commissioner of Indian Affairs, who reversed Morgan's approach, insisting that no children would be removed from any reservation without the parents' and agent's approval, and that their consent must be voluntary.[66]

By 1893 events both on and off the reservation pointed to the fact that mixing white communities and goals with those of the Indians was like trying to blend oil with water. There certainly had been progress over the relatively short span of time, given the scale of change forced upon the Ute people, but friction still abounded. With off-reservation Ute warriors acting "sassy" and challenging cowboys that they were ready to fight; with "a very large number of bad white men… [who] are ready at any time to murder a few

Indians to get their ponies;" with the troubles around McElmo and in southeastern Utah; with the porous borders of the reservation; with some Weenuche Utes under Johnny Benow living off the reservation and having "the appearance of extreme poverty, looking half-starved, are nearly naked, and [some] are subsisting upon rations issued to the Southern Utes;" with a large number of "renegade Paiutes" under no one's control, much to "the annoyance of settlers and stockmen;" and with all of the friction raised by two different cultural communities living in close proximity, it was time for a change—a change that had been discussed for years.[67]

As early as 1885 the Ute chiefs had approached Stollsteimer with demands for such change—a new reservation that met their needs and would keep them away from disputes with white men. The agent took a delegation of leaders with him to Washington, who returned "full of hope that their wishes would be gratified" and that they would be removed to a better reservation.[68] Nothing happened, turning their hope "into a constant clamor and muttering," translated into daily expressions of discontent coupled with threats. Two years later the government took steps to reduce the entire concept of reservations when on February 8, 1887, the General Allotment, or Dawes, Act passed Congress. By providing individual Indian ownership of the land, it took those holdings from existing reservations, gave male heads of families 160 acres, single males 80 acres, and male minors 40 acres, and then opened remaining undistributed lands to settlement as part of the public domain.[69] There were other amenities added for those who participated, but fundamental to the act was the belief that private ownership would get the Indian out from under the "blanket," an item of clothing worn constantly and with pride by reservation denizens. On the eastern end of the Southern Ute Reservation there had been limited agriculture and some construction of irrigation ditches. On the western end,

Johnny Benow (*right*), an "off-reservation Indian," made his home in Montezuma Canyon and had a side canyon named after him. This photo was taken after he and a companion rode into Professor Byron Cummings's camp during his 1907 expedition in San Juan County and insisted that the archaeologist leave Montezuma Canyon; Cummings refused but remained unharmed. (Courtesy of Smithsonian National Anthropological Archives)

where the Weenuche lived, not a single foot of ditch existed, their efforts being tied into livestock. They did not know if there was sufficient water to grow crops on an individual basis, how that water would get to one's allotment, or if the weather and soil were suitable enough to make it profitable. Stollsteimer agreed it was far too much of a gamble and supported the Weenuche Utes' refusal to initiate the process.[70]

To Coloradoans anxious to get the Southern Utes out of their state, sending them to the Uintah Reservation, where they had sent the Northern Utes, seemed practical. After all, they were the same people. The Southern Utes heartily disagreed. For the past thirty years these two groups had been locked in "a deadly feud" with "bad blood" stemming from an unknown issue.[71] Given the antics of Bridger Jack and others, friction kept the animosity smoldering, removing the possibility of the two groups peacefully sharing the land. Add to this the already strained relations between the Utah Uintah Utes and the recently implanted White River Utes from Colorado, and frictions between the Muache/Capote and the Weenuche Utes, the concept of joint ownership offered little chance of success.

A new reservation was still in the offing. As people cast about for a place to move the Utes, southeastern Utah appeared to be the least inhabited and would provide a minimum of disruption to the people of Colorado and the expansive Navajo Reservation. Indeed, in previous discussions, it became apparent that the commissioner of Indian Affairs was not even aware that there were white settlements in that part of Utah. The official position of the Mormon Church was that it did not want to give up Bluff or its other holdings. For the people of this settlement to move to Mancos or Yellow Jacket, Colorado, would require the Mormons to relinquish control of the area and ask people to give up their improvements and a promising economy.[72]

Some of the Indians had their own ideas. Bridger Jack requested that the government establish a reservation near Blue Mountain, where his people could receive agricultural supplies and assistance building ditches. Stollsteimer responded that the government probably would not establish a little reservation next to the Southern Utes, but how would Bridger feel about moving the Southern Utes to Utah? He was fine with that, and Mariano chimed in, saying that a reservation for both Utes and Paiutes in that location might work.[73] Shortly after this discussion Washington formed a three-member

Southern Ute Commission to initiate steps to purchase all of San Juan County for a reservation. The dialogue that this action prompted continued for seven years, with all the drama of a first-rate political brouhaha.[74]

The Ute Commission had the responsibility of reporting all improvements made by settlers in Bluff so that the government could reimburse them when relocated. Francis A. Hammond accepted the task of determining the extent of improvements, their value, and how much the government should pay. This he did for both Mormon and non-Mormon settlers. Still, no one seemed thrilled with the initial prospect of moving. After insinuating mistrust of the government and outlining considerations it should take, Hammond wrote:

> I trust you will consider all these matters, and the great trouble and expense connected with the removal of our people from this section to God only knows where, to found new homes and give up our homes to the Indians. Some of the families who will have to move are not able to, unless they are paid for their claims, as they are about all they have of this world's goods—not even teams to move with.
>
> We have been here some nine years struggling hard to hold and redeem this country; standing guard as it were, on the outpost, to protect our more wealthy populous counties from the raids of Indians and renegade white men, white renegades being far the worst. We have had heavy and constant tax upon us of about three hundred Paiutes and renegade Indians from other tribes to feed and partially clothe since ever we located here; previous to our settling here life and property were not safe anywhere in this section, but owing to our pacific treatment of the Indians and our constant watch of the cattle and horse thieves, the country is now full of large cattle, sheep, and horse herds.[75]

Still, the residents were not disheartened with the possibility of moving because they believed the government would pay full value for lost property. Hammond's wife wrote her husband that "it is amusing to hear the sisters [LDS women] talk that they all hope and pray that this place will go in to Indian reservation."[76] The Mormon Church counseled them that if they did have to move, not to move too far, so that they could continue to "more effectually carry out the object of their mission in looking after and caring for the interests of the Lamanites [a *Book of Mormon* term] — the Navajos as also the Southern Utes."[77]

The commission, with seven members from the three bands, left on October 14 for a tour of the lands in southeastern Utah under discussion. That night Hammond chanced upon their camp on the Big Bend of the Dolores River and was invited to stay with them.[78] He learned that the Indians were disgruntled with the "representations made to them by the Commissioners" and were thinking of ending the trip that night. Later that evening Buckskin Charlie invited Hammond to attend a private council with him, Ignacio, Benow, and the other chiefs; he was a friend and had always been truthful with them. Hammond advised them, as their friend, to accept the new reservation because it was better than the one they had, and to ask for $100,000 also. He feared that if they did not, "the Government would take them in hand and forcibly remove them, possibly to Florida or some other undesirable location," as it had with other tribes. Following further discussion, the chiefs agreed that the suggested terms were best, following which they seized Hammond "by the hands and indicated their pleasure at what I had said and their willingness to accept my advice."

Entering Utah near Piute Springs, thence moving on to the Carlisle Ranch, Verdure, and Bluff, the visitors were impressed with the quality of grazing land.[79] However, Aguilar, one of the travelers, became sick on a storm-filled day, convincing him that the "Great Spirit" was angry with him for coming on the trip — a misguided venture to remove him from his lands. On October 19, Mancos Jim, Hatch, and Whiskers joined the party

The San Juan Co-operative Company, 1914. A notable landmark in Bluff, the store served as a trading post, community center, and, during two episodes in the early 1900s, as a place for Ute captives. The Utes sitting outside the store are observing members of Professor Byron Cummings's expedition team. (Courtesy of San Juan County Historical Commission)

and expressed their willingness to have the Colorado Utes come and live with them so that they could become incorporated as part of the tribe. Eventually the group separated into three elements that reconvened later back at Ignacio. By now a few things were clear. The Southern Utes had no desire to move to the Uintah Reservation but were happy with the San Juan area. The twenty Anglo families in Bluff, the twelve in Monticello, and the six in Verdure held few legal claims to the land and would have to go, which could be accomplished for less than $30,000. And finally, the Utes wanted Moab added to the suggested holdings; the commission felt that was beyond their prerogative but would inquire.

By November 13, 1888, three-quarters (253) of the male Indians on the Southern

Ute Reservation had signed an agreement that relinquished their lands to the public domain, set aside the lands of San Juan County for a new reservation, provided $50,000 to be paid in ten annual per capita payments, promised $20,000 worth of sheep, gave them hunting rights around the La Sal Mountains, and removed all settlers within San Juan County. A fourteen-point petition written and signed by Coloradoans in the southwest corner of their state encouraged immediate passage of the legislation. Appearances indicated that most were in favor. The Senate passed a draft of the bill on February 25, 1889, but it was defeated three days later in the House and sent back for revision.[80]

Discussions continued, with every side taking a position from which it would benefit. Starting with the Territory of Utah, the governor and legislature sent a petition to Congress condemning any action that would move the Southern Utes to Utah. The gist of their reasoning was that public lands should be open to "industrious and law-abiding citizens" who could develop mining claims or promote the livestock and agricultural industries. Already established homesteads would have to be abandoned. But most important: "When it is remembered that quite a large portion of the limited amount of land available for settlers is now embraced within two Indian reservations in Utah, it will, I think, be admitted that Utah has now her share of Indians and should not be made to receive more at the selfish behest of a neighboring state."[81]

Citizens of Colorado remained in direct opposition, although they used similar arguments to buttress their case. Two sworn affidavits from Colorado cattlemen attested to the fine range and agricultural possibilities that the land held. Benett Bishop, who headquartered at Cross Canyon, provided estimates of present cattle companies to show potential grazing rights that the Utes would receive when they occupied the land: those belonging to John Reid (3,000), Henry Goodman (2,000), Lacey Cattle Company (10,000),

Lee Kirk (900), John McLain (100), the Mormons (2,000–3,000), Pittsburgh Cattle Company (10,000), and the Carlisles (15,000). As for sheep, the Bluff Co-op had 11,000 and William O'Connel 10,000–15,000.[82] Agricultural land was also plentiful.

Citizens provided sworn statements from eight Southern Utes, including Ignacio and Buckskin Charlie, which were translated through an interpreter and attested to by agency farmer Allen S. Griswold. They spoke of the poor grass on their current reservation, how in the summer they needed to go to the mountains for grazing but were prevented by Mexicans and Americans who hemmed them in, how whiskey would not be as readily available to their people, and how the Indians just wanted to be left alone. They were very familiar with the proposed reservation because their people had stayed there often, and they wanted to see the exchange performed quickly.[83]

Francis Hammond was very much in-between. Charged with getting a fair price for those who would be removed and yet not anxious to contravene church authority, he had the unenviable task of also working with Washington bureaucrats. In explaining just what the Indians would get, he pointed out that this new reservation would have 1.7 million acres more land, three times the acreage of the present one. Mountain resources of all kinds were plentiful, the San Juan River and mountain-fed creeks and streams offered sufficient water for extensive agricultural undertakings, and the land currently cultivated proved that it could be done. As for the "renegades," Hammond explained that they "always consulted [with Ignacio] in matters of importance and his counsel is as closely followed as by the Utes under his immediate supervision. Again, during the season of 1888, some of these renegades, among them Mancos Jim, Hatch, Little Whiskers, Old Bally, the terror of the whites, aided by the whites actually raised a fair crop of corn, squash, and melons on Big Cottonwood

Creek."[84] The only complaint from Hammond was that the government was offering the settlers only half of a fair price for the holdings they would abandon.

The people of San Juan County were resentful. Although they were willing to do the bidding of the government and move in order to settle the Indian issue, they also realized that they held no titles to the land other than by right of presence. Little legal work had ever been filed. For the previous two years they had been unable to apply for the land because of the pending transaction. Now that Senator William Dawes, chairman of the Senate Committee on Indian Affairs, was frowning on the transfer, Hammond felt the government should move things out of limbo. Indecision would kill any kind of progress for all concerned. He reported, "The Utes cannot understand the slothful way in which the government is acting in the case, they themselves having done everything they could to effect a ratification of the treaty. The settlers of San Juan fully expect that unless speedy action is taken, much trouble will arise with the Indians, who are becoming impatient."[85] Indeed, relations between the Indians and Mormons were deteriorating. The Utes were returning to "their old custom of several years ago," stealing horses, butchering cows, and generally aggravating the settlers because of the frustration they felt.[86]

The same was true on the reservation. Bartholomew wrote to Morgan that the Utes had acted "quite ugly for the last three weeks owing as they state to the fact that the U.S. Government was acting in bad faith with them."[87] They had made a treaty, and the provisions of it had not been carried out. In one month's time, if they had not heard anything, they were going to go anyway. On ration day they gathered in large groups, with both men and women on horseback, and "discussed the question vehemently…neglecting for hours to come and receive their rations." Once they got them, they "dispersed as if by magic" instead of spending the time until dark, as they usually did, in dancing. Extreme excitement prevailed.

Nothing happened. Bartholomew noted in his annual report for the next year, 1891, that Congress's inaction had created an "unsettled condition of mind" among the Utes. There was no motivation to make improvements, engage in agriculture, or send their children to school. The only result was that they no longer had any trust in the government's word and placed no faith in strangers representing the dominant society.[88]

1892 was no better. In 1893 the new commissioner of Indian Affairs, Daniel M. Browning, recognized that five years had elapsed, and the agreement was still unratified. The situation was doing more to retard advancement on behalf of the Utes than any other issue. "It prevents the work of allotment and creates a general disinclination to agricultural pursuits or home-making, except of the most temporary character."[89] Something had to be done.

CHAPTER 10

The Replevied Present

San Juan County, the Southern Utes,
and What Might Have Been, 1895–1900

I do not know anything about selling land, and I do not know how to sell it. I
do not know any other land that will suit me better than this.... I was born and
raised on this land, and have lived up to this day on this same land, and of course
I do not want to see any other land, but want our land as it is now.... I would
only like to talk once, and what I say once is forever, and it will be all right.

Cabeza Blanca's Son, 1888

December 1894 was bitterly cold, with snow sweeping across "the Great Sage Plain," piling high at the foot of Blue Mountain. Blustery south winds dispersed the smoke as soon as it left the chimneys of the dozen homes braced against the Monticello winter. The Mormon settlers went about their daily tasks of feeding livestock, chopping wood, and hauling water, but something was weighing heavily on their minds. True, Christmas was in the air, and there were preparations to be made and presents to get ready for the children. The adults, however, were soon to be involved in their own preparations for something that had been discussed for years, but most never believed would happen. There were now hundreds of Utes either already in southeastern Utah or on their way from Colorado to claim their own present—all of San Juan County—as they believed that had been promised by the U.S. government. The settlers would soon be looking for new homes.

Preparation for this month had started years ago, in 1888, in the meetings of the Southern Ute Commission, then empowered to modify land agreements promised in previous treaties.[1] Beginning on August 9 and ending on November 13, a series of eight councils interspersed with visits to both the reservation and southeastern Utah were held with representatives of the Capote, Muache, and Weenuche bands. Most prominent for those representing the Weenuche Utes were Ignacio and Mariano, with Cabeza Blanca's Son also in attendance. Buckskin Charlie spoke for the Muaches, and Severo for the Capotes, with forty-five chiefs and subchiefs also attending the agency in Ignacio.

Excerpts of the dialogue from these various meetings are instructive.[2] They provide insight not only into what the Indians were thinking, but also their agreement with government officials, which laid the groundwork for what would later become an explosive situation. Ignacio, the chief spokesman, echoed the sentiments of many when he suggested that he was not sure he wanted to leave his established home.

Ignacio: I am very glad that I have talked to my friends, and am also glad that my friends are talking to me. It is all right that you come to talk to us

186

about this business. This is my land. The Great Father has told me before that this is my land. Consequently, I do not know how to sell it. I do not know myself what to do, or how my people will go into business. I do not know whether any other place is better than this. Also, because I was born here, was raised here, and have lived here all this time, this is the only place we have had to hunt for a longtime. We have done everything according to what the government has ordered us to do. I have done nothing wrong. All I have done is just as I have been told.[3]

Other leaders expressed similar concerns, but once the issue of removal to southeastern Utah arose, a number of new questions surfaced. Buckskin Charlie feared being pushed onto increasingly undesirable land.

Buckskin Charlie: Out there [San Juan County] there is no large river; there is no river like the Animas; there is no river like the Los Pinos or the Piedra. This land is worth a great deal of money; why should we wish to sell it? I have been here ten years farming and getting my family; the first year I did not like it, but the second year I liked it a little better because I got used to it. Here we have watermelons and muskmelons, and all kinds of fruits and vegetables, and here the children are happy and are satisfied, and if we go away we cannot farm, and what shall we eat?

The reason you say that it is a good idea for the Utes to go out there in the Blue Mountains is because it is a desert; but all the same, we are willing to go if you will give us what we ask. Afterwards, too, if we make a treaty with you, we have nothing to say. Here you cannot come and say we have got a farm, we have got a mighty good country then to farm in. Then you will not have to say, "Get out of here, Utes; you have got too good a land." No other commission will have to say that. That is the reason I say now, and that the Utes all say, too, that we will take that land that you will not have to drive us out of there.[4]

Buckskin Charlie had other concerns. He was well aware of the conflict existing be-

Buckskin Charlie and his wife, Emma Naylor Buck, dressed in traditional Muache attire, 1890s. Among the best-known Southern Utes, Buckskin Charlie served as their leader until his death in 1936 at the age of ninety-five. He owned allotted land, followed closely the government plan for his people, and became a model for the "progress" envisioned by white society. (Denver Public Library, Western History Collection, Nast, X-30447)

tween the Utes/Paiutes and the white settlers in San Juan County, and feared even more trouble once the Southern Utes moved into that region.

Buckskin Charlie: When we leave this land you will have plenty of money. We want Rio Colorado, and want those Mormons taken away from there, for the Mormons have cattle and horses. As long as they are there and have cattle and sheep, they are bound to bother us on the reservation. If the Mormons are kept there the horses and cattle will go on the reservation, and then the Mormons will lie to the Utes and say the Utes stole their horses. And they will say I am lying and that the Utes killed it. If there are no Mormons there to interfere with us it is better.[5]

Mariano, a frequent visitor to southeastern Utah, wanted to know what would happen to the Indians already living there.

Mariano: There is where I understand the Paiutes live, there in the Blue Mountains, and those
Paiutes do not receive any money at all from the
government. And when the snow comes, that is
the place we go in the wintertime. We are together
there. And there are also Paiutes living on the side
of the San Juan. That is the reason that I say all
these places have people.

What I am telling you now is more for my
people, not for me personally. I would like to have
it always the same as it is, that we can go down
south if we want to in the winter and come up
here in the summer.

Chairman: We know you own this reservation, but
it is not wide enough for you, and just as soon
as more white people come in they will object to
you doing this, and the Utes will have to live on
this reservation. The Paiutes have no reservation
out there, and we can go out there and lay out
a reservation large enough for all of you, both
Utes and Paiutes. And you can sell this land to
the government.

Mariano: I understand that where the Utes live is
their own land. I understand that this land is not
surveyed, but that is all their land.

Chairman: No, it is not. The Great Father can give
you a reservation out there large enough for you
to live on and he will drive all the cattle away from
there and give it to the Utes and Paiutes. (That is,
he will drive the cattlemen away.)

Mariano: Then what will you do with these Paiutes;
they were born and raised there, and they live
there? I understand that that land belongs to the
Paiutes and it has always been known as their land.

Buckskin Charlie agreed and feared further consequences associated with removal.

The government always lies to us. When we lived
over on the Cimarron they told us we could come
here and live forever, we and our children and
grandchildren, and that all could live here and die
here, and we would never be bothered, and now
they come and try to bluff and scare us out of
here. They also said there were not cattle here, nor
Mexicans, nor anybody else; but when we came
here we found the country full of cows and people.

The government says: "Move from there over
here. There will not be any Americans or anything
to interfere with you." As long as the Mormons
stay, there will always be lies going back and forth
with letters to Washington. If the Utes go there
to that new country, the Americans will be very
contented here.… You probably do not hear, but I
hear; that is the reason the Utes want it that way.
If they are by themselves, nobody will make any
complaint against them.[6]

Following a visit to San Juan County, the
commission and the Ute delegation agreed
that it was a desirable move and concluded
their talks with an understanding that the
settlers located at Bluff, South Montezuma
Creek (Verdure), Dodge Spring, Monticello,
and Indian Creek, lacking legal claim to the
unsurveyed land, would be removed. These
white men recognized the government's right
to do so.[7] Commission chairman J. Mont-
gomery Smith concluded his report of the
negotiations by stating, "This is considered
a very fair and favorable treaty both for the
Government and the Indians by all who have
any knowledge of it."[8] From all appearances,
but especially from the Ute perspective, an
agreement had been reached, was binding,
and ready to set in motion. Years of congressional haggling and disinterest lay ahead—
a modus operandi difficult for the Indians
to fathom.

Ironically, even though indications from
the Ute perspective seemed highly favorable
for such a move, those who wished to protect
them felt duty-bound to prevent a terrible
mistake. Beginning with Indian commissioner Thomas J. Morgan, a feeling arose that
coercion and power politics were forcing the
Indians into one more bad deal. He offered
seven reasons for his opposition: the Utes
had reluctantly agreed by coercion to the
move; any progress previously made toward
civilization would be negated; the government would find protecting the Indians more
difficult; the allotment process would be put
on the shelf, returning to the reservation sys-

tem of land held in common; administration of the Indian program would face greater difficulties; it would be more difficult for them to become self-supporting; and shifting the responsibility from Colorado to Utah would just slow the civilizing process.[9] Besides, they "numbered less than two thousand" and did not require that much land.

The strident voices of members of the Indian Rights Association (IRA), headquartered in Philadelphia, sounded a frequently loud warning cry. Founded in 1882, this organization, along with the Lake Mohonk Conference of Friends, beginning in 1883, were two watchdogs whose purpose was to advocate for education, support legal protection, and promote the general welfare of various Indian groups. Based in the East, members traveled often to the West for inspection tours, gathering the necessary ammunition to fight Indian political battles in Washington. Herbert Welsh, founder of the IRA, outlined clearly in a letter to influence congressional representatives that the Southern Utes should remain where they were, their lands allotted in severalty, and the remainder added to the public domain for settlement. The Indians' reservation, with its water and agricultural land, could support the necessary civilizing process as outlined in the Dawes Act, frequent contact with sympathetic neighboring whites provided role models, and to place them on lands that were so "mountainous and inaccessible as to furnish a powerful temptation to lawlessness" was ill-advised. At the core of this view was the government's "weightiest of obligations… to civilize Indians—to permit them no longer to live as Indians, and to require them to live as white men."[10]

Charles C. Painter, an investigative agent for the IRA, provided Welsh with much of his information and additional insight. After showing how the government had abandoned many of the precepts of the 1880 Agreement, Painter argued that the present reservation did not bar contact with the

white citizens of New Mexico and Arizona, but served more as a positive opportunity to interact with the Utes. Although the government was supposedly teaching them how to farm and get away from hunting, it had expended a huge effort on their behalf so that they could hunt in the La Sal Mountains, off reservation, and maintain their old customs. After providing a detailed list of areas in San Juan County where agriculture was possible, Painter pointed out that other than the area around the San Juan River, which had been proven by the Mormons as unyielding to large-scale agricultural efforts, there was limited arable land compared to holdings in Colorado. Livestock provided the only practical industry, yet the end of the open range made profitable grazing under that system no longer possible. He next cited the fact that the government had received "more than eight hundred petitions" (signatures) from both Colorado and Utah protesting the removal, and that more than three hundred industrious taxpayers would be displaced if the Utes took these lands.[11] Finally, there was the mixing of the Southern Utes with "renegade Paiutes," who had already had a fight. Citing the death of "Hatch, one of the Paiute chiefs, and two Utes, Cowboy and Kid…[whose] bodies were by the side of the road two days after the fight, when the writer of this article passed through that country," Painter cast aspersions at the "savage cut-throats" in this wild territory.[12] Civilization against savagery played as theme throughout his article.

Another IRA representative, Francis F. Kane, traveled through the Southern Ute Reservation and much of San Juan County between August 24 and September 25, 1891. His detailed account is given with an eye to the land's resources, noting every spring, homestead, and parcel of agricultural land encountered along the way. Surprisingly, he saw few Indians, but he did leave some impressions of the white men he met. With only a few exceptions, both Coloradoans and Utahans—white and Native American—felt that the Utes truly wanted to move to Utah. They viewed the Utes as a generally agreeable people and felt Ignacio was a good man who faithfully paid his debts and always picked the poorer cuts of meat, allowing his people the better part. He had promised that if the government supported the desired move, he and Mariano would send the Weenuche children to school; as for the Mormons, they spoke well of their Ute neighbors and had no problem with the Southern Utes bringing their livestock off the reservation into the county; still, many of them were not eager to depart.[13]

A trader named "Gillett" (Peter or Herman Guillet?) owned a post at the confluence of McElmo Creek with the San Juan River. He told of the constant traffic of Utes traveling up and down the canyon, always inquiring if the government would keep its word. Many of them said that they were going to go regardless, but wiser heads prevailed. The trader felt that "the best Utes never went to the Los Pinos Agency, for instance Benow, whom [the trader] seems to regard as perhaps the most powerful chief among the Southern Utes. Gillett seemed to think that the more self-respecting and energetic Weeminuches were ashamed now to go to the government agency to be fed."[14] As a side note, he pointed out that some of his Ute customers were redeeming cartridges, indicating that ammunition was used in place of money while gambling and "probably passed through his hands hundreds of times."

Gambling in Washington took a different form. Letters to the public from the IRA urged that removal was synonymous to the "destruction of the Indian" and the civilizing process. Other bureaucrats countered that it was best for all concerned and that the Utes supported the transaction.[15] A letter from Ignacio written to "Our Great Father" gave the Ute perspective. They wanted to go to Utah; "We are not children yet you treat us as such"; the Americans' cattle ate all of their grass, Ute livestock would do better in Utah, the agent needed to live closer to the people,

and they had agreed five years ago to this move and still nothing had happened.[16] It had also been five years since, on November 15, 1888, the government had withdrawn the disputed territory from the public domain, and now the Utah settlers demanded through petition that it be remanded and opened for filing claims.[17]

At the end of 1892 and the beginning of 1893, a gold rush erupted along the San Juan River, adding another voice to the white population who favored keeping the Utes where they were.[18] The *Mancos Times* hinted of the motivation for dispossessing the Indians, saying, "For the life of us we are unable to see just what great good can come from the removal outside of the few ranches that will fall into the clutches of the old ring that is still in existence in Durango."[19] Part of that "ring" very well could have been tied to David F. Day, the new agent for the Southern Utes, appointed in the fall of 1893, who served for the next three and a half years. Prior to holding this position, Day worked as an editor of the *Solid Muldoon*, published in Ouray, and was very aware of the issues swirling about Ute removal. When he transferred to Durango in 1892, he continued in the publishing business, starting the *Durango Weekly Democrat*, through which he fostered additional business ties. As a newspaper editor, he took a combative stance on local issues, an approach hearkening back to his earlier years. During the Civil War he had been wounded four times, slashed once by a sword, was a prisoner of war three times, and received the Congressional Medal of Honor, all before his discharge at age nineteen.[20] Thus, when it came to Ute issues, he was not afraid of a fight.

F. A. Hammond recognized what he called a "cabal among a certain class in and about Durango" who, through their agent, had sent the Utes to southeastern Utah. In July he wrote of the sullenness of roving bands of Indians who had been subjected to a "conspiracy" to deceive them and that "this systematic deception is having its desired effect in arousing a resentful feeling among these deluded Indians." All of this was due to the urging of their agent and land speculators waiting for the Indians to vacate their old reservation.[21] Others chimed in, saying that "Mr. Day…is not a fit man to be in such a position" and that it was an outrage that the people of San Juan County "should be at the mercy of a lot of scheming land-grabbers of Colorado."[22] The settlers on the ground in Utah believed that Day had denied them their right to protection and had instructed the Utes that the whites had no call to be in that land, that speculators had convinced the Indians that they had already ceded their lands in Colorado, and that "the average Southern Ute mind evidently has been shrewdly educated" to believe that belligerence was justified. Day's response: If there was going to be trouble, it would start with the cowboys, and since the land had been withdrawn from settlement and use, all of the cattle companies grazing herds on the public domain were trespassing; it was up to the commissioner of Indian Affairs to decide what to do. Meanwhile, because of vague boundary lines on the eastern edge of the Colorado reservation, "sooners" were claiming lands that were not theirs, but which also could not be denied because of boundary questions.[23]

With the advent of the fall hunting season, matters became increasingly grave. Ignacio and Mariano had moved many of the Weenuche Utes to Blue Mountain, leaving their livestock with their Capote and Muache relatives. Ignacio sent word to Day that he would not return; Day countered that his leaving negated the treaty of 1880, which would leave him homeless and without annuities. According to Day, Ignacio's response was that the "President, Commissioner, and General Armstrong say 'all right' when he was in Washington [recently] and I [Day] am like a 'warrior when big Chief talk' or in other words 'I can saw wood.'"[24]

Petitions, one with more than 150 signatures, flowed from the citizens of Grand and San Juan Counties to Utah governor Caleb W. West and thence to Washington. Their complaints were literally at the grassroots level—which had been poor that year because of drought. Livestock was hard-pressed to find feed; the Indians, estimated at 500, were camped around waterholes, denying access to the cowboys' cattle; Day had directed the Utes to go to Utah but claimed innocence; the Indians threatened to call in the military (what a reversal) if the county residents interfered; Ute livestock had now appeared in large numbers (4,000 horses and 10,000 sheep and goats), but the women had left and more men were arriving, ready for a fight; there were 300–400 warriors, who outnumbered 120 white men spread throughout the county in a defenseless posture; plus there were 200 to 300 Navajos ready to ally with the Utes to drive the whites out for good.[25]

Major General A. McCook, commanding general of the Department of the Colorado in Denver, based his response to these allegations on Day's position, saying that the Utes had always wintered in San Juan County, were quiet, and these reports were fabricated by cowboys who were themselves the trespassers. There was no need for military intervention.[26] This was no comfort to Mormon bishop F. I. Jones, who wrote to West following a conference with Ignacio and four subchiefs. The Indians' position was clear. "Ignacio says their Agent sent them here and he further says that he will not leave even though the government commands him to. Our danger as settlers lies in their driving their stock down on the cattlemen's winter ranges. Some of these men, commonly called cowboys, are hot-headed and may either shoot some of the Indians or their stock and thus bring on a war which would be very disastrous to our defenseless settlements."[27]

If there was going to be a war, it would start first in the newspapers. A Salt Lake paper sported headlines of "Indians—Utah Invaded by the Blood-thirsty Utes, Driving the Settlers Out."[28] Citing documents from government correspondence, the writer put an additional spin on it, claiming that "The militia of Utah is ready and willing, however, to go to the front at any time in behalf of the citizens of the Territory… [and were] ready to call out at a minute's notice." Colorado papers, on the other hand, took an opposite stance. Day wrote that white use of reservation land had left little more than sagebrush, with the interloping cattle driving the Utes to greener pastures. He added that the Indians had only 600 ponies and 200 sheep, had far fewer than 300 warriors, had brought their families with them, and that President Grover Cleveland himself had told Ignacio during his spring 1893 visit to Washington that "he didn't care a damn" if he took his people to Blue Mountain. To Day, the whole problem fell squarely on Congress, which had consistently dragged its feet in ratifying the agreement.[29] These sentiments should not be confused with those of another Colorado camp, who accused the Indians of slaughtering deer, killing cattle, and acting "saucy." There were bound to be cattlemen who, in their words, would "make some good Indians" (meaning they would kill them). To these people, "Truly Uncle Sam has in these Indians another case of the 'white elephant'. They won't work, and they are not good to eat. They are simply an expensive ornament to the lands and beyond that are of no earthly use."[30]

As the December weather turned bitterly cold, the controversy gained heat. Conflicting reports and constant finger pointing did little to ease tension. Everyone had an opinion, many of which were at odds. For example, one person reported that the Indians could muster two hundred men in six hours, while another pointed out that they did not fight in cold weather, had brought all of their women and children with them, and now had all their livestock there, none of which portended war. This was countered by those who said the Utes were coming in large numbers to winter in Utah, something never done before, and although they were quiet, "so is a burglar" when invading a house and taking one's possessions.[31] Some said the Utes were peacefully camped in Dry Valley drying meat, but others claimed that Indians were threatening to claim Grand Valley and the La Sals as well as San Juan County.

While hoping for a peaceful solution, the people of Grand County requested one hundred rifles and eight thousand rounds of ammunition from Governor West, who pulled them from National Guard units and delivered them to the Moab County Courthouse.[32] Rumor had it that on December 15 the cowboys would initiate hostilities and that they had gone to the Mormon settlements requesting thirty men from each "to jointly go in and dislodge the Indians" if something were not done.[33] Day, swearing that "my Indians will not be shot down to gratify transgressive cowboys," wrote to West and asked that he do "all in your power to protect my squaws and papooses who are ignorant of impending danger as well as the infirm and unarmed warriors who seek only grass upon unsurveyed lands for their starving herds."[34] As for the Utes, Ignacio promised, "Soldiers can only kill me. I shall die in Blue Mountain," the "old homestead," underscoring the Indians' "earnest desire for removal" to Utah.[35]

Enough. Leaders representing the various factions needed to see for themselves. On December 7 Governor West boarded a train in Salt Lake City headed for Thompson Springs before disembarking to Monticello. That same day General McCook ordered Lieutenant Colonel H. W. Lawton, inspector general of the army's Colorado Department, to head for the same location. Not surprisingly, Day soon boarded the Denver and Rio Grande and sped off to the same appointment.[36]

LDS leader Brigham Young Jr., on assignment to southeastern Utah, had met with Ignacio, Benow, Mariano, and Colorow in

Durango on December 4. They were there seeking letters of support from people who were aware of their previous trip to Washington and who would vouch for the veracity of their claim that President Cleveland had said they could stay in San Juan County. "Ignacio prides himself upon always telling the truth," and so Young wrote a letter giving tacit approval for their staying in Utah for the winter.[37] Ignacio also said that he had no choice but to keep his cattle there because there was no grass or water on the reservation. But "when the weather moderates and the snow melts so as to have water on the reservation, he will return." Before parting, Young noted that all four swore to the president's authorization, that Ignacio was "very friendly, especially with the Mormons," and that Young summarized the situation as "All the Colorado Indians want peace; the renegade band of Utes would like a brush with the cowboys, I believe, and would like to rope in the Colorado Utes; [and] some of the cowboys would like to fight the Indians and rope in the Mormons to aid them. We [Mormons] have all to lose and they have nothing to gain."[38] Unbeknownst to all, two days later the commissioner of Indian Affairs directed Day to return the Indians to the Colorado reservation immediately.

Leaders were still descending on Monticello in the most adverse conditions. Lawton and Day give an apt description of what travel at this time of year meant. As soon as Lawton reached Dolores by train, he hired a buckboard, met the agent, and started for the meeting. "The weather was very cold, snow deep [six to eighteen inches] and still snowing and a blizzard blowing."[39] Fifteen miles out of Dolores, the rear wagon axle broke, so they rigged a pole under it and continued; ten miles farther the front axle went. The two men unhitched the horses, left everything behind, and rode bareback most of the night until they encountered a lone man with a wagon camped on his way to Monticello. The

three hunkered down against the cold, awaiting daylight, and then traveled until noon before reaching their destination and ending their thirty-two hour fast.

On December 12 a discussion started in the log building that served as both school and church. Besides Hammond, Tatlock, and Lawton, there was special interpreter Joseph Smith, who would later take Day's place as agent. He had been there for a few days to gather information. Also there was Governor West, who had arrived from Moab about the same time, having arranged for fifty volunteers from Grand County to be on call as militia. In his buckboard lay a chest of rifles and ammunition, and he was escorted by a group of men from San Juan County.[40] He had already gone on record as saying that the Indians must leave immediately; that if the federal government would not act, he would call out the territorial militia; and that Day and the government were responsible. "This speech put additional 'pep' into about thirty well-armed cowboys, some of whom had been drinking freely" and who were known participants in the Beaver Creek massacre ten years before. Hearing the cowboys were ready "right now," West realized that he had aroused the wrong sentiments and turned on them, threatening arrest if they did not quiet down.[41]

There were fourteen Indians present, Ignacio, Mariano, and Benow being the most prominent. They were convinced that the meeting had an already-agreed-upon agenda to move them, although they had received no official word. West's opening remarks increased the tension. Soon the Indians branded him as "Little Capitan the Mormons had found," which shut him down and opened the floor to Lawton and Day, "Washington's Big Capitans."[42] Ignacio was adamant that orders for his return to Colorado were a trick, and he would not do it. There was no way that the Weenuche Utes could go back without Herculean efforts and

This log church and school, built in 1888, served as the central meeting place for most activities in Monticello, Utah, until it was replaced in 1912. The main twenty-by-forty-foot room was where federal and state officials, settlers, and the Utes held their conference in 1894. Given the town's population, this photo probably includes most of its residents. (Courtesy of San Juan County Historical Commission)

loss of livestock and possibly people. Lawton realized that if soldiers were needed, there were two troops of cavalry available in Logan and four at Fort Wingate, but their involvement would "entail great expense and also suffering for the Indians."[43] Lawton assured his commander that the Utes had peaceable intentions, that the settlers did not fear them unless the cowboys started something, that troops would not be necessary, and when a move occurred, "that every facility be given these Indians."[44] As for those who had always been here, the Paiutes and Utes, he had no intention of moving them to Colorado, but if he did, it would be a different matter. He reported that Benow's group had fifteen lodges, or about ninety-five people, and the Paiutes approximately eighty. "Benow's band belongs to the agency but has never resided there and do not now propose to move there.... Troops only could move them."[45] The colonel agreed

with Day that West had made a big mistake in "arming additional cowboys when they are the hostile element" who could trigger what all hoped to avoid.[46]

The discussion became more heated. The Indians accused Day of having a "forked tongue," and interpreter Smith, although respected, was not perceived as defending the Indians' rights. Consequently, Christian Lingo Christensen became the main translator, using both Ute and Navajo to ensure understanding. Accusations of Ute depredations led to a further "bedlam of voices."[47] The Indians reiterated at every opportunity, "The land of their forefathers where they lived and died had been taken from them by the whites; their deer, elk, and antelope had been killed. They nearly foamed at the mouth when engaged in speaking on these subjects."[48] Mariano went further: "Washington City man tell us to come here, sit down, we sit down. All over this country it is ours. Now you say get out and go back to your reservation. What's the matter now? Our fathers, our grandfathers have hunted here for many, many snows. We love this country; it is our 'happy hunting ground' for us here on earth. We feel the Great Spirit wants us here. Washington City man says all right so we stay."[49]

Around 4 p.m. Lawton received an official dispatch that the Utes must return to Colorado. "The air was filled with exclamations of 'liar, traitor, split tongue,' and many other Indian expletives." Ignacio was incensed. He held up his fingers to represent telephone poles and said, "Mebbe so wire talk from heaven, mebbe so from hell." Citing his impression that everything that came from Washington became garbled and misunderstood, "this message was dead and had gone into the ground."[50]

Noting the tenor of the meeting, Hammond arose to urge the Utes to peacefully accept the directive and leave; Ignacio lashed out with an epithet and told him to sit down. He followed up by saying, "We were both in Washington; I sat in the president's chair; you never sat in that chair; you are not fit to take part in this important move."[51] Day offered to help with food (two beeves) for the Indians and hay (seven tons) for the livestock, which he bought from Mons Peterson's store. The store was also doing a brisk business in Winchester cartridges—"legal tender at all stores in San Juan County"—in exchange for about a hundred deer and goat hides. This was on the same day that Governor West's arsenal arrived.[52] Hammond and West became increasingly assertive, while Lawton sent a messenger to summon troops for the removal and to break the angry stalemate.

According to Christensen's detailed account, the translator spent the rest of the night trying to persuade the Indians of the futility of resistance. They felt he had been a failure because he had not convinced the white leaders that the Utes should stay in San Juan County. Christensen sat around their campfire, piled up sand to represent all of the whites in the United States, used his thumb to represent all of the Indians in America, and argued that the Indians had no chance at resistance.

> They said, "We can whip cowboys. Whip soldiers. Mormons no fight. Mormons mostly good friends."
>
> Christensen replied, "Yes there are not many cowboys to fight you, and the Mormons do not want to fight if they can avoid it. But Washington's soldiers are like the sands of our great rivers… countless."
>
> As he talked he took the sand in his hand and let it run slowly through his fingers.
>
> "It would be useless for you to fight against Washington's people. Go back to your reservation and Washington will be good to you. Stay here and it will mean death to most of you."[53]

Ignacio, having been to Washington and stayed in a seven-story building where people on the street looked like ants, agreed. Another turning point was when the interpreter suggested that "buffalo soldiers" would arrive; "they wilted, for they have an extreme dread of colored troops."[54] They responded, "Go wake up 'Black Eye' Lawton. Tell him we will go in the five days allowed us to move."[55] The colonel countermanded the order for troops.

There were some happy people. Governor West left Monticello on December 14 for the railroad depot, ninety-five miles away, secure in the knowledge that he had put on a good show and prevented anything from tarnishing the escutcheon of the soon-to-become forty-fifth state in the Union. The cattle companies—the Carlisles with their 20,000 head, Pittsburgh with their 12,000, and L.C. with its 10,000—were assured that the grass remained theirs.[56] The Mormons, for better or worse, held onto their settlements, waiting for other opportunities to sell to the government in the future. The military was glad that they had saved their department the costly effort of shipping cavalry troops in the dead of winter with all of the attendant inconvenience.

Among the whites most dissatisfied with this agreement was David Day. As the other officials left, he penned a letter to the Commissioner to explain how "-------- ridiculous this entire proceeding" had been from the start.[57] The Indians were now trying to gather their livestock in the midst of a blizzard. The agent swore that he would get them back on the reservation as cheaply as possible because he regretted having to leave even a dollar in San Juan County. "The entire affair has been a shameful imposition" on many, "enlisting the disgust of the blanket Indian[s]," who really were the ones to suffer. Not so for the cowmen, who got their grass, or the governor, who would receive "political preferment when statehood was achieved." Day later wrote that Mormon Nephi Bailey swore that the cowboys had forced the settlers to sign the petitions that brought on the affair.[58] While this statement should be weighed against other actions, including the visits of San Juan and Grand County residents in Governor West's office, it does illustrate the tack that Day took following the incident. And it would continue months after, when he and Tatlock opened a vehement dialogue, blaming each other for the problem, the diatribe being serialized in the *Solid Muldoon*.

Another enemy made that day was Johnny Benow, son of Benow, who believed that his father and the other chiefs were cowards for backing down and pulling out. He preferred to fight and felt his large herds of horses and livestock had as much right to graze on Utah grass as any cattle company owned by white men. He would later be involved in a number of altercations with cattlemen, law enforcement, and settlers, causing Christensen to claim that he "annoyed us many times since [and] is usually the instigator of all our troubles with the Paiutes."[59]

Despite the rations for the Indians and feed for their livestock the "condition of weather made it exceedingly dangerous for travel with women and children at this season."[60] Snow fell for the next twenty-four hours, adding another eighteen inches and forcing the Indians to take a more southerly return route. Day agreed to have hay, flour, and beef brought to the travelers in sheltered canyons along their way to Sleeping Ute Mountain. Although he recognized that the movement would be very slow due to the women and children and weather, he was anxious to get them moving; a delay might prove dangerous "as the Paiutes and renegade Indians urge the Utes to stay."[61]

By Christmas Eve, Lawton and Day, having spent six days in the saddle checking routes and Indian locations, were back in Dolores.[62] Each went their separate way, hoping that the affair was over. The new year proved it was not. Representatives from Grand and San Juan Counties were in West's office claiming that the Southern Utes had not returned to Colorado, were eating the white men's cattle, and that Day had told them to remain in Utah but out of the way. Something needed to be done. On January 5, 1895, the governor issued orders to Captains George W. Gibbs (Battery A) and John Q. Cannon (Troop C) of the National Guard to determine the truthfulness of these allegations, as well as the number and composition of the Indian camps—both Southern Ute and "renegade." The next evening the two men boarded the train heading for Thompson Springs.[63] In Moab the officers, dressed as civilians, picked up a guide and horses and started their fact-finding tour.

At first together and later with their own individual guides, the two men covered much of both counties, rendezvousing roughly two weeks later at Moab before returning to Salt Lake. The results of their findings, discussed in Chapter 2, indicate many of the Indians' wintering spots, how meshed the Southern Utes were with the San Juan County Utes, and the large size of the Indians' herds. They also provided important ethnographic and histor-

Even lower elevations such as Dry Valley, north of Monticello, Utah, were deep in snow during the winter of 1895. Large herds of horses; travois loaded with children, tepees, and equipment; lack of food and forage; very cold temperatures; and continuing storms made returning to southwestern Colorado difficult at best. (Used by permission, Utah State Historical Society, all rights reserved.)

ical details that point to the complexity of the situation. For instance, the first Indian camp they encountered, approximately nine miles below Moab on the Colorado River, belonged to Bridger Jack (a "renegade"), head of one lodge, and one-legged Dave Root, a Southern Ute who spoke English well and presided over five tepees. There were fifteen men, fifty people total, and five hundred horses, as well as five hundred sheep and goats.[64]

Cannon described Root as talking freely, explaining that Agent Day had encouraged them to stay in Utah for the forage, but to remain inconspicuous. In the spring they planned to perhaps go to the Uintah reservation, but not to Colorado; they wanted nothing more to do with their agent. This same conversation was echoed in other camps, where the warriors were "sullen and full of curses against the agent and [who] reiterated the story that they had been deceived by him [so] would not go to Colorado…their ponies will hardly need much more moving for scores of them are surely about to die of starvation."[65]

Following the dialogue with Root and Bridger Jack, Cannon made the mistake of unbuttoning his coat to get at his pocket watch, exposing his army belt and pistol. The ever-observant Indians noticed the distinctive hardware

> …and instantly took the form of clam-like silence.… We were soon to learn that, travel as rapidly as we might — and we rode strong, grain-fed horses — the news of our presence and the nature of our inquiries had preceded us, and we found the transients uncommunicative and guileful. Only a few hours later, on arriving at Monticello sixty miles away, the storekeeper told me he had heard his Indian customers talking mysteriously about a "Mericat [American] Capitan" who was in their midst fishing for information.[66]

Cannon was baffled as to how this communication occurred. Both officers feared that the Utes would withdraw into even more inaccessible terrain once they realized people were interested in their whereabouts. That may be one reason that Gibbs and Cannon put a rush on a camp as soon as it was found. Once they located the tepees, they hastily rode into their midst, "dismounted instantly, and without ceremony entered the various lodges and began census-taking. Often times we were met with ugly looks but never was there any resistance, though on many occasions we could have been easily overpowered."[67] They found the Southern Utes "generally fat and contented, having obtained supplies from the agency but not yet having crossed into Colorado"; their livestock, however, was not as fortunate, "dying by the hundreds. In one day's ride over toward the Colorado boundary, I [Cannon] counted no less than sixty ponies which had perished on the trail."[68] The White Mesa Utes also were not faring well, being "poverty-stricken and their condition generally is deplorable. There is absolutely no game to be had and any depredations they or the Southern Utes may make upon the cattlemen's and settlers' herds are easy to account for."[69] They also did not have many animals. Final tally for both groups: Southern Utes—238 men, women, and children, with 1,779 horses and 1,225 sheep and goats; the White Mesa Utes—125 total, with 132 horses and forty sheep and goats.[70] The former, despite their angry denials, were making their way back to Colorado, while the latter remained where they were. Thus ended the nine-hundred-mile midwinter odyssey of the two captains. Two months later Cannon became the adjutant general of the Utah National Guard, promoted to the rank of brigadier general.[71]

If for no other reason, the removal of the Utes to Utah heightened awareness that the whole Indian question needed to be answered. Following acrimonious debate among Coloradoans, congressional members, IRA activists, and the commissioner of Indian Affairs, President Grover Cleveland signed the Hunter Bill on February 20, 1895, separating the Muache and Capote Utes on the eastern end of the reservation from the Weenuche Utes on the western end. When

put to a vote of the 301 males living on the eastern end, 158 voted to accept the agreement, which made the entire group eligible for allotment and the other provisions of the Dawes Act. Within a short time 358 Southern Utes had signed the necessary paperwork to receive their individual holdings and become U.S. citizens; four years later, with the opening of nonallotted lands for settlement, the number rose to 374 Utes accepting allotments.[72] For the Weenuche Utes under Ignacio, the western end would not be allotted, and a new agency would be established at Navajo Springs. The passage of this act also allowed the lands in southeastern Utah, which had been tied up for years, to be opened for settlement following a six-month waiting period.

Through it all, Agent Day received high marks for fairly representing the Indians, ensuring that they had a clear understanding of policy and were not badgered into agreeing to something they did not want. Consequently, he became a target for expulsion from his position, but he stood firm. In his words, "The novelty of a Western man, a resident of this section who believes the Indians have rights and is willing to maintain them was too sudden for this people and as a result of my efforts in battling for law and justice as against prejudice and falsehood, I have won a degree of unpopularity in this vicinity that can only be duplicated by a 'sound money' advocate."[73] His feelings, however, about the Weenuche Utes—whom he referred to as "Chief Ignacio and his western worthless following"—were still colored by the recent Utah episode.[74]

The Weenuche Utes remained on what was then being called the "diminished reserve." By April they were suffering from hunger, making demands at cabin doors, and refusing to go to the agency at Ignacio, not only because of distance, but also because of enmity with the Muaches and Capotes. Indeed, when a Weenuche named Ta-wee-ah (Tawíya'—"All of Us") died, they blamed it

The Navajo Springs Agency, 1908. Established at the southern end of Sleeping Ute Mountain in 1895, the agency remained in operation for twenty-three years. The location proved difficult because of erosion, its exposure to wind, and inconsistent sources of water. (Denver Public Library, Western History Collection, H. S. Poley, P-76)

on witchcraft from the other bands because they had refused to go to Utah. The Indians attributed two other deaths to supernatural means after the construction of a schoolhouse. Buckskin Charlie warned that any retribution against his people would be punished by the government.

Ignacio still resented schools, agriculture, and his agent.[75] Nevertheless, he was a leader who cared. Although the Muaches and Capotes said he did not think about his people, others knew differently, reporting that "he never has a dollar of his own, as he gives with a lavish hand to the needy of his tribe. Probably he is as poor a man in stock and money, as can be found among the Utes, and he has never been known to break a promise."[76] The *Mancos Times* reported, after a prejudicial diatribe about issue day on the reservation, that Ignacio counted every sack of flour going to his people. When there were some without, he ordered his share distributed to them until it was gone, and then he and his wife went to Mancos, sold a beautiful pair of beaded moccasins for three dollars, and bought a one-hundred-pound sack of flour for themselves. An observer questioned his

doing this and received the reply, "My people are hungry. They must not want." The article concluded by saying, "That sort of a chieftain is fit to lead. Would that America was presided over by such a grand, noble man."[77]

As new boundaries and then allotments began to appear on maps, Ignacio met with Meredith H. Kidd, the Southern Ute commissioner charged to carry out the entire allotment and new reservation process. They counseled at the southern end of Sleeping Ute Mountain with the Weenuche Utes and more than 100 Indians from Blue Mountain who had been there "ever since the Meeker massacre and only a few of whom have been enrolled in the census."[78] The four-day meeting confirmed that all of those present wanted a reservation and nothing to do with allotment. Those from Blue Mountain felt similarly; Mancos Jim and Red Rock, their leaders, asked that the commissioner point out where their houses would be and when construction could start. Kidd mentioned their poverty, insisted they were "in fact a part of the Southern Utes of Colorado," and should be treated as equals. All present signed the roll.

The land that the Weenuche Utes had agreed to live on was primarily desert, sparsely covered with grass, and had only three springs—Willow, Navajo, and Mariano—none of which offered a significant flow for man or beast compared to the rivers on the eastern end. Local whites called all the land west of the La Plata River "the Dry Side," which fully encompassed the lands on the west end of the reservation.[79] Still, the weather was warmer, the snowfall lighter, and it was home. By the fall of 1896 construction of the agency buildings at Navajo Springs was moving forward, but haltingly due to insufficient funding. Materials shipped by the Denver and Rio Grande traveled forty miles by wagon from Mancos, while other necessary supplies for the adobe and corrugated roof construction came from even farther away. The water from the spring there was as insufficient as the money, and not enough to handle the demands of the agency and the Utes. Consequently, the Indians either drove their cattle to the mountains to save their herds or traveled to Utah to visit the White Mesa Utes. Those who grumbled, such as Mariano, "who has been the leading spirit in advocating indolence and denouncing schools and farming," were taken off the police force and replaced by others who supported the agent's plan.[80]

Agent Day also found himself on his way out. In the fall of 1896 he concluded his annual report by stating that it could very well be his last. His final paragraph summarized his feelings about the last three years: "The task of an Indian agent is a thankless one; he is labeled as a 'thief' when his bond is filed, and no matter how earnest his efforts, how sincere his aims, he is hounded and defamed in his immediate section from start to finish, and by a class whom Hades would experience more or less trouble in duplicating."[81] Six months later, the *Mancos Times* reported that the new agent, William H. Meyers, was hard at work constructing buildings at Navajo Springs and pushing forward many of

the projects that Day had started. Most important to both agents was the issue of water.

The allotted Utes had their holdings closely clustered together so that land not occupied could be opened for white settlement. The seven rivers on or bordering these allotments provided ample water for agricultural purposes. For the Weenuche Utes, the greatest concern remained obtaining it from off their reservation. Meyers, a thirty-year resident of Colorado, characterized the 308,000 acres of the "diminished reserve" as "the most valuable section [of land] in our state," with soil and an altitude suitable for raising all kinds of vegetables, cereals, grasses, and fruits. Without water, however, nothing could grow, and the Indians would continue to leave.[82] Meyers, Day, U.S. Indian inspector J. G. Wright, and others met in August 1897 to address the problem. The Dolores River, miles away from the reservation, was the only dependable source. The Montezuma Valley Canal Company could deliver the water in sufficient volume to irrigate between 10,000 and 15,000 acres of land at a rate of $900 per cubic foot, or $150,000 per year.[83]

The plan sounded good, but nothing happened. For the next two years the irrigation ditch remained only on paper. In the meantime approximately 300,000 acres of unallotted land of the Muache and Capote Utes in La Plata and Archuleta Counties were about to open for a land sale. Selling at 50 cents down and not more than an eventual payment of $1.25 per acre, settlers were lining up for the May 4, 1899, rush. The Denver and Rio Grande handed out pamphlets "which they distributed broadcast over the country" to prospective participants.[84] On opening day "several thousand ranged themselves along the Ute line" as soldiers patrolled the eager participants until noon, when the ceded lands officially became part of the public domain and open to claim.[85] Durango assumed a holiday air as new settlers filed paperwork in the public land office, firecrackers exploded about the town, and banquets feted visiting dignitaries. The Wee-nuche Utes sat on their lands and wondered why the canal was taking so long.

The western end of the reservation saw little change. The Utes there were still "in the blanket," attempting to live a communal life and maintain traditional ways. Some Navajo families drifted onto the Ute reservation with their large herds of sheep and then refused to leave. Ignacio, through his agent, requested they be removed. A local paper carried an article announcing gold on Sleeping Ute Mountain, but fortunately, little seemed to develop from the news, while speculators anxiously rubbed their hands at the prospect of what a canal with water would do for lands both above and on the reservation that could be leased to white farmers.[86] Many Utes still drifted from the agency in search of resources on the public domain. There was little to draw those living in southeastern Utah into the difficult living conditions of southwestern Colorado.

The Weenuche Utes continued to survive among the settlements and on the ranges of Utah. Conflict never seemed far away, and at times arose among the Utes themselves. On November 12, 1895, Ute warrior John Tobias returned from a hunting trip near the Big Bend of the Dolores and reported finding two dead Utes assassinated in a tepee on Chicken Creek.[87] Blame immediately fell on local cowboys but soon shifted to "Paiute" Jimmie Hatch from Utah. Following a thorough investigation, he confessed the deed in detail. He had camped with the man, his wife, and a young boy the evening before. The two men got into an argument over the woman, so Hatch arose early the next morning, shot the man as he slept, killed the boy when he awoke, stole what he wanted, and then took the wife and three horses and traveled towards Mancos. Hatch stopped at noon, built a fire, and shot the woman after she claimed that with her husband dead, "she had nothing in the world to live for."[88] The jury found him guilty, and so did the Utes, who wanted to

see the man hanged and requested that their own representative, Severo, who had testified in court, be there to witness the execution. On October 25, 1896, law officers carried the sentence out.[89] For the next few years things in Utah remained quiet.

As 1899 came to a close, it served as a time to reflect on the past. Rapid change had overtaken the Utes in the Four Corners region. Thirty years before they had owned the western third of the territory of Colorado and had two agencies in New Mexico. Their traditional lifestyle of hunting and gathering, which they had known for centuries, had expanded over an extensive region with the introduction of the horse. Now all of the northern Colorado Utes were in exile in Utah, most of the Capotes and Muaches had accepted individual allotments, and the Weenuche Utes were confined to a small corner in southwestern Utah, awaiting the miracle of water to transform their land into something livable. The White Mesa Utes had remained in their homeland but were surrounded by cattle operations and growing settlements, while their old way of life was fast disappearing. Although most were now enrolled at the Navajo Springs Agency, there was little incentive for them to live there. The new century did not hold much promise, but the White Mesa Utes were still not ready to give up the traditions of their fathers.

Even to the most casual observer of events over the preceding thirty years, change had become inevitable. The question has always been direction and rate. In 2004, Frances Leon Quintana published *Ordeal of Change: The Southern Utes and Their Neighbors*, in which she analyzed the effects of change on Southern Ute economy (fixed residence, subsistence, individual enterprise, and acquisition of private property), politics, education, religion, and medicine.[90] Looking at the period from 1877 to 1926, the author focuses primarily on the Southern Utes on the eastern end of the reservation. Their experience was dramatically different from that of the Weenuche Utes due to the Southern Utes' historic as well as contemporary interaction with Hispanic neighbors, acceptance of allotment and subsequent loss of land, access to constant sources of water for agriculture, willingness to assimilate Hispanic and Anglo practices into cultural institutions, receipt of individual payment with a decrease in the barter system, as well as their painfully hesitant adoption of white education. While the Southern Utes held on to many distinctive cultural beliefs and institutions, they moved away from many traditional practices of the Weenuche Utes, who became known as the Ute Mountain Utes. The result becomes abundantly clear in Richard K. Young's *The Ute Indians of Colorado in the Twentieth Century*, which provides dramatic evidence of the different but intertwining paths each group took over the next one hundred years.[91] The dramatic split began in 1899, as the Muache and Capote bands stepped onto the trail to assimilation, while the Weenuche Utes headed for preservation of a more traditional lifestyle and limited adoption of white ways. Neither group would be totally satisfied in the end.

CHAPTER 11

"Only Bullets Talk Now"

Turmoil and Dissent in a Shrinking World, 1900–1915

I am a very old man now and would like to have some of those things the government has promised me before I die, but it has always been mañana, always mañana. The white man has big mines and big ranches where we used to live and they could help these people if each one would give a little, but they laugh at us instead.... We will not sign any more papers to give up any more of the land we have left.

Ignacio, September 1903

The dawning of the twentieth century over Sleeping Ute Mountain was anything but bright. Shrouded in the depressing pallor of the two preceding decades of broken promises, conflict, and degradation, the next two decades followed suit. For the Weenuche Utes gathered at Navajo Springs, their new agent, Joseph O. Smith, was now the only person in position to voice their needs loud enough for bureaucrats in Washington to hear. The Utes were drowning in misery in a high country desert with few outsiders ready to toss a lifeline. Smith faced the problems squarely and did what he could for those on the reservation, but the Utes and Paiutes in southeastern Utah were on their own with their white neighbors.

Smith's first task was to continue the effort to bring irrigation water to the Ute Mountain Ute Reservation. He noted that the Indians had been fairly prosperous until removed to Navajo Springs in 1895, but with "each succeeding year until now [1900] they are compelled to exist on roots, prairie dogs, and bark."[1] Building canals, headgates, and other irrigation infrastructure

would require too much time to help the Indians, who were leaving the reservation in search of water and pasturage. Smith had planned on improving three springs, but an extremely hot summer had left them dry. Consequently, the annual barrage of letters from stockmen complaining about Indians using water and grass in the public domain ensued, with the usual threat of armed conflict if something were not done. Smith notified his superiors that the Utes were well-behaved, could not return to the reservation until conditions improved, and if there were trouble, it could be laid at the feet of the white men.[2]

Until the Indians could feed themselves, the government dole, as promised by treaty, was necessary for survival. State laws circumscribed off-reservation hunting, defined specific seasons, and became increasingly restrictive due to scarcity of game. Ration days at the beginning and middle of the month thus became crucial for survival. S. F. Stacher, the agent at Navajo Springs from 1906 to 1909, wrote a particularly detailed description of what it was like.

Ration day at Navajo Springs, 1908. Agent S. F. Stacher took this photo and also wrote a graphic description of this bimonthly event that conveys a sense not only of the Utes' eager anticipation, but also of their desperation to sustain themselves on a reservation where life was so difficult. (Courtesy of Colorado Historical Society, Indian tribes — Ute — Places — Navajo Springs, Scan no. 10040267)

On the first of each month the contractor would deliver to the corral near the slaughterhouse 12 to 15 head of fat steers or dry cows for slaughter and under the terms of his contract such animals had to remain overnight in the corral before being weighed. Early the next morning I would weigh them up and shoot them down as fast as the Indian butchers could drag them into the slaughterhouse. There they bled, skinned, and removed the entrails, then the carcasses were hung high with block and tackle, there to remain until next morning. Paunches and offal were shoved through a small door at the rear, where the Indian women took over. They emptied the paunches and intestines and if there were children that were restless and needed entertainment, the mother would cut off a strip of intestine and give it to the child to chew on.

At daylight the next morning the butchers were ready to cut up the meat and the agency team and wagon hauled it to the commissary a half mile distant. The net meat was weighed and the amount to go to each person was determined. There was the same number of butchers as there were animals to be slaughtered and each one received a hide for his work. By 10 o'clock most of the Indians were gathered about the commissary, all with sacks in which to put their rations.

Everything in readiness, the Indians lined up, the doors opened and they were given supplies in order named: flour, baking powder, sugar, salt, soap, and fresh beef. No beef was issued at the middle-of-the-month ration day, but salt pork and beans were substituted. Each family presented ration tickets, which were punched on days of issue; there never was any argument over anyone not receiving his rations. Taking care of the issue required about two hours time with the assistance of five or six Indians.[3]

The remainder of the day featured horse racing, card games such as monte and coon-can, and feasting amidst a number of cooking fires aromatic with cedar smoke, roasting meat, and boiling coffee. The three-quarter-mile racetrack south of the agency attracted large groups — Ignacio's followers on one side, Red Rock and Mariano's on the other. The opponents selected a horse (Ignacio's horse was named Joe and won often), placed their bets of money, jewelry, beadwork, blankets, and saddles on a blanket, the competitors matched stakes, and the race was on, winner take all.[4] The Indians spent the rest of the day socializing before life returned to normal.

Agents Stacher and Smith both shared other concerns. A smallpox epidemic in 1900 resulted in fifty-five deaths; how many more went unreported is unknown. Only eight births were recorded during the same period.[5] Rations had to be increased by at least a third to prevent starvation; the annual issue of clothing had to be reinstated; and Ignacio, who was then living in "a miserable little tepee close to the agency," needed to be recognized for his faithful support of the government and given a home and pension in his old age. Stacher commented that many of the Utes blamed him for their bad situation, and some even threatened to take his life, since he had encouraged them to accept the plans of the commissioner of Indian affairs in the past. This faction opposed Ignacio and his followers in many things, but sending children to a white man's school they saw as particularly onerous. Mariano summarized these feelings when he pronounced that "Ignacio talks like a white man."[6]

At least some people in the white community became aware of Ignacio's circumstances when the *Montezuma Journal* announced how "the old warrior is off by himself at a little water hole pondering upon the veracity of the average paleface. The Utes have most certainly encountered the warm end of every government treaty and promise."[7] Although he did eventually receive a cash bonus and a two-room house built a half mile from the agency, it was little comfort given the trials of his people.[8] Mariano and Red Rock continued their assaults on his chieftainship, with Red Rock complaining to Ignacio, "What's the matter, no ketchum money."[9] Stacher suggested that the whiner Red Rock climb Sleeping Ute Mountain so that the agent would not have to listen to his crying.

The Ute Mountain Ute Agency saw little change between 1900 and 1915. With the exception of two major events—the loss of Mesa Verde and the relocation of the agency—the reservation remained in the doldrums. The superintendent's annual reports highlight the issues, the most critical of all continuing to be water. In 1901 Smith wrote, "[Irrigation] is the most important matter pertaining to the advancement of the Indians"; ten years later the annual report continues Smith's monologue.

> No agricultural or horticultural operations are possible without irrigation.... From my observation ten acres will cover all the land on the reservation cultivated by Indians including gardens. A number of Indians occupying sections along temporary streams have expended a good effort of labor trying to get enough water to make small gardens but their efforts have been almost unavailing on account of lack of water.... Water is the only solution.[10]

Three years later it was the same story. By 1913 the agent admitted defeat, having spent a "considerable sum of money on a ditch from the Mancos River," which he had to give up because "this river goes dry by July 1st."[11] Compare this to what developed on the Southern Ute Reservation, fed by five streams, with funds for irrigation, and greater assimilation through its school and off-reservation business activity. Their more traditional Weenuche neighbors had a much different story to tell.

Leasing part of their land to the Montezuma Stock Growers Association, with whom they had struggled in the past, appeared to be their only option. As many as 4,500 cattle grazed on land that was meted out in a one animal to thirty acres proportion.[12] Due to lack of water, this was practical only as winter range, so at the same time that the Indians were using reservation land, the cowboys were renting it, too. The money received, even though the contract was "secured in the first place through gross misrepresentation.... worked no hardship" as far as the agent was concerned and became a necessity.[13] Ironically, when the Indians went off the reservation in the summer and into the public domain, the livestock owners were leery and thought it best that they stay on their own lands.

Education was another issue. In 1903 Special Agent Conser from the Indian Service visited both agencies to see how enrollments were faring. At Navajo Springs there was not a single unallotted Ute child in school. Smith promised to get twenty-five children for the agency day school, but felt strong parental resistance to sending the students to Fort Lewis. In 1913 there were no Indians attending white public school, spotty attendance at the reservation day school, with only 20 out of an eligible 180 school age children enrolled, and still "[there were] not two Indians on the reserve who can speak intelligible English although the day school has been here for a number of years."[14] Anthropologist Robert Lowie agreed. When he visited Navajo Springs in 1912 to study traditional culture, he was caught in a dilemma. He felt that the Utes there were the "most promising," but were "so little touched by civilization that [he] had to leave after a short stay for lack of any even half-way acceptable interpreter."[15] The agents shared the belief that what was really needed was a boarding school with capacity for a hundred students. This seemed the only answer to preventing potential students from traveling with their families while herding livestock far from the agency's doors.

In the government's eyes, Indian education was the door to civilization and the only real answer to an improved reservation situation. Learning a trade could lead to employment and getting off the dole. Learning to read and write English would lead to a better lifestyle, greater understanding, and the possibility of voting and citizenship. Assimilation of the "vanishing Indian" could save the few that might survive. But to the Ute Mountain Utes, education meant losing children who entered the doors of the boarding school in the fall and never returned. Death from disease was a real concern. Loss of traditional practices that tied the people to the land and their religion removed the foundation of what had allowed them to survive. It was one thing to herd cattle, plant crops, and wear white men's clothes, but an entirely different thing to lose the land of one's fathers, deny traditional religion, and accept a foreign social and political structure. Change would require time.

On December 18, 1888, ranchers Richard Wetherill and Charlie Mason had sat atop a canyon rim gazing for the first time at Cliff Palace, one of the Ancestral Puebloan ruins at what would later become Mesa Verde National Park.[16] At that time a sizeable portion of Mesa Verde was on reservation land, but the ruins had remained untouched by the Weenuche because of their spiritual concerns. Publicity and exploitation followed, and by 1901 the Colorado Cliff Dwellers Association, among others, were lobbying the federal government to establish the park, protect its resources, and construct roads to some of the Mokwič dwellings.[17] The Utes agreed to a ten-year lease with the understanding that further negotiations would follow for a more permanent agreement.

On September 1, 1903, Agent Smith held a council with Ignacio and other leaders to discuss the matter. What follows is part of Ignacio's statement, "taken down as nearly verbatim by the clerk as possible," giving a sense of the betrayal felt by the Weenuche Utes.

> These Indians were once a great people. They occupied and roamed over a great country. They were brave and strong. We used to fight much and we were never beaten by any other tribes.... After a while the white man came and we made friends with him. We never fought the white man because we thought him our friend and we had no friends among the other tribes of Indians. When they were

at war with the whites we used to help the soldiers and it was my people that whipped the Navajos back when they were about to beat the soldiers. Pretty soon the white man came to the mountains in great numbers and we crossed to the western slope and in a little while they came there and my people began to grow ugly. The white man made a treaty with us by which we were to receive large sums of money. We got rations for a while that were sufficient, also some money. From the sale of those lands we now receive about $15 each, annually and there are still large sums due us which the government has never paid. Still, we have never fought with the white man and we never will for I have long known that we would lose and if we were to go to war we would not know what to do with the squaws and children for the white man is on every side of us....

We did not like the Muache and Capotes for [accepting allotments] and drew off to ourselves. The man from Washington promised us that if we would remain on this [west] end of the reservation, the government would build ditches for us and give us plenty of water so that we could farm our lands by ourselves. That was eight years ago and we have no water or anything else. The land here is dry with no grass and we are poorer than we ever were before and getting poorer all of the time. The only grass that we have for our ponies is on Mesa Verde and now they tell us to give that up and I feel sure that if we did we would never get what would be promised us for it.... Mesa Verde is the only place we have left to live on where there is enough water to drink and some grass for our ponies and we will not sign any more papers to give up any more of the land we have left.[18]

Red Rock followed, asking what the white man was going to do with "those old houses where people used to live." If the white man really wanted to take care of them, then they should leave them alone, because the Indians never bothered them and they had been there for a long time. Bigger problems would be the Indians' loss of wood and grass, and the friction over livestock. The white men "would take their guns and shoot everything around there so that not even any birds would be left. No, if the white man will just let those old houses alone, we will take care of them."[19] Mariano agreed, arguing that entrepreneurs were really after the coal that was there and would tear down the "old houses" to get what they wanted. Acowitz spoke next, avowing that the Utes had already signed enough papers, "too many now," and they had gotten nothing. "You tell Washington we say no."[20] All other speakers agreed, resisting any land sale.

This attitude did nothing to deter the government from pursuing its park. In June and August 1904 Superintendent William M. Peterson of the Fort Lewis School approached the Utes on behalf of the government and received the same answer. He had offered a land swap with comparable acreage along the Dolores River, but it was narrow canyon country, buried deep in snow during the winter, and could not be irrigated in the summer.[21] In 1910 the superintendent of the Navajo Springs Agency, U. L. Clardy, well aware that legislation to designate Mesa Verde a national park had passed Congress in 1906, approached the Indians, who again refused. With the ten-year lease drawing to a close and public pressure to consummate an agreement, F. H. Abbott, assistant commissioner of Indian Affairs, and James McLaughlin, U.S. Indian inspector, held talks in May with both Ute groups and formulated an exchange of two parcels of land. To the Ute Mountain Utes went 19,520 acres in close proximity to their agency, which was the only reason a majority vote of 65 of the 108 men on the agency rolls passed it. Even the two government men, charged to make the deal but also to look out for the welfare of the Indians, noted that "the Ute Mountain tract is of little value, being rough and mountainous and largely devoid of vegetation."[22] On June 30, 1913, the government officially received what it wanted and transferred the lands.

Less than six months later Ignacio lay dead. The eighty-five-year-old warrior died

In 1918 the agency at Navajo Springs moved to Towaoc, two miles distant. Closer to Sleeping Ute Mountain and less exposed to the elements, the site soon boasted a boarding school that served both Ute and Navajo children. In 1915 the Ute Mountain Utes had become a separate subagency with its own leadership. (Courtesy of Colorado Historical Society, Indian tribes — Ute — Places — Towaoc, Scan no. 10040266)

from diabetes and old age, but certainly his most recent hardships of land loss and the struggles of his people had added to the stress. Born in the vicinity of Cimarron, New Mexico, where he spent his younger years, he died on December 8, 1913, at the Navajo Springs Agency, having seen much. Newspapers noted that his passing was met with sadness in both the Indian and white communities, who "deeply mourned."[23] It was also the end of a life that spanned the remarkable change foisted upon Ignacio's people, beginning with the Mexican period, the Navajo and Plains wars, the expulsion from New Mexico, and the loss of thousands of acres of land to the Americans. When his family members buried him in an unspecified location east of the agency, they also interred a symbol of a way of life that had all but disappeared.

There was another change afoot. In 1915 the government officially recognized the Ute Mountain Utes as a separate subagency of the Southern Ute Agency in Ignacio.[24] Physical problems with the Navajo Springs Agency begged for solutions, that called for an entire move. Government agents selected a new spot two miles to the north and closer to Sleeping Ute Mountain that was out of the path of flash floods and dust storms. Issues with culinary water could also be solved by creating a new reservoir and installing pipes. Government inaction slowed the process, so it was not until 1918 that sufficient — though incomplete — construction allowed the new agency to begin functioning. But given the problems at Navajo Springs, it is not surpris-

ing that the new site received the name of "Towaoc" (Tagw-yak), meaning "Just Fine" or "It Is Good."

Across the Utah state line the period from 1900 to 1915 witnessed even greater, more unsettling change. No doubt the Ute people living there were intimately aware of what was going on at Navajo Springs and wanted nothing to do with it. Unwilling to relinquish their freedom, they continued to hunt and gather in the mountains, canyons, and desert of southeastern Utah while preying upon the livestock herds grazing on public land. Both activities proved grounds for conflict. Complaints from Colorado Fish and Game and white residents of southeastern Utah accused the Utes of killing large numbers of deer and grazing big herds of livestock to the detriment of white interests. Agent Smith spent a week chasing down the rumors and obtaining statements to the contrary showing that the Utes had little livestock and were peaceful.[25]

In 1903, however, a pattern emerged that for the next twenty years centered around Posey, who by now was in his early forties. Briefly introduced in Chapter 9, this Paiute man born near Navajo Mountain has become a well-known symbol of the resistance and conflict that characterized the first two decades of the twentieth century. Made famous by Albert R. Lyman in his historical novel *The Outlaw of Navaho Mountain*, Posey had been a chief participant in every major conflict up to this time. The historic record suggests that he may well have acted as an agitator against white encroachment earlier, but the first documented account of his activities begins in 1903 with the theft of a horse.

On July 28 Lyman found Posey's son, Fatty, riding one of the settler's family mares and was told that Posey was the one who had taken it. Lyman later retrieved the horse from some Navajos who had bought it, but when the same thing happened again, he filed a complaint against Posey, following a heated exchange. The Paiute also refused to leave his camp a half mile from town to come in and talk to Sheriff Arthur Wood, so a posse of twelve men went to fetch him. Each member stood by an Indian to prevent gunplay; after a rousing scuffle, the sheriff brought the handcuffed miscreant to town. Word of the trial drew fifty to one hundred armed sympathizers to oppose the twenty white men then in Bluff. Following a preliminary hearing that directed Posey to appear in district court, he rode back to his place of confinement, speaking Ute to his angry tribesmen along the way.

The next day James B. Decker, who had also had issues with Posey over a stolen horse, took him to the San Juan River to bathe. The Indian stayed in the water for some time, slowly edging away from his guard. When Decker told him to come back, he dove and swam, managing to escape with only a flesh wound in the leg before mounting a horse his brother Scotty had waiting for him on the far side. From there it was Navajo Mountain, ensuring a clean flight from the pursuing posse.[26] Two years later he sent word promising not to cause any more trouble if Lyman dropped the charges, which he did.[27] In reality, Posey was only waiting for the next round.

Over the following four years the friction continued to smolder. Agents, local law enforcement, ranchers, and settlers all had their beliefs about what was really going on with the Utes in southeastern Utah. At one point two hundred Indians from the Uintah, Southern Ute, and Navajo Springs Agen-

cies were reported to have joined Navajos to prey upon the stockmen's herds and evade any kind of control. Navajo and Ute agents made lengthy trips to investigate, only to find there was little substance to the complaints. Those grazing their livestock were doing so peacefully and legally.[28] There were, however, "Piutes or renegade Utes living near the Blue Mountains [who] are in the habit of killing and stealing stock belonging to farmers and stockmen."[29] The land was such that they were impossible to root out and control, creating definite potential for future conflict.

White expansion continued. In 1905 Lyman and his family pitched a tent in what would soon become the town of Grayson, later renamed Blanding. Not only did this remove a favorite camping spot from the Ute inventory, but it also served as another jumping-off point for additional cattle interests. More people, more livestock, more lost range further increased the pressure on Indian resources. By 1907 Grayson, Monticello, and Bluff had become nodes of Mormon ranching and agriculture, and a growing irritation for the Utes. Two incidents the fall of that year reveal the attitudes on both sides.

On October 30 in Grayson, Lyman received word from some passing Utes that Polk's horse was grazing in one of the settler's pastures. Lyman tied the horse to a fence near a store and sent word for Polk to come and get it. In a short while the Ute's son Tsene-gat (Činigatt — "Silver Earrings"), also known as Everett Hatch, retrieved the horse and put it back in the pasture.[30] Lyman confronted him and again secured the horse to the fence, but before too long, Polk and son loomed out of the darkness. They berated Lyman in the best broken English they could muster while sticking the barrel of a Winchester rifle in his face. There was little that Lyman could do, and so the horse went back into the pasture until morning. The angry settler went to Monticello to get the sheriff but eventually dropped the charges. Sore feelings continued to fester even after Lyman

Tse-ne-gat (Činigatt—"Silver Earrings") was born in 1888 and died in 1922. During his short life he created a stir that brought attention to southeastern Utah from as far away as the White House. Both whites and Indians feared his father, Polk, which Tse-ne-gat capitalized on for his own benefit. (Courtesy of San Juan County Historical Commission)

talked to Mancos Jim, the recognized leader in the area, who condemned Polk's actions.[31]

Montezuma Canyon, which stretches east of Monticello and Blanding, was the site of the second occurrence. That fall four cowboys, Dick and John Butt, Johnny Scott, and Jake Young, all from the KT outfit, were driving cattle from Tin Cup Spring toward Nancy Patterson Park. The cowboys had destroyed a brush fence made by the Utes and were moving the cattle to greener pastures. The Indians, who included Johnny Benow, Polk, Posey, Wash, and Mancos Jim, were camped at Nancy Patterson. As the cows approached their village, the Indians mounted horses, waved blankets, and yelled, turning the cattle back down the trail. One cow fell to its death, and both groups became increasingly irate, exchanging hot words over the cowboys' claim to Ute pasturage. Benow drew his rifle,

while Dick Butt moved forward quirt in hand. Cooler heads prevailed as one of the cowboys grabbed Butt's reins, turned the groups' horses around, and followed the cattle down the canyon. Butt wanted to try again the next day, but his companions refused to become further entangled in the dispute.[32]

A flurry of letters followed, providing a glimpse of Ute life as well as attitudes. J. F. Barton, one of the owners of the KT, wrote to the governor of Utah, John C. Cutler, asking that something be done to remove the "Colorado Utes" from San Juan County. Barton considered the incident in Montezuma Canyon representative of the Indian problem that had been "worked on for several years."[33] The unstated problem was how to obtain use of Ute grasslands. Utah senator Reed Smoot contacted the governor, advising him and the commissioner of Indian Affairs, Francis E. Leupp, that "They [Indians] have a perfect right to go from one place to another the same as any other citizen."[34]

In the meantime, Sheriff J. H. Wood from Monticello started an investigation he hoped would bring the offending Utes to justice. When he arrived in the canyon with his posse, he found the families and their livestock, but no leaders. The Indians claimed that their agent had said they could live off the reservation, which to Wood and others from San Juan County smacked of dereliction of duty. The sheriff asserted that the Indians had leased their reservation lands to Colorado stockmen and then traveled to Utah to "prey upon the property, especially sheep and cattle, of the citizens of this county."[35]

The Utes, however, reacted out of what they considered justifiable reasons to maintain their holdings, and interestingly enough, a number of whites agreed. For instance, in September 1908, J. S. Spear, the superintendent of the Fort Lewis School, visited Montezuma Canyon and reported his findings. He talked to Johnny Benow, who said that the Indians had lived in the canyon all of their lives and that it was far better than being on the reservation. They grew small crops, had about 1,500 sheep and goats, were prosperous, and "well spoken of except by those who have filed complaints."[36] Spear suggested the reason for the disagreements was that they provided convenient excuses to remove the Indians to obtain rangelands, even though he believed the members of Benow's band had not given any trouble to white citizens.

No verbatim transcript exists of Benow's interview, but Spear provided a summary. After denying that he had killed cattle or horses, Benow said that the Mormons were trying to drive him out of the canyon by fencing the land. The Utes retaliated by doing the same, which led to threats to put them on the reservation. Benow refused to move. The superintendent closed by generally agreeing that the Indians had as much, and probably more, right to be there than the ranchers.[37]

It is not surprising, given the events of 1894, that Governor John C. Cutler, prompted by a petition signed by 108 citizens of San Juan County, launched his own investigation. The petition complained that Navajos on the south and Colorado Utes on the east were using lands that did not belong to them and that there were also two bands—Johnny Benow's in Montezuma Canyon and Mancos Jim's in Allen Canyon—that needed to be removed to the Southern Ute Agency. By keeping the Indians on the reservation, they would be better served, plus learn respect for the law.[38] A. W. Ivins, as a representative of the governor's office, recommended exactly what the citizens requested, with a caveat that if the Indians were not placed on the reservation, they should at least be given lands away from white settlements and have a government agent to supervise them.[39]

The federal government sent its own investigator, Special Inspector Levi Chubbuck, to work alongside Ivins and Spear in late April and early May of 1908. Chubbuck took thirteen sworn statements, two from Indians, and when added to five others taken earlier by Superintendent Spear, they provide documentation of not only the issues but also the people's daily lives. Too lengthy to cite in its entirety, a few fragments from Spear's work follows: Cattleman L. L. Morrison said he was "well-acquainted with Wash, Brooks, Mike, Henry, and John Benow…[and] I consider them as good Indians as I have ever known." They made their living by working for cattlemen and "do not steal a little bit." F. M. Ottaway testified, "I have heard the Utes say that the Mormons are trying to get them out of the Montezuma so they (Mormons) could get the range, and accuse them of killing cattle, but they have never done it. Wash has come to my house and talked to me until late at night, telling me how the Mormons had mistreated them."[40]

Chubbuck's sworn statements netted the following comments: Willard Butt estimated Benow's camp at fifteen lodges and 65 "souls." Nephi Bailey said, "They have signals that beat telegraphy and telephoning…. Benow and his band I consider pretty good Indians…. Trouble between whites and Indians arises largely from a desire upon the part of the whites to acquire more grazing lands…. The old Indians are 75% better than the young ones." J. P. Nielson and his two brothers owned 800 cattle and 10,000 sheep, while George Adams testified that there were 95,000 sheep and 40,000 cattle in San Juan County. Nielson went on: "In the past I think the Indians stole and killed a great many cattle but I do not think there is very much stealing now." George A. Adams said, "The county commissioners have told the sheriff not to arrest Indians as we are not strong enough to cope with them," even though he estimated there were 150 Utes and 1,000 whites spread over San Juan County at the time. In a letter to Commissioner Leupp, Utah governor John C. Cutler wrote, "Cattle do not like Indians. Indians always have a lot of dogs that run the cattle…. Navajos sympathize with the Utes when they get in trouble with the whites. Had it not been for this sympathy, I think Posey could have been put in jail at Bluff when the officers had him.... Polk asked if his boy would be arrested. I told him yes; he said the Indians would fight and not permit the arrest."[41] This last point is particularly instructive given events that occurred between 1914 and 1915.

Johnny Benow's statement is presented here in its entirety, providing a different perspective of events and attitude.

> I live on Montezuma Creek. I moved around from place to place for about fifteen years when white men told me I ought to settle down. Five years ago I went to Montezuma Canyon. Four years ago I located where I now am. My children will not herd my sheep and horses. I have to make fences to keep them in. I had no trouble with cattlemen so long as they kept their cattle off the mesa where I and my friends live. I went to the reservation and when I returned the cowboys had burned my fence. I said "What is the matter? I never burned anybody's fence; why do my friends burn my fence?" I sent a man to see what the cowboys had to say. When the cowboys came with more cattle I let them. I had a gun but it was not loaded. I was just bluffing. Mr. Spear and Mr. Holley [a trader in McElmo Canyon] had told me it was alright for me to remain in Montezuma Canyon. The Mormon captain at Grayson also told me it was alright. The cowboys said those men know nothing about the country. This is white man's country. The Indian belongs on the reservation. I thought the talk of the cowboys no good. I told them if they would go with me to the agency, we would go and see the agent about it. I do not want to live on the reservation because the Indians there are stingy with their grass and water and for the further reason that the medicine men make bad medicine. I am afraid they will kill me. I and the Indians who are with me have about 350 sheep and goats and about 100 horses. There are about sixty-five Indians at my camp, including men, women, and children. I have no complaint to make against the white people. They have always treated me properly.[42]

The government was stymied. With no clear infraction of the laws, the Indians resistant to distant relocation, and pressing issues already a concern on the two reservations, there was not a lot of enthusiasm for removal. Chubbuck and Agent Stacher held a meeting on February 26, 1909, with Polk, Posey, and Benow's band members in Bluff, many of whom were in tepees and wickiups, having left the deep snows in Allen Canyon for the winter. The government proposed to the Allen Canyon group that the La Sal National Forest provide some of the land that the Utes had just left for their summer camp. Although the quality of the land was highly questionable from an agricultural standpoint, they were happy with it. Winter homes could also be established on ten- to fifteen-acre parcels in Bluff on the west side of Cottonwood Wash, with an agent stationed there to supervise. All of the Utes felt this was acceptable, but Indian Affairs never acted on the suggestion.[43] Although a local agent was not appointed, part of the national forest was "set aside [as] the allotment for the said Mancos Jim and his little band of Indians and all trespassers will be dealt with according to law." At the beginning of November 1913, Bluff cattlemen drove their livestock from the Blue Mountains through the Utes' property on the way to winter range. After some cattle broke down fences and trampled crops, Mancos Jim showed one of the trespassers the permit but was laughingly told, "Heap crazy talk; no government papers" and then ignored.[44] Carl Stockbridge, assistant forest ranger, threatened with a federal trespass suit if it continued.[45] But there were larger storm clouds looming on the horizon.

Polk and Tse-ne-gat provided the impetus for a string of events that eventually attracted attention from the White House and President Woodrow Wilson, at a time when the country was embroiled with incidents along the Mexican border and Europe was fighting World War I.[46] The affair started simply enough in mid-May of 1914, when two Utes approached Superintendent Claude C. Covey, stationed at Navajo Springs. They reported a body buried in a wash southwest of Cowboy Springs, six miles north and six miles east of the New Mexico and Utah state lines.[47] The agent, a coroner, and an attorney went with a group of Indians to determine the man's identity and cause of death. Articles on the body quickly confirmed that he was Juan Chacón, a Hispanic herder returning home to New Mexico with a large paycheck earned in Utah. He had fallen in with some Utes, spent the night at Mariano Springs (called Salt Water) in successful gambling, and then was ambushed by a member of the group he had played cards with. That man turned out to be Tse-ne-gat.

Ute testimony from five individuals painted a detailed picture of how events unfolded.[48] One man, Ca-vis-itz's son, told of returning from the agency and having Tse-ne-gat rein in next to him and inquire if he had seen Chacón and how far ahead was he. When told the Mexican had passed that way just a short while before, Tse-ne-gat said he was going to kill him. When asked why, the Ute replied that it was for the large amount of money Chacón carried. Three other witnesses testified that while they were looking for cattle near Sleeping Ute Mountain, they heard three rapid shots from a .30-30 rifle and hastened to see what was happening. They ascended the crest of a hill in time to see Tse-ne-gat pulling and pushing something into a ravine, but once he realized he'd been spotted, he mounted his horse, took in tow a second animal, and quickly rode toward the agency. Upon investigation, the three Utes found the body of Chacón lying face up in the wash with three bullet holes in him. They did not report their find because the agent was on a trip, and they "were afraid of this Indian and his father as they are known as bad men, the father, Polk having killed a number of Indians, including two of Rooster's sons and that we now fear that he will try to kill us for having told this;…we believe that Polk knows that the Mexican was murdered, that Polk and his son have said

that they would kill Indians or white men who tried to arrest them."[49] Other witnesses confirmed all that had been told, one man reporting that when he ran into Tse-ne-gat heading toward the agency, he said, "I did not think anybody saw me."[50]

Superintendent Covey sent word for Tse-ne-gat to come in to discuss the matter. He and his father almost did, but turned around before reaching Navajo Springs and returned to Allen Canyon. Polk, or Billy Hatch, as he was known on tribal rolls, struck fear into the hearts of the Utes at Towaoc and was believed to hold supernatural power that made him bulletproof.[51] "Billy Hatch is said to have killed five or six other Indians. The Indians living here received word that the Hatches, with a number of friends, were coming to the agency in force and if an attempt was made to arrest young Hatch and take him away they will kill anyone making the attempt."[52] The agent realized that the Indian police would be totally ineffective in a situation like this and could not officially operate off the reservation, so he suggested that a U.S. marshal serve the warrant to arrest Tse-ne-gat.

In September Deputy Marshal David Thomas appeared in Bluff and confronted Tse-ne-gat in Frank Hyde's store, but decided not to arrest him, fearing there would be an uprising and bloodshed. The locals believed this would just embolden an already impudent father and son, especially considering that there were "thirty men ready to help the marshal if necessary and that they could have taken him without serious resistance."[53] From the marshal's perspective, however, the townspeople were "unwilling to cooperate… for fear that if assistance was rendered, revenge might be taken on some of the people later," and so he returned empty-handed.[54] Tse-ne-gat was allowed to go back to his camp with the understanding that he would surrender the next day, but when the time came, he refused and said he would resist any attempt to take him. The marshal, feeling unsupported by the white community and outgunned by the Indians, chose discretion and departed.[55]

Mormon Stake president and cattleman L. H. Redd then met in Salt Lake with Lorenzo D. Creel, special agent for the scattered bands of Indians in Utah, and Governor William Spry to determine what could be done. Creel had met Tse-ne-gat on several occasions and concurred that something needed to be done before serious conflict resulted. Louisa Wetherill, who with her husband John was a trader in Kayenta, knew Tse-ne-gat well enough to go to Bluff with a group of Paiutes from her area to ask him to surrender. He absolutely refused. Local papers questioned how the murderer of Juan Chacón could hold the authorities at bay for eight months with no decisive action. Around this same time James E. Jenkins replaced Covey as superintendent at Navajo Springs, inheriting a pot of trouble about to boil over.[56]

By now the commissioner of Indian Affairs, Indian agents in both Colorado and Utah, the U.S. Marshals Service, Governor Spry, and local citizens were well aware of the Indian resistance, more symbolic than real, mounting in San Juan County. The threat posed by Polk, Tse-ne-gat, and perhaps thirty followers needed to be stopped before infectious resistance spread, and it needed to be done quickly and with stealth. But stealth would be nearly impossible. Colorado and Utah journalists soon became aware of actions under way and reported any plans they heard about in great detail, some of which was fiction but made interesting reading. Portraying the conflict as an old-fashioned Indian war, the yellow press leaped into action, and any type of operational security flew out the window.

In the early part of February, Marshal Aquila Nebeker went to Cortez to raise a force he could deputize and move into Utah without alerting the Indians. Its mission: Capture the twenty-seven-year-old Tse-ne-gat and avoid fighting the estimated twenty-five warriors who sided with Polk. The marshal ex-pected a hard battle. The number of Indians who might resist was quickly inflated to 50, then 75, and eventually 150 as newspapers amplified their stories.[57]

The marshal next traveled to Grayson (which soon became Blanding) to recruit some local men, many of whom were ranchers, and to be closer to his objective. He sent five men on to Bluff to spy on the Indians and track their movements. In the meantime, twenty-six Colorado volunteers under Deputy Sheriff A. N. Gingles camped in McElmo Canyon during a major snowstorm. Many of these men had been involved in brushes with the Utes and were ready to polish their tarnished record of previous defeats. Rumors were rampant, declaring that the Indians had been forewarned, were digging entrenchments, and had vowed to fight to the last man — all of this despite Nebeker "having taken elaborate and effective measures to conceal the fact of his destination from everyone but those sworn to secrecy when he left Salt Lake."[58] He apparently forgot to swear in the newspapers revealing his every move. Fortunately, most of the Utes could not read.

The storms, said to have brought the heaviest snowfall in twenty years, continued blowing in over the next week, leaving an accumulation of four feet in some parts of northern San Juan County. Jenkins had traveled from Colorado in this weather and was the first Indian agent to arrive in Bluff on February 22, the day after, as he put it, "the eggs had been scrambled," while Lorenzo Creel traveled by train to join him. Jenkins felt that he could get Polk and Tse-ne-gat to come in to the agency peacefully, but if Nebeker was going to do something, he should at least wait for the weather to mellow. The agent assumed responsibility for the two Utes and their band, although he recognized that they were not on the Navajo Springs rolls. One of his primary goals was to separate visiting Colorado Utes from the resident Utes and Paiutes who had never enrolled on the reservation. Estimating that there were about fourteen adult males in Polk's group, comprised primarily of the Hatch, Whyte, May, and Posey families, Jenkins complained that "it was a serious mistake to permit other departments to undertake the handling of Indians. They don't understand the Indians and the Indians resent the interference of officials other than their own agents."[59]

Wayne H. Redd from San Juan agreed. He knew the Polk and Posey groups, who had worked for many of the people in Bluff. He told one reporter, "The Indians are known to be friendly and there are only a few perhaps who would fight. The Indians are in no condition to aid Tse-ne-gat to resist arrest. Their ponies are poor at this time of the year and the snow on the ground leaves them with no surplus food sufficient to last them in a siege."[60] Contrary to reports of entrenched Indians preparing for battle, and Polk selecting defensive terrain, the Utes were actually strung out over a three-mile stretch from Sand Island to Bluff. Many of their camps occupied the south-facing sand dunes below the bluffs, where snow did not accumulate for any length of time. If Polk was expecting trouble, he did not show it since his camp was just to the west of Bluff, and some of his people were living near the Navajo Twin rock formation on the other side of town.[61]

Ignoring those suggesting a more cautious approach, Nebeker moved forward with his plan. He placed strict censorship on the use of phones by civilians and posse members in Grayson and Bluff, greeted the deputized Colorado volunteers on February 20, traveled that night to Bluff, and began a partial encirclement of Polk's camp on the west side of Cottonwood Wash at first light on February 21.[62] Chester Cantsee recalls his parents returning from Bluff to their camp near Posey's home at Sand Island the day before the attack. They commented that there were "different kinds of horses" in town but did not attach any particular significance to them until the events of the next day.[63] Ac-

cording to Gingles, when the marshal's force reached the wash, it split, with half heading north and the other west in order to encircle the small camp where Polk and Tse-ne-gat had been playing cards most of the night. The converging elements awoke the camp dogs, whose barking gave the first indication that something was amiss. Gingles tells of "Polk and his boy in front of the wickiup dancing, whooping, and yelling" before they opened fire on the posse and then dashed with another Indian up the wash to take a position behind a sandbank.[64] From there they delivered steady fire as members of the posse maneuvered into place.

Joseph C. Akin crawled to a high part of an embankment and raised his head to get a fix on a target. In the split second before he was able to lift his rifle, a bullet entered his skull over his left eye and lodged behind his right ear. Less than two minutes later he was dead. Years later Polk claimed the kill, telling trader Ira Hatch how he still had the old Model 35 Winchester that he had used. The man was far away, so Polk "used all of his sights and the bullet landed on line but about twenty-five yards short. The next time he shot he used the end of his barrel for a sight and shot the man right between the eyes."[65]

The rest of the posse, west of this fighting, encountered Posey and others coming from their camp at Sand Island. Once Posey was in range, he shot José Cordova through the torso and began skirmishing against the rest, eventually breaking contact to return to the women and children. Frank Pyle recalled that "the rest of that morning there was no organization, white men and Indians were just shooting everywhere.... Posey's men cut five of the white men off from their horses and took them. The five men escaped and walked back to Blanding."[66] Uriah Butt, a young boy at the time, remembers how the "cowpunchers" did not want to remain out there much longer and so came to his house for breakfast. When Polk realized he was not under pressure, he and others gained a

The deputized Colorado posse poses in Bluff during one of the many lulls in activity during the 1915 Tse-ne-gat incident. They had already "scrambled the eggs" before any Indian agents arrived. These men failed to announce their purpose or who they were before attacking a group of Utes at dawn, something that Polk and others later criticized. (Special Collections, University of Nevada—Reno Library)

defensive advantage by climbing into some nearby rocks. "Those three Indians stood up there on the hill and motioned to the Bluff people to come up and fight. A whole bunch of us fellows were out in the street; I was just a kid, but I was out there among them, and the Indians could have shot all of us. They could have killed some of us if they had kept shooting, but they didn't keep shooting."[67]

There were also fatalities among the Indians, some of whom had just wanted to stay out of the fracas. Chicken Jack, unarmed, was making his way to town, crossing Cottonwood Wash, when he ran into members of the posse who gunned him down. Alma Jones recalled, "He was a favorite Ute in this area. He was friendly to everybody. He was no trouble; he never did get into any trouble at all."[68] During the initial outburst Jack Ute dashed into the open to rescue his six-year-old daughter, who had been caught between the two skirmishing sides; both sustained wounds. Fortunately, other Indians were allowed to surrender and come under protective custody. Eventually six men—Jack Ute, Havane, Joe Hammond, Jack Rabbit Soldier, Noland May, and a Mexican Bruno Seguro—were incarcerated in the dance hall on the second floor of the San Juan Co-op.

Two days after the fight began, Havane, who like Posey was Polk's son-in-law, felt threatened by the white men's talk and behavior. Convinced he was about to be murdered, he slipped off his handcuffs and ran to the window, hoping to leap to the ground twenty feet below. A guard named Honaker shot and mortally wounded him with a .45 caliber revolver, the concussion from which was powerful enough to blow out all of the kerosene lamps on that floor and to leave a gaping wound in Havane's kidney and spleen. Twenty-three-year-old Charles Burke from Cortez, working as a reporter for the *Rocky Mountain News*, went to Doctor E. E. Johnson, who had also arrived from Cortez, and obtained a hypodermic needle filled with sedative. He recorded the scene.

I went down there [Co-op] and he was lying on the floor. I said, "Havane, how are you?"

"Oh heap sick, heap sick, heap sick."

And I said, "Well I'm going to give you something to make you sleep. Pretty soon sleep." I rolled up his sleeve and gave him a shot.…

"You my friend," and I said yes. I told him as best I could that I wasn't there to do any fighting. I was not a friend of the white man, a friend of the Utes, see.

Notoriety from the Tse-ne-gat incident continued to follow four of the Utes who were involved, shown here in 1915 with Robert Martin, a Navajo interpreter from Shiprock. *Left to right*, Martin; Posey, sporting corporal stripes, a man known for his temper and strong conviction that the Utes were being mistreated; his son Jesse, who followed his father's lead; Tse-ne-gat, who went to Denver to stand trial for murder but beat the rap; and Tse-ne-gat's father, Polk, always quick to fight and believed to have strong supernatural powers. (Courtesy of San Juan County Historical Commission)

> He said, "Well you kill 'em. Me heap sick, you kill 'em me, please kill 'em me."
> It was a pitiful scene.[69]

After Havane died three days later, Alma Jones noted that "There were two peaceful, unarmed harmless men who lost their lives."[70]

Some posse members were actively searching for and questioning local Utes who might be assisting "the hostiles" or at least know what they were doing. Edward Dutchie was just a toddler but remembers the fear that four men brought to his home as he, his brother, sister, and mother stirred at daylight.

> Early in the morning my mother awoke me. She got me on her lap and held me down. She told me to keep quiet and don't cry. I saw riders outside... four people on horses with guns lying across their saddles. Before I could say anything, holler or anything like that, my mother put her hand over

> my mouth.... She was afraid the white men were going to kill her. She thought they might take us away or maybe kill us right there. So that is when we moved out.[71]

By the day after the attack, all of the Utes were gone, having fled down the San Juan River to Comb and Butler Washes, where they remained for some time without further engagements.[72]

A second group of "106 friendly Utes" who had been camped nearby in Butler Wash then moved to town to avoid association with those fighting. Navajo scouts from the Northern Navajo Agency in Shiprock escorted them. As the Indians conversed, the "friendlies" learned that they were actually slated to only pass through Bluff on their way to the Ute reservation. "They halted in their march and refused to come in. Leaders of the band declared rather than leave their ancestral hunting grounds they would resist the white authorities and join Old Polk and his bunch of renegades."[73] Further suggestion of their removal was quickly swept under the rug.

Nebeker began depending on local help and recruited the services of Mancos Jim, whom he sent to ask the fighters to surrender peacefully. They instead let it be known they would fight to the death. One eyewitness said of Mancos Jim, "He was one of the Mormon's main men to trust. He'd come in to town and then he'd go back and tell what they wanted him to tell some of these Indians. He always worked in the dark [because] he didn't want anybody to follow him."[74] Nebeker also sought help from Grayson and Monticello, the former providing seventeen men and the latter twenty-nine ready to fight, raising the total posse size to more than seventy. Newspapers carried the word that Bluff was surrounded, in imminent danger, and help needed, encouraging people from southwestern Colorado to further mobilize. Nebeker contacted Superintendent William T. Shelton at Shiprock to request twenty Navajo policemen to assist with tracking. They arrived in Bluff on February 25, just as Nebeker suspended field activities to give Jenkins and Creel an opportunity to work with the Utes.[75] Besides, now that the initial hysteria was over, the telephone lines between Bluff and Grayson cut by the Utes restored, and the flight of the Indians to the west an accomplished fact, the white posse members felt comfortable remaining close to Bluff for the next two weeks, regardless of what the press was churning out for a good story. Newspapers also falsely reported that Posey had killed his brother Scotty, who wanted to go to Bluff to surrender.[76]

The night of the initial attack Lorenzo Creel had arrived in Moab. Spurred on by the news, the agent "traveled alternately from stage to stage by wagon, sled, sled to wagon, through mud often hub deep, and again in snow from three to four feet deep, with but little sleep until we reached Bluff on the night of the 24th."[77] The next day he, Jenkins, interpreter Jim Allen (a Ute), and "Catombet," a Ute policeman, went in search of noncombatant Indians. Creel found evidence strewn along the trail of a hasty flight, which convinced him that they had fled in sheer terror, since "the posse and citizens did not seem able to draw the line between combatant and peaceful Indians."[78] Fifteen miles outside of Bluff the party encountered an old Indian acting as a lookout. Once he determined this group meant him no harm, others joined them, shaking hands all around and then listening to Jenkins's message that the Navajo Springs Agency was a refuge with food and assistance readily available. Eventually, all but Mancos Jim agreed to go, but the next day he too fell in with the departing group of sixty Indians under Jenkins's and Ute police supervision. Creel bid farewell and returned to Bluff to collect the Utes' property and livestock, as well as the sick Utes left behind by those fleeing. He also urged that regular troops be brought in to handle the situation, feeling that the posse members were "a bunch of greenhorns out for glory."[79] Before that happened, a better solution appeared.

On March 1, 1915, Nebeker summarized the situation in a letter to the attorney general. He believed he was now facing 50 Indians under Polk and Posey, 15 to 20 of whom were warriors, the rest women and children. Mancos Jim's band numbered 115, while another group of about 50 in the McElmo area was peaceful. All of these groups "commingled."[80] Those at large, however, had checkmated the posse. The same day that Nebeker made his assessment, Brigadier General Hugh L. Scott, army chief of staff, was implementing his own plan of action. He had received plenary powers to draw upon the resources of the War Department and Office of Indian Affairs, and legal rights granted by the Justice Department in order to convince the Indians to surrender of their own volition. He also requested that the Navajo Bizhóshí, whom he had arrested the previous

White captors and Indian captives in Bluff, 1915: *standing, left to right,* Willard Butt, Gene Powell, unidentified, Joe Hammond, Jack Ute, unidentified, unidentified, Henry Ince; *kneeling,* Havane, Bruno Seguro (a Mexican living with the Utes), Jack Rabbit Soldier, and John Noland (May). (Special Collections, University of Nevada — Reno Library)

year, meet him at Bluff to assist in negotiations. A living testimonial of Scott's character and veracity could go a long way. With President Woodrow Wilson directing his subordinates to support these efforts, Scott started to the field on March 3 with approvals in hand, arriving in Bluff with his aide Lieutenant Colonel Robert E. Michie and orderly Private Paul Randolph on March 10.[81] Nebeker received word of Scott's role; the newspapers, noting the shift, congratulated their "boys who have done their full duty and done it well"; and the five manacled prisoners boarded the Denver and Rio Grande Railroad for Salt Lake City to stand trial.[82]

Now it was Scott's turn to assess the situation. Louisa Wetherill, who had been in communication with Polk's group, sent a telegram asking for assurance that the father and son would not be hung if they surren-

dered. Could Scott guarantee them a fair trial? Creel and Jenkins reported that the Indians had crossed the San Juan River and were now around Douglas Mesa. The people in Bluff were afraid for the general and quoted what a Navajo had heard Polk promise to Nebeker — "Only bullets talk now."[83] Undaunted and unarmed, Scott set off the next day with John Wetherill, Bizhóshí, and four other Navajos, as well as the two agents and his aides.

Hardy Redd, son of L. H. Redd of Bluff, predicted failure, saying that the Indians would withdraw and that when the weather cleared, they would go to Navajo Mountain, where they would never be found. But Redd was holding a grudge; the previous summer Posey had drawn a gun on him when the cattlemen let down the bars of the Indian's fence in order to drive livestock through.

Participants in the surrender at Arthur Spencer's trading post in Mexican Hat, 1915: *left to right*, Robert Martin, Agent Lorenzo Creel, General Hugh L. Scott, Polk, unidentified, Lieutenant Colonel Robert Michie, Posey, Agent James E. Jenkins, and (*kneeling*) Jim Allen (Ute). (Special Collections, University of Nevada — Reno Library)

His take: "We would like to see the Indians driven out of this country."[84]

Redd was right about one thing: it would be some time before Scott encountered the Utes. The general established a headquarters at Mexican Hat and waited for a parley. In the meantime Nebeker bid farewell to his posse, who returned home on March 19. The next day Scott sent a telegram to the secretary of war: "Successful. Have four Paiutes desired by Marshal Nebeker, and at their desire am personally conducting them to Salt Lake to turn over to Marshal Nebeker."[85]

People were elated. Scott explained what had happened, and how Bizhóshí had played an important part. At first the Navajo and his two sons hesitated to go, reciting a story about how since the beginning of time Paiutes were mean. Scott cajoled him into agreeing after promising "that when we were both killed we would be buried together."[86]

Once the party reached the trading post

at Mexican Hat, they found only Arthur H. Spencer and family. Eventually Wetherill and Scott recruited a Paiute from Kayenta to find Polk and Posey, and invite them to come in for a talk. Several days elapsed before the messenger returned with news that the next day the "outlaw Indians," about thirty in number, would be at the post. They were, but not before carefully glassing the situation from afar and posting armed lookouts on the surrounding mesas.[87] After listening to their complaints, Scott asked them what they were going to do and was glad to hear them reply, "We are going to do just what you tell us to do."[88] With this music in his ears, Scott agreed to accompany the four recalcitrants to Salt Lake City to ensure a fair trial and see that Tse-ne-gat successfully arrived in Denver for his hearing. In the general's mind, he was going to "prevent those four Indians from being legally murdered."[89] Just as clear in Scott's mind was the belief that when the posse attacked these Indians, they had made no attempt to identify themselves, show a warrant, or give any explanation. The Colorado cowboys had attacked the Indians, and they had just defended themselves. John D. Rogers, a local cattleman, later told of how Polk had explained this fact to him long after the incident was over.[90]

Praise poured in for Scott, who had enjoyed the dramatic situation. The secretary of war sent congratulations, as did the adjutant general of the army, commissioner of Indian Affairs, and president of the United States. The Indian Rights Association was also quick to applaud, believing "the red men" had an advocate looking out for their welfare. But the Utes captured even more of the spotlight. From the time they arrived in Moab, and then Thompson to board the train for Salt Lake, press coverage ran continuously. The train ride was a new experience, and the reporter played on the "curious savage theme." Scott, "the White Father," assumed a paternal role with the Indians, who admired him and depended on his friendship, remaining close to his side. The large crowd at the station jockeyed for position to catch a glimpse of the prisoners, who were sporting dark glasses when they got off the train.

Their reunion with the other Utes awaiting them in their cell was a "genuine joy" countermanded only by the sadness they felt at Scott's eventual departure for the East. There were car rides in a Studebaker Six, church services in LDS and First Church of Christ chapels, and a deputy marshal caught by reporters learning the Ute "war dance." The daily walks about the city were enjoyable, except for Polk, who suffered from rheumatism. And a few weeks later, when Tse-ne-gat went to a hospital in Denver for treatment of tuberculosis, the newspapers were sure to report his reaction to a white female nurse—"Me no sabe white woman. She funny, she heap pretty—no got man."[91]

On a more serious side, the government released the seven Indians in Salt Lake to return with Superintendent Jenkins after they promised to remain at Navajo Springs, forsake their connection with southeastern Utah, encourage others in their band to join them, send their children to school, and no longer carry weapons.[92] All signed or placed their thumb print on the paper in agreement. "Old Polk put his hand on his heart and declared he now saw clearly that he had been blind before, that his heart was bad, but that he now knew his duty and would do it."[93] The group went to what had by then become Towaoc.[94] Tse-ne-gat, still facing trial and very ill with tuberculosis, departed for Denver, where he went to Saint Anthony's Hospital and received a prognosis that he had five years left to live.[95]

Although Tse-ne-gat's trial is an interesting study in the complexity of external sources affecting the legal system, several other salient points are worth considering. Both sides made every effort to exert pressure through expert testimony that played well in the press as well as the court. Before the trial started, U.S. District Attorney General Harry B. Tedrow traveled to Towaoc and Bluff to gather evidence and evaluate the strength of his arguments. He correctly divined that if it were just a matter of presenting evidence, he had a very strong case. He was also a realist. He recognized that the murder victim had been a Mexican, that Scott was a hero who supported Tse-ne-gat, that the Ute people were afraid of Polk, that the interpreters had struggled to make their points, and that the defendant was gravely ill—which all added up to an emotionally biased case in favor of the defense. "The old time prejudice against Indians has been replaced in the locality of the trial by a general feeling distinctly in the defendant's favor. Denver representatives of Eastern Indian Societies [Indian Rights Association] are much interested in Hatch [Tse-ne-gat] and his case."[96] All of the evidence indicated Tse-ne-gat was guilty, but convincing the jury would be another story.

The Ute prisoners and government agents on their way to the trial in Salt Lake City, 1915: *left to right*, Agent Lorenzo Creel, Lieutenant Colonel Robert Michie, General Hugh L. Scott, Aquila Nebeker, Polk, Jesse Posey, Posey, Tse-ne-gat, and A. B. Apperson, superintendent of the Denver and Rio Grande Railroad. (Courtesy of San Juan County Historical Commission)

During the collection of eyewitness statements in Bluff, Polk, Posey, and twenty other men appeared at the hearings and intimidated those providing information against Tse-ne-gat. Jenkins was supportive of the two leaders, even suggesting that they might become part of the agency police force, while at the same time publicly declaring his opinion that the defendant was innocent. The agent could also take no actions against witchcraft or other "methods peculiar to themselves [Indians] to intimidate witnesses," giving an open hand to Polk's faction.[97] Indeed, some white men were afraid to testify against Tse-ne-gat, knowing full well that both Polk and his wife might appear on behalf of the defense. The attorney general in Washington, DC, intervened to ensure Jenkins would keep the two testifying sides separate at all times and would not allow them to influence each other.[98]

The trial started on July 6, with Judge Robert E. Lewis presiding and Henry McAllister Jr. and Charles L. Avery serving for the defense. The latter's strategy was to discredit the witnesses, who testified about Tse-ne-gat's actions on the day of the murder. From Tedrow's perspective, the defense received a great deal of help from Jenkins, who took one of the Indians, Harry Tom, to Avery's office and coached him. Antonio Buck, interpreter for the defense, offered him money; Jenkins had made his pro-defense position clear, which endangered the Indians under his charge; and Tom became confused with some of the questions, responding to only the parts he understood. The prosecutor also claimed that Jenkins had not followed instructions and had brought only a portion of the information requested from the agency files. The superintendent also went to the scene of the crime, fired a rifle three times, and then reported in court that the person accompanying him, stationed at the place where the body was found, could not hear the shots, discrediting the Indian witnesses. Finally Jenkins claimed that the three Utes testifying for the prosecution belonged to Mariano's faction, were untrustworthy troublemakers, and at odds with Polk's band. Subsequent testimony by Covey, the previous agent, and local whites countered this assertion, saying these men were of good character and entirely credible. Tedrow concluded that Jenkins had done this because of his promise to Polk that the trial would turn out favorably for his son; if it did not, the Indian would exact revenge, a recurring theme during the trial.[99]

The defense enjoyed a strong ally in the press. Billed as "the most thrilling criminal trial ever held in Denver," activities inside and outside the courtroom grabbed the public's attention. Titles and subtitles captured the imagination: "Mother of Tse-ne-gat Braves Terrors of Railroad Engines to Be at Son's Side" (Polk was subpoenaed to appear but refused); "Mournful Eyes Turn on Mother"; "Indian Simplicity Baffles the Court" and "Existence of Feud Admitted by Agent" — all of which fueled the fires of public spectacle. Written like a dime novel, the text bubbled with description.[100]

'Ma Polk' mother of the defendant [was] brown, worn, aged; this Indian mother watched the opening proceedings ignorant of what was being said, what was being done, her twinkling black eyes fixed steadily on the melancholy face of the young man at the head of the table in the middle of the room. Now and again Tse-ne-gat turned his mournful eyes toward his mother. For long moments they gazed at each other then the glance was broken, not by a smile of sympathy, but by a woman lifting the loose end of her red calico sleeve and wiping her lip. 'Ma Polk' is dressed to kill in turkey-red calico edged with orange yellow. She wears white leather moccasins and her bronze colored hands are covered with silver rings set with stunning turquoise.[101]

Nine days after the trial started, the twelve-man, all-white jury reached a verdict of not guilty following seven hours of deliberation. Tse-ne-gat and his mother remained

unmoved after the pronouncement, but they were the only ones. Juan Chacón's widow "sprang up like a tigress and went for Tse-ne-gat," only to be stopped by a deputy; Antonio Buck, interpreter for the defense, grasped the hand of his friend; Mary Baker, a graduate of Haskell and the court interpreter, smiled broadly; and each juror shook Tse-ne-gat's hand in congratulations. Crowds of people in the corridors surged around the Indian, giving an ovation, and no doubt the "women in Denver [who had] sent red neckties and pink stockings, love notes and sweetmeats," were elated.[102] When Scott received the news that night, he also expressed approval, declaring that he had known Tse-ne-gat was innocent. As for Tedrow, he fumed and demanded an investigation into Jenkins's behavior, and those who had testified for the prosecution shuddered at what this tacit approval would mean back in southeastern Utah.[103]

All that remained was a dramatic farewell from Denver. Tse-ne-gat boarded the train the next day with a "string of cheap medals pinned on one side of his breast," no doubt as he had seen Scott attired, and an American flag draped over his other shoulder. "Ma Polk" sported a new dress that had safety pins attached all over the front. In one hand she carried an American flag and in the other a bag in which well-wishers, many of whom were women, had placed presents and food. Her son took a position on the rear of the last car to bid farewell to the people of Denver while, according to the newspaper, "Polk, his father, wait[ed] in the front of his tepee, his aged eyes shaded from the sun, watching for his son."[104]

Polk may have been facing east and awaiting his son, but where he had pitched his tepee was becoming an issue. The Utes who had gone to Salt Lake City returned to the reservation but soon traveled with Jenkins to San Juan County to get their wives and possessions. Polk declared that he was going to stay in Utah until he heard how his son had faired in the trial, and others remained as well. They retrieved their hidden arms and obtained ammunition from caches and Navajo friends, but were hesitant to go to the reservation. Since their livestock was in poor shape, Jenkins left them to return on their own, estimating they would be back in a week or ten days.[105] The white community, unhappy that the Indians were still around, felt the whole incident had been handled poorly. As reports of events in Salt Lake City and then later Denver filtered back, many believed the vocal advocacy of the Indian Rights Association and federal bungling were at the roots of their problems.

When Tedrow had been in Bluff on May 6 collecting information for the upcoming trial, he learned that Posey and his group were sullen and outspoken about how they did not want to go to the reservation and did not intend to stay long once they got there. One young warrior grabbed Kumen Jones, a Mormon bishop and an elderly advocate for Indians, and shook him with frustration. Still, to their credit, all of the Utes except Polk arrived at Towaoc a day ahead of the appointed time. Ten days later Jenkins reported that all of the Bluff Indians were present for ration day, and that the fuss about their being off the reservation was just more "yellow press" encouraged by "vicious white men anxious to make trouble for Indians."[106]

By the next day, however, in a telegram to the commissioner of Indian Affairs, the superintendent had changed his tune. That morning a group of travelers had encountered Posey and fifteen Utes leaving the reservation for Allen Canyon, driving their sheep. "He is very untruthful and irresponsible and should be disciplined for breaking parole.... Recommend marshal be notified and requested to apprehend Posey and return him to jail.... Posey is half Mexican and half Piute; very unpopular with rest of tribe; his arrest and incarceration would have wholesome effect."[107]

For the public, however, Jenkins maintained an image of control. He went on

record in mid-June stating that the rumors of friction in Bluff were false, and that he had given the Indians permission to go off the reservation temporarily to collect possessions and pick up their families. He also "estimated that it may take a year or two to complete the transfer of all effects and people to the agency but it will be accomplished as fast as possible."[108] Besides, he had "many letters from residents of Grayson, Monticello, and other places from people who desired he send them Indians to help on ranches."

Like the Ute story of the Creator learning that people were let out of the bag and now lived about the land, the federal government began to realize that getting Posey and Polk to stay on the reservation was becoming an impossible mission. Polk, camped near James M. Holley's store in McElmo Canyon, showed up on the reservation for ration day but the rest of the time went where he wanted. Mancos Jim had left Towaoc with a dozen people in search of water and grass for their livestock. Posey did not even pretend to be on the reservation. Bluff, Allen Canyon, Mexican Hat, Douglas Mesa, Navajo Mountain—he returned to all of his haunts with his band of twenty-five to thirty followers and took up his old practices of demanding food at cabin doors and appropriating cattle for dinner. The men in Bluff feared leaving their families to go out on the range to tend cattle and wondered if the previous fight had accomplished anything.[109]

As 1915 came to a close, people tallied the results from the past fifteen years. Important lessons had been learned—but not necessarily the ones desired. The Utes in southeastern Utah were living in an untenable position. Lacking water and other resources, the reservation could not support them, and the Indians already there were not eager to receive them. At the same time the Utes' hunting and gathering way of life had been shattered, forcing the Indians to depend on white settlements, where they were not welcome, to provide food and commodities. The Utes' livestock were also in direct competition for grass and water on the public domain. Although the Utes' ties to the land were just as strong, much of it was now inaccessible because of cattlemen, federal agencies, and farmers who did not understand and had little sympathy for the native inhabitants.

Indeed, from the white man's perspective, the Indians were a nuisance at best and a threat at worst. The recent conflict bore testimony that outside help only made matters worse, that people beyond the Four Corners area did not really understand the wards they were championing, and that the Utes had become more aggressive since they had beat the white man on his own terrain—the

courtroom. Albert R. Lyman, one of several witnesses called to Denver to testify for the prosecution, summarized what he had seen during the trial, writing, "All the evidence was minimized, overlooked, or ignored by the daily papers. I was never so thoroughly disgusted with a court procedure in my life. The Indian Rights people had no eyes to see, ears to hear, nor hearts to consider the sorrowing parents and the broken hearted wife [of Juan Chacón]."[110] The failure to resolve these problems had created what Lyman called "scoff-law killers." Only the future would tell how the conflict, exacerbated by recent events, might be resolved.

CHAPTER 12

Posey and the Last White Uprising

Ending the Cycle of Violence, 1915–1923

...at some future time it may be that even Old Posey, an intrepid, determined Ute and the leader of a local war in Utah, as well as Tecumseh, Pontiac, Black Hawk, Sitting Bull, and Chief Joseph, will be recognized as truly national figures in our history.

Wilbur R. Jacobs, historian, 1973

Smoldering coals of resentment remained from the fires started by the conflict in 1915 between whites and Indians in Bluff. For the next eight years participants fanned them in their own peculiar ways. Not until Posey lay dead in an alcove near Comb Ridge was Ute resistance doused sufficiently to prevent further armed conflict. In the interim each group involved—Indians, agents, settlers, ranchers, Indian Rights activists, Bureau of Indian Affairs appointees, and special-interest groups—gnashed their teeth over real and perceived wrongs, and then took action. None of them seemed to have faith in any other group to solve problems other than their own. With cooperation in short supply, unilateral actions were taken, with each faction condemning what it believed to be the incorrect approach of others. Conflict resulted until a final solution—not necessarily the best, but definitely final—eliminated the problem: in this case, putting the White Mesa Utes into a restricted area under local federal government supervision. Until that time contention reigned.

In 1916 the most strident voices sounded from the newspapers. Still sulking over Tse-ne-gat's acquittal and the return of Polk and Posey to their haunts in southeastern Utah, the people of Bluff and Cortez felt betrayed. But worse, white people were still advocating for the Indians, saying that the whole incident was the fault of the dominant society. Activist M. K. Sniffen, secretary of the Indian Rights Association, headquartered in Philadelphia, poured gas on the fire with a report he submitted following a visit to the Four Corners area in September 1915. He got some of his information wrong, quickly branded posse members as "rough-necks and tin horns," and selected events that showed little balance in reporting what happened. The Indians, painted in a most positive light as oppressed victims who had made huge progress in establishing farms and making other advances in civilization, were now about to lose their lands, which were being ogled by the cattlemen of southeastern Utah. Sniffen explained the killing of Havane using information gained from one of the other prisoners, who said "the guards indulged in the 'gentle' pastime of holding guns to their heads and against their bodies, at the same time threatening to shoot."[1] In Sniffen's view the whites had made no discrimination between good Indians and bad, the public domain was just that, the Utes were following instructions to establish their own homes off the reservation, which showed them progressing toward mainstream society, and all they needed was a "white man's" chance.

This capsule summary of a complex affair, sprinkled with inaccuracies, did not sit well with the locals. For over a month, starting in mid-January 1916, the *Cortez Herald* posted weekly diatribes against the evil Sniffen. The newspaper was quick to point out things that he could have and should have done, but neglected. There were the usual snide remarks filled with venom; however, there were also clouds with silver linings. In responding to different issues, the editor was receiving very detailed information from someone at the Towaoc Agency. For instance, he mentions that Tse-ne-gat had been recently appointed as a policeman, even though he had reportedly beaten his wife and child to death; the construction boss building the new school at Towaoc had received threatening notes of "Utes want no school, Utes shoot to kill" and had actually been wounded; twenty cattle purchased by the government for the agency had starved to death, wasting the Indians' money; Indian babies had a higher infant mortality rate—more than 30 percent—because they breastfed longer and once put on regular coarse food, "die with alarming frequency"; and while accounting for past killings, the editor wrote: "Wash killed Bridger Jack; Old Hatch killed Rooster's two boys; Polk's brother killed two bucks and a squaw on the Mancos, William Hart killed Polk's son-in-law; Posey killed his wife, Polk's daughter; Tse-ne-gat killed his first squaw and Juan Chacón."[2] While much of this information was negative and misleading, it not only shows prevailing attitudes but also some very real concerns.

By August 1916 "General Scott's Indians" had abandoned every pretense of being on the reservation and were again entrenched in San Juan County. Posey attracted "eight or nine rather surly young bucks," who along with Polk's faction were buying ammunition and returning to their old practices.[3] In January 1917 the federal government wished to examine again the continuing unrest. Special investigator Major James McLaughlin arrived on January 1 and remained for eighteen days, interviewing the Indians at Towaoc, Montezuma Canyon, and Bluff. An unbiased source, he presented findings that clearly showed the destitute conditions and fear felt by many living in the area.

McLaughlin hoped that the Utes would journey to the agency to meet with him, but James C. Wilson, an assistant of Samuel Rentz, who owned a small trading post and home in Montezuma Canyon, wrote a letter on behalf of the Indians saying that the trip would be too great a hardship. These Utes, Wilson insisted, were afraid to go to the agency; many were sick, most without sufficient clothing, some were walking barefoot in the snow and living in shelters made of "old rotten canvas full of holes," and their horses were too worn to travel.[4] They were, however, very eager to talk with McLaughlin.

The inspector departed the agency and first bumped down McElmo Canyon by auto, then traveled by wagon up Yellow Jacket Canyon and across Cahone Mesa to the Rentz trading post, where he arrived on January 9 and stayed for two days. He met with all of the adult male Indians living in the area, whose total population he estimated at 160, with another 50 around Bluff. All of the Utes were enrolled at Towaoc. In attendance from Montezuma were John Benow, estimated at forty-five years of age, who was born and raised in the canyon and served as spokesman; George Brooks, a medicine man often associated with Cross Canyon; and Old Polk, then age sixty. The seven-hour conference was a cordial opportunity to air past grievances, but Benow refused to move or even consider the offering of a 146,000 acre tract of land in the southeast corner of the reservation. His band had 55 male adults, occupied good land in the canyon for their 600

William Posey, early 1920s. Posey became the most famous of all the White Mesa people by chance. Caught in the conflict over loss of land and resources, he defended his rights and property, and provoked, irritated, and fought with those who sought to take them away. The vest with what appears to be a U.S. military belt buckle was one of his trademarks. (Courtesy of San Juan County Historical Commission)

sheep and 1,200 goats, and willingly shared this area with Mancos Jim and his followers.[5]

The fifty-five-year-old Posey, with his Bluff contingent of ten men, met with McLaughlin the next day and expressed the same anxiety about moving to the reservation.[6] When asked why he had not honored the agreement he had signed to remain at Towaoc, both he and Polk denied ever agreeing to it and said James Allen, the Ute translator, had not made anything of that nature clear. Subsequent discussions with Allen, however, indicated that they had in fact understood the agreement. The settlers in Bluff

also talked to the inspector and gave him a list of suggestions that were no surprise. The basic themes of this dialogue were that the Utes were a "law-unto-themselves" they should be put on the eastern (farthest) end of the Southern Ute Reservation, their leaders should be moved away from the main body of people, and they should be rounded up in winter, when the Indians were less mobile.[7]

Although McLaughlin appears to have made a favorable impression on both the Indians and Mormons, future correspondence suggests that he viewed the ultimate solution to be the removal of the Utes to Colorado. Superintendent A. H. Symons later visited with Benow, who was waiting for the commissioner of Indian Affairs to call upon them and ensure the Indians' rights to remain where they were. The agent, on the other hand, knew that the opposite might happen and so asked that his soon-to-arrive replacement be given the responsibility of moving them so that it could be blamed on the military and not him. His explanation: "If a new man were in charge here, they [Utes] would not attach the blame to him and would start with a clean slate."[8] The move, however, did not occur.

The remainder of 1917 and the next six years were fraught with friction. With each of the Ute groups that McLaughlin had visited, turmoil seethed beneath the surface, eventually erupting into small conflicts. Starting with Montezuma Canyon, troubles festered at Rentz's trading post. One time, when Polk and Tse-ne-gat were camped nearby, Polk went to the store to redeem a belt he had pawned but questioned the amount of goods he had received in the exchange, believing the belt worth more. Rentz acquiesced to the Ute's claims and gave him additional supplies. A few days later Polk and Tse-ne-gat entered the store to eat dinner and became increasingly boisterous in their demand for bread and coffee. Although out of baked goods, the cook made more and gave it to the Indians, who crumpled it in their hands and tossed it under the table. Rentz ordered them to pay for their meal and get out, whereupon Tse-ne-gat reached for a pistol in his boot, only to go down under the blows of the trader. Polk tried to help his son by grabbing a knife from the table, but he too went down. The white man threw them out of the store, listening to their threats of vengeance as they left for camp. Tse-ne-gat returned and took a shot at Rentz from one of the canyon walls. Later Polk arrived at the post with his warpaint on and demanded $100 reimbursement for having been wronged in the incident. Some Navajos who were nearby eventually got Polk settled down, but Rentz, fearing retribution, took his family to Dove Creek, then went to Monticello to report the incident to the sheriff. The trader did not lodge a formal complaint, believing that in a few months the Indians would be moved to the reservation and cease to be a problem.[9]

Yet there were other whites who lived and worked with the Utes in Montezuma Canyon on a daily basis and valued their friendship. Henry McCabe was one of them, having herded cattle in the area since 1910. His appreciation, bordering on admiration, was fostered by the understanding that his cows were ranging on Ute lands. He often asked permission, made payments of meat and skins, and shared friendly visits. McCabe recalled camping one fall in the north part of Cedar Park, where he had stored 1,500 pounds of oats plus sugar, flour, honey, and canned goods under a sheltering overhang. He left the food unguarded when he went to Dolores on a week-long trip, and returned to find a well-worn path in the eight to ten inches of snow that had fallen. The Utes who were camping a quarter mile away had been curious as to what they could see in the cave, but not one of them entered or disturbed a thing. Another time a Ute named Short Hair showed his admiration for McCabe by taking one of his Indian ponies and placing it in the white man's herd. Nothing was said, just a mutual acceptance of friendship. The cowboy

later went so far as to suggest that the Utes served as guards and would warn him if anything were to bother his cattle.[10]

Compare this to an event two years previous in the same area when in 1915 the KT outfit was camped in Montezuma Canyon. Eighteen Utes approached, their leader suggesting to the foreman that since the cowboys had just killed a cow for supper and there was usually meat left over, the white men should give the Indians some. The foreman bluntly told the Utes, "Yes, we leave it for the coyotes and the skunks. We think more of them than of you." The Indians departed peacefully up the trail, found some cattle, and shot one for supper. Most of the men in the cow camp supported what the Utes had done and believed that the foreman was too scared to say anything to the Indians.[11]

The same type of low-grade friction grated at the nerves of Utes and white people around Blanding. A quick perusal of articles that appeared in the last four months of 1917 in the *San Juan Blade*, precursor of the *San Juan Record*, provides a glimpse of this irritation. One of the most common transgressions was Ute ponies in farmer's fields, eating grass and destroying crops. Other infringements included unwelcomed harvesting of gardens, robbing ranchers' sheep camps on north Elk Ridge, buying large quantities of ammunition from Navajos and Mexicans with a stated purpose of war preparation, stealing money and a watch from a ten-year-old boy, and hopping on a car driven by a lone and frightened white woman to demand a ride. The whites were also causing problems, charging Utes for livestock grazed in their fields, putting livestock on White Mesa Ute lands, and voicing subdued threats.[12] Many of these articles mention Posey's involvement in some way. His growing reputation, whether warranted or not, placed him in the spotlight, suggesting that he was behind a growing resistance.

Two other issues—World War I and the influenza epidemic—created additional unrest during the next two years. For the Ute people, the Great War raised the issue of citizens serving overseas. Registration for the draft, at first for those between the ages of twenty-one and thirty-one, and later between eighteen and forty-five, was required for all males, regardless of whether they were citizens or not. This included the Utes in the Four Corners area. Unfortunately, the date selected for registering in Durango coincided with the Bear Dance, so only six of the twenty-five men required to register did so. Reported in the papers as having spent "most of the day dancing war and 'bear' dances in native costume," the Utes had a poor showing.[13] A ten-day extension increased the numbers to nineteen, and eventually all twenty-five registered for the draft. Edward E. McKean, their newly appointed agent, explained that the Utes had not understood that registration did not mean they were being drafted, that they had a special deferment as Native Americans and noncitizens and thus were not required to serve but could volunteer.[14]

There was a particularly strong response among the Southern Utes in Ignacio. They signed a petition allowing the government to use their money in the treasury to fight the war, but also asked what would happen to their ranches if they went to fight.[15] Indeed, the Indians at Ignacio were the first in their county to go "over the top" in subscribing to war bonds. That was in April; by August there had been a definite shift in attitude. Whether it was disgruntled white men looking for an opportunity to boost their own importance, visiting Utes from the Uintah Reservation, ranchers and farmers attempting to exert more control on the Indians, or German agents, as one article suggested, the Southern and Ute Mountain Utes were faltering in their support of the war effort. Colorado newspapers claimed "Utes Opposed to Registration and Army Draft," "Indians Burn and Raid in Montezuma County — Angered by Proposed Draft," "Utes Leave Reservation and Clash with White Settlers in Southwest of State Are Feared," and "Open Rebellion over New Draft Extension."[16] There was little substance to any of it.

What is interesting, however, is that the Colorado papers felt that the resistance would most likely come from Polk and Posey, citing the 1915 fight as its example, while also mentioning Mariano. The *San Juan Blade* joined in, saying that the Utes were happy to see the young white men being drafted, thus evening the odds if they wanted to exert their own pressure. Even some of the friendly Indians, such as Mancos George, who had been a friend of the Mormons for thirty-five years, was said to be fomenting trouble among his people, who "nurse a special dislike for draft regulations."[17] McKean, after investigating all of the rumors, sent a statement from Buckskin Charlie that summarized the "present attitude of most of the Indians of this jurisdiction." Charlie, after tracing a brief history of early government-Indian relations and the signing of peace treaties, went on to say:

> We buried our arrows and tomahawks and guns, and we have never dug them up. We spread a white sheet over them to cover up all the black things that had been done. Now the government asks us to dig these up and to fight again. We do not want to go back to the old ways; we do not want our young men to register or to be taken away. Congress and the government who made this war did not ask the Indians about it. We feel like a man who has had a long sleep and who has awakened and been told things that are going on at the present and things that will be going on in the future…. I have heard that you have made out a paper with all the young men's names from eighteen to forty-five. I want you to rub those names off that paper. I do not want any of these Utes to register.[18]

Cato Sells, commissioner of Indian affairs, insisted that the Indians had to register but did not have to serve. The whole issue became a moot point a few months later with the signing of the armistice terminating World War I on November 11, 1918.

Following hard on the heels of the war was an influenza pandemic that took a huge toll of life across the United States. The Utes felt its grasp. On November, 14, 1918, the clerk at the Southern Ute Boarding School reported that all forty-five students were kept in school, not quarantined, and later sent home after being exposed. "Now there is or has been someone sick in nearly every home. To date there has been seventeen deaths from 'flu' all but one since the fourth of this month. As it is now, the sick are scattered over a radius of several townships, making it impossible to give them the attention necessary."[19] But by December 27, there had been only a few deaths because the Utes had "yielded readily to medical treatment and seemed to suffer much less than their Indian neighbors."[20] Another possible explanation is that the Utes' traditional curing practices did not require large groups of people to congregate in order to perform ceremonies, as did the Navajos. In fact, "When the flu was bad, most of the Indians left the agency, some going to Mesa Verde and some to other parts, and their ponies are so poor and weak they can neither ride nor drive them."[21]

The Utes did not, however, entirely escape the effects of the illness. They fled from their homes when someone died inside, and some fell prey to the elements and disease. Many had trouble understanding how white men could get sick, take medicine, and get better, while the Indians took the same medicine and died. By the end of the epidemic, white doctors had trouble treating Utes, who suggested "maybeso medicine given Indian was coyote bait (poison)."[22] The Indians had turned so mistrustful that they ran from their camps to hide when a white man approached, fearing he might be a doctor.

The Paiute people living around Navajo Mountain were decimated by the disease.

Perhaps one reason is that many of them did follow Navajo healing practices that encouraged people to congregate, and also there was far less medical attention available due to isolation. Anecdotal accounts suggest the overall impact. Fred Yazzie, a Navajo living in Monument Valley, recalls that groups of Paiutes and Utes traveled from Navajo Mountain to the Allen Canyon area, dying along the way. "The sick slowly made their way here. Whole Paiute and Ute families died off. Some babies had no effect from the sickness. In one place a mother had died two days before and the baby was still sucking on her. That is how the baby was found."[23] Because the two groups often visited, some Navajos believed that they had contracted the illness because of their interaction with the Paiutes. Gilmore Graymountain tells of going to the Oljato trading post and meeting a Paiute who begged for help. He went to his camp and found only a brush enclosure under a tree with two women close to death and two other women with children barely weathering the conditions. Cold, wind, exposure, and hunger took its toll; some were left behind as others moved on.[24] By February 21, 1919, the epidemic had subsided, and the dying ended; government officials held hearings to ensure that affected families received a fair inheritance of property from those who had died from the flu.[25]

During the remainder of 1919 and 1920, the same low-grade friction continued beneath the surface of everyday life. The cattlemen in San Juan County had no patience for Indians who appropriated livestock because their wild game had been depleted and living off the land was impossible. In 1919 Superintendent Axel Johnson visited with the white ranchers and other locals to talk about their long list of grievances. They accused the Utes of killing and mutilating cattle. They said the Indians would pitch their camps in the midst of the grazing grounds, select fat calves to kill, and then bury the bones so that all the cowboys found were mother cows with udders filled with milk. When they occasionally located a calf tied in a camp, the Indians would deny taking it.[26]

L. H. Redd estimated that he lost $1,000 to $2,000 in livestock each year, including purebred Herefords that had been killed or so badly mutilated that they had to be. One cowboy who asked some Indians where they had gotten the side of beef hanging in their camp were told "Lem's [Lemuel H. Redd] beef." Hanson Bayles was angry about six purebred ewes worth $200 each that had been taken from his corral and served up for dinner. When Bayles confronted the Indians for stealing the sheep, their reply was, "You see me steal um?" Reply: "No." "Me no do it."[27] Other complaints centered on the Indians denying access to summer range and water holes, running cattle until they were injured, stealing traps, and destroying poison coyote baits that also killed Indian dogs. Petitions and letters from local and state authorities to stop this behavior met the official stance from Indian Affairs that there was insufficient proof, that removing the Indians would just intensify the conflict and lead to bloodshed, and that those suggesting actions against the Indians were prejudiced and just looking for an excuse to get rid of them; finally, since Indian Affairs could not punish them for crimes committed off the reservation, prosecution of wrongdoing would have to be left to the state.[28] To the opposing side: "There seems to be no good reason offered by the Indian Department for allowing the Indians to rove at large."[29] Posey, not Polk, was now the one headlined in the papers and viewed as the main source of conflict.

It was just a matter of time before another incident occurred. On May 25, "Joe Bishop's Little Boy" and "Dutchie's Boy" stole one of John Rogers's calves, killed it, ate part of it for lunch, and dumped the remains in a wash. Polk, who had chastised these young men for doing it before, reported their act to Sheriff J. E. Powell in Bluff, who contacted Sheriff R. Lynn Hyde and County Attorney Fred Keller. They formed a posse of eight men from Blanding and then went to arrest the two Indians. What followed began as a carbon copy of the 1915 fight. The Indian camp, one mile west of Bluff, was taken by surprise. The posse surrounded it in the early morning and demanded the surrender of the two men, who fled toward the river, jumped a twenty-foot embankment, and hid in the bushes. When the sheriff pursued them, the Indians opened fire and then swam across the San Juan River, except for Dutchie's Boy, who had fallen on a sandbar in the river after receiving a slight wound under his left arm and a serious one in the knee. John Rogers and Gene Powell carried him to shore so the sheriff could evacuate him to Blanding for medical care and then arrest him.[30] Hints of further contact forced the white men to leave, but they later returned for their prisoner.

Again, yellow journalism had a field day. Newspapers reported that a man had been killed, the Bluff telephone and telegraph wires cut, the Indians were planning an uprising, Tse-ne-gat was gleeful for another opportunity for trouble, and a posse was en route, comprised of "cowboys from southwestern Colorado, eager to avenge the slaying of companions by Piutes" during the 1915 fight. To add to the surreal déjà vu, Marshal Nebeker was on his way.[31] Only a few false echoes of clashes occurred before the posse returned home from the nonexistent war. Mancos Jim, still the recognized leader of the Utes in Allen Canyon, came to Blanding with others and assured the townspeople that all of the Utes desired peace. The wounded Dutchie attempted to escape but succeeded only in losing a lot of blood before regaining his "hospital" bed.[32]

Further talks in Blanding, the surrender of Joe Bishop's Little Boy, and promises by Posey and Polk to end the theft of livestock quieted the uproar. Still, an estimated 1,500 steers and "a considerably larger number of sheep" had been stolen over the past year,

On a visit to Natural Bridges National Monument in 1921, Governor Charles R. Mabey stopped in Cottonwood Wash to visit with the Utes. He promised that if they behaved themselves, they could remain in the area and not have to move to Towaoc. *Standing, left to right*, Tse-ne-gat, Washington Dutchie, Joe Bishop, Anson "Scotty" Cantsee, unidentified, Posey, Governor Mabey. (Used by permission, Utah State Historical Society, all rights reserved.)

and some type of punishment needed to be exacted.[33] Governor Charles R. Mabey, on a tour to Natural Bridges National Monument, first met with the Indians in Blanding and the next day in Cottonwood Wash, near Allen Canyon, to cash in on the political bravado that headlines could provide. He directed Posey, Polk, "their chief medicine man [Joe Bishop]," and Tse-ne-gat to cease and desist with any theft, promising that if they behaved themselves, they could remain in the county. The two recently imprisoned young men had by then escaped by digging their way out of the log cabin jail in Monticello and were believed to be hiding in the Allen Canyon area, but according to the Utes living there, the two had not been seen. Both sets of parents, however, said they would urge their sons to follow the law.[34] When Governor Mabey returned to Salt Lake City, he approached Senator Reed Smoot about the possibility of the federal government purchasing Bluff and turning it into an Indian school for the Utes. Otherwise, "the San Juan situation is a powder magazine which may be exploded at any minute."[35]

Next on the docket was a trial in early June for the two young men, who had surrendered at the urging of their people. Christian Lingo Christensen, the interpreter from the 1894 meetings in Monticello, and trader John Hunt served as interpreters for this case, providing a description of the four-day courtroom drama. Christensen and Hunt translated from English to Navajo, and John Soldiercoat from Navajo to Ute. The defense spent the first day trying to show that both of the defendants were juveniles. One Bluff resident claimed to have spent twenty-three years throwing rocks at "Bishop's Boy" and vice versa; another mentioned that this Ute had a wife and three children, to which came the reply, "My boy married a Navajo widow with three small children; they are not his but belong to Haskeyninney's [Hashkéninii's] Son who died with the flu."[36] After other questionable testimony, the court accepted the fact that the boys were at least one month shy of being eighteen and therefore juveniles, and should be judged accordingly. Polk testified against them, saying that he had found them doing this type of thing before and was told to "shut up" and mind his own business. The Utes also complained that a number of their people had been killed in San Juan County and there had been no trial, but now there was a big fuss over a "little calf the navel of which was not yet dry from its recent birth." After three hours of deliberation the Monticello jury acquitted the boys of stealing the calf and burning two bridges. As for the charge against Dutchie's Boy of shooting at law officers, that would have to go to juvenile court.[37] Little resulted, and so to the local white populace, this was just one more example of the guilty going free.

Time for another special investigating agent from Office of Indian Affairs to visit southeastern Utah. Governor Mabey's suggestion of turning Bluff into an Indian school had resonated with some in Washington. By mid-July the commissioner of Indian Affairs had decided to send a new inspector to meet with the local people and Indians to determine the best course. On August 1 Elfego Baca received the appointment and was given four objectives to accomplish: (1) get the Indians' side of the story and their feelings about a reservation in Allen Canyon, (2) listen to the white settlers' complaints, (3) see how the lands around Allen Canyon were being used, and (4) determine if Indians were using the land called the Paiute Strip south of the San Juan River or if it could be withdrawn from reservation status and returned to the public domain for oil exploration (See chapter 14).[38]

By September 1 Baca was on the ground taking notes. The value of his work is in the testimony gathered and observations made of the Utes' situation. Too lengthy to cite in detail and repeating much of what has already been said, the report adds a few details to the general picture of their life. It is clear that they were living on the edge of poverty and feeling vindictive as "have nots" who had been pushed into an ever-shrinking corner and who were aggressively taking retribution on those who had put them there. A few examples will suffice. W. H. Redd testified

about two Ute boys who broke into the Nielson Cash store in Blanding and stole overalls, shoes, money, and groceries; local law enforcement eventually captured them and received confessions, but the two never paid a fine nor were otherwise punished. Twenty Indians surrounded H. C. Perkins while on Elk Ridge, struck him on the head with a rifle and beat him with a quirt while threatening to kill him. Others broke into the Mexican Hat trading post and stole clothing and jewelry but were later forced to return it. Indian men threatened white women at home and at work, requiring them to provide food and other supplies.[39]

Baca's report also captures the level of threats that had become a daily occurrence. The language is amusing now, but the fear it generated was real. "Mebbe so you go cow, huntem; me rock set down (waiting for you); me killem you." "Gimme bread, me shoot." "Me no scairt; Washington way up [far off]." Tse-ne-gat summarized his 1915 experience for the locals as: "Pretty good. Killem white man; Washington takem long way on the cars; give good chineago [Navajo for "food"], good bed, good time. Mebbe so Washington give em white squaw. Me killem more white man, get more ride and a good time." Finally Ione Hunt, wife of Marion Hunt, who was working at the Kigalia ranger station, told of how an Indian had demanded food when her husband was gone. She offered a dollar and dinner for hoeing the garden, but after fifteen minutes he was finished and demanded both. When she refused, he threatened, "All right, three days me go Elk Mountain, mebbe so you no see em your man any more.... Washington man way off, no savvy Bluff." Then, as he left, he told her six-year-old son that he was on his way to kill the boy's father.[40]

Baca's report includes some insight into the Indians' lifestyle and motivation. The investigator visited the camps in Allen Canyon and noted that the only tools the Indians had for gardening were digging sticks; they lived in shacks and had no provisions or

Inspector Elfego Baca visited the Utah Utes in 1921 on a fact-finding tour to determine the reason for continuing conflict and dissent. *Back row, left to right,* Mancos Jim, Posey, Baca, unknown, Jim Mike, Washington Dutchie, Anson Cantsee, Posey's Little Boy, Jesse Posey, and Joe Hammond; *front row,* Johnnie Peterson, Johnny Cockeye's wife and baby, Charlie (interpreter), Jack Fly, Joe Bishop's Little Boy, Havane's Son, and Johnny Cockeye. (Courtesy of San Juan County Historical Commission)

blankets, only a few sheepskins and rags. Kumen Jones mentioned that in the winter they added brush to the outside of their homes and then dirt, which kept them quite warm. They absolutely refused to be moved from Allen Canyon and blamed their pitiful state on the loss of game after the white man entered their territory. The young men killed livestock for food and mutilated it for revenge, which the elders condemned, but they were still in collusion with them. L. B. Redd testified that "They are in such a destitute and degraded condition that about the only way they can live is to steal, and they have no way of making an honest living."[41] The Indians were afraid of soldiers, and Kumen Jones recommended that if they were going to be removed, it would be best to do in winter, when they congregated. Baca felt it would be easier to invite them to Blanding, trap them while they were in town, and take them to a place far removed. Otherwise, it would take a hundred soldiers just to keep them wherever they were relocated to.[42]

The idea of Bluff becoming a school and reservation community was short lived. Following Baca's report, Major General Hugh Scott, serving as chairman on the Board of Indian Commissioners, visited Towaoc and its newly completed boarding school. His findings were caustic, calling into question why a $200,000 facility capable of handling two hundred students had been built for the forty-one Ute and seventeen Navajo students then enrolled. "It is outrageous that such an expensive plant should have been constructed with such a large portion of the Ute capital…when it is well known that the small size of the tribe, 456 in all, could never furnish many children to the school."[43] Scott felt that the funds should be used to get all Ute families a herd of sheep, build hogans, teach the women to weave, and basically turn them into Navajos, who at this point appeared to be eminently successful. As for a school in Bluff, Scott made no mention, but no doubt government officials had lost their appetite for such a venture at this point.

As the eventful year of 1921 faded into history, 1922 appeared to be a respite. Tse-ne-gat died of tuberculosis on February 1; six months later Superintendent McKean took charge of the Ute Mountain Agency; and the people in Allen Canyon continued their marginal existence.[44] There was no solution in sight to many of the issues raised recently. What can be said with surety is that the white residents of southeastern Utah were tired of the conflict and loss they were feeling from a handful of Indians, whom they felt should be on the reservation or at least controlled. The government had continually failed to find any solution with permanence, and despite the investigative committees, reports, and plans, nothing happened. Indeed, between the Indian Rights Association, the government agents, General Scott's support, and newspaper advocacy, the Utes' position for causing trouble had been enhanced. On the Indians' side, their poverty was a direct result of the white invasion that had removed everything they had depended on to survive. Their way of life had been destroyed, their people attacked in peaceful camps — in 1881, 1884, 1915, and 1921 — which to many of them seemed unprovoked, and although their Mormon neighbors were certainly better than the Colorado cowboys and non-Mormons (forty of whom now lay in San Juan soil), there was still plenty of friction. Again, it was only a matter of time.

The new year, 1923, began without incident. But as with previous outbreaks of violence, small acts mushroomed into larger events. While history does not repeat itself, patterns of history do, so no one was surprised to hear that Joe Bishop's Little Boy and Sanáp's Boy visited the sheep camp of Desidirio Chacón (a relative of Juan Chacón, killed by the Utes in 1915), evicted the tenant, and then helped themselves to food and other items before departing.[45] Chacón reported the theft, and after much discussion between the Indian and white communities, the two young men, now in their early twen-

ties, surrendered in Blanding to stand trial.[46] Sheriff William Oliver accepted their gesture and turned them over to Deputy Sheriff John D. Rogers to watch for a few days before the proceedings. Rogers kept them nearby while he was building a house, indicating that he expected little trouble. That first night, however, two men with rifles showed up to stand guard, and the Indians became noticeably alarmed. Joe Bishop and Sanáp, the boys' fathers, came from the Ute settlement at Westwater to Rogers's house and protested, refusing to leave. "Me seeum now," said Sanáp. "All night men with two guns watch, watch, watch. Me too, all night, watch, watch, watch."[47] Rogers said that shortly after these words were spoken, the guards went outside to help gather firewood, leaving their unattended rifles in the house with the Utes. If escape had been part of the boys' motives, they did not take advantage of their opportunity.

A few nights later Joe Bishop's Little Boy ate some scalloped potatoes and became violently ill. Rogers indicated that the young man may have been faking, but he let both prisoners go to their homes at Westwater with a promise that they would return for the trial. The next day Joe Bishop's Big Boy, a brother, appeared at the settler's home and actively complained of his sibling's treatment to Rogers's wife. "'All night boy shook like poisoned coyote,' he shouted at her. He waved his arms and shook himself violently. 'Mebbe so die! Me talk to Posey and he say cook potatoes and milk make heap poison.'"[48] It seems strange that if the two prisoners were intent on escaping that this man would have protested. Equally strange is the fact that on March 19 the two boys arrived at the trial as promised, Joe Bishop's Little Boy limping into court on a stick, apparently feeling the after-effects of his "poisoning."

There were other unsettling points for the Utes to consider. First, Joe Bishop was concerned about his son. He realized that his boy had been antagonistic toward the settlers and that there were strong feelings against him.

Lyman Hunter, a visitor to San Juan County who ended up staying for a few years, said, "I think his father had a lot of trouble with him from the way Joe Bishop talked with me about what he had tried to do. Joe Bishop talked with me just like an ordinary father who is having trouble with his son that was growing up, and he just didn't know what to do with him."[49]

A second problem was that Fred Keller, the prosecuting attorney, was the same man who had shot Dutchie's Boy two years before. Despite these drawbacks the Indians' attitude was that "they thought something ought to be done.... The [Indian] people would talk to the kids about it there in jail, and they [the prisoners] would tell them all about how they did it. They were hungry.... [but] these old Indians were on the side of the law this time."[50]

The trial went without interruption until lunchtime. The jury found the prisoners guilty, and since six hours had to lapse between verdict and sentencing by the judge, Sheriff Oliver waited for the courtroom to clear before taking the defendants to get something to eat. Whether it was the anticipated light sentence of ten days in jail or a desire to push the issue further, the young men changed their attitude of cooperation as they left the basement of the schoolhouse where the trial had been held. Here the statements of eyewitnesses vary greatly, but most of them indicate that Joe Bishop's Little Boy hit Oliver with his stick, the sheriff drew his pistol, which twice failed to fire, and Bishop's Little Boy grabbed the gun, mounted his horse, and as he rode out of town, turned and fired at the sheriff, wounding his horse. Chester Cantsee recalls: "Suddenly there came a rider galloping past me on a horse that looked like it belonged to a white man. It was one of Joe Bishop's boys. In his hand he held a pistol. Following right behind him was the sheriff. He was holding a gun. The sheriff fired a couple of times but Joe Bishop's son got away."[51] Sanáp's Boy, in the mean-

time, went with Posey, who was blamed by most whites as being at the bottom of this incident, and fled to Westwater.[52]

The fight was on, first shots fired, so news spread quickly as "every man dropped what he was doing and ran for his horse and gun then rushed to volunteer."[53] The rapid mobilization caught many by surprise. With a nucleus of six World War I veterans, Oliver sealed off the town and rounded up all the Indians within its limits. One man told how Dave Black brought in Joe Bishop, who insisted that he did not want trouble and would make every effort to bring his boy back. Black let Bishop go, but when the Indian thought he was out of sight, "He just whirled and took off as hard as he could ride. Black caught him then commanded, 'You old son-of-a-bitch. You turn around and go back or I'll let your guts out right here.'"[54] A sweep of the area netted about forty Ute men, women, and children, approximately half of the Westwater population, caught totally unaware.[55] This fact counters the belief of many white participants that the entire episode had been planned, food cached for an anticipated flight, and that Posey had plotted and directed the events. The great Indian uprising—or "Posey's war," as it is often billed—appears to have been more of a white uprising spurred by past grievances.

Initially, those captured stayed in the basement of the schoolhouse where the trial had been held. Described by Superintendent McKean as "warmed by a furnace and a stove...and fairly well-lighted and ventilated," the structure served as a temporary jail until the townspeople completed a one-hundred-square-foot stockade with ten-foot-high barbed wire fences closer to the center of town. The basement, initially crammed with forty people, whose numbers swelled to almost eighty, proved to be much too close of quarters for the Utes. They not-so-lovingly dubbed the edifice "the shithouse" since buckets in the corner were all they had to relieve themselves.[56]

The stockade built in the center of Blanding in 1923 had two hogans, some tents, a water spigot, and an outhouse. Guards patrolled the perimeter, townspeople brought food in daily, and occasionally a Ute received permission to leave the stockade to care for the prisoners' livestock. Treated as if they had started a war, these captives were really just victims of circumstance. (Courtesy of San Juan County Historical Commission)

Edward Dutchie remembered the day of his capture and subsequent stay in the basement. Just six years old, he had been in town and was on his way home with a group of friends when they spied several horsemen approaching through the trees near the Westwater Ruin. The children scattered "just like ants," jumping down into the canyon and scurrying under flat rocks where a space had eroded away. Some white teenage boys appeared, throwing rocks to scare the Utes out of hiding, but everyone remained under the boulders. After the searchers departed, the children were continuing on to their camp when "a lot of riders came out with their guns. Everybody knew there was trouble then. Some white guys got off and pushed the women around. They pushed us kids around, too."[57] Everyone who was cornered was brought to the school. Once they were put in the basement,

> each one of us took a place there. Maybe a woman and child or two or three kids all in one place. Men were pushed in with guns shoved in their backs. They were locked up and those that were still out were chased in, too. Some were out for something when they came home and found nobody there so

they went back into town. The [white] men would find them and take them. That thing was full. When they started using the restroom, it was into buckets. Boy, the smell would kill you in there.

> What I heard as a child was that they were going to take us away from our parents and the older people's heads [would be] cut off. Some of them were crying. One guy said, "What are you people crying for? You are crying because they are going to cut your head off? Why cry for it?" he said. "Let it come. Let them cut your head off and forget about yourselves. Try to be brave," he said, "maybe it won't happen." So everybody quieted down. That was the rumor going on among the Utes.[58]

Local men, with help from some Navajos, built the World War I-style barbed-wire stockade. The Navajos also constructed two large hogans, which with several tents sheltered the eighty captives for a month until Posey's fate was determined.[59]

Soon after the fracas began, a group of settlers visited Polk's camp in Montezuma Canyon to see if he had any intention of joining Posey's group. He said he had no desire to be a part of it, and told them that "if you fellows shoot Posey, pretty good alright."[60] McKean was convinced that the reason for this response was because the Ute horses were in a weakened condition from the poor winter range and so could not get the warriors to the scene of conflict. Another reason was that many of the rifles owned by Polk's men were in hock at the Montezuma Canyon trading post for supplies already purchased.[61] Polk's response also may have been prompted by a desire to please the posse; at any rate, he never entered the fight.

Members of the Ute community who had not been initially captured began fleeing, first to Murphy's Point, five miles south of Blanding, and thence west, most likely heading for Navajo Mountain, a traditional sanctuary during times of trouble. The exodus was not a well-planned retreat. As women and children moved away from Blanding with some of the men, others spread the word to outlying groups, while still others served as a rear guard. They watched to see if they were being followed, discovered they were, and fought a delaying action. Oliver took the opportunity to make the proceedings legal by saying, "Every man here is deputized to shoot. I want you to shoot everything that looks like an Indian."[62]

Not everyone in the posse shared that sentiment. Alma Jones, when later asked what his feelings had been toward Joe Bishop's Little Boy, said, "He was just friendly. He would shake hands with me and talk.... I just asked myself, 'What am I doing here? What would I do if I did come face to face with that boy and had to choose between shooting him or letting him shoot me.' It would be just like shooting one of your friends."[63] Posey, among others, returned fire with his .30-06 rifle, outgunning members of the posse at Murphy's Point and other places along the route. John D. Rogers had his horse shot out from under him, and three other men had a near miss when a bullet passed through the Model-T Ford they were riding in. The day concluded with most of the posse returning to Blanding, but ten men remained close to the trail at Fred Lyman's cabin, on the road

eight miles south of Blanding.[64] That night, guards stationed there spotted cedar bark torches being tossed high in the air to the west, signaling other Utes to come and join those who were fleeing. Little did they know that the other Utes were imprisoned in the school basement.[65]

The next day a posse of about fifty men renewed its efforts with an increased determination fostered at the previous night's town meeting. "We all knew that Old Posey wasn't going to be taken alive, and there was not one dissenting vote about what we must do."[66] As they advanced, they occasionally found spots where the Indians had "barricaded themselves behind rocks and banks" to use as fighting positions if the posse approached too close and threatened the escape of the women and children fleeing ahead with the goats and ponies.[67] By noon the whites spied the Indians' campfires across Butler Wash, at the head of what is now called Posey's Trail. The men dismounted, leaving their horses hidden and under guard in Butler Wash, spread out, and moved through the trees toward the camp. Dave Black and Bill Young reached the crest of Comb Ridge ahead of the others moving upslope. Below, gunshots rang out, and warriors emerged from the wash, taking the enemy under fire before retreating. Black, as leader of the group, ran downslope to better assess the situation, leaving Young at the top of the ridge. Posey emerged from the north, began firing, and then used his horse as a shield, riding in the opposite direction, possibly heading for a trail farther north, where Highway 95, when constructed, dropped off Comb Ridge near the mouth of Arch Canyon.[68]

Meanwhile, Bill Young held his position on the crest. After spying Joe Bishop's Little Boy and Sanáp's Boy riding toward his location, he moved downslope to avoid detection. The Indians spotted him anyway, whipping their horses into a run. Realizing that he could not outdistance them, he moved behind a bushy juniper and waited.

The two Utes rode on either side of the tree. Young sighted his rifle on the button of Joe Bishop's Little Boy's coat through the branches and fired. As the Indian toppled off his horse, Young moved to the other side of the tree to engage Sanáp's Boy, now in full retreat. Not wanting to kill needlessly, Young let him go, determined that the other man was dead, and rejoined his party. One testimony claimed that Young said, "There's one good Indian up there." Another person said he reported, "It was no fun to kill an injun." But probably the most realistic and sensitive account came from Alma Jones, who remembered, "It wasn't long until he came down. He was upset. He said, 'I have killed a man.' He just kept saying that. That wasn't like Bill Young at all. He is one of the most calm and collected men that you ever saw. He was really upset."[69]

The men in Butler Wash determined that at least one of the Indians, Jack Fly, had been released from Blanding for some reason. He was in their rear, sporadically firing at targets of opportunity. Fearing that all of the Ute prisoners had been freed, the posse returned to town, only to learn that townspeople had turned Fly loose to care for his livestock, but he then chose to help those resisting. In the meantime the Indians returned to the top of Comb Ridge and spent the night reclaiming their livestock and baggage before moving to a more defensible position. A second town meeting reaffirmed the whites' desire to either kill or capture the Indians not already incarcerated and end the issue. The next day forty men from Blanding rendezvoused with twenty from Bluff and then traveled up Comb Wash. Standing at the foot of Posey's Trail, the united party spied the Utes on top of "the Island," a high mesa a half mile wide.

Only two paths traversed the mesa's easily defended steep slopes. Splitting the force, the posse sent a handful of men to seal off the rear trail while the rest spread out and assaulted the heights. They encountered no resistance. There was only an abandoned camp,

cooking fires still burning, and food in some frying pans. The Indians had "found a treacherous trail on the opposite side of the mesa, jumping their horses down four and five foot ledges, managing to scramble to safety just ahead of us."[70] Oliver reminded his posse, "Now men, when you see the horse tracks separate and the good horses with the big feet go this way, don't follow them. You follow the squaw tracks on the little horses. The bucks come back to them every night."[71] But finding the Indians' trail became increasingly difficult. They had taken every precaution to stay on rock and had eventually descended a steep incline at night, illuminated by cedar torches, carrying only their weapons. The posse at first could find no tracks, making it "look like the red men had simply 'riz' in the air." Eventually they spotted an impossible place to descend, found a dog who had refused to go down, and lowered some of the posse members on ropes before again finding tracks along the base of the rimrock above the talus slope.[72] The chase resumed.

As evening approached, the Utes were holding the next mesa to the west; Posey had exchanged shots with Black the previous day, had been wounded, and had not been seen since. The posse had no desire to wage war in the dark and so spent the night at Frank Karnell's ranch at the mouth of Arch Canyon, sending volunteers to Blanding for food. Sunrise saw the vigilantes riding toward where they had stopped the chase the previous day. The Utes had disappeared through a crack in the rim into Dry Wash. The posse pursued. In the Utes' tracks and tied on trees, white pieces of cloth indicating a desire for peace fluttered in the canyon breeze. By evening the whites had them surrounded within a three-mile radius at the head of Dry Wash. A small boy with a white flag approached the camp first. Posse members sent him back with the message that everyone should come down and surrender, or else the whites would go up and "kill them all."[73]

That night the Indians came down from

Ute prisoners, 1923. Instructions were clear: shoot the man in front of you if there is any sign of danger or if given the command. With that, these Utes were marched down Comb Wash until a truck arrived to transport them to Bluff and then Blanding. (Courtesy of San Juan County Historical Commission)

above on different trails, carrying cedar bark torches to light their way, which the posse interpreted as an attempt to signal Polk in Montezuma Canyon to come to their defense. The Indians arrived without weapons. When asked to surrender them, they refused until Anson Posey went back up the hill with Dave Black and showed where they had been buried or hidden in cracks in the rocks. Black learned that they were totally out of ammunition and could no longer defend themselves.[74] With that the Utes settled down for the night around the campfire, Mormon guards kept watch, and all prepared for the next day's march down Dry Wash and into Comb Wash, where trucks were to transport the captives to Blanding via Bluff. The uncertainty of the situation took its toll on the people; they were nervous, afraid of what might happen, but also realized resistance was futile. Only one incident marred the truce, when "Sanáp's Boy became frightened and suddenly bolted from the fire and escaped into the darkness. John W. Newman from Bluff, who had formerly been sheriff in Arizona, fired a shot at him as he vanished

into the darkness. He was quite upset to find that he had missed his mark."[75] The Indian fled all the way to the San Juan River and a Navajo camp, where the people took him in.

The next afternoon only one of the two requested vehicles arrived. Oliver squeezed on the women and children and as many men as possible and started it rumbling on its way down Comb Wash. When the eight remaining Utes became restless, the sheriff feared trouble and ordered the remainder of the posse to get the prisoners moving. Rogers recalled,

> We lined the Indians up abreast in the bottom of Comb Wash, and a man with a gun got behind each Indian. The sheriff on his horse rode out on one side of the wash, and I on my mule rode out on the other side. We told the Indians that if Posey attacked or any trouble started, the posse men would immediately each kill an Indian without any questions. The sheriff and I were to fire shots if Indians were sighted or any trouble encountered. This would be the signal for the others to shoot the prisoners. If we had fired a shot for any reason at all, those eight Paiutes would have been killed.[76]

Fortunately, after two or three miles the second truck arrived and took all but the men who remained with the horses to Bluff, where they spent the night. Sixteen-year-old Ellen Lefler remembers walking through the encampment, where the captives sat around several campfires. Many of the women were crying. "It broke my heart because the tears were streaming down their faces.... It was a sad thing. These people had lost some of their loved ones. We walked out among the campfires. We thought maybe some of them would talk to us but they didn't. They hung their heads in grief and kept on crying. Their feet had been bleeding also."[77] Guards remained posted throughout the night.

That evening in Bluff the white men thought it would be useful to interrogate the eight prisoners individually in order to find out where Posey was located. Joe Bishop's Big Boy was the first to be separated from the group and questioned. Next the men took Anson Posey. His response was immediate: he "braced his hands against the door and refused to go in. The sheriff hit him on the fingers with his gun," four or five men wrestled him down, and then they started the interrogation.[78] He yelled, "'Me know! White man kill Joe Bishop's Little Boy and skin him now! Mebbe so kill me and skin me too!'"[79] Although no such incident occurred, the Indians viewed their captors as being capable of such actions.

Posey, the man whose name became synonymous with this fracas, was still at large. Last seen fighting around the large mesa to the west of Comb Wash, he never surrendered. During the month after the Utes were rounded up and imprisoned in the stockade in the middle of Blanding, his signal fires appeared on Comb Ridge, close to where he had disappeared. Posey spent his last days in a small alcove near the mouth of Mule Canyon. When the signal fires stopped, his people, thinking that he was dead, guided Marshal J. Ray Ward to where he had been hiding, and where Ute friends had visited

him. He had died of blood poisoning from a gunshot wound through the hip. That was the white man's explanation. The Utes, however, thought that he had been killed by poisoned Mormon flour. Jim Mike, Harry Dutchie, and others believed that the settlers could not find him and so laced a sack of flour with poison so that people released from the stockade to tend Ute animals would give it to him. He had made bread from it and died. The Utes who visited Posey, including his son Jesse ("Goatee") and Jack Fly, had unwittingly brought the poisoned flour to his camp. They say that later, after the settlers found his body, they shot it so that they could claim that was how he had died, but the white flour and bread in his hands showed what had really happened.[80]

Ward and some of the Utes who had led the marshal to the body buried Posey secretly. The law officer returned to Blanding and assured the townspeople, "Boys, I want to announce to you that Posey is dead and no other white man will ever know besides myself where he is buried. I buried him today and the tracks are covered up."[81] John Rogers remembers the marshal saying, "I have given the Indians my word that I will not tell where Posey is buried, but I assure you he is dead... and I ask that you take my word for it."[82] But the people of Blanding resented the "high-handed manner" with which the law had treated the situation. The next day, after a brief search, some townspeople exhumed the body, which happened at least three times during the next two weeks — once by Agent McKean from Towaoc, and twice by local settlers — to verify his death. It happened at least one other time; five years later the body had disappeared.[83] Thus forty years of physical conflict between the Utes and Paiutes and the white invaders was over, consigned to history.

The so-called Posey war was a product of its time, not only as the end of a long chain of events, but also as a commentary on contemporary affairs. Talk of electrified fences and aircraft armed with machine guns and bombs, the use of prisoner stockades and the dissemination of volatile propaganda, combined with tracking Indians using Model T Fords and horse-mounted posses, and engaging in old-fashioned gunfights, made this outbreak dramatic if not unique. As the old frontier passed away, modern inventions marked a new era dominated by machines and technological advances. Not only the equipment, but also the approach used by men who had been introduced to the military regimen of World War I played a part. While not showing tremendous skill in applying either, the white settlers in San Juan County were resolved to bring the existing situation to a close. Ironically, however, as Bill Young noted, "the Utes were as friendly after the war as before."[84]

As with other recent conflicts, the press irritated the situation by publishing inaccurate, overly dramatic, and inflammatory information. The month between the initial outbreak and the discovery of Posey's body provided the newspapers with yet another field day. Two reporters—one from the *Chicago Tribune*, the other from the *Salt Lake Tribune*—fired off press releases with only a thin veneer of truth covering a mass of outright lies. Under such headings as "Piute Indians Again on War Path; Attack Southern Community" and "Piute Indians are Reinforced," C. F. Sloane of the *Salt Lake Tribune* had Blanding besieged during "thirty-six hours of terrorism"; Indians in warpaint riding the streets; Posey, "the red fox," forming a "mobile squadron"; a well-planned Paiute conspiracy, which included robbing the San Juan State Bank; and finally "sixty men skilled in the art of the mountains awaiting the call of service."[85] In the best tradition of yellow journalism, and reminiscent of the lively reporting of World War I, reporters gave the town a military character: "Blanding since the outbreak has become more or less an armed camp. It wears the aspect of a military headquarters. The arrival and departure of couriers from the front is a matter of public interest."[86] When the citizens of Blanding kidded the reporters for their coverage, they replied, "We're not ready to go home yet and if we don't keep something going, we'll be getting a telegram to come home."[87]

Personalities from the past also inserted themselves at the first sign of conflict. The day after the trial and escape, General Scott offered his services to quell the problem, inasmuch as he had "very good relations with them [Utes], and if considered suitable, I feel that I can settle the matter now without further bloodshed."[88] Request denied but appreciated. Members of the Indian Rights Association offered to intervene and promoted the possibility of using Scott. Charles Burke, commissioner of Indian Affairs, felt that Superintendent McKean was sufficient.[89] Instead of Aquila Nebeker, U.S. Marshal J. Ray Ward appeared on March 22 as the law enforcer. He proved equally ineffective, unable to gain the trust of the local whites. He did hire a dozen men as deputy marshals to search for Posey for almost two weeks and to guard the stockade, but still he was an outsider. When the Utes finally guided him to Posey's body, he did his best to hide the grave and cover the tracks, but the townspeople learned of the Indian's death, questioned the white men who had been involved with the marshal, and located the site, contrary to Ward's instructions.

The predominant theme throughout the entire incident was that the settlers would allow no outside interference in settling this problem. The results from the 1915, and to a lesser extent 1921, disturbances would not be repeated. While the Indians at first believed that the Mormons would take a passive role as in the past and were surprised at the reaction, the whites were determined to find a solution. Albert R. Lyman captured the feeling when he wrote:

> We built a barbwire stockade, a 'bullpen,' and put them in it as a bedraggled bunch of piñon busted steers. Standing on the outside of the corral and

Bundled against the cold March weather, women and children receive rations in the stockade, 1923. This "bedraggled bunch of piñon busted steers" were held captive in these conditions for over a month. (Courtesy of San Juan County Historical Commission)

looking them over, as we had long been wont to do after a successful roundup, Bishop Wayne H. Redd remarked, "This is the first time these fellows have been stopped since the days of Gadianton."[90]

The Office of Indian Affairs, however, empowered Superintendent McKean to act. He concentrated on two goals. The first was to get the Ute prisoners to accept individually owned or allotted lands. Allen Canyon had been in the discussion for some time, and since McKean knew of the resistance of both groups of Indians to moving the Utah Indians to Colorado, a local subagency appeared practical. He was not convinced that Allen Canyon would serve as a good site during the winter, but he did feel that local supervision of the Indians, the creation of a local school, and local economic development could create a situation tolerable for all.[91] The agent had "talked personally with nearly all the people of Blanding," and "they do not wish them [Utes] banished from the country but they do insist that they should be confined to a certain area of land and have some

government supervision and assistance."[92] By mid-April, Special Allotting Agent A.W. Simington appeared and began dividing the land in Allen Canyon and surrounding area for individual use.

The second concern was getting the educational process started for the many children who had never darkened a classroom door. McKean gathered the adults together and explained that he could forcibly take the children to Towaoc, but that he would rather have the family and children decide to go. He sent them home to think about it; the next day eighteen children voluntarily boarded the school car and a hired automobile, leaving for the agency "in the best of spirits."[93] Edward Dutchie's recollection of the experience is not so pleasant. He had been in the stockade for a little more than a week when he and other children were given clean, donated clothing and "hauled away."[94]

After a full day's travel the children were put in boarding school beds for the first time. In the morning school workers came in yelling, got them out of bed, and then marched

Ute children in the stockade, 1923. One of Agent Edward McKean's main goals was to get the Ute children of southeastern Utah into school, something that had been avoided thus far. Some of the children were marched directly from the barbed-wire enclosure to an area where they received a hurried cleaning and haircut, after which they boarded vehicles bound for Towaoc. (Courtesy of San Juan Historical Commission)

them down to a long "trough" where they were to wash. The children had never seen soap before, and "some were looking up with that soap in their eyes. We didn't know what it was." The same problem with bathroom facilities: urinals and toilets were totally foreign to these children, who had been raised outdoors. Afterward the boys and girls were marched separately to the dining hall and seated at different tables. Edward recalled, "We helped ourselves. We had to eat because we did not have much to eat…. So I got used to going to school. They marched us in that school just like old time soldiers. The principal was an old veteran of WW I. I guess it was his way of doing it, to line us up that way. Later I got used to it. I went to school for eleven years."[95]

A new type of battle now confronted the Utes. The age of warriors, of the Posey and Polk era, had ended, with the Utes' former leaders either dead or aging rapidly. The rising generation no longer had to face armed conflict, but the new frontier being shaped by the dominant society. The previous forty years had been characterized by land loss, gunfights, and friction over resources; the next forty years would be characterized by cultural loss and dependence on a foreign society. In the end the Utes would have to face total immersion in white American culture. Armed conflict had ended, giving way to a different type of struggle for the Utes: to maintain their culture's traditional beliefs and practices.

CHAPTER 13

Avikan

Remembering the Homeland, 1923–1941

We have lived in this country many years. In this land our grandfathers and
our fathers and our families are buried. Our wives and our children have lived
and died here long before any white men came.... The white men are driving
us back and we are driven around the country like coyotes. When white men
settle in a country and have their many families there, they build a school. We
want a school built at the mouth of Allen Canyon where our children can go.

Mancos Jim

So spoke Mancos Jim to Ute Mountain Ute
superintendent Edward E. McKean on January 15, 1923, in a council held in Montezuma
Creek. Ute representatives from Bluff, Allen Canyon, and Montezuma Canyon were
present, and they elected Mancos Jim as
spokesman to discuss issues of land loss and
sovereignty. Thus, even before the Posey war
erupted, people on both sides of the canyon
were seeking a solution that would allow
the Utes to remain in the area while freeing white ranchers from having to deal with
conflicts over ranges and livestock. In Mancos Jim's eyes, there were two types of white
men inhabiting the country: the cowboys
who did not like Indians and drove them
away, and the farmers who wanted the local
Utes and Navajos to help clear the land and
perform chores. McKean felt that something
needed to be done to quell the intensifying
conflict between the two sides. If the land
could be allotted, a government farmer provided to give direction, and a school built,
the Utes would "make greater progress and
cease to become a source of trouble to the
government and a menace to the surround-

ing country."[1] The first two came relatively
quickly, but the school did not materialize for
another seventeen years. Even after McKean
transferred to the Rosebud Agency in South
Dakota in 1928 and E. J. Peacore assumed
responsibility for the Allen Canyon–White
Mesa and Towaoc Utes, little was done.[2]
The opportunity to wed education and economic development in Allen Canyon had
disappeared.

Two months after the discussion of allotments, the Posey incident exploded, sending
the captured Utes of the Allen Canyon faction to the stockade, while Polk's followers
in Montezuma Canyon watched the conflict
from the sidelines. Both groups felt the back-
lash of the escalating push toward a permanent solution to the so-called Indian problem
to prevent future incidents. Both groups also
were in the way of the stockmen, who did
not want to lose access to any land in Montezuma or Allen Canyons. Since this was public
domain, it was open to fair use by both the
whites and Indians, but the Blanding cattlemen "do not look upon it in that light, but
in the light that the Indian is a trespasser."[3]

McKean noted that the Utes' flocks of sheep and goats, which at one time had prospered, were now greatly diminished. Even though this was the most practical livelihood for these people to sustain themselves, it also put them clearly in competition with their white neighbors. Not welcomed on the Ute Mountain Ute Reservation in southwest Colorado, these Utah Utes had no desire to be uprooted from their ancestral lands. Given the options, local allotments were the only real choice.

As the Utes emerged from the stockade, the government had already determined their destiny. The complex of canyons west of Blanding—including parts of Whiskers Draw and Cottonwood, Hammond, Allen, and Dry Wash Canyons (which to the Utes became collectively known as Allen Canyon)—were targeted for allotment to the one hundred plus members of Posey's band.[4] Anderson Cantsee, born in 1870, recalled that his mother had been born in Allen Canyon, that both his grandparents were buried there, and that he had spent his entire life either there or in Blanding.[5] His family was one of ten who were living in the canyon during the 1860s as the Navajos' Long Walk period unfolded. Thus Allen Canyon, or Avikan, meaning "A House (or Home) of Rest" (*avi* = lie down; *kan* = house), fit very much into what Mancos Jim had described earlier.

Polk's group laid similar claim to the Montezuma, Yellow Jacket, and Cross Canyons region. Small allotted sections of these areas became available for Polk's group of about eighty-five members. For what was now being identified in agency correspondence as "Posey's Band," a subagency, or "the station," was to become the hub of activity in Allen Canyon, with a school and an agent to assist with economic development. Polk's group, on the other hand, received many of its services directly from Ute headquarters in Ignacio, which had recently subsumed Towaoc, sixty-five miles away.[6] Allen Canyon's four-month growing season between frosts, water available from plentiful springs

and intermittent streams, and its location next to Forest Service holdings offered lands desirable for both agriculture and livestock. Since the Indians had lived there "for at least seventy years" and had become a "stumbling block" for the Forest Service because of their hunting and grazing activities, the agency enthusiastically agreed to part with some of its border lands to get the Indians settled with an agent assigned to keep control.[7]

The task of dividing the lands fell to McKean and Special Allotting Agent A.W. Simington in March. The commissioner of Indian Affairs removed Simington from his assignment on the Navajo Reservation to facilitate putting the front-page Ute issue to rest. Important stipulations included making sure that all white improvements were honored, and that any driveways used to move livestock to summer and winter ranges remained open. To rancher Lemuel H. Redd, this point was crucial. Allen Canyon was his main thoroughfare for moving sheep from the winter lambing grounds in Cottonwood Wash to the Blue Mountains. As far as he was concerned, the Utes should be removed to Colorado and the lands kept open.[8] Most of the other townspeople in Blanding were not as concerned; they did not want to see the Indians punished or relegated to continuing abject poverty, just kept out of the way.[9] Simington and McKean sought an even ground.

On April 22, McKean, who was coming from Ignacio, and Simington, from Gallup, New Mexico, met in Aztec, New Mexico; they arrived in Blanding three days later. On April 28, accompanied by Jesse Posey, Indian Mike, Charlie Ute, and an interpreter (most likely Edwin Z. [or "E.Z."] Black), they visited the Allen Canyon area to better grasp their assignment. McKean was happy to find the prospects of a future community better than expected. He felt that early seasonal irrigation dependent on runoff from the mountain could be developed to an even greater capacity than had been done by previous occupants. There was sufficient land for allotment in 160-acre parcels, water at a shallow depth held promise for wells, a road from Blanding could be quickly built to haul construction materials for the agency, and a site for a school with support facilities was nearby. McKean made clear his intentions of starting the allotment process immediately for "the benefit of the Indians and the least inconvenience to the white stockmen," but each side would have to make concessions. Simington rented a house in Blanding, sent for his family, and began work—first on the Allen Canyon allotments, then those in Montezuma Canyon. The Utes from both groups urged the government agents to get the process under way.[10]

According to the General Allotment Act, each Indian qualifying for land could receive up to 40 acres of irrigable or 80 acres of nonirrigable farmland, or no more than 160 acres of grazing land. The head of a family could also select land for their children, thus adding to a larger family holding. The Forest Service provided part of this acreage, while part came from the public domain in order to keep family property contiguous. The Utes accompanying the survey party knew which families had been living in various locations and so had a voice in the allotment process. McKean estimated that the survey would be completed by July 10. One priority was identifying a school site central to all of the holdings.

The agent envisioned building a house for a couple, with the man to serve as farmer and economic developer, and the wife as teacher. Although rock was abundant, after considering labor and costs, McKean felt frame buildings would be most practical. Materials could be shipped from Blanding, twenty-two miles away, and what was not available could be ordered from Dolores. Although Indian trails crisscrossed the land, some of which undoubtedly fed more directly into Allen Canyon from Blanding, any shipping would have to be done on the road that dropped into Cottonwood Wash about five miles south of town. By 1925 a work crew had cut a more direct route across Brushy Basin. Some of the hills on this new road were steep, requiring a "four-horse team [to] pull an ordinary two-horse load." As for the agency, it was estimated that a three-room cottage could be built for $3,000 and a two-room school for $4,000.[11]

The deciding factor in selecting a site for "the station" was water. One tentative spot supposedly had a spring that never went dry—but it did that year. A second place, at the mouth of Hammond Canyon, had a large spring less than two miles upcanyon that promised never to go dry, was capable of producing a large volume of water, and was accessible through pipes.[12] That is where the agent chose to build the facility. In the surrounding canyon complex were an estimated 730 acres of irrigable, 480 acres nonirrigable agricultural, and 3,850 acres of grazing land. At present there were only 39 acres under cultivation, which the Indians prepared by burning the sagebrush when high winds blew, leaving the remainder of the work for hoes and shovels. There were only ineffective brush fences on a few plots to keep animals out of the gardens. Simington felt that within two or three years the inhabitants would be self-supporting and meet their occupancy requirement for ownership.[13]

There were still issues. Anglo livestock owners, such as Redd, did not want to see their "driveways" to the Blue Mountains cut off by Indian ownership of the thirteen sections being withdrawn for their purpose. The Forest Service agreed that existing trails needed to be maintained, but without hurting Indian homes, gardens, and grazing areas. The agency believed that there would not be a lot of animals—just "saddle and pack animals and a few head of cattle"—and that if the travelers stayed in the streambed, there would be little damage. If a few spots where falls and rock ledges could be dynamited out, the wash would be a suitable thoroughfare.[14]

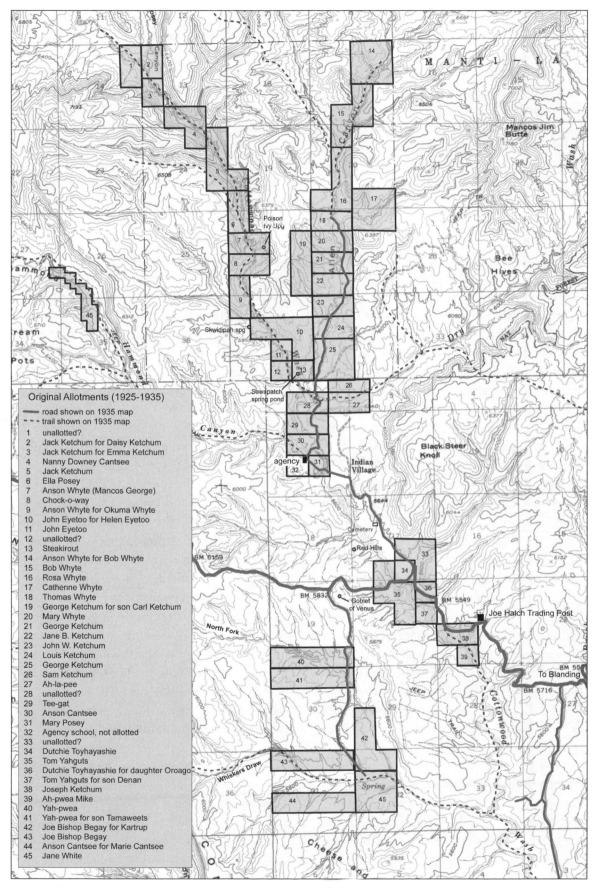

Original Allotments (1925-1935)

——— road shown on 1935 map
- - - trail shown on 1935 map

1   unallotted?
2   Jack Ketchum for Daisy Ketchum
3   Jack Ketchum for Emma Ketchum
4   Nanny Downey Cantsee
5   Jack Ketchum
6   Ella Posey
7   Anson Whyte (Mancos George)
8   Chock-o-way
9   Anson Whyte for Okuma Whyte
10 John Eyetoo for Helen Eyetoo
11 John Eyetoo
12 unallotted?
13 Steakirout
14 Anson Whyte for Bob Whyte
15 Bob Whyte
16 Rosa Whyte
17 Catherine Whyte
18 Thomas Whyte
19 George Ketchum for son Carl Ketchum
20 Mary Whyte
21 George Ketchum
22 Jane B. Ketchum
23 John W. Ketchum
24 Louis Ketchum
25 George Ketchum
26 Sam Ketchum
27 Ah-la-pee
28 unallotted?
29 Tee-gat
30 Anson Cantsee
31 Mary Posey
32 Agency school, not allotted
33 unallotted?
34 Dutchie Toyhayashie
35 Tom Yahguts
36 Dutchie Toyhayashie for daughter Oroago
37 Tom Yahguts for son Denan
38 Joseph Ketchum
39 Ah-pwea Mike
40 Yah-pwea
41 Yah-pwea for son Tamaweets
42 Joe Bishop Begay for Kartrup
43 Joe Bishop Begay
44 Anson Cantsee for Marie Cantsee
45 Jane White

Map 6. Allen Canyon allotments. (Courtesy of Winston Hurst)

McKean urged the stockmen to go around the allotted sections instead of through them, but Cottonwood was a natural thoroughfare and main artery for travel. Some officials suggested that if the west side of Cottonwood Wash were open, that would be sufficient, but once they understood that both sides held allotted lands, they realized this would not work. Others felt that the livestock drives, held twice a year, coming and going, would not be much interference and nothing to worry about. Still others suggested fencing the north and south ends of the allotted area, granting Indian approval and access for specific occasions.[15] The final solution lay in granting stockmen access to the wash without improvements, but also not requiring approval.

Another tit-for-tat game played out over water. One means of effectively stopping the allotment process was to file on the area's major water sources. Springs and ponds in question included Paiute Canyon and Douglas Mesa, two other areas under survey for Indian use, as well as Allen Canyon. Clark L. Bayles, a Blanding livestock owner, filed upstream claims for his ranch at the head of Allen Canyon. The state engineer announced it in the Salt Lake City newspapers, and Bayles sat back to watch what would happen. The Office of Indian Affairs knew that if the state engineer approved the claims, "all of our work and effort towards improving the condition of the Indians in the Allen Canyon region would be lost."[16] H. F. Robinson, supervising engineer of the U.S. Indian Irrigation Service, did his homework. He showed that Bayles had claimed the use of far more water than he needed, that he had only sixty acres of irrigable property, and that his intent was to thwart Indian settlement of lands used by stockmen. The government triumphed, his claim was modified, and on October 12, 1923, Calvin Coolidge signed an executive order setting aside Allen Canyon for Ute allotment; on May 31, 1924, H.R. Bill 2882 became law, making available forty acres of unallotted land for the school and farmer's station.[17]

Skipping ahead for a moment to the issue of the school, a primary reason for the sub-agency's existence, one finds that throughout the years when the station was a vital part of the community, no one ever built one. Allen Canyon children were sent instead to Ignacio, Towaoc, or Blanding, a story told fully in Chapter 14. Not until around 1940 did the government build a school in Allen Canyon, but by then the station had been abandoned, no teacher would sign a contract to live in the "wilderness," and World War II was looming on the horizon. The attempt to operate the school was short-lived, with few if any children attending. By the fall of 1946, when Albert R. Lyman opened a school outside of Blanding, at Westwater, to educate Ute children, the Allen Canyon School had been closed for years.[18]

During Simington's allotment process, Polk's band in Montezuma Canyon did not fare well. Its members faced issues somewhat similar to those encountered by the Allen Canyon group, but on a larger scale. In early July, when the allotting agent undertook the task of partitioning lands in Montezuma and Yellow Jacket Canyons, he found them already claimed. "From Rentz' Store in T. 39 R. 24 to the mouth of Montezuma Creek the land is all occupied by Navajos who live here all of the time and make good use of the land. From the store up the creek for seven miles all the land in the valley has been filed on by white men. These are not recent filings but have been of record for years; there is a home and family on nearly every homestead."[19]

Simington increased the previous estimate of the size of Polk's band to 125 or 150 Utes, found that they had no place to settle, and discovered there was no access to water. The Utes had made no improvements on any property, were transient enough to have not claimed any particular location, "were the most primitive Indians in the country," and were not ready to accept the idea of having individual holdings. Polk deemed none of the land satisfactory, so only George Brooks and two others received small allotments in Cross Canyon. Simington was clear: "I offer no recommendations as to its solution"; he had completed his task as best he could. McKean had no solution either. He met with Polk's discouraged band, which was still determined to remain in Montezuma Canyon. The only hope the agent offered was that perhaps the white homesteaders would be willing to sell their holdings, but he feared that their price would be too high.[20] He told them he would get back to them once he had a solution. Some did not wait, instead moving to Towaoc, while others, such as James Morris, Lewis Collins, and Harry Lang, took their families to Allen Canyon.[21]

With the survey completed, McKean began looking for a man who could devote his full attention to the Allen Canyon subagency. Edwin Zemira (or "E.Z.") Black, from Blanding, having already assisted with surveying and fluent in Ute, received the job and the official title of "stockman." Known to the Utes as Pannápiġyet ("Glass Eyes" or "The One Who Wears Glasses"), "Blue Eyes," and "White Father," Black was also a farmer, engineer, and man-for-all-seasons. He began working with his charges immediately, but construction of the station was slow in coming. Bids went out for men and materials, but changing fiscal years, a lack of carpenters, poor roads, and winter weather pushed construction into 1924, then 1925. Tools and machinery, barbed wire, and lumber came from as close as Blanding and as far away as the railroad in Durango, but to get it to Allen Canyon required good transportation.[22] The distance over the circuitous and difficult route through Cottonwood Wash was shortened by following part of an old Indian trail that went west of Blanding through Big Can-

Edwin Z. ("E.Z.") Black, 1930s. Black spoke the Ute language, truly cared for those he worked with, and had the patience necessary to assist during a difficult period of transition. Ute elders today have fond memories of this soft-spoken agent, recalled as "a good man." (Courtesy of Nada Black)

yon (known to the Utes as "Deep Canyon"), Brushy Basin Wash ("Clay Valley"), and thence Cottonwood Wash to the agency site at the mouth of Hammond Canyon.[23]

At least one person did not wait for the completion of the shortcut. E.Z. enlisted his son, Allan, to haul lumber down the old route in Cottonwood as the new road crew labored in Brushy Basin. Sandy roads, a heavy load, and difficult terrain made it a tiring two-day trip. Allan returned to work on the road crew until E.Z. had another shipment of lumber to add to the accumulating pile of materials that eventually turned into a cottage. He made the trip with another driver, but on the way home he spotted the road crew in the bottom of Brushy Basin and decided to traverse a new, unexplored route. Against the protests of his companion, Allan started his team downslope. In his words:

Old Red and Brownie were pulling the wagon and I started down through the trees. I picked a ledge about three and a half feet high and went off from that, rolling over rocks as I went. Willard [Young] was behind me. When we got down to the bottom, those guys could hardly believe we came down that way. I was the first fellow to cross Brushy Basin in a wagon.... When I got up on this side, there was old Scotty Ute and three older Utes. Scotty was kind of a witty old devil. He looked at me with a twinkle in his eyes and said, "Hum. Where are your wings?" He knew that I had been out at Allen Canyon and that there was no road down the other side, but we had saved a whole day by coming across that way.[24]

By the late spring of 1926, three years after E.Z. had begun working with the Utes, the station was ready for occupancy. What follows is a composite picture of events and accomplishments during Black's tenure, which ended when he left in the spring of 1938 to assume stockman responsibilities in Towaoc for the next three years. Three distinct voices explain what daily life was like during Black's sojourn in Allen Canyon. The first is that of Black's own family, who moved into the cottage that spring and remained there until the fall and the start of school, when the family returned to Blanding. The Ute people lend the second voice. Many of them established a pattern of living in Allen Canyon in the summer and then returning to their Westwater or White Mesa encampments to put their children in school, get out of the deep winter snow, and use winter range for livestock. The third voice is that of Joe and Stewart Hatch, who in 1931, at the request of the Ute people, established a trading post on the boundary of the allotted lands. The store remained there for ten years, until much of the activity in the area ceased. All three voices add perspective to the picture of daily life at the subagency.

E.Z. and his wife, Chloe, had six children at the time, two of whom—Allan the oldest and Zelma the second youngest—have shared their experiences.[25] Zelma, or

"Jawma," as the Utes pronounced her name, also known as "Blue Eyes' Daughter," recollected the family's first move to the agency. The family horses and cows went in front of the two wagons, groaning under the weight of a piano and all of the clothes and some of the food needed for the next three or four months. Tied to the sides were dynamite boxes with screen lids to contain the chickens inside, while the children fit in where they could. The road was rough and steep, demanding nine hours of travel.

The next year, 1927, the government provided a Model T Ford, and in 1929 Black received a new Ford truck for hauling children to school, the sick to Towaoc and Ignacio, and commodities for distribution.[26] This decreased the travel time and effort, but still the roads were a constant concern. They washed out and gullied with intense rainstorms, becoming slick with wet clay or blocked by sliding rocks and debris. Indeed, few people traveled the road after it had snowed or rained because it was so treacherous. When Black did attempt it, his greatest concern was Clay Hill, coming out of Brushy Basin. To many it was "a road to be fearful of."[27] Ute men often walked on both sides of the vehicle to prevent it from slipping off the path and careening down the hill. Although motorized traffic increased over the years, the agency maintained a team of mules and wagon for general use, available to residents with special needs. Stella Eyetoo, as a young girl, made several trips to Bluff in the wagon with Pochief Mike and other women to pick sumac for baskets.[28]

Over time the agency expanded. At its zenith, in 1938, there were several buildings that met a variety of needs. The wooden cottage had three rooms—a living room and kitchen, each with an outside door, and a bedroom. Screened porches on the south, east, and north provided comfortable visiting and sleeping accommodations during the warm summer months. A propane refrigerator cooled the food, a wood stove cooked it and provided central heat, a cement-and-dirt dugout on the side of the hill preserved large quantities of family food, and the outhouse south of the home completed the food cycle. Black distributed rations and supplies from Towaoc twice a month, storing them in a large wooden building. There was also a combination blacksmith, machine shop, and tool shed. North of this stood a corral for the horses and the Jersey cow, whose "milk was so rich it made butter on the side of the pail."[29] East of the cottage lay a communal garden flanked with apple, plum, and other fruit trees. Corn, melons, squash, and beans were popular; the beets were not, described by the Ute farmers as tasting like dirt.

Water was absolutely critical to the agency's success. A well with a windmill-driven pump set in operation in 1930 provided cool water that was so hard it reeked of iron.[30] Unpalatable and too hard to even use for laundry, the water went to irrigate crops and quench the thirst of livestock. The spring in Hammond Canyon, however, provided excellent drinking and irrigation water. The problem was maintaining sufficient elevation so that it could reach the house. E.Z. asked for the assistance of his father, Ben Black, in Blanding, who was not only a self-taught engineer but handy with a stick of dynamite. The two drilled holes in the rock wall to the west of the house, packed them with explosives, and watched the rock slough off the face of the hill, making room for a wooden flume to carry the water. Eventually the land met the flume, and from there water could be ditched or piped. One of E.Z.'s biggest projects was bringing irrigation water to individual Ute gardens spread throughout Allen Canyon and Cottonwood Wash. Concrete headgates, pipes, plowed ditches one and a half to two feet deep, and diversion dams laced the canyons' floor, bringing a more dependent source of water to supplement summer rains and stagnant pools left from spring runoff. Beyond these ditches, in the more southerly parts of Cottonwood Wash and Whiskers

Draw, either short family-made ditches from springs or pot irrigation had to suffice.

A few excerpts from E.Z.'s daily logs give a sense of the stockman's life at the Allen Canyon Agency during the last six months of 1925. As early as that January Black had requested a team of horses to plow ditches and sixty-five acres of unbroken soil, and then another forty acres on Ute farms that had failed to produce the previous year. He could use this same team to haul supplies from Blanding, since McKean was not too keen on employing a Black or a Redd because of the expense and what he considered poor service.[31] E.Z. ordered dynamite and seeds for corn, beans, potatoes, onions, melons, and a variety of squash in preparation for the summer's work. By July, when planting should have been well under way, measles broke out in the stifling heat, preventing any meaningful labor. Black spent three weeks visiting the camps and putting up fence while people recuperated. Joe Bishop Jr. and Mary Cantsee's camps burned to the ground, destroying everything.

On August 1 Black reported, "The crops are nearly all dead except some we got irrigated and they are looking fine. We have been able to save two pieces of alfalfa and part of two more besides forty or fifty acres of corn, some potatoes, squash, and melons."[32] A week later he went to Monticello to see if he could obtain any of the guns that had been confiscated during the Posey fight two years earlier because the owners wanted them back for hunting season. None were located. He next brought a woman to the Towaoc hospital, where she died of venereal disease, and then returned to Allen Canyon and lectured the men about not being so hard on women. By September Black had recruited eighteen children from sixteen camps to go to school in Towaoc; fixed the road that was badly eroded; made a casket for Ellen Eyetoo Hatch, "a favorite among the Utes as well as her family," and then buried her in the Allen Canyon cemetery; checked out the range

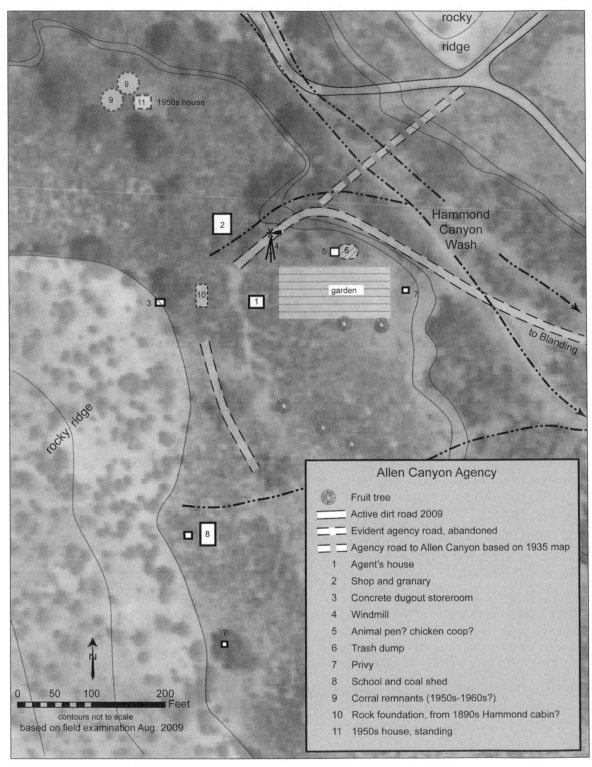

rocky
ridge

Hammond
Canyon
Wash

1950s house

garden

to Blanding

rocky ridge

N

0   50   100   200
                            Feet
contours not to scale
based on field examination Aug. 2009

Allen Canyon Agency

Fruit tree

Active dirt road 2009

Evident agency road, abandoned

Agency road to Allen Canyon based on 1935 map

1   Agent's house
2   Shop and granary
3   Concrete dugout storeroom
4   Windmill
5   Animal pen? chicken coop?
6   Trash dump
7   Privy
8   School and coal shed
9   Corral remnants (1950s–1960s?)
10 Rock foundation, from 1890s Hammond cabin?
11 1950s house, standing

Map 7. Allen Canyon Agency. (Courtesy of Winston Hurst)

"E.Z." Black teaching spring planting techniques in front of the station at Hammond Canyon, 1930s. The garden, whose produce was shared by all in the community, augmented individual family plots. Other efforts included caring for livestock and planting alfalfa and hay, as well as a large number of fruit trees, some of which remain today. (Courtesy of San Juan County Historical Commission)

near Blanding to see what feed would be available for the sheep and horses in the winter; and worked with various families for a week to surrender the children who had run away from Towaoc, a hundred miles away, and had recently returned to Allen Canyon.

October was just as busy.[33] E.Z. again repaired roads damaged by intense rainstorms; drove five men to Blanding to work in a uranium mine in Dry Valley; helped bury a child who had died of "summer complaint"; used the few men not heavily involved in deer hunting to again fix the road and put up fence while most of the women picked pine nuts; and again obtained and issued rations. One event out of the ordinary was Black's trip to Blanding to obtain the body of Elsie Whyte, Jack Ute's wife, who had died and was to be buried at Allen Canyon. "After I had got there,

she revived and was two days longer dying so I stayed to look after her removal." He spent November plowing before the ground froze, continuing to teach his charges how to work a team and plow, "for they don't know anything about horses, only to ride, but most of them are willing to try so I think they will learn"; he also traveled to Butler Wash to have Jim Mike and Joseph Ketchum move their camp to Allen Canyon and off the white men's cattle range, and then followed orders from Towaoc to find two men scheduled to appear in court in Pueblo, Colorado. He located them in Towaoc and spent the next week completing that assignment. At the end of November and beginning of December he traveled to Fry Canyon and elsewhere to find missing cattle that belonged to Jim Mike and Herbert Stacher. He made three trips to Blanding to obtain enough lumber for a sheep-dipping vat and then met with the district forest supervisor and local stockmen to discuss obtaining more range on the forest lands, but was unsuccessful. He ended the year by responding to McKean about how he was going to dispense the 8,000 pounds of hay and 1,500 pounds of oats to Indian livestock.[34] Thus ended a typical six-month period.

Chloe Black was just as busy but less mobile than her husband. She assisted with the large community garden and also spent much of her time teaching the women how to can and dry fruit and vegetables, make quilts, and use the treadle sewing machine provided by the Indian Service to fashion layettes for the babies and clothing for the people. When the sewing machine was first introduced, many of the women "stood back and really watched the needle go up and down through the cloth.... After they were around it for a while, got used to it, and saw that it really wasn't going to hurt them, she was able to teach them to sew and a number of them got quite handy at it."[35] Chloe also assisted as a midwife and nurse, delivering babies and providing simple medical instruction on caring for wounds, preventing pneumonia, and curing bronchial infections. One time a family argument ended with serious injuries to a woman's head, which Chloe sewed up with a needle and white thread; she also adopted two daughters, Mollie and Katie Deer, who lived with the family for years until they were married. They always called the Blacks "Mother" and "Father."

The Ute people reciprocated with friendship. Every fall one woman, Tazhunie, brought a gift of a one-hundred-pound sack of piñon nuts to the station, and at other times a fine basket or beadwork. E.Z. often received a hind quarter of deer meat, sometimes identified as a leg of goat during the nonhunting season. The Utes' love of children won Zelma's heart through Anson Cantsee, known as Scotty. He would sit on the porch and hold her in his lap and teach her Ute

words. Life in the camps was primitive, and lice were common, but Zelma did not care about these new "friends" — even after her mother washed her hair with kerosene and combed it with a fine-toothed tin comb accompanied by a gentle scolding. It did not matter. As soon as Scotty was back, Zelma was up in his lap learning Ute. Another close friend was Mancos George, who assumed the responsibility of resident policeman and truant officer, lived near the agency, and was ever attentive to the Black family's needs. Zelma recalled: "Mancos George, whose house was about three blocks away, always came and slept on the ground at the front of the house and looked after [her brother] Greg's and my safety. I'm sure I never felt afraid.... I don't think my dad ever hesitated for a minute to leave the two of us there alone. These would be overnight trips to Ignacio and sometimes he'd be gone as long as three days, as we stayed there to do the chores."[36]

Still, not all was peace and light. One of Joe Bishop's older boys, Navúü ("Copy Cat" or "Imitator"), who had lost a brother in the Posey conflict and resented white influence, transferred his hostility to Black. He notified the agent that on a certain day he was going to come to the station and kill him. Early in the morning of the appointed day, he arrived with a .30-30 in hand and took up a position on a knoll across from the house. E.Z. was very much aware of his presence, but despite Chloe's pleading went about his chores outside from sunup to sundown knowing there was a rifle aimed in his direction. Black reasoned that if he showed fear, he would have to put up with a disagreeable situation for the rest of his sojourn in Allen Canyon. His gamble paid off; the incident ended peacefully with no more said.

As a teenager, Zelma also had a run-in, this time with Johnny Soldiercoat, who took pleasure in giving her a hard time. She customarily helped her father distribute rations, and on one particular day Johnny became so irritating that Zelma picked up a big rock, let fly, and hit him squarely in the head, knocking him unconscious. People started yelling for the agent, who came on the run to find an unrepentant daughter. "My dad nearly skinned me for that. He really gave me a talking to. After awhile that old boy woke up and he stayed pretty clear of me from then on." For years to come, many Ute witnesses kidded her about the incident and seemed to feel it was justified given the teasing she had taken. Her father was not so sure.[37] These two examples were exceptions to the general feeling of peace and cooperation that existed between the agent and his family and the Ute people.

Although Ute oral history confirms a general admiration for Black and what he accomplished — Indian accounts often ending with "He was a good man" — there were definite differences as to what the people felt important. The agent pointed out that the Utes were transitioning from a lifestyle demanding mobility for survival to the sedentary ways of agriculture. The size of the population served by the agency ranged from a low of 45 to a high of 120 people. In the 1928 through 1931 censuses 63 people labeled "Pahutes" were living there, and another 103 categorized as Utes.[38] Because some of them were part of what was then called Posey's band, they were classified as Paiute even though they were Ute. Intermarriage confused the picture further, with Paiute people marrying Utes who were picked up on the Towaoc census, while still others from Polk's band ended up on both rolls. Add to this the heavy visiting and friendly relations between the groups, and then sprinkle in some Navajo relatives, and one finds a homogenized mix of people. What can be said with certainty is that the life lived and the beliefs practiced were Ute.

What was this life like? Medicine men played an important role in the community. Among the practitioners were Joe Bishop, Washington Dutchie, Mike Jim (Jim Mike's uncle), Mormon Joe, and George Ketchum.[39] These men specialized in protection and healing, and there is some indication that

Navajos traveled to Allen Canyon to be cured by Ute healers, whom they viewed as more powerful than their own medicine men.[40] George Ketchum, for instance, would bless a newborn boy by wrapping him in a freshly killed mountain lion or bear skin so that the child would have it as his guardian spirit, giving him power to fight for and protect his people.[41] Others, through dreams and as a spiritual gift, healed patients by sucking out supernaturally implanted objects. Mormon (or "Merman," as the Utes pronounced it) Joe performed this on Stella Eyetoo, who described having a pain in her head that "felt like my head would break."[42] Mormon Joe prayed and sang and sucked out what was bothering her — a bloody mass — and by that evening she felt a lot better and on the road to recovery. Mormon Joe became wealthy through his practice, rode a large white horse, and lived on a bench southwest of the Hatch trading post. When he died, the people buried him in the rocks on the west side of Cottonwood Wash, and his family killed all of his sheep and horses to be with him in the afterlife. As Stella said on a number of occasions, "He was a good medicine man."

Zelma and her father witnessed a similar ceremony in Joe Bishop's hogan. Bishop chanted as he leaned over a man with acute stomach pain. Around the healer's neck hung a buckskin thong strung with "little feathers and little cloth pouches probably filled with powdered herbs or colored clay, and there were great big animal claws, probably bear claws…. Finally…he raised up and started pulling little rocks and pieces of wool out of his mouth."[43] Despite these efforts, the patient died.

Women also practiced medicine as herbalists and midwives. Bonnie Mike Lehi and Stella both gave birth in the traditional way — a practice taught by Sináwav, the Creator, in the beginning. When people had approached him to ask what should be done when a baby is born, he instructed them to erect a large forked stick in the ground inside a shelter, suspend a strip of cloth from the fork, form a depression lined with a blanket close to its base, and have the expectant mother kneel or squat over the blanket. Stella's family set up a tent under a large cottonwood tree, where she delivered a son with the help of a midwife who pushed down on her stomach to ease the baby out. After the delivery the woman bound Stella's stomach with a wide cloth and gave her warm water to drink, since cold water clotted the blood. Stella vomited. Next the midwife gave her a shaved oak stick a foot long for her to push downward on her stomach if she had abdominal pains. "People got after her" if she did not follow instructions—for thirty days she could not eat meat, someone else had to comb her hair, and she could drink only warm water. Her husband also had restrictions, but just for ten days. Following the birth of the baby, the husband bathed, changed his clothes, drank warm water, and gave a present, such as a beaded belt or bracelet, to someone.[44]

As with Agent Black, water was a primary concern for the Utes living in Allen Canyon. While the agent's efforts centered on harnessing this resource for gardens, the Utes had additional concerns. Informants today speak of dangers involved. Flash floods in the summer quickly arose from storms in the mountains that spread water through a canyon system that greatly multiplied its volume by the time it reached Allen Canyon. At the head of Hammond Canyon was an area called Slickrock that was a particularly heavy contributor. What may have started as a dry day could end with a seething mass of brown, roiling water six to eight feet high careening down Cottonwood Wash as a wall of destruction that tore out cottonwood trees, irrigation systems, and anything else in its path. Today trees and tamarisk impede rampaging waters and secure the wash's sides; in those days there was less to stop floodwaters, so the banks caved under its force.[45] There are no known fatalities from these summer floods for a good reason. Many people said

that long before the water arrived, they could hear large boulders and hefty trees scraping along the bedrock and against the banks, sounding like an approaching train. Others mentioned how they could smell the water as it neared, and once it roared into sight, there was a fine spray of dust that preceded the wall of water forcing air before it. Within minutes the wash would fill, and within hours the flood would subside, leaving a two-foot-high stream of mud as a reminder.[46] These rains also filled the rock cavities, or *tinajas*, in the sandstone ridges, and these could hold water for days. Called by the Utes "frog's home," these basins provided water for sheep and their herders away from more developed sources.[47]

Accompanying summer rain was lightning, something to be feared. When a storm blew in, adults cautioned children to get under shelter, a rock overhang if nothing else, and sit quietly. Bonnie Lehi, as a youngster, herded her family flock of goats and sheep on the hills and in the canyons, but once the thunder and lightning started, she moved to safety and gained control of the herd later. Both thunder and lightning can be quieted through prayer, but once a tree or object is struck by it, sickness, even from the smell of the burned wood, can result. Adoline Eyetoo agrees. Lightning struck a pole at her house, and now her body is crippled.

One sultry June day in 1926, Scotty had just enough time to get his animals home under the large cottonwoods. When the storm hit, lightning struck a tree nearby, killing eleven goats and a sheep. He would not touch the carcasses, so E.Z. had him dig a trench for burial, but the agent was the one who had to place them in their grave. Before doing so, he removed the bells worn by the lead goats and offered them to Scotty, who would have nothing to do with something struck by that power. He warned Black that lightning would kill him because of the things he had touched. The agent waited until the next electrical storm and then worked outside the entire time. The lightning did not strike him, convincing many of his neighbors that he had strong protective powers.[48]

Water also demanded respect in a different way at "Green Pool," located at the mouth of Allen Canyon. Larger then than it is today, the deep, spring-fed pool also filled with runoff from the canyon during flood stage. It provided a constant source of water, but also held *paá'apači* ("water babies"), which could pull swimmers down into its depths. Annie Cantsee remembers swimming with Nedra Ketchum one day when something began pulling Nedra down. Annie swam out to assist as the desperate girl kept sinking and then bobbing to the surface. Wrapping her arms around Annie's neck, the two were both in danger of going under, but Annie managed to get her friend to shore. Not surprisingly, "We never went back."[49] For that same reason, Pochief Mike, who lived near Green Pool most of her life, cautioned her grandson Aldean Ketchum never to go swimming there alone or at night because the water babies would capture him and take him to their home. The locals say that at night one can hear them crying at the pool.[50]

Another source of concern was snakes, Allen Canyon having an abundance. The large bull snake that the Blacks allowed to remain in their food cellar stayed with permission in order to keep the mice population down. And the rattlesnake that E.Z. rolled around with his foot in the garden, thinking it was a piece of wood, was not a major concern.[51] But when Charlie Ute visited the station and sat down on a box to talk to Black and an unmistakable rattle sounded, he became wary. The viper was nowhere to be seen, so the conversation continued until a second warning rattled. The agent had Charlie Ute get off the box, kicked it over, and out slithered a large snake. No mention was made as to whether it escaped in deference to the Ute belief that these creatures should not be killed around a home site because its mate and family members would return to bite someone from the offending party.[52]

This was no concern to fourteen-year-old Zelma, who one day during ration issue heard a commotion behind the storehouse. E.Z. sent her outside to investigate, and she found a large, coiled rattler in the base of a cottonwood tree. She lopped off its head with a shovel, causing great concern among the Utes. During lunch there was another fuss out in the yard—the same problem, different snake, same solution. Zelma recalls: "That just shook the whole tribe up; they were really stirred up about it."[53] That evening she drove the cows down from Hammond Canyon to be milked. One of them proved obstinate, jumped a ditch, and started off on the other side. The young herder jumped into the streambed in pursuit and faced her third rattlesnake of the day. She brought the rattles home but started to believe that there really might be something to the Ute belief of snake family members seeking revenge.

From various sources of water came vegetation, an important aspect of life in Allen Canyon. The various plants used by the Ute people, many of which are still being consumed, are discussed in chapter 2. This is not to suggest that there were not dietary changes: beef and sheep had replaced deer; flour and other government commodities as well as canned goods from the trading post were an increasingly important part of daily fare; and livestock played a major role in the cash economy. Nevertheless, traditional, natural foods important in Ute culture continued to be used. Elders today still look at the land with its abundance of resources and are concerned that these plants and the knowledge of their use are not being passed on to future generations. Adoline and Stella Eyetoo, aunt and niece, respectively, share an extensive understanding of how they used plants during this time. The white flowers of the serviceberry, Mormon (or Brigham) tea, mountain mahogany, and sagebrush were steeped and used as different types of

A camp in Allen Canyon, 1927. In the summer many Ute families used the shade of a juniper or cottonwood as their basic shelter. Warm days and cool nights did not require extensive cover. (Special Collections, J. Willard Marriott Library, University of Utah)

tea; sagebrush was also inhaled for colds. Chokecherries were a favorite; once picked and ground on a metate, pit and all, cakes were formed to dry in the sun before storing. Chokecherries were an excellent cure for diarrhea. Annie Cantsee remembers finding these berries as large as the tip of her little finger near Red Top Ridge in Allen Canyon and near the Bears Ears. Piñon nuts, harvested around Zeke's Hole Point and elsewhere, were eaten raw, ground into a consistency like peanut butter and then spread on tortillas, or roasted and added to stews. Piñon pine's sap was used to pull infection from wounds and coat wicker baskets, and also served as chewing gum.

Berries from the sumac bush, also known as squaw brush, were eaten as picked or ground to make "Indian lemonade," and its branches were woven into baskets. Although sumac and willow were preferred, rabbitbrush was also used if nothing else was available for basketry. Women used sumac to form the shade hood on a cradleboard and to make pine pitch-covered water jugs with a carved cottonwood stopper. Elders say these

containers kept the water cool and sweet. Women harvested Indian ricegrass by beating the seeds into a woven basket, burning the stems off, removing the chaff, grinding the seeds to a consistency of flour, and then placing the meal in boiling water to form a batter to bake as bread. These seeds were also added to gravy. The prickly pear cactus fruit, once cleaned of spines, provides a sweet meat, as does the phloem peeled from beneath the bark of a cottonwood or pine tree. The Eyetoos preferred cottonwood because it was sweeter and did not have a piney taste. As Stella explained, "Everything has got sugar in the springtime." Yucca provides a variety of necessities: its leaves can be fashioned into strong cordage; its points serve as needle and thread; roots, when crushed and swished in water, provide soap and shampoo; its stalk, once cooked, tastes like celery; and its fruit or banana is sweet. Cliffrose bark can be rubbed on a spot that hurts, and its bark, when dried and shredded, can be used as a diaper, as could juniper or cedar bark that was worked to a soft pliable tissue and also served as toilet paper. Some people claim

Rock structure in Allen Canyon, 1924. Hogans and rock structures were practical for winter use, although many inhabitants of Allen Canyon moved to the rim of Westwater Canyon, outside of Blanding, to get out of the heavier snows near Elk Ridge and the Blue Mountain. (Special Collections, J. Willard Marriott Library, University of Utah)

that the bark has qualities that prevent diaper rash. Cedar berries were eaten plain or added to food once they turned brown. Cooks added roasted cedar leaves to ground cornmeal mush for a tangy flavor. Rocky Mountain beeplant had to be cooked and rinsed several times before it was eaten like spinach. Oak trees provided acorns that were leached of their tannic acid before being ground into a meal; the Utes preferred oak leaves and limbs as roof covering on their summer shades because they shed rain well.[54]

Summer encampments in Allen Canyon were simple. Most of the people lived in brush shelters and four-post shades or tents pitched under cottonwood trees. Although a 1929 account of the Towaoc Utes mentions their living in tepees, these were fast becoming outdated.[55] By the mid-1930s no one in Allen Canyon was using them, but mobility to range flocks was still a necessity. To replace the traditional structure, they purchased white canvas tents, either eight by ten or ten by twelve feet, from trading posts, such as the one located near Allen Canyon. In the winter, many who remained,

as well as those who returned to Blanding, built hogans, introduced by the Navajos. In some camps there might be an east-facing sweat lodge covered with canvas or blankets stretched over a frame of cut and bent saplings. Participants brought rocks heated in a fire outside to create an intensely hot sauna. The same form of structure for menstruating women might be found a short distance from a family camp. Other women brought food and cared for the women, who would remain segregated from men for five to seven days, until considered "cleansed."[56]

Cooking was done over a fire with a wire mesh grill, Dutch oven, frying pan, and a galvanized pot for boiling potatoes and beans. Sagebrush was readily available, burned quickly, and provided enough heat for summer cooking. Women hung food in sacks tied to tree branches, and used a box on the ground to store cooking and eating utensils. People sleeping in the canyon purchased quilts and cotton blankets at the post for warm summer nights that became chilly by morning. A four-post forked frame with cross pieces overlaid with small logs or

A Ute camp in Allen Canyon, 1925. Tents and brush shelters were practical for families on the move. This campsite belonged to Mancos Jim, seated in front of the tent. (Special Collections, J. Willard Marriott Library, University of Utah)

brush served as a bed to keep a person off the ground and away from insects and critters. To keep flies and mosquitoes away, a slow-burning fire of sheep or cow manure was kept smoldering around the dwelling, or people moved onto a ridge for the breeze. Most camps had six or eight dogs to keep them clean.[57]

A primary source of food and cash that grew in importance over the years was livestock. Following the Posey incident, the Utes lost most of their sheep and goats. One of Black's major responsibilities was to reintroduce livestock into Ute culture with the hope that this would lead to self-sufficiency, much as it had for the Navajos following their stay at Fort Sumner. Ute flocks, however, never approached the size of their neighbors'; flocks in Allen Canyon reached a high of around a hundred sheep, with a similar number of goats. Still, to McKean, "This was one of the most encouraging features connected with Indian industry. The Indian is brought face to face with the fact that there is money in ... selling wool and good rams."[58] The government took its responsibility seriously, provid-

ing infusions into the herds at various times. In 1929 the Utes at Towaoc received 2,000 sheep, and the residents of Allen Canyon 1,000 to add to individuals' growing flocks.[59] Black monitored the progress, ensuring that the animals were free of scabies and ticks, and that the herders alternated ranges and followed appropriate breeding practices.

What this translated to on the ground for Black was a lot of work. His field notes paint a picture of intense interaction with his charges. In January 1926 he noted that the Utes camped around Blanding and others at Allen Canyon were not moving their flocks often enough, and so he had to keep after them. He continued to visit their camps, cautioning them to "take the bucks from the herds after service." The Indians became irritated, turned the bucks loose, and allowed them to scatter. For two and a half weeks, Black's entries spell out his frustration: "Hunting for those lost bucks ... found tracks.... There are so many small canyons with large boulders.... Went to Allen Canyon to see if bucks had gone back ... looking below Allen Canyon.... Went down Cotton-

Joe Hatch's trading post in Allen Canyon, which operated from 1931 to 1941. The vertical post construction, called by the traders "stockade style," was common for small trading posts. Built primarily with native materials taken from the site and Ute labor, the interior had a bull pen and counter space as well as domestic quarters. *Left to right*, unidentified woman, Joe May, Joe Hatch, and unidentified man. (Courtesy of Stewart Hatch)

wood.... Hunting for the bucks again, found two.... I finally found the lost bucks and the Indian John Sanup says he will take care of them."[60] Black also traveled to Bluff, Montezuma Creek, Cahone Mesa, Mexican Hat, Douglas Mesa, and Oljato with sheep inspectors to evaluate the state of other Ute, Paiute, and Navajo flocks while also looking for additional grazing lands. At the same time he visited the Utes at Yellowjacket and Montezuma Canyon, and encouraged them to start making land improvements if they wanted assistance from the government. Not much seemed to happen.

Life at that time was not easy for the Utes either. Friction over grazing lands with the livestock owners of Blanding bubbled under the surface.[61] The problems of water in the summer and grass year-round multiplied as the Taylor Grazing Act of 1934 placed greater restrictions on access to both. The weather sometimes compounded the problem. Stella remembers that in the early

1930s, when she was around six years old, she was at Jim Mike's camp with two other families—Billy Mike's and Abe Lehi's—on the west side of Westwater Point. The windswept, sagebrush-covered plateau provided little shelter from the biting wind and driving snow, which piled up against her tent and the two hogans. Any plants to graze were buried, so the families cut pine boughs for the sheep to eat. Despite their efforts, many starved or froze to death, and the area became known as "Where They Cut the Pine Trees."[62]

Economic development brought opportunities in the form of a trading post, which the Utes requested.[63] Built on Bureau of Land Management property by Joseph Hatch Sr., Joseph Jr., and an Indian work crew, this post followed the same pattern as the 1926 Hatch trading post in Montezuma Canyon, which also served Utes and Navajos in that area. Constructed of trimmed cedar posts chinked with mud and sunk three feet into the ground, the post had a flat roof made of boards covered with six inches of soil. The building had two rooms: the store and a sleeping quarters/kitchen area. The bullpen boasted a fitted sandstone floor, a potbellied stove squatting in the center, and benches lining the periphery. One long wooden counter stretched most of the building's width, with shelves behind holding food and hardware. Located next to the road, the post became an important feature in the life of Allen Canyon residents between 1931 and 1941.

Joe Hatch Jr. acted as proprietor. Representing the third generation of family traders who had bartered on both Navajo and Ute reservations, he knew what it took to keep customers happy. On the shelves sat canned goods—corned beef, Vienna sausages, peaches, pears, creamed corn, regular corn, and string beans. Large, one-hundred-pound sacks of sugar and flour, containers of salt pork and bacon, cases of Arbuckle coffee, bolts of cloth—the brighter the better—were stacked next to the cans or under the counter, with a scale at the end to weigh purchases. Each customer had his or her own account kept on a paper bag on which Joe tallied the items until he ran out of room. Very little credit needed to be extended since his Ute customers received monthly payments from Ignacio. Joe and E.Z. worked together with them to keep careful track of expenses.

Outside the store was a place for sacking wool, which was usually purchased in the spring, as well as a shade to store the seven-foot-long burlap bags. After three or four of them had accumulated, a pickup hauled them to the Montezuma Creek post, manned by Joe's brother, Ira. A fenced canyon provided forty acres to graze sheep, mostly wethers, which Joe bought in the fall at an average of thirty head per family. He developed a spring close to the store so that there was plenty of water, owned a small flock of chickens to keep the bugs down and the snakes away, built a guest hogan for travelers, made a sweat lodge for himself, and created a large

flat area in front of the post for Allen Canyon residents to play games and tie their horses.

People from Blanding, San Juan County, Ignacio, and the Midwest Oil Company pooled resources in 1926 to make travel easier for ever-increasing automobile and truck traffic.[64] Men from the Ute community pitched in to maintain the road system, a constant task. E.Z. recorded in his "Monthly Time Book" that he employed twenty-six men whose work totaled 217 days of labor at a daily rate of two dollars in March 1933.[65] As the road improved, a small customer base developed of tourists headed toward Natural Bridges National Monument, as well as workers from the Midwest Oil Company who were developing an oil field near the Bears Ears. But the primary flow of traffic through the post door was Ute and Navajo visitors.

What, then, passed across the counter from the bullpen to the trader? In addition to the wool and sheep, there were products for which the White Mesa—Allen Canyon residents are still famous: baskets and beadwork. Baskets were particularly profitable. In his 1925 annual report, McKean wrote, "The Indians of Ute Mountain and of the Polk and Posey Band manufacture more beadwork and baskets than any other. For these they find ready sellers and are able to provide considerable food supplies and clothing for their families."[66] Black encouraged the industry, and the women of Allen Canyon rose to the occasion. Collecting sumac at places like Hammond Canyon, Elk Ridge, Cottonwood Wash, Montezuma Creek, San Juan River, and Comb Ridge, the weavers went to work and became some of the most successful basket makers in the Four Corners area. Black described just how successful in 1937, when he reported that the goal of having twenty-six women weave twenty-five baskets in a year's time had been surpassed twofold. Instead of the anticipated 650 baskets, they wove 1,200.[67] He then cited John and Tazhunie Dutchie as a "source of inspiration to all their Pah-Ute relatives and also to the white people of that territory." They were not on the annuity roll, so John did beadwork and she made baskets for their income. In addition to harvesting the sumac that often grew a long distance from Allen Canyon, the Utes also had to peel, split, cure, and dye the materials, which took seven days. E.Z. estimated that "a woman can make ten baskets in forty days, averaging $2.50 per basket, the income for forty day's hard work would be $22.50. During the past year Tazhunie has woven 109 baskets." [68]

Ninety-year-old Stewart Hatch, Joe's brother, who helped operate the post in Allen Canyon, had a lifetime of experience in dealing with Navajo and Ute crafts. He recalls that the Posey family made the best baskets, selling for $3.50. The two colors used to dye the willows or sumac were black and brown, and came either from natural sources or were purchased at the post. There was no red as used today. A few baskets had different designs, with animals or geometric forms, but the vast majority followed the traditional wedding basket design since they were used in ceremonies by Navajos, favorite customers of the Utes.

Another popular item exchanged between the two cultures was deerskin. Stewart believes that few other people have mastered the technique of tanning hides as well as the Utes. Every camp in Allen Canyon had a hide-processing area. When a hunter killed a deer, he removed the meat from the bones and piled them along with the antlers in one place for animals to eat. He skinned the deer completely, leaving the skin of the head and the tail attached, wrapped the meat in the hide, and brought it home. He then placed the green hide in a pit with moistened cedar ashes on the fur side and left it buried for a while. The tanner later removed the skin and placed the still wet hide on a pole a foot in diameter that was leaned against a tree; a rock or knife was used to scrape off the

This young Ute girl, photographed in Allen Canyon in 1936, exhibits the traditional skill of basket making. The following year twenty-six women produced 1,200 baskets. Willow and sumac, cut at the right time of year, were in constant demand. (Special Collections, Sherratt Library, Southern Utah University)

fur, which now came off easily. The tanner worked the hide before putting it back in the hole and burying it again. When it was taken out, it was rubbed with either deer or sheep brains and, as the final stage, with white clay to remove any smell and brighten the finished product. All of the hides sold at the trading post had the tail and face with fur on the skin; there could be no knife cuts in it if it were to be used for Navajo ceremonials. Joe bought these skins for eight to twelve dollars and sold them for twelve to eighteen, and he was always able to move his inventory quickly. [69] The Hatch trading post also sold lots of beadwork, sewn on everything from cradleboards, belts, moccasins, and gloves to rabbit foot lucky charms for the tourists.

Joe Hatch (*standing*) observing a game outside his trading post circa 1940. Having traded before with the Hatch family in both Montezuma Canyon and Montezuma Creek, the Ute people in Allen Canyon requested that this store be built. Hatch supported and participated in many community activities. (Courtesy of Stewart Hatch)

Allen Canyon folks also found time for recreation. Two favorite events—horse racing and card playing—involved gambling. Racetracks, a couple hundred yards to a quarter mile long, were located near the Bears Ears, Kigalia Springs, Chippean, the mouth of Hammond Canyon, along Cottonwood Wash west of the trading post, and between the mouth of Dry Wash and Allen Canyon—actually, any place there was a flat stretch of land. Stella recalls how spectators sat on the rocks near Dry Wash and watched two to no more than four riders race to a finish line at the south end of the flat. Nearby was "Under the Cottonwood Tree," where others watched while trying their hand at cards—usually monte, also known as "squaw poker".[70] Joe Hatch would show up to sell candy, cookies, and canned goods out of the back of his pickup. Favored jockeys such as Edward Dutchie and Avon Rabbit would kick off their boots for a better feel of the horse, mount bareback, and race to the finish line. Coins or small items changed hands with those who bet. Navajos also raced their horses, which were easily distinguished from those of the Utes. Navajo mounts had long

"broom" tails that nearly touched the ground, while the Ute horses' tails were cropped to a foot and a half in length.[71]

Twice a month, starting at nine in the morning and lasting all day, the station issued rations as E.Z. and Zelma provided another opportunity for betting. Sugar, salt, flour, bacon, beans, coffee, soap, cans of tomatoes, peaches, corned beef, and mutton became the stakes when the cards came out. Only the women played "squaw poker," and two of them—Jane and May Whyte, Jesse Posey's wives—were consistent winners. According to Zelma, these two would end up with all the rations for each family by the end of the day. Even Chloe's big kettle of vegetable soup and homemade bread and canned peaches were not enough to calm the excitement. E.Z. tolerated the activity until tempers boiled; then he would sort out the mess and make sure that each family had enough to eat until the next issue. Zelma, when recounting the situation, chuckled, "This went on every month. I'll tell you, they'd rather play poker than anything."[72]

There were other games of chance. Hand games, wrestling matches, foot races, and later baseball became popular. The flat area west of the trading post was a favorite spot for both men and women to play shinny. With curved sticks in hand, opposing teams faced off with a goal line at each end of the field. Stewart remembers seeing balls made out of leather, rubber, and a tin can, which after a little use became rounded. "It was kind of dangerous. The players would get in close quarters, swinging their stick and hitting. Somebody would hit that can and it would soar by like a bullet."[73]

Without a doubt, the biggest community event was the Bear Dance, occurring once in the spring and again in the fall after hunting season. Performed at Towaoc, White Mesa, Montezuma Creek, and elsewhere, residents of Allen Canyon have particularly fond memories of those held at the site a hundred yards west of the trading post. A flat, cleared area embraced by the flanks of a hill held the brush enclosure, or "Cave of Sticks." Annie Cantsee remembers Utes coming on horseback and Navajos in wagons to attend the three- or four-day festivity, with twenty-five people dancing at a time. Utes from Montezuma Creek and Towaoc, as well as a few families from Ignacio and White Rocks, also attended.[74] Stewart estimated as many as five hundred may have participated, although this figure seems high.

The post was a major sponsor of the dance. The store donated canned goods, two or three lambs, a hundred pounds of flour, shortening, and lard for bread, and stocked more perishables than usual. Cinnamon rolls were a fast snack, but particularly popular were the large bunches of bananas removed from crates and then suspended on a roof beam in the post. Customers cut off as many as they wanted and paid ten cents each at the counter. Perhaps this is how Joe Hatch received the Ute name "Weece Neece," *weece* being Ute for "banana" (the meaning of *neece* is unknown). The post also became the destination for white visitors who wished to attend the Bear Dance. When Civilian Con-

servation Corps Company 3241, stationed in Blanding, held a barracks inspection and Barracks Number Six won, the government transported two truckloads of young men to the dance. "The boys who went enjoyed the ceremonies very much, something that an Easterner hears about but seldom sees."[75] The same occurred in June 1940, when ninety CCC men in three Grazing Service trucks attended.[76] For all concerned, it was a chance to make new acquaintances.

The Bear Dance also provided a semi-annual opportunity for men and women to meet and contemplate marriage. While there were several ways of practicing courtship, one of the more romantic forms employed the flute. Stewart, when a young boy traveling with his father, Joseph Sr., on a trading expedition near Ute Mountain, spied a flute tied in a tree close to Mariano Spring. He wanted to get it, but his father cautioned him to leave it alone, explaining the custom behind the hanging flute. In the old days, a prospective husband who had identified a potential wife carved a flute and then found a place in the rocks above her home. For three days he played his instrument, notifying the girl and her family that he was interested in marriage. Previous contact had made the identity of the suitor evident, so the woman had time to decide. If she accepted his offer, she collected her possessions and walked into the rocks to meet her future husband, who had horses waiting. If she declined and did not go to him by sunset of the third day, before departing he would tie the flute in a tree to weather and decay.[77]

When asked whether marriages in Allen Canyon had been initiated this way, Stewart was unsure, but he was positive that there was an abundance of flutes that were played often, and that the trading post did a lively business in buying them for three or four dollars before selling them at Mesa Verde National Park and elsewhere. Although many men, including Mancos George, could make flutes, Billy Mike was particularly well known for this skill. Allan Black reminisced, "When he makes a flute, he will blow on it and the tone has to be just right. If it isn't, he will take it apart and do something to it until he gets the right tone. They used to tell me that if I saw a young Ute blowing on one of those, he was trying to get a [wife]. If the [woman] came to him that was the one he took."[78] Each young man composed a distinct tune associated with the woman he was courting. He also could attach to his flute a lock of the woman's hair, have a medicine man bless the instrument, and hope the song's power persuaded the woman to go with him.[79]

For fifteen years Allen Canyon hummed with activity as the station implemented programs for improvement. Then, in the spring of 1938, the Indian Service transferred Black to Towaoc. The Ute people still owned their allotments, still traveled back and forth to Blanding and White Mesa in the fall and Allen Canyon in the spring, but times were changing. George Gravelle and his wife, Josephine, stationed in Blanding, focused on the children attending school there and seemed

to have no interest in living in Allen Canyon. They did not have the same knowledge and skills that Black had brought to his job as a resident stockman. Within a few years they were transferred, and the station began to fall into disrepair.

Grazing herds of sheep and goats and later cattle still dotted the hills. Individual family farms continued, but maintenance of the irrigation ditches slowed, the issuance of supplies stopped, and the close supervision of agricultural and livestock endeavors declined and then halted. People continued to live in Allen Canyon; the tribe had five or six new homes built on individual allotments in the late 1950s and early '60s.[80] Today they are abandoned. Avikan, however, is still a place of rest, a refuge, a homeland to the White Mesa Ute people, and provides roots in a world that moves much faster now than it did in the 1930s. Those who recall the early days there do so with pleasure. Remembering the homeland gives a sense of connectedness with the land and the Ute people's heritage, both of which are important for the future.

CHAPTER 14

Education, Economics, and Integration

Establishing the White Mesa Community, 1923–1960

I once thought the white people were very bad people and that they did much wrong; and the whites thought the Indians were very bad people and did much wrong. But I think different now for I understand more of the laws that came from God....I believe that when all peoples know what God meant, they will all be friends with each other.

Buckskin Charlie

To catch wisdom you must have a spider web of learning.

Mancos George

Life in Allen Canyon was only half the story. As the Ute people forged a path into the future, change lay all about. For the forty years following their release from the stockade in 1923, their life became one of transition. The fight to hold on to the traditional lifestyle of hunting and gathering was over, and in its place lay the path of education, economic development, and integration into the dominant culture. Although assimilation held benefits, the Weenuche were determined to maintain elements of the past. The challenge was to blend traditional practices with contemporary demands.

One of the greatest challenges for the Utes was education. Shortly after the children walked out of the stockade in the spring of 1923, they were on their way to the boarding school at Towaoc to join the 173 pupils already enrolled in the four grades.[1] Agent Edward McKean intended to establish schools at both Allen Canyon and Monte-zuma Creek for Posey's and Polk's bands, but the concept proved unviable. Even though Polk had enrolled his grandchild in school, many of the Indians were reluctant to follow suit because of problems with trachoma and tuberculosis, and the distance the children were from home—more than 100 miles if at Towaoc, and 160 miles when at Ignacio. Polk begrudgingly agreed to have other children from his band attend school, but leaders from both Ute groups requested something closer. Given the three-year delay in getting the station operational, it is not surprising that the issue of attendance in San Juan schools dragged on for another four years.

By 1925 the students at Towaoc were voting with their feet. E.Z. Black reported that he had visited all eighteen Ute camps in Allen Canyon, rounding up children who had run away from the boarding school because they wanted to be with their family. At that point there were twenty-five enrolled, and another ten who should have been, but their experience at the school and the necessity of helping with camp chores convinced parents that they should remain home.[2] Washed-out roads, rainy nights in the open, broken vehicles, and cool temperatures were other reasons that students were slow to return. Herbert H. Stacher, a Ute "writing in behalf of my tribesmen," urged the government to build a school in Allen Canyon. He reasoned that the distance from the current school was too far, parents wanted to be able to see their children during the nine-month school year, the pupils would be less likely to run away if they were near their families, and there were enough Navajo and Ute students near Towaoc to fill it to capacity.[3] McKean, who knew of Stacher, did not agree, stating that during the fall and winter most of the Utes were scattered anywhere from a few to fifty miles away from Allen Canyon herding livestock and so would not be available. What was needed was a less expensive solution that would keep them closer to home. Public schools, anxious for the tuition that Indian children would pay (the same rate as out-of-state residents), might consider accepting them.[4]

Not until 1930 would that agreement be in place. In the meantime, getting the children into school meant sending them to Towaoc, which proved hard on everyone. The 26 families comprised of 118 men, women, and children living in Allen Canyon promised that if there were a local school, all would be enrolled. Black summarized his efforts by saying, "I don't feel very well satisfied with my school work this year [1928]. I thought I would be able to get all delinquents in school in my district, but have had plenty of opposition from the parents and relatives; they have all kinds of excuses."[5] The main reason: distance. Still, in 1928 there were 37 children ranging in age from six to sixteen in attendance in the six grades then available at Towaoc. Not all stayed. Avon Rabbit and Joe Whyte from Allen Canyon escaped on

November 17, took two horses, and started for home. The school sent search parties, one of which caught Avon in Blanding and returned him to Towaoc for interrogation. He finally admitted that he had left his cousin, Joe, on Sleeping Ute Mountain, where they had camped when they first ran away. The boys slept under a tree one night but when Avon awoke, Joe appeared dead. Avon hastened away but then went back and found that Joe had moved, but now really appeared to be dead. A search party found the body and determined he had died from exposure. Officials held his funeral at the school.[6]

A year later Indian Education Supervisor F. H. Hammond investigated the practices of Wayne W. Burns, disciplinarian at the Towaoc Boarding School. Staff and students had brought charges against him for such things as having children wear logging chains for punishment, hitting and kicking the boys, taking too much interest in certain girls, and being lax in his duties. A lengthy investigation followed, resulting in a recommendation that Burns and his wife be transferred. Of greater interest are some of the details concerning treatment of White Mesa children that shed light on why parents were reluctant to send them to school. Burns incarcerated Avon Rabbit in the clothes room for a lengthy period of time. Johnny Benow, or Green Ute, called the disciplinarian a "Comanche," saying "too much kick, too much box him the boys." The investigator found that many of these charges were not supported by fact, although he considered Burns "somewhat of a martinet"; still, returning students brought their perceptions with them when they went home.[7]

The demand for a school in Allen Canyon, despite heavy snowfalls, the herding of livestock far from it, and the expense of maintaining a facility for small numbers, persisted. Forty-nine parents signed a petition promising to put all of their children in the school once it was built, citing sickness and deaths at Towaoc as their main reason for changing

Teacher Orpha Brown (*center*), surrounded by Ute students, 1935. Integration of Indian children into the public school system was a challenge for all concerned. It would be another thirty years before true educational assimilation began in earnest, but in the meantime there were a variety of attempts to increase learning. (Courtesy of San Juan County Historical Commission)

the status quo. Black supported their wishes, pointing out that for $4,000, a school built with Forest Service lumber would meet the needs of the twenty-four school-age children living within five miles of the station. Agent Edgar J. Peacore was convinced it would not work, but believed if the Utes were forced to do otherwise, they would fight. He hoped to convince the county to build a facility that would also encourage the Utes to accept permanent homes.[8] Each faction had an idea, but shared little common ground.

Time slowly softened the hearts of both Ute parents and school administrators. In 1926 government officials felt it would be a number of years before public school could accommodate Indian children, but the next year students from Ignacio enrolled in off-reservation schools. For the next two years the parents of the Ute Mountain and Allen Canyon groups resisted placing their stu-

dents anywhere off the reservation, but by 1930 the door of the public school in Blanding swung open for their admittance.[9] There were a number of contributing factors. The previous year the government had begun surveying lands eleven miles south of Blanding as allotments for Utes who were in need of winter range and not staying in Allen Canyon. Once settled, the Indians would receive a small schoolhouse staffed by a teacher paid for by San Juan County. The white community preferred this solution since the Utes were "living in tents and [were] not clean enough. I [Peacore] am afraid I will not be able to overcome this opposition and will not be able to enroll a single one in the public school."[10] Some people in Blanding were more supportive, especially when Black announced he was looking for a place nearby to build a small Indian school for $7,000 to $10,000. One article in the *San Juan Record* saw the issue as part of a democratic process that everyone should support.[11] Certainly, the thirty-five cents per day per student was welcome income during this time of the Great Depression. It added up. Just for the first year (1930–1931) the government paid $26,000 for the dorms and the people who lived there, all of which went into the pockets of Blanding citizens, with another $2,000 going to the school district. D. L. Bayles, in an article in the *San Juan Record*, wrote, "We should lay aside our race prejudice and rejoice over the real avenue for increased business and the splendid opportunity to preach the Gospel to the Indians."[12]

The problem was resolved by what became known as the Blanding Ute Dormitory. In the early 1920s, Hanson and Evelyn Bayles had built a three-story brick house with a wrap-around porch, large downstairs rooms, and spacious five-beds-per-room quarters upstairs, later capable of housing around twenty-two students. Hanson passed away in 1922, and by 1930 Evelyn was seeking a buyer; the government bit. In September E. Z. and Chloe Black assumed the responsibility of managing the ten boys and ten girls scheduled to attend public school in Blanding.[13] Peacore, pleased at their progress, said that not only did he hope to increase the dorm's capacity to thirty, but to have similar setups in Monticello and Bluff. He later changed his mind because Bluff showed little progress, with the homes there in "terrible condition."[14]

Chloe Black died the next year at the age of forty-one; E.Z. remained the stockman for Allen Canyon, lived in his home in Blanding during the winter, and remarried, but his connection to the dorm was only in working with the children and not in running it.[15] A series of caretakers continued to watch after the children, the most notable being George and Josephine Gravelle, who had worked in Towaoc between 1930 and 1935, and then transferred to Blanding for the next six years. The couple were Chippewas from

Mancos George (George Whyte), mounted and ready for business, was a familiar sight to Ute children playing hooky from school. "We were told that a policeman on a big horse was coming but he could not catch us. They said he had a rope. But people liked him. He was a nice man." (Courtesy of San Juan County Historical Commission)

Minnesota and thus well suited to their roles as employees of the Indian Service. Among their duties was ensuring that the twenty to twenty-five students received food, clothing, and accommodations comparable to those of a boarding school. The public school education was academically oriented and considered excellent, but many of the industrial trades and crafts available at Towaoc were missing. Some of the children still ran away, but now the parents or a local truant officer could bring them back.[16]

The dorm may have provided a caring atmosphere, but the Ute experience in public school could be harrowing. Helen Shumway, who attended elementary school in the late 1930s, described what it was like. Her teacher, Mable Peterson, had sixteen Ute children in

George and Josephine Gravelle (*top right*) and Ute students on the porch of the Ute Dormitory, late 1930s. Both of Chippewa descent, the Gravelles had a reputation for being strict but fair with their charges and were well-accepted in the white community. Their main interest was in helping the children in school, so they did not have the same responsibilities and rapport with the adults as "E.Z." Black did. (Courtesy of San Juan County Historical Commission)

class. Many of them were older and too big for the small seats, which encouraged them to find opportunities to be up and about. Peterson became so frustrated that she got hammer and nail and fastened one girl's dress to her seat. Another time she put one of the boys in a closet as punishment; when she opened the door at noon, she found that he had consumed all of the lunches stored there. Emmett Posey was also incarcerated in a dark closet, but he managed to find a stack of books and whiled away the time carving different animals from their hard covers. The children enjoyed having them once the teacher let him out. Dan Posey, like the other children, was not allowed to chew gum in school and so parked it on his head, leading to amusing impromptu haircuts. There were also a sufficient number of fights among both boys and girls to keep people on edge. The east side of the school was particularly famous as a sparring ring. The Ute girls were

fascinated with the white girls' blonde hair, running their fingers through the golden tresses, but this admiration could also lead to confrontation.[17]

Some of the children never made it to school, instead escaping through the dorm windows and heading for Westwater or Allen Canyon. Mancos George and Platte May, truant officers, went in pursuit. Myers Cantsee ran away seven times but always ended up back in his second-grade class.[18] Stella Eyetoo also recalls running away from the dormitory: "We [Stella and Alice Posey] ran away from Mancos George and went to Montezuma Creek. We were told that a policeman on a big horse was coming but he could not catch us. They said he had a rope. But people liked him. He was a nice man."[19] One story about runaways tells of two boys who sneaked out of the dorm one night and on their way to Allen Canyon entered an alcove where they found a large Ancestral Puebloan olla filled with jade beads. The runaways loaded their pockets and then continued the journey until the truant officer intercepted and returned them to Blanding. After a few days they started to display their find, and others became interested, but even though one of the fathers accompanied the boys, they were unable to relocate the cave with its treasure. People from Blanding continued to search without success, but as late as 1952 there were those who hoped to find it.[20]

By 1941 the government had built a small day school in Allen Canyon and stopped sending children to Blanding, depriving the school district of the annual infusion of BIA money into its coffers. The Gravelles left Blanding for Sacaton, Arizona, and their new assignment working with Pima children. But having built the long-awaited school in Allen Canyon, the Indian Service wanted it put to use. Any use was short-lived. Besides a few terse statements in a Blanding history, there was little notice. "In 1941 an Indian agent took a notion to move the school to Hammond Canyon in the wilderness country of the Paiute. The Gravelles protested that it would mean the end of the school…[it was] a futile and expensive effort to set up the school beyond all essential facilities where no teacher could be induced to stay and go through the motions.… Six [officially three] years after that school had been doomed to perish in the solitude of Hammond Canyon, the camps beyond Westwater had a rising generation of hillbilly boys and girls unable to speak English."[21] The effect of not having an education in an increasingly white world was explained by ninety-plus-year-old Lizzie Jacket from Towaoc. Interviewed in 1993, she explained the impact of not having an education: "I did not attend school.… I do not understand English. I just listen to my family talk very loud."[22]

This was also a time of flux for the Ute Mountain Ute School at Towaoc. In 1935 the government closed the boarding school, leaving only a day school to provide education.

By 1942, with World War II raging, the facility closed entirely, and the students were encouraged to attend the Ute Vocational School in Ignacio. In March 1943, less than a year after the boarding school at Towaoc was shut down, the school in Allen Canyon shared a similar fate, presumably for the same reasons—"a shortage of water, non-attendance of pupils, and an inability to secure adequate personnel."[23] This, coupled with the nomadic lifestyle fostered by the livestock industry, kept Ute students from formal education and on the fringe of white society. The hogan and tent community of Westwater expanded over the years, but at this point the Ute children were not attending school in town.

Ever since the first settler's home arose in 1905 in what was first known as Grayson and later Blanding, Utes and Navajos seeking employment descended on its outskirts. Indian families settled in to trade and perform menial chores such as chopping wood, clearing brush, herding livestock, weeding gardens, and a host of other tasks. While these subservient roles helped them to eke out an existence, the Utes did not prosper. Forming a separate community, the Utes had Navajos as neighbors, but only a few families were accepted in both groups. Westwater Canyon also became a general dividing line between the whites living on the east side and the Indians on the west, with the Ute settlement pattern extending all the way to the head of Big Canyon, three miles away. Springs in Westwater were critical—one at the north end of town and the other in the middle, or slightly to the south of the western edge. Likewise, the Navajo community was on the southern end of the Ute area, with their dispersal pattern extending much farther south and west than the growing town's immediate size suggested.[24]

By 1944 the Westwater community was clearly, but unofficially, the "other side of the tracks" (or canyon). The Utes lived in three places, with Allen Canyon primarily used in the summer. In the fall people with livestock in need of winter pasture moved to White Mesa, and those with children or other reasons to be near town went to Westwater. In all three places poverty was apparent. Albert R. Lyman writes of how in January 1944 he and his wife, Gladys, rode their horses into the hills west of Blanding,

> [visiting] about thirty camps within a radius of three miles, one section occupied by Piutes, the other by Navajos. We were depressed in contemplating the conditions in which we found them; they had wretched hogans, old tents, and doubtful shelters. Some of their children ran barefooted in the snow. We saw no worth-while stoves, nothing resembling a white man's house, and no attempt at convenience in their homes or surroundings.[25]

Another time, he said, "We rode back and forth among the cedars, hunting Indians as far as the rim of Big Canyon. The farther we rode, the more depressed we felt — not only at their destitute condition but at the spiritless and cheerless way they hovered over their fires, living as it were because life was thrust upon them."[26] Four months later Lyman and his wife began a five-year mission to the Indians of the Southwest for the Mormon Church.

In less than two years, however, Lyman was back in Blanding to help those he had left behind. The couple felt that the greatest impact they could have on the future was to assist with education. By this time the Blanding school had lost interest in doing anything for the local children not fortunate enough to be enrolled elsewhere. In fact, when Lyman approached the school board about the possibility of educating Indian children, he faced stiff resistance: they said the Navajos were present in the largest numbers; the white community felt that it was their tax money, and that the Indians had contributed nothing to support the town; the school system would be overwhelmed by the sheer number of those needing education; dirt, disease, and friction would create a poor learning and living environment; and Indians were not smart enough to learn "white man subjects" anyway.[27] Suddenly there was no land for sale in or around town, and if there were, it became exorbitantly expensive. Some efforts to derail the purchase of land were subtle, others overt: "I know what you're after and the answer is 'No.'"[28]

Lyman realized that the school would have to locate beyond city limits, so he identified a spot across Westwater Canyon a mile from his home and set to work. The Mormon Church donated the first $500, but as word spread, people throughout Utah began to contribute, including kind-hearted folks from Blanding. The missionaries obtained enough money for construction materials, and local people labored to build the one-room schoolhouse with an adjoining room to serve as kitchen to prepare the noon meal. Lyman built benches, seats, tables, and other furniture from scraps of lumber, clothes were donated, and Gladys bought or scrounged limited educational supplies. One man bulldozed a road through the cedars so the school was accessible by car, while another person drove the Lymans during the winter so they would not have to fight through the snow with the children's lunch. Further local support arose. The husband and wife team opened the door, ready to provide instruction, on November 15, 1946.

They intended at first to teach only Navajo students, but as their efforts became known, local Utes asked if their children could participate. They were welcomed. The twenty to thirty pupils ranged in age from three to eighteen years; few spoke much English, all received clothing, and some got haircuts. One of the ongoing problems was the friction between Navajo and Ute children. The latter were fewer in number, often smaller in size, and the recipients of generations of animosity. Adoline Eyetoo, who attended the school for two years with other Ute children — including Anna Lee Rabbit, Calvin Welsh, James Mill, Annie Taylor,

Shirley Ketchum, and some Dutchie children — remembers that the Lymans treated them right and prevented the Navajos from causing trouble. "The Navajos did not want us to go to school, but he [Albert] was praying for us. The Navajos were mean and used to beat us up after school. The Utes called them 'Pagáwič' which means 'To Have a Knife in Your Hand' and the Navajos called us 'Payŭche' or Paiute."[29]

More than names went back and forth. One time Gladys, standing at the blackboard, saw out of the corner of her eye a fourteen-year-old Navajo boy spit in the face of a little Ute child. She reared back and slammed an eighteen-inch ruler across the offending boy's cheek and then "roasted" him for his behavior. After school some of the older Navajo boys would waylay Ute children on their way home to their "wickiups." Fistfights erupted right in the classroom; it got to the point that during the noon break following lunch, the Navajo children were chasing the Ute children home. Lyman adopted the practice of having the Utes wait in the classroom with the doors locked until instruction resumed at one o'clock.[30]

For two years Albert and Gladys Lyman worked tirelessly to keep the children progressing. The constant toil took its toll on their health, and although many local people supported the effort, resistance continued. Lyman eventually located a piece of land on the edge of town and had the school moved in one piece onto the lot. This in itself was an amazing feat, accomplished by putting a large solid log through both rooms then lifting the structure and moving it over the rough terrain and across Westwater Canyon. Later, when classes became too large, Lyman procured a second building from the Civilian Conservation Corps camp in town and moved it onto the property. As hearts softened and the school "began to melt down the mountains of heathen prejudice in town," opportunities to enroll in the local public school increased.[31] The next step, once the Indian students were in Blanding, was for the school board to accept responsibility for their education, which it did by providing teaching staff. Two or three years later the board abandoned segregation and began integration.[32] Lyman noted, "Within four years of the time that school began beyond Westwater, it was superseded by better schools far and near who absorbed not only the Blanding Indian children, but hundreds of others. From that time it has become increasingly popular for children of all tribes to attend the Blanding schools."[33]

Other forms of progress followed. Lyman repeated the same trip he had made seven years previous to survey the conditions of the Indians and now found seventeen houses made of lumber with windows and doors and board floors. Sewing machines, radios, stoves, and cars were also present.[34] Two years later, in 1953, the Mormon Church built a $17,000 chapel on the north end of town and began the Indian Branch for Navajos and Utes. Nine years later the *San Juan Record* reported a meeting in Blanding of over fifty individuals from the BIA, Utah State Board of Education, the Ute and Navajo tribes, and state welfare agencies to discuss who should be responsible for Indian education. With 200 Indian children enrolled in San Juan County public schools, 140 of them in Blanding, there needed to be a clear understanding. Those in attendance noted language barriers and problems arising from different cultural and social backgrounds, but these issues could no longer be used as excuses. The mandate was clear: "The Bureau of Indian Affairs has responsibility for educating Indian pupils who live on a reservation and who are not close to a public school or a public school bus route. School districts are responsible for schooling students who live off reservations that are close to public schools or school bus routes."[35] By the early 1960s education had provided a major thrust toward integrating Indian people into the white society of southeastern Utah.

Other elements of the push for integration had originated in the 1920s, most under the general rubrics of economic and political development. The broad spectrum of what these developments entailed for the Ute Mountain Utes, with whom the White Mesa Utes were grouped, is covered in Richard K. Young's *The Ute Indians of Colorado in the Twentieth Century* and will only be briefly referenced here.[36] What is important to understand is that in 1923 the Southern Ute Agency in Ignacio subsumed the administrative structure of Towaoc, placing the government headquarters of the Consolidated Ute Agency at a greater distance. Not until 1968 did the Ute Mountain Utes regain their autonomy.[37] The presiding agent now administered federal programs for all three bands.

Katherine M. B. Osburn wrote about a portion of this same period (1887–1934), specifically focusing on the effect of government policy on Southern Ute women.[38] Osburn notes, "Acculturation pressures at Ute Mountain were far fewer than those at Southern Ute because of the lack of allotments," but still the times were changing, and the traditional roles of Ute women in the home were shifting.[39] Wage labor, male participation in government, brittle marital bonds, decrease in kinship roles, and a general second-class position within the dominant society took its toll on women's status. Still, "Ute women did not suffer a serious decline in status and power among their people."[40] Since these pressures were more distant for the women of White Mesa — twice removed from the Ute Mountain Ute experience — their role continued to be one of a shared partnership with their husband in sustaining the family. Ute women maintained their position as a significant force in their family economy and raising children.

Central to problems facing the Utes was the government's control of their money. Previous treaties had promised annual funds and rations to be paid per capita to the Indians for land cessions. In 1913 a new policy required that the Utes work for their money, that the annuity process stop, and that when the government issued equipment or livestock, payment for it came from tribal or individual, not government, funds. Much of the money for individuals went into bank accounts with controlled access by the agent. McKean bluntly stated: "We discourage the issuing of rations to strong men and they are getting to be ashamed to ask for them. We do not miss a chance to stress the importance of work, being the only thing that will raise their standards of living and supplying the wants of life."[41] Sheep were to be the financial answer, and for the "Paiute families in Allen Canyon…not far from their location is found some of the best flocks of sheep in America. These flock masters are united in their opinion that the sheep industry offers the Ute people the only avenue for industrial life."[42]

The entire system was bewildering, even eighteen years after the government began implementing it. Chief Buckskin Charlie of the Muache met with a congressional investigative committee in 1931 and presented his understanding that the government was making the Utes pay twice with their resources: through the initial land sale, and again when the government issued something and then took payment from the Utes' account. He explained that "George Washington made a treaty with his people" and he wanted to know why there was so much confusion. After being corrected by Senator Lynn Frazier that it was Lincoln (actually Andrew Johnson) who had signed the agreement, and that there was $268,000 of Ute money "sitting in Washington," Charlie queried, "Did they bury Mr. Lincoln with the treaties that this tribe made?"[43] He was told to just give his statement.

Another source of funding came from claims made against lost lands. The Utes entered the first of a number of court cases in 1910, a process that continued into the 1950s. The federal claims court rendered a verdict a year later awarding the Confederated Bands

Sam Ketchum herding sheep in Allen Canyon. Problems with livestock and availability of range were two of the biggest issues that faced the Ute people. With enforcement of the Taylor Grazing Act, government control of land, and shrinking grazing areas, competition sharpened between Indian and white ranchers. (Courtesy of San Juan County Historical Commission)

of Ute Indians $3,305,257 at 4 percent interest.[44] For the Ute Mountain and Allen Canyon people, this meant $797,820 for their 462 members, with most of the settlement going to the Uintah-Ouray Utes, and the remainder to the Southern Utes. Congress still pulled the purse strings, but by 1925 the Weenuche had received $555,000, with $289,000 of it being in per capita payments, leaving a balance of $268,000. The point to ponder was what would happen when it was gone.

A congressional hearing in 1931 provides a detailed snapshot of Weenuche life on the reservation. E. J. Peacore, who had by then been at Ignacio for two years, testified that he presided over 444 people between the Ute Mountain and Allen Canyon groups, 44 of whom were "Piutes." Each family had a flock of sheep ranging from 25 to 150 animals, totaling 17,000. There were only twelve wooden ten-by-twelve-foot homes on the Ute Mountain Ute Reservation, with everyone else living in tents or brush shelters furnished primarily with sheep pelts. In addition to their livestock, each man, woman,

and child received a per capita payment of $50 a year, dramatically decreased from the $200 they had received a few years before. Peacore felt the money a bad idea, creating unnecessary dependency.[45]

E. Z. Black also testified. The committee asked if those living in Allen Canyon would be willing to move to the reservation, to which the stockman replied that perhaps a third of them would do so, but the rest would not want to leave the forty allotments they now held. Sustaining the operation required $10,000 to $15,000 a year, and with only 300 acres under cultivation, one can sense the importance of husbandry.[46] Ninety percent of the Weenuche families owned livestock, with a cumulative total of 11,015 sheep and 520 horses on a reservation that lacked water for agriculture but was ideally suited for grazing.[47] That was one reason Black favored the plan to have the Allen Canyon Utes move to Towaoc.

But there was another reason. The issue of White Mesa Ute removal again raised its ugly head, based on an issue, although peripheral, that had simmered for years. To grasp the complexity of it, one needs to understand the politics of the "Paiute Strip," an area west of the 110th degree longitude, encompassing Monument Valley, Navajo Mountain, and the lower area by the San Juan and Colorado Rivers before they cross the Utah-Arizona state line. President Chester A. Arthur gave this and other lands to the Navajos by executive order in 1884, but when a gold rush on the San Juan River began in 1892, the strip returned to the public domain, only to be given back to the Indians, Paiutes this time, in October 1907. The Paiutes, numbering fewer than one hundred, who were living in this area had their name attached to the land, but Navajo families filtered in to stay and graze their sheep. The BIA agent in charge of the Paiutes, Levi Chubbuck, visited these people, who "claim the territory in which they live (the lower San Juan River country on both sides of the stream [near Navajo Mountain and Paiute Canyon]) as theirs and deny somewhat aggressively the right of whites or other Indians to locate there."[48] Even so, Navajo families continued to settle in the area with their livestock, while oil prospecting in 1921 pressured the government to once again return the strip to the public domain.[49]

Agent Byron A. Sharp from the Tuba City Agency, responsible for assisting the Kaibab and San Juan Paiutes, traveled to see how the Indians were using the land of the Paiute Strip. His investigation took him to Monument Valley and surrounding areas, and he determined that the eighty-six Paiutes who had been living there in 1907 were now gone. Some still inhabited Douglas Mesa, but many had died during the 1918 influenza epidemic, others had moved to Blue Mountain, and only forty-eight lived in Paiute Canyon. The agent determined that they had "sufficient land within their own reservation to care for their needs," so he could "see no objection to throwing it open to settlement."[50] In 1922 600,000 acres returned to the public domain. Although these Paiutes had definite

connections with the Weenuche living in Allen Canyon, many of their concerns had taken a different direction.

The Navajos, with their exponential expansion in livestock, were constantly seeking new grazing lands and often came into direct conflict with Paiutes living near springs with their own herds. For instance, on Douglas Mesa, A. W. Simington had registered some individual allotments to Paiutes in 1923, when he had been working in Allen Canyon. Jim Mike received one of them. Two years later Jim had fisticuffs with a Navajo named Whitehorse who had torn down Mike's fence and several Paiute hogans because he was being blocked from using a spring that he had made improvements on but which was located on Paiute land. The Paiute fencing of trails that led to public pasturage was another concern, especially since it was Mormon livestock under their care, while the Navajos were being denied access. All of these conflicts ended amicably, but they provide an example of the growing importance of rangelands and resulting friction.[51]

These early incidents were hints of even greater conflicts to come concerning the entire Paiute Strip and the role of the Navajos. In 1929, not only Indians but also whites were using these public lands for winter range. Trouble arose. At the same time, Navajos were herding their flocks across the San Juan River to the Bluff, Montezuma Creek, and Aneth areas, and in the latter they had filed for personal allotments on the public domain. The white ranchers felt threatened and angry, believing that the Navajos should stay on their reservation. The entire issue came to a head in 1933, when the Paiute Strip became part of the Navajo Reservation, the Aneth extension was added to the 1905 Aneth acquisition, and the Navajos relinquished their individual allotments north of the river with a promise that they would not seek more in the future.[52]

During this time of turmoil, the Anglo stockmen were casting furtive glances at the

Allen Canyon Utes. The Indians' grazing lands on the National Forest and Bureau of Land Management holdings were just one more challenge to their livestock operations. Take, for instance, the Whyte family, who in the summer lived near Cottonwood Wash, corralled their animals there, and ranged them out in a four-loop cloverleaf pattern to graze. At the end of the summer and harvest, the sheep ate what was left of the garden, small cottonwood trees cut for feed, and the flocks were moved to the winter range of White Mesa. The May family, on the other hand, also used the cloverleaf pattern, but started from their camp and moved their livestock up Cottonwood Wash, stopping for a few weeks at different spots as they headed toward the national forest boundary. Once they arrived, it was time to move back down the wash, the flock grazing along the way until it reached the main camp. With fall waning, the animals were herded to White Mesa, Black Mesa, and Butler Wash for the winter ranges.[53] Multiply these two families by the number in the Ute community, the intense pressure placed on the land during all seasons, and the increasing competition with the white ranchers seeking the same resources, and one can see the problem that Peacore and other agents faced.

In mid-September 1930 superintendents from various agencies, including Peacore, representing the Consolidated Ute Agency, traveled throughout southeastern Utah on a fact-finding expedition. From this confab came the recommendation that those living in Allen Canyon "should be encouraged to return to the Ute Mountain Reservation where range could be had to meet all their needs."[54] Peacore missed a follow-up discussion in Monticello due to illness, but Black made a presentation and later reported how discouraged he was at the suggested removal. Peacore agreed: "I do not think that is a fair deal at all for the Paiutes and Ute Indians who live around Blanding.... If these people are moved away, a number of them will have

to be moved in coffins.... I am sure that these people will never consent to going down on the [Paiute] Strip, and they will never consent without a fight to be taken back on the Ute Mountain Reservation."[55]

Charles Redd, the leader of the livestock association in southeastern Utah, continued to wear away at the Indians' arguments. He insisted that less than a third of the Utes and Paiutes living around Blanding were related to the original inhabitants, and the rest had recently moved there. The old tune that Coloradoans were just trying to keep the Indians in Utah had a tired but familiar ring, as did the purported interference of the Indian Rights Association, "who has been particularly mischievous in thwarting our efforts... much to the detriment of the Indians."[56] Removal would be "a God-send to the Indians." If they remained, they would be confined to the Allen Canyon area, and if any expansion took place, it would have to be on the Ute Mountain Ute Reservation.[57]

Peacore began to relent. On December 13 he and Black met with the stockmen in Blanding who were pushing for a specific place of confinement for the Indians' livestock. The two men left the meeting convinced that if a solution was not found soon, there would be trouble. The Indians wanted more sheep, refused to move to the reservation, and argued that this had "been their home for many years and that is the place where they are going to live and die."[58] The cattlemen, on the other hand, were "doing everything in their power to persuade the Indians to make this move," while the local paper announced "if the plan as outlined works out, the Utes who now inhabit Allen and Montezuma Canyons will be moved on the new addition to the reservation."[59] Peacore looked at land on the reservation and found some under lease that would soon be renewed. The lease holders, the Decker Brothers, were willing to share the 120,000 acres. Peacore envisioned dismantling the station in Allen Canyon and hauling it to a site on Mancos Creek near Towaoc, and then moving the 113 Allen Canyon residents there.[60]

It never happened. The size and scope of the power politics involved with the Navajo and Anglo land exchange overshadowed all else; by the time the different parties signed the agreement that became House Resolution 11735 (passed on March 1, 1933), it appeared that the only stipulation that affected the Utes was the requirement to fence their allotments.

Land became even more precious to stockmen during the Great Depression and John Collier's administration of the BIA. With passage of the Taylor Grazing Act in 1934 and its system of allocating rangeland by animal unit month (AUM)—the forage necessary to feed one cow, one horse, or five sheep for one month on a specific piece of ground—a control to prevent overgrazing moved into place. Even though the CCC hired Utes and Navajos to work on their reservations to develop roads, fences, water sources, and pest control measures, the people were still trying to eke out an existence on a shrinking land base now measured by the new system. For the Allen Canyon Utes this was particularly true of the forty-five allotments made by Simington in 1930 on White Mesa. These were filed three years before the bill had worked its way through Congress, giving the Paiute Strip and other lands to the Navajos. This later became an important point since the bill stipulated that no further Indian allotments or homesteads could be made north of the San Juan River. Even though preexisting, they remained frozen for nine years.

In 1939, as White Mesa became an increasingly important part of the Utes' economic base, they believed they had secured these lands.[61] But Charlie Redd claimed there was an understood, but unwritten, agreement that those allotments in the pipeline had become null and void in 1933. "We were battling for the elimination of the forty-five applications made for the Utes in the area

just south of Blanding. In fact, it was the one important concession made by your party, and we are planning to resist to the utmost the patenting of these lands."[62] J. M. Stewart, director of lands for the BIA, pointed out that neither he nor the former commissioner had the power to cancel individual filings by Indians if done properly, and that the livestock committee could not have influenced that process either. A drought followed by deep winter snows in Allen Canyon made the patient Utes even more anxious to determine their allotment status.

To add insult to injury, one rancher claimed to have a permit to graze his animals on the land in question, and others destroyed all of the hogans built on it when the Utes filed in 1930. The livestock owners warned the Indians to just stay off. Superintendent S. F. Stacher was irate. "If the Indians are within their rights in claiming their allotments, as we believe they are, and your office [BIA] so advises us to this effect, we will immediately mark out the boundary and take possession of same and will prevent trespass on this land."[63] The commissioner of Indian Affairs wasted little time responding. First there were no minutes kept in the 1932 meeting; second, there was definite misinterpretation of the wording and intent of the agreement; third, it had been decided in that meeting that previously valid filings would be honored; fourth, the Ute and Paiute people had gained nothing from the land transfer, while the Navajos had; and finally, the Utes had filed appropriately and should "proceed to patent at the earliest practicable date."[64]

The stockmen countered through the courts, dragging the litigation on for another year. Because the land was technically individual property, the government could not fence it to keep trespassers out. In a meeting held in Blanding in December 1940, the Ute Mountain Council passed a resolution that the Indian Office should accept the deeds from those who had filed, making the land government property and protected accordingly.[65] The White Mesa community had received its start, but in his annual report for that year, their superintendent, Floyd MacSpadden, still classified them as "paupers and [they] are still a definite problem from either the range or social standpoint.... [They are faced with] difficult and intensive opposition from the large Mormon livestock interests in southeastern Utah...[who use] the Grazing Service as a disguise to conduct their avaricious oppositions."[66] Not until 1948 were all the allotments accepted and the tribal fencing of White Mesa gotten under way.[67]

In 1936, during Collier's administration of the BIA, the Southern Utes and Ute Mountain Utes accepted provisions in the Indian Reorganization Act that required each to approve a new tribal constitution to include a council voted into office, thus decreasing the power of the traditional chieftainship. The Southern Utes adopted it that year, but for the more traditionally minded Ute Mountain and Allen Canyon Utes, who after Chief John Miller's death had replaced him with an equally strong leader, Jack House, it would take another four years.[68] Anson Whyte represented the people of Allen Canyon during this time, and in a meeting in Moab on May 10, 1938, he shared their views. Concerned about the new constitution, he said: "Our children are not educated enough to handle our problems, as well as you [Southern Ute and Uintah Ouray] people. We were going to adopt the constitution and bylaws but after thinking it over we changed our minds and thought it best to remain as we are. My friends, I am telling you because I'm sure you would like to know why we refuse to adopt it."[69] In the same speech he notified Superintendent Stacher that his people refused to move from Allen Canyon, which the agent had urged, because "we do not like to do that [move and farm] since we like our place regardless of how hopeless it is and we aim to remain there." While the council agreed with this position, there was not necessarily strong admiration for the Allen Canyon Utes'

involvement. In a meeting that November, the council wanted to add another member but did not want one selected from Blanding, "as they would rather not have anything to do with these Utes. They stated that these Utes have their own leader and for him to take care of their own affairs."[70] Not until May 8, 1940, was the constitution approved by a 91 to 12 vote, signaling its adoption and guaranteeing a position for one member from Allen Canyon to serve on the council.[71]

Different problems loomed on the horizon as World War II began. The doldrums of the Great Depression gave way to a national economy that consumed goods and materials at an unprecedented rate. Cattle and sheep sold at competitive prices, encouraging tribal members in the livestock industry. Of even greater future impact were the ninety-four Ute men from the Southern and Ute Mountain Ute reservations who enlisted in the armed forces.[72] From White Mesa, Nolan May, Phillip Posey, and Edward Dutchie served their country and returned home safely.[73] These veterans returned with skills and experience that were later put to use in tribal government and general leadership of their community.

Another major step toward integrating Indians into white society began in 1938 with the Indian Claims Commission Act, which gave the Utes a second opportunity to air grievances and receive reimbursement for lost lands. Four different claims, backed by expert testimony and the astute leadership of the Salt Lake–based lawyer Ernest L. Wilkinson, netted the Utes a victory on all four counts. On July 13, 1950, the federal government awarded $31,761,206 for the more than six million acres lost between 1891 and 1938.[74] Division of the funds was based on reservation populations, with 60 percent going to the Uintah and Ouray Utes, and 40 percent to the three bands of Southern Utes. The Ute Mountain people were eventually awarded $6.2 million, but even after the amount had been determined, there were still things they had to do. Chief among them was to outline and have approved a rehabilitation plan showing how the money would be spent. On August 12, 1953, Congress passed it.

The Ute Mountain Rehabilitation Plan called for a per capita cash payment of $500 and an additional $3,000 set aside for each person in the form of a financial grant that would in some way improve an individual's standard of living and general economic position. In 1951 the Ute Mountain Ute Planning Committee canvassed the people in Towaoc and Allen Canyon to determine their needs. The combined population around this time was approximately 625, including 125 Allen Canyon Utes.[75] Just how great their needs were at midcentury became apparent. The average Ute family had four members, and families lived in homes ranging from frame houses (31, 24 of which were one room) to tents (143), hogans (7), and brush shelters (12). There were 960 acres of land under cultivation, and 897 cattle, 1,705 sheep, and 309 horses being grazed on the reservation, but the education and skills needed to operate in the dominant society were sorely lacking.[76]

For its long-range goals in economic development, the Ute Mountain Utes set aside $1 million to purchase summer range, another $1 million to boost the livestock herds, and $40,000 to develop springs. Irrigation water was another concern, and three sites were targeted for development: the Mancos River, Navajo Wash, and Cottonwood and Hammond Canyon Creeks. By this time, many of the ditches had fallen into disrepair, been washed out, and abandoned. The people of Allen Canyon wanted their five hundred acres of irrigable land restored to productive use. Ditches, flumes, and headgates were all part of this restoration project, to the tune of $23,000.[77] On October 10, 1952, all of the Allen Canyon Utes met with government officials interested in determining future residence. After much discussion, the forty-one members voted. Nineteen of

them wished to live in Allen Canyon and encouraged further development, while eight agreed to move from Westwater to a place near Blanding where there was more and better land. Arthur Dutchie, Helen Eyetoo, and Myers Cantsee formed a committee to assist with relocation.[78]

Superintendent Elbert J. Floyd visited Allen Canyon the following April and determined that a headgate dam four feet high and fifty feet long, along with a smaller one in Hammond Creek, would meet the residents' needs. He was especially eager to build the dams because "there has been very little tribal work for the Utes in Utah."[79] The project would not only help those interested in agriculture, but also provide an opportunity for paid labor. The next fiscal year offered additional opportunity with another appropriation of $50,000. The target this time was a well to supplement the natural irrigation water during the dry months of July and August. Tribal funds were also used to purchase a tractor, scraper, dump truck, and a pickup to work the estimated 200 acres of farmland that had been subdivided into small tracts "to provide gardens for the 12 to 18 families who insist on living in this area."[80] Upon completion of the work, which was to be finished before the planting season of spring 1954, the entire project would be turned over to the Allen Canyon residents.

The reaction to all of this from the white community is instructive. While little was said about the farm improvements, the per capita payments took direct fire. Even before the local Utes determined the amount to be received, the *San Juan Record* reported, through a syndicated press release, Northern Ute activity around Fort Duchesne. In part the article told of how "The 'Great White Fathers' in Washington plunked down a $400,000 first installment to begin squaring things with 2600 Ute Indians the palefaces beat on a land deal back in the 1880s.... The red men decided to pick up the cash in payments of $1,000 for each brave, squaw, and

Myers Cantsee and Edward Dutchie circa 1950, when Utes began receiving the first claims settlements for loss of traditional lands. The money that poured in allowed the people of White Mesa to purchase things that they had never been able to before. Recalling this time, many Utes say that the wealth could have been handled better, but they also recognize that many people were understandably caught up in the euphoria of their new buying power. (Courtesy of San Juan County Historical Commission)

papoose.... If they blow it on firewater or other unnecessary items, Uncle Sam will possibly hold back on his future installments."[81]

There was just as much innuendo in Blanding when a per capita payment arrived in mid-April 1952. After noting that each person had received $500 which should have gone to the parents and grandparents of yesteryear, a reporter wrote:

> The stores and streets were so full of money spenders, it was almost impossible to get up and down the sidewalk. One woman was carrying checks amounting to more than $4,000.
>
> The Indians are all driving automobiles now, and they were all hunting for better second hand or new cars to buy. By night time a good part of the checks had changed hands and the merchants and car dealers were carrying them around. The men were wearing new boots and the women had material for new silk dresses. The whole tribe guzzled pop and ice cream continuously. Perfume and talcum powder must have been sold by the gallon judging from the odors that were so prevalent.
>
> Piutes sat in cafes and ate beef and hamburger steaks while their neighbors, the white people, ate hamburgers. Car dealers from other towns were in Blanding to try and get their share of the car sales. New cars had been ordered from as far away as Dolores, Colorado. The Piutes ride back and forth from their little homes at Westwater. They ride in to the picture shows and for the present at least, their life is one of luxury.[82]

Bonnie Mike Lehi agrees that some of her people "spent their settlement money silly," buying things like television sets before there was electricity on White Mesa, not to mention consuming increased amounts of alcohol, which, along with its attendant ills, many elders still condemn today.[83] The newfound wealth opened doors in ways that a few years earlier would not have been possible, but there was much to learn. Drivers' licenses, for instance, became an issue after twenty-five Utes in the Blanding area purchased cars in 1952. Driver education classes, then an oral exam with an interpreter, if necessary, prepared them for the road. In one course of instruction, all twelve participants passed with an excellent average.[84] Once tremendously marginalized, the Ute people now held purchasing power and a position in local society that they had never experienced.

Other funds were arriving from oil and gas leases on the Ute Mountain Ute Reservation. In June 1952 a government official asked some of the people how they were planning to spend all this money flowing in. One woman replied, "A house with a window and a cook stove. A cow and some hay and a horse. No, two horses."[85] To this point there had been five per capita payments of $1,025, or an aggregate sum of $151,700, to the 148 Indians living in the Blanding area. But the Ute woman's dream of a comfortable home, a cow, and two horses was, in reality, no closer than when the first royalty payment came in January 1950.[86] The tribal council, however, had recently approved giving $8,000 to each person from the rehabilitation fund for the construction of a home, meaning an average family of four would receive $32,000 — enough to build "a home with a window" and much more.

But where? The Utes insisted that they did not want to settle where they were not wanted, but they also wanted all the modern conveniences of other Americans. The people of Blanding and Superintendent Floyd wrestled with the concept at a meeting on October 24, 1952. While the community "exhibited a splendid attitude toward this question," it was divided between two alternatives.[87] One group encouraged the purchase of individual lots in town where white neighbors could help the Indians build their homes. The other group, which included a unanimous vote from the city council, wanted the Utes to purchase a tract of land

nearby where electricity and water would be made available. City plots were expensive and limited, so this approach seemed more practical. There was no mention of separation or segregation, but it is interesting to note that in the movie theater, for instance, the Indians always sat on the left side, whites on the right.[88] Whether this was directed or self-imposed is not clear, but it certainly illustrates prevailing attitudes. Not until the 1960s and the general civil rights movement did this pattern shift.

Most Ute people agreed that Allen Canyon was too distant for a central community because of the growing emphasis on education and the need for school facilities. Westwater was too rocky for farming, but several men herded livestock for residents, tended gardens, chopped wood for whites, or labored in the mines. To move too far from Blanding would hamper these opportunities to work. Although the "attitude of the Blanding people was very fine," Floyd also recognized that change "will take some time but it is not impossible by any means."[89] The answer lay eleven miles to the south, at White Mesa. It offered the best of both worlds with its allotted lands and room for expansion, yet it was close enough to form a community and provide access to the services of Blanding, including schools. Here the Utes could establish a distinct community and maintain their identity beyond the reach of the city's government.

This was not new territory. For years the Utes had lived in camps at White Mesa and used it as winter range for livestock, freeing them from the deeper snows of Allen Canyon and providing road access to Blanding and Bluff. A favorite camping spot just below it in Westwater Canyon, known as Coyote's Nose, had a spring and trees that offered welcomed shade to herders with their flocks of sheep.[90] Stella Eyetoo's family had been on the move when she was born there. Blanding, on the other hand, elicited no feelings of fondness

Johnnie Peterson (a.k.a. "Steve Hatch") holds young Gordon Redd's hand on the porch of Parley Redd's Store in Blanding, Utah, 1929. Despite all of the conflicts and turmoil, there were many close ties and goodwill shared between Utes and whites. (Courtesy of Finley Bayles)

or connection. After they abandoned the Westwater camps, few had a desire to return. Edward and Patty Dutchie tried living with white neighbors but eventually left. Patty said of White Mesa, "It was big enough to move around where I could do whatever I wanted, like cooking outdoors and doing things like grandma used to do instead of being looked at by white people. Whenever I did things I would get embarrassed when they looked at me and they might think I am dirty."[91]

In the latter part of September 1954, Slavens Incorporated, a construction company in Cortez, Colorado, began building the first of eighteen two-room homes on White Mesa.[92] For thirty years, until 1984, this company was a major contractor for building Ute housing, not only on White Mesa but in Blanding (homes for Edward and Arthur Dutchie) and Allen Canyon (four homes). Paid for with rehabilitation funds,

these homes represent the first concerted effort to provide the White Mesa Utes with living conditions comparable to those of their white neighbors. With concrete footers, wood construction, siding, and a standard floorplan, these structures took only a couple of months to build. Soon standardization gave way to customer wishes, and the homes became bigger and more elaborate. Slavens also built thirty sheep-camp tent frames with wood and linoleum floors and doors, over which a ten-by-twelve-foot canvas tent could be erected. As times changed and amenities such as running water, indoor plumbing, and electricity became available, Slavens also contracted for the remodeling.[93] In 1976, with fifty homes already dotting the grasslands of White Mesa, twenty-five Housing and Urban Development homes equipped with water, plumbing, and electricity were added to the community. Today more than a hundred buildings rest atop the mesa.

Other improvements came fast on the heels of home construction. In 1956 Highway 191 between Blanding and Bluff, and passing through White Mesa, received its first coat of tar.[94] Travel became easier, with less wear and tear on vehicles, making it possible to bus schoolchildren. Initially the tribe paid for water to be hauled from Blanding, but by the mid-1950s, a well near Edward Dutchie's house in the center of the community provided sweet-tasting water that was pumped into a truck and delivered to metal tanks or concrete cisterns outside each home.[95] The water still entered the house in buckets; not until 1976 did piped plumbing on a centralized water and sewage system become the standard, with a 100,000-gallon storage tank standing sentinel at the northern end of the community.[96] Electricity replaced kerosene lamps in 1964, when tribal leaders in Towaoc determined that the Utah Power and Light Company lines would not burn down the homes and that it was safe to install the system on White Mesa.[97] The tribe also provided money for a community worker, police protection, a recreation program, and a community workshop.[98]

When one considers the enormous change that occurred over thirty years, or roughly one generation, in the life of the White Mesa Utes, it is apparent that this period was crucial to their entry into white society. While many of the preceding decades had been characterized by loss—of land, traditional values, and way of life—this time the Utes' losses were being replaced at a rapid rate with Anglo-American culture. This is not to suggest that their distinct identity had been lost, but only that the Weenuche embraced many of the ideas and material goods of the twentieth century and began the struggle to adapt to the dominant culture. This was not always easy, given the rate of speed and direction in which change occurred. Starting with the Posey conflict and continuing through the allotment process, the Allen Canyon and livestock efforts, the boarding and Blanding school experiences, the Great Depression, the Indian Reorganization Act, the Taylor Grazing Act, World War II, Tribal Land Claims settlements, and the establishment of the White Mesa community, one can see the turbulence and challenges confronting the Ute people of southeastern Utah. There was more ahead, but perhaps in no other period in their history had the White Mesa Utes been faced with so much, so fast—a constant bombardment by the forces of integration. Considering what these people encountered, they handled their situation remarkably well.

CHAPTER 15

People and Perception

Neighbors' Views Across a Chasm, 1860–1960

These days, I think some people would have called Posey an ecologist.
He was somewhat concerned about preservation of the land. He told me,
and Mancos Jim told me a time or two before, how the country had been
when Posey was a boy. And their expression always was something like the
grass would grow up to the belly of the ponies. He said there was lots of
grass and lots of deer and there was hunting.

Lyman Hunter, San Juan cowboy, 1920–1922

The people of White Mesa have long had rocky relations with their neighbors. In the earliest recorded observations, made during Hispanic control of the Southwest, Navajo and Ute interaction was characterized by periods of peace frequently broken by betrayal and war. Anglo-American associations followed a similar pattern. All three cultures operated from a bank of perceptions that categorized, explained, and then initiated what seemed appropriate responses. Indeed, highly subjective perceptions, based on everything from mythology to event, opened the doors to motive, then action. This chapter examines three cultural scenes: Ute-Navajo relations, trading post interactions, and Ute-settler relationships — to provide a variety of views concerning these complex associations. As expected, negative feelings still arise when people recall past wrongs, yet there is also a surprising amount of understanding and appreciation. In more than one instance, the neighbors of the White Mesa Utes shared friendship and provided assistance to local Utes they had come to know well.

Navajo tradition teaches that the origin of the Utes hearkens back to the creation of the world, when Coyote, the trickster, sought to marry his daughter. Feigning death, he left instructions for his wife and child to place his body on a drying rack and move away from their home, and for the daughter to marry the first man she met. After completing Coyote's wishes, the two women gathered their belongings and began looking for a new home. Along the way they encountered a man, actually Coyote in disguise. The daughter married him; his wife soon recognized the imposter, but too late, for her daughter had conceived. Following the birth, the young mother tossed her baby boy into a badger's hole, leaving him to die. A mother owl rescued and raised the child, but her husband grew jealous and chased the now-grown man away to his own people, who also rejected him. As he fled, he uprooted spruce, ash, sumac, mountain mahogany, and other plants that became the ancestors of the Utes, who were personified as arrows.[1] Born through trickery and deceit, related to Coyote, and associated with night and death, the progenitor of the Utes established the characteristic foundation of one of the Navajos' great competitors.

Another version of Ute origin tells of a young man who killed two Navajo children with arrows while playing and then fled.[2] As the Navajos pursued him, they discovered that at each of his camps another man joined him. The story suggests that the boy actually created these people from the trees previously mentioned. Realizing that they were outnumbered, the Navajos returned home. In another version the boy makes arrows as he looks for his relatives, and these become the Utes.[3] The boy's rejection and pursuit by the Navajos resulted in the creation of enemy warriors derived from tough mountain plants. Wooden arrows, as symbols of war, represent the hostile relations between the two tribes.[4]

All of these stories, unflattering to the Utes, provide insight into the Navajos' fear and mistrust of their neighbors. Coyote, although a sacred being with extensive power, also exhibits negative behavior and characteristics abhorred by the Navajos. Incest, deceit, uncontrolled passion, excess, and fighting among relatives were all to be avoided. Owl is also a dangerous creature associated with death. Thus, the Ute-Navajo conflict was often interpreted as being as much a spiritual contest between good and bad as it was a physical contest. The enemy and what he stood for could be confronted on a physical and a spiritual level. With such a long history of feuding, rooted in the beginning of time, it is not surprising that Navajos referred to the Utes as "the Enemies You Continually Fight With" and "the Arrow People."[5]

Navajo storytellers tie events in their stories to specific geographical sites. As Florence Begay shared her version of the origin of the Utes, she added detail that left no doubt that the land of the Weenuche figured heavily in her telling. When Coyote faked his death, he said that he wanted to be buried just as the warrior who lies as Sleeping Ute Mountain was buried, covered with sticks and leaves. He instructed the mother and daughter not to look back, but one of them did and saw the impostor arise from his grave, which appeared much like the brush shelters the Utes later made. Another site with two large rocks near Sleeping Ute Mountain is the place where Mother Owl picked up the offspring from Coyote's union with his daughter. She took the baby to her home at Mesa Verde, but her husband eventually became jealous of the boy and cast him out. He returned to the Navajos but was not accepted.

So the Owl People are the Utes. That is why the Utes' necks are like this [short and stocky]. They do not have necks. They [Navajos] started to chase him and he had his bow and arrows. He cut four different branches and these were used to make the shaft of the arrows. When he cut these, this was the way the Utes came into being in Dolores. Then into the mountains nearby the Utes were scattered all over this way. I have asked the Utes about the mountain and they say that Ute Mountain is like their mother and when they die, they will go back into it.... So from Mancos Creek to Montrose, the Utes were planted.[6]

Navajo teachings also differentiate between Utes (Nóóda'i) and Paiutes (Báyóodzin), who have their own place of origin specified—Navajo Mountain. During the time of creation, when monsters roamed the earth, two Navajo twins—Monster Slayer and Born for Water—received supernatural powers to destroy these troublesome, evil creatures. One of these monsters was He Who Kicks People Off the Cliff (Tsé dah Hódziiłtáłii) who lived on the side of the mountain. Monster Slayer walked a narrow trail high upon the cliff where this being sat with his legs drawn up, ready to kick. After four fruitless attempts to send the hero over the precipice, the monster innocently suggested that he was just trying to stretch his legs. Monster Slayer carved him up with his large knife, threw his body into the canyon, and then descended to the desert floor to kill the creature's twelve children. He did not destroy the last one because it was so ugly and dirty; instead it was left in exile at Navajo Mountain because "it was a barren land, where you will have to work hard for a living, and will wander ever naked and hungry."[7] This creature was the progenitor of the Paiute people.

Local Navajo lore adds variety and detail to the main version, which expresses contemporary relationships. When Monster Slayer descended to destroy the children, they said, "No, you will not kill us. In the future, the people [Navajo] will use us." Monster Slayer shot one of them to Blue Mountain, and they were told not to eat anymore people. "They have become the Utes. Now they have become men and we have helped each other. The Utes make ceremonial baskets. That was the agreement from the past."[8] Another version tells of how the children ate their father when he fell below and then raced away before Monster Slayer could trap and destroy them. After a lengthy chase, these "proto-Paiutes" finally faced Monster Slayer and some Navajo people near Kayenta, where they lost their power and were almost destroyed. The Paiutes "pleaded with the People [Navajo] to stay and live there; they promised to keep the Navajos for as long as they lived. That is how some of these Utes ended up living on the side of Navajo Mountain."[9] Thus, Navajos generally recognize the differences and similarities between the Utes and Paiutes and treat them accordingly.

Utes are often associated with war, especially during the Fearing Time of the 1850s and 1860s (see chapter 5). A typical story from this era tells of a Navajo woman who eventually triumphed over her captors. A war party seized her as she herded sheep, slaughtered the flock, and traveled north to Ute country. Eventually the warriors separated, and she rode off with her captor, sitting on the back of his horse. As they camped, he sharpened a stick to clean his ears. Waiting for the right moment, she slammed his hand, driving the stick into his skull and toppling him. The woman grabbed a rock, hit him on the head, and proceeded to hammer his skull "just as one tans leather."[10] Taking his horses, she crossed the San Juan River and met her maternal uncle, who had been tracking the enemy. In other stories the Utes tie their female captives with leather thongs or place them under large buffalo robes and sleep around its edges. The only times that women had any possibility of escape was when the men were asleep or allowed them to gather wood or water.

Wolfkiller recalls returning from a trading expedition to find that the Utes had raided his camp. Gathering some men, the party went to retrieve the captured women, children, and livestock. Because there were only a few raiders, the Utes were able to herd their spoils faster, intent on escape rather than fighting the Navajos. As the pursuit wore on, the Utes released the sheep and many women and children, but killed some of the older ones and babies during the hard drive. The enemy made good their flight. Warrior Girl was among the women that the Utes kept. She arrived in the enemies' camp and was immediately put to work, hauling wood and water for her captors. If the women were unable to complete their chores, the Utes would beat them with a buckskin whip until they bled.

Many captive women became wives, which angered the jealous Ute women. They told the new arrivals that their husbands would soon tire of them and sell them to the Mexicans as slaves. The Ute women encouraged them to escape before it was too late, wanting to be rid of their competitors. After a failed escape by another Navajo woman, the Utes bound Warrior Girl's hands and feet each night when she went to bed. One night, however, the wife cut Warrior Girl's bindings, gave her some food, and sent her on her way. She ran all night and the next day. The men were in no hurry to recover her because they did not believe she could cross the San Juan River, which was full from the late spring runoff. They finally caught sight of her at the river and scornfully laughed, believing that she would drown. To their surprise Warrior Girl used a cottonwood log to cross safely and then eluded her pursuers. She traveled for many days before reaching her home, starved and exhausted, but having successfully escaped.

As in many of these captivity narratives, Navajos escaped either through supernatural means or sheer grit. On the other side, Rachel Eyetoo learned of when a group of Ute women were picking berries at the head of Allen Canyon and Navajos attacked, scattered, and killed some. One woman ran all the way to the Bears Ears, where she met a group of Ute warriors who then chased and killed many of the guilty Navajos.[11]

Following the Long Walk era, animosity and conflict continued. One Navajo story tells of how the Utes "sang songs against the Navajo," stole Navajo horses, and drove the animals into a deep canyon for safekeeping. The Navajos asked for them back, were refused, went home and performed their own ceremonies, and then returned to find the horses freed and the Utes gone.[12] One time Joe Bishop's Little Boy and Joe Bush's Boy stole two Navajo horses, placed them in an alcove, and fenced them in with rocks. Two days later the owner found his missing property, stole the bridle and rope the Utes had placed on his animals, and fled to the reservation, where the two Utes soon accosted him and demanded their property back. Tension almost led to a fight, but the Utes relinquished control.[13] Another time conflict arose over bets placed on a horse race, followed by a shooting. Navajo medicine men "knew a great deal of sacred things performed against the Paiutes, who moved out of Paiute Canyon [near Navajo Mountain]. Many died when moving out this [Monument Valley] way. They moved to Douglas Mesa. Some died while they were moving."[14]

A newspaper article mentions how Scotty and Jesse Posey (William Posey's son) cornered a Navajo named Mustache, taunting and physically restraining him outside the San Juan Co-op (Bluff) trading post. Seven or eight Navajos learned of his plight and came to his rescue, capturing Scotty but missing Jesse, who ran to his father's camp on Cottonwood Wash. Upon hearing the situation, Posey ran full-tilt to the cluster of Navajos, dispersing them and freeing Scotty by viciously slashing at the captors with a large knife. "They parted before him like sheep before a coyote," having had enough for that day.[15] These types of incidents, multiplied many times but often unreported, give a sense of the tenor of relations.

As these "Wild West" practices quieted, conflict continued over land use. The aggressors here were the expansionist Navajos, who herded their flocks of sheep onto Ute reservation lands in search of pasture. The Ute council, with the encouragement of their agent, sought Ute families who would move to the affected areas with their livestock to lay claim to the land. Albert H. Kneale and Edward E. McKean, the Navajo and Ute superintendents, respectively, formulated a plan to prevent the problem from spreading, but the Utes moved faster than their agent realized, rounded up some of the Navajo stock, and killed some of their horses. A meeting between the Navajos and Utes at Towaoc (called by the Navajos Kin Dootł'izhí — "Blue House"), presided over by McKean, allowed the participants to work out the issues. This resulted in hiring a Navajo policeman to handle Navajo infractions, and a general agreement between both groups. At other times riders patrolled the fence lines and reported any unauthorized trespass.[16]

There were also friendly relations fostered through trade, marriage, and shared proximity. In exchange for baskets and buckskins, the Paiutes of Monument Valley and Navajo Mountain received horses and ceremonial services. They believed that the Navajos had

A Navajo in Allen Canyon in August 1935 trading for tanned buckskin, the quality of which the Utes were famous for. Navajos also traveled the long distance to Ute territory to participate in the Bear Dance, seek medicinal cures, and purchase woven baskets. (Special Collection, Sherratt Library, Southern Utah University)

strong supernatural healing powers and so asked them to perform different curing rites. Fred Yazzie remembers his father conducting ceremonies and curing the sick. "Lots of Paiutes said my father's ceremonies were real and got well from them.... In this way we had gotten to know them."[17] Paiutes also herded sheep, carded and spun wool, cared for Navajo gardens, and performed general chores. They traveled back and forth to Blue Mountain, although "their horses were usually skinny with sores on them."[18] As expressed in the myth, the Paiutes who were left unharmed promised to be an asset to the Navajos; they "have lived here ever since and our people [Navajo] have learned to weave baskets through them. We have mastered their trade and now make a living from this 'asset.'"[19]

The Utes played a somewhat different role for the Navajos. Slim Benally remembers trading with the Utes in Bluff, Montezuma Creek, and Aneth. "They used to ride among the Navajo, bartering for sheep, corn, and other kinds of food and paying in money."[20] Ella Sakizzie, as a young girl, participated in Bear Dances under the cottonwood trees at Ira Hatch's trading post in Montezuma Canyon and often saw Utes and Navajos gambling in card games. "I used to see them ride their horses carrying bundles of long sumac stems tied to their saddles behind them. I did not know what they were for back then, but now I make baskets out of them, too."[21] Centenarian Maimi Howard remembers Navajos and Utes calling each other by kinship terms as relatives. "They used to live together in the same place and they loved each other.... They shared their knowledge with others. They got together for the Enemyway Ceremony and made the ceremony work easier. They were very good at it, too."[22]

Gambling, a favorite pastime in both cultures, provided many stories of jackpots lost and won. John Holiday, a medicine man from Monument Valley, told of the Utes and

A group of Utes south of Mexican Hat Rock playing cards, probably either monte or coon-can, circa 1920s. Games of chance were a favorite pastime of the Utes, who also enjoyed horse racing, stick games, shooting contests, and feats of strength. (Courtesy of San Juan County Historical Commission)

Navajos meeting at the Bluff trading post with high stakes—woven rugs, hides, wool, livestock, and other valued items—to use for bets. The Navajos lost everything; the Utes were elated. A Navajo named Continuous Hills climbed the hill where the cemetery is located and shot his rifle at the center of a prominent white rock. He later joined the gamblers and asked for a shooting contest with the stakes being all that had been lost plus additional property. Each side provided their representative, winner takes all. Posey was the marksman for the Utes. He was well-known by all—the Navajos called him Hooghan Binaanish ("I Am Working on the House"), a name received for helping a white man build a home. The Utes gave him their own names: "Moccasin Shoestring" because of the type of moccasins he wore, "Chaps" for his fringed leather leg protection, and by the Utes at Towaoc, "Soft Part above the Hip."[23] The Navajo shot first, and then Posey, who hit the dirt near the edge of the rock. All the Navajos cheered and claimed that their man had hit the rock in the center, and when two riders went to inspect the rock, they saw

the mark actually left earlier by Continuous Hills. With their goods returned plus the buckskin dresses, beaded items, and concho belts won from the Utes, the Navajos stayed longer and gambled more.[24]

One of the most pronounced qualities that the Utes even today attribute to the Navajos is the strength of their witchcraft powers. The type most often mentioned is the Navajo skinwalker, who is able to acquire superhuman qualities, such as running with lightning speed, and can sicken victims with corpse poison, use prayers to curse an individual, and obtain other people's wealth by shrinking and then stealing it.[25] Rachel Eyetoo in 1971 spoke extensively about how a Navajo medicine man became angry with a Ute medicine man who was helping a Navajo woman. He died. She went on, "The Navajos are the only ones who are witching us because they want to take our land. That is why my people are going crazy from witchcraft."[26] Lola Mike agrees. When asked why Navajos were now living on lands that had previously belonged to the Utes, she felt that their witchcraft was so strong that it had forced her people to move away to escape its power.[27]

Rachel had been shot by an object that penetrated her shoulder through supernatural means. It required a Hopi medicine man to suck out the offending substance. When asked if all the Utes were afraid that Navajos were witching them, she replied, "Yes, [but the Utes] don't know how [to retaliate]. Nowadays, the Utes are dying all over. There are no Utes…because the Navajos are witching them."[28] Her grandfather, Scotty Cantsee, was also a target of this animosity. "He was witched by a Navajo, too. I guess they did it to him through his horse [which] was witched and it went to him. He died without any sickness in a hospital. He talked about the Navajos coming to him and said, 'They are going to get me.' That is the only thing he talked about until he died, which took maybe one or two hours."[29]

Rachel went on to say that Ute children today are "going crazy" because Navajo men, women, and children are working their evil against them. The only preventative measure to keep witchcraft away, often indicated when the dogs start to whine at night "because they are scared," is to put soap in a frying pan, heat it on the stove, and then pour it on a certain plant called Ghost Brush. The smoke from doing this is enough to "scare anything away, even the owl." At the same time a special whistle is blown in the smoke four times, a cure said to also have been used by the Mokwič. She learned these protective measures from her grandfather, who was a medicine man and understood the problem. Most other Utes did not know about witchcraft and how to protect themselves.

One place where the Utes and Navajo were on equal footing was the trading post. The Four Corners area between 1880 and 1940 saw a proliferation of posts that served the Indians in a burgeoning business built primarily on wool and its manufactured products. Ute and Navajo clientele traded in Bluff, Montezuma Creek, Hatch, Ismay,

Blanding, Allen Canyon, Aneth, McElmo, Four Corners, Tanner Mesa, Mancos Creek, Towaoc, Cortez, Mexican Hat, Monument Valley, Kayenta, Navajo Mountain, and elsewhere. Many of these posts were on the edges of reservations, avoiding the stricter government regulation required for those on Indian land. Each store depended on the whims of the mainstream economy and characteristically had a large turnover of proprietors with a convoluted history of ownership. Although a great deal of information exists about posts serving Navajos, whose volume of business and beauty of product became nationally known, little has been said about Ute trading. Limited space does not allow each post's story to be told here, but a generalized picture of operation speaks of their importance.

Strategically located to capture the flow of customers traveling along trails, visiting a source of water, or grazing livestock, most posts sprang from the land to meet a need. Many initial structures were built of wood. Billy Meadow's trading post, located on the south side of the San Juan River north of Shiprock, is a good example of one made of piñon logs, similar to the early posts in Montezuma Canyon, Allen Canyon, and Oljato. Earle R. Forrest visited it in 1902, describing it as "a building as primitive as I have ever laid eyes on."[30] The long, narrow structure with a "bull pen" for its customers, a flat roof covered with six inches of dirt to keep out heat and moisture, and a livestock corral was very much like Joe Hatch's post (described in chapter 13). Other stores, such as those in Aneth (1885), Four Corners (pre-1884), and Mancos Creek (1923), used locally quarried sandstone for their building material. The Four Corners store, for instance, had an L-shaped configuration, with a western wall 117 feet long comprised of rock over 2 feet thick and 11 feet high, while the short stem of the "L" was 65 feet long. Eight large windows dotted the walls, with firing ports in places where there were no doors or windows.

Adobe covered the walls, and three fireplaces heated the spacious rooms. Utes and Navajos frequenting this store must have been impressed with its comfortable and spacious accommodations.

Trading posts on and off the reservation employed men and women who spoke both Navajo and Ute, understood these cultures, and were respected friends. For example, during the Tse-ne-gat fight Louisa Wetherill, from Kayenta, camped five days with the Utes in Bluff, urging them to surrender. Even though her "hypnotic influence over the Indians and great confidence in her ability to persuade [them]" was insufficient, this incident certainly shows the respect that the Ute men had for this Anglo woman.[31] During the same incident trader Arthur Spencer, at Mexican Hat, found that as soon as the conflict started, the Utes lost all of their food and "would come down on me and, of course, their being broke and no other tribes to help them, they had to eat. The only thing I could do was to feed them and take a chance on getting the money out of them when they were able to pay it. In doing this they eventually left a bill of several hundred dollars which I never could collect."[32] Trader-customer relations were paramount to continued post operations.

Rather than sift through a myriad of names of the men and women manning these posts, one can look at Oen Edgar Noland as an example of one of the most successful traders to the Utes. His interactions with these people spanned more than forty years, and his activities illustrate the concern he had and the variety of ways he was able to serve them while maintaining positive relations. Born September 25, 1852, in Independence, Missouri, he arrived in Colorado in 1873 to work as a miner and freighter until 1882. That year he took out a loan of $10,000 to open a post on the San Juan River with the understanding that he would sign over a life insurance policy of $35,000 as collateral. One of the lenders, Pete Schifferer, warned, "The

Utes and Navvies are bad; that region is Hell's own backyard," to which Noland replied, "I'm going down there to be a trader, not a hired gun buzzard after bounty scalps."[33]

He first established a post in Riverview (today's Aneth), but when the flood of 1884 swept the building down the river, he moved upstream thirteen miles and built the Four Corners trading post. During that time he married Caroline (Callie) Mitchell, daughter of Henry L. Mitchell, another trader—which gave Ed his Navajo name of Bidoni (Baadaaní) Son-in-Law. He had five children with Callie before she died in 1895. Seven years later he married Lolla Kutch, bought a home in Mancos, hired people to alternate with him behind the counters in the Four Corners and Navajo Springs (1895) trading posts, and was considered "the best equipped of any man on the border to carry on an Indian trading post...[since] he has the confidence of the entire tribe [of Utes].[34]

Noland knew and served the Ute people, who brought him success. In 1900 he sold them more flour and clothing than the government issued, while advocating that the reservation system should be taking care of its charges. He and interpreter Joe Smith "are looked upon by them as being their only friends," even though the newspaper insisted the "Navajo Springs Utes are a better dispositioned people than the same number of whites would be under similar circumstances, else they would have long been on the warpath."[35] Two years later he rescued eleven children on their way to the school at Fort Lewis. They had left the Navajo Springs Agency crammed in a wagon with no blankets, food, or bedding for this mid-December trip, moving at a rate of twenty miles per day. After spending a frigid night around a fire in a clump of piñon trees, the children arrived in Mancos, where Noland learned of their situation, took them out to eat, and paid their train fare for the rest of the way.[36] He was also an advocate for the Utes with the government, encouraging the agents to work

The Hatch trading post in Montezuma Canyon, mid-1930s: *left to right*, Joe Hatch, Ira Hatch, Joseph Hatch Sr., and Hugh Rentz. Joseph Hatch Sr.—the father of Joe Hatch, who ran the Allen Canyon trading post—built this store in 1926. Located approximately twelve miles from the San Juan River, it served Utes living at the north end of the canyon as well as Navajos to the south. (Courtesy of Stewart Hatch)

harder on getting irrigation water for the reservation while affirming that the Indians would be more than willing to prepare and plant the land if they had something to work with. He accompanied the Ute delegation to Washington, DC, when the Mesa Verde deliberations were under way and worked to get crooked agents out of the Indian Service.[37] Little wonder that when a man from Oklahoma shot Noland three times and permanently blinded him, the Utes went in search of the miscreant in Cortez, "and made a raid down there on the jail, but there were guards…[who] would not let the Indians get a hold of him."[38]

A few more examples of Noland's treatment of the Indians show why they trusted and loved him. In his posts he taught them how to keep their own records. To each customer he gave a little book to log expenditures. He used symbols and dots to represent fifty cents, seventy-five cents, a dollar, and so on, and made sure that his book and theirs were compatible. The same practice took place at ration time, when he sold the cattle he had bought from the Indians to the agency. All the meat was cleaned, carefully divided, and distributed in fair shares. Lolla recalled that one Christmas, as she put the final touches on a massive dinner for a house full of guests, Ed asked if she had enough food for eighteen Utes "dressed up in their feathers and blankets, beautiful reds and everything," whose horses were tied along his fence in front of the house in Mancos.[39] She emphatically said no, which set him in motion. He went to the store and purchased food baskets with bread and other assorted goods, canned meat and peaches and tomatoes, coffee, and sweet syrup and then set up sawhorses with planks for tables surrounded with chairs and stools in the backyard. "They had the biggest Christmas that anybody ever heard of. Everything under the sun. They were just tickled to death," right down to the last cookie.[40] Ed died at the age of eighty-eight, respected by the people to whom he had devoted his life.

Most traders were not nearly as wealthy and influential as Noland became in his later years. The number of clientele they served varied—the Bluff trading post operated by

Frank Hyde served sixty-five Utes and 950 adult Navajos who came in from a sixty sixty-mile radius, while the Hatch trading post in Montezuma Canyon served twenty-three Navajo and twenty-two Ute camps.[41] When asked which ethnic group they enjoyed dealing with the most, traders had varied but definite opinions. Parley Oscar Hurst, after forty-three years of running a store in Blanding, had no doubt as to whom he trusted — and that was the Utes. "There was many a time when one came in that I had to leave him alone in the store. If it was a Navajo, I didn't dare leave. I could just say to a Ute, 'You look after it until I get back.' The Ute has a personality that is different from a Navajo. They're more jovial and can see a joke."[42] Frank Pyle, a trader in Towaoc, allowed Utes who had traveled long distances by horse or wagon to sleep in the post's bull pen overnight, with much of the store's merchandise unsecured. He never lost a thing.[43] Ira Hatch agreed that the Utes were generally trustworthy, but his brother, Stewart, who worked in the Allen Canyon post, did not see much of a difference between them and the Navajos.

On the other hand, Alan Whitmer felt the Utes, as a people, were more aggressive than the Navajos.[44] Ray Hunt also fell into this camp. He tells of moving to Bluff with his father in 1919 and having to learn "ways of buying that I was not accustomed to."[45] The things they bought were similar to what the Navajos purchased, but they were "loud and over-bearing at times." His father, John, "knocked one Ute down because he wanted to come in back of the counter and took him to the floor and grabbed him by the heels and dragged him out. Then people said, 'We knew very well we shouldn't have sold this store to you; you should not treat people like that.' My father said, 'All you have to do is give me my money back. I didn't want the damn place anyway, but as long as I own it, I am going to run it.'"[46] Perhaps the best summary of these varying opinions is the *Cortez Sentinel*'s statement that "The Indian as a rule is as conservative a buyer as the white man and he can be depended upon to pay his bills just about as well as does his pale face brother. A great amount of credit is extended the tribes by the posts and very few accounts are lost."[47]

Some posts serving primarily Navajos used tokens to keep their clientele tied to a particular store, but those trading mostly with Utes did not generally use them. When pawning became necessary, the Utes offered some colorful items. Earle Forrest described the pawn he encountered in the backroom of the Meadows' post in 1902.

> Before we went to bed, the trader showed me the finest collection of beaded buckskin clothing and war bonnets I have ever seen. There were coats, vests, moccasins, and buckskin and red flannel chaps or full-length leggings, all covered with colored beads, dyed porcupine quills, and long fringe. The finest coat in the collection was decorated with scalp locks of enemies killed in battle, and the buckskin leggings with it adorned with long fringe and scalp locks, evidence that the owner had been a great warrior in his day. All this material had been pawned, and when the Indians wanted it for some dance or festive occasion, they borrowed it, just as the Navajos borrowed the pawned medicine basket from Billy Meadows.[48]

Stewart Hatch recounted the mutual respect of those involved in a pawning situation when Baby Deer entered the Allen Canyon Post and approached Joe Hatch about releasing his pawned .22 rifle, then in hock for two or three dollars. Joe agreed and also gave Baby Deer ammunition. In three hours the hunter was back. He returned the rifle and the box of bullets with one missing, gave a choice piece of deer meat to the trader, and went home with the rest of the deboned meat wrapped in the hide.[49]

The ethnographic scene in a trading post — where two cultures met to barter — provides additional insight into the values of the participants. Navajo interaction at trading posts has been discussed elsewhere, and even though some traders noted little difference between the Navajos and Utes during exchanges, some indicate otherwise.[50] Trading for both groups appeared leisurely, each customer purchasing one item at a time and then resting. Some store owners, however, felt Ute trade was more direct. A husband and wife would enter the store, bring their items to the counter, and work together with the trader to reach a satisfactory price. If there were no products to sell and it was necessary to pawn an item, then the couple might discuss what to do before deciding, whereas Navajo ownership was more individualized. On the other hand, an eyewitness account of Ute trading given by John Q. Cannon in 1895 shows that it was comparable to the Navajo approach.

> In the Monticello store I had an illustration of the Indian manner of trading. Their sole medium of exchange seemed to be buckskins, of which each family of purchasers had a goodly number lying in a heap at their feet or in a sack upon which they kept vigilant watch. The trading was done principally by the squaws and the white man's side of the negotiations was certainly a test of patience. The native woman would produce one skin at a time, which the storekeeper spread out upon the counter, examining it for bullet holes or knife cuts, after which — perhaps taking the additional precaution to weigh it — he would indicate by a show of fingers how much he was willing to pay. If the figure was acceptable, the squaw pushed the skin out of her way and proceeded to specify the various articles she wanted in exchange. These consisted nearly always of a small supply of tobacco, a scoopful of flour, two or three yards of bright-colored calico, ten or fifteen cents worth of sugar, etc., until the storekeeper signified her capital was exhausted; whereupon the counter would be cleared off; the purchaser placing her parcels in her pack, the merchant tossing his buckskin under the counter. Then the former would produce another buckskin and exactly the same procedure would be repeated, the buyer investing in precisely the same goods and to the same amount of quantity. Thus at the end of the transaction — which usually required the better part of half a day for each purchase — the storekeeper would have all her buckskins and she would have perhaps a dozen pieces of the same kind of calico, a dozen little parcels of flour and sugar and tobacco, etc., in like proportion. There was no use trying to hurry her or force upon her anything that she did not want, nor would any success have attended the effort to induce her to trade in two or more buckskins at once.[51]

While some traders spoke both Ute and Navajo, and a few traders only Ute, Navajo was the lingua franca when broken English would not suffice. Even in gambling or transactions solely between Navajos and Utes, the Navajo language prevailed. Alan Whitmer, who traded with both groups, estimated that 75 percent of the older Utes he knew spoke Navajo, but he did not know of many Navajos who spoke Ute.[52] Trader Ray Hunt agreed, saying that he never bothered to learn Ute because "all the old time Utes spoke Navajo."[53] There was, however, some Ute vocabulary that entered in at different times. For example, the Navajo classified money by appearance, so that a penny was "a red," a nickel "a yellow," and a dime "a blue." For the Utes a dime was *pavó-qač*, a nickel *tupwí-ker*, a penny *aká-tupwí-ker*, fifty cents *türágwako*, and a dollar *suíspanáqar*, or "one metal." Whenever they requested an item in English, the patron tacked on the word "mont" after it, as in "coffee — mont" and "shoes — mont".[54]

Depending on the period of history, buckskin, beads, baskets, and later wool and sheep hides were the primary objects of trade. As government per capita payments from land settlements became available, cash served more as a medium of exchange. Because the Navajos did not receive individual payments, they remained much more on a barter system until they entered the wage economy beginning in the 1940s and 1950s. As money and barter mixed, the Utes separated the two in their transactions in the Hatch trading post near Allen Canyon. They purchased food with money, but when baskets or deer hides went to the trader, their value bought clothing or other hard goods. "They did not pay their [food] bill with baskets. Maybe he [Ute customer] could get a new pair of Levis or a shirt…. Navajos always bought Pendleton shawls, but the Utes wanted a thinner, different type, made back East. The Ute shawl was altogether different than the Navajo shawls. They were really colorful, which the Utes really liked."[55]

The women were deliberate in their purchase of cloth to make dresses. They selected four yards of soft, colorful cloth. Four yards was immutable. "That is exactly what it took to make a dress, two in the front and two in the back. I sold a lady four yards of cloth and in a little while she came back into the store wearing a dress she had just pinned together with safety pins. It was always four yards of cloth, which held true when we were in Towaoc, too."[56] Once they were ready to sew the dress, the garment came together quickly.

Ute women developed a high level of craftsmanship in beadwork. Traders evaluated their products in a systematic way, just as Navajo woven blankets were scrutinized for certain qualities. The smaller cut-glass beads had sharper angles that reflected light and could be more closely sewn together than the rounded seed beads. Purchased in large hanks by the traders and then broken into smaller amounts for sale, the beads added color to a variety of objects. Everything from cradleboards, belts, moccasins, purses, pants, shirts, and dresses to rabbit's feet acquired unique Ute artistry. If the beadwork was sewn on hand-tanned hides, as opposed to commercially tanned, the value of the object increased. The Utes used many of these objects for themselves, but the rabbit's feet were strictly for whites who wanted good luck. The people of Allen Canyon made hundreds of these key-chain fobs, each with an individualized beaded pattern, and then strung them, a dozen to a cord, to sell to the trader, who in turn moved them to the general economy.[57]

The third cultural scene involved the daily interactions between Utes and white neighbors. Although some of these have already been noted from correspondence and newspapers, those writings tend to offer just one side of the equation. Local papers and daily recollections are also sources of important information about Ute individuals and lifestyle that would have otherwise been lost. Albert R. Lyman recorded particularly good observations in serialized form in two newspaper columns in the *San Juan Record* — "The Old Settler" and "San Juan and Its Piutes," which ran for years — and two books, *The Outlaw of Navaho Mountain* and *Indians and Outlaws*.[58] These generally untapped sources of information, along with oral interviews, are too extensive to be fully examined here, but a sampling follows.

Before proceeding, it is useful to note Lyman's and other Mormons' beliefs concerning Native Americans in general, and the Utes in particular. Born in 1880 and dying in 1973, Lyman lived through the tumultuous years of early settlement, the final gasps of Ute freedom, the Allen Canyon experience, and the topsy-turvy 1950s, when the Utes finally started receiving payments for lost land. While often sympathetic to the Ute situation, Lyman, during his early life, can be generally characterized as steeped in conflict with his Indian neighbors, whom he viewed through religious glasses. The clearest link he and others made connecting the Utes and Paiutes to Mormonism is reflected in his article "A Relic of Gadianton: Old Posey as I Knew Him," which appeared in 1923, the same year the so-called Ute problem was settled. Posey was a Paiute who had become a symbol of all of the pent-up frustration of these early years, and Lyman painted him in the shadows of events depicted in the *Book of Mormon*. Therein, the Gadianton robbers, an outlaw band formed through secret oaths and bloody misdeeds, prey upon the righteous (and sometimes not so righteous) people. Posey and his following, according to Lyman, descended from this line of thieves and cut-throats. The "Old Settler" wrote, "From the time that his fierce ancestors, of the Gadianton persuasion, swept their pale brethren from the two Americas, his people had known no law, but in idleness had contrived to live by plundering their neighbors. Posey inherited the instinct of this business from robbers of many generations."[59] Thus, Lyman cast all of the events that surrounded the Utes' efforts to maintain their lifestyle in the light of a cosmic struggle of good versus evil that had started centuries before. The Utes were characterized as depraved, with an "unyielding hatred of law," while living as "spoiled children."[60]

By the end of the 1940s, however, Lyman had served in the Southwest Indian Mission for the Mormon Church, and his sometimes sympathetic approach to the Native American dilemma had burgeoned into full-fledged advocacy for his "red brother," spurred on by a desire to do well by them. Analyzing his changing perception goes beyond the focus of this chapter, but it is important to understand the context in which much of his writing took place.

Of all the White Mesa Utes, Posey was the most notorious, thanks primarily to Lyman's writing. Although Mancos Jim and Polk received at least equal press, Posey captured the imagination due to Lyman's "Wild West" portrayal. Yet sandwiched in among the sometimes balanced but often florid prose, characteristic of the writing style of this era, are nuggets of observation about the Ute people and their life in this difficult time in their history. Of Posey, Lyman said, "[He] charmed me. He was magnetic. I loved him regardless of my pronounced prejudices and his native ignorance…[yet I] had to recognize he was an inveterate thief."[61] The cowboy often visited the Paiutes' camps in Peavine, near Cottonwood Wash, and at the end of Long Point on Elk Ridge. When Posey

and Lyman worked as a team to herd livestock, Lyman "could not have found a more willing and capable helper. He knew how to fry meat, bake bread, unpack at night, find our horses early in the morning, how to replace the packs, and move the herd."[62]

Lyman was in tune with Indian practices. He mentioned that they had a "fixed tradition" that they would not kill a San Juan Mormon who in turn would not kill a San Juan Paiute or Ute. When the 1923 incident occurred, he believed that the Indians were totally taken by surprise since their neighbors had never before been engaged with them in an armed conflict. In all of the other fights, the Mormons had been observers. He also commented on how each fall at the Bears Ears, "They started fires in the grass to make clearings in which they could see game the next season." He told of how Grandma Broken Arm took charge of a little orphaned baby, later named Maudie, and fed her small pieces of masticated meat, which "she took in her withered old fingers and put in the dainty reaching mouth of the baby…. smiling through all of the criss-cross furrows of her wrinkled face." And when death stalked the Utes' camps, he noted that the Indians cut their hair, wailed loudly, and "employed expert howlers to join them, as was the custom among their people." According to Lyman, when the elderly and infirm could no longer take care of themselves, they were left to die on their own. The food supply ended, the warmth of a wickiup and bedding were removed on a cold night, or the person might be abandoned in a desolate area. Life was hard, and people understood that their time had come.[63]

Many of Lyman's observations about Ute culture related specifically to Posey's life. Following the accidental shooting of his first wife, the Paiute made amends with his father-in-law, Polk, by sending several horses to his camp. There was also the spiritual side. "Strange fears haunted him wherever he went and often he would move his bed as many

Utes from White Mesa participating in a Fourth of July parade in front of Parley Redd's store, 1940s. Daily life in Blanding provided new learning experiences on both sides of the cultural fence. Although whites could be patronizing toward the Utes and their culture, there were also shared, friendly experiences. (Courtesy of San Juan County Historical Commission)

as five times in one night to get away from the devils that swarmed around him."[64] On the other hand, he had a sense of immunity from harm, declaring "'Me all the same Jesus Christ' and went on to explain that if a bullet were fired directly at him, it would either turn out around him or fall to the ground." He also had a sense of humor. When John Hammond arrived in Posey's camp hungry and tired, the Paiute followed the same etiquette that whites showed his people and handed John an ax and told him to go chop some wood. The cowboy saw the humor in the situation, fulfilled his task, but did not get supper until Posey asked, "Whatsa matter; you heap lazy," and sent him back for more wood.[65] Another time he rode to Allen Canyon with a small group of men, among them the portly Elfego Baca. Despite Baca's reputation as a gunfighter in his earlier years, Posey had a grand time mimicking how the heavy man sat in his saddle astride his horse.[66]

Stories about Posey from other settlers abound. Three will suffice here. While Lyman claims that he intentionally created what was known in those days as a "Posey fence" — one that was rickety and open for invasion by livestock so that a claim against the owner for ruined crops became possible — there

are others who indicate this was not really the case. Lyman P. Hunter came to San Juan County to work as a cowboy between 1920 and 1922. During that time he often interacted with the Utes and brought an outsider's perspective to a situation. He tells of camping at Kigalia and having Posey ride into camp extremely angry. Hunter invited the Indian to have some biscuits, bacon, and coffee, hoping this would quiet his temper. There would be no eating until the white man called the county commissioner, "Georgie Perkinuts" (George Perkins), about the cattle that had broken through his fence, destroyed his crops, and ruined his camp. Hunter reported, "He said for me to tell Georgie Perkinuts, that they would have a fight, the 'Mormonee's and the Paiutes, and that whoever won that fight could have the country around there. He said, 'No soldiers.' He did not want any soldiers, just the Indians and the Mormonees."[67] A call from the phone in the ranger station soothed the situation, with Perkins promising to make amends, but to Hunter this was one more example of what he called "a distinct lack of cordiality on both sides."

Posey's first attempt to use the phone by himself occurred in Blanding when he needed to communicate something to his son in Bluff. At first aloof from the strange contraption, he let the switchboard operator do the talking. Eventually she got the phone in his hand, put the receiver to his ear and the transmitter to his mouth, and let him speak. At first he used English, but when he realized that the machine, or "hurry-up talk," could also "understand" Ute, he was amazed. Indian words came from the other end. "He ventured a native grunt [characterized by A. R. Lyman as "guttural grunts, inarticulate groans and 'toowitchchamoorooroouppi'"] and the answer came clear in classical Piute. He took a more confident grip on the thing—if it cou'd talk Piute it could be trusted, and he poured into it his best dialect of the hills."[68]

John D. Rogers recalled how Posey and Polk would come to Bluff and challenge the young men to a shooting contest. "I saw them get out in the street in front of the old Co-op store and pick out a black spot or something up on the hill north of Bluff. They would shoot at it. If they knocked a rock loose, they would kind of see where they hit. Those Indians would bet with them if they had a quarter or fifty cents or a dollar bet.... They were pretty good shots. They could hold their own with any of those white fellows shooting at any of those rocks."[69] Brig Stevens remembered Posey as a "shark," but always friendly, and "kind in whatever conversation I had with him. He acted like he had a special friendship for me. I don' know why he did," but "most of the people of Blanding were scared to death of him."[70]

Polk was another Ute whom everyone seemed "scared to death of." Tse-ne-gat's passing "came as a death-blow," and he became "violently disagreeable" with many of the members of his band, including his wife, who abandoned him in his camp at Yellow Jacket and moved to Westwater.[71] He spent his last years visiting trader Ira Hatch at the Montezuma Canyon trading post. Hatch considered him a good man and described him as having no fear of anything.

According to Polk, conflict with the Mormons began when they first arrived in Bluff, and the Navajos provided them with corn and the Utes with game. Both felt comfortable with the initial settlement, but when livestock began to take over the ranges, the Utes became increasingly uncomfortable. There was an agreement that if the Indians allowed the settlers to continue to use the ranges, they would "give the Utes their beef every two weeks for putting them [Indians] out of their way."[72] When the Indians visited them in the fall, the Mormons refused to honor the agreement, thus beginning the antagonism that dragged on for forty years. In 1935 the *San Juan Record* reported that Polk had died in Towaoc at the age of seventy-eight, "his later years filled with suffering and sorrow due to illness and blindness." His wife, "Gramma Polk," who had been living with Joe Dutchie for the past ten years, died exactly one year later and was buried near her wickiup on the brink of Westwater. Even in death Polk and Posey were not separated in the public mind, the paper's editor wishing that "their bones lie unmolested and their spirits soar to places of greater spiritual enlightenment."[73]

Mancos Jim was another Ute who was there to meet the initial onslaught of settlement. In the 1880s he was well-known for his role in the Pinhook Draw and Soldier Crossing fights, but by the 1890s he had chosen a more pacific role. Indeed, whenever there was trouble, the white men called for Mancos Jim to calm the situation. His name grew synonymous with the Allen Canyon area, where he, his father, "Fatty," and his son Mancos George would eventually be buried. Despite his friendly demeanor, Mancos Jim represented the old, traditional way of life. His home in Hammond Canyon and his presence along its trails caused Lyman to view him as another part of nature, "somebody who was native to its rugged rocks as the fish were native to its sparkling water."[74]

One night Amasa Redd was resting by a campfire after a day's work of building a fence across an old trail that went from Allen Canyon to Indian Creek on Blue Mountain. He constructed a gate farther down the fence in what he considered a reasonable line of drift. Suddenly, out of the dark on the mesa above camp, he heard, "Oh Jesus Christ; oh God damn, Mormonee son-of- bitch."[75] Mancos Jim had hit the fence, stopping abruptly his travel to Allen Canyon. Redd invited him down for something to eat, explained that there was a gate for him to go through, and spent part of the evening calming the frustrated Indian, who continued on his way.

Mancos Jim had another encounter with a fence as he traveled out of Brushy Basin. Again, the land he thought was open was not only fenced but had a threshing machine on it bailing hay. He dismounted, crawled under the wire, and stood amazed at how the machine was clicking, clacking, and tying hay into neat bundles. One of the workers approached Jim to get his response about what he saw. In his best English, he retorted: "Whatsa matter, white man all of it savvy— everything savvy! Whatsa matter, damn son em a bitch Piute no savvy nothing."[76]

Mancos George, Jim's son, was highly respected for his trustworthiness and helpfulness. Both Zelma Acton and Fern Simpson recall his kind ways with them and the white children living in Allen Canyon. If he knew that the parents were not around, he would turn visitors away from the station to protect the children. One time he approached Lyman about borrowing a horse to go to a "medicine dance" sixty miles away. The settler, who had had extensive conflict with other Utes over livestock, agreed that it would be all right to take the horse; he reported later, "No white man could show more appreciation for the use of that blue mare than George expressed then and ever afterwards. He never forgot."[77]

His physical appearance was striking, Lyman suggesting that he had a profile worthy

Jim Mike, shown here in the 1950s, became famous for his involvement in the "discovery" of Rainbow Bridge. Highly respected in Blanding, he was a deeply religious man whose experiences are still discussed among the people of White Mesa. (Courtesy of San Juan County Historical Commission)

to be on a nickel as a stereotypical Native American. His long braids added to the image, but his wife insisted that he cut them off, which he did. After being shorn, "he always felt bad to think that he had cut his hair. It just took something away from him spiritually and his looks, too."[78] When he passed away in the first week of July 1949, his obituary referred to him as "Mancos George, Nobleman" and noted his extreme friendliness. "Mancos George had nobility and dignity not found in enough of the human race, whether they be white or red."[79]

Jim Mike also made his mark in history. Born in 1872 near El Capitan rock in Monument Valley, he was most often associated with the area around Blanding, Allen Canyon, Navajo Mountain, and Douglas Mesa, where he held an allotment. His father— known as Moencopy Mike, or Mike Ute, or Sore Heel—was far more aggressive than his son in his relations with white neighbors.

Jim worked as a cowboy for Jacob Adams, married young and lost his wife and many of his children at an early age, and spent much of his time herding his own flock of sheep. Pochief and Billy Mike were his only surviving children, and he lived with them in his later years after trachoma took its toll on his eyesight.[80]

Lyman characterized Jim in his earlier years as "an authority on the beliefs and history and traditions of his people and he knows the old trails of this country as they may never be known again."[81] No doubt this knowledge is one of the reasons he is linked to the official "discovery" of Rainbow Bridge.[82] Jim had spent thirty-six years in the Navajo Mountain area and knew of the monolith's existence. When the Byron Cummings and William B. Douglass expeditions set off in August 1909 to locate the bridge, Jim Mike led the combined party along with Nasja Begay, another Paiute. Accounts from both Cummings and Douglass attest to a spirited rivalry between the two leaders as to who would be the first to see, and then pass under, the bridge, claiming the right of discovery. According to Douglass, Jim Mike received the credit; Cummings said it was Nasja. In 1927 Richard Wetherill and others placed a plaque east of Rainbow Bridge recognizing Nasja's effort, and the claim remained uncontested until the 1970s, when several articles mentioned Jim Mike's role. A desire to rectify the situation became entangled in National Park Service bureaucracy and unfulfilled plans until September 30, 1997, when a ceremony officially emplaced a second plaque of equal size denoting the role of both Paiutes in the official discovery of Rainbow Bridge.[83]

During this same time period, Joe Bishop, whose recalcitrant son died on Comb Ridge, served as a medicine man and was a friend to the whites. Superintendent J. E. Jenkins, during the 1915 fracas, wrote of "'Dutchy' and Joe Bishop and their family connection, probably 15 to 20 in all. The former belongs

on the Navajo reservation and the latter is a mixed Paiute-Navajo belonging to the Kanab reservation. They are perfectly harmless but I got them to promise to return to their reservations and endeavor to establish homes for themselves and their families."[84] Bishop's connection to southwestern Utah provides a partial explanation as to why he considered himself "Heap Mormon, tree times baptizem."[85] Born in 1872, his Paiute name was Mana-vi ("Tumbleweed"), but he later received the Bishop appellation because of his large stomach, which seemed to go with that ecclesiastical position.

The white community viewed Joe Bishop as a good man who was worried about his son. Lyman Hunter sat on a front porch and talked to him at length about what he could do to help his son stop the lawlessness. Bishop had counseled the young man that "if he wanted a shooting contest with the white fellows, they should put up a mark and shoot at it, not at each other."[86] But the father's love for his son was not enough to avert tragedy. The evening that his son was killed, during the Posey incident, Joe Bishop watched through the basement window of the schoolhouse, where half of the Ute community was being held. Members of the posse rode to the building with two hats tied to their saddles. The first one belonged to Jack Fly and had two bullet holes through the crown, but Jack had escaped unharmed. The second hat belonged to Joe Bishop's Little Boy and had no hole, but his father surmised what it meant before anyone said a word. The old medicine man "lifted his voice in a long, bitter cry: he cried with loud abandon of a broken-hearted child—the lament of a man which is seldom heard in modern times. Joe Bishop himself was never a bad man, but a book could be written about the cussedness of his sons."[87]

There are many other stories about the Ute people, told by Navajos, traders, and white neighbors, that give a sense of how they were viewed. The stories provided here are enough to show that they were neither relics of the Gadianton robbers nor innocent angels being categorically destroyed by evil white men. Instead, they were real people with real problems, watching a new way of life unfold before them. Outside perspectives do not always take into account previous issues and experience, but rather focus on a problem at hand. Even so, settlers like Lyman and Hunter, traders like Noland and Hatch, and Navajos like Fred Yazzie and John Holiday talked and wrote about their Ute neighbors with insight and humanity. Ranging anywhere from adulation to grudging respect, these outside perspectives gained from across the chasm of culture provide additional understanding of the White Mesa Utes.

CHAPTER 16

Circles, Trees, and Bears

Empowering the Weenuche Universe

Spirit means everything. In the trees, the animals, the insects, the grass,
the ancestors. I saw the grass move, like there were people walking toward
the center. [He] saw it too. They were dancing with us. It will grow and grow.
It will never be lost. So I think of it in a good way for the people.

Anonymous Northern Ute Elder

The townspeople of Green River were curious as to why a white man and an Indian
were traveling together in the same car. To
William R. Palmer, whose avocation included
the study of Southern Paiute culture, this was
not strange at all. He was on his way to Allen
Canyon with translator Woots Parashont
to visit a group of Indians that he and the
main body of Southern Paiutes living around
Cedar City had had little contact with and
knew even less about. Directed by the Mormon Church in 1935 to determine the needs
and status of the Indians living in southern
Utah and Nevada, Palmer decided that a
visit to this mysterious group would answer
a number of questions. First on the list was
to determine whether these people were Paiute, Ute, or some kind of combination mixed
with Navajos. If they were Paiutes, why had
they left the main group in southwestern
Utah? And what effect had this separation
had on their language, customs, and stories?
What did they know about the Anasazi?
And what characterized their relations with
white neighbors? All Palmer knew was what
he had read in the newspapers about past
friction. It was time for him to gain his own
perspective.[1]

On August 22 the men arrived in Blanding, and after making initial contact with
Stake President Wayne H. Redd and Agent
"E.Z." Black, they bumped their way over the
rough roads to Allen Canyon with Jim Mike
as their guide. Parashont went to work when
they arrived around five o'clock, calling the
people near the station together to explain
what he and his white companion wanted.
Palmer spoke enough Paiute to understand
what was being said, but he wished to keep
this talent secret so that he could get a grassroots impression of what people were feeling. A leader identified as "Paddy" (Anson
Whyte) stepped forth with a few questions
of his own. Was the white man a government man? (They were tired of them.) What
did the two want to know, and how much
would they pay for that information? (There
had been a long string of broken promises,
so payment needed to be up front.) Both
replies were negative: no government man
and no pay. One does not pay a friend for information, but the visitors had a lot to share
that all would find interesting. Following
some deliberation, relations warmed, and
everyone agreed to meet around a campfire
that evening to discuss things while giving a

chance for others in the Allen Canyon area to join them.

In the meantime Palmer and Parashont gathered some of the simpler answers. The physical arrangements for life here were primitive. All of the Indians were poorly dressed; one man was wearing part of some overalls for shoes, while others went barefoot. When asked where their homes were, a person pointed to a cottonwood tree and said, "This is the best house we have. We can only make brush wickiups for we are too poor to make homes."[2] A sheepskin served as bedding, bread tortillas were the mainstay in the diet, and small game was all that was hunted. Woots suggested that they go out and kill some deer — "raise a fuss" — so that the government would provide more and better food. Palmer tacitly approved, noting that "The Indians in San Juan are right where our Cedar [City] Indians were thirty-five years ago."[3]

Other answers came that evening. The oldest member of the approximately seventy Indians assembled swore that his people had not had any contact with the Paiutes in the Cedar City area within his lifetime. That was why Palmer was "surprised, almost amazed to find this long isolated band speaking more nearly pure Pahute than some of the clans that attend the tribal saparovan [storytelling fest held] every year and do much visiting back and forth every summer. Their words for water, grass, mountain, tree, fire, camp, man, woman, sun, moon, stars, and scores of other things were the same as the Pahutes at Cedar City."[4] He was even more surprised when he began to tell the story about the North Star.

In Paiute mythology, "the heavens are an inverted world with great rivers and valleys and mountains, the peaks of which are pointing down toward us. Many of the stars we see are [beings] glorified by the gods for special deeds of courage or bravery."[5] Palmer told the story of Nahga, Mountain Sheep, who accepted the challenge of climbing

Mancos George (*center*), Woots Parashont (*right*), and an unidentified Ute man at the station in 1935. Parashont and William Palmer determined during their visit that the purity of the language and teachings of the Allen Canyon people was equal to, and in some instances surpassed, that of the Southern Paiutes in southwestern Utah. (Special Collections, Sherratt Library, Southern Utah University)

the tallest peak, persevering under difficult circumstances. Shinob (Sináwav) watched his efforts and then rewarded him by positioning him as the North Star and giving him a set of large earrings, which are his horns. This allowed him to provide direction like a compass and divide the sky at three angles into parts — morning, midday, and afternoon. Partway through telling the story, one of the elders interrupted and said that he already knew it; Palmer had him complete it and found it to be identical to his version. Other tales followed with similar results.

Palmer attributed this accuracy to the way the stories were told. Each group would have one man responsible for relating the narrative on an annual basis, but if anyone disagreed with part of what was being said, he could interrupt the speaker and call for clarification and group response. "The fact that I found the same stories so faithfully preserved in these two branches of the Pahute tribe that have had no chances of comparing their legends since time out of memory of any living Indian proves their fidelity in this tribal trust."[6] In addition to gaining this understanding, Palmer purchased a medicine pouch from Jane Lehi, an elder who at first did not want to sell it. She warned that it would bring bad luck, perhaps kill the white man, whose spirit would then return to trouble her. Palmer persisted, she relented, and later he sent a nicely beaded pouch "filled with good luck medicine" to her.

This last incident perhaps characterizes Palmer's work. He was intellectually invested in learning about the Paiutes and successful in accomplishing it, even to the point of being "adopted" with full, formal approval of the tribe. He learned early on that he must "never laugh at anything they told me however absurd it might seem to me. Now I had their legends and I wanted to try them out among the distant Indians who had never heard of me before."[7] But as with the medicine pouch, Palmer missed the real point: the spiritual power invested in the stories. Consequently, he has preserved a series of "Just So" tales that are delightful to read but void of the guidance and power associated with deeply believed and spiritually felt conviction.[8] Like a string of pearls detached from a necklace, they stand alone, interesting and informative in their own way, but missing cultural efficacy. Even John Wesley Powell, in collecting materials from different Numic groups, fell into the same pit, unable to see the connected pearls of teaching strung together to make a complete necklace threading through the culture. Consequently, few historians or anthropologists have used these teachings to interpret elements from the past.

The southern portion of the Colorado River in Arizona is the general area of the Numic-speaking Chemehuevi, often characterized as the most southern of the Southern Paiutes. While their culture and history are far beyond the scope of this chapter, these people were fortunate enough to have an individual, Carobeth Laird, assist them in collecting and recording many of their early teaching tales while they were still "strung" together in a cohesive interpretation of their worldview. Married to George Laird, a full-blooded Chemehuevi, she spent much of her adult life recording, with her husband's help, the teachings of his people.[9] Her approach, rooted in the mythology of the Numa, offers insights into the work of Powell and Palmer, tying separate, seemingly unconnected pieces of information together and allowing a more complete interpretation. Her approach and some specific details are utilized here to better explain the beliefs of the White Mesa Utes mentioned in earlier chapters.

Laird, Powell, and Palmer have recorded the same characters in similar stories. Supreme above all is Tavwoats, often referred to as Elder Brother and portrayed in both an anthropomorphic form and as Wolf. Sináwav, the Younger Brother, can also assume an anthropomorphic shape, as well as that of Coyote, and is at times referred to as a trickster and imitator. These two personalities figure heavily during the time of creation called "When Animals Were People," which serves as the setting for most of their experiences, explaining how the Numic people should live. Both characters have human traits and lack the omniscience assigned to the Christian deity. Wolf, however, has superior knowledge, making him close to an ideal man, with strong supernatural powers. Coyote, on the other hand, "embodies all the human traits: cowardice and incredible daring; laziness and patient industry or frantic exertion; foolishness and skillful planning; selfishness and concern for others. If he were simply the dark shadow of Wolf, the People would not have said, 'We followed Coyote.'"[10]

This is Laird's position. Powell generally agreed, noting some minor differences between the two, but placing Tavwoats as the creator and as one who directed his associate. Sináwav has the responsibility to ready the world for mankind, as much through trial and error as purposeful design.[11] Powell actually identifies two Sináwav brothers, Skaits (Sahkaič—"Younger Brother") and Pa-vits [Pavíč—"Older Brother"), with Tavwoats as a third superior deity. Regardless of the combination, there are more stories about Sináwav than Tavwoats. Palmer does not give "Tobats" the same kind of power and recognition, referring to him more as an "idle genius" who "has no patience for irritating detail" and depends on "Schinob," his brother, to set events in motion.

> Between the powers of these two great ones, there is an essential difference. The works of Tobats are everlasting, eternal. He builds [with] massive stone and the products of his hands are enduring. He cares little for artistry or color and does his work in bold and mighty sweeps. Schinob his brother god is artful and tender. He is the author of life and light and love.... But alas! The touch of Schinob is a blighting touch. Whatsoever his hand falls upon shall perish and its days are ephemeral and fleeting. It will take the mighty work of Tobats to call back into being such perished creations as he shall deem worthy of preservation.[12]

Both Bonnie Mike Lehi and Adoline Eyetoo of White Mesa noted that Sináwav's name is used only in stories and is not connected in prayers to "The One Who Created the Earth," although they could not give a reason for this.[13]

The Ute creator is often represented in a variety of stories, dances, and ceremonies that have intense, powerful value for the Ute people. The Bear Dance and the Sun Dance (discussed briefly in chapter 3), as well as the Worship Dance, share recurrent symbols of deity and power. The circle, a center pole, the Bear, Sináwav, and Tavwoats are part of this unified complex that speaks to important values. The Bear and Sun Dances have been explored in a number of publications and will be examined briefly here; the Worship Dance, which is now performed only by a White Mesa elder, Jack Cantsee Sr., will be looked at in greater detail below. All three ceremonies share similar values expressed in different ways. One should also note that while some of these practices are older than others, some reaching back to antiquity, there have been different interpretations of their form and meaning over time. For instance, with the introduction of Christianity, some Ute people changed the names of Tavwoats and Sináwav to God and Jesus Christ, and assigned them a function and meaning similar to that of the old pair. At this point there will not be any attempt to separate the two, assign a chronology, or advocate for any particular position on why these changes occurred.

The origin of the Bear Dance, unique to the Utes, is explained in at least a half dozen stories with variations. In some narratives the bear is a male, in others a female; the hunter who stays with the bear is alone or accompanied by a friend; he willingly submits to going with the bear during the winter or is forced into captivity; the list goes on. But common to all is a bear, a cave, a tree, and the distinctive back-and-forth step learned by a man and practiced in the dance. The setting of the story is in the mountains, where Bear oversees its domain. Whether male or female, the bear emerges from hibernation in a den and performs bear actions that foretell the coming of spring. The first rumble of thunder, duplicated by the sound of the bear's jawbone, or morache (*muurači*) in the dance arena, is part of the preparation that makes available the high country's resources to the Ute people. Some elders believe that the Utes shared direct kinship with bears as their ancestors during the time of creation, before they changed into humans, perhaps another reason that they refer to themselves as the Mountain People.[14]

The bear plays a prominent role in many Native American cultures, is often referred to as "Grandfather," and is admired for its

Singers and participants on the west side of the "cave of sticks" at a Bear Dance on White Mesa, 1993. The five singers are holding moraches, which are played with a stick to produce a sound representing the growl of an awakening bear or the sound of thunder, both associated with spring and the availability of mountain resources. (Courtesy of White Mesa Ute Council)

powers in both the physical and supernatural realms. Anthropologists who have collected Ute teachings containing stories about bears include Robert Lowie, Anne M. Smith, and Tom Givón.[15] Lynda D. McNeil, a specialist in comparing Ute and Siberian Native beliefs of bear mythology, finds close relationships between these people and their narratives. Among the points she makes about Ute practices are that (1) when bears are killed, they are addressed as "Grandfather" or "Grandmother"; (2) in early times, smoke from fires (and more recently from a group of men smoking *kinnikinnick* [tobacco] during the Bear Dance) communicates with dead ancestors and prevents sickness; (3) the bear ancestor returning from hibernation was restored to health and moved from symbolic death to resurrected life; (4) the dancers either used their hands in a motion that reenacted a bear scratching a tree or hugged their partner as they moved back and forth in the "cave of sticks"; (5) the women are the ones

who get to choose their partner and are the "aggressive" ones, as was the mythical female bear in her relationship with the hunter; and (6) in the past, those who were sick could be healed by certain events in the dance.[16] Forming two lines, the men and women move back and forth, reenacting this male-female dichotomy. The bear held a variety of powers for the benefit of both genders, who in turn respect its role.

During the first three days, dances are held during the day, but the one on the last day continues through the night. Before the final, or "endurance," dance begins in the evening, there is the event known as "the Coming." In the past a man accompanied by a woman dressed in complete bearskins entered the dance arena and interacted with participants.[17] The person imitating the bear was sometimes accompanied by another man or woman who assisted. The spectators in the enclosure had special songs to welcome and bless the bear, who confronted the people on its "hind legs" with paws up. If someone moved, he would advance to that person and make clawing gestures and "attack."[18] Some accounts suggest that at one point the bear was ceremoniously killed and skinned, symbolic of the sacrifice it was making as keeper of the mountain domain for the Utes. Other accounts stress that the purpose of the dance was to restore good health to the bear so that it would assist the people in food collection. Following this part of the dance, an elder talked about those who had been at the dance in previous years and had since died and gone to the next world. "The people would cry and mourn for this individual.... It was a speech in their memory that this person would talk and of course it was kind of a sad moment there for everyone."[19] Following this the endurance dance began and continued until sunrise, the start of the new day and the new season.

The circular "cave of sticks," or dance arena, represents the place of hibernation from which the bear emerges. Made of green juniper boughs whose branches point skyward, the enclosure's opening faces east. To Jack Cantsee Sr., a Bear Dance chief at White Mesa, there is a special reason why juniper (locally called cedar) is used to build the structure. "That tree has got its own blessing. It has roots that go far into the ground.... [My Grandfather] taught me that the cedar tree is a very sacred tree that can live anywhere. Before cutting it down, you have to offer a prayer and tell the Creator why you are doing it, and if you cut it good, the prayer goes with it."[20] Evergreen trees, unlike those that are deciduous, have an "ever green," or not-dying, quality that accompanies the coming back to life aspect of the bear's return.

Aldean Ketchum, also a Bear Dance chief, tells of the origin of the corral, explaining how a medicine man went to the mountains seeking supernatural assistance. He encountered a bear, which had smelled him approaching, but seeing that the man was unarmed, the bear decided to talk to him.

The animal stood on its hind legs, faced the sun, sang a number of healing songs, and then instructed the man to return to his people and teach them what he had heard. He was also to "build a corral as a symbol of the world and all that is connected to it, point the tops of the cedar trees used in the corral towards the heavens, and at the end of four days, have a feast. The people should dance for health and to bless others in the enclosure.... The songs tell of a female bear rustling the bushes and who is coming because she wants to dance."[21]

There is other tree symbolism. In keeping with the story of the bear dancing back and forth to a tree, there has in the past, and in some Bear Dances today, been one or two poles placed in the enclosure either near the entrance or in the back. These trees serve several different functions. McNeil believes that the pole is a conduit between the spirits and powers of the world that restores the natural environment through the prayer and dance activities. It also facilitates communication with the dead and allows the bear to serve as a messenger between this world and "the Land Beyond."[22] Southern Ute Bear Dance enclosures use two trees on the east entrance, one representing a male, the other a female, where prayers and offerings are left. "The people at Ignacio still use them to bless themselves with the branches that come from those trees in the enclosure, just as they do in the Sun Dance."[23] Today the people at White Mesa do not have the two entryway posts, although Adoline Eyetoo remembers standing between two posts of a Bear Dance lodge entrance near Joe Hatch's trading post while praying to the east.[24] There is also a live cedar tree near the entrance of the White Mesa Bear Dance arena where people pray and leave offerings today.

A number of rock art petroglyphs in the Four Corners area are of ancient origin and depict a bear dancing toward or climbing a tree. Indeed, Northern Ute elder and historian Clifford Duncan commented that the tree in these petroglyphs may be more symbolically important than the bear.[25] He said that medicine men could use the power of the tree to heal the sick, and that when the first thunder sounded in the spring, a young person's arms would be stretched so that they would grow—all through the power of the bear. While the "cave of sticks" is considered more a female domain—just as the tepee or wickiup is a woman's space—the pole used in the Bear Dance, as well as in the Sun Dance lodge, is male space with male power. Duncan points out that the moving lines of men and women in the Bear Dance "take turns being the tree" before they break into individual pairs.[26] In many enclosures today, there is a Bear Dance flagpole with an image of a bear, tree, and dancer in some combination. The staff that supports the flag serves the same function as the pole(s) in the past and is considered male.

While many people refer to the Bear Dance as solely a social event, it is apparent that for others the meaning behind it has not been lost. The generation of power, through its symbols, is real. Jack Cantsee tells how the beat of the drum, the songs, and the movement forces the energy out "all over your body. You can feel the song, what they're singing, carrying you off like that. Sometimes you feel like you are floating. You believe in the Bear Dance and yourself; you believe that you can do it, the same way that the Bible tells the white people that they are going to be this way."[27] His son, Jack Cantsee Jr., agrees. When he sings during the dance, he feels empowered. "I feel that spirit, the bear spirit, going through me. A lot of the [other singers] there feel that bear strength come in. I can feel that strength come in.… You can do anything you set your mind to with that spirit of the Bear."[28]

The Sun Dance has never been performed at White Mesa, although some of its residents, such as Edward Dutchie, have participated in ones held at Towaoc, Ignacio, and White Rocks. A brief survey of the teachings and symbols of this dance, however, shows how it has been adapted to reflect Ute values already discussed. According to Terry G. Knight, Sun Dance chief of Towaoc, only men who have received a vision or served in the military are to dance.[29] Reasons for participating include seeking a vision and guidance, to gain knowledge, to heal someone who is sick, bring good fortune to the people, and rejuvenate the world. Joseph G. Jorgensen, who has studied Ute and Shoshone Sun Dance practices extensively, believes that the Ute Mountain Utes, and perhaps the Northern Utes, hold more closely to the original form, as it was first introduced to them around 1900, than any of the other groups. "The historical integrity with which the Ute Mountain dance has been preserved may justify the opinions of the Ute Mountain Ute people who say that theirs is the correct dance."[30]

For three or four days and part of the nights, dancers move forward and backward toward a center pole housed within a cottonwood branch and sapling enclosure, open to the sky except for at least four, and often twelve, rafters representing the cardinal directions and a small arbor. They radiate out from the center post to the edge of the arena. Around the circumference of the enclosure, known as the "thirst house," are twelve poles integrated evenly in the structure, equidistant from the center pole. Filling in beside them is the sapling and branch wall that goes around the circumference except for the open, east-facing door. The arbor covers the eastern half of the corral, where the drummers and spectators sit, while the western portion is open and serves as the sacred dance space.[31] A sacred fire pit is located just east of the center pole out of the dance area.

Jorgensen summarizes the ideology underlying the ceremony as the accumulation of power as the dancers move between a physical and spiritual state, characterized as going from "dry to wet" and "hot to cool." Beyond the abstinence from food and water during the dance, the participants move sym-

The interior of a Sun Dance lodge built at White Rocks in 1911, with the traditional center post, brush arbor, and poles radiating out from the middle. The Creator, Sináwav, participates in this sacred rite, which challenges participants spiritually and physically to move close to the "center" and be near God. (Used by permission, Utah State Historical Society, all rights reserved.)

bolically from ignorance to enlightenment, receiving a vision and blessings. A man who has participated for twelve years in the dance can "fan" or provide a blessing for someone seeking one. Spiritual empowerment is the motivation and final outcome. The center pole, like the dancer, is a "participant" in that it also has to be dried out before it can attain its full potential of radiating and offering its spiritual power. As with a person's life, its existence is short, enters the world (enclosure) through song and prayer, and will see the fulfillment of its purpose before returning to Mother Earth. It has, however, passed on its legacy, as old people do to the next generation, making the world a better place.

The Utes address this center pole as Sináwav, the Creator. There are other names and teachings by which it is known, and for nonbelievers that might be confusing at best and proof of insincerity at worst. Jorgensen points out that the multiplicity of meanings is additive, citing a Northern Ute dancer as

saying: "No one knows the true meaning or what the whole dance means. Even the chiefs who have danced for a long time know only parts of it. They are always learning more about it through the dreams that that Man gives them."[32] Movement toward the pole is said to make a person feel good, whereas movement away, or distancing oneself from the Creator, does not.[33]

Thus, the pole may depict "life, the sacrifice of power so that others may live, a man's heart, Jesus Christ, Jesus' crucifixion, God's brain, power itself, water, [and] Sinawaf." Stripped of its bark, the pole is painted with the four colors representing different aspects of the earth and sky, as well as the number of days the dance will last. Red represents the ground, yellow the light and sun, white daylight, and black the night. The pole faces east, as does the Sun Dance chief in the morning when saying prayers. Its forks, one pointing north and west, the other south and east, have cloth scarves attached to them as offerings to the powers of the four directions.[34] They are also offerings made to the "old people" who have gone to the Land Beyond, asking them to assist the living and provide good health. A nest of willow branches placed in the crotch of the center pole can represent water, life, Jesus's body, and sacrifice for others.[35]

Connor Chapoose, a Northern Ute Sun Dancer, believes that the posts and rafters represent the twelve men who work with the Creator, and that the rafters radiating out from the center pole are the messages he is sending to them for the universe.[36] The westernmost post is said to symbolize the backbone of the arena, personified as a living being, while the others are ribs, Christ's apostles, and the months of the year.[37] The saplings and branches of cottonwood, willow, and aspen that provide substance to the outer wall also add their power and blessing to those dancing within. The "drying" of the saplings, like that of the dancers, is recognized as part of the renewal process that brings forth new life through sacrifice. Even the dirt that forms an altar at the base of the pole becomes dry while sacrificing for others: "Each year things are born and things die; all of these things get their power from the dirt — that's where life comes from. That's why those doctors take the dirt from around Sinawaf [center pole]. It gives good health to everybody and cures the sick people who need new life."[38] Dusting oneself with this dirt is a blessing. Thus, the Sun Dance ceremony, from the ground to the sky and everywhere in between, is replete with power.

This is also true of the Worship Dance, which employs many of the same symbols and embodies many of the same teachings found in the Bear Dance and Sun Dance. The ceremony today is performed only by the White Mesa Utes under the direction of Jack Cantsee Sr., who has kept its practice alive. Historically, it has been known by another name — the Ghost Dance — and has been the topic of a number of significant works that explain its origin and its impact on not only the Numic-speaking peoples of the Great Basin and Colorado Plateau, but also Plains tribes such as the Sioux and Arapaho. Much of this is far beyond what can be discussed here, but a brief overview of its practice corroborates its relationship to what the White Mesa Utes now perform.

The earliest ethnographic reports of Paiute and Ute dances speak of the Great Basin Round Dance, in which participants interlocked arms or hands and danced in a circle to give thanks for gathered food, to celebrate a war victory, bring rain, cure the sick, or mourn the dead. The Paiute "Cry," or Mourning Dance, held three months to a year after a relative has passed away, shared some common elements with the later Ghost Dance, such as concern for the dead and dancing in a circle, but it was, and is, more of a funerary rite to send the deceased on their way with the things that they will need in the Land Beyond.[39] The destruction of goods is sometimes part of this "send-off"; the Ghost Dance had no such elements and nothing to do with postburial experience. Palmer described a Cry he attended in 1924, held as part of a funeral rite for Anthony W. Ivins, a friend of the Paiutes in southwestern Utah.

The Indian Sing begins at sunset and continues until sunrise. They have a string of songs that come in proper sequence through the night. At certain places the chant stops and everyone surrounds the dead person and weeps and wails. They explained to me that the songs were like a string that runs all through the night. Here and there all along there are knots in the string and every time they came to a knot, they must stop and cry — a very apt illustration….Their chants go on for about two hours before they come to the first cry [which lasted about a half hour]…. As the chant went on anyone who wanted to say anything about [the deceased] arose and spoke to the song accompaniment, for the chant never stopped until they came to another cry time.[40]

The Mourning Dance is still practiced today on White Mesa. It starts in the evening and ends at sunrise with a final prayer that sends the departed on their way to the spirit world. The ceremony begins with the "Cry" performed in the dead person's house. The ceremonial leader offers the opening prayer, burning sweetgrass or sage and "mountain cedar" (Rocky Mountain juniper) as incense to carry the words to the Land Beyond. Aldean Ketchum of White Mesa explained, "Spirits live in a smoky fog and so [these plants] are burned to prevent a spirit from entering a person's mind and body and possessing it. It keeps them at bay so that the deceased can make the transition from this world to the next, while preventing evil spirits from harming the living."[41] Following the Cry, mourners move outside, form a dance circle, hold hands, and move in a clockwise direction around the leader, who stands in the center. Aldean did not recall a tree in the center, but said that a staff with feathers could be used to tie the people of the earth to the land of the spirits. With the approach of the sun, the deceased begin their journey. Thus the Mourning Dance focuses on the departure of a specific individual; in a sense, it is the opposite of the Ghost Dance, which greets a multitude of the dead who are returning to assist the living.

The first Ghost Dance movement, taught and led by Wodziwob, began in 1870; the second, under Wovoka (also known as Jack Wilson), arose in 1888. Both men were Northern Paiutes who were intimately familiar with the Round Dance, attended Mourning Dances, and held strong beliefs about an afterlife.[42] What made these ceremonies different from previous expressions were the underlying tenets of the faith. Among the teachings were: the Indian dead would return in a glorified, resurrected form to assist the living in restoring the old way of life; white men would decrease in prominence and even disappear; the earth would assume its earlier "pristine" state; and all this could be accomplished through practices outlined in revelation by these two prophets.

While some of the more eastern Plains tribes in the late 1880s developed a more militant interpretation, introducing the idea of bulletproof shirts and invincibility, this was not part of the original message. In addition to the revelations of the two prophets, part of the origin of the dance is attributed to the Paiute Round Dance and the influence of Mormon missionaries teaching about the return of the dead, the earth receiving a paradisiacal glory, and during the 1890s Ghost Dance, wearing undergarments with protective powers.[43] Scholars who have studied both movements generally agree that these teachings arose in response to the tremendous economic and cultural pressures facing Indians in the West. As the old lifestyle deteriorated and tribes were exiled to reservation "islands," the people sought a solution to their plight through religious revitalization. A survey of seventy tribes in the West and Southwest shows that of the forty-five who adopted the Ghost Dance, most of them were traditionally hunters and gatherers who had watched their way of life disappear and the world turn ugly.[44]

Wodziwob's influence over the dances in the 1870s was short-lived. His message—"our [deceased] fathers are coming; our mothers are coming; they are coming pretty soon. You had better dance"—lasted until 1872 and was over.[45] But during that time, as noted in chapter 6, Indian groups, including Navajos and Sheberetch, Elk Mountain, and Weenuche Utes, headed north to join the Northern Utes, who were sponsoring a gathering near Sanpete, Utah. James Mooney, an ethnologist on the scene for the 1890s dance, received testimony that Paiutes from southwestern Utah had also traveled to Nevada, visited the Paiutes living there, and received the new belief, which included "a dance performed at night in a circle with no fire in the center, very much like the modern Ghost Dance."[46] The practice garnered some attention by outsiders, but relatively little mention of it made its way into official reports or newspapers compared with the movement twenty years later.

Wovoka's influence over the Ghost Dance as a widespread phenomenon started in December 1888; the movement had petered out by 1892, although he lived until 1932 and continued to teach to the end.[47] During the height of the practice, newspapers, government agents, anthropologists, and apologists studied and reported various tribes' adoption of the beliefs, especially around the time of the 1890 massacre at Wounded Knee, South Dakota. A year before that, many Indian groups sent delegates—reportedly as many as 1,600, including Utes, Navajos, and Paiutes—to Nevada to learn the doctrine and dance.[48] Although the Cheyenne and Sioux sent representatives to Wovoka, the Sioux credit the Utah Utes as the ones who really taught them. Testimony gathered in 1891 indicates the powerful influence they had upon the Sioux, who returned to speak of a messiah and share the dance they had learned. This included dancing in three or four concentric circles with fingers interlocked moving clockwise around a thirty-foot pole with a white strip of cloth at the top to represent purity, and the wearing of shirts of white muslin or skin painted with Ghost Dance symbols. The dancers would stop briefly as the leader prayed, "Great Spirit, look at us now. Grandfather and Grandmother have come," while people prayed, wept, and left offerings at the sacred pole.[49]

Other tribes, such as the Navajo, did not embrace the dance. The Utes and Utah Paiutes provided the primary impact in the Shiprock-Tohatchi region, on the northern part of the Navajo Reservation. But fear of the dead, a major tenet of Navajo beliefs, encouraged leaders such as Manuelito to tell his people to avoid this type of practice, saying, "We know that ghosts are bad," and "If they do appear we will have to get rid of them."[50] While Numa also avoid the dead, the messiah had said through Wovoka that they were returning to assist in the approaching millennial state and so it was a positive blessing.

The *Salt Lake Tribune* triumphantly reported in December 1890 that "Utah Has a Ghost Dance" at the same time that Wounded Knee was making national news. The article claimed that the White River Utes "no doubt believe in the coming of Shin-ob (Christ) and the resurrection of their dead friends.... The dance is performed by the half-naked and painted bucks around a high pole ornamented with wolf scalps and one eagle feather.... The dance lasts for days at a time and in many respects is similar to the 'ghost dance' of the Northern Indians."[51] A week later, however, the newspaper claimed that there was no Ghost Dance, although specific details in the first report indicate strong familiarity with Ute practices. Elders later said of this era that they were very much involved in the Ghost Dance. Six different informants testified: "My people used to dance the Ghost Dance."[52] The Utes called the ceremony the Jesus or God Dance because "They wanted to see Sinapi (Wolf, God)" and encourage the dead to come back to life. Characteristic features of the dance included the interlocking of fingers, moving clockwise in a circle around a tree or stick, and dressing in white. These same features were present in the Ghost Dance practiced by the Utah Paiute and Arizona Pai people. Participants wore white clothing or robes and danced around a center pole with eagle feathers tied at the top, a brush fence enclosed the 150-foot-diameter dance ground, the circle of dancers communicated with the dead, and the ceremony lasted four or five days.[53] While there were local inconsistencies with some elements, the general pattern existed throughout.

In southeastern Utah, the record of the early 1890s is silent. The Indian agents' annual reports make no mention of the Weenuche Utes paying any attention to what was going on with groups to the north (Northern

Utes), east (Plains tribes), and West (Paiute and Pai people). Not until 1915, during testimony given by Tse-ne-gat, is there reference to a dance of this nature, one held on the night of Juan Chacón's death. "There was to be a Spirit Dance or 'Dance to God' near Sam's [Ramon] place, and that's why I [Tse-ne-gat] changed from boots to moccasins and went to the dance and danced all night."[54] Little else was said.

As in the case of the Northern Utes, substantive information about the practice surfaced only during later interviews as witnesses spoke of their involvement. Edward Dutchie, born in 1918, recalled the practice in detail.[55] He spoke of attending "what some of them called a Ghost Dance" around 1932. "They took this person over to a place to join in a dance called a Circle Dance, a religious dance they called the Ghost Dance at that time. They secretly called it a Ghost Dance." This one was held in Allen Canyon, but other places for this ceremony were at the base of the Bears Ears, the spring at Kigalia ranger station, Indian Creek, Camp Jackson, Babylon Pasture, White Mesa, Squaw Creek, Cross Canyon, Mariano Spring, Montezuma Creek, Towaoc, and Ignacio, as well as in the La Sal Mountains. All of these sites are quiet and have water and enough space for an encampment, but of primary importance was that it "had to be more spiritual" in order to "celebrate spiritual ways." Mountains were particularly favorable.

Edward noted that "the dance was for everything—rain, the people, what Mother Earth gives," but most importantly "they prayed to the Lord." A sick person can be healed, said Patty, Edward's wife, adding, "It's like talking to your Creator and his answer you can hear. His answers are what he is saying to his people. There is a main person who knows what the Creator is saying so he tells his people what is going to happen, what is going to be in the future. It was for that purpose." She later said, "The spirit is always coming to us when we pray. In our grandpar-

ents' time, prayers were always answered. He [her grandfather] would hear a person."

Edward described the 1932 dance in detail:

They [the White Mesa Utes] went up to the mountain and cut down a pine tree, like a Christmas tree, and stood it in the ground where it is level. People had come on horseback or walked. The people came around and some of them started—maybe four or five of them. They have this certain person who leads off in song after offering a prayer. He said he was going to start this going around with about three or four songs. When he began singing, some people dressed in white blankets came in. When they stopped singing, some more would come in and make a bigger ring, then another one had a song.

He made up this song right there.... This song he was singing was from a spiritual way. He said that the songs he sang didn't come from him but from around here. "In my sleep," he said, "I dreamed. I dreamed there was a nice place, nice level place, and beyond a hill I saw dust coming up and I walked over that bump and saw lots of people. They were having a dance like this. The people were singing. I joined in." This man was singing that song and was telling the people about it. That is where he said he got that song. "It didn't originate here," he said. "I carried it back here so I could sing it to you." Then he sang.

It mentioned the earth being round, and at the end of the earth was a fire still burning. On this side there is a big water—waves coming. That is what the song was about. It was naming these things and then again it tells the story about what has taken place. This man did not talk English. He couldn't write his name, but he translated what those people up there told him to tell these people.

Today we could believe what that song said. The fire started from the edge—from California. Over here [east] it talked about the water down in Florida. So it makes me think back to that song and what it is saying. So that is what the dance is for, to pray for the people. All of us, not just the one that put up that spiritual dance, but to pray for everybody who walks the earth today. That is what he was praying for at that time. I was listening.

There was a lot more to it, but that is what I remember that took place at the beginning of the Circle Dance or Ghost Dance or Round Dance or however you call it. The dancers had white sheet blankets. Some made their blankets out of flour sacks sewn together. I guess it belongs to that spiritual dance. As the years go by, I have not seen it anymore. I do not hear mention about what will take place later, but at that time, I heard it. The song starts the fire going around, high waves over there, tornadoes coming everywhere. That is what the song mentioned. It was going to come later. I guess it was foretold to him up there somewhere; I don't know where. That is what he told all of the people. We listened to him.

The dance was held at night and illuminated by a large fire. When asked the meaning of the tree placed in the center of the dance area, Edward insisted that it had to be an evergreen because it never changes, and the people "want to live like that. It might have grown way up towards the Creator because that is the only one that is tall—tallest anywhere, pine.... Through that tree they might reach the Creator somehow." He went on to explain that the "Creator of All Things" should not be confused with Sináwav, or Coyote, who performs miracles but also is involved with wrongdoings on earth. "Sináwav is the Coyote and his brother the Wolf. A big wolf. The two make laws and tell how it is going to be. Sináwav is the one who goes ahead and gets everything started, then runs away or steals something." Edward later stated, "The one who created him [Sináwav] and Mother earth, that's the Creator.... Those old people prayed to the Creator of All Things, wherever he is. He might be right here talking to me.... The one who turns this earth, seasons, changes—puts different coats on it, nice things, that is who I am talking to. That is who they used to pray to, those old people, before the white man brought his paper over—the Bible."

Elders at White Mesa remembered other Ghost Dances, or as they prefer to call them today, Worship Dance ceremonies, performed until the 1960s. While there are slight variations in their accounts, they generally corroborate what Edward described. Bonnie Mike Lehi tells of a cedar tree with medicinal healing power erected with prayers in the middle of the dance circle. The tree had the same function and meaning as the Sun Dance pole and is believed to connect the living with the dead. The people danced in a circle, offered prayers for well-being, and sang songs that belonged to families and were passed down to future generations—"they had a song for everything."[56] She also recalls hearing of people dressed in white clothing but did not see that. Clifford Duncan, a Northern Ute tribal elder, also heard his mother speak of people wearing white shirts and going to a special place that the spirits knew. There they erected a tree in the center and danced all night. In the morning, "everyone scattered and allowed the sun to purify the place where the dancers had been communicating with the dead."[57]

Stella Eyetoo remembers the dancers wearing white clothing or blankets made of flour sacks. They prayed when they danced: "All night they dreamed the songs and saw them [visions]. They dreamed about it as they danced."[58] She recalled one Worship Dance held in McElmo Canyon for Polk's people that drew participants from Montezuma Creek, McElmo, and Towaoc, and that Mancos George used to conduct the dances. Like many of the elders, Stella said that the last Worship Dance was in the 1960s, when soldiers stationed with a missile project on Black Mesa attended. During that dance the participants did not use white blankets. Stella's aunt, Adoline Eyetoo, said the last Worship Dance was held for her grandfather, Anson Cantsee, but it was before the soldiers participated. During the dance "people felt happy. They were thinking about Jesus who is Sináwav. Everybody was dressed in white in the old days. They put a cedar tree in the middle of the circle because they were thinking about Jesus."[59] She related the cross, tree of life, and the Sun Dance pole

Jack Cantsee Sr. of White Mesa, 2009. Cantsee is the only practitioner capable of conducting the Worship Dance. He is frequently invited to other Ute reservations to lead and direct the dance. Behind him is a cedar (juniper) tree from which he cuts branches to use in purification ceremonies. (Photo by author)

to the tree erected in the circle and then explained: "They pray when they put the tree in the ground and then pray to the tree for the people on the earth. It gives us good things to think about. They prayed for those in danger and to do what is right." As many as two hundred people may have been in attendance, all praying in unison.

Annie Cantsee said that either a pine or a juniper tree could be used, and she vaguely remembered that the dancers wore white clothing or blankets with moons and stars painted on the back. They also put red clay on their cheeks, a practice done for the deceased at funerals. "It connects the dead with Sináwav."[60] The dance is performed for the sick, but the prayers are for everyone. The songs could be either extemporaneous or ones passed down within the family. "Some of the songs are about birds flying. People feel better when they sing the worship songs." The Utes held the dance in the spring, summer, and fall, but the winter was too cold.

Despite the claims of many elders that the last Worship Dances were in the 1960s, they are still held today under the direction of Jack Cantsee Sr., who has conducted them at Towaoc, Ignacio, Roosevelt, and White Mesa. He received his teachings initially from his grandfather, Anson Cantsee (a.k.a. Scotty Ute [1868–1966]). As a young man he saw the people dancing around a cedar tree all night, singing and praying until morning, when his grandfather lined them up to face the rising sun and to fan them off with eagle feathers. Jack did not know how to sing, but he watched and listened as the dance unfolded. At one ceremony some of the people came to him and "put a sheet over me and said 'initiated into the Worship Dance.' I went with them singing all through the night."[61] He continued to participate until Anson died in 1966, taking with him the knowledge and practice of the Worship Dance.

For a while Jack left the ceremony alone. Eventually, however, "all those songs started coming up and coming up, different ones, different ones, singing, singing, and singing those songs by myself." He went to Towaoc and sang, and again at Ignacio, and then realized that he knew enough to perform the ceremony, and there was no one else who would keep the tradition alive. The origin of the dance was as important as the practice, and so he "backtracked" based on what his grandfather had told him. He arrived at the time of creation with Coyote and Wolf. "They were the ones who were the rulers of the world at that time. My Grandfather used to talk about it." He then proceeded to tell a story with unmistakable detail that linked it to the Chemehuevi myth "How Wolf and Coyote Went Away," recorded by Carobeth and George Laird sometime between 1920 and 1940. The antiquity of the story is real, unquestionably connected as the final episode in the Wolf-Coyote cycle of the Numas' creation stories.[62]

The narrative is long and detailed. Briefly, the plot and characterization follow the same pattern as the other stories, with Wolf being the wise, omniscient older brother, and Coyote the imitator who fails to follow instructions, creates problems, and foreshadows the patterns that man will practice. The story begins with Wolf, "who always spoke in a chant," sending Coyote on an errand to obtain grass seed from their aunt, Bear. Not surprisingly, Coyote meddles with some of Bear's offspring, angering her, and receives a grievous wound before escaping. Wolf heals Coyote and sends him with poisoned food to kill Bear and specific instructions on how to destroy her property and kin, but Coyote again fails to follow directions. Bear is killed, but her relatives seek revenge. Wolf and Coyote prepare for war by making arrows and putting on different types of protective armor, are able to defend their cave from the enemy host, and almost succeed in defeating the bears, but Coyote again does not follow instructions, and as he flees, turns around to see how Wolf was winning the battle. Even the armor Wolf wore, said to be so bright that the "light dazzled the eyes of the bear warriors," was not enough to counteract Coyote's disobedience, causing the enemy to kill and utterly destroy the older brother.

Coyote was devastated. Still, curiosity got the best of him, and he returned to their cave, where he went through Wolf's belongings before burning them as part of the mourning practice. He opened a series of buckskin wrappings, one inside the other, and unintentionally released Night. Only after several attempts did he succeed in restoring daylight. He then went to the scene of battle and collected what little scraps of Wolf he could find, placing them under a basket. Coyote next made a lot of bows and arrows, as many as "he could possibly carry," and cached them along his route as he searched for the Bears with his brother's scalp.

Coyote's supernatural powers allowed him to detach his penis to act as an alter-ego that communicated and thought just as he did. As the two approached the bears' camp, they disguised themselves with paint. Penis advised that they kill two old women carrying wood for the evening's dance, get inside their bodies, and infiltrate the enemy's domain. Af-

ter learning from them how they should act and what they should say, Coyote and Penis killed the old ladies and succeeded in fooling everyone in the camp so they could participate in the Scalp Dance. Each dancer placed Wolf's scalp on their head and then passed it around the circle. Coyote and Penis, still disguised as the old ladies, positioned themselves for a quick escape. Penis received the scalp first and gave it to Coyote, who sprinted out of the circle while Penis reattached in the proper place. Coyote fought a delaying action with the bows and arrows he had prepositioned, and evaded his pursuers using his supernatural powers. The bears finally gave up but caused a snowstorm to blanket the ground both day and night. To no avail. Coyote was safe and warm in a snug cave.

The next day Coyote shrank himself to fit into a little puffball that the wind carried back to his home. After regaining his normal size, he placed Wolf's scalp under the basket with the other body parts and left to rest. At midnight he awoke and listened; shortly before the Morning Star arose, he heard his brother's voice and knew that he had returned from the dead. "Coyote listened intently. He was happy, because this time he had done everything exactly right. Now that his brother had come back to life, they would go on living together in the cave, and everything would be as it had always been." But Wolf's howls were heading to the "North, the Storied Land where the Ancient Telling starts and ends," not back to the cave, as Coyote had hoped. He decided to follow him, and the two have not been seen since.

This story of resurrection—returning everything to how it had always been—answers questions and raises possibilities not previously explored. For example, an earlier report of a dance of the White River Utes mentioned wolf scalps and an eagle feather tied to the top of a pole in a Ghost Dance arena. Other accounts talk about painting faces and the significance of the pole as a device for communicating with the Land Beyond, but that could also be interpreted as Coyote's penis; the story also tells why the dance was held at night and ends at daybreak, and most important, it notes the connection of the dead with the living. Jack recalled that an old medicine man who spoke no English and knew nothing of Jesus "started to sing one song that talked about a stick standing with something on top of it. He said 'thees' [Jesus?] and the blood was dripping down from that. He didn't say Jesus Christ, but he said the blood is dripping from there." While Jack did not know what was on the pole, he was sure it was still alive and could communicate.

The wearing of a white blanket or painting the face or body with white clay suggests various interpretations. The color white could represent Wolf's armor, which shone with dazzling light, and although protective Ghost Dance shirts were a Plains Indian phenomenon, the parallel with protection exists. The snowstorm conjured by the bears is another possibility, as is Jack's suggestion that the blankets symbolized Christ's robe. The strongest possibility, however, is that it is associated with the spirit world. As mentioned previously, smoke and incense represent the realm of the spirit. Scholars working on various aspects of the Ghost Dance confirm this belief. Judith Vander quoted Emily Hill, a Shoshone elder, as saying "The soul is like a fog when it gets out of the body," and later states, "If we consider the soul's journey out of the body, first as foggy breath and then as dusty whirlwind…fog-soul is closest to life either as it leaves or returns to it."[63] Vander also points out that Great Basin shamans painted patients with white clay or paint as part of healing the sick, mourning following a burial, or recovering after a bad dream. Havasupai Ghost Dancers covered themselves with white clay before dancing.[64]

Mooney, who earlier observed the Shoshone, noted that at the end of the dance the "performers shook their blankets in the air, as among the Paiute and other tribes before dispersing."[65] He also cites a description of a "Walapai" Ghost Dance: "The dancers,

Jack Cantsee Sr. wearing a stole signifying leadership in the Worship Dance. At a dance he attended when he was eight years old, some participants covered him with a woven white blanket which was later given to him, signifying his initiation and right to participate. The staff he holds has a real bald eagle's head and represents the leader of a group. (Courtesy of Jack Cantsee Sr.)

to the number of 200, clad in white robes with fancy trimmings, their faces and hair painted white in various decorative designs, moved slowly around in a circle, keeping time with a wild chant, while 200 more stood or crouched around the fires, awaiting their turn to participate."[66] Jorgensen tells how "participants shook the blankets in order to bring good health and to get rid of any lingering ghosts."[67] Michael Hittman, who studied extensively the life of Wovoka, arrived at a highly complex explanation, too lengthy to examine here, of the significance of the color white. He concludes: "Thus, the color white = thunderclap = rifles = Tibo'o [white man] = the Prophet's invulnerability = Wovoka's ability to doctor gunshot wounds = the white horse = the prophecy of the white horse = the Messiah = Wolf = God = Our Father = Sun = Thunder = clouds = rain =

The Rainmaker = water = eagle feather = shamanic curing = ebe (white paint)."[68] The many interpretations of the color white and other aspects of the Worship Dance, as with the Sun Dance and Bear Dance, are in keeping with the tendency for Native American symbols to be polysemic, or expand in meaning, and mulitvocal, evoking a variety of responses and teachings.

As a dance leader Jack Cantsee has his own explanation of the importance of the tree and the eagle. The individual directing the dance brings a person in need of a blessing to the cedar in the center, where he prays for him or her. The recipient holds on to the tree and is fanned from head to foot, which brushes away any problems through the power of the eagle. "He comes out through that tree, the center, and fans him off." Two or three eagle feathers will do, but they must be eagle "because it has more power than anything" and can see and hear things that other creatures cannot. "He has the power to carry a message to the Creator." This same power is transmitted during the Sun Dance through an eagle bone whistle. When it is blown, the message goes to the Creator, who connects with the person in need of help. One time, after getting a phone call that his son had been in a car accident in Yakima, Washington, and had been given only a 50 percent chance of survival, Jack walked outside of his home in White Mesa carrying an eagle bone whistle. He offered a prayer and then blew it four times. Word came that his son would live. Jack then drove to his bedside and used an eagle feather to fan him; a few days later the son walked out of the hospital on his own power. "That kind of a miracle can happen."

The tree placed in the center of the dance area is "respected just like a person." The cedar tree "brings out a lot of people singing. You can see the cedar tree moving when the wind blows. It does a lot of different things like move around, and they say that [with] that cedar tree, those worship songs get into your head. You see and feel what is there and what it is." After his explanation of the tree, Jack continued with his thoughts on the spirit world, connecting the two. Although he did not know where it was located and said that nobody really knew about it, he identified the land of the dead as a "dream land." "I dream about the people who are gone. I see them at a distance.... I see my brothers who are gone. I see my grandmothers who are gone. I see them in the spirit world, in dream land. There is no land around here like that."

Jack also suggested that people wore white in the past because spirits can connect and help a person in a positive way if one can be seen and recognized. He felt that the good spirits are present at the dance and ready to assist, while the bad ones — the ones usually feared at night — do not attend. The assistance from the spirit world makes a person feel good, "feeling that something has come over you — the energy comes over you and makes you cry and think of somebody." Central to obtaining this feeling are the songs. Jack sings many that he heard his grandfather use, but new ones also come to him from the spirits. The songs are revealed but have been present for a long time. "The songs just travel around, travel around with the air.... All the songs are nothing but the Creator and the creation of mankind on this earth. The Ute people. So that is a good part of it."

Thus, the Worship Dance, Sun Dance, and Bear Dance share many teachings and symbols common to Numic speakers. Each ceremony is unique and performed for a variety of reasons, but the common ground between them cannot be missed. Healing the sick, renewing the necessities of life, connecting spiritually with ancestors for assistance, communicating with the Land Beyond, establishing patterns of prayer and worship, and sharing symbols that unify religious expression characterize the faith of the White Mesa people. Circles, trees, bears, and other emblems are not just tokens of past beliefs but still empower the universe today.

CHAPTER 17

Adoption, Adaptation, and Abandonment

Changing Weenuche Religious Practices, 1900–2010

When the people lived in Allen Canyon, [Utes] from Towaoc came over and held Native American Church meetings. That is when I was healed.... There were [also] a lot of different medicine men. Half were good and half were bad. The Native American Church came in and started getting rid of all the bad people. So today, all the people are good.

Jack Cantsee Sr.

Today there are no traditional Ute shamans, or medicine men, living on White Mesa. The loss of this powerful force within the community can be attributed to several causes, as the statement above suggests. Native Americans in general have undergone rapid change over the past century, but some elements within the White Mesa Ute community have persisted, even as new elements have been adapted or adopted outright. Many of the old ways have fallen out of practice, but others, such as the Bear Dance and Worship Dance, continue. Among those traditions that are no longer practiced is shamanism, which can use both positive spiritual power to heal or negative power to kill. A new religion—espoused by the Native American Church—has replaced both uses of power with a different form that has no provision for sorcery or other types of witchcraft. Religious change rests at the heart of this story.

Spiritual power invests the Ute universe. *Puwá-v* is a good power used to heal the sick, whereas *üvü puwa-gat* is associated with sorcery. Both can be wielded by the same person. Chapter 3 explained how the

spirits chose a medicine man, how he used the power that they gave him, and told of personal experiences of those who benefited from someone's healing abilities. Those who held this type of power were well-known to the community and appreciated by the spirits. The power was not taken lightly. Connor Chapoose recalls hearing of medicine men being challenged as fakes. "In later years when they had guns, I have heard of some of them taking these rifles and shooting a medicine man. He would tell them to 'Go ahead and shoot me. If I'm not what I am telling you, representing what I am, you kill me. But' he says, 'if it's true, you won't hurt me.' I have never heard of anyone being killed."[1] However, as early as 1859, Charles H. Dimmock, who was with the Macomb Survey, reported that the Capote Tamuche had wives who "when sick were attended by...Indian medicine men who were killed when failing to cure. The last one Tamuche put out of the way before his wife died."[2]

Those who held this power had to behave well, control it in an acceptable way, and be obedient to whatever practices accompanied receipt of it. Failure to do so would lead to sickness or death.[3] Healing ceremonies were open events where one or more medicine men gathered to help and work with a patient. Members of the community observed, assisted with songs, and later testified of the power they had witnessed. Clifford Duncan explained that a medicine man learned "how to deal with spirits, the types of spirits there were, and how to control this or that…. You have to have control of that side too, the mind. It seemed that at that time, the mind and body had to be balanced out."[4]

These beliefs were deeply entrenched within Ute culture and provided guidance in working with the intangible, invisible world of spirits and sickness. Tribal chairman John Miller testified before a Senate subcommittee in 1932 of the difference between sending an ill Indian to the white man's hospital and using Native healers.

> There are a lot of Utes who do not understand English. They may be sick or something else and the [white] doctor might give them different medicines than what the sickness is. You people are white people; you make your own medicines; you understand for what purpose you take it and my Indian doctors know something about this sickness this fellow got and they might help him out in case he is sick.[5]

To the agents and the medical staff in the hospital at Towaoc, there was nothing further from the truth. From their perspective the world of disease, germs, and sanitation was the only reality; the rest was a relic of the past and should be forsaken. Superintendent W. F. Dickens believed, "In the Ute Mountain section and in Polk and Posey's Band, considerable difficulty is experienced in combating the evil influence of the different Indian medicine men, and I believe that to overcome this influence it will take a number of years in order to show, especially to the older Indians, the superior benefit to be derived from patronizing the white doctors."[6] A year later he continued his diatribe, pointing out that

these same groups "are very superstitious and backward. There are many complaints against the Indian alleged to have given some unfortunate Indian 'bad medicine.' This is a common complaint, though I do not think it is sincerely believed by many of the tribe."[7]

The superintendent was wrong. This dark side of spiritual power—*üvü puwa-gat*, or sorcery—was a very genuine problem, and just as real as any issues being wrestled with by the white medical profession. Although it could not be put under a microscope, *üvü puwa-gat* had been a concern of the Ute community long before contact with whites. Whereas the germ theory of disease speaks of contagion, the type of sickness caused by sorcery was caused just by thinking of an intended victim. Through songs and prayers, a small stick or rock could be shot into someone, sickness and death could be spread, food poisoned, or bad dreams sent. Those practicing *üvü puwa-gat* tried to remain anonymous and work their black art alone, but medicine men were always prime targets for accusation of witchcraft. Jack Cantsee Sr. suggested that since they worked to heal an individual using a person's sacred name given at childbirth and known only by family members or a person involved in healing, the shaman could use this knowledge to cure or curse someone. Cantsee explained, "The bad medicine people get rid of you right away. Utes have a Ute name which the Creator understands when a person asks for something. When they asked Him, the person said their name so He knows who you are. That's how they [evil shamans] used to use it to get rid of a person."[8] Without this knowledge the sorcerer might be able to create some pain in different parts of the body, but not kill the person.

There were also ways to ferret out those involved in *üvü puwa-gat*. Among those suspected of being practitioners were individuals who were mean and believed to be motivated by evil thoughts; those who became subject of widespread gossip; people who seemed suspicious based upon circumstantial evidence; anyone accused by another medicine man; and anyone who, once accused, showed fear and attempted to flee.[9] A medicine man combating sorcery had three options. Once he identified the person, he could speak to him, asking that he stop his practice and purify himself by bathing and praying to the sun. If that didn't work, he could remove the object bothering the patient through sucking or try to reverse the evil power through healing songs. Edward Dutchie explained, "The medicine man is going to sing that song to the part where it hurts. This song will tell him what it is and how to get it out, how it got in there, and ask if that is correct. You have to tell him the truth although he already knows it. The only thing he is going to do is suck out that bad thing, clean it all out, and then he will show it to you in his hand."[10] If a medicine man was found guilty of witchcraft, he became the scapegoat for many other things that heretofore had been unexplained. Traditional custom allowed for someone wronged by such an individual to take strong measures, including killing the witch. The evil person's family members could also come under this decree. While these steps were not desirable, often leading to interfamily and interband conflict, the community generally considered the initial act of killing an evil shaman justified.

Given the private nature of sorcery at a time (through the 1930s) when agents reported that even public dances were being held in secret, it is somewhat surprising to find a number of written reports in newspapers and government documents referring to sorcery. Part of the reason for this is the persistent nature of the problem, and partly because Ute traditional practices of eliminating the guilty party were now punishable under federal law. Those with a complaint turned to their agent for a solution. One incident, before there was tight control, illustrates traditional Ute law in full force.

In the early 1890s a local cowboy eased his horse through a winter storm of blowing, drifting snow outside of Monticello. Near the roadside an unnatural pile of snow caught his eye, only to reveal a four-year-old Ute girl, scantily dressed, huddling against the cold. There was no Indian camp nearby, so the rider brought the child to Edward Hyde, a good friend of the Utes. He cared for her for several months, but when the weather warmed, a band of Utes stopped at his place on their way to the mountain. When they spotted the girl, one of the men, Rooster, raised his gun to shoot; Hyde stopped him. Tension mounted, but Wash convinced Rooster to refrain from pushing the issue and let the girl live. Wash then explained that the girl's mother had been a witch and so was killed, and that this little girl, as a relative, had been abandoned in the snowstorm as part of the cleansing. Her death, not rescue, was in keeping with tribal custom. The Indians left, and the girl went to live with a woman named Baker, but the incident was not forgotten. A few months later Rooster and some other men reappeared, forcibly seized the girl, took her to a cliff, and tossed her over the precipice, shooting her several times to ensure the power within her could not return.[11]

In spring 1904 there were two reported killings of medicine men. The first occurred in the beginning of April, when William Heart (Magua) killed Kane, both Weenuche from Navajo Springs. The *Montezuma Journal* carried a short article commenting on "the murder of another Ute medicine man by one of his own tribe."[12] Because the crime occurred in San Juan County, Utah, local law enforcement became involved. It turned out that Kane, a medicine man, had failed to cure Heart's "friend," so Heart killed him. Sheriff J. H. Wood from Monticello declined to arrest him because he felt the Indian should come under federal jurisdiction. William M. Peterson, acting agent for Navajo Springs, felt equally hampered because he lacked an efficient interpreter, and his "police are useless in such a case," suggesting that the Utes condoned the action.[13]

All of this held true a month later when Wa'áp, or Nuu-viač, a Weenuche medicine man, met a similar fate. This fifty-year-old healer had practiced his trade for a long time and was considered successful. He lived below the La Plata River and was friends with Ignacio, who was on his way to the school at Ignacio with his son-in-law Wa-ra. As they traveled, the young man became increasingly ill, so they stopped at his brother E-woop's camp to rest and send for his uncle Wa'áp while Ignacio continued. The shaman arrived and mixed some "white-looking" medicine in water. After two days of vomiting and spitting blood, the patient died. Retribution followed.

Wa'áp's son Accuttetewap (Agöttu-tuwáp — "Big/Fat Pine Tree") felt the first pangs of revenge a few days later. He was visiting San Juan's (Samuel Johnson's) house when San Juan and his two sons, Conach (Kwanač — "Eagle") and Patricio, and Conach's wife grabbed him violently, threw him down, bound him with ropes, stomped on his neck, and threatened to cut his throat. They accused him of being in league with his father, but eventually relented and gave him an opportunity to help kill his parent. By now E-woop had joined the group, all of them setting off for Wa'áp's camp a mile and a half away. The party split, with E-woop, Patricio, and Wa'áp's son going directly toward the tepee while San Juan, Conach, and his wife rode around through the cedars. Wa'áp's son, with one bullet in his rifle to prevent resistance, shot first where he was directed. The others opened fire, and the second group joined in, pumping bullets into the tepee. Wa'áp's son recalled, "Father came out of the tent crawling on his hands and knees without speaking and they continued to shoot many times until he was dead. As soon as he was dead, San Juan went to my tepee and took my father's gun and a pair of leather saddle bags. All then rode away excepting Patricio

who stayed at my father's tepee and with my two sisters dug a shallow grave and buried my father on the spot where he was killed."[14] Patricio next warned that "no one [should] tell the Americans what had been done and if I told, they would kill me."

If good news travels fast, bad news travels faster. Agent Joseph Smith and some others visited the site of the crime, exhumed Wa'áp's body, counted eleven bullet holes, and began prosecution of those involved in the murder. Three found their way into district court, but the judge decided that his bench had no jurisdiction. A fourth defendant was brought before a grand jury in Denver and indicted, but he never stood trial and returned to the reservation.[15] Ignacio, who at first was sorry about the course of events, later felt that it was in keeping with traditional practices and a just punishment for Wa'áp. S. F. Stacher, commenting on his four years as an agent at Towaoc from 1906 to 1909, wrote, "Numerous times members of the tribe would come to me and complain that some certain Indian had made a few passes and shot a wolf tooth into the body of some member of the family and they wanted me to send a policeman to bring them in and put them in jail. Such cases were very hard to settle to the satisfaction of the complainant."[16]

Similar incidents occurred among the White Mesa Utes. In 1921 Posey and Scotty went to the county attorney in Monticello and complained that Jack Ute was killing people he did not like with a sunglass. Women and children in the community feared him, so Posey demanded that he be hanged, and when he was told that was not possible, he insisted that Jack be banished to the Navajo reservation and forbidden to return. Other "bad Indians" were said to spread coyote bait around, sickening and killing anyone who stepped on it. People said a man from Towaoc could flip a pebble into the air and then direct it to go long distances to harm the person he was cursing.[17]

The power of medicine men was a topic of

gossip and conversation that may have been based in real incidents, but which became exaggerated and embellished over time. In 1971 Rachel Eyetoo recalled events surrounding the killing of Bishop's Little Boy and other family members during the Posey incident of 1923. Joe Bishop, his father, and a notable medicine man had instructed Bishop's Little Boy in the practice. Rachel believed that when Bishop's son died, rather than being killed by Bill Young, he was actually captured by the posse and carved into little pieces. He had told his father that it was all right, that he willingly gave up his life to the God who gave it to him, and that was the only way that the white men could kill him. When the butchering commenced, his arms, pointed toward the sky, had blood running up them instead of down, testifying to his power as an apprenticed medicine man. "They cut him all up and he watched them. He said, 'Let them hit me. I don't care. What they want is my life. The God who made us — I am going to give my life to him. He will put something where I die.'"[18] This event occurred on Comb Ridge, where God placed a cedar tree that had no leaves but stood as a testament of what happened there.

Others were also accused of sorcery. Joe Bishop was said to practice witchcraft and have a "night bird" that spread his power to those he worked against. Posey feared that he might get cursed. Another medicine man lived in a hogan at the head of Allen Canyon. A man named "Brank" had a daughter who died from a curse placed upon her by this man. Brank and Sanáp went to his hogan, watched the man and his son eating supper, then shot them both and burned the bodies in their home. This did not end the matter. A curse descended on Brank that gave him a bad leg, and later his tent burned with him in it. His son also died a violent death as part of "God's punishment."[19] Mormon Joe, a Paiute living at Mariano Springs near Towaoc, and father in-law to Platt May, was also greatly feared. When his daughter

died, he commanded Platt to bury her and their living eighteen-day-old baby in the same grave. Platt feared the medicine man and did what he was told, so both went to jail. Agent McKean wrote, "Thirty or forty of the Utes came to me at Towaoc, while Mormon Joe was held in jail at Cortez, and protested against his ever returning to the reservation."[20] Following his jail sentence, he eventually moved to Allen Canyon.

Other incidents received only brief mention in local papers. An old medicine man, Moses Hamlin, appeared to have been poisoned as he traveled to cure a young girl living on Sleeping Ute Mountain. He died at Towaoc.[21] A year later the court arraigned Lloyd Cantsee and Truman Hatch for digging up the body of a Ute woman buried in Yellow Jacket Canyon, taking her fingers and toenails to be turned into powder for witchcraft that sickened and killed people. This "corpse poison" was well-known in Navajo witchcraft, and while these "Paiutes" pleaded guilty, there was no mercy shown by the White Mesa leaders — Paddy (also known as Anson Whyte), John Eyetoo, Jesse Posey, Mancos George, and Platt May — who wanted the two men "put away where they could do no damage to their enemies of the tribe."[22] While the defendants claimed to have done this just to scare people with their "bad medicine," the judge did not find it amusing and sentenced them to the state penitentiary with a provision that after four months of good behavior, they could be paroled.

When Chief John Miller died in 1936, accusations of witchcraft again came into play. He had attended the annual Bear Dance, during which the rain and cold brought on serious sickness. On his way home he pitched camp a few miles outside of Towaoc and sent for several Ute medicine men, who were later joined by some Navajo medicine men to assist in curing him. The agency physician also attended and pronounced the illness pneumonia, "but his presence was resented by the medicine men and also by the chief's family."[23] The illness progressed, Chief Miller ate his last meal of canned corn, canned pears, and Fig Newtons, and then passed away on his bed of sheep skins as the medicine men chanted and the family mourned around a campfire. At his funeral his favorite dogs and horses were killed to accompany him as he traveled to the Land Beyond.

But this was not the end. While on his deathbed, Miller proclaimed that his sickness had been caused by Henry Williams, a Paiute medicine man, and he instructed the tribal council to "get rid of him." "Williams, it seems, is held responsible by the Ute Mountain Indians for most of the deaths among that tribe in the past few years and, when drunk, has bragged of the Indians he has killed."[24] The council requested that he be incarcerated in a prison two to three thousand miles away so that they would be out of reach of his bad, sickness-producing medicine. Removing him to the Paiutes living around Cedar City was not far enough. Superintendent D. H. Wattson recognized that federal law had no provisions for something like this, but also that "medicine men have been killed here in the not too distant past and we shall be fortunate if it doesn't happen again."[25] Williams visited the Uintah and Ouray Reservation for a short time but then returned to Towaoc. What happened to him after that is unknown.[26] Certainly, what Clifford Duncan later explained held true with the Ute people of this time: "What God gave the people here to use for their benefit—the people's benefit—were I to use it against another person—it's wrong—so therefore I will have to pay for that with my own life."[27]

None of these examples are given to suggest that all medicine men were bad or that traditional beliefs became corrupted. What these incidents indicate is the tremendous pressure that each shaman felt during the performance of healing ceremonies. While some may have reveled in the wielding of spiritual power to threaten antagonists, there certainly were others going about their business only to be falsely accused of malpractice and sentenced to death. Unlike the white man's medicine, concerned with physical, tangible efforts to heal, medicine men worked in the intangible spiritual realm, leaving their practices open to a wide range of interpretations of good and evil, appropriate or malicious, life-saving or death-dealing.

In this same period of history (1930s–1940s), much of the Utes' cultural knowledge and many traditional practices were disappearing as external pressure to change from white society encouraged the Indians to adopt new ways. The old way of life was becoming a thing of the past. Some cultural elements, such as the Bear Dance and Mourning Ceremony, persisted because of their more socially acceptable appearance, whereas the performance of shamanistic healing rites drew closer scrutiny. Internal pressure within the community discouraged new apprentices from learning the trade, especially when the consequences of failure were so apparent. An Ignacio Ute told anthropologist Marvin K. Opler in 1937, "Today, the Indian doctors are not so good because they live in houses. They forget the old ways. The young people go to the White hospital, thinking that the White doctors can cure Indian sickness. In the old days, everyone knew that the Indian doctor alone could cure Indian sickness and they believed him.... They took him in a serious way. Today they laugh when they see him. The póo-gat forgets."[28]

Exactly when the last of the medicine men at White Mesa disappeared is hard to say, but Jack Cantsee Sr. thought it was in 1947, with the passing of Washington Dutchie.[29] When asked why he thought no one had followed in the traditional footsteps, Cantsee said it was "scary," and that in order for a medicine man to be effective, he needed to know both the "good and bad side" of the practice, which in itself was dangerous. Terry Knight, the Ute spiritual leader at Towaoc, agrees that there are no traditional medicine men there today.[30] Regardless of when the last shaman passed away, the result is aptly summarized by Duncan, who saw a similar change among the Northern Utes: "The power doesn't die out, just the people who [use it]. It is a matter of learning how to control it. The power and the things that they [use] like their medicine men are still here, but the Indians of today do not know how to harness it, therefore they do not know how to use it."[31]

Even before the practice of shamanism began to decline, a new rising star was gathering increasing strength as a way to express cultural values: the Native American Church. Growing out of a pan-Indian movement gradually sweeping the country, the new religion provides a way for Indians to incorporate important traditional values in their lives. While the Utes were somewhat latecomers compared to the Plains tribes of Oklahoma, they nevertheless embraced and then transmitted the new practice. The Native American Church, also referred to as "the peyote religion," had its inception in the late 1880s among the Kiowas and Comanches, who taught many of the physical practices and much of the general spiritual teachings to other Native American groups. Oklahoma, with its multiplicity of tribes, became a missionary center for the new religion, spreading the faith through various means to Indians throughout the United States. The three bands of Southern Utes received the ceremony at different times and in different ways.

Some people suggest that the new religion started as a less militant form of the 1890 Ghost Dance to revitalize Indian culture, following hard on the heels of that movement, but the initial impact was slow in reaching the Utes. Others believe that Buckskin Charlie was the first Ute to promote interest in the movement, and so went with a group of Southern Utes to the Cheyenne and Arapaho Agency in 1896 to receive instruction. Four years later an Arapaho visited Ignacio to conduct ceremonies, as did a Northern Cheyenne in 1910, but the teachings had yet to take hold.[32] In 1916 a Sioux practitioner called Sam Loganberry, or Cactus Pete, arrived at Towaoc to gather a following, but "his ways were crooked and he did tricks with peyote not in the straight Indian way."[33] Chief John Miller, a shaman and leader in the later peyote movement, explained that there was not much interest at this time because Loganberry preached Christianity, but the Weenuche wished to maintain traditional ways. At Ute Mountain the first "roadman" or "road chief" to conduct a peyote ceremony on home turf was James Mills, who started leading ceremonies in 1917 and was joined by three other Utes during the 1920s.[34]

From 1914 to 1931 Towaoc reported little growth in the number of converts, not enough to concern the superintendents, whereas the Northern Ute agent reported half of his charges were enrolled members.[35] What was not apparent to the agents was that there was continuous proselytizing by Wee'tseets' (Wičí — "Bird") from the Uintah Basin and peyotists from Oklahoma, who not only conducted meetings at Towaoc but hosted visitors on their own reservations. Herbert Stacher, a peyote priest, reviewed the tribal census roles and identified the increasing involvement of the Ute Mountain people. In 1925 he estimated that 33 percent were involved in the religion; by 1940 the number had risen to 85 percent, comparable to that of the Northern Utes.[36]

As with other religious practices, the Utes believed that what went on was not really the concern of white society. Eventually, however, government officials became increasingly aware of the growing religious movement. In 1923 McKean felt there was "a small following of Indians here who at times use peyote, but the practice has not grown."[37] A year later, in his annual report, the superintendent stated that peyote was coming from Oklahoma, Nebraska, and the Northern Utes at Fort Duchesne, but that the number of users was dwindling. For the next two years McKean waged war against

This photo, probably taken in the 1930s or '40s, is the earliest one known of a Ute practitioner in the Native American Church in southeastern Utah. Holding a gourd and an eagle feather fan, two important symbols of the church, the unidentified man represents a growing influence that spread throughout Ute and Navajo culture in the early twentieth century. (Courtesy of San Juan County Historical Commission)

the trafficking of the hallucinogenic cactus through the mail, and by visitors arriving from northern Utah. At one point he wrote to the agent of the Uintah-Ouray Agency to explain that he was sending back Sidney Bluewater and his wife, who had been distributing "considerable peyote to the Indians at Ute Mountain," and that as agent he was "very anxious to prevent its introduction among them."[38] The commissioner of Indian Affairs, Charles H. Burke, encouraged these efforts to curb peyote use, worked with the postal service to stop shipments, discouraged any type of recruitment, and supported the agents with prosecutions in court. Even searching personal mail and working against a religion that should have had constitutional protection did not seem inappropriate.[39] One interesting observation that came out of McKean's anti-peyote campaign was that the Indians involved in the practice were "among the better class, both from the point

of industry and abiding by the law," and that there were "small grounds for alarm of its spreading among these Indians."[40]

The agents' efforts failed. A Cheyenne named John P. Hart was making regular visits to the Ute Mountain Utes before 1918 and continued teaching the tenets of the faith, leading many Utes to consider him "our first teacher."[41] Anthropologist Marvin K. Opler did field research in 1936 and again in 1937 expecting "to find the cult at Towaoc struggling in the sub-rosa light of illegality. Instead one found the older, and from the native point of view, more respected and colorful members of the Weminutc band exerting a profound moral influence through mechanisms set up in the cult for preaching the virtues of native supernaturalism and native sentiments."[42] His informants insisted that the main impetus had come from the Northern Utes, beginning in 1931, and the religion now fostered a new way to express values of Ute traditional culture, and freed them from the restraints of Christianity that were incompatible with Indian beliefs. While the peyote religion filled this niche for the people of Towaoc, involvement among the Southern Utes was declining. For traditionalists the religion answered questions and provided opportunities; to the people at Ignacio, it seemed like a step backward. By the time Opler concluded his research, he determined that "at Towaoc, almost all of them use [peyote]."[43]

The spread of the Native American Church to the people of White Mesa can be traced to the 1930s. Edward Dutchie recalls peyote being used when the agency was at Navajo Springs, but after it moved to Towaoc in 1918, the people from Allen Canyon went there to participate. Around 1938 Blue Mountain Henry, whose Ute name meant Falling Leaves, brought the practice to southeastern Utah.[44] That same year San Juan County charged two men — Harry Wall and Hays Clark from Towaoc — with possession of peyote. Authorities had become aware of the drug's presence after two miraculous cures had spurred a growing interest in ingesting cactus buttons. Law officers seized a large supply from Hays Clark in a hogan in Westwater, and both men readily admitted owning it while demanding its return. The sheriff released the two defendants until April 12, the date of the trial. Chief Jack House promised to have them there at the appointed time, and they were. Since neither spoke English and had only a court-appointed lawyer, the judge postponed the trial until February. The court permanently released the men after learning that the federal government recognized the right of Indians to use peyote as part of their religious practices and that the Northern Utes had recently won the legal right to hold meetings.[45]

That same year the Ute John Cuthair reported that only fifty people at Towaoc did not use peyote, and that at Blanding "very few in that locality do not use it."[46] The White Mesa Utes had a growing number of road men to perform the ceremony, including Myers Cantsee, Arthur Dutchie, and Edward Dutchie, as well as people from Towaoc.[47] Ten years later anthropologist Omer C. Stewart estimated that 90 percent of the people at Towaoc used peyote, but only 10 percent of those at Ignacio, supporting Cuthair's estimate.[48] By the early 1990s there were thirty road men on the Ute Mountain Ute Reservation, and about half of the residents were participating, if only off and on, in Native American Church meetings; at Ignacio, only those on the "fringes of Southern Ute society" participated.[49] Jack Cantsee Sr., vice president of the Native American Church of White Mesa, estimated in 2010 that slightly more than a third of the people on White Mesa belonged to the organization, and that he and his son, Jack Junior, were the only two road men practicing from the community.[50]

Continuous historic interaction of the Utes with the Navajos helped spread the Native American Church. David Aberle and Omer Stewart's *Navaho and Ute Peyotism* is an in-depth study of this practice, which is only summarized here. What is obvious is that the White Mesa people played a part. The Utes of Towaoc were the main conduit through whom the religion entered the northern part of the reservation. Mancos Creek and Aneth were two prime locations, due to proximity and roads, where Navajos interacted with Utes on a daily basis. In the 1930s many Navajos worked on the Ute Mountain reservation as herders for Ute families and in the Civilian Conservation Corps. Navajos also depended on Ute medicine men to heal them from witchcraft practices, feeling that they had strong cures and that "sucking" was highly effective in removing foreign objects. Washington Dutchie and Joe Bishop were both mentioned as shamans who advocated the use of peyote for healing.[51]

Eventually there were enough trained Navajo road men to spread the religion south of the San Juan River, despite the Navajo tribe's legislative opposition to the sale or use of peyote. Considered a "devastating erosion on Navajo land, the peyote evil is fanning all parts of the Reservation from the Ute country on the north."[52] Aneth, Montezuma Creek, Hatch's store in Montezuma Canyon, Mancos Creek, and Bluff all had converts using peyote in the 1920s, and by the mid to late 1930s these communities had turned into hotbeds of Native American Church activity. The movement became so strong that in 1936 peyote priests confronted Navajo bootleggers who had dominated these areas for some time and drove them out of the country.[53] From there the religion moved south of the San Juan River, and its adoption proved unstoppable. Aberle and Stewart found that "the only significant source of initial transmission of peyote to the Navaho is by or through the Towaoc Ute."[54] Since the 1920s the Weenuche living in Allen Canyon had been involved with peyote, and there is little doubt that they also influenced its acceptance by the Navajos.

The experience of Navajo Oshley, a Navajo resident of Bluff and Blanding during the late 1930s, provides a good example of what it was like to be introduced to the Native American Church at Allen Canyon. "Wooden Foot," a Ute from Blanding, invited Oshley and two other Navajo men to attend a ceremony.

> I went to the ceremony and all the people who said they would be there were. People were preparing a lot of food and there were a lot of Utes, some of whom were from Towaoc-Cortez area. A lot of them I did not know. They were a handsome bunch, looked well-fed, and their hair was neatly combed and braided. We all went in and began to smoke, after which the singing started. Both men and women sang, the drum and songs sounding really loud.
>
> The peyote took effect and I started hallucinating. The people looked as if they had big fat lips, their eyes were distorted and very funny in appearance. I thought they were looking only at me, and I felt like urinating, but when I tried, nothing would come out. I asked a Ute why I could not urinate, and he told me I should confess my wrongdoings and feelings; then I could. He also said that some other thing might be blocking it, and that I would probably come across it if I thought about it. Then I would get relief.
>
> It was almost dawn when we went out again. I saw a red rock and a ceremonial tool, but for what ceremony I did not know. The singing was very loud. This was when I started to relieve myself with urine splashing over the red rock....
>
> Two days later [it seemed] we were playing cards again, and I won twenty five dollars from him [Red Rock Springs]. I just backed out of there, even though people were still playing and urged me to continue. This was what I was hallucinating about. I went out again [from the ceremony] and heard two people talking in the woods. The two of them appeared and they looked like Utes. Right where they were walking, a coyote appeared. It was a big one and he was standing in the direction of Ute Mountain where the Utes were living. I thought it was like this, and I stood there and watched, but it did not change so I just went back inside. This was what happened in the peyote ceremony.[55]

Oshley did not accept this religion, but he remained a good friend of many of the Ute people in the area, living with them in the Westwater community for several years.

While the Native American Church is a pan-Indian movement accepted by dozens of tribes as a spiritual expression of their traditional beliefs, it is also an excellent example of syncretism infused with traditional Ute values. The ceremony, paraphernalia, symbols, and teachings are a hand-in-glove fit to elements associated with the Round Dance, Sun Dance, Bear Dance, and Worship Dance discussed in the previous chapter. There are, of course, differences, such as the use of peyote, the lack of dancing, and symbols such as the crescent-shaped moon altar, rattles, and a large cactus button called Father Peyote. Many of the traditional Ute symbols were modified to fit time, place, and circumstance.

Still, there are so many comparable elements that one can see why this ceremony is considered so powerful, and why it was so readily adopted.

A brief summary of events in a typical peyote meeting provides the context for this interpretation.[56] Whenever possible, the ceremony should be held in a tepee, although hogans and Anglo-type dwellings can also be used. An altar in the shape of a crescent moon is fashioned from dirt inside the meeting place and becomes an important resting spot for Father Peyote and other objects used during the ceremony. The road man carries a three-foot staff, an eagle bone whistle, an eagle fan with twelve feathers, and dried juniper leaves for purification. Other ceremonial items include a water drum, drumstick, rattles, tobacco (either store-bought or wild), and a bag of peyote. A fire, built east of the moon-shaped altar, provides light. Moccasins often replace store-bought shoes, and in the past a "few of the older men painted their faces and the part in their hair with red 'Indian paint,'" the significance of which has been noted previously.[57]

At dusk the participants, preceded by the road man, enter the tepee following an opening prayer. All movement within is in a clockwise direction; the leader sits on the west side with the chief drummer on his right, the cedar man on his left, and the fire chief on the north side just inside the entrance. Prayers for the group invoking protection from evil, bad dreams, ghosts, and the Devil start the meeting, with the leader praying out loud and the others accompanying him silently. Participants rub sagebrush on themselves for purification; juniper smoke blesses and cleanses the people and paraphernalia. The leader starts with an opening song, the first of four mandatory chants—Opening Song, Midnight Water Call, Morning Water Call, and Quitting Song—sung during the night. He begins by holding the staff and fan, but later, when others wish to pray and sing, they receive the staff. Just as there are

four required songs, that same number is repeated in the purification of ceremonial objects, the times an individual blesses himself with juniper smoke, the number of peyote buttons taken at the beginning, the songs sung by an individual as leader, how often a person drums for the person to his left, the times the road man blows the eagle bone whistle before the Midnight Song, and how often he blows the whistle to the cardinal directions when he leaves the tepee alone to pray. The ceremony ends at dawn, when participants emerge to greet the sun. The ceremony is followed by a feast for participants and community members.

Many elements of the peyote ceremony tie in to traditional Ute values and practices. The most fundamental is the seeking of a dream or vision for guidance—an experience induced by song, which connects the spirit world to that of the living. Each individual is able to receive his or her own guidance or assistance in interpreting the unknown. That help from beyond—whether in healing the sick, blessing a person with immediate assistance, or learning about the future—functions much like dreams did in the past. The road man who directs the ceremony and understands how to connect the physical with the spiritual world is similar to the traditional *póo-gat*. Aberle and Stewart, in their study of the Native American Church, described a "smooth working relationship between the two types of cures: peyote and sucking" and noted that the first peyote priests, although not drawn from the ranks of practicing medicine men, were not opposed by them.[58] The two belief systems, while not conflicting, were also not integrated for most people. However, Washington Dutchie performed both healing methods in the same meeting, so it was possible to be a medicine man, a road man, or both.

An example of what the two ceremonies were like when combined is provided by a Navajo man, called here "Joe" (to preserve anonymity), whose wife was sick and needed to be healed.[59] They went to Towaoc and met with Herbert Stacher, who in the 1920s and early 1930s was living in Allen Canyon but was carried on the tribal census sometimes as a Paiute and at other times a Ute. Stacher's father treated a Navajo woman who was suffering from blindness, using the sucking cure on the back of her head and above her eyes to remove "white stuff like paper, a big wad of it, and from above her eyes something red and black, two finger joints long." There was no immediate cure, but the Stachers gave her some peyote, and within a month she felt better. The couple returned to Towaoc, where Herbert Stacher conducted a regular ceremony for mostly Ute participants. He prayed in English. Joe received an extensive vision, and by the end of the experience he had decided to join the Native American Church.

Opler's research in the mid-1930s suggests that integration of the peyote religion was not nearly so smooth for those at Ignacio. He found tension between the traditionalists and the peyotists rooted in the fundamental belief of the power of the shaman. The Utes believe that inside of each healer lived a small man, human in form, who controlled the power that allowed the shaman to commune with spiritual forces. If this being did not like peyote when eaten, he might become sick, angry, and kill the person he was dwelling within. Jack Cantsee Sr. provided a description of this spirit in a story about Mormon Joe, so called because the Mormons had incarcerated him, who returned as a good medicine man. Anson Cantsee, Jack's grandfather, said that when Mormon Joe died, "Whatever power he had came out of his mouth. It was green, green. About that long [six to eight inches]. It looked like a lizard coming out of his mouth. That was the power he had."[60]

Traditionalists often opposed the introduction of peyote, dividing the Utes into factions. "A good shaman could look right through another doctor, they say. He'd see the power another doctor had inside. In peyote meetings they could fight back and forth in this way. That is why the peyote members died off quicker than the *póo-gat* at Ignacio. They were always fighting because the peyote members claimed they could see right through you."[61] In some meetings the shaman who took peyote saw the Devil in the middle of the tepee during the ceremony, providing one more reason to not accept the hallucinogen. On the other hand, as mentioned in this chapter's introduction, many believed that there were both good and bad medicine men, but the Native American Church triumphed by getting rid of those who practiced evil. "So today, almost they are all good."[62] Ignacio, who had much stronger ties with Christianity and infused those teachings into the ceremony, struggled much more with the peyote movement than those at Towaoc, who did not preach Christianity and so readily syncretized the new religion with traditional beliefs.

Other elements that melded past teachings with the new included an east-facing tepee, repetition of elements in groups of four, moving people and objects in a clockwise manner, using herbs to cure, fanning a person to remove evil and provide a blessing, praying to heal the sick, seeing into the future, and bringing happiness into a person's life.[63] The cane, sometimes referred to as the cane of Christ by those who mix Christian symbols into the ceremony, functions much as the tree or bear flag pole of the Sun and Bear Dances, connecting the unseen spiritual realm with the participants. The person singing holds the cane and directs the activity until it is passed on.

Teachings are transmitted through the ceremony. The tepee becomes important because the Creator watches through the smoke hole and provides answers; it is like a mother's womb, where there is protection and good things happen. The poles are the mother's ribs, and so one should not lean against them. When people emerge in the morning, they are "born again" to life's possibilities. The entire ceremony is compared

The tepee is a prominent symbol and meeting place for members of the Native American Church. Pictured in this 1960s photo taken at White Mesa are (*left to right*) unidentified, Bonnie Hatch, Myers Cantsee, Jack Cantsee, and Paul Dutchie, all members of the church. (Courtesy of San Juan County Historical Commission)

to life: it is hard to sit all night and eat bitter medicine, but sometimes life is like that. The crescent moon provides a visual representation of Mother Earth, or the female from which life comes, and so the line drawn from one tip of the moon to the other is the road of life to old age as well as the circle of life. The drum sends prayers to the Creator, while the water mixed with charcoal inside represents rain, thunder, and clouds. Water is a cleansing, purifying agent, and alone it symbolizes womanhood. Fire and water are elements that all people depend on. Juniper represents all the green plants that live upon the earth, but this one never dies. Sage, the gourd, and staff are objects that communicate to and through the spirit world. Indeed, one reason that the symbols of the Native American Church are so well accepted is that they allow room for individual interpretation and expression, increasing the depth of meaning based upon a participant's ideas.

As Clifford Duncan, leader of the Native American Church on the Uintah-Ouray Reservation, said, "I've always looked at peyote as a way of life, tied in with the culture of each tribe for generations and generations.... We understand in a way that goes back thousands of years."[64]

Today the Native American Church on White Mesa is directed by members of the Cantsee family under a charter renewed in 2002. Meetings are held on any number of occasions that can include many of the Christian or national holidays, such as Easter, Christmas, and Thanksgiving, or when someone is seeking a blessing or celebrating a birthday. The size of the meeting varies, but thirty-five in attendance is fairly typical. When older residents participate, the language of choice is Ute, but if younger people are present, English is used. Often people talk of Christ, but at White Mesa the Bible is not part of the service. Instead, symbols such as the fire, staff, earth, and the Creator provide the teachings used in songs or prayers intoned by the leader or participants. Either store-bought or mountain tobacco, as well as sage and sweetgrass, carry the prayers to the holy beings.[65] The church, based on Ute symbols, provides a connection to traditional beliefs that resonate with past practices.

The Church of Jesus Christ of Latter-day Saints (Mormons) is also present on White Mesa. As noted in chapter 14, the efforts of Blanding missionaries visiting Allen Canyon in the 1920s, as well as the educational and religious labors of Albert R. Lyman in the 1940s, bore fruit in the 1950s with the creation of the Indian branch of the Mormon Church in the north part of town. While church records lack information concerning the development of the White Mesa Saints into a local church or branch, there appears to have been a consistent missionary effort by white members to encourage participation. Clessa Black and her husband, Anthon, served as missionaries in the late 1960s and early 1970s. This included bringing people in to attend meetings. One time Anthon brought a passel of twenty-two children to Blanding for services. He thought the branch would have a good congregation that day, and it did, until the car stopped, and all but three headed for town.[66]

On a more serious note, John and Jane Dutchie attended the Indian branch with their daughter. After a meeting a car accidentally hit the girl and killed her; the people of White Mesa stopped attending. Those serving on missions for the Mormon Church realized that they needed to start holding services on White Mesa and offering programs such as Mutual, which provides religious instruction and activities for youths; Primary, which does the same for younger children; and Relief Society, which teaches homemaking skills to women. As long as spiritual lessons accompanied the activities, it could all be counted as part of the missionary effort. The big question was where

to hold these meetings. One option was the home of the late Carl Ketchum, whose family had abandoned the structure after he died there. After several Mormon women had spent a day on White Mesa trying to find a place to meet, this remained the only possibility. Older Utes in the community refused to go there, but two or three community members said they were not afraid of the spirits inhabiting the structure and so would attend. The goats and sheep that had domiciled in the building now found themselves outside as the women set to work fixing it up.

Arthur Dutchie and his wife, Ruth, were among the first to attend, and although they never joined the Mormon Church, they made sure that their sons participated regularly. Three times a month Relief Society sisters brought quilting pieces to the house and showed the Ute women how to cut, sew, and tie quilts. On the fourth visit of the month there were cooking lessons, in which the recipes and skills of both cultures were shared. One Saturday morning each month the Primary held activities for the younger children, and on weekdays there were Mutual meetings. Sunday meetings became possible after Lorenzo Hawkins became the first branch president in the early 1970s. This ecclesiastical unit was classified as a dependent branch, affiliated with the Second Ward in Blanding. The priesthood leadership and their families comprised the core of those attending. On the Ute side it became apparent that some families would not participate if certain other families were present; however, two Utes—Delbert Begay and James Morris—served as branch presidents in the early to mid-1980s. Stella Eyetoo recalls, "It was good because they prayed. They prayed for everybody."

Where to meet continued to be a problem. At one point a house on the north end of the community looked like a possibility, although it too had been abandoned after a death. After members cleaned and prepared it, but before a meeting could be held, someone poured ashes down the chimney, send-

The Blanding Indian Branch of the Church of Jesus Christ of Latter-day Saints in the 1950s. Predominantly Navajo but with a good sprinkling of Ute members, the branch was an early attempt to gather Native Americans into a setting where they would feel comfortable and could learn church leadership. Eventually Ute members began meeting on White Mesa. (Courtesy of Gary Shumway)

ing the message that the Mormons were not welcome. Church members sought another place. They met in two other houses and the White Mesa Community Building in succession until in 1981 local builder Scott Hurst, also a high councilman, hauled a large trailer from Arizona and set it up close to the main road to serve as a chapel. Attendance continued to fluctuate between a low of ten and a high of fifty, the former number being closer to the median. Some were nonmembers, such as Patty (Mills) Dutchie, who maintained traditional ways but served faithfully as a counselor in Relief Society. In October 1979 the Indian branch moved to independent status, realizing autonomous leadership, but the need for a more permanent building persisted.[67]

Years took their toll on the trailer. The hollow core door barely functioned, mice ran rampant, and the water pipes froze regularly. Things had deteriorated to the point that Kent Tibbitts, local LDS stake physical facilities representative, began to press church authorities for a better structure.[68] Following approval by Stake President Preston Nielson, he began working with church leadership in Farmington, but they disapproved of paying for materials and enlisting a volunteer labor force for construction. There was a counteroffer of a prefabricated Boise Cascade home that could be delivered to the site, but that did not seem best. The branch had reached the church's target goal of an average quarterly attendance of fifty people, signifying sufficient need. Following a series of meetings, none of which were overly optimistic, a short phone call from Salt Lake headquarters said that sufficient funds remained at the end of that building year for one more chapel of

Construction gets under way for the new chapel on White Mesa, 1987. The old trailer on the right served as the meeting house for years but fell into disrepair. As membership expanded, a more permanent structure became necessary. (Courtesy of Steve Lovell)

the desired size, but that the application had to be filled out and accompanied by a $5,000 check sent to Salt Lake in less than a week. Kent spent two days filling out the detailed form, while Preston Nielson and his two counselors went to every ward in Blanding that Sunday and solicited donations. At the end of the day, the stake president wrote a check for the desired amount to accompany the paperwork, just in time to meet the deadline. White Mesa would soon have its chapel.

Tibbitts approached Cleal Bradford, executive director of the White Mesa Ute Tribal Council, and community members about buying some land where the trailer now sat and constructing a permanent chapel. He submitted a request for two acres, was initially denied, but then received permission to lease the property for twenty-five years. The proposed building was to have vinyl siding, but concerns with durability and potential vandalism led church authorities to grant special permission for a brick exterior. Final inspection of the completed edifice brought a welcome surprise. The infamous "punch lists" that accompany a final inspection of a building before turning it over to the owner often contain many items that need to be fixed. But Ernie Sondregger's Construction Company had performed flawlessly: there was not one

correction or addition that needed to be made, something that the church architects had never witnessed before.

On November 1, 1987, the day of the White Mesa Chapel dedication, more than a hundred people from the community and Blanding crammed into the meeting house, designed for sixty-six, filling the chapel and spilling into the hallways and rooms. Stan Bronson, a local musician, wrote a special hymn called "The Saviors of Avikan," sung by a Ute and Anglo choir. Its refrain urged: "Arise, arise the Grandfathers whisper, / Their voices are heard in the land. / Arise, arise, the Shepherd is calling / the saviors of Avikan."[69] Branch President Steve Lovell used the song as a text for his sermon and explained much of the "inspired" meaning behind the words.[70] There had been no vandalism of the old trailer, although it was certainly flimsy enough to stop no one, and there would be no vandalism of the chapel either. Kent Tibbitts and Lovell both affirm that the people "really respect that building." Perhaps one reason for that is the story told in the community about the following summer, when a half dozen crows for a couple of months delighted in pecking at the weather stripping on the front door and at the windows. Their activity in the area made quite a mess, but most important, it symbolized to some that evil had failed to break into the chapel. Crows, as scavengers, eat dead refuse and are associated with bad things. But after "They wore their beaks out," they gave up.[71] It truly seemed a sacred place. Record attendance reached a peak in 1996, when ninety-nine people participated in a sacrament meeting; normal attendance was closer to fifty or sixty, but funerals could draw as many as three hundred.[72]

Beyond the physical and economic challenges of obtaining a trailer and then a chapel were spiritual ones. Delbert Begay and James Morris, church members from White Mesa, served as branch presidents during the first half of the 1980s. The membership accepted both men, but there were other problems. As early as 1983 Morris requested that Stake President Preston Nielson, his counselors, and the High Council come to White Mesa "for the purpose of dedicating the community of White Mesa for the growth and spiritual prosperity of the struggling branch."[73] Kneeling in prayer, the group, through President Nielson, "rebuked the evil spirits and cast Satan out of the area. All evil actions that weaken and destroy spiritual growth were denounced," and unity in the branch encouraged.

Similar issues faced other branch presidents. Steve Lovell remembers calling five families in the community to begin attending church. Every one of them, at some point, complained of evil spirits stopping their progress, physically bothering them, inflicting them with serious sickness, and tormenting their children. Prayers and blessings for the sick followed, and each situation was resolved. Attendance now fluctuated between twelve and forty people, and many participated in the two-acre garden planted in Blanding for members. Even with all of the ups and downs in the weekly, monthly, and yearly activities, Lovell summarized his three years as branch president as "absolutely beyond

any other spiritual experience I ever had because it dealt with the powers of the priesthood to the people. In the process, the bonds of love developed when spiritual things took place. There is no question that the people are deeply spiritual people and they are bold to ask for blessings through the power of the Spirit. God loves them through a way that they can receive it."[74]

Even today residents talk about spirits in or near the community. Some people believe that when funerals are held in the community recreation center, a spot for sports and not consecrated for religious purposes, evil spirits may attend. Their presence is not only sensed but observed. One person said that she had been pushed by a spirit, while others testify to the unexplainable opening and slamming of doors, lights turned on and off, and voices from the unseen. The only explanation given for these phenomena is that the building, unlike a church, has not been blessed, and so "there are a lot of spirits that dwell there."[75]

North of White Mesa, not too far from the UMETCO (now Dennison) mill, a powerful medicine man is buried. At night his spirit is believed to roam about and follow people walking in the area.[76] Jack Cantsee Sr. had such an experience with that spirit. One day he and a friend were making their way back from Allen Canyon after getting their car stuck. As they neared this spot in the twilight, a sudden chill came over both men, stopping them from moving. A bird on the road kept hopping toward them, "just sneaking around," coming closer, closer. Edward Dutchie pulled up in his car, and the two jumped in before Dutchie could even ask what was wrong. When they told him the feelings they had just experienced, he said, "You guys are walking where the bad spirit is. There is a bad man buried just over that hill in that bowl near White Mesa Mill. A Ute was buried there who was a bad man and used to do witchcraft."[77] Jack believed that

Patty Dutchie—holding a beautifully beaded leather cradleboard with a wicker frame and sunshade—stands before the completed LDS chapel on White Mesa, early 1990s. Although she never joined the church, continuing with traditional ways, Patty served faithfully in the Relief Society. (Photo by Carol Edison, courtesy of Utah Arts Council)

the bird was a physical manifestation of the evil medicine man, who had the power to curse those he found.

Stella Eyetoo explains what she sees as the connections between the old beliefs and those of the Mormon Church. In her eyes, Sináwav and Heavenly Father (God) are the same person, and so there is no difference in using either name. The Worship Dance was a "stepping stone" provided in the past to prepare the Ute people for what was to come, when their language and old ways were lost. It was "a way of recognizing a spiritual way that people would come to know God."[78] Now that the younger generation is losing the Ute language and living more like Anglos, they do not participate in the Worship Dance but instead follow the religious path provided by the Mormon faith. Loretta Posey says that she converted to Mormonism because she "felt comfortable with the feeling and the prayers."[79] But it was her experience with a priesthood blessing that healed her niece's hip that convinced Loretta that this was the church for her.

Lola Mike and Stella once told me an often repeated story and then asked to have it told back to them to make sure it was accurate and understood. The story goes that once, in Allen Canyon, there was a group of Ute people playing cards. When they looked up, a man with long hair and dressed in a robe stood watching them. When he walked, he left no footprints. The man said that he was Jesus Christ, the caretaker of this world, and that Heavenly Father had sent him to watch over the people. He then went down Cottonwood Wash, where he encountered Jim Mike and Harry Mike and repeated the message. At first the men and their horses were startled, but after settling down, Jim Mike asked if he was hungry, but learned he was not. Jesus told Jim that he would come again, and that Jim would live for a long time, which he did. Stella was in the hospital with Jim Mike when he died at the end of his very long life. He said, "Where are my shoes? I am leaving." He put them on and died.[80]

Pochief and Billy Mike told a slightly different, more detailed version of this event. In August 1920 Jim and Harry Mike, with Jack Fly and another man, met Jesus, who called Jim by his sacred, secret name. The men conversed, asking where the Savior had come from, did the hot sand near Cottonwood Wash burn his bare feet, and was he hungry. Jesus then showed them scars from his crucifixion and said, "I want you to know, you would not have done this to me."[81] The group continued on its way, noting that a Model T Ford was traveling in the same direction that the Savior had gone. Upon their return, the men followed the tracks, which indicated he had ridden a ways in the car, gotten out, crossed some sand dunes, and then disappeared. Some Navajos living on Douglas Mesa told of his arrival in their camp a few weeks later, how he healed a sick person and then left, his tracks again vanishing after a

short distance. This story has become an important link between the past and the beliefs of some Latter-day Saints living on White Mesa today.

Considering the long religious history of the Weenuche Utes, particularly the events of this last century, one sees recurring threads that course throughout. The Utes are a deeply spiritual people, invested as much in the unseen, spiritual world as they are in the material one. During the past hundred years, whether looking at the loss of traditional medicine men (abandonment), the introduction of the Native American Church (adaptation), or the adoption of the Church of Jesus Christ of Latter-day Saints, underlying values of respect for the individual, love of family, appreciation of nature, thankfulness for the Creator, and reverence for spirituality have persisted. There is also recognition of evil and those who practice it. The Utes have been dealt with harshly. If this past is any indicator of the future, the people of White Mesa will continue to invest their lives in faith sprung from a tradition of spirituality.

CHAPTER 18

Ironic Industries and Traditional Ties

Shifting Fortunes of the White Mesa Utes, 1950–2010

Deep inside of me I am still with my Indian ways and a lot of times I can't make up my mind. I'm sitting alone and I just can't hold myself down. Sometimes I want to go back and I always dream about my old times of wandering, roaming, walking, and horseback riding and all the free time I had at home. You know, seeing lots of animals and plants and whatever I used to know. I miss all of that and sometimes think I am tied down.

Patty Dutchie

History, as a discipline, offers a longitudinal perspective over time that often ends with irony. What was opposed in the past becomes readily adopted in the present, providing what the dictionary explains as an "incongruity between what might be expected and what actually occurs" — or irony.[1] This final chapter in the history of the White Mesa Utes provides a glimpse of where the people are today — and how few would have guessed one hundred, or even sixty, years ago where they would end up given their previous history. Still, with all of the shifts and change, a rich heritage continues to course through their culture and community, providing guidance and stability at a time when all the world is on an accelerated path of transformation. The past as prologue prepares those in the present for the future.

Starting in the late 1870s and continuing through the 1920s, the Utes of southeastern Utah struggled against the white livestock industry. In the early years this meant combat with the Colorado cowboys, resulting in the Pinhook Draw fight (1881), the Soldier Crossing fight (1884), the Beaver Creek massacre

(1885), and the Tse-ne-gat Bluff incident (1915), not to mention an ongoing low-grade conflict with Mormon and non-Mormon ranchers in Utah over grazing rights and subsistence living. So to think of the Utes eventually becoming cowboys themselves may seem strange. But it happened. The White Mesa Utes, with Towaoc's assistance, launched into the cattle industry, adding significant herds to their small flocks of sheep and goats.

On October 27, 1955, the Ute Mountain Utes bought 800 acres of private land in Comb Wash with grazing permits for surrounding public lands from Earl H. Perkins and his wife, Tamar. That next May, fifteen residents of White Mesa formed the Allen Canyon Ute Cooperative Livestock Association, a nonprofit organization, and purchased the couple's cattle and forty acres in Comb Wash adjacent to the tribal land.[2] Raising and marketing cattle became their goal. What had been the Perkins's ranch, at the entry to Arch Canyon, was now in the hands of the Utes whose ancestors had fought against the advent of the cattle industry seventy years before. The tribal land had a reliable water source—either running or pooled—throughout the year. There was also good bottom land, as well as shelter for the livestock, making it an excellent winter range. Surrounding areas provided additional grazing; soon the new cattle company was in business.

Another point of irony was that the Allen Canyon Cooperative was fifteen years ahead of similar organizations at Towaoc. As land settlement money rolled in to the tribe between 1953 and 1954, to the tune of slightly less than $1.5 million, and again between 1967 and 1971 in amounts totaling $980,000, the people of White Mesa wanted to invest.[3] The cattle industry decreased in importance during this time, with only twelve Ute Mountain members identified as full-time ranchers, but their neighbors looked at the new industry as an opportunity. Not until 1970 did Towaoc own a cooperative enterprise, the Ute Mountain Pottery Corporation, which employed tribal members.

Dependent on mutual cooperation, the Allen Canyon Livestock Association and the Ute Mountain Ute Tribal Council sat down with the Bureau of Land Management (BLM), the Soil Conservation Service, and the Bureau of Indian Affairs (BIA) to draft a use plan. Scientific land management for the cattle industry, as first introduced in the Taylor Grazing Act, had reached new levels of sophistication. By 1968, when the group convened, there were high expectations, especially from the growing environmental movement. The grazing area sprawled over 115,000 acres—65,000 belonging to the BLM, 41,000 to the Forest Service, 7,000 to the state, and 1,500 to the tribe.[4]

The Utes held grazing privileges for 527 cattle (3,951 AUMs) based on the concept of winter-summer range rotation. By controlling the base property and the permit, tribal members ran their own cattle under the Allen Canyon Livestock Association with BIA advisers. The problem was that 67 percent of the range was classified as in either poor or bad condition, with only 2 percent in good condition.[5] Severe erosion caused by overgrazing took its toll. To prevent losing the grasses beyond recovery, the BLM divided the land into six pastures with a limited time allotted for each one. Indian ricegrass was the key species on native ranges. Upper Comb–Arch Canyon Pasture served as the gathering and drift way to and from the forest and other surrounding locations. The BLM and the livestock company shared joint responsibility to make the plan work and improve the ranges.

The Allen Canyon Cooperative hired Harry Lang, who for years mended fences, pushed cows, maintained pasture and water sources, and generally "rode herd" over the operation. It was a daunting task given the size and nature of the range, as well as the fact that except for two annual round-ups when owners assisted, he had sole responsibility. But even Harry, whose sense of humor earned the epithet of "the Bob Hope of White Mesa," had to admit that there were times when the job was tough.[6] A snapshot from 1976–1977 illustrates what he faced. The BLM files tell of grazing trespass after grazing trespass: March 8—180 cows; December 15—9 cows; February 21—44; March 16—21; March 24—7; April 14—10; April 26—18; April 27—24; July 2—4; August 31—10; and November 9—52. Charges based on AUMs followed.[7] Threats to entirely remove grazing privileges were also made. The livestock company worked hard to stay apace with its cattle, rotating the herd to its different pastures, while the BLM tried to be good neighbors yet uphold the schedule.

As time went on, the cattle company grew. At one point there were six employees and 700 head of livestock. Contributing to this growth was new financial management under the White Mesa Ute Council. By the mid-1980s this organization had purchased from the still-remaining ten owners their shares of the herd and placed its care and profits under a single institution that used

The Allen Canyon Livestock Association provided employment and income for tribal members, but as southeastern Utah became increasingly popular for its scenic beauty and prehistoric ruins, the practices of the livestock industry were continually challenged. (Courtesy of White Mesa Ute Council)

the proceeds for the welfare of all the people on White Mesa. Edward Dutchie Jr. served as their representative on the tribal council at Towaoc, as well as chairing the newly named White Mesa Cattle enterprise committee. Familiar with livestock and aware of local needs and tribal politics, Edward did an excellent job in meeting expectations.[8] An additional permit on North Elk Ridge, a favorite camping area in the old days, provided expansion for a combined herd of 725 cattle.

Still, there were people who objected to this venture. Environmental groups led the list. Their growing activism, combined with increased tourism, led to direct conflicts with stockmen grazing cattle in highly traveled areas, especially Comb Wash, with its five tributaries of Arch, Mule, Fish Creek, Owl, and Road Canyons. By 1989 enough manure had been splattered in the wrong places that a lawsuit was filed.[9] Familiar players drew the line in the sand. The National Wildlife Fed-

eration, Southern Utah Wilderness Alliance (SUWA), and law professor Joseph M. Feller were arrayed on one side. On the other side of the stream stood the BLM, American and Utah Farm Bureau Federations, Public Lands Council, National Cattlemen's Association, American Sheep Industry Association, and the Ute Mountain Ute Tribe.

The charges against the BLM and its co-respondents were many and varied but fell into three main categories: (1) the BLM was not a wise steward because of a poor assessment of the land's potential in its environmental impact statement (EIS); the land was badly abused and needed a plan for recovery; and the cultural (Mokwič) and recreational resources were being destroyed. Experts from various disciplines testified on both sides as to what they saw happening.[10]

The debate dragged on into 1993, when the court reached a settlement. There would be no cattle grazing in the five tributary

In the 1980s the headquarters of the White Mesa Ute Council was a renovated house that also served briefly as an LDS chapel. Another home became a learning center. In these humble circumstances, the council wrote grants and developed programs that began to improve the community's quality of life. (Courtesy of White Mesa Ute Council)

canyons. The BLM agreed that given the topography and the high rate of recreational visitation, it would not pursue the avenue left open to them of developing an EIS for each canyon so that they could be used for grazing. Given the canyons' recreation value, cattle were not compatible with this environment.[11] As for Comb Wash, roughly the northern two-thirds remained open to Ute cattle, but political winds blew in new leadership that changed the profitability of the business, and the size of the herd shrank along with the Ute land base. The White Mesa Cattle Company sold its stock to the tribe in 2000 and got out of the cattle business, but not before it had served as a major contributor to other investments.

The last quarter of the twentieth century brought additional challenges requiring organization and sophistication. What had been handled historically by group leadership in the form of strong personalities such as Mancos Jim, Johnny Benow, Polk, and Posey gave way to committees and councils. There was no doubt that opportunities lay ahead, but how to access and implement them was another question. The people of White Mesa had for twelve years watched the Utah

Navajo Development Council in Blanding provide services, obtain grants, and generally improve the lives of their people by using oil royalty money and a wide variety of different sources. Under the direction of Cleal Bradford, this organization had proven its worth. He had lived his whole life in San Juan, knew its people, and worked to improve conditions for all. So it was not surprising that Edward Dutchie Sr. contacted him in December 1977 to tell him that the people of White Mesa had recently formed a nonprofit corporation called the Allen Canyon Ute Development Council (ACUDC). He then asked if he would consider heading their organization to direct "community development, job development, and improve services."[12]

Discussions and groundwork continued for another year and a half, with Bradford receiving pay of a dollar a month until the organization obtained enough funding for his salary. Cleal went to work, and on April 1, 1979, officially stepped into the office of executive director. There was plenty to do. The council's office space was an old home that had been doubling as a church building on Sunday. The front door hung on one hinge, every pane of glass sported either a hole or had disappeared, graffiti covered the walls, and the rags stuffed in the windows barely slowed the winter wind. The executive director's twelve-foot-square office required seven coats of paint to cover the writing on the wall.[13] Towaoc empowered ACUDC to "act for the benefit of members of the community of White Mesa," to form a seven-member board while retaining membership with the Ute Mountain Utes, and enter into direct contracting for services with the Bureau of Indian Affairs and Indian Health Service, as well as other state and federal agencies.[14] A year later the organization's name changed to the White Mesa Ute Council (WMUC).

Over the next fifteen years WMUC acted as the central agency for developing the White Mesa Ute community's economic, social, educational, and political opportunities. The budget grew from close to zero to over a half million dollars by 1994. The many activities and enterprises over this period were varied and demanded people with specialized skills and interests. In 1979 the community opened a new recreation center that made it possible to play indoor sports such as basketball, boxing, volleyball, and tennis, as well as outdoor sports such as softball so that White Mesa could become "a daytime community not just a place to sleep at night."[15] Summer youth programs, adult education, Headstart, and a community paper, *The Whispering Sage*, provided supplemental educational experiences. Four gatherings each year celebrated the Bear Dance, a Christmas dinner, White Mesa Ute History Day, and the Posey Trail Hike, bringing people together through shared experiences. Medical and dental teams provided services in a small clinic made available through the council's efforts. James Morris became the first full-time police officer in 1982, receiving assistance from county and Blanding law enforcement upon request. By mid-1983 WMUC employed twenty-five to thirty Ute local residents to provide various services, where just three years before there had only

been two employees.[16] The new enterprise of White Mesa Pottery began in 1981, employing local talent who two years later moved into Blanding as business expanded to join another ceramics operation, Cedar Mesa Pottery.[17] In June 1984 the citizens of White Mesa walked through the doors of the mesa's first gas and grocery store, built by and leased from the Ute Mountain Tribe.[18]

A full-page, front-page article in 1991 in the *San Juan Record* summarized the council's latest accomplishments. Sixteen new houses funded by Housing and Urban Development (HUD) were under construction; fifteen miles of protective fence had been built along the highway to prevent further accidents, following the death of two children on the road; and paved streets paid for by the BIA now connected individual homes in the community. Representation at Towaoc had also improved. Myers Cantsee held the first three-year term as representative of White Mesa on the Ute Mountain Ute Council starting in 1982; three years later Thomas Morris held the first position for White Mesa on the Ute Mountain Housing Authority; and the next year Myers Cantsee assumed a position on the roads committee. Councilman Edward Dutchie Jr., as the representative of White Mesa in Towaoc, pointed out, "Some tribal chairmen have been sympathetic and helped us. Others have been indifferent to our needs." Still, there can be no doubt that with increasing representation in various governmental positions, the voices of the people of White Mesa sounded louder.[19]

The last quarter of the twentieth century saw many dramatic changes, but none greater than those in education. Again, the situation is fraught with irony. Considering the Utes' struggles with boarding schools, the dormitory experience, Lyman's Westwater venture, and local resistance to integration in the 1950s and early 1960s, it is gratifying to see what has since been accomplished. A 1977 survey shows just how bleak the situation had become. In the White Mesa com-

The skyline of the White Mesa community changed with the addition of power lines. Hogans and shades sit beside new housing, marking the transition. (Courtesy of San Juan County Historical Commission)

munity there were thirty-two children not attending school, and forty others in court-ordered foster care, detention, or LDS Placement, with not one in high school.[20] By the end of the fourth grade, all the children had quit. The people at Towaoc were not faring much better, reporting that in 1980 the average education of community members was six years; nine years later, only 30 percent held a high school diploma, and only two of those had graduated from college.[21]

The White Mesa Ute Council went to work. Serving as a hub for community discussion, the council learned that many Ute parents were unfamiliar with how the San Juan School District operated. They believed that if a student was sent home for disciplinary problems, it was a final, no-return situation. There was also not a lot of effort to bring them back; however, times were changing. In 1975 two Navajo chapters (local reservation governing entities) filed a lawsuit known as *Sinajini v. The Board of Education* to determine what responsibilities the local

school district held as opposed to those of the BIA and tribal educational organizations.[22] By 1979 the answer was clear. The San Juan School District was the prime caretaker of Indian education in the county—and that included the Utes. The council opened a steady dialogue to learn what needed to be done to get the children back in school and keep them there. The district reciprocated and increased its efforts toward that goal.

Early in the process the council implemented after-school tutoring, varied services in its educational center, and a series of rewards applied consistently. For instance, the June 1981 *Whispering Sage* announced, "Winners of the attendance contest have had a week of good activities. On Saturday, May 23, about 32 winners showed up at the skating party for an evening of fun. Wednesday, May 27 saw 31 winners going to Mesa Verde for a day of hiking, eating, and educational experience. Thursday June 2 was a night of camping for 14 students who won top prize for excellent attendance the last

Pochief Mike (*left*) watches Frank Beeson install a television with rabbit-ear antennas in her hogan, 1964. Other improvements followed. (Courtesy of White Mesa Ute Council)

three months of school."[23] As the system bore fruit, it was not uncommon to find months where fifteen to twenty students were in attendance 100 percent of the time. The district did its part by supplying materials and training to local tutors on White Mesa who could reinforce the lessons learned in school. Five years after implementing these efforts, the council pointed to the fact that 42 percent of the White Mesa community was involved in some type of public or higher education, all Headstart-eligible students were enrolled, and almost all of the K-12 students were, too, with twenty-eight of them in high school. "In 1984, seven White Mesa youths graduated from high school. Up to that time, total White Mesa high school graduates numbered seventeen."[24] Bradford proudly proclaimed, "There was not one child from White Mesa who was out of the community on court placement. They were back home. There was not one on LDS Placement. They were back home. There was not one cut loose. One hundred percent were attending school. That was a result of

the community group who just said, 'Hey. Our community is in crisis and we've got to do something about it.' And they did."[25]

Maintaining this record of enrollment with stabilized students was not easy. Reports concerning school district success showed how difficult it could be. In 1989 University of Utah professor Donna Deyhle published "Pushouts and Pullouts: Navajo and Ute School Leavers," based on research in San Juan County going back to 1984. Using both quantitative and qualitative investigative techniques, she painted a dismal picture of high school students who dropped out. Sometimes separating but often conflating Ute information with that of the Navajo, Deyhle tracked a total of 1,489 youths using a database that encompassed eight years. While she does not specify how many were Utes, instead stating her calculations in scaled percentages, another report covering approximately the same time period suggests a total population of 98 Ute students with a drop-out rate of 34 percent (33 students).[26]

The White Mesa Learning Center, mid-1980s. The center offered a variety of services from driver's education to high school tutoring to college classes. As a result, many students' academic records greatly improved. (Courtesy of White Mesa Ute Council)

Deyhle's focus was on those who left school and never returned. Summarizing her data, she found, among other things, that of the Ute students, 78 percent felt the teachers did not care, 88 percent that the teachers did not help, and 64 percent that school was irrelevant; 78 percent had no parental support, and 92 percent had problems at home.[27] Ethnographic comments were just as damning. "The Ute complained bitterly that their teachers did not care about them or help them in school.... 92% of the Ute said problems in the form of alcohol or drug abuse, crowded homes, fighting parents, and unemployment existed in their homes.... The Navajo and Ute, however, were not silent when expressing their sense of racial discrimination, isolation, and of being 'unwanted' by many in the Anglo community."[28]

White Mesa Ute Council education staff questioned the Deyhle report, believing there were actually more positive relationships within public education. The school district found her results an especially bitter pill to swallow. Conversations with district employees who worked with Deyhle during her research implied that the data were skewed, questions were designed to obtain a desired response, and that the whole effort had the intended outcomes prevalent during this era of championing an "underdog" and "white bashing." Whether this was the case or not, Deyhle's conclusions paint a picture of social disruption and the challenges that the White Mesa community faced.

Youth from the most disjointed and fractured culture, the Ute, were most likely to feel school to be either a threat to their identity or irrelevant to their lives. None of the Utes spoke Ute. They had a 64% dropout rate from high school. Less than a handful had ever been to college. The unemployment rate on their reservation is over 80%. They were confrontational in their stance to school and many teachers expressed fear and discomfort with them in their classrooms. Facing a school that refused to acknowledge their "Uteness" in any positive contemporary light and coming from homes that transmitted little of "traditional" Ute culture, these youth clearly were living in the margin.[29]

Ten years later, in 1999, the school district paid for an external evaluator, Carolyn Shields, to conduct another study. Her two-hundred-page report focuses on the 578 White and 563 Navajo students who responded to her survey. The responses of the twenty-six Utes in the Blanding middle and high schools were dwarfed in comparison, but do provide information about what was occurring at White Mesa. Among the Utes, 100 percent lived in homes with electricity and had television; 96 percent had running water; 84 percent had phones; 81 percent spoke English; 84 percent considered themselves good readers, compared to 41 percent of the Navajo students; 70 percent said their family followed traditional beliefs and practices of their culture; and 80 percent planned to teach those traditions to their children.[30] They also colored a different picture than Deyhle about what was taking place in the schools. Of the combined responses from both schools, 75 percent felt that the teachers cared about their learning, 84 percent felt respected, 80 percent cared about learning, 72 percent respected their teachers, and 78 percent felt their cultural heritage was accepted.[31] The students gave lower percentages to teachers for making the subject interesting (33 percent), understanding the student (45 percent), and having high expectations (64 percent). While these figures do not reflect the feelings of students who dropped out, as did Deyhle's, the survey shows that those who stayed in school came away with a generally positive impression.

Blanding offered further educational opportunities. In 1978 the College of Eastern Utah in Price opened a full-time campus. Small numbers of Ute students began attending, so the college reciprocated by teaching three courses—psychology, English, and physical education—in White Mesa in 1981. A year later Jeanette Badback became the first Ute student to receive a certificate of completion in clerical studies. Two years later Joe Lehi, Mary Jane Cantsee, Bernadine Dutchie, and Jennie Morris earned their associate's degrees.[32] The number of students fluctuated over the years, but its highest enrollment, in 1991, was thirteen in various programs.[33] When one considers previous enrollments in high school, these numbers indicate that more Utes were pursuing higher levels of education than ever before.

Even more miraculous, and equally ironic, is the educational endowment that the White Mesa Ute Council supported through their executive director's urging. One of the early issues in Ute education in Blanding had been who was going to pay for it. Funds from Towaoc had paid for teachers, supported the dormitory experience, and hauled students to boarding schools. But when that money dried up, so did the opportunity for education. The endowment actually secured funding for all Native Americans and qualified Anglos in San Juan County who wished to enroll in higher education without leaving home.

The process started with application for a federal Title III challenge grant that would match local funds at a two-to-one ratio. The San Juan Foundation, another nonprofit organization for which Cleal Bradford was executive director, accepted the major role of obtaining local funds from various organizations, the White Mesa Ute Council being one of them. The College of Eastern Utah—San Juan Campus acted as applicant. The council had already been providing limited scholarships to college-bound students, but the amount required at this time surpassed anything they had yet dreamed. Starting with $20,000 of existing scholarship funds and $5,000 from cattle company profits, the group approached Towaoc to see if they would like to participate by matching funds that would open higher education opportunities in San Juan County for any

Ute Mountain Ute student who would like to attend. The tribe was not interested but loaned $25,000, with the council's cattle herd as security. Additional funds came from county PILT (payment in lieu of taxes) money and funds granted by the state legislature, and when federal matching funds were added, the total amount available for the White Mesa Ute part of the endowment was $710,000.[34] The total corpus was $6 million, the remainder being divided among three other subfunds: the Cal Black Memorial, Native American Scholarship, and Utah Navajo Scholarship. In 1993 the first scholarships were awarded. Today, because of reinvestment of interest, the White Mesa share of the fund is over $2 million.[35]

What this did for the people of White Mesa, who invested $50,000, was ensure that any Ute residing in San Juan County had guaranteed funding as long as they maintained a C average (2.0). Funds to do this came from the interest earned by the corpus, which could be withdrawn at a rate of 11 percent each year; recently that percentage has increased to 13 percent. The people of White Mesa operate their own screening committee for applicants, have representation on the college's scholarship committee, and are debt-free from any previously incurred loans. Ironically, their participation made it possible for the entire project to move forward at an increased level, assisting students of Native American, Anglo, and other ancestry to apply for the other subfund resources as county residents.

With all of this progress, however, came change, which sometimes cuts like a two-edged sword. The White Mesa community, made up of roughly seventy families, has always exhibited a flair for individuality and strong opinions. Issues can prove divisive as families and groups cluster around what they feel important. Change and political maneuvering to accomplish an objective are not always welcomed, and when combined with forceful personalities, can rupture relationships. Add this to unemployment rates that were at least as high as those reported at Towaoc—between 57 percent and 80 percent in the 1980s—and conflict over solutions was bound to erupt.[36] That is what happened in White Mesa in the fall of 1994.

A few miles north of White Mesa is a uranium processing plant then called Energy Fuels, which had been in operation for fourteen years. In the old days the general vicinity became known as Yucca Sitting About (Wíisi-vü garü´) because of the profusion of yucca, wild onions, and tea-producing plants, while the area to the south end of the mesa was called White Mesa because of the clay found for pottery.[37] The owners of Energy Fuels were more interested in their own geological additions by amending their license to receive old mill tailings from a federal Superfund clean-up project underway in Monticello. The hauling of radioactive material, expansion of the operation, and danger of contamination stirred many residents of San Juan County as well as outside environmentalists to oppose this activity; others, however, welcomed increased potential for employment and saw no particular threat. Some of the people of White Mesa, however, had definite concerns and set events in motion to stop further action. Stella Eyetoo, for one, was born just to the west of the mill, had lived in the area much of her life, and did not like the smell produced by the mill. On September 19 seventy White Mesa Utes joined Navajos from Blanding, people from Towaoc, and Anglo sympathizers in a march to protest plans to increase the mill's storage capacity to allow 2.6 million yards of additional radioactive material. The group swelled to two hundred protesters under the direction of Norman Begay from White Mesa as they marched along Highway 191. Arriving at the doors of the mill, they offered prayers and speeches.

That afternoon in Monticello, Begay and his attorney, Cullen Battle, met with officials from Energy Fuels; their attorney, Hank Ipsen;

and federal administrative judge James P. Gleason to determine if there were sufficient grounds for a hearing to dispute the expansion. The protestors had a petition with "signatures of nearly every Native American over 18-years-old living in White Mesa and Westwater."[38] The opposition presented three main concerns: desecration of ancestral burials, contamination of groundwater, and increased traffic. According to Begay, the excavation of Mokwič remains fourteen years before had been a sacrilegious act that should not be repeated. "We respect our burial grounds and want the same respect from the Anglos. If they okay this mill tailings haul they will have to dig more pits and desecrate more graves. We don't want that and we don't want them to make us a waste dump."[39] Ipsen countered that on February 7, 1979, White Mesa officials had signed a letter agreeing to the construction of the mill, and that no mention had been made about this concern. Neither side addressed how the Mokwič were related to the Utes. Begay also charged that drinking water on White Mesa had become spoiled and now had to be hauled from Blanding. He presented no proof of this claim. As to the anticipated increased traffic, there was no doubt. There definitely would be more trucks hauling materials—an estimated 110,000 round-trips over a three-year period—which could be a problem for the community and other traffic along the route.[40] By January 1995 the debate had ended. Assistant Energy Secretary Thomas Grumbly decided to bury the materials near Monticello and forego the potential risk of hauling.

Two weeks after the fall protest there were further rumblings, this time on White Mesa. In a 5 to 2 vote, the council board discussed releasing Bradford from his position as executive director. This was made possible by the loss of two members in a local election that empowered two new people, not on friendly terms with Bradford, one of whom was Norman Begay. He publicly announced that "the community has wanted this for a long time" and that was why he was elected.[41] From his perspective, Bradford had gone against the wishes of the people of White Mesa by supporting the mill's expansion; by stifling the growth of new business in the community, including the removal of the pottery business to Blanding; and by supporting Energy Fuels in not allowing a water pipeline to cross its property unless the community agreed to the company's conditions. The owner of Cedar Mesa Pottery flatly denied that he had left White Mesa because of anything that Bradford had done—it was purely a business decision. Energy Fuels also felt that allegations against them were "absolutely untrue." But at this point it did not matter—Bradford was out of office.

On the other hand, Cleal felt that he had served well, had voiced the desires of the people, and was interested in making a smooth transition. He offered to resign, which the council accepted, and also offered to assist the person taking his place for a period of two weeks to six months; in a little over a week he was gone. The tribe started to withdraw its different programs to manage them from Towaoc. Even the livestock owned by the White Mesa Cattle Company came under tribal control. Over the next five years, after which Bradford returned as executive director, the herd dwindled to less than 150.[42]

Bradford's replacement, Mitchell Kalauli, did not fair much better. He did not assume office until February 1995, when he began a ninety-day probation period. At the end of May he received a very positive evaluation, but the next month the board placed him on administrative leave. A flurry of accusations and counter-accusations followed. At the bottom of it all were issues between families who controlled power and others who wanted to. Norman Begay and other members were removed from the White Mesa Ute Council board; the chairwoman of the Ute Mountain Ute Tribal Council, Judy

Knight-Frank, leveled charges of corruption; unorthodox voting procedures plagued the entire political process; and program funding became endangered. To Kalauli, "This board has placed itself in jeopardy both legally and in its legitimacy as the voice of the White Mesa community."[43] A month later, after garnering two-thirds of the community's support, the board reinstated him and relieved two council members.

While community members hailed these moves as proof that the "democratic process still works," things did not get any better for Kalauli. In August the council formally reinstated him as executive director, but by November it had released him.[44] He complained of powerful factions using the council for personal agendas, lack of cooperation with the leaders in Towaoc, illegal political procedures, and a deaf ear turned to the people. No matter. For the next four years the councils at Towaoc and White Mesa remained in turmoil due to internal and external forces. Issues not only remained but compounded. In 1997 International Uranium Corporation, which was then in charge of the mill north of White Mesa, offered to accept radioactive waste originating from a Nevada test site. Begay and others protested. By the time the legal process ended, the materials had already arrived at the mill and been processed, and Begay had died in a car accident.[45] Reversing the mill's action was impossible, but future deals would come under closer scrutiny and be appealed in court. In 2003 and again in 2006 environmental protesters and some White Mesa Utes raised the same issues of airborne and waterborne contamination, and desecration of burial grounds, but with no apparent effect.[46]

In 1999 the tribe approached Bradford to see if he would like to again become a part-time employee of the White Mesa Ute Council. He accepted and began to pick up the pieces from five years of conflict. A little later Dennison Mines merged with IUC and began to seek better relations with the

Cleal Bradford, executive director of the White Mesa Ute Council, 2005. Noted for organizing and building partnerships, Bradford has served in this position for more than twenty-five years; his efforts have influenced many aspects of life on White Mesa. (Courtesy of White Mesa Ute Council)

Utes. For the next three years the company offered scholarships to White Mesa students, but as cooperation warmed, a new concept emerged. In order to help community members, improve relations, and provide employment, a new organization—White Mesa Incorporated (WMI), a for-profit company—emerged. The concept behind it was that the mill would contract with this organization for workers, and WMI would handle payroll and administrative matters for its employees. From this came a percentage of the payroll that would be paid to individual shareholders. For a couple of years this proved successful, but since the shareholders were primarily White Mesa Ute Council board members, problems with conflict of interest arose. By 2006 the council had bought all of the shares, and the for-profit company became a subsidiary of the nonprofit council, with all proceeds assisting the people of White Mesa.[47]

The success of WMI surpassed all expectations. Who would have thought at the outset that it would become one of the biggest employers (not including state or federal programs) in the county. But it was; and the irony of the situation is evident. Compare two articles written ninety years apart. The *San Juan Blade* of Blanding published one entitled "Indians Help on White Mesa; Noble Redman Works Best on Empty Stomach" in 1917. The gist of it told of how twenty to thirty Utes cleared sagebrush, threshed beans, cut corn, or hoed weeds in a ten-mile swath around the city. "Nearly any one of them will work by the day or on a small contract, especially if he is hungry."[48] The remainder of the article pointed out how they labored with "real nip" the first day, but after they ate, serious efforts ceased, leading to a poor wage.

In 2008, headlines read, "White Mesa Inc. Now One of County's Largest Employers."[49] The company had just surpassed placing over one hundred workers at the mill, with a two-week payroll of $156,000.[50] By the end of the year this figure had climbed to over $3 million, with 117 employees, as the facility processed 1,700 tons of uranium a day.[51] The workforce was 60 percent Navajo and Ute, 33 percent Anglo, and 5 percent Hispanic. Applicants passed their drug tests and were ready for work at a time when Utah and the rest of the nation were suffering from layoffs and cutbacks, and many job candidates were failing screening tests. At the height of this mill run WMI employed twelve Utes simultaneously.

Success not only breeds success, but also envy. The lack of acceptance, at times, of the White Mesa people by other Ute groups extends back to the time of Ouray and before. Sometimes viewed as outcasts, as "Paiutes," and as renegades, the people of White Mesa have had to chart their own course. Although relations with Towaoc have been generally cordial, in 2004 there was a divisive split based on success, resulting in the expulsion of the council from White Mesa. To understand why, one must return through a convoluted past to 1969. That year the federal govern-

ment dissolved the Consolidated Ute Agency and formed two separate entities: the Southern Ute Agency in Ignacio and the Ute Mountain Ute Agency in Towaoc, under whose supervision White Mesa fell. This move empowered the people of Towaoc to determine tribal membership, which for the Ute Mountain Ute certificate of Indian blood (CIB) is one-half.[52] There was the ever-present undercurrent among the tribe that the people of White Mesa were historically more Paiute and Navajo than Ute, and so were not as deserving of tribal services, even though several White Mesa/Allen Canyon families were now living in Colorado. Distance between the two communities and limited representation on the council also did not help.

When problems arose on White Mesa, factions developed, with some looking to Towaoc for support, while others sought local assistance. To muddy the waters further, there were also issues with jurisdiction — not just tribal, but also state and federal. The roughly seven-mile-long and five-mile-wide White Mesa community has three different types of land. Generally, those in the center of the community are tribal, those on the periphery are individual allotments, and those on the outskirts are fee lands that the tribe has bought and pays taxes on, unlike those in the other two categories. Technically the tribe does not have control over individual allotments unless that right has been given over to it. If the residents do not pay taxes, their land is considered trust land under tribal and federal supervision. For all practical purposes, Towaoc and the federal government control all activities on White Mesa. This can be both a blessing and a curse.

Perhaps the biggest rub comes with law enforcement. In 1975 Emeline Casey won a lawsuit that determined that "she was subject to the 'exclusive jurisdiction of the United States or the Ute Mountain Tribe' and not the state of Utah," and so consequently she did not have to enter a court-ordered foster home.[53] This ruling removed the ability of

Original members of the White Mesa Ute Council, 1984: *standing, left to right*, Barbara Morris, Mary Jane Yazzie, Loretta Posey, Stella Eyetoo, and Anna Marie Nat; *seated*, Myers Cantsee (who also served on the Ute Mountain Ute Council), Annie Cantsee, and Shirley Dennetsosie. (Courtesy of White Mesa Ute Council)

local law officers to go on reservation land and assist its citizens unless approved by tribal authority. The BIA soon realized that this created a protection vacuum, which the agency filled by contracting with law enforcement to assist tribal police, and providing a court for adult offenders. The FBI handles major crime investigations, as it does on other reservations. All of these jurisdictional decisions came from Towaoc, with White Mesa having a limited say.

The tribe assisted in the formation of the White Mesa Ute Council in 1979 with support from the Ute Mountain Ute Agency. As a nonprofit organization, the council received a series of responsibilities contracted by the tribal council, some of which they reaffirmed when Bradford assumed the position of executive director in 1999. Among the council's tasks were to hire staff; hold annual elections; develop community-supported projects; act as liaison with state, county, and local officials; administer contracts; and establish future programs.[54] As seen with the

development of the educational endowment and WMI, in some cases the council was meeting its objectives with dazzling results.

The Ute Mountain Ute Council had also been working hard to raise money and lower its unemployment rate. On Labor Day weekend in 1992 it opened the doors of the 30,000-square-foot Ute Mountain Ute Casino to a capacity crowd of 1,000 people who played at the 300 slot machines and 14 blackjack and poker tables. The business employed 250 people, 79 of whom were tribal members, and had an estimated payroll of $3 million.[55] Other tribally owned businesses, such as the Ute Tribal Park and Sleeping Ute RV Park, brought in additional income. So it should not be surprising that the efforts of the White Mesa Ute Council, which had been empowered by the Ute Mountain Ute Tribal Council, might also be considered part of their dealings. As Bradford explained, "There have been the tribe's attorneys, executive director, and a couple of members of the Ute Mountain Tribal Council who expressed the position that since they authorized the creation of the White Mesa Ute Council, it means they own it and all of its assets. White Mesa feels that since it is a Utah nonprofit organization functioning on the reservation by contract, that it was independent of tribal oversight, except as the annual agreement required."[56] This difference of opinion led to the split.

In March 2004 Tribal Chair Judy Knight-Frank resigned her position halfway through her term.[57] Vice President Harold Cuthair assumed her responsibilities and began to exert pressure on the council to conform to his desire for total control of their organization. Resistance followed to the point that the tribe requested that the council dissolve and turn over its assets to the Towaoc administration. Under the guise of challenging, and thus endangering, the council's sovereignty, the tribe demanded an end to its activities. The White Mesa Ute Council saw no justification for this position and had no desire to cease and desist.

There were a few options, the best one being to take the council's activities off reservation land. By doing so, it freed them to function as a nonprofit, Utah-based organization, exempt from any control by the tribe yet able to develop economic opportunities for the Ute people without impinging on tribal sovereignty. Program participation in a partnership or under supervision of the council included Headstart, San Juan Family Learning Centers, the Four Corners Enterprise Community, the Americorp VISTA Program, White Mesa Inc., and the White Mesa educational endowment. The tribe had signed previous memorandums of understanding about the council's role, but at this point refused to meet with its members for any discussion. Instead it told them to move off reservation lands and stop operating. On July 19, 2004, the White Mesa Ute Board members notified Cuthair that they had received correspondence ordering them to dissolve, vacate any tribally owned space, and close out financial

dealings with the tribe. The group abandoned the office space, severed ties with tribal support, and moved the operation to Blanding, where it remains today.[58]

White Mesa continues to have a representative on the six-member tribal council (plus chair) in Towaoc, and the White Mesa Board continues to administer its own programs, but the Ute Mountain Ute Council does not recognize the other organization's legitimacy and believes it should relinquish its assets. That is why when the White Mesa Ute Council sold forty acres of land near Arch Canyon to a private businessman in 2008, the tribe called foul. Past agreements and actions concerning the defunct cattle company surfaced, with issues of control moving to center stage.

The Ute Mountain Utes, apart from the White Mesa Utes, had their own way of adding to certain historical ironies in San Juan County. Looking back at the 1870s and 1880s, one recalls the fear and absolute hatred the Utes felt toward surveyors. The conflict with parties from the Hayden mapping crew in 1875 in Dry Valley attests to these feelings. So it is ironic that today the tribe is a major contributor to a $4 million building project at the Four Corners Monument, an edifice based solely on survey lines marking where the states of Colorado, Utah, New Mexico, and Arizona intersect. Three Utes participated with four Navajos and one Anglo on the eight-member planning committee, which in turn worked with the fifteen-member Four Corners Heritage Council board, which also enjoyed Ute representation. But it was not just about representation. The tribe put in $200,000 toward the project and was a unifying element when disagreements with other partners arose. Bradford, who had been involved with the project since its inception in 1995, commented that "the Ute Mountain Utes' involvement in this project has been great. Everybody from Ute Mountain who has participated in this has been aggressively seeking to have a project there. They feel certain they own a quarter of that monument site."[59] The discussions and implementation dragged on too long, with different tribal and state concerns interfering with the construction, but constant throughout, with no delay, the Ute Mountain Utes were consistent contributors. On September 17, 2010, Utes and Navajos joined with state and federal officials to dedicate the new, improved monument.

An equally ironic but more significant situation clusters around concerns with medical care. To understand how significant, one needs only to recall the 1950s. Historian Gary Shumway, who was born and raised in Blanding, was familiar with the circumstances at that time concerning Indian health care.[60] His mother, Grace, was not a professionally trained midwife but cared about the Navajo and Ute people living in Westwater. Traditional birthing practices usually worked well for the Indians, but when complications arose, they sent for Grace. A knock on the door at night, a hastily scribbled note, and she was on her way to deliver one of the 165 babies she helped bring into this world. There were times, however, when her skills were not enough. The first line of resolving the problem meant going to the doctor's house in Blanding with the expectant mother in the Shumways' car. The physician would come out to the vehicle and examine the patient and either correct the problem by turning the child or do what he could to make the woman comfortable. If he could not help, the next step was a torturous ride over dirt roads to Shiprock, New Mexico, the closest IHS hospital.

Twelve times Gary drove his mother and an expectant mother in a hell-bent-for-leather race between birth and death to the hospital doors. On one occasion they had a Ute woman who made it as far as Cortez, but Grace realized that even the relatively short distance remaining to Shiprock was too far. Gary pulled into the hospital, and Grace prevailed on administrators to save the woman's life by delivering the baby in the hospital. "They were not very happy about it" but re-

lented, and both child and mother survived. On another occasion, a Navajo woman from Westwater could not even make it to Cortez.

> Before we got to Monticello, Mom said, "She's not going to make it. We're going to have to go to the hospital." I said, "Mom, we've already tried that." She said, "Here's what we are going to do. You do exactly what I tell you. We're going to drive up to the hospital and you're going to run in the front doors. There's going to be a gurney sitting there. You get that gurney and bring it out to the car." So I did. We loaded the woman onto the gurney and brought her in. As soon as the doors opened there were nurses and other people running towards us so that they could get that Indian woman out of there.
>
> "You can't bring her in here; you know you can't. What are you doing?"
>
> My mother just looked at them, I remember very clearly, and said, "You've got two choices. You can let this person die right here in front of all these people in the waiting room or you can take her into the pediatrics and help her have her baby. She needs that and deserves that."
>
> They just started cussing like mad, but they took her in, and we were only there for fifteen minutes before the baby was born. This woman decided when they asked her what the baby's name was she said, "It's Gary."[61]

The purpose for recounting this incident is not to emphasize the prejudice of yesteryear, but to contrast attitudes of the past with those in the twenty-first century. In 2002 a joint Native American and Anglo project, the Blue Mountain Hospital in Blanding, was launched. A major proponent of the concept was Donna Singer, chief executive officer of the Utah Navajo Health Systems, a private, nonprofit organization. From this business came an initial $800,000, which the Ute Mountain Ute Tribal Council matched. The Utes entered into an agreement only after meeting with the people of White Mesa, who saw it as an opportunity to have services closer than Shiprock, more jobs, and a place for training future nurses. Although this was a tribal business venture, with the Ute participants being "tough, astute businessmen [and] excellent to work with," Singer felt that uppermost in their minds was what would be best for their people. There was also no doubt that without their initial investment, and that of the Navajos, none of the loans that made the structure possible would have been secured.

By the end of 2006 all the project loans were in place. Construction continued through 2007 and 2008, and the hospital was dedicated on July 4, 2009. Cost for the facility: $23 million, with $3.8 million coming from the Ute Mountain Utes, $3.8 million from the Utah Navajo Health System, and the remainder primarily from HUD-secured loans.[62] Prevalent health concerns, including cardiovascular disease, diabetes, obstetrics, and emergency medicine, are being addressed and will be further developed as IHS carves out funding and transfers it to the facility. Singer says, "The people of San Juan County, especially those in Blanding, should be very grateful and aware of the role that the Ute Mountain Utes and Navajo people played in increasing availability of medical services in this area. If it had not been for their support, this hospital would not be here."[63] As far as Stella Eyetoo is concerned, the facility "takes care of us and we do not have to go a long way," referring to the days when contracted services, other than emergencies, came primarily from Ignacio or Santa Fe.[64]

Perhaps the biggest development and change between 1950 and 2010 has been in the hearts of the people—both Ute and Anglo—of San Juan County. Their intertwined history has been a love-hate relationship, with a growing acceptance over a chasm between cultures. Both groups were products of their time and circumstance, and so should not be judged by twenty-first-century standards. Indeed, today's trend toward political correctness was bred in the turmoil of the 1960s and 1970s, when equal rights, Black Power, and the American Indian Movement (AIM) sought change through strident voices, aggressive action, and court or legislative decisions that encouraged racial and cultural acceptance. A few vignettes from the past illustrate how people and events have closed this chasm.

Thell D. Black, grandson of "E.Z." Black, recalled living in Allen Canyon in 1935 and playing with the Ute boys his age. "Those Utes were all my very best friends."[65] So one can imagine how he felt when one of the local men in Blanding tried to run Phillip Posey out of a dance in the 1950s. The Ute veteran had seen action on World War II battlefields and stood his ground, replying that "he had already been fighting for the white man and he was not going to leave." And he didn't. Posey met similar resistance when he entered an establishment for a haircut. The barber told him, "I can't cut your hair. If you have bugs, it will drive all my customers away." Phillip replied, "You cut my hair, and if you find one bug in there, I will pay you twice for what your haircut is worth." He paid the normal price. Jim Slavens, who ran the local movie theater, remembers that the Indians all sat on one side, the whites on the other.[66] This was not enforced segregation, just how people from both races felt comfortable. Black summarized the times by saying, "It was kind of rough for them [the Utes]."[67]

The times, however, were changing. In 1972 Gary Shumway and some students from the University of California encountered a group of AIM activists one night in a Blanding campground. By the end of the evening the two sides were moving toward open aggression until one of the students went for the police. The activists departed, and the next day a number of the local Indians went to authorities and renounced the outsiders' actions, saying they wanted nothing to do with AIM.[68] This incident is mentioned only to show that the mood of the era did not bypass southeastern Utah. Other things such as education, economic development, shared experience, and increased cultural sensitivity played a part in shifting perceptions.

While there were those in town who looked down on the Utes, many others were friends and lovingly gave assistance through the years. There is a certain irony in the way that Blanding fostered this love-hate relationship by creating a special place in its heart for Posey and what has become known as the Posey war. Billed as the last Indian uprising in the United States, and totally blown out of proportion, the man and the incident that carries his name are all that many people know of the White Mesa Utes. In the late 1950s and early 1960s, this enthusiasm for local history took the form of a pageant called "Echoes from the Rimrocks," staged on the east side of Westwater Canyon, with the western rim lined with cars filled with onlookers. The climax of the production was the "roundup" of the "Indians" (played by Utes, Navajos, and some Anglos) as the "cowboys" chased, captured, and incarcerated the willing participants.[69] Although everyone involved in this local morality play did it for fun and enjoyed it, the underlying perception of the Ute people was an inaccurate stereotype.

Returning to Posey as an example, the man has emerged bigger than life. Boy Scouts marked "the Posey Trail" and erected a monument where "Chief Posey shot John D. Rogers' horse during the Indian uprising in 1923"; a local singer, Stan Bronson, wrote romantic songs about the man accidentally killing his wife and the trials of his life; in 1981 dramatist Steve Lacy wrote *Posey*, a play performed in the streets of Blanding and the surrounding area with a cast of all-white actors; four years later he was involved in a presentation for *Prime Time Access* called "The Posey Wars"; and in 2007 he published the book *Posey: The Last Indian War*.[70]

The White Mesa Ute Council frequently sponsors a Posey Trail Day for the public that starts with a sumptuous breakfast. Hikers then traverse the narrow defile to the bottom of the canyon, and then ride back to the cooking site for a steak dinner and more stories. When asked why the council sponsors a hike that draws up to a hundred participants but centers on a difficult time in Ute history, Bradford replied, "Any recognition is better than none," and noted that the Ute people and guests all enjoy the outing.[71] Loretta Posey, great-great-granddaughter of the local icon, adds further perspective: "It is good for people to enjoy themselves and helps them to get along. When I am there I am not thinking about his death, but rather that he was a strong man. He stood up for his land which we still have. We still have our lands now."[72]

The attitude today shows just how far the two cultures have moved in this new direction. In September 2009 a full-page article by Buckley Jensen — born, raised, and still living in San Juan County — appeared in the *San Juan Record*. He presented a good deal of the Ute view, and then concluded by admitting that he had known primarily only the Anglo version of the Indian's life.

> My view of Chief Posey is now of a man who loved his family, his nation, and his birthright. His core values are not unlike those of many of my heroes like George Washington, Lincoln, and Churchill. He was willing to fight and die for what he believed.
>
> Where the actual truth lies is a matter of personal conjecture. However, I have come away from this project with a healthy respect for this Indian leader who gave his life that future generations would be able to retain their ancestral lands, maintain their rich culture, and eventually assimilate into the larger society of the state of Utah.[73]

Rarely does a year go by without some white student writing a paper about "Chief Posey," often placing well in a local or state history fair competition. There is nothing tired about the man's personality and the historical situation he found himself in. It also offers an opportunity to champion an "underdog" who stood bravely in the face of overwhelming odds. As Jensen notes, "where

Adoline Eyetoo working on a wedding basket. Today there are fewer than a dozen basket makers on White Mesa. Elders complain about how rheumatism and other ailments prevent them from continuing the craft, but they are eager to share their knowledge with the rising generation. (Courtesy of Rebecca Stoneman)

the actual truth lies is a matter of personal conjecture," but the answer must also be buttressed with historical fact tempered with cultural understanding.

Ties to the traditional past continue to lace through the community. Billy Mike, born in a tepee on Douglas Mesa in 1905, learned the art of flute making from Sam Ketchum when he moved to Allen Canyon. For years he was the sole craftsman continuing the art and playing the instrument. In 1990 his grandson, Aldean Ketchum (Lightning Hawk), with the help of a Utah Arts Council grant, apprenticed to the master flute maker and learned the trade; he now makes flutes and composes his own music. He has since traveled with the Utah Opera Company (1998), conducted workshops throughout the Four Corners region, and in 2002 performed in the opening ceremo-

nies of the Winter Olympic Games in Salt Lake City before an estimated audience of 2.5 billion people.[74] Aldean today shares his music on CDs, serves on the White Mesa Ute Council, assists in a language preservation project, and acts as one of the four Bear Dance chiefs for the annual event.

Aldean's wife, Wanda, practices another traditional skill, that of beadwork. She and other women, including Mary Jane Cantsee, Alice May, Adoline Eyetoo, Shirley and Sheila Denetsosie, Sarah Owl, and Diane Hungry, ply their craft with finely cut glass beads that form intricate designs on clothing, cradleboards, and a variety of objects ranging from key chains and stethoscope covers to elaborate powwow regalia. A wide band of beadwork may also stretch across the crown of a cradleboard, still used by Ute mothers. Boys are put in cradleboards made with white tanned hide and beads, while girls are slipped into cradleboards of yellow leather. The baby's umbilical cord is still placed in a pouch, often beaded and attached to the carrier, symbolizing the child's ties to its home and family.[75] Annie Cantsee, Alice May, Adoline Eyetoo, and Shirley Denetsosie keep this craft alive through knowledge and practice.

White Mesa has always been famous for its woven baskets. Weavers who still practice the art include Stella and Adoline Eyetoo, Bonita and Bonnie Lehi, Lola Mike, Janet Ketchum, Amanda May, Francis Lehi, and Imogene Pelt. Each fall, when the sumac are best, they get into a senior citizen van or private car and head for Moab or Farmington, New Mexico, to see what they can find. Sumac are not as readily available as they used to be because of property restrictions and development, and arthritis has crept into the joints of some of the older women, but the craft continues. Adoline is also one of the few who still makes woven, resin-covered water containers.[76] Selling their wares at trading posts such as Stewart Hatch's in Farmington, the elders remember his friendship, formed in the post near Allen Canyon in the 1930s. Hatch bemoans the fact that "Towaoc doesn't weave. They quit a long time ago. In fact, we don't buy very many baskets [from Ute people] now, just once in a while from White Mesa, which is about the only place."[77] While there are many Navajos involved in the craft, the number of Ute basket makers is dwindling.

One of the most important, yet most difficult, aspects of heritage to preserve is language. In 1975 the Southern Ute Tribal Council contracted with an outside linguist to create a written alphabet and dictionary to prevent language loss. Richard Young cites the council as saying, "If the language is not written, the language will surely die, as not too many members of the tribe under 30 years of age speak their native tongue."[78] The same was true for the people at Towaoc and White Mesa. The linguist produced a dic-

tionary in 1979 that the tribe made available to every household on the reservation, and the Ute Mountain Utes later worked on some language projects and offered classes to assist with preservation.

At White Mesa, Jack Cantsee associates this loss with the end of the world. He remembers Baby Deer, his grandfather, warning that "all the tribes, [including] the Ute tribe, are going to lose their ways, their language. They are going to lose all their language and become one with the white man's language. It is coming to that now.... We are losing it and our culture. We need to teach our kids how to talk their language."[79] Stella agrees, saying that the weather and seasons are changing; there are many earthquakes, caused perhaps because "the Navajos and Anglos are increasing and the Utes are not— maybe they are getting too heavy on the earth"; and the Ute language is fading away.[80] The young people cannot translate for the few remaining elders on White Mesa.

In 2008 the White Mesa Ute Council hired linguist Brian Stubbs to develop a White Mesa dictionary and language lessons specific to their dialect. The project is well under way and has now become a 250-page manuscript that will be made available to the Ute people in 2011 and eventually to the general public. Stubbs, specializing in Uto-Aztecan languages, has determined that the dialect spoken at White Mesa is one of the oldest stocks among all the Ute dialects in Utah and Colorado, and that there is also a mix of Ute and Paiute pronunciation. He hopes to eventually work with other Ute groups to explore and expand upon linguistic and cultural roots and derivations. At the center of the issue is the understanding that the language must be maintained in order to preserve the Ute worldview captured within.

Today, on a hill overlooking Westwater Canyon in Blanding, sits a modern wood- and fiberglass-sheathed tepee, home of the White Mesa Ute Council. Dedicated on March 20, 2010, by Aldean Ketchum in his native tongue, this structure symbolizes the future as much as the past. The now five-member board meets monthly to plan for future economic development as they sit where canvas tepees and brush shelters used to be. A door faces east, the direction of new beginnings, but another faces west, in the direction of the Bears Ears and Allen Canyon, both significant in their history. The council, presided over by Mary Jane Yazzie, who has served as chairman and board member numerous times in many organizations, encourages links to the past as well as bridges to the future. Their task is not easy, but necessary, and appreciated by some, but questioned by others. Wherever the future may take them, it will be their traditional ties that carry them through. The people of White Mesa can be proud of their distinctive heritage, rooted in the land they love.

Epilogue

Remember the days of old, consider the years of many generations;
ask thy father, and he will show thee; thy elders and they will tell thee.

Deuteronomy 32:7

October 10, 2009: Two dozen cars and trucks wend their way down the freshly graded one-lane road leading to the mouth of Hammond Canyon. As they descend a steep slope covered with piñon and juniper trees and enter a sagebrush flat, there are no signs of habitation except an occasional dilapidated barbwire fence. Gnarled apple trees, remnants of a bygone era, are interspersed among a grove of taller, smooth-bark cottonwoods lining the bank of the wash. The travelers climb from their vehicles, stretch, and take in the surroundings—bright yellow leaves shimmering in the sunlight, a pile of weathered boards that used to be Harry Lang's cabin, and a toppled outhouse with no sign of a pit. Across the wash, the blades of a tilted windmill creak with the breeze, but its ability to pump water from the ground is long gone.

Lawn chairs come out, a card table is set up to hold maps of the former station and surrounding irrigation systems, and photographs taken ninety years before that tell an old story in a different time. The seventy-five visitors settle in for an hour-long Utah Humanities Council program about the heyday of the Allen Canyon subagency, its agent, E. Z. Black, and Ute life in the 1920s and '30s. Some of Black's descendants sit next to people from White Mesa, sharing the past culled from written records and oral history. Prior to this, Ute elders had spent days recording their memories of what it was like when Allen Canyon hummed with activity.

Now, with the exception of the speaker's voice and an occasional squeak from a lawn chair, the site is as quiet as it was when first abandoned. Following the presentation, groups armed with maps and photos wander around the remnants of the once bustling agency, parts now covered with six-foot sagebrush. An hour later members of the White Mesa Ute Council board serve a lunch of hamburgers, hot dogs, and fry bread and then prepare to leave. As the caravan makes its way out of the canyon, the red dust settles into the ruts to await the next White Mesa Ute History Day in this spot, perhaps five or ten years hence. Like the warm sun and yellow leaves that will soon give way to winter, this event is but a fleeting moment captured in memory and a few pictures.

Time continues to flow, but not in a necessarily predictable pattern, as this White Mesa Ute history shows. Even Albert R. Lyman, who lived ninety-three years in San Juan County, did not get it right. He wrote:

The Piutes of San Juan are on their way out. As a tribe and a people they are on their way out of this tangible world. To the people who have lived as neighbors to them for seventy-two years, the people who have learned to love them in spite of all their early disagreements, this is a matter of sorrow.

One of the youngest participants at the commemoration of White Mesa Ute History Day, October 10, 2009. Never too young to learn about their people's proud heritage, Ute children and teenagers are encouraged to remember the past in preparation for the future. (Courtesy of Heather Young)

In the [eighteen] eighties and nineties, the Piutes moved in long processions across the country, dragging their tent poles behind them as they rode. With their bleating goats and sheep, their barking dogs, their loose ponies, their rattling tin-ware, and their calling back and forth one to another, they made an imposing company that could be heard for a long distance. Their camp occupied a considerable area, and if they stayed long in one place, they stripped the country like a swarm of grasshoppers. They numbered hundreds then where they number tens now. Their hundred and twenty at the present is but a faded remnant of what they were sixty years ago.[1]

Certainly there has been loss. A drive through White Mesa today takes one past houses abandoned due to death. But Stella Eyetoo can still be found outside on a warm spring day watering her trees, other senior citizens loading into a van for a trip to Towaoc or to pick sumac, and Jack Cantsee preparing the brush enclosure for the Bear Dance. But the young people look to the future, not the past. With iPod in ear, cell phone on belt, and laptop computer in hand, they have entered the twenty-first century. When one considers the changes that Lyman saw, spanning seven years shy of a century, and what lies ahead in the next hundred years, one wonders about the direction and rate in which this change will take place. What will be its themes, and with what values will they be met?

History does little good unless remembered. Learning from the past is important only when applied. No doubt there have been difficult times for the people of White Mesa. Whether considering the Spanish and Mexican periods and the burgeoning slave trade that affected so many tribes; the introduction of horses and other livestock, which both blessed and cursed the Ute way of life; encroachments on Ute land by Mormons and others, and the competition for resources; the conflicts that followed, where many of the battles were won but the war was lost; the early reservation years on allotments in Allen Canyon and later White Mesa; or the challenges of the 1950s to the present—the people of White Mesa have remained true to a number of core beliefs. One is the importance of the land. Through good times and bad, like the pole in the Sun Dance lodge, the people return to their center: the land. When Billy Mike, speaking of the old days, said, "It was as if the land owned us," he was not just talking about seasonal quests for food. He meant also a spiritual relationship established by the Creator, reflected in daily beliefs and religious practice. The future, with all of its uncertainty, still lies ahead. May the people of White Mesa greet it facing the early morning sun. Then they will remember.

Notes

Introduction

1. Albert R. Lyman, "History of San Juan County, 1879–1917," Special Collections, Harold B. Lee Library, Brigham Young University, Provo, UT.

2. Lyman, *Indians and Outlaws: Settling of the San Juan Frontier* (Salt Lake City: Publishers Press, 1980); and *The Outlaw of Navaho Mountain* (Provo, UT: Albert R. Lyman Trust, 1986).

3. Adoline Eyetoo, interview with author, July 25, 2009.

4. Forbes Parkhill, *The Last of the Indian Wars* (New York: Crowell-Collier Press, 1961).

5. Steve Lacy and Pearl Baker, *Posey: The Last Indian War* (Salt Lake City: Gibbs Smith, 2007).

6. Virginia McConnell Simmons, *The Ute Indians of Utah, Colorado, and New Mexico* (Boulder: University Press of Colorado, 2000).

7. Robert W. Delaney, *The Ute Mountain Utes* (Albuquerque: University of New Mexico Press, 1989).

8. Richard K. Young, *The Ute Indians of Colorado in the Twentieth Century* (Norman: University of Oklahoma Press, 1997).

9. Nancy Wood, *When Buffalo Free the Mountains: The Survival of America's Ute Indians* (Garden City, NY: Doubleday, 1980); Jim Carrier, *West of the Divide: Voices from a Ranch and a Reservation* (Golden, CO: Fulcrum, 1992).

10. *Early Days of the Ute Mountain Utes* (1985), *Ute Mountain Utes: A History Text* (1985), *Ute Mountain Ute Government* (1986), and *Ute Mountain Ute Stories, Games, and Noise Makers* (1986), all published by the Ute Mountain Ute Tribe, Towaoc, CO.

11. University of Utah's American West Center and Utah Division of Indian Affairs, *Utah Indian Curriculum Guide* (Salt Lake City: University of Utah Print and Mail Services, 2009).

12. William A. Haviland, *Anthropology*, 9th ed. (New York: Harcourt College Publishers, 2000), 29.

13. Stella Eyetoo, conversation with author, May 4, 2001.

14. "An Indian friend," cited in Marvin Kaufmann Opler, "The Southern Ute of Colorado," reprinted from Ralph Linton, *Acculturation in Seven American Indian Tribes* (New York: D. Appleton-Century Company, 1940), 119.

Chapter 1

1. This version of the Ute creation story came from Buckskin Charlie in 1904. The translator referred to Sináwav as "Manitou or great He-She spirit," and used no Ute name. Other accounts specify that Sináwav was the Creator's name and so is used here. This story is cited in Nancy Wood, *When Buffalo Free the Mountains: The Survival of America's Ute Indians* (Garden City, NY: Doubleday, 1980), xiii–xiv. A very similar version is provided by anthropologist Albert B. Reagan in "Wickiup Wonder Tales—Ute Legend of Creation," *San Juan Record*, May 7 and 14, 1936, 5.

2. "The Ute Indians of Southwestern Colorado," unpublished manuscript compiled by Helen Sloan Daniels, 1941, Public Library, Cortez, CO.

3. Uintah-Ouray Tribe, *Stories of Our Ancestors: A Collection of Northern Ute Indian Tales* (Salt Lake City: University of Utah Press, 1974), 22.

4. Fred A. Conetah, *A History of the Northern Ute People*, ed. Kathryn L. McKay and Floyd A. O'Neill. (Salt Lake City: Uintay-Ouray Tribe/University of Utah Press, 1982), 20.

5. William R. Palmer, "The Pahute Fire Legend," *Utah Historical Quarterly* 6 no. 2 (April 1933): 62–64.

6. Albert B. Reagan, "Mother Nature," Albert B. Reagan Collection, Special Collections, Harold B. Lee Library, Brigham Young University, Provo, UT, 64–65.

7. Coyote, as with all of the animals mentioned in Ute creation stories, is personified. They all think and act as humans and are participants with each other during the creation. Coyote, particularly, has an enduring role in establishing patterns for people. Ute teachings indicate confusion as to whether he is in animal form or that of a man, but most agree that he has supernatural powers that allow him to affect an individual's destiny, often in a negative way. See Connor Chapoose in Y. T. Witherspoon, ed., *Conversations with Connor Chapoose, A Leader of the Ute Tribe of the Uintah and Ouray Reservation*, Anthropological Papers no. 47 (Eugene: Department of Anthropology and Oregon State Museum of Anthropology, 1993), 110–114.

8. Patty Dutchie, "The Seasons of the Year," in Ute

Mountain Ute Archives, American West Center, University of Utah, Salt Lake City.

9. See also Chapoose and Witherspoon, *Conversations*, 110–111.

10. William R. Palmer, "The Paiute Indian," January 1954, William R. Palmer Collection, Special Collections, Gerald R. Sherratt Library, Southern Utah University, Cedar City, 4–5.

11. Palmer, "An Indian Legend," Palmer Collection, 1–2.

12. Ralph Cloud, "The Ute Creation Story," cited in Talmy Givón, *Ute Traditional Narratives* (Ignacio, CO: Ute Press, 1985), 9–16. In another version there are two brothers, Sináwav Pavits and Sináwav Skaits. In still other versions the name *Tavwoats* (also spelled *Tovwoats*) is used for Wolf or the older brother who is wise and directs Sináwav. He is more of a creator figure and less likely to err. Sináwav in this setting, either wittingly or unwittingly, causes turmoil. In Cloud's narrative, Pavits (Pavíč — "Big Brother Who Was Wolf") directed Skaits (Sahkaič — "Younger Brother Who Was Coyote") not to open the bag. The younger brother did, and those who remained he placed in the Four Corners area. See Don D. Fowler and Catherine Fowler, *Anthropology of the Numa: John Wesley Powell's Manuscripts on the Numic People*, Smithsonian Contributions to Anthropology 14 (Washington, DC: Smithsonian Institution, 1971), 78.

13. Here, Sináwav is the Creator, comparable to Wolf, while Sunawiga is comparable to Coyote. (See note 12.)

14. Anne Smith noted during her extensive work in oral tradition that "All strange Indians were called [a word] which was usually translated as Sioux. Further questioning was needed to identify the 'Sioux' as Arapaho, Comanche, or Sioux." Smith, *Ethnography of the Northern Utes*, Papers in Anthropology no. 17 (Albuquerque: University of New Mexico Press, 1974), 239.

15. Variations of the name by which the Utes call themselves are "Nutc" or "Nunts."

16. Emmitt, "Creation," n.d., "Ute Legends," on file in Northern Ute Archives, American West Center, University of Utah, Salt Lake City.

17. Pamela A. Bunte and Robert J. Franklin, *From the Sands to the Mountains: Change and Persistence in a Southern Paiute Community* (Lincoln: University of Nebraska Press, 1987), 227.

18. Fowler and Fowler, *Anthropology of the Numa*, 78.

19. Brian D. Stubbs, *Uto-Aztecan: A Comparative Vocabulary* (Blanding, UT: self-published, 2008), 3–4.

20. Ibid.

21. Sidney M. Lamb, "Linguistic Prehistory of the Great Basin, *International Journal of American Linguistics* 24, no. 2 (1958): 95–100.

22. James A. Goss, "Culture-Historical Inference from Utaztekan Linguistic Evidence," paper presented at Plenary Symposium on Utaztekan Prehistory of the Society for American Archaeology and the Great Basin Anthropological Conference, May 1966, 11, 27.

23. James A. Goss, "Traditional Cosmology, Ecology, and Language of the Ute Indians," in *Ute Indian Arts and Culture: From Prehistory to the New Millennium*, ed. William Wroth (Colorado Springs: Colorado Springs Fine Art Center, 2000), 36.

24. Ibid., 28.

25. Minette C. Church, Steven G. Baker, Bonnie J. Clark, Richard F. Carrillo, Jonathon C. Horn, Carl D. Spath, David R. Guilfoyle, and E. Steve Cassells, *Colorado History: A Context for Historical Archaeology* (Denver: Colorado Council of Professional Archaeologists, 2007), 62, 69, 72.

26. Alan D. Reed, "Ute Cultural Chronology," in *An Archaeology of the Eastern Ute: A Symposium*, ed. Paul R. Nickens, CCPA Occasional Papers no. 1 (Denver: Colorado Council of Professional Archaeologists, 1988), 80–81; archaeologist Winston Hurst, conversation with author, September 9, 1992.

27. Robert C. Euler, "Southern Paiute Archaeology," *American Antiquities* 29 (January 1964): 380; Reed, "Ute Cultural Chronology," 82; Fowler and Fowler, "The Southern Paiute: A.D. 1400–1776," *The Protohistoric Period in the North American Southwest, A.D. 1350–1700*, ed. D.R. Wilcox and W.B. Masse, Anthropological Research Papers no. 24 (Tempe: Arizona State University), 129–162. See also Church et al., *Colorado History*, 29–57; Steven G. Baker, Jeffrey S. Dean, and Richard H. Towner, "Final Report for the Old Wood Calibration Project, Western Colorado" (Montrose, CO: Centuries Research, May 1, 2008).

28. Goss, "Culture-Historical Inference," 33–34.

29. Goss, "Traditional Cosmology," 29.

30. S. Lyman Tyler, "The Yuta Indians before 1680," *Western Humanities Review* 8 (Spring 1951): 157, 160.

31. Donald G. Callaway, Joel C. Janetski, and Omer C. Stewart, "Ute," in *Handbook of North American Indians*, vol. 11, *Great Basin* (Washington, DC: Smithsonian Institution, 1986), 339; Virginia McConnell Simmons, *The Ute Indians of Utah, Colorado, and New Mexico* (Boulder: University Press of Colorado, 2000), 21–22.

32. William Wroth, "Ute Civilization in Prehistory and the Spanish Colonial Period," in *Ute Indian Arts and Culture: From Prehistory to the New Millennium*, ed. William Wroth (Colorado Springs: Colorado Springs Fine Art Center, 2000), 57–58.

33. Ibid., 366. The entire issue about the use of "Weenuche" and "Weeminuche" is still unclear. Some elders felt that "Weeminuche" was fine and that

"Weenuche" referred more to the prehistoric Ute people. Edward Dutchie explained it this way:

"Weeminuche" is the tribal name for the Ute Mountain Utes. It means they lay on their stomachs. But some guys joke about it and [say] that they are turned towards the ground. But actually it means they lay like the Ute Mountain…. When the government began handing out land, the Southern Utes liked the arrangement, but some of the Ute Mountain Tribe members did not. So they laid around with their faces to the ground. The Southern Utes made a joke of it, calling them lizards. They said they looked like lizards laying on a flat rock with their stomachs going up and down [as in intercourse]. The Ute Mountain Tribe is called "Weeminuche" or Si-sügǘ'nawüči — "gray lizard". That is where the name Weeminuche started.

While allotment began much later in the historic record, the play on words catches why the White Mesa people wish to avoid it. By request of the White Mesa Ute Board and elders of the historical committee, "Weenuche" will be used in this book.

34. Isabel T. Kelly and Catherine S. Fowler, "Southern Paiute," in *Handbook of North American Indians*, vol. 11, *Great Basin* (Washington, DC: Smithsonian Institution, 1986), 368, 396.

35. Robert A. Manners citing Isabel Kelly, *Paiute Indians* vol. 1, *Southern Paiute and Chemehuevi* (New York: Garland, 1974), 230.

36. William R. Palmer, "Utah Indians Past and Present: An Etymological and Historical Study of Tribes and Tribal Names from Original Sources," *Utah Historical Quarterly* no. 1 (April 1928): 52.

37. Omer C. Stewart, *Culture Element Distributions vol. 18: Ute-Southern Paiute* (Berkeley: University of California Press, 1942), 236.

38. William R. Palmer, "San Juan Indians," Palmer Collection, 32.

39. Anne M. Smith, *Ute Tales* (Salt Lake City: University of Utah Press, 1992), xxi; Bunte and Franklin, *From the Sands to the Mountains*, 1; Smith, *Ute Tales*, xxvi.

40. Bunte and Franklin, *From the Sands to the Mountains*, 183, 232. Historical accounts by careful observers underscore these differences by saying that at times the Utes from the Montezuma Canyon — southwestern Colorado area would help whites control the Allen Canyon group and that the general term "Paiute" was given to the latter, while those people nearer Colorado were "Utes." See Lyman Hunter, interview with Michael Hurst, February 21, 1973, Charles Redd Center for Western Studies, Brigham Young University, Provo, UT, 2; Kumen Jones manuscript, Utah State Historical Society Library, Salt Lake City, 106; Stella

Eyetoo, interview with Aldean Ketchum and author, December 21, 1994.

41. Martha C. Knack, *Boundaries Between: The Southern Paiutes, 1775–1995* (Lincoln: University of Nebraska Press, 2001), 31.

42. J. A. Jones, "A Reinterpretation of the Ute-Southern Paiute Classification," *Anthropological Quarterly* 27, no. 2 (April 1954): 53–58.

43. Fowler and Fowler, *Anthropology of the Numa*, 38.

44. Joe Pinnecoose and Clifford Duncan (Utes), cited in Richard E. Fiske and H. Blaine Phillips II, *A Nineteenth Century Ute Burial from Northeast Utah*, Cultural Resource Series no. 16 (Salt Lake City: Bureau of Land Management, 1984), 91.

45. Goss, "Traditional Cosmology," 33, 47–48.

46. Terry Knight, spiritual leader of the Ute Mountain Utes, interview with Mary Jane Yazzie and author, December 19, 1994.

47. Marvin Kaufmann Opler, "The Southern Ute of Colorado," in *Acculturation in Seven American Indian Tribes* (New York: D. Appleton-Century Company, 1940), 141–142; Fowler and Fowler, *Anthropology of the Numa*, 66; Knight interview.

48. William R. Palmer, "The Religion of the Piutes," *The Improvement Era* 39, no. 9 (September 1936): 536.

49. Chapoose and Witherspoon, *Conversations*, 95–96, 110–111.

50. Florence Begay, interview with Nelson Begay and author, April 29, 1988; Ira S. Freeman, *A History of Montezuma County* (Boulder, CO: Johnson Publishing Company, 1958), 166–167; Russell Lopez and Merry Palmer, "Legend of the Sleeping Ute Mountain," Ute Mountain Ute Tribe (Blanding: Utah State Office of Education and San Juan School District Media Center, 2006).

51. Edward Dutchie Sr. and Patty Dutchie, interview with author, May 13, 1996.

52. Conetah, *History of the Northern Ute People*, 20.

53. Fowler and Fowler, *Anthropology of the Numa*, 67–76.

54. Even though the name "Water Boy" indicates that the water babies are male, there are often female creatures too, but according to Stella Eyetoo, the masculine term is used for both.

55. James Jefferson, Robert W. Delaney, and Gregory C. Thompson, *The Southern Utes: A Tribal History* (Ignacio, CO: Southern Ute Tribe, 1972), 74–75; Patty Dutchie interview; Smith, *Ute Tales*, 110.

56. Smith, *Ute Tales*, 39, 109–113; Jefferson et al., *Southern Utes*, 74–75.

57. Stella Eyetoo and Adeline Eyetoo, conversation with author, December 9, 2008.

58. Edward Dutchie interview.

59. William F. Hanson, "The Lure of Tam-man Nacup, Springtime Festival of the Utes," unpublished master's thesis, 1937, Special Collections, Harold B. Lee Library, Brigham Young University, Provo, UT, 51–52.

60. Chapoose and Witherspoon, *Conversations*, 77.
61. Patty Dutchie interview.
62. Åke Hultkrantz, "Mythology and Religious Concepts," in *Handbook of North American Indians*, vol. 11, *Great Basin* (Washington, DC: Smithsonian Institution, 1986), 633.
63. Smith, *Ethnography of the Northern Utes*, 155.
64. Edward and Patty Dutchie interview.
65. Stella Eyetoo, interview, November 16, 2005.
66. Aldean Ketchum interview, 2009.
67. Stella Eyetoo and Adoline Eyetoo interviews, 2009.
68. Edward Dutchie interview; Carla L. Knight, "The Utes and Their Environment," unpublished paper, 1986, used with permission, in possession of author.
69. Lola Mike, interview with Aldean Ketchum and author, November 16, 2005.
70. Chapoose and Witherspoon, *Conversations*, 91–92.
71. Harriet Johnson, cited in Joseph Gilbert Jorgensen, "Functions of Ute Folklore," unpublished master's thesis, 1960, University of Utah, Salt Lake City, 115.
72. Ibid., 93.
73. Fowler and Fowler, *Anthropology of the Numa*, 66.
74. Jack Cantsee Sr., interview with author, September 24, 2009.
75. Patty Dutchie interview.
76. Hultkrantz, "Mythology and Religious Concepts," 633.
77. Fowler and Fowler, *Anthropology of the Numa*, 66.
78. Jack Cantsee interview.
79. Goss, "Culture-Historical Inference," 29–30.
80. Anne M. Smith, *Ethnography of the Northern Utes*, Papers in Anthropology no. 17 (Albuquerque: University of New Mexico, 1974), 16.
81. David M. Pendergast and Clement W. Meighan, "Folk Traditions as Historical Fact: A Paiute Example," *Journal of American Folklore* 72, no. 284 (April–June 1959): 128–133.
82. Edward Palmer, "Notes on the Utah Utes by Edward Palmer, 1866–1877," in *Anthropological Paper no. 17*, ed. R. F. Heizer (Salt Lake City: University of Utah, May 1954), 3.
83. Edward Dutchie interview.
84. Henry McCabe, *Cowboys, Indians, and Homesteaders* (self-published, 1975), 183.
85. Frank McNitt, *Richard Wetherill, Anasazi: Pioneer Explorer of Southwestern Ruins* (Albuquerque: University of New Mexico Press, 1966), 22.
86. Lola Mike interview.
87. William H. Jackson, *William H. Jackson: Frontier Photographer Diaries, 1866–1874* (Glendale, CA: Arthur H. Clark, 1959), 316–319.
88. McCabe, *Cowboys, Indians, and Homesteaders*, 6.
89. Buckskin Charlie, cited in Wood, *When Buffalo Free the Mountains*, xiv.
90. Ibid.

91. Sunshine Cloud-Smith, Mary Inez Rivera, and Everett Burch, "The Southern Ute Beliefs about the Ancient Anasazi," on file in the BLM—Anasazi Heritage Center Library, Dolores, CO.
92. Patty Dutchie interview.
93. Stella Eyetoo interview.
94. Patty Dutchie interview.
95. Edward Dutchie interview.
96. Jim Carrier, *West of the Divide: Voices from a Ranch and Reservation* (Golden, CO: Fulcrum, 1992), 113.
97. Greg Johnson, "Echoes in the Canyons: 'Superstition' and Sense in Ute Conceptions of Anasazi Things," draft, April 14, 1994, on file in the BLM—Anasazi Heritage Center Library, Dolores, CO.
98. Ibid., 34.
99. William R. Palmer, Field Notes, Palmer Collection, 44–45.
100. Hultkrantz, "Mythology and Religious Concepts," 631.

Chapter 2

1. Billy Mike, interview with Aldean Ketchum and author, October 13, 1993.
2. Stella Eyetoo, interview with Aldean Ketchum and author, December 21, 1994.
3. Billy Mike interview; Edward Dutchie Sr. and Patty Dutchie, interviews with author, May 7 and 13, 1996; Chester Cantsee, interview with Aldean Ketchum and author, September 6, 1994; Alfred N. Billings, "Memorandum, Account Book, and Diary of Alfred N. Billings, 1855," Special Collections, Harold B. Lee Library, Brigham Young University, Provo, UT, 14.
4. Harold Lindsay Amoss Jr., "Ute Mountain Utes," doctoral dissertation, University of California, 1951, 34.
5. Eyetoo interview; Edward Dutchie interview; John W. Van Cott, *Utah Place Names* (Salt Lake City: University of Utah Press, 1990), 264; Cantsee interview; Edward Dutchie interview.
6. Edward Dutchie interview.
7. Lizzie Jacket, interview with author, May 30, 1991; E. L. Hewitt, "Field Notes 1906–09," photocopy, Edge of the Cedars Museum, Blanding, UT; Chester Cantsee interview; Eyetoo interview; William R. Palmer, "Indian Names in Utah Geography," *Utah Historical Quarterly* 1, no. 1 (January 1928): 21.
8. Hewitt, "Field Notes"; Eyetoo interview; Mike interview; Edward Dutchie interview.
9. Edward Dutchie interview; Eyetoo interview.
10. Stella Eyetoo, interview with Aldean Ketchum and author, November 16, 2005.
11. Mike interview; Edward Dutchie interview.
12. Lola Mike, interview with Aldean Ketchum and author, November 16, 2005; Eyetoo interview, 2005.

13. Hewitt, "Field Notes"; Eyetoo interview, 2005; Edward Dutchie interview.

14. Edward Dutchie interview.

15. Stella Eyetoo, interview with author, July 11, 2009; Adoline Eyetoo, interview with author, July 25, 2009.

16. Stella Eyetoo interview, 2005; Cantsee interview; Mike Lola interview; Edward Dutchie interview.

17. Mike Lola interview; Stella Eyetoo interview, 2005; Billings, "Memorandum," 14.

18. Jack Cantsee, interview with author, September 24, 2009.

19. Ibid.; Edward Dutchie Sr., conversation with author, May 13, 1996; Aldean Ketchum, interview with author, July 30, 2009.

20. Julius S. Dalley, "Mancos Jim Mesa — San Juan County," Utah Writers' Project, August 11, 1942, Utah State Historical Society Library; Eyetoo interview, 2005.

21. William B. Douglass, U.S. Deputy Surveyor, "Field Notes of the Survey of the Reservations Embracing the Natural Bridges National Monument, Cigarette Cave, and the Snow Flat Cave," October 3, 1908, copy in Grand Gulch — Wetherill Collection, Edge of the Cedars Museum, Blanding, UT, 3.

22. Ketchum interview.

23. Amoss, "Ute Mountain Utes," 90; Ute Mountain Ute Tribe, *Early Days of the Ute Mountain Utes* (Salt Lake City: University of Utah Printing Service, 1985), 6.

24. James A. Goss, "Traditional Cosmology, Ecology, and Language of the Ute Indians," in *Ute Indian Arts and Culture: From Prehistory to the New Millennium*, ed. William Wroth (Colorado Springs: Colorado Springs Fine Art Center, 2000), 47–48.

25. Mike Billy interview.

26. Don D. Fowler and Catherine Fowler, *Anthropology of the Numa: John Wesley Powell's Manuscripts on the Numic People*, Smithsonian Contributions to Anthropology 14 (Washington, DC: Smithsonian Institution, 1971), 53.

27. Chester Cantsee, interview with Floyd O'Neil and Gregory C. Thompson, March 22, 1980, White Mesa Ute Oral History Project, American West Center, University of Utah, Salt Lake City, 35.

28. Frank Silvey, "Information on Indians," September 26, 1936, Library, Utah State Historical Society, Salt Lake City, 1–2. While Silvey's work addresses this topic specifically, many of the sites mentioned are known from a scattering of historical documents that span a hundred years.

29. James T. Gardner, "The Old Man of the Mountains," *Rocky Mountain News*, September 22, 1875, F. V. Hayden Collection, American Heritage Center, University of Wyoming, Laramie, n.p.

30. George B. Chittenden, "Report," *Ninth Annual Report of the United States Geological and Geographical Survey of the Territories Embracing Colorado and Parts of Adjacent Territories, 1875* (Washington, DC: Government Printing Office, 1877), 357.

31. Goss, "Traditional Cosmology," 38.

32. William R. Palmer, Field Notes, William R. Palmer Collection, Special Collections, Gerald R. Sherratt Library, Southern Utah University, Cedar City, 5.

33. Silvey, "Information on Indians," 1.

34. Ibid.

35. Frank Silvey, "Pioneer Personal History Questionnaire," September 10, 1936, Silvey File, Utah State Historical Society Library, Salt Lake City, 4.

36. Omer C. Stewart, *Culture Element Distributions*, vol. 18: *Ute Southern Paiute*. Anthropological Records 6, no. 4 (Berkeley: University of California Press, 1942), 240. This is an excellent source of information on traditional Ute cultural practices. Tables in the study include the Gosiute, eight Ute bands, four Southern Paiute bands, and the northwestern Navajo. Answers from at least one and sometimes two or three elders from each group delineate practices observed in the past. For this book I included elements primarily if they were done in common by both Weenuche Utes and the San Juan band of Paiutes. While some anthropologists may criticize this source because the informants did not observe the same practices, at least some of the Utes/Paiutes did. Unless otherwise noted, material from this section came from this study.

37. Carla L. Knight, "The Utes and their Environment," March 19, 1986, unpublished manuscript, used with permission.

38. Adoline Eyetoo, interview with author, July 25, 2009.

39. Amoss, "Ute Mountain Utes," 55.

40. Anne M. Smith, *Ethnography of the Northern Utes*, Papers in Anthropology 17 (Albuquerque: University of New Mexico Press, 1974), 46–53.

41. Edward Dutchie interview.

42. Frank Silvey, "Indians in San Juan," June 10, 1940, Silvey File, Utah State Historical Society Library, Salt Lake City, 4; Annie Cantsee interview with author, August 4, 2009.

43. Annie Cantsee interview; Palmer, Field Notes.

44. Uintah-Ouray Ute Tribe, "The Ute People" (Salt Lake City: University of Utah Printing Service, 1977), 13.

45. Stewart, *Cultural Element Distributions, vol.18*, 279–283; Smith, *Ethnography of the Northern Utes*, 70–77.

46. Verner Z. Reed, *The Southern Ute Indians of Early Colorado* (Dillon, CO: Vistabooks, 1991), 8–9.

47. Silvey, "Pioneer Questionnaire," 2.

48. Smith, *Ethnography of the Northern Utes*, 50.

49. Edward Dutchie interview.

50. Stewart, *Cultural Element Distributions, vol.18*, 242; Goss, "Traditional Cosmology," 42, 46.

51. Silvey, "Pioneer Questionnaire," 1.

52. Stewart, *Cultural Element Distributions, vol.18*, 246–247.

53. Edward Dutchie interview, May 7 and 13, 1996. Some elements of this story are unclear, but there is no missing that it was told as an example of why people need to be very respectful of snakes.

54. Ibid.

55. Fred A. Conetah, *A History of the Northern Ute People*, ed. Kathryn L. McKay and Floyd A. O'Neil (Salt Lake City: Uintah Ouray Tribe, 1982), 9; Florence Hawley et al., "Culture Process and Change in Ute Adaptation—Part I," *El Palacio* (October 1950): 325; Smith, *Ethnography of the Northern Utes*, 61–62, 64.

56. Marvin Kaufmann Opler, *The Southern Ute of Colorado* (New York: D. Appleton-Century, 1940), 137–138, 140.

57. S. Lyman Tyler, "Before Escalante: An Early History of the Yuta Indians and Area North of New Mexico…," unpublished doctoral dissertation, University of Utah, 1951, 66.

58. Frank Raymond Secoy, *Changing Military Patterns on the Great Plains: 17th Century through Early 19th Century*, American Ethnological Society Monograph 21 (Seattle: University of Washington Press, 1953, 1971), 28.

59. For a current, in-depth discussion of the horse and the Utes, see Minette C. Church, Steven G. Baker, Bonnie J. Clark, Richard F. Carrillo, Jonathon C. Horn, Carl D. Spath, David R. Guilfoyle, and E. Steve Cassells, *Colorado History: A Context for Historical Archaeology* (Denver: Colorado Council of Professional Archaeologists, 2007), 59–63.

60. Smith, *Ethnography of the Northern Utes*, 21.

61. Amoss, "Ute Mountain Utes," 66–68; Stewart, *Ute-Southern Paiute*, 274; Silvey, "Pioneer Questionnaire," 1–2.

62. Silvey, Pioneer Questionnaire," 2

63. Amoss, "Ute Mountain Utes," 55–61; Ralph V. Chamberlain, "Some Plant Names of the Ute Indians," *American Anthropologist* 2 (January–March 1909): 27–37.

64. To understand just how dependent Ute and Paiute people were on many plants found in this general environment and how they were processed, see Percy Train, James R. Heinrichs, and W. Andrew Archer, *Paiute Indians*, vol. 4, *Medicinal Uses of Plants by Indian Tribes of Nevada* (New York: Garland Publishing, 1974), 30–150; see also Margaret M. Wheat, *Survival Arts of the Primitive Paiutes* (Reno: University of Nevada Press, 1967).

65. Uintah-Ouray Ute Tribe, "The Ute People," 7.

66. Amoss, "Ute Mountain Utes," 37–38; Chamberlain, "Some Plant Names," 27–40; James Jefferson, Robert W. Delaney, and Gregory Thompson, *The Southern Utes: A Tribal History* (Ignacio, CO: Southern Ute Tribe, 1972), 72–73; Ute Mountain Ute Tribe, *Early Days*, 13–16.

67. Patty Dutchie interview.

68. Stella Eyetoo interview, November 16, 2005.

69. William W. Dunmire and Gail D. Tierney, *Wild Plants of the Pueblo Province, Exploring Ancient and Enduring Uses* (Santa Fe: Museum of New Mexico Press, 1995), 156.

70. Annie Cantsee interview.

71. Ibid., 190, 124–126, 119, 106–107.

72. Edward Dutchie interview, May 7 and 13, 1996; Smith, *Ethnography of the Northern Utes*, 269–270.

73. Marilyn A. Martorano, "Culturally Peeled Trees and Ute Indians in Colorado," in *Archaeology of the Eastern Ute: A Symposium*, ed. Paul R. Nickens, CCPA Occasional Papers 1 (Denver: Colorado Council of Professional Archaeologists, 1988), 5–21; and "So Hungry They Ate the Bark off a Tree," *Canyon Legacy: A Journal of the Dan O'Laurie Museum* 1, no. 1 (Spring 1989): 9–12.

74. Ibid.

75. Leann Hunt, conversation with author, October 15, 2008.

76. Hunt conversation; Winston Hurst, archaeologist, conversation with author, October 14, 2008; Don Irwin, Forest Service archaeologist, conversation with author, October 15, 2008.

77. Edward Dutchie interview, May 7 and 13, 1996.

78. Martorano, "So Hungry They Ate the Bark," 12.

79. Hunt conversation.

80. Goss, "Traditional Cosmology," 38.

81. Ibid., 43.

82. William W. Dunmire and Gail D. Tierney, *Wild Plants of the Pueblo Province: Exploring Ancient and Enduring Uses* (Santa Fe: Museum of New Mexico Press, 1995), 33.

83. See Alan D. Reed, "Ute Cultural Chronology," in *An Archaeology of the Eastern Ute: A Symposium*, ed. Paul R. Nickens, CCPA Occasional Papers no. 1 (Denver: Colorado Council of Professional Archaeology, 1988), 80–82, for a discussion of the Utes' entrance into the Four Corners region.

84. Edward Dutchie interview, May 7 and 13, 1996.

85. Stewart, *Ute-Southern Paiute*, 258–275; Ute Mountain Ute Tribe, *Early Days*, 23; Palmer, Field Notes, 113.

86. Edward Dutchie interview, May 7 and 13, 1996.

87. Stewart, *Cultural Elements Distributions, vol. 18*, 257, 259; L. B. Titus, interview with Sandra Caruthers, March 24, 1967, n.n., Doris Duke Oral History Project, Special Collections, Marriott Library, University of Utah, Salt Lake City, 6.

88. Church et al., *Colorado History*, 51.

89. Winston B. Hurst, "The Blanding Navajos: A Case Study of Off-Reservation Navajo Migration and Settlement," master's thesis, Eastern New Mexico University, May 1981, 236–237.

90. Cited in Smith, *Ethnography of the Northern Utes*, 33.
91. Lizzie Jacket, interview with author, May 30, 1991; Stella Eyetoo interview; Edward Dutchie interview.
92. Smith, *Ethnography of the Northern Utes*, 37–39.
93. Dan A. Freeman, *Four Years with the Utes: The Letters of Dan A. Freeman* (Waco, TX: W. M. Morrison Company, 1962), 2.
94. Edward Dutchie interview, May 7 and 13, 1996.
95. Ibid., 40; Amoss, "Ute Mountain Utes," 50.
96. Stella Eyetoo interview; Reginald and Gladys Laubin, *The Indian Tipi: Its History, Construction, and Use* (New York: Ballantine, 1957), 63–74.
97. "Official Report of Captains Gibbs and Cannon," *The (Ogden, UT) Standard*, January 30, 1895, 1.

CHAPTER 3

1. Donald G. Callaway, Joel C. Janetski, and Omer C. Stewart, "Ute," in *Great Basin*, vol. 11 of *Handbook of North American Indians* (Washington, DC: Smithsonian Institution, 1986), 354.
2. Anne M. Smith, *Ethnography of the Northern Utes*, Papers in Anthropology no. 17 (Albuquerque: University of New Mexico Press, 1974), 137–138; Omer C. Stewart, *Culture Element Distributions*, vol. 18: *Ute-Southern Paiute*. Anthropological Records 6, no. 4 (Berkeley: University of California Press, 1942), 303.
3. Bonnie Mike Lehi, interview with author, July 20, 2009.
4. Bertha Groves, interview with Ginger Bigsby and Barbara Beasley, April 18, 1991, Southern Ute Oral Histories, Center of Southwest Studies, Fort Lewis College, Durango, CO, 2.
5. Ibid., 4.
6. Stewart, *Cultural Elements Distributions, vol. 18*, 303.
7. Stella Eyetoo, interview by author, July 11, 2009; Annie Cantsee, interview by author, August 4, 2009; Bonnie Mike Lehi interview.
8. Groves interview, 1–2.
9. Stewart, *Cultural Elements Distributions, vol. 18*, 306–307; Smith, *Ethnography of the Northern Utes*, 139–142.
10. Marvin Kaufmann Opler, "The Southern Ute of Colorado," in *Acculturation in Seven American Indian Tribes*, ed. Ralph Linton (New York: D. Appleton-Century Company, 1940), 138.
11. Edward Dutchie Sr. and Patty Dutchie, interview with author, May 21, 1996. Other interviews with them were conducted on May 7 and 13, 1996. These interviews are referenced as one collection under either Edward or Patty Dutchie, depending on who offered the information.
12. Stewart, *Cultural Elements Distributions, vol. 18*, 307–308; Smith, *Ethnography of the Northern Utes*, 143; Connor Chapoose, *Conversations with Connor Chapoose*, ed. Y. T. Witherspoon, Anthropological Paper 47 (Eugene: University of Oregon, 1993), 42.
13. Groves interview, 4.
14. Ute Mountain Ute censuses on file in the Family History Center, Church of Jesus Christ of Latter-day Saints, Blanding, UT; Chester Cantsee, interview with Floyd O'Neil and Gregory Thompson, March 22, 1980, White Mesa Ute Oral History Project, American West Center, University of Utah, Salt Lake City.
15. Adoline Eyetoo, conversation with author, December 9, 2008.
16. Opler, "The Southern Ute of Colorado," 132.
17. Smith, *Ethnography of the Northern Utes*, 144–145.
18. Harold Lindsay Amoss Jr., "Ute Mountain Utes," doctoral dissertation, University of California, 1951, 77–81; Ute Mountain Ute Tribe, *Early Days of the Ute Mountain Utes* (Salt Lake City: University of Utah Printing Service, 1985), 29.
19. Edward Dutchie interview.
20. Ibid.
21. Don D. Fowler and Catherine Fowler, *Anthropology of the Numa: John Wesley Powell's Manuscripts on the Numic People*, Smithsonian Contributions to Anthropology 14 (Washington, DC: Smithsonian Institution, 1971), 51.
22. Henry McCabe, *Cowboys, Indians and Homesteaders* (self-published, 1975), 86–88.
23. Groves interview, 14.
24. Edward Dutchie interview.
25. Ibid.
26. James A. Goss, "Traditional Cosmology, Ecology, and Language of the Ute Indians," in *Ute Indian Arts and Culture, From Prehistory to the New Millennium*, ed. William Wroth (Colorado Springs: Colorado Springs Fine Art Center, 2000), 39–40.
27. Ibid., 41.
28. Groves interview, 8.
29. Smith, *Ethnography of the Northern Utes*, 146–147.
30. Steven G. Baker, "Historic Ute Archaeology: Interpreting the Last Hour Wickiup," *Southern Lore* 69, no. 4 (Winter 2003): 22–23.
31. Adoline Eyetoo, interview with author, July 25, 2009.
32. Stewart, *Cultural Elements Distributions, vol. 18*, 309–311.
33. Groves interview, 7; Ute Mountain Ute Tribe, *Ute Mountain Utes: A History Text* (Salt Lake City: University of Utah Printing Services, 1985), 19.
34. Opler, "The Southern Ute of Colorado," 140. The killing of coyotes, although not part of traditional practice, perhaps became acceptable as part of protecting livestock.
35. Stewart, *Cultural Elements Distributions, vol. 18*, 311–312.
36. Chapoose and Witherspoon, *Conversations*, 24–25.

37. Jack Cantsee, interview with author, September 24, 2009.

38. Smith, *Ethnography of the Northern Utes*, 43–44; Stewart, *Cultural Elements Distributions, vol. 18*, 259–260.

39. Adoline Eyetoo interview.

40. Edward Dutchie interview.

41. Goss, "Traditional Cosmology," 45–47.

42. William Wroth, "Ute Civilization in Prehistory and the Spanish Colonial Period," in *Ute Indian Arts and Culture: From Prehistory to the New Millennium*, ed. William Wroth (Colorado Springs: Colorado Springs Fine Art Center, 2000), 66–67.

43. Joseph G. Jorgensen, "Ghost Dance, Bear Dance, and Sun Dance," *Great Basin*, vol. 11 of *Handbook of North American Indians* (Washington, DC: Smithsonian Institution, 1986): 663.

44. Groves interview, 26.

45. Verner Z. Reed, *The Southern Ute Indians of Early Colorado* (Dillon, CO: Vistabooks, 1991), 12.

46. Groves interview, 6; Smith, *Ethnography of the Northern Utes*, 131.

47. Amoss, "Ute Mountain Utes," 82.

48. Chapoose and Witherspoon, *Conversations*, 123.

49. Ute Mountain Ute Tribe, *Ute Mountain Ute Stories, Games, and Noise Makers* (Salt Lake City: University of Utah Printing Services, 1986), 2–5.

50. Stewart, *Ute-Southern Paiute*, 296; Groves interview, 6; Smith, *Ethnography of the Northern Utes*, 131–134.

51. Reed, *Southern Ute Indians of Early Colorado*, 13.

52. Stewart, *Ute-Southern Paiute*, 298.

53. Callaway et al., "Ute," 352.

54. Edward Dutchie interview.

55. Amoss, "Ute Mountain Utes," 73–74; Opler, "The Southern Ute of Colorado," 165; Stewart, *Ute-Southern Paiute*, 301–302.

56. Fowler and Fowler, *Anthropology of the Numa*, 37–38.

57. Amoss, "Ute Mountain Utes," 85–87.

58. Elmer Denver, Louise Cuch, and Hazel Wardle, interview with Susan Denver, "Native Cures," in "Ute Legend Materials" folder, American West Center, University of Utah, Salt Lake City; James Jefferson, Robert W. Delaney, and Gregory C. Thompson, *The Southern Utes: A Tribal History* (Ignacio, CO: Southern Ute Tribe, 1972), 72.

59. Edward Dutchie interview.

60. Ibid.

61. Opler, "The Southern Ute of Colorado," 142.

62. Patty Dutchie interview.

63. Smith, *Ethnography of the Northern Utes*, 154–155.

64. Stewart, *Ute-Southern Paiute*, 315.

65. Opler, "The Southern Ute of Colorado," 137.

66. Joseph G. Jorgensen, "The Ethnohistory and Acculturation of the Northern Ute," unpublished doctoral dissertation, Indiana University, 1964, 37–38, 351.

67. Amoss, "Ute Mountain Utes," 37.

68. Stewart, *Ute-Southern Paiute*, 315–317.

69. Martha C. Knack, *Boundaries Between: The Southern Paiutes, 1775–1995* (Lincoln: University of Nebraska Press, 2001), 25.

70. Edward Dutchie interview.

71. Opler, "The Southern Ute of Colorado," 143.

72. Reed, *Southern Ute Indians of Early Colorado*, 15.

73. Knack, *Boundaries Between*, 26.

74. Edward Dutchie interview.

75. Edward and Patty Dutchie interview.

76. Joseph G. Jorgensen, *The Sun Dance Religion: Power to the Powerless* (Chicago: University of Chicago Press, 1972), 24.

77. Ibid., 305–340.

78. Ibid., 318–320.

79. Aldean Ketchum, interview with author, July 30, 2009.

80. Stewart, *Ute-Southern Paiute*, 319; Smith, *Ethnography of the Northern Utes*, 151.

81. Edward Dutchie interview.

82. Adoline Eyetoo, conversation with author, December 9, 2008.

83. Opler, "The Southern Ute of Colorado," 146.

84. Stewart, *Ute-Southern Paiute*, 312–314.

85. Reed, *Southern Ute Indians of Early Colorado*, 15.

86. Palmer, Field Notes, 64, 125; and "Indian Life and Lore," William R. Palmer Collection, Special Collections, Gerald R. Sherratt Library, Southern Utah University, Cedar City, 10.

87. A. J. McDonald, cited in Paul R. Nickens, "An Overview of Ethnographical and Archaeological Data for Ute Burial Practices," in *A Nineteenth Century Ute Burial from Northeast Utah*, ed. Richard E. Fike and H. Blaine Phillips II, Cultural Resource Series 16 (Salt Lake City: Bureau of Land Management, 1984), 96–97.

Chapter 4

1. For a comprehensive overview of this period and what was happening to all of the Ute groups, see Virginia McConnell Simmons, *The Ute Indians of Utah, Colorado, and New Mexico* (Boulder: University Press of Colorado, 2000).

2. Ned Blackhawk, *Violence over the Land: Indians and Empires in the Early American West* (Cambridge, MA: Harvard University Press, 2006), 49.

3. Marvin Kaufmann Opler, "The Southern Ute of Colorado," in Ralph Linton, *Acculturation in Seven American Indian Tribes* (New York: D. Appleton-Century Company, 1940), 170.

4. Two excellent works for an overview of borderland history are David J. Weber, *The Spanish Frontier in North America* (New Haven, CT: Yale University Press, 1992); and John Francis Bannon, *The Spanish Borderlands Frontier, 1513–1821* (Albuquerque: University of New Mexico Press, [1963] 1974).

5. Minette C. Church et al., *Colorado History: A Context for Historical Archaeology* (Denver: Colorado Council of Professional Archaeologists, 2007), 61.

6. Frank Raymond Secoy, *Changing Military Patterns on the Great Plains: 17th Century through Early 19th Century* (Seattle: University of Washington Press, [1953] 1971), 28–29.

7. Opler, "The Southern Ute of Colorado," 156–163.

8. This summary is based on S. Lyman Tyler, "The Spaniard and the Ute," *Utah Historical Quarterly* 22, no. 4 (October 1954): 343–361.

9. Blackhawk, *Violence over the Land*, 35–54; Opler, "The Southern Ute of Colorado," 161–162.

10. Alfred Barnaby Thomas, trans. and ed., *Forgotten Frontiers: A Study of the Spanish Indian Policy of Don Juan Bautista de Anza, Governor of New Mexico, 1777–1787* (Norman: University of Oklahoma Press, 1932), 75.

11. The most complete regional summary of this era is found in David J. Weber, *The American Frontier, 1821–1846: The American Southwest under Mexico* (Albuquerque: University of New Mexico Press, 1982).

12. S. Lyman Tyler, cited in Blackhawk, *Violence over the Land*, 30; Opler, "The Southern Ute of Colorado," 162–163.

13. Church et al., *Colorado History*, 63–65.

14. Blackhawk, *Violence over the Land*, 64.

15. Tyler, "The Spaniard and the Ute," 355.

16. Ibid., 356.

17. Blackhawk, *Violence over the Land*, 74.

18. Opler, "The Southern Ute of Colorado," 158.

19. Billy Mike, interview with author, October 13, 1993.

20. The best overview of this troubled time is provided by Blackhawk in *Violence over the Land*. See also L. R. Bailey, *Indian Slave Trade in the Southwest* (Los Angeles: Westernlore Press, 1966).

21. David J. Weber, *The Taos Trappers: The Fur Trade in the Far Southwest* (Norman: University of Oklahoma Press, 1968), 23.

22. Steven G. Baker, "Trails, Trade, and West-Central Colorado's Gateway Tradition: Ethnohistorical Observations," *Southwestern Lore* 74 no. 1 (Spring 2008): 1–41.

23. Ibid., 9.

24. Ibid., 20.

25. Austin Nelson Leiby, "Borderland Pathfinder: The 1765 Diaries of Juan Maria Antonio de Rivera," unpublished doctoral dissertation, 1984, Northern Arizona University, Flagstaff, 115.

26. Ibid., 129.

27. Ibid., 133.

28. Ibid., 136–139.

29. Ibid., 182–184.

30. Austin Leiby places the travelers farther to the east, in western Colorado, while G. Clell Jacobs ("The Phantom Pathfinder: Juan Maria Antonio de Rivera and his Expedition," *Utah Historical Quarterly* 60 [Summer 1992]: 201–223) has them going more through Utah, in the area of the La Sal Mountains and Moab. Of the two, Leiby's interpretation appears more likely, not only because of Rivera's carved cross being found by Domínguez and Escalante, but also because the Ute groups named were known to reside in that region of Colorado.

31. Ibid., 196.

32. Ibid., 214.

33. Donald G. Cutter, "Prelude to a Pageant in the Wilderness," *Western Historical Quarterly* 8 (January 1977): 4–14; F. A. Barnes, "A Journey to the Rio del Tizon," *Canyon Legacy* 9 (Spring 1991): 16–22; F. A. Barnes, "Update—Rivera's 1765 Expedition," *Canyon Legacy* 10 (Summer 1991): 31.

34. Fray Angelico Chavez and Ted J. Warner, ed., *The Domínguez-Escalante Journal: Their Expedition through Colorado, Utah, and New Mexico in 1776* (Provo, UT: Brigham Young University Press, 1976), 26–33.

35. Ibid., 90.

36. Ibid., 21.

37. Ibid., 101.

38. Ibid., 101–104.

39. Joseph J. Hill, "Spanish and Mexican Exploration and Trade Northwest from New Mexico into the Great Basin, 1765–1853," *Utah Historical Quarterly* 3 (January 1930): 5, 21–23.

40. Weber, *Taos Trappers*, 27; Bailey, *Indian Slave Trade*, 143.

41. Bailey, *Indian Slave Trade*, 144; Hill, "Spanish and Mexican Exploration," 17–18.

42. J. Lee Correll, *Through White Men's Eyes: A Contribution to Navajo History*, vol. 3 (Window Rock, AZ: Navajo Heritage Center, 1979), 141, 147, 149, 154, 179–180.

43. Uintah-Ouray Ute Tribe, *A Brief History of the Ute People* (Salt Lake City: Uintah-Ouray Tribe and the University of Utah Press, 1977), 6.

44. James H. Knipmeyer, "The Old Trappers Trail through Eastern Utah," *Canyon Legacy* 9 (Spring 1991): 10–15.

45. Some historians claim that it was Wolfskill and Ewing Young, not Yount, who opened the trail. Yount was Wolfskill's partner in a fur and trading enterprise in Taos, but he had traveled to California earlier in 1830 by a different route and so was not present at this initial opening of the entire Spanish Trail. See Weber, *Taos Trappers*, 144.

46. C. Gregory Crampton, "Utah's Spanish Trail," *Utah Historical Quarterly* 47 (Fall 1979): 361–382; Steven K. Madsen, "The Spanish Trail Through Canyon Country," *Canyon Legacy* 9 (Spring 1991): 23–29. For a detailed account of the Spanish Trail see Leroy R. Hafen and Ann W. Hafen, *The Old*

Spanish Trail: Santa Fe to Los Angeles (Glendale, CA: Arthur H. Clark Company, 1954); Steven K. Madsen, "A Letter Concerning the Location of the Ute Crossing of the Colorado River," in *Spanish Traces* 6, no. 2 (Spring 2000): 33. For a guidebook on today's landscape see C. Gregory Crampton and Steven K. Madsen, *In Search of the Spanish Trail, Santa Fe to Los Angeles, 1829–1848* (Salt Lake City: Gibbs Smith, 1994).

47. Bert Silliman, "The Orejas del Oso Trail or Bears Ears Trail," "Writings" folder; Dean Brimhall, interview with Charles Peterson, May 1, 1970; both located in Utah State Historical Society Library, Salt Lake City.

48. Duflot de Mofras, cited in Hafen and Hafen, *The Old Spanish Trail*, 187.

49. David M. Brugge, *Navajos in the Catholic Church Records of New Mexico, 1694–1875*, Research Report no. 1 (Window Rock, AZ: Navajo Tribe, 1968), 37.

50. G. Douglas Brewerton, "A Ride with Kit Carson through the Great American Desert and the Rocky Mountains," *Harpers New Monthly Magazine* 8 (April 1854): 312–313; Conway B. Sonne, *World of Wakara* (San Antonio, TX: Naylor Company, 1962), 135.

51. Martha C. Knack, *Boundaries Between: The Southern Paiutes, 1775–1995* (Lincoln: University of Nebraska Press, 2001), 35.

52. See Sonne, *World of Wakara*, for the Ute chief's life history. Variations of his name and its translation are found on pages 2, 6.

53. "Doctor Lyman," cited in William J. Snow, "Utah Indians and Spanish Slave Trade," *Utah Historical Quarterly* 2 no. 3 (July 1929): 76.

54. John C. Frémont, *Memoirs of My Life* (Chicago: Clarke and Company, 1887), 385–386.

55. James Jefferson, Robert W. Delaney, and Gregory C. Thompson, *The Southern Utes: A Tribal History* (Ignacio, CO: Southern Ute Tribe, 1972), 15–21; Ute Mountain Ute Tribe, *Ute Mountain Utes: A History Text* (Salt Lake City: Ute Mountain Ute Tribe and the University of Utah Press, 1985).

56. See Sondra Jones, "The Trial of Don Pedro León," *Utah Historical Quarterly* 65 no. 2 (Spring 1997): 165–186, and "'Redeeming' the Indian: The Enslavement of Indian Children in New Mexico and Utah," *Utah Historical Quarterly* 67 no. 3 (Summer 1999): 220–241.

57. *Acts, Resolutions, and Memorials, passed at Several Sessions of the Legislative Assembly of the Territory of Utah* (Salt Lake City, 1855), cited in Hafen and Hafen, *The Old Spanish Trail*, 274–277.

58. Lieutenant E. G. Beckwith, "Report of Exploration of a Route for the Pacific Railroad near the 38th and 39th Parallels of Latitude," U.S. Congress, House Document 129 (1855), 57.

59. Ibid., 68.

60. Gwinn Harris Heap, cited in Steven K. Madsen, *The Spanish Trail: A Compilation of Spanish Trail Diaries and Maps* (self-published, 1992), 6.

61. Ibid.

62. McConnell Simmons, *The Ute Indians*, 90.

63. Richard D. Poll, Thomas G. Alexander, Eugene Campbell, David E. Miller, *Utah's History* (Provo, UT: Brigham Young University Press, 1978), 133–134.

64. See Kenneth Lee Petersen, "Tabehuache and Elk Mountain Utes: A Historical Test of an Ecological Model," *Southwestern Lore* 43 no. 4 (December 1977): 5–21.

65. Isabel T. Kelly, *Southern Paiute Ethnography*, vol. 1, *Eastern Bands*, cited in Robert A. Manners, *Paiute Indians*, vol. 1, *Southern Paiute and Chemehuevi* (New York: Garland, 1974), 230.

66. Julian H. Steward, *Basin-Plateau Aboriginal Sociopolitical Groups*, Bureau of American Ethnology Bulletin 120 (Washington, DC: Smithsonian Institution, 1938), 228–229.

67. Julian H. Steward, *Ute Indians: Aboriginal and Historical Groups of the Ute Indians of Utah*, vol. 1 (New York: Garland, 1974), 18.

68. Ibid., 19–20.

69. Ute Mountain Ute Tribe, *Early Days of the Ute Mountain Utes* (Salt Lake City: Ute Mountain Ute Tribe and the University of Utah Press, 1985), 2.

70. J. W. Powell and G. W. Ingalls, "Utes, Paiutes, Gosiute, and Shoshonean Indians—Special Report," February 23, 1874, *Report of the Secretary of the Interior*, 1st Sess., 43d Cong., H. R. Exec. Doc. 157, 17.

71. Ibid.

72. Alfred N. Billings, "Memorandum, Account Book, and Diary of Alfred N. Billings, 1855," Special Collections, Harold B. Lee Library, Brigham Young University, Provo, UT, 3.

73. John McEwan to Henry McEwan, June 17, 1855; *Deseret News* (vol. 5, no. 190), Salt Lake City.

74. Ibid.

75. John McEwan to Isaac Higbee, June 21, 1855, *Deseret News* (vol. 5, no. 191); "Elk Mountain," July 17, 1855, *Deseret News*, Salt Lake City.

76. Billings, "Memorandum, Account Book, and Diary," 7.

77. William B. Pace, "Diary of William B. Pace during the Elk Mountain Mission, 1855–1856," Utah State Historical Society Library, Salt Lake City, 12.

78. Ibid., 14.

79. Billings, "Memorandum, Account Book, and Diary," 8–11; Pace, "Diary," 15–17.

80. Ethan Pettit, "Ethan Pettit Diary, Aug. 6–Sept. 12, 1855," Pettit File, Utah State Historical Society Library, Salt Lake City, 1–5; Billings, "Memorandum, Account Book, and Diary," 13–17; Andrew Jenson, "The Elk Mountain Mission," *Utah Genealogical and Historical Magazine* 4 (1913): 189.

81. Pace, "Diary," 14.
82. Pettit, "Diary," 2.
83. Billings, "Memorandum, Account Book, and Diary," 17–19.
84. The following account comes from Billings, "Memorandum, Account Book, and Diary," 19–24.
85. Ibid., 22.
86. "Massacre near Elk Mountains," October 10, 1855, *Deseret News*, Salt Lake City, 2.

CHAPTER 5

1. For an excellent overview of the entire history of struggle for the Utes, see Ned Blackhawk, *Violence over the Land: Indians and Empires in the Early American West* (Cambridge, MA: Harvard University Press, 2006).
2. P. David Smith, *Ouray, Chief of the Utes* (Ouray, CO: Wayfinder Press, 1986), 47–49.
3. Commissioner of Indian Affairs to James L. Collins, November 24, 1857, Office of Indian Affairs, New Mexico Superintendency, 1857, "Letters Received," National Archives, RG 75, Washington, DC (hereafter cited as Indian Affairs, NM—Letters Received).
4. David Meriwether to George Manypenny, January 1, 1857, Indian Affairs, NM—Letters Received; Henry Kendrick to William Nichols, February 11, Records of the U.S. Army Commander, Department of New Mexico, 1857, National Archives, RG 98, Washington, DC (hereafter cited as Army—Letters Received).
5. *Gazette*, March 13, February 27, and April 10, 1858; J. Lee Correll, *Through White Men's Eyes: A Contribution to Navajo History* (Window Rock, AZ: Navajo Heritage Center, 1979), 115, 117, 122. This six-volume set of compiled original documents is a rich source of correspondence concerning the Navajos from Spanish times through the treaty of 1868. Hereafter it will be cited by names and dates of correspondence, *TWME*, and the page number. Correspondence is chronologically ordered as follows: vol. 1: 1540 to June 1855; volume 2: July 1855 to April 1860; volume 3: May 1860 to December 1863; vol. 4: January 1864 to December 1864; vol. 5: December 1864 to October 1867; and vol. 7: November 1867 to June 1868.

   William Brooks to Assistant Adjutant General, March 20, April 4, and May 30, 1858, Army—Letters Received.
6. U.S., Congress, Senate, *Report of the Secretary of War*, John Garland to Army Headquarters, January 31, 1858; J. G. Walker to Commander, September 20, 1859; S. Exec. Doc. 2, 36th Cong., 1st Sess., 339–340.
7. Captain J. G. Walker and Major O. L. Shepherd, *The Navajo Reconnaissance: A Military Exploration of the Navajo Country in 1859*, ed. L. R. Bailey (Los Angeles: Westernlore Press, 1964), 85, 89.
8. John G. Walker to John Edson, September 20, 1859, *TWME*, 298, 300.
9. James L. Collins, "New Mexico Superintendency," August 30, 1857, *Report of the Commissioner of Indian Affairs* (Washington, DC: Government Printing Office, 1857), 273 (hereafter cited as *RCIA*).
10. Samuel M. Yost to Collins, November 23, 1858; John Garland to Lorenzo Thomas, January 31, 1858; *TWME*, 206, 108.
11. William Brooks to Assistant Adjutant General, July 15, 1858, Army—Letters Received.
12. Dixon Miles to William Nichols, September 8, 1858, Army—Letters Received.
13. Thomas T. Fauntleroy to Winfield Scott, January 29, 1860, Army—Letters Received.
14. Edward Canby to Assistant Adjutant General, September 19 and November 17, 1860, Army—Letters Received.
15. Albert H. Pfeiffer to Canby, October 16, 1860, Army—Letters Received.
16. See L. R. Bailey, *The Long Walk: A History of the Navajo Wars, 1846–68* (Pasadena, CA: Westernlore Publications, 1978); Peter Iverson, *Diné: A History of the Navajos* (Albuquerque: University of New Mexico Press, 2002); Broderick H. Johnson, ed., *Navajo Stories of the Long Walk Period* (Tsaile, AZ: Navajo Community College Press, 1973); Lawrence C. Kelly, *Navajo Roundup: Selected Correspondence of Kit Carson's Expedition Against the Navajo, 1863–1865* (Boulder, CO: Pruett Publishing, 1970); and Gerald Thompson, *The Army and the Navajo: The Bosque Redondo Reservation Experiment, 1863–1868* (Tucson: University of Arizona Press, 1982).
17. John Ward to Canby, September 2, 1862; José Francisco Chaves to Gurden Chapin, September 8, 1862; Army—Letters Received.
18. Testimony of James H. Carleton, July 3, 1865, Indian Affairs, NM—Letters Received.
19. James L. Collins, "New Mexico Superintendency," August 30, 1857, *RCIA*, 1857, 274.
20. Florence Charley, p. 148; John Tom, p. 178; Dugal Tsosie Begay, p. 13; Hascon Benally, p. 229; as cited in Johnson, ed., *Navajo Stories of the Long Walk Period*.
21. Martha Nez, interview by Baxter Benally and author, August 10, 1988.
22. Yellow Horse, cited in Will Evans, *Along Navajo Trails: Recollections of a Trader* (Logan: Utah State University Press, 2005), 65.
23. Ibid.
24. George Littlesalt, cited in Johnson, ed., *Navajo Stories of the Long Walk Period*, 159–168.
25. Wolfkiller, as cited in Louisa Wade Wetherill (recorder) and Harvey Leake (editor), *Wolfkiller: Wisdom from a Nineteenth-century Navajo Shepherd* (Salt Lake City: Gibbs Smith, 2007), 67.

26. Wetherill and Leake, *Wolfkiller*, 80.

27. Ibid., 81.

28. Ibid., 84.

29. Hashkéninii Begay, cited in Charles Kelly, "Chief Hoskaninni," *Utah Historical Quarterly* 21 no. 3 (Summer 1953): 219–226.

30. Ibid., 221.

31. Hashkéninii Begay, cited by Charles Kelly, "Notes," Charles Kelly Papers, Special Collections, J. Willard Marriott Library, University of Utah, Salt Lake City.

32. "Old Man Bob," Testimony, January 27, 1961, Doris Duke #734. All Doris Duke Indian Oral History Project materials cited are in Special Collections, Marriott Library, University of Utah, Salt Lake City.

33. "Old Ruins" (Kit'siili), Testimony, January 18, 1961, Doris Duke #704.

34. Eddie Nakai, January 21, 1961, Doris Duke #23.

35. Ibid.

36. "White Sheep" Testimonies, March 15, 1953, and January 6, 1961, Doris Duke #687A and 687B; Frank McNitt, *Navajo Wars, Military Campaigns, Slave Raids, and Reprisals* (Albuquerque: University of New Mexico Press, 1990), 80.

37. Charles Dimmock, cited in Steven K. Madsen, *Exploring Desert Stone: John N. Macomb's 1859 Expedition to the Canyonlands of the Colorado* (Logan: Utah State University Press, 2010), 67, 155–156.

38. Ibid., 89.

39. Henry Dodge to Meriwether, April 19, 1856, *TWME*, 32–34.

40. Lorenzo Labadi to Meriwether, August 7, 1856, *TWME*, 50.

41. Asa Carey to Assistant Adjutant General, May 10, 1864; Joseph H. Eaton to Benjamin C. Cutler, February 8, 1865, Army—Letters Received.

42. Carleton to no addressee, February 15, 1865, *War of the Rebellion*, series I, vol. 48, pt. I, 864–865; John Ayers to Cutler, March 20, 1865, Army—Letters Received.

43. Edmund Butler to Assistant Adjutant General, January 18, 1866, Army—Letters Received.

44. Paul Goodman, January 6, 1961, Doris Duke #689.

45. "Warrior Woman" (Desbaa'), Testimony, January 18, 1961, Doris Duke #703.

46. Ibid.

47. W. W. Hill, "Navaho Trading and Trading Ritual: A Study of Cultural Dynamics," *Southwestern Journal of Anthropology* 4 (Fall 1948): 377, 380.

48. Mabel Dry, Testimony, July 25, 1967, Doris Duke #110.

49. George Martin Sr., March 22, 1961, Doris Duke #913.

50. Paul Jones, January 19, 1961, Doris Duke #712.

51. Maggie Holgate, interview with Gary Shumway, June 13, 1968, Doris Duke #956.

52. For a discussion of friendly relations with the local Utes and Paiutes living in the Bears Ears area, see testimony of Billy Holiday, July 21, 1961, Doris Duke #668; George Martin Sr., March 22, 1961, Doris Duke #913; Cecil Parrish, January 6, 1961, Doris Duke #667; Paul Goodman, January 6, 1961, Doris Duke #689; Pat Shortfinger, January 11, 1961, Doris Duke #694; and Anderson Cantsee (Ute), January 28, 1961, Doris Duke #739.

53. Billy Holiday, Testimony.

54. John Smith, as cited in Johnson, ed., *Navajo Stories of the Long Walk Period*, 137; Charles Kelly, "Interview notes with Hoskaninni Begay," Charles Kelly Papers, Special Collections, Marriott Library, University of Utah, Salt Lake City.

55. Fred Descheene, as cited in Johnson, ed., *Navajo Stories of the Long Walk Period*, 210.

56. Howard W. Gorman, as cited in Johnson, ed., *Navajo Stories of the Long Walk Period*, 28.

57. Ibid.

58. Major Albert Pfeiffer to A. K. Graves, December 10, 1866, Indian Affairs, NM—Letters Received.

59. William Davidson to Southern Ute Agent, April 11, 1889, Indian Affairs, NM—Letters Received.

60. J. L. Collins, "Annual Report of the New Mexico Superintendency," October 8, 1861, *RCIA—NM*, 125–126.

61. Collins, "Annual Report," October 10, 1862, *RCIA—NM*, 240; Collins to William P. Dole, November 8, 1862, *RCIA—NM*, 245–246.

62. Michael Steck, "Annual Report," October 10, 1864, *RCIA—NM*, 181–182.

63. Steck, "Annual Report—Abiquiu," September 23, 1863, *RCIA—NM*, 231.

64. Felipe Delgado, "Annual Report—New Mexico Superintendency," September 10, 1865, *RCIA—NM*, 163.

65. Gregory Coyne Thompson, *Southern Ute Lands, 1848–1899: The Creation of a Reservation*, Occasional Papers of the Center of Southwest Studies, no. 1 (Durango, CO: Fort Lewis College, 1972), 4.

66. Virginia McConnell Simmons, *The Ute Indians of Utah, Colorado, and New Mexico* (Boulder: University Press of Colorado, 2000), 115.

67. John Alton Peterson's *Utah's Black Hawk War* (Salt Lake City: University of Utah Press, 1998) is an excellent study of the war and its causes. Unless otherwise specified, this portion of the chapter dealing with the Elk Mountain Utes is dependent upon this source.

68. Ibid.; see also 68 n. 89, R. N. Allred to Brigham Young, April 11, 1865.

69. Agent Franklin H. Head, cited in Peterson, *Utah's Black Hawk War*, 185.

70. Head, "Utah Superintendency," 1867, *RCIA—UT*, 174–175.

71. Peterson, *Utah's Black Hawk War*, 96.

72. Collins and W. F. M. Arny cited in *Utah's Black Hawk War*, 186.

73. Ibid., 186, 196–197.

74. Ibid., 345, 350.

75. Henry Mercure to Carleton, January 15, 1866, *TWME*, 294.

76. A. B. Norton to D. N. Cooley, July 29, 1866, *Report of the Secretary of the Interior*, 39th Cong., 2d Sess., House Exec. Doc. 1, 152.

77. "Report of Special Agent J. K. Graves," 1866, in *Report of the Secretary of the Interior*, 39th Cong., 2d Sess., House Exec. Doc. 1, 152, 132; Archuleta to Graves, January 1, 1866, *Report of the Secretary of the Interior*, 39th Cong., 2d Sess., House Exec. Doc. 1, 152, 141.

78. Arny to A. B. Norton, "Abiquiu Agency Report," June 24, 1867, *RCIA—NM*, 206.

79. Thompson, *Southern Ute Lands, 1848–1899*, 5.

80. Charles Kappler, "Treaty with the Ute, 1868," *Indian Affairs—Laws and Treaties* (Washington, DC: Government Printing Office, 1913), 990–996.

81. Arny to Charles E. Mix, October 3, 1868, Indian Affairs, NM—Letters Received.

82. Navajo Council with Military in February or March, 1866, *TWME*, 139.

83. William T. Sherman in Council on May 28, 1868, *TWME*, 133.

84. Arny to Commissioner of Indian Affairs, August 30, 1868, *Report of the Secretary of the Interior*, 40th Cong., 3d Sess., House Exec. Doc. 1, 632–633.

85. Arny to Luther E. Webb, May 31, 1868, Indian Affairs, NM—Letters Received.

86. Arny to N. G. Taylor, March 19, 1869, Indian Affairs, NM—Letters Received.

87. Arny to Ely S. Parker, July 16, 1869, Indian Affairs, NM—Letters Received.

88. J. B. Hanson to William Clinton, October 13, 1869, Indian Affairs, NM—Letters Received.

89. Frank T. Bennett to J. C. French, October 26, 1869, Indian Affairs, NM—Letters Received.

90. Arny to Parker, July 7, 1869, Indian Affairs, NM—Letters Received.

91. Arny to Parker, July 19, 1879, Indian Affairs, NM—Letters Received.

92. Bennett to Clinton, December 23, 1869, Indian Affairs, NM—Letters Received.

93. N. H. Davis, "Annual Report—Indians," 1869, *RCIA—NM*, 255.

94. William A. Pile, "Memorial," January 24, 1870, Indian Affairs, NM—Letters Received.

95. John Ayers to Commissioner of Indian Affairs, March 31, 1869, Indian Affairs, NM—Letters Received.

Chapter 6

1. Ignacio, cited in W. F. M. Arny, *Indian Agent in New Mexico: The Journal of Special Agent W. F. M. Arny in 1870*, ed. Lawrence R. Murphy (Santa Fe, NM: Stagecoach Press, 1967), 23.

2. William R. Palmer, Field Notes, William R. Palmer Collection, Special Collections, Gerald R. Sherratt Library, Southern Utah State University, Cedar City, 39.

3. Leroy R. Hafen, "Historical Summary of the Ute Indians and the San Juan Mining Region," n.d., unpublished manuscript, Utah State Historical Society Library, Salt Lake City, 18–19.

4. Cited in ibid., 20.

5. Arny, *Indian Agent*, 17.

6. Ibid., 19.

7. Ibid., 24.

8. Ibid., 29.

9. Arny to William Clinton, June 28, 1870, Letters Received by the Office of Indian Affairs, New Mexico Superintendency, 1870, National Archives, RG 75, Washington, DC (hereafter cited as Indian Affairs, NM—Letters Received).

10. J. B. Hanson to Nathaniel Pope, January 5, 1871, Indian Affairs, NM—Letters Received.

11. Hanson to Pope, February 28, 1871, Indian Affairs, NM—Letters Received.

12. Hanson to Clinton, July 4, 1870; Arny to Eli S. Parker, July 19, 1870; Indian Affairs, NM—Letters Received.

13. Hanson to Pope, "Annual Report," September 1, 1871, Indian Affairs, NM—Letters Received.

14. John S. Armstrong to Pope, March 30, 1872, and May 6, 1872, Indian Affairs, NM—Letters Received.

15. John Alton Peterson, *Utah's Black Hawk War* (Salt Lake City: University of Utah Press, 1998), 362 n. 53.

16. Eveline M. Alexander, *Cavalry Wife: The Diary of Eveline M. Alexander,*" as cited in Peterson, *Utah's Black Hawk War*, 364.

17. Pope, "New Mexico Superintendency," October 10, 1872, *Report of the Commissioner of Indian Affairs* (Washington, DC: Government Printing Office, 1872), 299 (hereafter cited as *RCIA*); Armstrong to Pope, June 2, 1872, Indian Affairs, NM—Letters Received; see also Norman J. Bender, "The Battle of Tierra Amarilla," *New Mexico Historical Review* 63, no. 3 (July 1988): 241–256.

18. Francis A. Walker, "New Mexico Agency—Navajos," November 1, 1872, *RCIA*, 53.

19. Charles Adams, "Los Pinos Agency," September 6, 1872, *RCIA*, 291; Arny, "Navajo Agency," September 9, 1872, *RCIA*, 303.

20. *Report of the Commission to Negotiate with the Ute Tribe of Indians*, (Washington, DC: Government Printing Office, 1873), 46.

21. John S. Littlefield, September 5, 1872, *RCIA*, 288–289.

22. Hafen, *Historical Summary*, 21–22.

23. U.S. Congress, House, "Negotiations with Ute Indians," January 6, 1873, *Report of the Secretary of the Interior*, H. Exec. Doc. 90, 42d Cong., 3d Sess., 2.

24. Ibid., 5–6.

25. Ibid., 7–8.

26. Ibid., 2.

27. *Report of the Commission to Negotiate with the Ute Tribe of Indians*, October 15, 1873 (Washington, DC: Government Printing Office, 1873), 6.

28. Ibid., 19.

29. Ibid., 22.

30. Ibid., 31.

31. George W. Manypenny, *Our Indian Wards* (New York: Da Capo Press, 1972), 418–419.

32. Ferdinand V. Hayden, *Ninth Annual Report of the United States Geological and Geographical Survey of the Territories Embracing Colorado and Parts of Adjacent Territories: Being a Report of Progress of the Exploration for the Year 1875* (Washington, DC: Government Printing Office, 1877), 1–6.

33. Ibid., "Report of William H. Holmes, Geologist of the San Juan Division, 1875," 238–239.

34. James T. Gardner, "Ute Warriors," *Rocky Mountain News*, September 5, 1875, 4. Unless otherwise noted, newspaper accounts will not have page numbers cited because they are retyped manuscripts from the F. V. Hayden Collection, Special Collections, American Heritage Center, University of Wyoming, Laramie.

35. Cuthbert Mills, "The Hayden Survey," *New York Times*, September 9, 1875. See also Albert C. Peale, "Diary," F. V. Hayden Collection, Special Collections, American Heritage Center, University of Wyoming, Laramie, 14–15.

36. See John N. Macomb, *Report of the Exploring Expedition from Santa Fe, New Mexico, to the Junction of the Grand and Green Rivers of the Great Colorado of the West in 1859* (Washington, DC: Government Printing Office, 1876).

37. Mills, "The Hayden Survey," September 9, 1875.

38. The Dreyse Needle Gun received its name from its long firing pin, which struck a percussion cap and ignited the black powder charge, sending a .61 acorn-shaped round at a muzzle velocity of one thousand feet per second. This breech-loading, bolt-action rifle increased the rate of fire over muzzle-loading weapons in a five-to-one superiority, leading eventually to a standardized cartridge. This rifle was used in both the Austro-Prussian and Franco-Prussian Wars. By 1871 the Prussian military replaced it with improved weaponry, but surplus needle guns made their way to the United States. From "Franco-Prussian War: Dreyse Needle Gun," http://militaryhistory.about.com/od/smallarms/p/needlegun.htm?p=1.

39. Peale, "Diary," 16.

40. Mills, "The Hayden Survey," September 9, 1875.

41. David Grey (Aldrich), "The Hayden Survey," *The Daily Inter-Ocean*, September 8, 1875, F. V. Hayden Collection, Special Collections, American Heritage Center, University of Wyoming, Laramie.

42. Gardner, "Ute Warriors," *Rocky Mountain News*, September 5, 1875, F. V. Hayden Collection, Special Collections, American Heritage Center, University of Wyoming, Laramie.

43. Mills, "The Hayden Survey," September 9, 1875.

44. Ibid.

45. Grey, "The Hayden Survey," September 8, 1875.

46. Mills, "The Hayden Survey," September 9, 1875.

47. Grey, "The Hayden Survey," September 8, 1875.

48. Peale, "Diary," 17.

49. Peale, "Chain and Level — The Hayden Geological Survey," *Philadelphia Press*, September 9, 1875, F. V. Hayden Collection, Special Collections, American Heritage Center, University of Wyoming, Laramie.

50. Gardner, "Ute Warriors," September 5, 1875.

51. Grey, "The Hayden Survey," September 8, 1875.

52. Mills, "The Hayden Survey, A Rescue Expedition," *New York Times*, September 25, 1875, F. V. Hayden Collection, Special Collections, American Heritage Center, University of Wyoming, Laramie.

53. Gardner, "The Sierra La Sal Utes," *Rocky Mountain News*, September 17, 1875, F. V. Hayden Collection, Special Collections, American Heritage Center, University of Wyoming, Laramie.

54. Mills, "The Hayden Survey, A Rescue Expedition," September 25, 1875.

55. William H. Jackson and Howard R. Driggs, *The Pioneer Photographer* (New York: World Book Company, 1929), 249.

56. William H. Jackson, "Diary — June 22, 1875 thru October 6, 1875," August 23, 1875, microfilm, Colorado Historical Society, Denver.

57. Jackson and Driggs, *The Pioneer Photographer*, 266.

58. Ibid., pp. 267–268.

59. William H. Jackson, *Time Exposure: The Autobiography of William Henry Jackson* (New York: G. P. Putnam and Sons, 1940), 241.

60. Ibid. This is somewhat confusing since Polk of later years would be young at this time. According to the 1915 Ute census, "Old Polk," a.k.a. "Billy Hatch," was born in 1857 and had the phonetically spelled Ute name of "Poco Narraguinip" — "Slow Storyteller." If this is truly his father, then perhaps this name and the responsibility of being a storyteller had been passed down for a number of generations. It also could be an entirely different person.

61. Ibid.

62. Gardner, "The Sierra La Sal Utes," *Rocky Mountain News*, September 17, 1875, 2.

63. Holmes, "Report," 239.

64. "The Murderous Ute Outlaws," *Rocky Mountain News*, September 21, 1875, 2.

65. Gardner, "Ute Warriors," September 5, 1875.

66. Mills, "The Hayden Survey," September 9, 1875.

67. "The Hayden Expedition," *Philadelphia Inquirer*,

September 28, 1875, F. V. Hayden Collection, Special Collections, American Heritage Center, University of Wyoming, Laramie.

68. Grey, "The Hayden Survey," September 25, 1875.

69. Henry R. Crosby to Hayden, November 26, 1876, F. V. Hayden Collection, Special Collections, American Heritage Center, University of Wyoming, Laramie.

70. John Pope, "Indian Affairs—Utes in Colorado," September 26, 1876, *Report of the Secretary of War*, H. Exec. Doc. 1, pt. 2, 44th Cong., 2d Sess., 449.

71. Edward Hatch to Assistant Adjutant General, September 30, 1876, Indian Affairs, NM—Letters Received.

72. S. A. Russell, "New Mexico—Abiquiu Agency," August 16, 1876, *RCIA*, 102–103.

73. Henry R. Crosby to Thomas W. Patterson, April 13, 1876, Letters Received—Adjutant Generals Office, 1871–1880 (hereafter cited as AGO—Letters Received).

74. H. F. Bond, "Los Pinos Agency," September 30, 1876, *RCIA*, 19.

75. See J. T. Biggs Family, "Our Valley" (Mesa, AZ: self-published, 1977); Thomas Rickner, *The History of the Pioneers of the Mancos Valley* (Mancos, CO: self-published, 1910); John Franklin Palmer, "Mormon Settlements in the San Juan Basin of Colorado and New Mexico," unpublished master's thesis, 1967, Brigham Young University, Provo, UT; Frank Silvey, *History and Settlement of Northern San Juan County* (self-published; n.p., n.d.); Lee Emerson Deets, "Paradox Valley—An Historical Interpretation of Its Structure and Changes," *Colorado Magazine* 11, no. 5 (September 1934): 186–198; Paul M. O'Rourke, *Frontier in Transition: A History of Southwestern Colorado*, Cultural Resource Series 10 (Denver: Bureau of Land Management, 1980).

76. Petition to William T. Sherman, February 14, 1877, AGO—Letters Received.

77. James J. Hefferman et al. to President of the United States, May 25, 1877, Letters Received—Colorado, 1857–1907, National Archives, RG 75.

78. No name, Second Lieutenant, Third Artillery, "Relations between the Utes and Settlers in the San Juan Region," November 13, 1877, AGO—Letters Received.

79. S. A. Russell, "Abiquiu Agency Report," August 15, 1877, *RCIA*, 154, and August 7, 1878, *RCIA*, 106.

80. Secretary C. May(?) to Secretary of War, March 2, 1878; E. A. Hayt to Secretary of the Interior, March 18, 1878; Hayt to Secretary of the Interior, April 5, 1878; John Pope to Philip H. Sheridan, April 18, 1878, AGO—Letters Received.

81. Sheridan to Sherman, May 3, 1878, AGO—Letters Received.

82. William W. Belknap to Sherman, July 13, 1878, AGO—Letters Received.

83. Pope to Sheridan, April 20, 1878; Hayt to Secretary of the Interior, April 30, 1878; Special Orders 82, May 8, 1878, Headquarters, Department of the Missouri, Fort Leavenworth, KS; William Leeds to Secretary of the Interior, July 8, 1878; William Whipple to Adjutant General, July 19, 1878; Edward Hatch to Assistant Adjutant General, July 19, 1878; AGO—Letters Received.

84. F. H. Weaver, "Annual Report—Southern Ute Agency," August 18, 1878, *RCIA*, 16–17.

85. Ibid.

86. Weaver to Hayt, April 3, 1878, AGO—Letters Received.

87. Weaver to Hayt, April 5, 1878, AGO—Letters Received.

88. Weaver to Hayt, April 3, 1878, AGO—Letters Received.

89. S. D. Axtell to Carl Schurz, May 28, 1878, Indian Affairs, NM—Letters Received.

90. Frances Leon Quintana, *Ordeal of Change: The Southern Utes and Their Neighbors* (Walnut Creek: Altamira Press, 2004), 28.

91. John Pope, "Report of General John Pope," October 4, 1878, *Report of the Secretary of War*, 45th Cong., 3d Sess., 1878, 41; Acting Commissioner of Indian Affairs to Weaver, June 26, 1878; "Articles of Convention and Agreement," November 9, 1878; Edward Hatch to Assistant Adjutant General, November 25, 1878; Ute Commissioner to Assistant Adjutant General, December 4, 1878; AGO—Letters Received.

92. Duane A. Smith, *A Time for Peace: Fort Lewis, Colorado, 1878–1891* (Boulder: University Press of Colorado, 2006), 7–10.

93. Henry Page, "Annual Report," August 28, 1879, *RCIA*, 16–17.

94. Ibid. Page to Hayt, May 29, 1879, Letters Received—Colorado, National Archives, RG 75.

95. "The Indians," clipping from Cimarron, NM, newspaper, September 18, 1879, attached to letter by Charles Parker to Southern Ute Indian Agent, September 19, 1879, AGO—Letters Received.

96. The best detailed account is by Marshall Sprague, *Massacre: The Tragedy at White River* (Lincoln: University of Nebraska Press, 1957); Robert Emmitt, *The Last War Trail: The Utes and the Settlement of Colorado* (Norman: University of Oklahoma Press, 1954); Charles S. Marsh, *The Utes of Colorado: People of the Shining Mountains* (Boulder, CO: Pruett Publishing, 1982); P. David Smith, *Ouray, Chief of the Utes* (Ouray, CO: Wayfinder Press, 1986); Virginia McConnell Simmons, *The Ute Indians of Utah, Colorado, and New Mexico* (Boulder: University Press of Colorado, 2000); and Robert Silbernagel, *Troubled Trails: The Meeker Affair and the Expulsion of the Utes from Colorado* (Salt Lake City: University of Utah Press, 2011).

97. Sheridan to H. McCrary, October 3, 1879; Hatch

to Adjutant General, October 16, 1879; AGO—Letters Received.

98. Page to Hayt, October 13, 1879, AGO—Letters Received.

99. Valois to Assistant Adjutant General, October 15, 1879, "Ute Indians in Colorado," *Letter from the Secretary of the Interior*, S. Exec. Doc. 31, 46th Cong., 2d Sess., 87.

100. Ibid., Page to Hayt, October 21, 1879, 163.

101. For both a personal experience of a man stationed at Pagosa Springs during the conflict and an example of the rapidity with which he and his unit were deployed, see Robert G. Athern, ed., "Major Hough's March into Southern Ute Country, 1879," *Colorado Magazine* 25, no. 3 (May 1948): 97–109.

102. Pope to Sherman, December 31, 1879, AGO—Letters Received.

Chapter 7

1. See Ruth S. Clark, "The Founding of Dolores," *Colorado Magazine* 5 (Fall 1927): 60–63, for information on the development of Dolores and Big Bend.

2. Daniel K. Muhlestein, "The Rise and Fall of the Cattle Companies in San Juan, 1880–1900", unpublished manuscript, n.d., Utah State Historical Society Library, Salt Lake City, 2–5.

3. Robert W. Frazer, *Forts of the West: Military Forts and Presidios and Posts Commonly Called Forts West of the Mississippi River to 1898* (Norman: University of Oklahoma Press, 1972), 38.

4. Notes on file, "Fort Lewis—Calendar of Letters Received, 1880," Special Collections, Center of Southwest Studies, Fort Lewis College, Durango, CO.

5. Three major studies look at the role of Fort Lewis. In chronological order, they are: Robert W. Delaney, *Blue Coats, Red Skins, and Black Gowns: 100 Years of Fort Lewis* (Durango, CO: Durango Herald, 1977); Duane A. Smith, *Sacred Trust: The Birth and Development of Fort Lewis College* (Niwot: University Press of Colorado, 1991), and *A Time for Peace: Fort Lewis, Colorado, 1878–1891* (Boulder: University Press of Colorado, 2006).

6. "Against the Utes," *Dolores News*, May 29, 1880, 1.

7. The historical record provides two spellings of James Merritt's or Merrick's name. I have chosen to use the latter based on key documents written at the time by people who knew him.

8. See Robert S. McPherson, "Navajos, Mormons, and Henry L. Mitchell," *Utah Historical Quarterly* 55, no. 1 (Winter 1987): 50–65.

9. David E. Miller, *Hole-in-the-Rock: An Epic in the Colonization of the Great American West* (Salt Lake City: University of Utah Press, 1975), 92–94.

10. Galen Eastman to Commissioner of Indian Affairs, February 6, 1880, Indian Affairs, NM—Letters Received, National Archives, RG 75, Washington, DC.

11. H. L. Mitchell to Eastman, February 15, 1880, Indian Affairs, NM—Letters Received.

12. J. Carpenter to Carl Schurz, February 28, 1880, Indian Affairs, NM—Letters Received.

13. Mitchell to Eastman, February 27, 1880; Eastman to Commissioner of Indian Affairs, March 8, 1880; and F. T. Bennett to Acting Assistant Adjutant General, March 22, 1880; Indian Affairs, NM—Letters Received.

14. "Trouble near Home, and War in the Blue Mountains," *Dolores News*, November 13, 1880, 1.

15. "The Navajo Mountain Explorers," *Dolores News*, January 28, 1882, 1.

16. Albert R. Lyman, "History of San Juan County, 1879–1917," unpublished manuscript, Special Collections, Harold B. Lee Library, Brigham Young University, Provo, UT, 12.

17. Albert R. Lyman Testimony, July 30, 1968, Doris Duke Indian Oral History Project no. 395, Special Collections, Marriott Library, University of Utah, Salt Lake City.

18. Lyman, "History of San Juan," 20.

19. Muhlestein, "The Rise and Fall of the Cattle Companies," 31.

20. Lyman, "History of San Juan," 21–22, 31.

21. Ibid., 66–67; Albert R. Lyman, "San Juan and Its Piutes," *San Juan Record*, December 17, 1931, 5.

22. Lyman, "History of San Juan," 35–36.

23. Ibid.

24. George Manypenny et al., "Report of Ute Commission," January 20, 1880, *Report of the Secretary of the Interior, Indian Affairs* (Washington, DC: Government Printing Office), 260.

25. Ibid., W. H. Berry, "Report of the Los Pinos Indian Agency," September 10, 1881, 79.

26. Ibid.; Manypenny et al., "Report of the Ute Commission," 261.

27. Ibid., 263.

28. John Pope, "The Utes," September, 22, 1881, *Report of the Secretary of War*, vol. 1 (Washington, DC: Government Printing Office, 1881), 116.

29. For a longer version of this battle and surrounding events, see Rusty Salmon and Robert S. McPherson, "Cowboys, Indians, and Conflict: The Pinhook Draw—Little Castle Valley Fight, 1881," *Utah Historical Quarterly* 69, no. 1 (Winter 2001): 4–28.

30. D. D. Williams to Col. R. E. A. Crofton, May 2, 1881, Headquarters Letters Calendar 1881, Fort Lewis College Library, Durango, CO.

31. Henry Page to Crofton, October 24, 1880, Calendar of Letters Received, 1880, Fort Lewis College Library, Durango, CO.

32. A. W. Dillon, "Early History of Montezuma County," in *Dolores Star*, September 4, 1908, 1.

33. Mancos Minutes, La Plata County, CO, Septem-

ber 25, 1881, Special Collections, Marriott Library, University of Utah, Salt Lake City. Members of the Mancos and Dolores communities wrote this important document on September 25, 1881, and it was signed by many of the participants in the Pinhook Draw fight. Consequently, its information appears highly accurate, not being subject to vague recollection.

34. Events surrounding the Pinhook Draw fight have been discussed in a variety of sources: interviews, letters, newspaper articles, reminiscences, second- and thirdhand accounts, and secondary sources—many of which are conflicting. Materials gathered shortly after the fight from participants who later shared their story are used here. Not all of the conflicting information has been resolved, nor all questions answered. In a number of instances, what follows is the most logical explanation of what occurred based on primary sources, a walk of the battlefield, and the attitude of the times. Evaluation of some of the more prominent sources is given in future endnotes.

35. Wilson Rockwell, *The Utes: A Forgotten People* (Denver, CO: Sage Books, 1956), 220–221. This author validates his version of the May and Thurman killings from interviews and letters from the 1930s. Most of the testimony was given a long time after the event but seems plausible.

36. "Interesting Indian Intelligence," *Dolores News*, May 14, 1881, 1.

37. Agent W. H. Berry to Commissioner of Indian Affairs, July 18, 1881, Special Collections, Marriott Library, University of Utah, Salt Lake City.

38. Jones Adams, "In the Stronghold of the Piutes," *Overland Monthly* 22 (December 1893): 584; Jordan Bean, "Jordan Bean's Story and the Castle Valley Indian Fight," *Colorado Magazine* 20 (1943): 19; A. M. Rogers, "A True Narrative of an Indian Fight," *Echo of the Cliff Dwellers* (District 1, La Sal National Forest, U.S. Department of Agriculture, April 1912), 39.

39. Rockwell, *The Utes*, 221. Although Indians subsequently claimed that Smith had been killed, and several years later an unidentified body was found, he could have escaped. An article published in the *Dolores News* on May 25, 1883, tells of how Smith, who was in jail in Santa Fe, had been talking about his escape from Indians near the Utah-Colorado border.

40. Faun M. Tanner, *The Far Country: Moab and La Sal* (Salt Lake City: Olympus Publishing, 1976), 117. Tanner relied on multiple sources, including newspapers and interviews, and depended heavily on Frank Silvey's writings. One of her greatest original contributions is her interview of Joseph Burkholder, a member of the Moab contingent, which she cites in her book.

41. Platte D. Lyman, "Diary of Platte D. Lyman,"

Special Collections, Brigham Young University Library, Provo, UT, 39.

42. Ibid., 40.

43. Bean, "Jordan Bean's Story," 19; Mancos Minutes, 1881.

44. *Dolores News*, May 28, 1881, 2; Cornelia A. Perkins, Marian Nielson, and Lenora Jones, *Saga of San Juan* (Salt Lake City: Mercury Publishing Company, 1968), 238; Mancos Minutes, 1881.

45. Conflicting accounts written at the time or shortly after raise questions about accuracy. To see how far some of these stories can stray from actual events, read C. N. Cox, "Late Indian Troubles in the San Juan Country," *Colorado Magazine* 17, no. 6 (June 1940): 30–34.

46. Perkins et al., *Saga*, 238; Tanner, *The Far Country*, 119–120; Frank Silvey, *History and Settlement of Northern San Juan County, Utah* (n.p., n.d.), 13–14. Silvey is an oft-quoted source on the Pinhook battle, and though he was not a participant, his brother Jack was part of the rescue party from Rico. Some of Silvey's version is unsubstantiated by other documents or eyewitness accounts.

47. Bean, "Jordan Bean's Story," 20.

48. "A 'Quien Sabe' Case," *Dolores News*, June 11, 1881, 2.

49. "The Stronghold of the Paiutes," *Dolores News*, June 4, 1881, 1.

50. Ibid.

51. "Operational Returns," Fort Lewis, October 1878–August 1891, Microfiche M617, National Archives, Washington, DC; "War on the Border," *Denver Tribune*, June 25, 1881, 2; Silvey, *History*, 19; Bean, "Jordan Bean's Story," 19–20; "The Fight with the Utes," *Denver Republican*, June 29, 1881, 1.

52. Adams, "In the Stronghold of the Piutes," 586.

53. Jordan Bean, "Jordan Bean," unpublished account, May 14, 1941, in possession of author. Bean recorded his memories in several articles and interviews, most of which were written sixty years after the fight. Despite the lapse in time, his statements have proven to be quite accurate and verifiable using other sources.

54. Perkins et al., *Saga*, 240; Silvey, *History*, 20.

55. "The Fights with the Utes," *Denver Republican*, June 29, 1881, 1; Rogers, "A True Narrative," 40. Many of Rogers's minute details are accurate (e.g., the eclipse and the comet), but he injudiciously wrote his story as though he were a participant in the battle when, in fact, he has been verified as a member of the Rico rescue party. He gleaned much of his material from other sources and the participants as well as his firsthand experience.

56. Ibid.

57. Ibid., 46.

58. Ibid, 42; "Second Anniversary," *Dolores News*, June 16, 1883, 3.

59. Rogers, "A True Narrative," 41–42.

60. "Second Anniversary," *Dolores News*, June 16, 1883, 3.

61. Bean, "Jordan Bean's Story," 20.

62. Untitled, *The Idea* (Durango newspaper), June 16, 1886, 1.

63. Rockwell, *The Utes*, 222.

64. "The Indian Battle," *Denver Tribune*, July 9, 1881, 3. This appears to be a very accurate source, having been written within three weeks of the battle and whose contents were "acknowledged as reliable by the survivors who have returned and furnished the facts for the following." It is also interesting that it corresponds closely to what Mancos Jim, a Ute participant, claimed five years later.

65. Silvey, *History*, 17.

66. Ibid.

67. "War! With the Indians," *Dolores News*, June 25, 1881, 1.

68. Bean, "Jordan Bean's Story," 20.

69. Ibid., 20–21.

70. Silvey, *History*, 19.

71. "War!," *Dolores News*, June 25, 1881, 1.

72. "Second Anniversary," *Dolores News*, June 16, 1883, 3.

73. The actual number was probably closer to ten men from Moab. This is based on what Joseph Burkholder, a member of this group, stated in an interview with Faun Tanner (see note 39).

74. "Return of Rico's Reinforcements," *Dolores News*, July 9, 1881, 2.

75. Ibid.

76. Bean, "Jordan Bean," 3; Eliza Burr (Moab resident), Statement, November 30, 1948, in possession of author.

77. Ibid.; Jones, Kumen. Manuscript. Utah State Historical Society Library, Salt Lake City, 590.

78. "The Indian Battle," *Denver Tribune*, July 9, 1881, 3.

79. Ibid.

80. "Return," *Dolores News*, July 9, 1881, 1.

81. Operational Returns, Ninth Cavalry, Calendar of Letters Received, 1881, Fort Lewis College Library, Durango, CO.

82. Untitled, *The Idea*, June 16, 1886, 1.

83. Jones, ms., 591; Thomas Magraw to R. S. Mackenzie, June 25, 1881, RG 94, Letters Received, Adjutant General's Office, 1881, National Archives, Washington, DC (hereafter referred to as AGO — Letters Received).

84. Lyman, "History of San Juan," 22–23.

85. Lieutenant Colonel R. Crofton to Colonel Henry Page, June 9, 1881, RG 75, Bureau of Indian Affairs, Consolidated Ute Agency, Federal Records Center, Denver.

86. H. G. Cavanaugh to Commander, B Company Thirteenth Infantry, May 22, 1881, Calendar of Letters Received, 1881, Special Collections Fort Lewis College Library, Durango, CO.

87. Mount Tukuhnikivatz in the La Sal Mountains is the second highest peak in the range. The fact that a band of these "Sierra La Sal Utes" was named after it, or vice versa, indicates once again the practice of naming a group associated with the mountains in their tribal area.

88. Berry to Commissioner of Indian Affairs, July 18, 1881.

89. H. J. Crosby, Letter from the War Department with Enclosure from Colonel C. H. Smith, September 29, 1881, MS 109, Special Collections, Marriott Library, University of Utah, Salt Lake City.

90. Colonel R. S. Mackenzie to Assistant Adjutant General, Fort Leavenworth, Kansas, July 20, 1881, AGO — Letters Received.

91. Hiram Price to Secretary of the Interior, August 15, 1881, AGO — Letters Received.

92. Secretary of Interior to Secretary of War, September 29, 1881; Major General Jonathan Pope to Colonel R. Williams, November 22, 1881; AGO — Letters Received.

93. Pope to Adjutant General, Headquarters Division of Missouri, January 21, 1882, AGO — Letters Received.

94. Pope to Adjutant General, Headquarters Division of the Missouri, January 21, 1882; Price to Secretary of War, February 16, 1882; AGO — Letters Received.

95. Price to Secretary of the Interior, August 9, 1883; Assistant Adjutant General, Department Commander, to Adjutant General, U.S. Army, August 22, 1883; AGO — Letters Received.

96. Manypenny et al., "Report of the Ute Commission," 335.

97. Henry Page, "Southern Ute Agency Report," September 1881, *Report of the Commissioner of Indian Affairs* (Washington, DC: Government Printing Office, 1881), 81.

Chapter 8

1. Albert R. Lyman, "History of San Juan County, 1879–1917," Special Collections, Harold B. Lee Library, Brigham Young University, Provo, UT, 35.

2. Beatrice P. Nielson, "Settling of San Juan County," Special Collections, Marriott Library, University of Utah, Salt Lake City, 11.

3. Don D. Walker, "The Carlisles: Cattle Barons of the Upper Basin," *Utah Historical Quarterly* 32, no. 3 (Summer 1964): 269–270.

4. Ibid., 272.

5. "A New Military Post," *Dolores News*, October 29, 1881, 1.

6. For a longer discussion of Fort Lewis's military role in southeastern Utah, see Robert S. McPherson, "Soldiering in a Corner, Living on the Fringe: Military Operations in Southeastern Utah, 1880–1890," *Utah Historical* Quarterly 77, no. 2 (Spring 2009): 126–150.

7. See Robert S. McPherson, "Navajos, Mormons, and Henry L. Mitchell," *Utah Historical Quarterly* 55, no. 1 (Winter 1987): 50–65.

8. Assistant Adjutant General, District of New Mexico, to Commanding Officer, Fort Lewis, June 12, 1882, Calendar of Letters Received, Special Collections, Fort Lewis College Library, Durango, CO (hereafter cited as Fort Lewis—Letters Received).

9. "The Ute Reservation," *Dolores News*, March 4, 1882, 1.

10. Gregory C. Thompson, "The Unwanted Indians: The Southern Utes in Southeastern Utah," *Utah Historical Quarterly* 49, no. 2 (Spring 1981): 189–203.

11. "The Southern Utes," *Dolores News*, March 11, 1882, 3.

12. "Explorers," *Dolores News*, June 3, 1882, 1; "Lower Dolores," *Dolores News*, June 2, 1883, 1.

13. Colonel Stanley to Warren Patten, August 31 and September 1 and 2, 1883, RG 75, Bureau of Indian Affairs, Consolidated Ute Agency, Federal Records Center, Denver (hereafter cited as BIA—Ute Agency Records). After further investigation of this incident, blame for the murder was placed on a Navajo. Who actually killed Tracy is questionable. See David M. Brugge's unpublished manuscript "Navajo Use and Occupation of Lands North of the San Juan River in Present-day Utah," in author's possession.

14. For more information about this incident and others in southeastern Utah during this period, see Robert S. McPherson, *The Northern Navajo Frontier, 1860–1900, Expansion Through Adversity* (Logan: Utah State University Press, [1988] 2001), 46.

15. W. J. Forham, *Deseret News*, October 12, 1887, cited in "San Juan Stake History," unpublished manuscript, Historical Archives, Church of Jesus Christ of Latter-day Saints, Salt Lake City.

16. Petition from Mancos to Commanding Officer, Fort Lewis, March 18, 1884; Commanding Officer, District of New Mexico, to Commanding Officer, Fort Lewis, March 18, 1884, AGO—Letters Received; Warren Patten to Commanding Officer, Fort Lewis, March 24, 1884, Fort Lewis—Outgoing Correspondence, 1883–1885, Special Collections, Fort Lewis Colllege Library, Durango, CO.

17. Major R. H. Hall to Assistant Adjutant General at Fort Leavenworth, April 18, 1884, RG 75, Letters Received, 1881–1907, Bureau of Indian Affairs, National Archives, Washington, DC (hereafter cited as BIA—Letters Received).

18. Second Lieutenant J. F. Kreps to Post Adjutant at Fort Lewis, May 1, 1884, BIA—Letters Received.

19. Lieutenant Theodore Mosher to Christian Soffke, May 18, 1884, Fort Lewis—Outgoing Correspondence.

20. "The Ute Mountain Country," *Dolores News*, June 28, 1884, 2.

21. Ibid.

22. E. L. Stevens to Warren Patten, Esq., June 13, 1884, BIA—Ute Agency Records.

23. Sam Todd to Glen Hanks, "A Pioneer Experience," March 2, 1925, Utah State Historical Society Library, Salt Lake City, 1–5. Sam Todd is an interesting character. Born in Missouri in 1854, he soon moved to Texas, where he worked as a cowboy. By age eighteen he had contracted tuberculosis, and he ended a two-year bout with the disease by having a lung removed. Thereafter he always wore a pad under his coat to compensate for the caved-in left side of his chest. In 1880, at the age of twenty-five, he moved to the Disappointment country of southwestern Colorado, where he continued to ranch. He lived in this area until 1925, when he and his wife moved to Burbank, California. He spent the last four years of his life there, returning to Cortez, Colorado, in 1929 just long enough to breathe his last and be buried in the country that he knew and loved. "Sam Todd Never Bragged—Could Have," *Montezuma Valley Journal*, April 22, 1987, 10A.

24. See Robert S. McPherson and Winston Hurst, "The Fight at Soldier Crossing, 1884: Military Considerations in Canyon Country," *Utah Historical Quarterly* 70, no. 3 (Summer 2002): 258–281.

25. James Monroe Redd clarifies exactly where the two groups were located: "The cowboys were camped on the top of the hill just above Verdure where the dugway goes up. It's a pretty good road now. It used to be a narrow dirt road. The Utes were camped down in Verdure where the Barton home is now." James Monroe Redd Jr., interview with Michael Hurst, February 15, 1973, CRC-J4, Charles Redd Center for Western Studies, Brigham Young University, Provo, UT, 9.

26. Don D. Walker, "Cowboys, Indians, and Cavalry," *Utah Historical Quarterly* 34, no. 3 (Summer 1966): 254–262. This article is an annotated letter written by Harold Carlisle eleven days after the fight and published in the *Denver Republican* on July 29. Rich in detail, this is an important primary document.

27. Ibid., 257; Cornelia A. Perkins, Marian Nielson, and Lenora Jones, *Saga of San Juan* (Salt Lake City: Mercury Publishing Company, 1968), 242; H. L. Mitchell to Warren Patten, July 8, 1884, BIA—Ute Agency Records.

28. Perkins et al., *Saga*, 242.

29. "A Serious Conflict," *Dolores News*, July 12, 1884, 3; Lyman, "History of San Juan," 40.

30. Lyman, "History of San Juan," 41; Todd, "A Pioneer Experience," 1; "A Serious Conflict," 3.

31. "A Serious Conflict," 3.

32. Albert R. Lyman, *The Outlaw of Navaho Mountain*

(Salt Lake City: Albert R. Lyman Trust, 1986), 55–56.

33. Platte D. Lyman, "Diary of Platte D. Lyman," Special Collections, Harold B. Lee Library, Brigham Young University, Provo, 76.

34. "A Serious Conflict," 3.

35. Ibid.

36. Walker, "Cowboys," 257.

37. "Two More Victims," *Dolores News*, July 26, 1884, 3.

38. Walker, "Cowboys," 257; Report of Colonel L. P. Bradley to Secretary of War, *Report of the Secretary of the Interior*, 48th Cong., 2d Sess., vol. 1, 1884, 121.

39. "Two More Victims," 3.

40. Christian Soffke to Warren Patten, July 12, 1884, BIA — Ute Agency Records.

41. Anonymous to Patten, BIA — Ute Agency Records, n.d., 1884.

42. Patten to Hiram Price, Commissioner of Indian Affairs, July (blurred) 1884, BIA — Ute Agency Records.

43. "Capture of Six Indians," *Dolores News*, July 19, 1884, 3.

44. Walker, "Cowboys," 258.

45. It is unclear whether this is a literary device invented by Lyman, a metaphor similar to the "warpath" of Hollywood movies, or an actual physical trail imbued by the Utes with legend and lore from previous defensive and offensive campaigns, as Lyman asserts. In any case, the Utes were undoubtedly following familiar trails, components in a vast and complex network of ancient trails that spanned the region.

46. Identifying parts of this old Ute trail is difficult. In an attempt to tie Todd's account to the land, I spent two days looking for a trail off Elk Ridge. The most likely route followed by the Utes and their pursuers in 1884 is now a major, developed stock trail that heads in a corral on the rim of the Pushout and descends via a knifelike ridge with several level spots to the valley floor. This trail has been significantly improved and maintained over the years and remains in active use as a drive trail. Most other sections of the Pushout and adjoining lands that offer the view described by Todd are impassable or would be difficult to negotiate by pack stock, with ledges, talus, dense vegetation, and rock walls making movement very difficult or impossible. Todd's statement that two Utes, a half mile away from the rim, lit signal fires to warn the main body fits very nicely with a level plateau on the ridge approximately a half mile from the top. The place is clearly visible from the likely Ute encampment on the Cheesebox/White Canyon bench to the southwest, and would have offered easy access to the valley floor after the fires were lit.

47. Todd, "A Pioneer Experience," 2.

48. Ibid.

49. Walker, "Cowboys," 258; Todd, "A Pioneer Experience," 2.

50. Lyman, *The Outlaw of Navaho Mountain*, 59.

51. Todd, "A Pioneer Experience," 2.

52. Ibid. People who travel to the battle site will find the terrain formidable. The trail to Piute Pass is dimly etched in the land and is not associated with the recently rebladed, mid-twentieth-century uranium road that traverses another part of the slope at a gentler angle. After leaving the bench along which Highway 95 runs, the Utes' trail winds over a ridge with three steplike hills that ascend to the base of a steep talus slope approximately three hundred meters long. Ascending at a thirty-plus degree angle, the slope is covered with boulders, sagebrush, and piñon and juniper trees. At the top of the talus slope is the low saddle in the seventy-foot-high rimrock, through which Piute Pass slices. There is no level place at the top of the talus slope for the maneuver of units, and the trail traversing the talus is too steep. The aforementioned bladed road has cut through the pass and widened the gap, apparently obliterating the actual narrow defile where the old trail passed and significantly disturbing the position used by the Utes.

There are two interesting points for conjecture. First, two unfired .50-70 caliber bullets were found along the trail, one between the White Canyon bench and the upper talus slope, the other in a protected location in the Ute position at the top of the trail. These were made to be fired by either an obsolete (in 1884) U.S. Army Springfield rifle or a Sharps rifle. The placement of the bullets suggests the possibility that they may have been put in position as defensive "medicine" to invoke supernatural power in defense against the pursuers. A second issue is how the Utes brought all of their livestock up such a steep slope and through the narrow defile. Most likely they separated and tied the large horse herd into strings before leading them up the trail in groups. The ruggedness of the terrain would have precluded herding so many animals en masse.

53. Walker, "Cowboys," 258; Todd, "A Pioneer Experience," 2.

54. While the battlefield has been picked over by visitors to the site, the evidence that has been salvaged gives an indication of how both sides were armed. The soldiers carried .45-70 caliber trapdoor Springfield carbines with a maximum effective range of five hundred yards. The cowboys had .44-40 Winchester center-fire rifles with a maximum effective range of two hundred yards. The standing operating procedure for soldiers at this time was for each man to carry sixty rounds on his person and sixty rounds in his saddlebag.

The Utes had a greater variety of rifles, including a .45-60 caliber Winchester, a .44-40 Winchester, a Henry rifle, and a Sharps. This analysis is based on the ten pounds of lead and the shell casings found at the site. Obviously, there were other types and numbers of firearms involved in the fracas.

55. Todd, "A Pioneer Experience," 3.
56. Ibid.
57. "Incidents of the Indian Fight," *Dolores News*, August 2, 1884, 3.
58. Ibid.
59. Todd, "A Pioneer Experience," 4.
60. Lyman suggests that the Ute trail led across Mossback Mesa before "skirting the Colorado River" via Red Canyon. This is probably an error on his part, based on the mistaken impression that the scarp at Piute Pass is part of Mossback Mesa, which is actually miles to the south, beyond Fry Canyon. A much more likely route leads directly southwest from Piute Pass across Red Canyon to the Moki Canyon sand slide via Mancos Mesa.

   The Ute trail across the Moki Canyon sand slide was inferred by Lyman's informants from the later discovery there by Bluff stockmen of a pocket watch believed to have been taken from one of the Piute Pass victims and dropped on the trail by the Utes (Lyman, *Indians and Outlaws* [Salt Lake City: Publishers Press, 1980], 68). There is no independent evidence to support that inference.
61. Lake Pagahrit, or "Hermit Lake," was an ancient natural reservoir that had formed behind a massive falling dune in the drainage now known as Lake Canyon. This was a favorite camp area for both native people and Anglo stockmen prior to the failure of the dam and emptying of the lake in 1915, following several decades of severe impacts from cattle grazing. See David E. Miller, *Hole in the Rock* (Salt Lake City: University of Utah Press, 1959), 133, and photographs following p. 112.
62. Lyman, *The Outlaw of Navaho Mountain*, 62.
63. Todd, "A Pioneer Experience," 4.
64. Ibid., 5.
65. Major R. H. Hall, Twenty-second Infantry, Fort Lewis, "Post Returns, October 1878 to August 1891," *Returns from U.S. Military Posts from 1800 to 1916*, microfilm roll 624, National Archives, Washington, DC.
66. "Two More Victims," *Dolores News*, July 26, 1884, 3.
67. "The Mitchells Ordered to Leave," *Dolores News*, August 2, 1884, 1.
68. "Incidents of the Indian Fight," *Dolores News*, August 2, 1884, 3.
69. Ibid.
70. "Interesting Indian Intelligence," *Dolores News*, August 30, 1884, 1.
71. Ibid.; John H. Bowman to Warren Patten, August 26, 1884, BIA—Ute Agency Records.
72. Warren Patten, "Southern Ute Agency Report," August 25, 1884, *Report of the Secretary of the Interior*, 48th Cong., 2d Sess., H.R. Exec. Doc. 1, 62.
73. Ibid.
74. "Indian Crimes," *Dolores News*, October 18, 1884, 1.
75. Colonel Peter T. Swaine to Adjutant General, Fort Leavenworth, June 18, 1885, Fort Lewis—Letters Received.
76. Swaine to Adjutant General, Fort Leavenworth, June 19, 1885, Fort Lewis—Outgoing Correspondence.
77. Swaine to Adjutant General, District of New Mexico, August 10, 1883, Fort Lewis—Outgoing Correspondence.
78. Warren Pyle, "The Story of the Beaver Creek Incident," unpublished manuscript (Cortez Public Library, n.d.); Ignacio's statement cited in Earle R. Forrest, *With a Camera in Old Navaholand* (Norman: University of Oklahoma Press, 1970), 12–13.
79. Swaine to Adjutant General, District of New Mexico, June 22, 1885, Fort Lewis—Outgoing Correspondence.
80. Cowboy accounts testify of six dead; the Indians' account says seven. Perhaps the reason for the discrepancy is due to the "sentinel," who was said to have tumbled off a cliff when shot. If so, his body would not have been among those killed in the camp and so was not included in the count.
81. Swaine to Adjutant General, District of New Mexico, June 21, 1885; Swaine to Major David Perry, June 22, 1885; Fort Lewis—Letters Received.
82. Christian F. Stollsteimer, "Southern Ute Agency Report," August 18, 1885, *Report of the Secretary of the Interior*, 49th Cong., 1st Sess., H.R. Exec. Doc. 1, 241.
83. John H. Bowman to Southern Ute Agency, July 24 and August 1, 1885, Bureau of Indian Affairs, Ute Agency, "Intertribal Difficulties, 1879–1926"; R. E. Crofton to Acting Assistant General, Fort Wingate, July 28, 1885, BIA—Ute Agency Records.
84. Swaine to Adjutant General, District of New Mexico, June 25, 1885, Fort Lewis—Letters Received.
85. Swaine to Adjutant General, District of New Mexico, July 2, 1885, Fort Lewis—Letters Received.
86. Use of the word "Lo" is in reference to a quote by Alexander Pope, "Lo the poor Indian, whose untutored mind sees God in clouds, or hears him in the wind," written in the early to mid-1700s. In the latter part of the 1800s, the appropriated phrase, "Lo the poor Indian," was connected to humanitarian groups in the East such as the Indian Rights Association, which many westerners felt had misplaced sympathies and objectives.
87. No title, July 25, 1885, *Dolores News*, 2.
88. Ibid.; July 5, 1885, Fort Lewis—Letters Received.
89. Ketchum to Swaine, August 7, 1885; Swaine to Assistant Adjutant General, District of New Mexico, August 7, 1885; Fort Lewis—Letters Received.

90. Francis A. Hammond, "The Southern Utes Will Probably Be Removed to San Juan County," *Salt Lake Herald*, October 30, 1888, 1.
91. N. W. Osborne to Headquarters, Department of the Platte, October 26, 1885, AGO — Letters Received.
92. Swaine to Stollsteimer, November 26, 1885, BIA — Ute Agency Records.

CHAPTER 9
1. No title, *Dolores News*, August 25, 1883, 2.
2. The mention of fire may also be associated with low-intensity burns used to increase vegetation for grazing, for animals both hunted and grazed. There is a growing literature that looks at both the prehistoric record (see, for example, Thomas R. Vale, ed., *Fire, Native Peoples, and the Natural Landscape* [Washington, DC: Island Press, 2002]) and the historic record (see Stephen Pyne, *Fire in America: A Cultural History of Wildland and Rural Fire* [Princeton, NJ: Princeton University Press, 1982]).
3. Edmund S. Carlisle to W. M. Clark, October 1, 1884; Carlisle to Major Hall (Fort Lewis, Colorado), November 8, 1884; John F. Tapping to William Clark, December 16, 1884; National Archives, Records of the Bureau of Indian Affairs, RG 75, "Consolidated Ute Records," Denver Record Center (hereafter cited as BIA — Ute Agency Records).
4. Carlisle to Clark, October 1, 1884; Carlisle to Hall, November 8, 1884; BIA — Ute Agency Records.
5. Frank Silvey, *History and Settlement of Northern San Juan County* (n.p., n.d.), on file in the Utah State Historical Society Library, Salt Lake City, 33.
6. Ibid.
7. P. T. Swaine to Christian F. Stollsteimer, November 26, 1885; L. Richardson to Indian Agent, September 1, 1886; BIA — Ute Agency Records.
8. F. W. Knoege(?) to Honorable Secretary Lamar, September 9, 1887, National Archives, Records of the Bureau of Indian Affairs, RG 75, "Letters Received, 1881–1907," (hereafter cited as BIA — Letters Received).
9. Petition to Colonel P. T. Swaine December 16, 1886; Harold Carlisle to Stollsteimer 12 June, 1887; BIA — Ute Agency Records.
10. Harold Carlisle to Christian Stollsteimer, June 12, 1887; L. M. Armstrong to Stollsteimer, July 17, 1887; Armstrong to Stollsteimer, August 19, 1887; BIA — Ute Agency Records.
11. Thomas J. Morgan to Charles A. Bartholomew, September 25, 1889, BIA — Ute Agency Records.
12. Silvey, "History," 42; Cornelia Perkins, Marian Nielson, and Lenora Jones, *Saga of San Juan* (Salt Lake City: Mercury Publishing, 1968), 220.
13. Bartholomew to Commissioner of Indian Affairs, October 26, 1889, BIA — Ute Agency Records.
14. "The Southern Utes Not to Blame," *Durango Herald*, October 25, 1889, 1.
15. John M. Schofield to Secretary of War, October 28, 1889, National Archives, Records of the Adjutant General's Office, RG 94, "Letters Received," Washington, DC (hereafter cited as AGO — Letters Received.
16. George M. Williams to Post Adjutant, December 11, 1889, BIA — Letters Received.
17. Ibid.
18. Petition from Citizens of Grand and San Juan Counties to A. L. Thomas (Governor of Utah), August 14, 1890; Petition from Citizens of Monticello to Governor, August 14, 1890; BIA — Letters Received.
19. Bartholomew to David L. Shipley, October 13, 1890, BIA — Ute Agency Records; Bartholomew to the Navajo Indians, November 11, 1890, BIA — Letters Received.
20. Article (no title), *Creede Candle*, August 12, 1892, 1; Governor Davis H. Waite to President Grover Cleveland, May 9, 1893, BIA — Letters Received.
21. Bartholomew to Commissioner of Indian Affairs, May 16, 1893, BIA — Ute Agency Records.
22. Bartholomew to A. M. McCook, August 12, 1893, BIA — Ute Agency Records.
23. Ibid.
24. Walter Dyk, *A Navaho Autobiography* (New York: Viking Fund, 1947), 40, 75.
25. This issue of overhunting and destruction of resources is not limited to this time and place. As early as the 1600s the "beaver wars" that raged among the coastal Algonkians and the Iroquois centered on wiping out large animal populations and its effect on the Indians doing it. See Calvin Martin, *Keepers of the Game: Indian-Animal Relationships and the Fur Trade* (Berkeley: University of California Press, 1978) and a response to it by Shephard Krech III, ed., *Indians, Animals, and the Fur Trade: A Critique of Keepers of the Game* (Athens: University of Georgia Press, 1981). A similar approach to destruction of game occurred in the Southeast with the hunting of deer by the Five Civilized Tribes, as well as trapping and hunting of sea animals along the Northwest Coast.
26. "Destruction of Game by Indians," *Report of the Commissioner of Indian Affairs*, 1894, Office of Indian Affairs, Department of the Interior, Washington, DC, 66-67 (hereafter referred to as *RCIA*).
27. Brigadier General J. H. Carter (?) to Assistant Adjutant General, Division of the Missouri, July 7, 1886; E. D. Thomas to Assistant Adjutant General, Department of the Missouri, July 13 and July 18, 1886; C. G. Morton to Assistant Adjutant General, Department of the Platte, July 15, 1886; AGO — Letters Received.
28. J. B. Irvine to Commanding Officer, Fort Lewis, December 26, 1886, BIA — Ute Agency Records.
29. John Oberly to Thomas McCunniff, November 9, 1888; Morgan to Bartholomew, December 16, 1890; BIA — Letters Received.

30. F. W. Knoege (?) to Honorable Secretary Lamar, September 9, 1887, BIA — Letters Received.

31. Judge Milton T. Morris to Bartholomew, September 25, 1891, BIA — Ute Agency Records.

32. Morris to Bartholomew, October 1, 1891; "To Whom It May Concern" from Bartholomew, October 4, 1891; Bartholomew to John R. Pond, October 21, 1891; BIA — Ute Agency Records.

33. Stollsteimer to Adjutant General, Fort Lewis, January 11, 1887; Swaine to Irvine, January 16, 1887, "Fort Lewis — Calendar of Letters Received, 1880," Special Collections, Southwest Center Library, Fort Lewis College, Durango, CO (hereafter cited as Fort Lewis — Letters Received.

34. Assistant Adjutant General, Department of the Missouri to Swaine, January 22, 1887, Fort Lewis — Letters Received.

35. Albert R. Lyman, "History of San Juan County, 1879–1917," unpublished manuscript, Special Collections, Harold B. Lee Library, Brigham Young University, Provo, UT, 44.

36. Kumen Jones to Stollsteimer, September 23, 1886, Southern Ute Files, American West Center, University of Utah, Salt Lake City (hereafter cited as Southern Ute Files).

37. *Deseret News*, November 28, 1887, cited in "San Juan Stake History," n.p.

38. Lyman, "History of San Juan," 66–67.

39. Kumen Jones to Francis A. Hammond, June 1, 1887, Southern Ute Files.

40. Harold Carlisle to Stollsteimer, July 13, 1887, Southern Ute Files.

41. Irvine to Commanding Officer, August 8, 1887, AGO — Letters Received.

42. Stollsteimer to Swaine, July 14, 1887, Southern Ute Files.

43. Silvey, *History*, 32–33.

44. Silvey, "Historical Records Survey," September 10, 1936, Utah State Historical Society Library, Salt Lake City, 1–4.

45. Silvey, *History*, 43–44.

46. Ibid. In *The Outlaw of Navaho Mountain* (Salt Lake City: Publishers Press, 1986), Albert R. Lyman mentions on several occasions that the Utes killed Bridger Jack because of his involvement with "bad medicine," or witchcraft. I have chosen Silvey's account because of his intimate and long-standing involvement with Bridger Jack, the fact that Bridger lived more in the area of northern San Juan County, where the Silveys homesteaded, and because of the follow-up discussion with Wash years later.

47. Albert R. Lyman, "Willard Butt — 100 Percent Man," Special Collections, Harold B. Lee Library, Brigham Young University, Provo, UT, 27–30.

48. Lyman, "History of San Juan," 67, 74.

49. Ibid., 84.

50. Lyman, *Outlaw*, 30, 44.

51. Ibid., 115.

52. Lyman, "History," 99.

53. Based on a survey of the 1886–1893 Southern Ute Agency reports found in *RCIA*.

54. Charles A. Bartholomew, "Report of Southern Ute Agency," September 12, 1892, *RCIA*.

55. Survey, *RCIA*.

56. Stollsteimer, "Southern Ute Agency Report," August 18, 1886, *RCIA*; Stollsteimer, "Statement," 1886; Southern Ute Files.

57. John D. Atkins to Stollsteimer, July 6, 1886, Southern Ute Files.

58. Bartholomew, "Southern Ute Agency Report," September 18, 1888, *RCIA*; Bartholomew to Commissioner of Indian Affairs, December 7, 1889, Southern Ute Files; Bartholomew, "Southern Ute and Jicarilla Agency Report," September 24, 1890, *RCIA*.

59. Acting Commissioner to Bartholomew, February 21, 1890, Southern Ute Files.

60. Morgan to Bartholomew, March 13, 1890, Southern Ute Files.

61. Thomas McCunniff, "Gratuity List of the Southern Ute Indians," January 10, 1889, Southern Ute Files.

62. Morgan to Bartholomew, August 27 and November 14, 1892; Bartholomew to Morgan, November 21, 1892; Southern Ute Files.

63. For the history of Fort Lewis as an educational institution, see Robert W. Delaney, *Blue Coats, Red Skins, and Black Gowns* (Durango, CO: Durango Herald, 1977); and Duane A. Smith, *Sacred Trust: The Birth and Development of Fort Lewis College* (Niwot: University Press of Colorado, 1991).

64. Morgan to Bartholomew, March 2, 1892, Southern Ute Files.

65. Bartholomew, "Southern Ute Agency Report," September 12, 1892; H. B. Freeman, "Southern Ute Agency Report," August 1, 1893; *RCIA*.

66. Daniel M. Browning to Indian Agents, April 21, 1893, Southern Ute Files.

67. Jesse D. Williams to Bartholomew, November 20, 1887; J. F. Daugherty et al. to J. D. Adkins, June 3, 1888; Acting Commissioner to McCunniff, June 17, 1889; Southern Ute Files.

68. Bartholomew, "Southern Ute Agency Report," August 18, 1886, *RCIA*.

69. U.S. Congress, House, *Report of the Secretary of the Interior*, February 8, 1887, H. Exec. Doc. 1, 50th Cong., 1st Sess., 356–357.

70. Stollsteimer to Commissioner of Indian Affairs, May 28, 1887, Southern Ute Files.

71. Hammond, "The Southern Utes Will Probably be Removed," *Salt Lake Herald*, October 30, 1888, 1.

72. John Taylor to Francis A. Hammond, April 10, 1886; Wilford Woodruff to Hammond, October 3, 1887; Historical Library, Church of Jesus Christ of Latter-day Saints, Salt Lake City.

73. Bartholomew to Commissioner of Indian Affairs, February 6, 1888, BIA — Ute Agency Records.

74. For a brief summary of the issues surrounding the

Utes and Paiutes in San Juan at this time, see Robert S. McPherson, *A History of San Juan County: In the Palm of Time* (Salt Lake City: Utah State Historical Society, 1995), 145–169.

75. U.S. Congress, Senate, "Ute Indian Commission," Exec. Doc. 67, 50th Cong., 2d Sess., January 11, 1889, 79.

76. Martha Hammond to Francis Hammond, December 11, 1889, Historical Library, Church of Jesus Christ of Latter-day Saints, Salt Lake City.

77. Woodruff to Hammond, December 11, 1888, Historical Library, Church of Jesus Christ of Latter-day Saints, Salt Lake City.

78. Hammond to Commissioner of Indian Affairs, January 17, 1890, Southern Ute Files.

79. "Ute Indian Commission," 13–25, 48.

80. "Agreements with the Southern Utes in Colorado," 1889, *RCIA*, 76; La Plata County Committee, "Resolution" November 12, 1889, BIA — Ute Agency Records.

81. "A Memorial to Congress asking no change… Southern Ute Indians of Colorado," January 30, 1890, Southern Ute Files; U.S. Congress, House, "Report of the Governor of Utah," *Report of the Secretary of the Interior*, Exec. Doc. 1, 51st Cong., 2d Sess., September 9, 1890, 645.

82. Sworn Affidavits of Benett Bishop and John Reid, January 23, 1890, BIA — Ute Agency Records.

83. Sworn Affidavits of Southern Utes, January 24, 1890, BIA — Ute Agency Records.

84. Francis A. Hammond, "Additional Notes with Map in Support of House Bill No. 156," February 11, 1890, BIA — Ute Agency Records.

85. "The San Juan Country," *Deseret News*, June 14, 1890, 358.

86. Kumen Jones to Hammond, January 14, 1890, BIA — Letters Received.

87. Bartholomew to Commissioner of Indian Affairs, August 28, 1890, BIA — Ute Agency Records.

88. Bartholomew, "Southern Ute Agency Report," September 21, 1891, *RCIA*, 228.

89. Browning, "Southern Utes," 1893, *RCIA*, 96.

Chapter 10

1. Space does not permit including all of the congressional activity surrounding this twelve-year process of establishing the Southern Ute and Ute Mountain Ute Reservations. For a good summary of the political activities involving federal and state government and special interest groups, see Gregory Coyne Thompson, *Southern Ute Lands, 1848–1899: The Creation of a Reservation*, Occasional Papers of the Center of Southwest Studies (Durango, CO) no. 1 (March 1972), 37–59; see also Thompson, "The Unwanted Indians: The Southern Utes in Southeastern Utah," *Utah Historical Quarterly* 49, no. 2 (Spring 1981): 189–203.

2. All quotes from this meeting are found in U.S. Congress, Senate, "Ute Indian Commission," Exec. Doc. 67, 50th Cong., 2d Sess. January 11, 1889.

3. Ibid., 30.

4. Ibid., 43.

5. Ibid., 54.

6. Ibid., 55.

7. Ibid., 71.

8. Ibid., 72–73.

9. Thomas J. Morgan, "Southern Ute Agreement," *Report of the Commissioner of Indian Affairs*, (Washington, DC: Government Printing Office, 1890): xliii–xliv.

10. Herbert Welsh to general audience, February 25, 1890, Special Collections, Marriott Library, University of Utah, Salt Lake City.

11. Charles C. Painter, "Removal of the Southern Utes," *Lend a Hand* (magazine) 5, no. 4 (April 1890): 258–269.

12. Ibid., 267.

13. Francis F. Kane, "Diary of Francis F. Kane — Ute Removal, 1891," *Indian Rights Association Papers, 1868–1968*. Microfilm reel 8 (Philadelphia: Office of the Indian Rights Association, 1891), 10, 14, 19, 23, 81.

14. Ibid., 68.

15. Herbert Welsh, "The Case of the Southern Utes," *Harper's Weekly*, April 2, 1892, n.p.; Welsh to the Public, open letter, April 22, 1892; T. S. Childs, "A Statement and Appeal for the Southern Utes," n.d., n.p.; all in Special Collections, Marriott Library, University of Utah, Salt Lake City.

16. Ignacio et al. to Our Great Father, April 1, 1893, National Archives, Records of the Bureau of Indian Affairs, RG 75, "Letters Received, 1881–1907 (hereafter cited as BIA — Letters Received.

17. Caleb W. West to Hoke Smith, July 20, 1893, BIA — Letters Received.

18. See Robert S. McPherson and Richard Kitchen, "Much Ado about Nothing: The San Juan River Gold Rush, 1892–1893," *Utah Historical Quarterly* 67, no. 1 (Winter 1999): 68–87.

19. "The Ute Removal Bill," February 16, 1894, *Mancos Times*, 1.

20. Helen M. Searcy, "Col. Dave Day," *The Pioneers of San Juan Country*, vol. 1 (Durango, CO: Sarah Platt Decker Chapter, 1942), 76–82.

21. F. A. Hammond to Commissioner of Indian Affairs, July 16, 1894, BIA — Letters Received.

22. Charles H. Ogden to Commissioner of Indian Affairs, December 5, 1894, BIA — Letters Received.

23. David Day to Hammond, July 3, 1894; Day to Commissioner of Indian Affairs, July 19, 1894; BIA — Letters Received.

24. Day to Commissioner of Indian Affairs, October 15, 1894, BIA — Letters Received.

25. Willard Butt to Caleb W. West, November 23, 1894; C. J. Elliot to Frank Hobbs, November 24, 1894; A. Taylor to West, November 26, 1894; Ter-

ritorial Executive Papers, 1850–1896, Utah State Archives, Salt Lake City (hereafter cited as Territorial Papers).

26. A. McCook to Adjutant General, U.S. Army (telegram), November 29, 1894, National Archives, Records of the Adjutant General's Office, "Letters Received" (hereafter cited as AGO — Letters Received).

27. F. I. Jones to West, November 27, 1894, Territorial Papers.

28. "Indians — Utah Invaded by the Blood-thirsty Utes," November 27, 1894, n.p., on file, AGO — Letters Received.

29. "The Ute Scare," November 30, 1894, *Durango Democrat*, 1.

30. *Mancos Times*, November 30, 1894, 1.

31. West to Secretary of the Interior, December 4, 1894; C. J. Elliott to Frank Hobbs, November 24, 1894; Territorial Papers.

32. McCook to Adjutant General of the Army, December 1, 1894, AGO — Letters Received; Grand County Petition, December 3, 1894, Territorial Papers.

33. Day to Commissioner of Indian Affairs, December 5, 1894, BIA — Letters Received.

34. Day to West, December 5, 1894, Territorial Papers.

35. Day to McCook, December 3, 1894, AGO — Letters Received.

36. McCook to West, and West to McCook, December 7, 1894, Territorial Papers; Day to Adjutant General of the Army, December 4, 1894, AGO — Letters Received.

37. "Ignacio's Veracity," December 7, 1894, *Mancos Times*, 3.

38. Brigham Young Jr. to F. A. Hammond, December 6, 1894, BIA — Letters Received.

39. H. W. Lawton to McCook, December 13, 1894; Day to Commissioner of Indian Affairs, December 13, 1894; AGO — Letters Received.

40. Christian Lingo Christensen, "An Indian War Averted," *Improvement Era* 31, no. 9 (July 1928): 776–780.

41. Ibid., 777.

42. Day to Commissioner of Indian Affairs, December 14, 1894, BIA — Letters Received.

43. Day to Commissioner of Indian Affairs, December 13, 1894; Lawton to McCook, December 13, 1894 (both telegrams); AGO — Letters Received.

44. Lawton to McCook, December 13, 1894 (letter), AGO — Letters Received.

45. Ibid.

46. Day to Commissioner of Indian Affairs, December 8, 1894, BIA — Letters Received.

47. Christensen, "An Indian War," 777.

48. Ibid., 777–778.

49. Diary of Christian Lingo Christensen, Special Collections, Harold B. Lee Library, Brigham Young University, Provo, UT, 164.

50. Christensen, "An Indian War," 777.

51. Ibid.

52. Day to Commissioner of Indian Affairs, December 14, 1894, BIA — Letters Received.

53. D. L. Blake, "Indian Troubles Plague First San Juan County Settlers," December 29, 1955, *San Juan Record*, 6.

54. Christensen, "When the Utes Invaded Utah," *Times-Independent*, August 3, 1933, 1, 8; and "An Indian War," 779.

55. Christensen, "When the Utes Invaded Utah," 4.

56. Ibid.

57. Day to Commissioner of Indian Affairs, December 14, 1894, BIA — Letters Received.

58. Day to Commissioner of Indian Affairs, December 16, 1894, BIA — Letters Received.

59. Christensen, "An Indian War," 780.

60. Lawton to McCook, December 14, 1894, BIA — Letters Received.

61. Day to Secretary of the Interior, December 15, 1894, AGO — Letters Received.

62. Day to Commissioner of Indian Affairs (telegram), December 24, 1894, BIA — Letters Received.

63. West to George W. Gibbs and John Q. Cannon, January 5, 1895, Territorial Papers.

64. Cannon and Gibbs to West, January 28, 1895, Territorial Papers.

65. Ibid., 5.

66. John Q. Cannon, "When the Utes Invaded Utah," *Improvement Era* 32, no. 1 (November 1928): 42.

67. Ibid., 45.

68. Ibid., 44.

69. Cannon and Gibbs to West, January 28, 1895, Territorial Papers.

70. Ibid.

71. Heber M. Wells to President and Gentlemen of the Senate, April 5, 1896, Territorial Papers.

72. Francis E. Leupp, *The Latest Phase of the Southern Ute Question: A Report* (Philadelphia: Indian Rights Association, 1895), 24; Louis A. Knackstedt, "Report of Southern Ute Agency," November 29, 1899, *Report of the Commissioner of Indian Affairs* (Washington, DC: Government Printing Office, 1899), 285 (hereafter cited as *RCIA*).

73. David F. Day, "Report of Southern Ute Agency," September 15, 1895, *RCIA*, 141.

74. Day to Commissioner of Indian Affairs, December 30, 1895, BIA — Letters Received.

75. Day to Commissioner of Indian Affairs, April 19, 1895, BIA — Letters Received.

76. *Mancos Times*, April 26, 1895, 1.

77. *Mancos Times*, June 14, 1895, 1.

78. Meredith H. Kidd to D. M. Browning, May 23, 1895, BIA — Letters Received.

79. Helen Sloan Daniels, "Lo the Poor Indian!" *The Pioneers of San Juan Country*, vol. 3 (Durango, CO: Sarah Platt Decker Chapter, 1952), 130.

80. Day, "Report of Southern Ute Agency," September 25, 1896, *RCIA*, 132.

81. Ibid., 135.

82. William H. Meyers, "Report of Southern Ute Agency," August 9, 1897, *RCIA*, 123.

83. "For This We Are Indebted to D. F. Day," *Mancos Times*, August 27, 1897, 1; "The Journal's Work," *Mancos Times*, November 30, 1897, 3.

84. *Mancos Times*, April 14, 1899, 1.

85. "The Ute Reservation," *Mancos Times*, February 24, 1899, 2; "May 4 Is the Epoch," *Montezuma Journal*, April 7, 1899, 1; "The Ute Opening," *Montezuma Journal*, May 12, 1899, 1.

86. Thomas P. Smith to Constant Williams, May 22, 1896, BIA—Letters Received; *Mancos Times*, January 1, 1897, 1; "The Journal's Work," *Montezuma Journal*, November 30, 1897, 3.

87. Day to Browning, November 12, 1895, BIA—Letters Received.

88. "District Court—Hatch the Indian Killer Hangs," *Mancos Times*, May 8, 1896, 1.

89. Day, "Report of Southern Ute Agency," September 25, 1896, *RCIA*, 134; *Mancos Times*, October 9, 1896, 1.

90. Frances Leon Quintana, *Ordeal of Change: The Southern Utes and Their Neighbors* (Walnut Creek: AltaMira Press, 2004).

91. Richard K. Young, *The Ute Indians of Colorado in the Twentieth Century* (Norman: University of Oklahoma Press, 1997).

Chapter 11

1. Joseph O. Smith to Commissioner of Indian Affairs, May 8, 1900, National Archives, Records of the Bureau of Indian Affairs, RG 75, Consolidated Ute Agency, "Letters Received" (hereafter cited as BIA—Letters Received).

2. Smith to Commissioner of Indian Affairs, August 10 and September 24, 1900, BIA—Letters Received.

3. S. F. Stacher, "The Indians at the Ute Mountain Reservation, 1906–9," *Colorado Magazine* 26, no. 1 (January 1949): 56.

4. S. F. Stacher, "Memories of Chief Ignacio and Old Navaho Springs Sub-Agency," *Colorado Magazine* 17, no. 6 (June 1940): 212–221.

5. Report of Agent for Southern Ute Agency, *Annual Report of Department of the Interior, Fiscal Year Ending June 30, 1901* (Washington, DC: Government Printing Office), 205.

6. Ibid., 57.

7. Smith to Walter Graves, July 17, 1900, BIA-Letters Received; *Montezuma Journal*, June 8, 1900, 2.

8. *Mancos Times*, December 7, 1900, 1.

9. Stacher, "The Indians," 60.

10. Joseph O. Smith, "Report of Agent for Southern Ute Agency," August 25, 1902, *Reports of Agents and Others in Charge of Indians*, U.S. Congress, House of Representatives, 57th Congress, 2d Sess., (Washington, DC: Government Printing Office, 1902), 180; Annual Report, 1910, Superintendent's Annual Narrative and Statistical Reports from Field Jurisdictions of the BIA, 1907–1938—Navajo Springs Agency, microfilm 1011, roll 90 (hereafter cited as Superintendent's Annual Report).

11. Superintendent's Annual Report, 1913.

12. Superintendent's Annual Report, 1910.

13. U. L. Clardy to Commissioner of Indian Affairs, August 28, 1910, BIA—Letters Received.

14. William A. Jones to Secretary of the Interior, December 11, 1903, BIA—Letters Received; Superintendent's Annual Report, 1910 and 1911.

15. Robert Lowie, cited in William Wroth, ed., *Ute Indian Arts and Culture: From Prehistory to the New Millennium* (Colorado Springs: Colorado Springs Fine Arts Center, 2000), 69.

16. See Frank McNitt, *Richard Wetherill: Anasazi* (Albuquerque: University of New Mexico Press, 1966).

17. Helen Sloan Daniels, "Lo, The Poor Indian!" *The Pioneers of San Juan County*, vol. 3 (Durango, CO: Sarah Platt Decker Chapter, 1952), 130–131.

18. Smith to Commissioner of Indian Affairs, October 15, 1903, BIA—Letters Received.

19. Ibid.

20. Ibid.

21. William M. Peterson to Commissioner of Indian Affairs, March 3, 1905, BIA—Letters Received.

22. U.S. Congress, Senate, "Agreement with Weeminuchi Band Ute Indians, Colorado," January 21, 1913, Senate Report 1133, 62d Cong., 3d Sess., 1–4.

23. "Chief Ignacio is Dead," *Weekly Ignacio Chieftain*, December 12, 1913, 1.

24. Virginia McConnell Simmons, *The Ute Indians of Utah, Colorado, and New Mexico* (Boulder, CO: University Press of Colorado, 2000), 235–236.

25. Smith to Commissioner of Indian Affairs, March 21, 1901; J. M. Woodard to Commissioner of Indian Affairs, October 24, 1903; White Mesa Ute Oral History Project, American West Center, University of Utah, Salt Lake City (hereafter cited as WMUHP).

26. Sworn statement of James B. Decker, May 1908, in report submitted by John C. Cutler to Commissioner of Indian Affairs, June 3, 1908, WMUHP.

27. Albert R. Lyman, "History of San Juan County, 1879–1917," unpublished manuscript, Special Collections, Harold B. Lee Library, Brigham Young University, Provo, UT, 100–101.

28. Acting Commissioner of Indian Affairs to Smith, September 30, 1904; Acting Commissioner of Indian Affairs to William T. Shelton, September 30, 1904; William Peterson to Commissioner of Indian Affairs, October 14, 1904; Acting Com-

missioner of Indian Affairs to Charles H. Dickson, February 11, 1905; WMUHP.

29. Smith to Commissioner of Indian Affairs, January 21, 1905, BIA — Letters Received.

30. He was known by four names. The one used most often, Tse-ne-gat, is a misspelling of "Činigatt," translated as "Silver Earrings," which he often wore. I have chosen to use this name because it appears in the literature of the day. Some writers (e.g., Forbes Parkhill, *The Last of the Indian Wars*) have said it translates as "Cry Baby" a name he was given as a child after he fell into a fire. He was also known as Everett Hatch, Pa-woo-tach, and Coffee, the latter mentioned by Chester Cantsee in his interview with Gregory Thompson and Floyd O'Neil, March 22, 1980 (OH-00, 776, White Mesa Ute Oral History Project, American West Center, University of Utah, Salt Lake City).

31. Albert R. Lyman, *Journal, 1907*, October 30–31, 1907, Special Collections, Harold B. Lee Library, Brigham Young University, Provo, UT, 161–164.

32. Jake Young, interviewed by Amasa Jay Redd, as cited in *Lemuel Hardison Redd, Jr., 1856–1923, Pioneer-Leader-Builder*, compiled and edited by Amasa Jay Redd (Salt Lake City: published privately, 1967), 103 (hereafter cited as *LHR*).

33. J. F. Barton to Governor John C. Cutler, December 23, 1907, *LHR*.

34. Reed Smoot to Cutler, January 17, 1908, *LHR*.

35. J. H. Wood to Cutler, January 17, 1908, *LHR*.

36. F. E. Leupp to Cutler, January 11, 1908, *LHR*.

37. Ibid.

38. Petition to Governor John C. Cutler, Fall 1907, BIA — Letters Received.

39. Cutler to Leupp, June 3, 1908, BIA — Letters Received.

40. Leupp to Cutler, January 11, 1908, BIA — Letters Received.

41. Cutler to Leupp, June 3, 1908, sworn testimonies attached, BIA — Letters Received.

42. Ibid.

43. A. F. Potter to Commissioner of Indian Affairs, November 27, 1908, WMUHP; Stacher to Commissioner of Indian Affairs, November 23, 1937, BIA — Letters Received.

44. Howard M. Patterson to Commissioner of Indian Affairs, February 19, 1915, WMUHP.

45. Carl Stockbridge, "To Whom It May Concern," November 14, 1913, BIA — Letters Received.

46. Forbes Parkhill (*The Last of the Indian Wars* [New York: Crowell-Collier Press, 1961]) has written an entire account of the 1915 fight in Bluff. Heavily dependent on newspapers and containing no citations, the book introduces a number of errors but also provided new information. It is a good general overview, but not entirely accurate.

47. Claude C. Covey to Commissioner of Indian Affairs, May 14, 1914, WMUHP.

48. Covey to Commissioner of Indian Affairs, May 18, 1914, WMUHP.

49. Ibid.

50. Ibid.

51. According to Stella Eyetoo, who met Polk and knew of him, he had a "bulletproof power" called *tuppwíyu-puwa-ga-pügat*, which ensured that no matter how many times he was shot, the rounds would just bounce off of him.

52. Covey to Commissioner of Indian Affairs, June 29, 1914, WMUHP.

53. Kumen Jones et al. to Cato Sells, September 28, 1914; Covey to Commissioner of Indian Affairs, September 26, 1914; BIA — Letters Received.

54. Aquila Nebeker to Covey, December 4, 1914, BIA-Letters Received.

55. William W. Ray to Commissioner of Indian Affairs, January 2, 1915, BIA — Letters Received.

56. "Investigation into Depredations of Indian is Ordered," *Deseret Evening News*, October 24, 1914, 1; Covey to Commissioner of Indian Affairs, October 29, 1914, BIA — Letters Received; "Colorado State News," *Bayfield Blade*, December 25, 1917, 2; "New Agent at Navajo Springs Takes up Work," *Montezuma Journal*, December 3, 1914, 1.

57. "Nebeker in Pursuit of Indians at Bluff," *Salt Lake Herald Republican*, February 17, 1915, 1.

58. "Piutes Entrench to Battle Nebeker's Force," *Salt Lake Herald Republican*, February 18, 1915, 1; "Posses Seeking Indian Meet Tonight," *Salt Lake Evening Telegram*, February 18, 1915, 2; "Coloradoans Are on Way to Join Nebeker," *Salt Lake Tribune*, February 18, 1915, 4.

59. James E. Jenkins to Commissioner of Indian Affairs, February 19, 1915, BIA — Letters Received.

60. "Nebeker to Demand Surrender of Indian," *Salt Lake Herald Republican*, February 19, 1915, 1.

61. Gary L. Shumway, Jay Jones, Kay Jones, and Merle McDonald, *Cowboys and Indians: Interviews and Recollections of Marion Ashton and Alma Uriah Jones* (Flower Mound, TX: Shumway Publishing, 2009), 44.

62. "May Clash with Redskins Today," *Salt Lake Herald Republican*, February 21, 1915, 1.

63. Chester Cantsee interview, White Mesa Ute Oral History Project.

64. "Testimony of Mr. [A. N.] Gingles," March 1, 1915, WMUHP.

65. "Testimony of Mr. [J. B.] Douglas," March 1, 1915, WMUHP; Ira Hatch, interview with author, May 30, 1991.

66. Frank Pyle, "The Uprising of Polk and Posey in 1915," William Evans Collection, Special Collections, Harold B. Lee Library, Brigham Young University, Provo, UT.

67. Uriah Butt, interview with Ruth Meo, May 29, 1978, O.H. #1628, Southeastern Utah Oral History Project, Utah State Historical Society and California State University, Fullerton.

68. Shumway et al., *Cowboys and Indians*, 44.

69. Charles Burke, interview with Floyd O'Neil and Gregory Thompson, September 13, 1968, O.H. #374, Doris Duke Oral History Project, American West Center, University of Utah, Salt Lake City.

70. Shumway et al., *Cowboys and Indians*, 44.

71. Edward Dutchie Sr., interview with author, May 21, 1996.

72. Pyle, "Uprising."

73. "Friendly Utes May Join Polk," *Salt Lake Herald Republican*, March 3, 1915, 1.

74. John Perkins, interview with Charles S. Peterson, n.d., Utah State Historical Society Library, Salt Lake City.

75. "Testimony of Aquila Nebeker," n.d., BIA — Letters Received; "Posse of 29 Is on Way to Aid" and "Indians Surround Marshal's Posse," *Salt Lake Herald Republican*, February 22, 1915, 1; Gregory to Nebeker, February 26, 1915, BIA — Letters Received; "Indian Police Hurry to Bluff," *Salt Lake Herald Republican*, February 25, 1915, 3; "Five Indians are Killed in Battle, *Salt Lake Herald Republican*, February 23, 1915, 2; "Renegades Still Showing Fight 100 Miles West," *Montezuma Journal*, February 25, 1915, 1; "Postpone Effort to Hunt Out Redskins," *Salt Lake Herald Republican*, February 25, 1915, 1.

76. "Ute Reported Slain by Posey for Mutiny," *Salt Lake Herald Republican*, February 27, 1915, 1.

77. Lorenzo D. Creel to Commissioner of Indian Affairs, April 13, 1915, BIA — Letters Received.

78. Ibid.

79. Ibid.

80. Nebeker to Attorney General, March 1, 1915, WMUHP.

81. Secretary of War to Attorney General, March 2, 1915; Scott to Secretary of War, March 2, 1915; Woodrow Wilson to Secretary of War, March 2, 1915; Scott to War Department (telegram), March 11, 1915; National Archives, Records of the Adjutant General's Office, RG 94, "Letters Received," (Washington, DC) (hereafter cited as AGO — Letters Received).

82. Attorney General to Dewey C. Bailey, March 3, 1915, BIA — Letters Received; No title, *Montezuma Journal*, March 4, 1915, 2; "Reds Entrench in Narrow Pass," *Salt Lake Herald Republican*, March 5, 1915, 1; "Quintet of Captives Lodged in Local Jail," *Salt Lake Herald Republican*, March 6, 1915, 1.

83. Scott to Commissioner of Indian Affairs, March 11, 1915; Cato Sells to Scott, March 11, 1915; BIA — Letters Received; "Only Bullets Talk — Polk," *Salt Lake Herald Republican*, March 11, 1915, 2.

84. "Scott Unarmed Goes to the Piutes," *Salt Lake Herald Republican*, March 13, 1915, 1; "Indians will Soon Scatter," *Salt Lake Herald Republican*, March 16, 1915, 7.

85. "Scott Fails to Find Renegades," *Salt Lake Herald Republican*, March 17, 1915, 1; "Nebeker Posse Ordered Home," March 19, 1915, 1; Scott to Secretary of War, March 20, 1915, AGO — Letters Received.

86. Hugh Lenox Scott, *Some Memories of a Soldier* (New York: Century Company, 1928), 536; see also, "Persons in the Foreground," *Current Opinion* (May 1915): 323–324.

87. "Scott Arrests Renegade Indians," *Salt Lake Herald Republican*, March 21, 1915, 1.

88. Scott, *Some Memories*, 538.

89. Ibid.

90. John D. Rogers, interview with Michael T. Hurst, April 29, 1972, CRC-J6, Posey War Oral History Project, Charles Redd Center for Western Studies, Brigham Young University, Provo, UT, 5.

91. "Redmen are Lodged in Salt Lake Jail," March 25, 1915, 1; "Indians Will Say Farewell Today to 'Good White Father' General Scott," March 26, 1915, 14; "Scott Bids Reds Farewell," March 27, 1915, 12; "Indian Warwhoops Reverberate Through Corridors of Jail," March 31, 1915, 6; all *Salt Lake Herald Republican*. "Tse-ne-gat Tickled with Hospital," *Denver Times*, April 20, 1915, 10.

92. "Sworn Oath," District of Utah, witnessed April 10, 1915, BIA — Letters Received.

93. "Indians Agree to be Peaceful," *Salt Lake Herald Republican*, April 13, 1915, 28.

94. Jenkins to Commissioner of Indian Affairs, April 14, 1915, BIA — Letters Received.

95. Jenkins to Utah Attorney General, April 22, 1915, WMUHP.

96. Henry McAllister to U.S. Attorney General, May 6, 1915, BIA — Letters Received.

97. Jenkins to Commissioner of Indian Affairs, June 5, 1915, BIA — Letters Received.

98. Harry B. Tedrow to Attorney General, June 25, 1915, BIA — Letters Received.

99. Tedrow to Attorney General, July 15, 1915, WMUHP.

100. "Indian Accused of Murder Sits in Court of Paleface," *Denver Post*, July 6, 1915, 1; Hatch's Counsel Ready to Spring Surprise in Case," clipping found in BIA — Letters Received.

101. "Indian Accused of Murder."

102. "Tse-ne-gat is Freed by Jury," *Rocky Mountain News*, July 15, 1915, 1; "Jury Frees Tse-ne-gat, Ute Shows no Emotion," clipping found in BIA — Letters Received.

103. "Tse-ne-gat is Acquitted of Murder and Leaves for His Native Hills," *Denver Post*, July 16, 1915, 3; "Enraged Widow Rushes at Piute," *Rocky Mountain News*, July 15, 1915, 7.

104. "Tse-ne-gat is Freed by Jury."

105. Jenkins to Scott, April 28, 1915; A. H. Spencer to Scott, April 29, 1915; BIA-Letters Received.

106. Tedrow to Attorney General, May 6, 1915; Jenkins to David S. Cook, May 6, 1915; Jenkins to Commissioner of Indian Affairs, June 1, 1915; BIA — Letters Received.

107. Jenkins to Commissioner of Indian Affairs, June 2, 1915, WMUHP.

108. "Supt. Jenkins Denies Reports of Indian Troubles," *Montezuma Journal*, June 17, 1915, BIA — Letters Received.

109. W. W. McConihe to Commissioner of Indian Affairs, September 13 and October 22, 1915; Jenkins to Indian Office (telegram), September 23, 1915; BIA — Letters Received.

110. Albert R. Lyman, *Indians and Outlaws: Settling of the San Juan Frontier* (Salt Lake City: Publishers Press, 1980): 164–165.

CHAPTER 12

The epigraph quote is from Wilbur R. Jacobs, "The Indian and the Frontier in American History: A Need for Revision," *Western Historical Quarterly* 4 no. 1 (January 1973): 43, 54.

1. M. K. Sniffen, "The Meaning of the Ute 'War,'" November 15, 1915, Special Collections, J. Willard Marriott Library, University of Utah, Salt Lake City.

2. "Hot Air about Neglected Utes," January 13, 1916, 1; "More about the Neglected Utes," January 20, 1916, 1; "The Poor Innocent Indian," January 27, 1916, 1; "More Facts about Utes," February 3, 1916, 1; "More about Ute Indians," February 10, 1916, 1; "Creel's opinion of Mr. M. K. Sniffen," February 17, 1916, 1; all from the *Cortez Herald*.

3. "Piute Braves are Back in San Juan County," *Grand Valley Times*, September 1, 1916, 1.

4. James C. Wilson to Agent A. H. Symons, January 5, 1917, James McLaughlin Papers, microfilm no. 8, Denver Public Library (hereafter cited as McLaughlin Papers).

5. James McLaughlin to Commissioner of Indian Affairs, March 30, 1917, National Archives, Records of the Bureau of Indian Affairs, Consolidated Ute Agency, RG 75 (hereafter cited as BIA — Letters Received).

6. McLaughlin to Indian Commissioner Cato Sells, January 1 and 20, 1917, McLaughlin Papers.

7. Undersigned of Bluff to Major James McLaughlin, January 12, 1917, McLaughlin Papers; McLaughlin to Commissioner of Indian Affairs, March 30, 1917, BIA — Letters Received.

8. Symons to McLaughlin, February 3, 1917, McLaughlin Papers.

9. "Old Polk and Son Again on Warpath," *Times-Independent*, September 18, 1919, p. 1.

10. Henry McCabe, *Cowboys, Indians, and Homesteaders* (n.p., self-published, 1975): 183, 188–189.

11. Ibid., 184.

12. "Ute Indians Growing Ugly," September 4, 1917, 1; "Noted Indian Prepares for War," October 5, 1917, 1; "Indians Again Growing Bold," October 26, 1917, 4; "Ute Trespassers Made to Pay," November 2, 1917, 5; "Ute Indians Hold up Blanding Boy," November 3, 1917, 1; "Old Posey May Stir up Trouble," December 21, 1917, 1: all from the *San Juan Blade*.

13. "Indians Refuse to Give Names," *Ignacio Chieftain*, June 8, 1917, 2.

14. Edward E. McKean to Commissioner of Indian Affairs, June 11, 1917, and February 23, 1918, BIA — Letters Received; "Indians Are Registered," *Ignacio Chieftain*, June 15, 1917, 1.

15. James Bush to Commissioner of Indian Affairs, April 9, 1918, BIA — Letters Received.

16. "Utes Opposed to Registration and Army Draft," *Denver Post*, August 1918; "Montezuma Co. Ranchers Say Utes Troublesome and Petition for Their Removal," *Durango Democrat*, August 1918; "Indians Burn and Raid in Montezuma County," *Durango Democrat*, August 1918; "Open Rebellion Over New Draft Extension," *Denver Post*, August 1918: all attachments to letter from McKean to Commissioner of Indian Affairs, August 22, 1918, BIA — Letters Received.

17. "Open Rebellion," "Montezuma Co. Ranchers," "Ute Threatens Man with Gun," *San Juan Blade*, August 24, 1917, 1; "Ute Indians Growing Ugly," *San Juan Blade*, September 4, 1917, 1.

18. McKean to Commissioner of Indian Affairs, August 28, 1918, BIA — Letters Received.

19. Ray H. Car to Commissioner of Indian Affairs, November 14, 1918, BIA — Letters Received.

20. "The Influenza among the Utes," *Mancos Times Tribune*, December 27, 1918, 1.

21. "Superstitious Utes," *Mancos Times Tribune*, January, 10, 1919, 1.

22. Ibid.; "Influenza Very Bad Among Indians," *Mancos Times Tribune*, December 13, 1918, 1, 3.

23. Fred Yazzie, interview with Marilyn Holiday and author, November 5, 1987.

24. Gilmore Graymountain, interview with Marilyn Holiday and author, April 7, 1992.

25. "Hearings on Indian Estates," *Mancos Times Tribune*, February 21, 1919, 1.

26. Axel Johnson to Commissioner of Indian Affairs, April 23, 1919, BIA — Letters Received.

27. "Indians Molesting San Juan Stockmen," *Times-Independent*, May 20, 1920, 8.

28. Cato Sells to Reed Smoot, August 7, 1920; E. [Edgar] B. Meritt to M. H. Welling, September 2, 1920; Assistant Commissioner [Meritt] to Smoot, n.d., 1920; BIA — Letters Received.

29. Welling to Sells, August 14, 1920, BIA — Letters Received.

30. "Red Uprising Subsides, Says Bluff Report," *Deseret News*, May 30, 1921, 1; "Piutes Pull Off their Usual Rumpus," *Times-Independent*, June 2, 1921, 1; Phillip Hurst, interview with Michael Hurst, September 2, 1972, CRC-J9, Charles Redd Center for Western Studies, Harold B. Lee Library, Brigham Young University, Provo, UT, 3.

31. "Ute Indian Braves on Warpath," *Deseret News*, May 28, 1921, 1.

32. "Ute Indians Quit Warpath as Utah Posse Gets Busy," *Denver Post*, May 30, 1921, 2; "Ute Outlaws Quit Pow-wow; Hostile Again," *Deseret News*, May 31, 1920, 3; "Indians Quit; Conference Off," *Salt Lake Tribune*, May 31, 1921, 3.

33. "Editorial," *Salt Lake Telegram*, June 5, 1921, 8.

34. "Chiefs Promise Peace by Indians," *Salt Lake Tribune*, June 24, 1921, 1; "Governor Mabey Holds Pow-wow with Ute Renegades at Blanding," June 25, 1921, 3, and "Salt Lake Visitors are Delighted With their Visit to San Juan County," July 2, 1921, 1, both *Deseret News*; "Indians Promise to Cease Outlawry," *Times-Independent*, June 23, 1921, 2.

35. Charles R. Mabey to Smoot, June 29, 1921, BIA — Letters Received.

36. "Gives Account of Indian Trial," *Times-Independent*, September 8, 1921, 8.

37. "One Conviction, One Acquittal at Monticello," *Times-Independent*, August 25, 1921, 1; "Indians Freed of Larceny Charges by Monticello Jury," *Times-Independent*, September 1, 1921, 8.

38. Edward Finney to Secretary of the Interior, July 29, 1921, and Finney, "Memorandum for Inspector Baca," August 1, 1921, both White Mesa Ute History Project, American West Center, University of Utah, Salt Lake City (hereafter cited as WMUHP).

39. W. H. Redd Testimony, September 1, 1921, and "Memorandum Notes on San Juan County Indian Situation," June 24 and 25, 1921, both as attachments to Elfego Baca's report in WMUHP.

40. Baca, "Memorandum Notes."

41. L. B. Redd Testimony, WMUHP.

42. Baca, "Memorandum Notes"; Testimony of Aquila Nebeker, L. H. Redd, Kumen Jones, and Baca to Secretary of the Interior, September 29, 1921, WMUHP.

43. Hugh L. Scott to Board of Indian Commissioners, October 11, 1921, WMUHP.

44. "Supt. McKean Given Charge of Agency at Ute Mountain," *Ignacio Chieftain*, August 4, 1922, 1.

45. Lloyd Nielson, interview with Gary Shumway and Kim Stewart, July 14, 1971, Utah State Historical Society and California State University, Fullerton, 26.

46. McKean to Commissioner of Indian Affairs, April 9, 1923, BIA — Letters Received.

47. John D. Rogers, interview with Michael T. Hurst, April 29, 1972, CRC-J6, Posey War Oral History Project, Charles Redd Center for Western Studies, Harold B. Lee Library, Brigham Young University, Provo, UT, 13–14.

48. Ibid.

49. Lyman P. Hunter, interview with Michael Hurst, February 21, 1973, CRC-J5, Posey War Oral History Project, Charles Redd Center for Western Studies, Harold B. Lee Library, Brigham Young University, Provo, UT, 3–4.

50. Rogers interview, 10.

51. Chester Cantsee Sr., interview with author, September 6, 1994.

52. Westwater, where the Indians lived in those days, was called Ute Village or Ute Flats, and had a racetrack often used by the community. Living sites extended along the canyon for about a mile, with its northern limit at what was called Big Spring and the southern limit slightly north of the Westwater Ruin, left by Ancestral Puebloans. George Hurst, interview with Michael Hurst, February 24, 1973, CRC-J7, Posey War Oral History Project, Charles Redd Center for Western Studies, Harold B. Lee Library, Brigham Young University, Provo, UT, 4.

53. John D. Rogers, "Piute Posey and the Last Indian Uprising," in Lloyd L. Young File (A2022), Utah State Historical Society Library, Salt Lake City, 2.

54. Hurst interview, 12–13.

55. Billy Mike, interview with Gregory C. Thompson and James Schultz, May 22, 1980, WMUHP.

56. McKean interview, April 9, 1923; Edward Dutchie, interview with author, May 21, 1996.

57. Edward Dutchie interview.

58. Ibid.

59. McKean interview, April 9, 1923.

60. Ibid.

61. J. Ray Ward to Attorney General, May 1, 1923, WMUHP.

62. Hurst interview.

63. Alma Uriah Jones, interview with Gary Shumway, August 4, 1981, CRC-K157, LDS Polygamy Oral History, Charles Redd Center for Western Studies, Harold B. Lee Library, Brigham Young University, Provo, UT, 68–69.

64. The following account is from John D. Rogers, "Piute Posey and the Last Indian Uprising," appendix to John Rogers's interview with Michael T. Hurst, April 29, 1972, CRC-J6, Posey War Oral History Project, Charles Redd Center for Western Studies, Harold B. Lee Library, Brigham Young University, Provo, UT. There are dozens of interviews of people who gave their versions of what happened in this fight, but Rogers's is the most complete. He was an active participant throughout the incident, and participated in additional interviews for clarification of detail.

65. William R. Young, "The 1923 Indian Uprising in San Juan County, Utah," filed in Lloyd L. Young Folder, Utah State Historical Society Library, Salt Lake City, 2.

66. Rogers interview, 22; Rogers, "Piute Posey," 7.

67. Young interview, 2.

68. The conventional wisdom of many involved in the fight was that Posey took the old Indian trail through where Highway 95 would be built. Another possibility is that he went farther north to another, easier, and more manageable trail into Comb Wash from Whiskers Draw since he had just been wounded in the hip by Dave Black.

69. Young interview, 34; Fern Oliver Shelley, "The Life Story of William Edward Oliver, 1858–1935," in possession of James W. Oliver Jr., Mapleton, UT; Alma Jones interview.

70. Rogers interview, 35.

71. Leland W. Redd, interview with Louise Lyne, July 12, 1972, O.H. 1094b, Southeastern Utah Oral History Project, Utah State Historical Society and California State University, Fullerton, 7.

72. Albert R. Lyman, "San Juan and Its Piutes," *San Juan Record*, September 21, 1933, 8.

73. Ellen Lefler, "Sheriff Newman and the Posey War," *Blue Mountain Shadows* 4 (Spring 1989): 24–27.

74. Wiley Redd, "Redd Recalls Indian Uprising, A Personal Experience," *San Juan Record*, June 1969, n.p.

75. Rogers interview, 37.

76. Ibid.

77. Ellen Lefler, "Memories of the Ute Roundup," *Blue Mountain Shadows* 4 (Spring 1989): 28.

78. Redd, "Red Recalls."

79. Ibid., 38.

80. Jim Mike, interview with Gary Shumway and Anna Marie Nat, June 20, 1968, Duke no. 550 and Harry Dutchie, interview with Gary Shumway, July 15, 1968, Doris Duke no. 517, Doris Duke Oral History Project, Special Collections, J. Willard Marriott Library, University of Utah, Salt Lake City; Clarence Perkins, interview with Mary Risher, June 29, 1971, O.H. 790, Southeastern Utah Oral History Project, Utah State Historical Society and California State University, Fullerton, 44–45.

81. Leland Redd interview.

82. Rogers, "Piute Posey," 10.

83. Ibid.

84. Young interview, 3.

85. *Salt Lake Tribune*, March 21–April 5, 1923.

86. "Piute Indians Are Reinforced," *Salt Lake Tribune*, March 24, 1923, 1.

87. Rogers interview, 22.

88. Hugh L. Scott to Commissioner of Indian Affairs, March 21, 1923, BIA-Letters Received.

89. Herbert Welsh to Charles Burke, March 22, 1923; Burke to Welsh, March 24, 1923; Welsh to Burke, March, 27, 1923; Hubert Work to Welsh, March 28, 1923; BIA — Letters Received.

90. Albert R. Lyman, "History of Blanding, 1905–1955," unpublished manuscript, Special Collections, Harold B. Lee Library, Brigham Young University, Provo, UT, 77–78. The reference to "Gadianton" comes from the *Book of Mormon*, in which a group of robbers and thieves assumed this name from a man who had led them.

91. McKean interview, April 9, 1923; Burke to George B. Lockwood, March 29, 1923, WMUHP; Burke to H. R. Olcott, March 29, 1923, BIA-Letters Received.

92. McKean interview, April 9, 1923.

93. Ibid.

94. Edward Dutchie interview.

95. Ibid.

CHAPTER 13

1. Edward E. McKean to Commissioner of Indian Affairs, January 23, 1923, National Archives, Records of the Bureau of Indian Affairs, RG 75, Consolidated Ute Agency, "Letters Received" (hereafter cited as BIA — Letters Received).

2. "To Rosebud Agency," *Cortez Journal-Herald*, December 15, 1927, 1.

3. Evan W. Estep to Commissioner of Indian Affairs, January 30, 1923, BIA — Letters Received.

4. Early in the historical record the canyon's name was misspelled "Allen." Although named after John Allan and his son Peter, who claimed lands in it and at its mouth, the canyon's name is now widely accepted as "Allen" Canyon.

5. Anderson Cantsee, interview with Aubrey Williams, January 28, 1961, Doris Duke #739, Doris Duke Oral History Project, Special Collections, J. Willard Marriott Library, University of Utah, Salt Lake City.

6. "Piute Indians to be Allotted Land in Utah," *Ignacio Chieftain*, April 20, 1923, 1.

7. E. B. Spencer, "Boundary Change Report," June 25, 1923, BIA — Letters Received.

8. Ibid.; McKean to Commissioner of Indian Affairs, April 4, 1923, BIA — Letters Received.

9. Commissioner to E. S. Booth, March 26, 1923, BIA — Letters Received.

10. McKean to the Commissioner of Indian Affairs, May 4, 1923, BIA — Letters Received.

11. Hubert Work to Secretary of Agriculture, May 18, 1923; Rush L. Holland to J. Ray Ward, May 12, 1923; McKean to Commissioner of Indian Affairs, June 25, 1923; BIA — Letters Received.

12. McKean to Commissioner of Indian Affairs, July 7, 1923, BIA — Letters Received.

13. A. W. Simington to Commissioner of Indian Affairs, July 23, 1923, BIA — Letters Received.

14. O. A. Olsen to District Forester, January 7 and 23, 1924; District Forester (R. H. Rutledge) to *The Forester*, January 26, 1924; BIA — Letters Received.

15. Rutledge to *The Forester*, July 2, 1923; C. V. Marvin to Secretary of the Interior, July 14, 1923; McKean to Commissioner of Indian Affairs, August 18, 1923; Charles H. Burke to McKean, September 10, 1923; Burke to Simington, September 18, 1923; F. M. Goodwin to Secretary of Agriculture, November 25, 1923; Simington to Commissioner of Indian Affairs, November 5, 1923; BIA — Letters Received.

16. McKean to Commissioner of Indian Affairs, December 1, 1923, BIA — Letters Received.

17. Burke to Herbert F. Robinson, December 16, 1923, BIA — Letters Received; U.S. Congress, Senate, "Reservation of Certain Land in Utah as a School for Ute Indians," *Report of the Secretary of the Interior*, May 31, 1924, S. Rpt. 668, 68th Cong., 1st Sess., 1–2.

18. Albert R. Lyman, "History of Blanding, 1905–1955," Harold B. Lee Library, Brigham Young University, 31–32.

19. Simington to Commissioner of Indian Affairs, July 23, 1923, BIA — Letters Received.

20. Simington to Commissioner of Indian Affairs, May 29, 1923; McKean to Commissioner of Indian Affairs, July 26, 1923; BIA — Letters Received.

21. Stella Eyetoo, interview with Floyd O'Neil and Gregory Thompson, July 1, 1980, O.H. #780, White Mesa Ute Oral History Project, American West Center, University of Utah , Salt Lake City.

22. McKean to Commissioner of Indian Affairs, May 19, 1924; Secretary to McKean, June 7, 1924; McKean to Commissioner of Indian Affairs, August 8, 1924; Burke to Senator Reed Smoot, February 27, 1924; BIA — Letters Received.

23. Adoline Eyetoo, interview with author and Winston Hurst, July 25, 2009. This interview and those done with Aldean Ketchum, Bonnie Mike Lehi, Stella Eyetoo, and Annie Cantsee in 2009 were sponsored by the Utah Humanities Council and are available in the Utah State Historical Society Library, Salt Lake City.

24. Allan Black, interview with Gary Shumway, May 30, 1978, O.H. 1638, Utah State Historical Society and California State University, Fullerton, Oral History Program (hereafter cited as SEUOHP), 36.

25. Ibid.; Zelma Acton, interviews with Deborah Fellbaum and Shirley E. Stephenson, July 11, 1972, and July 21, 1974, respectively, O.H. 1196a, b, SEUOHP; Zelma Black Acton, interview with Floyd O'Neil and Gregory Thompson, July 2, 1980, O.H. #774, White Mesa Ute Oral History Project, American West Center, University of Utah, Salt Lake City; and Zelma Acton, interview with author, May 14, 2007.

26. "Towaoc," *Cortez Journal-Herald*, March 21, 1929, 2.

27. Ardelle Ostergaard, conversation with author, February 5, 2009.

28. Annie Cantsee, interview with author and Winston Hurst, July 20, 2009; Stella Eyetoo, interview with author and Winston Hurst, July 11, 2009. See note 23.

29. Ostergaard conversation.

30. "Blanding Department," *San Juan Record*, June 5, 1930, 3.

31. McKean to Black, January 16, 1925, BIA — Letters Received.

32. E. Z. Black, "Farmer's Weekly Report," August 1, 1925, White Mesa Ute History Project, American West Center, University of Utah, Salt Lake City.

33. Ibid., October 1925.

34. Ibid., November and December 1925.

35. Acton interviews with Fellbaum and Stephenson.

36. Ibid.

37. Ibid.

38. White Mesa Ute Census, 1915–1931, one reel microfilm, Family History Center, The Church of Jesus Christ of Latter-day Saints, Blanding, Utah.

39. Stella Eyetoo; Aldean Ketchum; Bonnie Mike Lehi; Billy Mike interview with Floyd O'Neil and Greg Thompson, May 22, 1980, O.H. #789; Harry Dutchie interview with Floyd O'Neil and Greg Thompson, May 30, 1986, O.H. 789, White Mesa Ute Oral History Project, American West Center, University of Utah, Salt Lake City, Utah; Anderson Cantsee interview with Aubrey Williams, January 28, 1961, O.H. #739, Doris Duke Oral History Project, Special Collections, Marriott Library, University of Utah, Salt Lake City, Utah.

40. Stewart Hatch interview with author, August 5, 2009.

41. Aldean Ketchum interview.

42. Stella Eyetoo interview.

43. Acton interviews with Fellbaum and Stephenson.

44. Stella Eyetoo and Bonnie Mike Lehi interviews.

45. Stella Eyetoo interview.

46. Ibid.; interviews with Adoline Eyetoo, Aldean Ketchum, and Stewart Hatch.

47. Aldean Ketchum interview.

48. Acton interviews with Fellbaum and Stephenson; Black, "Farmer's Weekly Report," June 5, 1926, White Mesa Ute History Project, American West Center, University of Utah, Salt Lake City.

49. Annie Cantsee interview.

50. Aldean Ketchum interview.

51. Ostergaard conversation.

52. Ibid.; Acton interviews with Fellbaum and Stephenson.

53. Acton interviews with Fellbaum and Stephenson.

54. Adoline Eyetoo, Stella Eyetoo, Annie Cantsee, and Hatch interviews.

55. L. A. Chapin, "Homes for Ute Indians," *Cortez Journal-Herald*, January 31, 1929, 1.

56. Adoline Eyetoo interview.
57. Hatch and Stella Eyetoo interviews.
58. "Ute Mountain Ute Annual Report," 1925, Superintendents' Annual Narrative and Statistical Reports from Field Jurisdictions of the BIA, 1907–1938, Consolidated Ute Agency, microfilm 1011, roll 29, National Archives, Washington, DC (hereafter cited as BIA Annual Report).
59. "Towaoc," *Cortez Sentinel*, December 12, 1929, 3; "Towaoc," *Cortez Journal-Herald*, December 12, 1929, 2.
60. Black, "Farmer's Weekly Report," January 9 to February 6, 1926, White Mesa Ute History Project, American West Center, University of Utah, Salt Lake City.
61. Annie Cantsee and Adoline Eyetoo interviews.
62. Stella Eyetoo interview.
63. Unless otherwise noted, all information on the Hatch trading post comes from Stewart Hatch interview.
64. Joseph B. Harris to McKean, February 25, March 4, April 23 and 30, June 9, 1926, Road Construction, U.S. Bureau of Indian Affairs, Consolidated Ute Indian Service Files, 1879–1952, Federal Records Center, Denver, CO.
65. Black, "Monthly Time Book," 1933–1935, Department of the Interior, U.S. Indian Service, in possession of Ardelle Ostergaard (Family), Blanding, UT.
66. McKean, "Industries," BIA Annual Report, 1925.
67. D. H. Wattson to A. C. Cooley, April 9, 1937, White Mesa Ute History Project, American West Center, University of Utah, Salt Lake City.
68. Ibid.
69. Hatch interview.
70. Stella Eyetoo interview; Acton interviews with Fellbaum and Stephenson; Hatch interview.
71. Hatch interview.
72. Acton interviews with Fellbaum and Stephenson.
73. Hatch interview.
74. Annie Cantsee and Stella Eyetoo interviews.
75. "Blanding CCC News," *San Juan Record*, June 23, 1938, 9.
76. "Blanding CCC News," *San Juan Record*, June 13, 1940, 9.
77. Hatch interview.
78. Allan Black interview.
79. LaVerne Tate, "Billy Mike and His Courting Flute," *Blue Mountain Shadows* 7 (Winter 1990): 42–43.
80. James Slavens, conversation with author, September 7, 2009.

Chapter 14
The epigraph quote from Buckskin Charlie is from Verner Z. Reed, "The Southern Ute Indians," *Californian* 4 (September 1893): 488–505. The quote from Mancos George is from William R. Palmer,
Field Notes, William R. Palmer Collection, Special Collections, Gerald R. Sherratt Library, Southern Utah State University, Cedar City, 41.
1. Annual Report, 1923, Superintendent's Annual Narrative and Statistical Reports from Field Jurisdictions of the BIA, 1907–1938—Consolidated Ute, microfilm 1011, roll 29 (hereafter cited as Superintendent's Annual Report).
2. E. Z. Black, "Farmer's Weekly Report," September 26, 1925, White Mesa Ute History Project, American West Center, University of Utah, Salt Lake City (hereafter cited as WMUHP).
3. Herbert H. Stacher to Charles Burke, January 27, 1926, National Archives, Records of the Bureau of Indian Affairs, RG 75, Consolidated Ute Agency, "Letters Received" (hereafter cited as BIA—Letters Received).
4. Edward E. McKean to Commissioner of Indian Affairs, August 10, 1925, and April 29, 1926, Letters Received—BIA; Black, "Farmer's Weekly Report," October 3, 1925.
5. Black, "Farmer's Weekly Report," November 29, 1927, and September 15, 1928.
6. W. H. Harshberger to W. F. Dickson, October 28, 1928; Harshberger to I. E. Bell, January 1, 1929; WMUHP.
7. F. H. Hammond to Commissioner of Indian Affairs, February 28, 1929, WMUHP.
8. Black to Edgar J. Peacore, March 23, 1929; Peacore to Commissioner of Indian Affairs, March 12, 1929; Peacore to Commissioner of Indian Affairs, November 26, 1929; WMUHP.
9. Superintendent's Annual Reports, 1926–1930.
10. Peacore to Commissioner of Indian Affairs, December 4, 1929, WMUHP.
11. "Local Indian School to be Built," *San Juan Record*, April 3, 1930, 8.
12. Superintendent's Annual Report, 1932; D. L. Bayles, "Indian Education is Paramount Question," *San Juan Record*, October 2, 1932, 8.
13. Jami Bayles, "The Blanding Ute Dormitory," *Blue Mountain Shadows* 9 (Winter 1991): 75–79; "Blanding Department," *San Juan Record*, September 4, 1930, 8.
14. "Blanding Department," *San Juan Record*, September 25, 1930, 3; Peacore to Commissioner of Indian Affairs, November 1, 1930, WMUHP.
15. "Well-known Indian Worker Dies after Brief Illness," *San Juan Record*, August 13, 1931, 1.
16. Superintendent's Annual Report, 1935; "Blanding," *San Juan Record*, November 28, 1935, 8.
17. Helen Shumway, "Elementary Memories," *Blue Mountain Shadows* 4 (Spring 1989): 29–31.
18. Cleal Bradford, interview with author, February 24, 2009.
19. Ibid.; Stella Eyetoo, interview with author, July 11, 2009.

20. Albert R. Lyman, "The Old Settler," *San Juan Record*, June 12, 1952, 9.

21. Minnie G. Bugg, "Blanding News," *San Juan Record*, July 31, 1941, 8; Albert R. Lyman, "History of Blanding, 1905–1955," unpublished manuscript, Special Collections, Harold B. Lee Library, Brigham Young University, Provo, UT, 32.

22. Lizzie Jacket, interview with author, May 30, 1991.

23. "A Plan for the Rehabilitation of the Ute Mountain Ute Indians through the Use of Land Claim Payments," November 21, 1951, WMUHP, 20.

24. See Winston B. Hurst, "The Blanding Navajos: A Case Study of Off-Reservation Navajo Migration and Settlement," unpublished master's thesis, 1981, Eastern New Mexico University, Roswell.

25. Lyman, "The Old Settler," *San Juan Record*, January 11, 1951, 1.

26. Lyman, *The Edge of the Cedars: The Story of Walter C. Lyman and the San Juan Mission* (New York: Carlton Press, 1966), 144.

27. Lyman, "The Old Settler," *San Juan Record*, August 17, 1972, 2.

28. Lyman, "Among the Indians," unpublished manuscript in possession of author.

29. Adoline Eyetoo, interview with author, July 25, 2009.

30. Lyman, "The Old Settler, *San Juan Record*, August 3 and 10, 1972, 2; Lyman, "Among the Indians," 27.

31. Lyman, "The Old Settler, *San Juan Record*, August 17, 1972, 2; Lyman, *Edge of the Cedars*, 147.

32. Ryan Roberts and Jenny Hurst, "Indian Education," *Blue Mountain Shadows* 9 (Winter 1991): 72.

33. Lyman, "History of Blanding, 1905–1955," 33.

34. Lyman, "The Old Settler," *San Juan Record*, January 11, 1951. He may be off in his chronology by a few years since construction of these homes did not begin until 1954.

35. "Indian Education Problems Discussed at Blanding," *San Juan Record*, March 22, 1962, 8.

36. Richard K. Young, *The Ute Indians of Colorado in the Twentieth Century* (Norman: University of Oklahoma Press, 1997).

37. Ibid., 59.

38. Katherine M. B. Osburn, *Southern Ute Women: Autonomy and Assimilation on the Reservation, 1887–1934* (Albuquerque: University of New Mexico Press, 1998).

39. Ibid., 115.

40. Ibid., 117.

41. McKean to Commissioner of Indian Affairs, January 6, 1928, BIA — Letters Received; Superintendent's Annual Report, 1928.

42. Chester E. Faris to Commissioner of Indian Affairs, April 28, 1928, BIA — Letters Received.

43. U.S. Congress, Senate, *Hearings before a Subcommittee of the Committee on Indian Affairs*, May 13, 1931, S. Res. 79, 70th Cong., 2nd Sess., 10679–10680.

44. E. B. Meritt to C. W. Wiegel, March 11, 1926, BIA-Letters Received.

45. U.S. Congress, Senate, *Hearings*, 10610, 10618–10621.

46. Ibid., 10650–10651.

47. Young, *The Ute Indians*, 85.

48. Levi Chubbuck, cited in Martha C. Knack, *Boundaries Between: The Southern Paiutes, 1775–1995* (Lincoln: University of Nebraska Press, 2001), 140–141.

49. See Robert S. McPherson, *A History of San Juan County: In the Palm of Time* (Salt Lake City: Utah State Historical Society, 1995), 135–140.

50. Byron A. Sharp to Commissioner of Indian Affairs, June 2, 1922, Western Navajo Agency, J. Lee Correll Collection, Tribal Archives, Navajo Nation, Window Rock, AZ (hereafter cited as Navajo Nation Archives).

51. E. E. McKean to Commissioner of Indian Affairs, April 22, 1925; Meyers to Commissioner of Indian Affairs, April 23, 1925; Navajo Nation Archives.

52. For a more complete explanation of the Navajo side of this conflict, see Robert S. McPherson, *Comb Ridge and Its People: The Ethnohistory of a Rock* (Logan: Utah State University, 2009), 174–179.

53. Edward Dutchie Jr., "Ute Winter and Summer Ranges," March 1986, student paper, used with permission.

54. Faris to Commissioner of Indian Affairs, September 23, 1930, BIA — Letters Received.

55. Peacore to Faris, September 25, 1930, BIA — Letters Received.

56. Charles Redd to Reed Smoot, September 30, 1931; Redd to Colton, October 13, 1930; Navajo Nation Archives.

57. Redd to Colton, November 17, 1930, Navajo Nation Archives.

58. Peacore to Commissioner of Indian Affairs, December 18, 1930, Navajo Nation Archives.

59. Peacore to Commissioner of Indian Affairs, October 19, 1931, Navajo Nation Archives; "Outlook Encouraging for Much Road Work," *Times Independent*, January 1, 1931, 5.

60. Peacore to Commissioner of Indian Affairs, October 10 and November 10, 1931, BIA — Letters Received.

61. S. F. Stacher to J. M. Stewart, March 28, 1939, BIA — Letters Received.

62. Redd to Stewart, March 30, 1939, BIA — Letters Received.

63. Redd to Stewart, June 30, 1929; Stacher to Commissioner of Indian Affairs, August 21, 1939; Abe Murdock to Fred W. Johnson, October 5, 1939; Stacher to Commissioner of Indian Affairs, November 28, 1939; BIA — Letters Received.

64. Commissioner to Johnson, December 26, 1939;

Memorandum for the Acting Assistant Secretary, May 11, 1942, BIA — Letters Received.

65. Floyd E. MacSpadden to Commissioner of Indian Affairs, December 9, 1940; Ute Mountain Tribal Council, Meeting Minutes, December 3, 1940, BIA — Letters Received.

66. MacSpadden, Superintendent's Annual Report, 1940.

67. Ute Mountain Tribal Council, Minutes, February 3, 1948, WMUHP.

68. MacSpadden to Commissioner of Indian Affairs, February 4, 1941, BIA — Letters Received.

69. Anson Whyte, cited in Young, *The Ute Indians*, 116.

70. L. B. Cutting to Stacher, November 3, 1938, BIA-Letters Received.

71. Young, *The Ute Indians*, 117.

72. Ibid., 129.

73. Chester Cantsee, interview with Gregory Thompson and Floyd O'Neil, March 22, 1980, OH — 00, 776, WMUHP.

74. Young, *The Ute Indians*, 141; "Uncle Sam Settles with Utes," *Salt Lake Tribune*, as cited in *Desert Magazine* 13 (September 1950): 39.

75. "Three Ute Tribes Number about 3,000 People," *San Juan Record*, February 17, 1955, 49.

76. "A Plan for the Rehabilitation of the Ute Mountain Ute Indians through the Use of Land Claim Payments," November 21 1951, WMUHP, 7–8.

77. Ibid., 13.

78. "Allen Canyon General Council Minutes," October 10, 1952, WMUHP.

79. "Ute Mountain Tribal Council Meeting," April 22, 1953, WMUHP.

80. Irrigation Branch, Albuquerque, to Commissioner of Indian Affairs, December 31, 1953, WMUHP.

81. "Utes Get $1000 as U. S. Starts to Repay Old Debt," *San Juan Record*, October 25, 1951, 1.

82. "San Juan Piutes Have Pay Day," *San Juan Record*, April 24, 1952, 3.

83. Bonnie Mike Lehi, interview with author, July 20, 2009.

84. "Indians Attend School on Traffic Problems," *San Juan Record*, May 1, 1952, 1.

85. "Ute Land Settlement Fund Allocation Set by Council," *San Juan Record*, June 26, 1952, 1.

86. Ibid.

87. "Indian Meeting at Blanding Takes Up Many Problems Facing Tribe Including Living Conditions in Area," *San Juan Record*, November 6, 1952, 1.

88. James Slavens, conversation with author, October 15, 2009.

89. "Rehabilitation of Indians to be a Reality," *Dove Creek Press* and *San Juan Record*, December 19, 1952, 1.

90. Stella Eyetoo, interview with author, July 25, 2009.

91. Patty [*sic*] Mills Dutchie, interview with Gregory Thompson and Floyd O'Neil, August 13, 1980, OH-00, 779, WMUHP.

92. "Ute Indian Tribe Building New Homes," *San Juan Record*, October 14, 1954, 6.

93. Slavens conversation.

94. "The Big Road Heads South from Blanding," *San Juan Record*, August 9, 1956, 1.

95. Stella Eyetoo interview; Slavens conversation.

96. "Progress on White Mesa," *San Juan Record*, January 29, 1976, 8.

97. Maureen Beeson, "Electricity Comes to White Mesa," *Blue Mountain Shadows* 8 (Summer 1991): 45–46.

98. Maude Head to Commissioner, Bureau of Indian Affairs, July 11, 1956, WMUHP.

CHAPTER 15

1. Washington Matthews, "The Origin of the Utes," *American Antiquarian* 7 (September 1885): 271–274.

2. Martha Nez interview with Baxter Benally and author, August 10, 1988.

3. Charlie Blueyes, interview with Baxter Benally and author, August 28, 1988.

4. Nelson Begay, interview with author, March 1, 1987.

5. Mary Blueyes, interview with Baxter Benally and author, July 25, 1988.

6. Florence Begay, interview with Nelson Begay and author, April 29, 1988.

7. Raymond F. Locke, *The Book of the Navajo* (Los Angeles: Mankind Publishing Co., 1976), 120–121; Linda Hadley, *Hózhóójí Hane'* (Blessingway) (Rough Rock, AZ: Rough Rock Demonstration School, 1986), 31.

8. Sally Manygoats, interview with Marilyn Holiday and author, April 8, 1992.

9. Harvey Oliver, interview with Baxter Benally and author, March 6, 1991.

10. Charlie Mitchell, "The Story of a Navaho Woman Captured by the Utes," cited in Edward Sapir, ed., *Navaho* Texts (Iowa City: University of Iowa, 1942), 335–337.

11. Rachel Eyetoo, interview with Gerald Scheib and Gary Shumway, July 12, 1971, O.H. 777, Southeastern Utah History Project, Utah State Historical Society, Salt Lake City, and California State University, Fullerton.

12. Lucille Hammond, interview with Sam Goodman and author, October 18, 1985.

13. "Piutes and Navajos in Altercation near Bluff," *Times Independent*, December 15, 1921, 8.

14. Tully Bigman, interview with Baxter Benally and author, April 15, 1993.

15. Albert R. Lyman, "San Juan and Its Piutes," *San Juan Record*, August 10, 1933, 8.

16. "Ute Mountain Ute Council Minutes," July 2, 1923; Edward E. McKean to Albert H. Kneale, September 17, 1923; McKean to Commissioner of Indian

Affairs, December 21, 1923; National Archives, Records of the Bureau of Indian Affairs, RG 75, Consolidated Ute Agency, "Letters Received," (hereafter referred to as BIA-Letters Received).

17. Fred Yazzie, interview with Louanna Adakai and author, November 1, 1985.

18. Gilmore Graymountain, interview with Marilyn Holiday and author, April 7, 1992.

19. Joe Manygoats, interview with Marilyn Holiday and author, December 18, 1991.

20. Slim Benally, interview with Baxter Benally and author, July 8, 1988.

21. Ella Sakizzie, interview with Baxter Benally and author, May 14, 1991.

22. Maimi Howard, interview with Baxter Benally and author, July 19, 1988. For a list of individuals and Navajo clans in the Monument Valley area, along with their Paiute relations, see John Holiday and Robert S. McPherson, *A Navajo Legacy: The Life and Teachings of John Holiday* (Norman: University of Oklahoma Press, 2005), 232–234.

23. Edward Dutchie, interview with author, May 21, 1996.

24. Holiday and McPherson, *A Navajo Legacy*, 234–235.

25. For further information, see Clyde Kluckhohn, *Navaho Witchcraft* (1944; reprint, Boston: Beacon Press, 1970).

26. Rachel Eyetoo interview.

27. Lola Mike, interview with Aldean Ketchum and author, November 16, 2005.

28. Rachel Eyetoo interview.

29. Ibid.

30. Earle R. Forrest, *With a Camera in Old Navaholand* (Norman: University of Oklahoma Press, 1970), 25.

31. Testimony of Aquila Nebeker before Elfego Baca, 1921, BIA — Letters Received.

32. A. H. Spencer to Secretary of the Interior, April 12, 1933, BIA — Letters Received.

33. D. B. McGue, "Ed Noland Insured His Life to Finance Indian Trading Post in Early Days," *Cortez Sentinel*, n.d., n.p.

34. *Mancos Times*, May 15, 1895, 4.

35. "Utes are Buncoed," *Mancos Times*, February 9, 1900, 2.

36. *Mancos Times*, December 26, 1902, 1.

37. *Mancos Times*, January 15, 1904, 3; Lolla Kutch Noland, interview by grandchild (family member), no date, in possession of Madeline Noland McCrum.

38. Madeline Noland McCrum, interview with author, June 24, 1993

39. Ibid.

40. Ibid.

41. E. A. Sturges to Adjutant of Black Mountain Expeditionary Forces, August 12, 1908, Records of the War Department, RG 98, Department of Colorado, U.S. Army Commands; Ira Hatch, interview with author, May 30, 1991.

42. Parley Oscar Hurst, interview with Sandy McFadden and Gary Shumway, July 17, 1971, O.H. 697, Utah State Historical Society and California State University, Fullerton.

43. Alan Whitmer, interview with author, September 12, 2001.

44. Ibid.

45. Ray Hunt, interview with author, January 21, 1991.

46. Ibid.

47. "Utes and Navajos Making Progress on Reservation," *Cortez Sentinel*, June 9, 1932, 1.

48. Forrest, *With a Camera*, 191.

49. Stewart Hatch, interview with author, August 5, 2009.

50. For a discussion of Navajo trading, see W. W. Hill, "Navaho Trading and Trading Ritual: A Study of Cultural Dynamics," *Southwestern Journal of Anthropology* 4 (Autumn 1948): 371–396; Robert S. McPherson, "Naalyéhé Bà Hooghan, 'House of Merchandise,' Navajo Trading Posts as an Institution of Cultural Change, 1900–1930," in *Navajo Land, Navajo Culture: The Utah Experience in the Twentieth Century* (Norman: University of Oklahoma Press, 2001): 65–83.

51. General John Q. Cannon, "When the Utes Invaded Utah," *Improvement Era* 32, no. 1 (November 1928): 41–46.

52. Whitmer interview.

53. Ray Hunt interview.

54. Stewart Hatch interview.

55. Ibid.

56. Ibid.

57. Whitmer interview; Stewart Hatch interview.

58. Albert R. Lyman, *The Outlaw of Navaho Mountain* (Salt Lake City: Albert R. Lyman Trust, 1986) and *Indians and Outlaws: Settling of the San Juan Frontier* (Orem, UT: Publishers Press, 1980).

59. Albert R. Lyman, "A Relic of Gadianton: Old Posey as I Knew Him," *Improvement Era* 26, no. 9 (July 1923): 791.

60. Ibid.

61. Lyman, "The Old Settler," *San Juan Record*, March 16, 1972, 2.

62. Ibid., March 9, 1972, 2.

63. Ibid., March 30, 1972, 2; Lyman, "San Juan and Its Piutes," *San Juan Record*, January 14, 1932, 5; February 18, 1932, 5; April 14, 1932, 5.

64. Lyman, "The Old Settler," *San Juan Record*, June 30, 1933, 5.

65. Ibid., August 24, 1933, 5; June 1, 1933, 5; June 8, 1933, 4.

66. Lyman Hunter, interview with Michael Hurst, February 21, 1973, CRC-J3, Charles Redd Center for Western Studies, Harold B. Lee Library, Brigham Young University, Provo, UT, 16.

67. Ibid., 15.

68. Lyman, "San Juan and Its Piutes," August 3 and 10, 1933, 8; "Ute 'All-Same-White-Man' with Telephone," *San Juan Blade*, October 5, 1917, 1.

69. John D. Rogers, interview with Michael Hurst, April 29, 1972, CRC-J6, Posey War Oral History Project, Charles Redd Center for Western Studies, Harold B. Lee Library, Brigham Young University, Provo, UT, 25.

70. Brigham Stevens, interview with Mary Risher, July 18, 1971, O.H. 1096, Utah State Historical Society and California State University, Fullerton.

71. Lyman, "The Old Settler," *San Juan Record*, August 12, 1971, 2.

72. Ira Hatch interview.

73. "Piute Leader Dead, 'Old Polk' Seeks Happy Hunting Ground," February 14, 1935, 1; "Blanding," February 13, 1936, 5; both in *San Juan Record*.

74. Lyman, "The Old Settler," *San Juan Record*, May 25, 1950, 1.

75. Amasa Jay Redd, interview with Charles Peterson, July 27, 1973, Charles Redd Center for Western Studies, Harold B. Lee Library, Brigham Young University, Provo, UT, 21.

76. Lyman, "San Juan and Its Piutes," *San Juan Record*, August 3, 1933, 8.

77. Lyman, "The Old Settler," *San Juan Record*, October 15, 1942, 1.

78. Fern Simpson, interview with Deborah Fellbaum, July 12, 1972, O.H. 69-7B, Utah State Historical Society and California State University, Fullerton.

79. "Mancos George, Nobleman," *San Juan Record*, July 14, 1949, 1.

80. Lyman, "The Old Settler," May 31, 1962, 2; "Jim Mike," May 11, 1972, 2; both in *San Juan Record*.

81. Ibid., May 31, 1962, 2.

82. For information swirling around the controversy of who discovered Rainbow Bridge, see Stephen C. Jett, "The Great Race to Discover Rainbow Natural Bridge in 1909," *Kiva* 58 (1992): 3–65; and Hank Hassell, *Rainbow Bridge: An Illustrated History* (Logan: Utah State University Press, 1999).

83. Zeke Scher, "Jim Mike: The Man Who Discovered Rainbow Bridge" and "Synopsis of Events Leading Up to Jim Mike Plaque Ceremony of September 30, 1997," *Blue Mountain Shadows* 19 (Fall 1997): 17–23.

84. J. E. Jenkins to David S. Cook, May 6, 1915, BIA—Letters Received.

85. Lyman, "The Old Settler," *San Juan Record*, April 6, 1972, 2.

86. Lyman P. Hunter, "San Juan Remembered," unpublished manuscript, Special Collections, Harold B. Lee Library, Brigham Young University, Provo, UT.

87. Lyman, "San Juan and Its Piutes," *San Juan Record*, September 14, 1933, 8

CHAPTER 16

The epigraph quote is from an anonymous Northern Ute elder cited in Mary Stephanie Reynolds,

"Dance Brings about Everything: Dance Power in the Ideologies of Northern Utes of Uintah and Ouray Reservation and Predominantly Mormon Anglos of an Adjacent Uintah Basin Community," vol. 2, unpublished doctoral dissertation, University of California, Irvine, 1990, Special Collections, Harold B. Lee Library, Brigham Young University, Provo, UT, 334.

1. William R. Palmer, "San Juan Indians," William R. Palmer Collection, Special Collections, Gerald R. Sherratt Library, Southern Utah University, Cedar City, 27–28.

2. William R. Palmer, Field Notes, "San Juan Trip, August 21–26, 1935," William R. Palmer Collection, Special Collections, Gerald R. Sherratt Library, Southern Utah University, Cedar City. The Ghost Dance did not involve destruction of goods and had nothing to do with a postburial experience.

3. Ibid.

4. Palmer, "San Juan Indians," 32.

5. Ibid., 34.

6. Ibid., 37–38.

7. Palmer, "Experiences in Gathering Indian Folklore," November 3, 1945, William R. Palmer Collection, Special Collections, Gerald R. Sherratt Library, Southern Utah University, Cedar City, 4.

8. For an example of these stories, see William R. Palmer, *Why the North Star Stands Still and Other Indian Legends* (Springdale, UT: Zion Natural History Association, [1946] 1978).

9. See Carobeth Laird, *The Chemehuevis* and *Mirror and Pattern: George Laird's World of Chemehuevi Mythology* (Banning, CA: Malaki Museum Press, 1976 and 1984, respectively).

10. Laird, *The Chemehuevis*, 231.

11. Don D. Fowler and Catherine S. Fowler, ed., *Anthropology of the Numa: John Wesley Powell's Manuscripts on the Numic Peoples of Western North America, 1868–1880* (Washington, DC: Smithsonian Institution, 1971): 78–91.

12. William R. Palmer, "Indians—Paiutes—Natural Science" notes, n.d., William R. Palmer Collection, Special Collections, Gerald R. Sherratt Library, Southern Utah University, Cedar City, 1–2.

13. Bonnie Mike Lehi, interview with author, July 20, 2009; Adoline Eyetoo, interview with author, July 25, 2009.

14. Lynda D. McNeil, "Recurrence of Bear Restoration Symbolism: Minusinsk Basin Evenki and Basin-Plateau Ute," *Journal of Cognition and Culture* 8 (2008): 80.

15. Robert H. Lowie, "Shoshonean Tales," *Journal of American Folklore* 37, no. 143 (January–June 1924): 1–91; Anne M. Smith, *Ute Tales* (Salt Lake City: University of Utah Press, 1992); and Talmy Givón, *Ute Traditional Narratives* (Ignacio, CO: Ute Press, 1985).

16. Ibid.; Lynda D. McNeil, "Climbing Bear, Spirit

Helper: Companion Petroglyphs at Shalabolino (Siberia) and Shavano Valley (Colorado, USA)," http://spot.colorado.edu/~lmcneil/Climbing Bear .pdf; Lynda D. McNeil, "Ute Indian Bear Dance: Related Myths and Bear Glyphs," http://spot.colo rado.edu/~lmcneil/UteBearDance.

17. William F. Hanson, "The Lure of Tam-man Nacup Springtime Festival of the Utes," unpublished master's thesis, 1937, Special Collections, Harold B. Lee Library, Brigham Young University, Provo, UT, 54, 73; Anne M. Smith, *Ethnography of the Northern Utes*, Papers in Anthropology 17 (Santa Fe: Museum of New Mexico Press, 1974), 220.

18. Connor Chapoose and Y. T. Witherspoon (ed.), *Conversations with Connor Chapoose, a Leader of the Ute Tribe of the Uintah and Ouray Reservation*, Anthropological Papers 47 (Eugene: Anthropology Department, University of Oregon, 1993), 50–51.

19. Ibid.

20. Jack Cantsee, interview with author, September 24, 2009.

21. Aldean Ketchum, interview with author, July 30, 2009.

22. McNeil, "Climbing Bear," 3, 6.

23. Lehi interview.

24. Adoline Eyetoo interview.

25. Clifford Duncan, conversation with author, September 11, 2009; Carol Patterson has worked extensively with Duncan in interpreting bear-tree symbols at Shavano Valley, Colorado, rock art sites. See Carol Patterson, "Shavano Valley Rock Art Site Protection and Interpretive Project" (Montrose, CO: Alpine Archaeological Consultants, 2005).

26. Clifford Duncan, conversation with author, September 18, 2009.

27. Jack Cantsee interview.

28. Ibid.

29. Terry G. Knight, interview reproduced in Mary Jane Yazzie, "Life Traditions of the Utes of Avikan," *Blue Mountain Shadows* 7 (Winter 1990): 27–28.

30. Joseph G. Jorgensen, *The Sun Dance Religion: Power for the Powerless* (Chicago: University of Chicago Press, 1972), 201.

31. Ibid., 183.

32. Ibid., 210.

33. Larry Cesspooch, conversation with author, July 15, 2009.

34. Knight cited in Yazzie, "Life Traditions," 28.

35. Jorgensen, *Sun Dance*, 211.

36. Chapoose and Witherspoon, *Conversations*, 55.

37. Jorgensen, *Sun Dance*, 211.

38. Ibid., 209.

39. Isabel T. Kelly and Catherine S. Fowler, "Southern Paiute," *Handbook of North American Indians*, vol. 11: *Great Basin* (Washington, DC: Smithsonian Institution, 1986), 383–384.

40. Palmer, "Indian Memorial Service for President Anthony W. Ivins," n.d., William R. Palmer Collection, Special Collections, Gerald R. Sherratt Library, Southern Utah University, Cedar City, UT.

41. Ketchum interview.

42. Alex K. Carroll, M. Nieves Zedeño, and Richard W. Stoffle, "Landscapes of the Ghost Dance: A Cartography of Numic Ritual," *Journal of Archaeological Method and Theory* 11, no. 2 (June 2004): 137.

43. Scholars disagree as to whether or not there was a Mormon influence in either of the two periods of the Ghost Dance. See John Alton Peterson, *Utah's Black Hawk War* (Salt Lake City: University of Utah Press, 1998): 360–363, purporting a connection, and Lawrence G. Coates, "The Mormons and the Ghost Dance," *Dialogue: A Journal of Mormon Thought* 18. no. 4 (Winter 1985): 89–111; Coates believes there was no transfer of ideology.

44. Russell Thornton, "Demographic Antecedents of a Revitalization Movement: Population Change, Population Size, and the 1890 Ghost Dance," *American Sociological Review* 46, no. 1 (February 1981): 88–96.

45. Paiute informant cited by Cora DuBois in Michael Hittman, "The 1870 Ghost Dance at the Walker River Reservation: A Reconstruction," *Ethnohistory* 3 (Summer 1973): 250.

46. James Mooney, *The Ghost-Dance Religion and the Sioux Outbreak of 1890* (Chicago: University of Chicago Press, 1896, 1972), 4.

47. Michael Hittman, *Wovoka and the Ghost Dance* (Lincoln: University of Nebraska Press, 1990, 1997), 102.

48. Virginia McConnell Simmons, *The Ute Indians of Utah, Colorado, and New Mexico* (Boulder: University Press of Colorado, 2000), 209.

49. "The Indian Movement," *Deseret News*, November 29, 1890, 1; James P. Boyd, *Recent Indian Wars Under the Lead of Sitting Bull and Other Chiefs, with a Full Account of the Messiah Craze and Ghost Dances* (New York: Publishers Union, 1891), 176–178, 186–190.

50. W. W. Hill, "The Navaho Indians and the Ghost Dance of 1890," *American Anthropologist* 46, no. 4 (October–December 1944): 523–527.

51. "Utah Has a Ghost Dance," *Salt Lake Tribune*, December 12, 1890, 1; "No Ghost Dance at Uintah," *Salt Lake Tribune*, December 19, 1890, 1.

52. Smith, *Ethnography of the Northern Utes*, 216–218.

53. Henry F. Dobyns and Robert C. Euler, *The Ghost Dance of 1889 Among the Pai Indians of Northwestern Arizona* (Tucson: Prescott College Press, 1967): 1–18; Steven A. Weber and P. David Seaman, *Havasupai Habitat: A. F. Whiting's Ethnography of a Traditional Indian Culture* (Tucson: University of Arizona Press, 1985): 137–138; Richard W. Stoffle, Lawrence Loendorf, Diane Austin, and Angelita Bulletts, "Ghost Dancing the Grand

Canyon: Southern Paiute Rock Art, Ceremony, and Cultural Landscapes," *Current Anthropology* 41 (2000): 11–38.

54. Forbes Parkhill, *The Last of the Indian Wars* (New York: Crowell-Collier Press, 1961), 108.

55. The following information comes from three different interviews with Edward Dutchie Sr., and his wife, Patty (Mills) Dutchie, held on May 7, 13, and 21, 1996. Unless otherwise noted, Edward provided the information.

56. Lehi interview.

57. Duncan conversation.

58. Stella Eyetoo, interview with author, July 11, 2009.

59. Adoline Eyetoo interview.

60. Annie Cantsee, interview with author, August 4, 2009.

61. Jack Cantsee interview. Unless otherwise noted, the remaining discussion about the Worship Dance comes from this interview.

62. What follows is a synopsis of "How Wolf and Coyote Went Away," in Laird, *The Chemehuevis*, 192–207. According to anthropologist Kay Fowler, who specializes in beliefs and practices of Numic people, other versions of this story are found among the Northern Paiutes and Shoshones (personal communication with the author, February 16, 2010).

63. Judith Vander, "The Shoshone Ghost Dance and Numic Myth: Common Heritage, Common Themes," *Journal of California and Great Basin Anthropology* 17, no. 2 (1995): 184.

64. Ibid., 185.

65. Mooney, 53.

66. Ibid., 59.

67. Jorgensen, "Ghost Dance, Bear Dance, and Sun Dance," 662.

68. Hittman, *Wovoka and the Ghost Dance*, 193–194.

CHAPTER 17

The epigraph quote is from my interview with Jack Cantsee Sr. on September 24, 2009.

1. Connor Chapoose and Y. T. Witherspoon (ed.), *Conversations with Connor Chapoose: A Leader of the Ute Tribe of the Uintah and Ouray Reservation*, Anthropological Papers 47 (Eugene: University of Oregon, 1993), 34.

2. Charles H. Dimmock, cited in Steven K. Madsen, *Exploring Desert Stone: John N. Macomb's 1859 Expedition to Canyonlands of the Colorado* (Logan: Utah State University Press, 2010), 59.

3. Beatrice Blyth Whiting, *Paiute Sorcery*, Publications in Anthropology 15 (New York: Viking Fund, 1950), 30–32.

4. Clifford Duncan interview with Floyd O'Neil and Greg Thompson, November 14, 1983, Ute Indian Interview #853, American West Center, University of Utah, Salt Lake City, 13–14.

5. U.S. Congress, Senate, "Hearings before a Subcom-

mittee of the Committee on Indian Affairs," May 13, 1931, S. Res. 79, 70th Cong., 2nd Sess., 10702.

6. Annual Report, 1927, Superintendents' Annual Narrative and Statistical Reports from Field Jurisdictions of the BIA, 1907–1938 — Consolidated Ute Agency, microfilm 1011, roll 29.

7. Annual Report, 1928, Superintendents' Annual Narrative and Statistical Reports from Field Jurisdictions of the BIA, 1907–1938 — Consolidated Ute Agency, microfilm 1011, roll 29.

8. Jack Cantsee interview.

9. Whiting, *Paiute Sorcery*, 33, 56, 65–66.

10. Edward Dutchie, interview with author, May 13, 1996.

11. "Indian Witchcraft," *San Juan Record*, February 1, 1962, 3.

12. *Montezuma Journal*, May 27, 1904, 2.

13. William M. Peterson to J. H. Wood, November 2, 1905; Peterson to Joseph Lippman, November 9, 1905; National Archives, Records of the Bureau of Indian Affairs, RG 75, Consolidated Ute Agency, Letters Received, (hereafter cited as BIA — Letters Received).

14. C. A. Bonfils to H. L. Hall, June 22, 1904, BIA — Letters Received.

15. Peterson to Commissioner of Indian Affairs, March 10, 1905; Joseph O. Smith to Earl M. Cranston, June 24, 1904; BIA — Letters Received.

16. S. F. Stacher, "The Indians at the Ute Mountain Reservation, 1906–1909," *Colorado Magazine* 26 no. 1 (January 1949): 55.

17. "Piute Indians Appeal to Attorney for Aid in Getting Rid of Tribesman Practicing Magic," *Salt Lake Tribune*, October 31, 1921, 3.

18. Rachel Eyetoo, interview with Gerald Scheib and Gary Shumway, July 12, 1971, O.H. 777b (not transcribed), Southeastern Utah Oral History Project, Utah State Historical Society and California State University, Fullerton.

19. Ibid.

20. Edward E. McKean to Commissioner of Indian Affairs, April 6, 1925, BIA — Letters Received.

21. "Medicine Man May be Victim of Foul Play," *Cortez Sentinel*, August 8, 1929, 1; "Ute Medicine Man Dies Mysteriously," *Cortez Journal-Herald*, August 8, 1929, 1.

22. "Medieval Rites Lead Utes into Trouble," *San Juan Record*, April 17, 1930, 1.

23. D. H. Wattson to A. C. Cooley, April 9, 1937, BIA — Letters Received.

24. Wattson to Commissioner of Indian Affairs, June 10, 1936, BIA — Letters Received.

25. Wattson to Commissioner of Indian Affairs, June 10, 1936, BIA — Letters Received.

26. Wattson to Zimmerman, August 11, 1936, BIA — Letters Received.

27. Duncan interview.

28. Marvin K. Opler, "The Southern Ute of Colorado,"

in *Acculturation in Seven American Indian Tribes*, ed. Ralph Linton (New York: D. Appleton-Century, 1940), 194.

29. Jack Cantsee Sr., conversation with author, January 26, 2010.

30. Evelina Lucero, "'Spirit Journey' Ute Mountain Elder Charlie Knight Dies," *Weenuche Smoke Signals*, November 1996, 6.

31. Duncan interview.

32. Bernard Barber, "A Socio-Cultural Interpretation of the Peyote Cult," *American Anthropologist* 43, no. 4 (October–December 1941): 673–675; Omer C. Stewart, *Peyote Religion: A History* (Norman: University of Oklahoma Press, 1987), 195–196.

33. Marvin K. Opler, "The Character and History of the Southern Ute Peyote Rite," *American Anthropologist* 42, no. 3 (July–September 1940): 465.

34. Richard K. Young, *The Ute Indians of Colorado in the Twentieth Century* (Norman: University of Oklahoma, 1997), 69.

35. Stewart, *Peyote Religion*, 197.

36. David F. Aberle and Omer C. Stewart, *Navaho and Ute Peyotism: A Chronological and Distributional Study*, University of Colorado Studies in Anthropology 6 (Boulder: University of Colorado Press, 1957), 23.

37. Annual Report, 1923, Superintendents' Annual Narrative and Statistical Reports from Field Jurisdictions of the BIA, 1907–1938—Consolidated Ute Agency, microfilm 1011, roll 29.

38. Annual Report, 1924, Superintendents' Annual Narrative and Statistical Reports from Field Jurisdictions of the BIA, 1907–1938—Consolidated Ute Agency, microfilm 1011, roll 29; McKean to F. A. Gross, December 30, 1924, BIA—Letters Received.

39. McKean to Edward L. Smith, September 29, 1925; Charles H. Burke to McKean, April 20, 1925; McKean to Smith, January 19, 1925; BIA—Letters Received.

40. McKean to Commissioner of Indian Affairs, June 9, 1926, BIA—Letters Received.

41. Opler, "The Character and History," 465.

42. Ibid.

43. Ibid., 467.

44. Dutchie interview.

45. "Piote a Pernicious Drug," *San Juan Record*, January 6 and April 14, 1938, 1; Karl K. Lyman to Lysle Cutting, March 24, 1938, and E. M. Kreutzer to Lyman, March 25, 1938, BIA—Letters Received; Omer C. Stewart, *Ute Peyotism: A Study of a Cultural Complex*, University of Colorado Studies in Anthropology 1 (Boulder: University of Colorado Press, 1948), 7.

46. L. B. Cutting to Herbert Stacher, October 24, 1938, BIA—Letters Received. Note that there are two Herbert Stachers: one the agent referenced here, the other a Ute man mentioned later. On several occasions a newborn baby received the name of the agent at that time, as did McKean Posey, another Paiute man living in Allen Canyon.

47. Aberle and Stewart, *Navaho and Ute Peyotism*, 24.

48. Stewart, *Ute Peyotism*, 6.

49. Young, *Ute Indians of Colorado*, 275.

50. Jack Cantsee conversation.

51. Aberle and Stewart, *Navaho and Ute Peyotism*, 32–41.

52. Howard Gorman, "The Growing Peyote Cult and the Use of Peyote on the Navajo Indian Reservation," 1938, Gladwell Richardson Collection, Special Collections, Cline Library, Northern Arizona University, Flagstaff.

53. Ibid., 7.

54. Aberle and Stewart, *Navaho and Ute Peyotism*, 27.

55. Robert S. McPherson, ed., *The Journey of Navajo Oshley* (Logan: Utah State University Press, 2000), 156–157.

56. Stewart, in *Ute Peyotism*, provides an excellent description based on observations and interviews with Native American Church members from Towaoc, Blanding, and the Uintah-Ouray Reservation. This source provides the overview given here based on information from pages 8–30. For other detailed accounts, see Aberle and Stewart, *Navaho and Ute Peyotism*, as well as Stewart, *Peyote Religion*.

57. Stewart, *Ute Peyotism*, 11.

58. Aberle and Stewart, *Navaho and Ute Peyotism*, 35–36.

59. David F. Aberle, *The Peyote Religion Among the Navaho* (Chicago: University of Chicago Press, 1966, 1980), 158–159.

60. Jack Cantsee interview.

61. Opler, "The Character and History," 467.

62. Jack Cantsee interview.

63. Ibid., 474; Opler, "The Southern Ute of Colorado," 193.

64. Bob Mims, "Peyote: When the Ancient Indian Way Collides with a New Age Craze," *Salt Lake Tribune* (August 12, 2000), C-1.

65. Jack Cantsee conversation.

66. Clessa Black, conversation with author, February 15, 2010.

67. Annual Reports (LR 13807-11, 14), White Mesa Branch, the Church of Jesus Christ of Latter-day Saints, Church History Building, Salt Lake City.

68. Kent Tibbitts, conversation with author, February 15, 2010.

69. Stanley W. Bronson, "The Saviors of Avikan" (self-published, 1987).

70. Steven Lovell, conversation with author, February 15, 2010.

71. Tibbitts conversation.
72. Bronson to Robert S. Bowring, April 3, 1997; Bronson to John Pressler, June 15, 1997; "Building Profile—White Mesa Chapel," December 14, 1998; all located in the White Mesa File, Blanding Utah Facilities Management Group of the Church of Jesus Christ of Latter-day Saints.
73. Donald V. Jack, Special Report, Annual Reports 1980–1983 (LR 13807–3), White Mesa Branch, the Church of Jesus Christ of Latter-day Saints, Church History Building, Salt Lake City.
74. Steven Lovell conversation.
75. Lola Mike, Stella Eyetoo, and Aldean Ketchum, conversation with author, March 17, 2010.
76. Aldean Ketchum, interview with author, July 30, 2009.
77. Jack Cantsee interview.
78. Stella Eyetoo, conversation with author, March 17, 2010.
79. Loretta Posey conversation with author, March 18, 2010.
80. Stella Eyetoo and Lola Mike conversation. Among other stories about Jesus visiting White Mesa residents, one tells of him appearing near Sugarloaf Rock on Lime Ridge, another about his walking on water in McElmo Creek, and others about visits to Cross Canyon, Colorado, and Douglas Mesa. The fact that Stella and Lola insisted that I read back to them what I had written—the only time they asked me to do that—indicates the importance of this story. Aldean Ketchum was also present and corroborated what was said as told to him by Billy Mike.
81. Stanley W. Bronson, *The Ute Spiritual Cross of the San Juan Mission* (self-published, 1999), 15–16.

Chapter 18

The epigraph quote is from an interview with Patty Mills Dutchie by Gregory Thompson and Floyd O'Neil, August 13, 1980, O.H., 779, American West Center, University of Utah, Salt Lake City, 17–18.

1. *American Heritage Dictionary*, 2d ed., (Boston: Houghton Mifflin Company, 1985), 677.
2. Transfer Deed, October 27, 1955, and March 29, 1960, Comb Wash Files, Bureau of Land Management Field Office, Monticello, UT (hereafter cited as CWF); "Ute Indians Plan Co-op Venture in Group Farming," *San Juan Record*, May 3, 1956, 1.
3. Richard K. Young, *The Ute Indians of Colorado in the Twentieth Century* (Norman: University of Oklahoma Press, 1997), 184, 188, 194.
4. "Ute Mountain Tribe (Perkins Ranch) Plan," June 13, 1968, CWF, 2.
5. Ibid., 3.
6. Cleal Bradford, interview with author, February 24 and March 10, 2009.
7. "Comb Wash Trespass," n.d., CWF.
8. Bradford interview.
9. The following information concerning this court case is taken from "National Wildlife Federation, Southern Utah Wilderness Alliance, and Joseph M. Feller (Appellants), versus Bureau of Land Management, (Respondents) American Farm Bureau Federation, Utah Farm Bureau Federation, Public Lands Council, National Cattlemen's Association, American Sheep Industry Association, and Ute Mountain Ute Indian Tribe," number UT-06-91-01, Office of Hearings and Appeals, U.S. Department of the Interior, CWF.
10. For a more detailed account of this court case and the arguments presented by competing sides, see Robert S. McPherson, *Comb Ridge and Its People: The Ethnohistory of a Rock* (Logan: Utah State University Press, 2009), 197–201.
11. Nick Sandberg, BLM associate field manager, phone conversation with author, April 11, 2008.
12. Edward M. Dutchie Sr. to Cleal Bradford, December 29, 1977, White Mesa Ute Council files, Blanding, UT (hereafter cited as WMUC).
13. Bradford interview.
14. Allen Canyon Ute Council, Meeting Minutes, September 27, 1978, WMUC; Bradford interview.
15. "White Mesa Recreation Program Aims to Improve Community Ties," *Deseret News*, August, 1979, n.p., WMUC.
16. "White Mesa Council Nominated for International Exposition," *San Juan Record*, July 21, 1983, 1.
17. "Crafts at Center Become Business," *San Juan Record*, January 29, 1981, 7.
18. "Grand Opening for First White Mesa Business," *San Juan Record*, June, 1984, WMUC.
19. "New Look, New Outlook at White Mesa," *San Juan Record*, August 7, 1991, 1.
20. Ibid.
21. Young, *The Ute Indians*, 265.
22. Agreement of Parties, *Sinajini v. Board of Education* case materials, on file at DNA Legal Office, Mexican Hat, UT.
23. *Whispering Sage*, June 1981, WMUC, 1.
24. "New Look," 1.
25. Bradford interview.
26. Patrick M. Macy, "The NAU Report on Native American Students in San Juan School District: A Ten Year Study, 1980–1990," October 25, 1993, in possession of author, 3.
27. Donna Deyhle, "Pushouts and Pullouts: Navajo and Ute School Leavers," *Journal of Navajo Education* 4, no. 2 (Winter 1989): 40.
28. Ibid., 39, 43, 46.
29. Ibid., 50.
30. Carolyn M. Shields, "A Study of the Educational Perceptions and Attitudes of Four Stakeholder Groups in the San Juan School District in 1998,"

February 1999, on file at San Juan School District Office, Blanding, UT.

31. Ibid., 134.
32. "CEU Graduates Should Continue to be Different," *San Juan Record*, June 9, 1983, 12.
33. Bradford interview.
34. Ibid.
35. Ibid.
36. Young, *The Ute Indians*, 260.
37. Stella Eyetoo, conversation with author, March 17, 2010.
38. "White Mesa Community Marches to Protest Mill Tailings Truck Haul—Washington Judge Hears Case," *Blue Mountain Panorama*, September 28, 1994, 1.
39. Ibid.
40. Brent Israelson, "White Mesa Utes Beat Back Super-fund Tailings," *High Country News*, January 23, 1995, 1.
41. "White Mesa Utes Fire Director Cleal Bradford," *San Juan Record*, October 12, 1994, 1.
42. Bradford interview.
43. "White Mesa Fires Another Director," *Blue Mountain Panorama*, July 12, 1995, 1.
44. "White Mesa Utes Face Uncertain Future," *San Juan Record*, September 6, 1995, 1; "White Mesa Citizens Reinstate Kalauli," *Blue Mountain Panorama*, August 2, 1995, 1; "Letter to the Editor," *Blue Mountain Panorama*, November 7, 1995, 3.
45. "Be Wary of Waste Processing near Blanding, Indians Warned," *Deseret News* (web edition), June 12, 1997; "Ute-Navajo Indian Group Will be Allowed to Appeal Decision on Nuclear Waste," *Salt Lake Tribune* (web edition), May 13, 1998.
46. John F. Harrington, "The Devil's Dirt, Southern Ute Tribe Fights for Removal of Toxic Waste from Ancient Burial Ground," *Salt Lake City Weekly* (web edition), May 29, 2003, 7 pages; "IUC Opponents Speak at Hearing," *Blue Mountain Panorama*, January 11, 2006, 1.
47. Cleal Bradford, conversation with author, March 11, 2010.
48. "Indians Help on White Mesa, Noble Redman Works Best on Empty Stomach. Many Farms Being Cleared by This Labor," *San Juan Blade*, October 12, 1917, 1.
49. "White Mesa Inc. Now One of County's Largest Employers," *San Juan Record*, July 2, 2008, 1.
50. Ibid.
51. Bradford interview.
52. Corina May (Ute Mountain Ute tribal government), telephone conversation with author, March 18, 2010.
53. "Conflicting Laws Leave White Mesa Community without Access to Juvenile Court," *San Juan Record*, September 9, 1976, 7.
54. "White Paper," May 1, 2004, WMUC.
55. Young, *The Ute Indians*, 209.

56. Bradford interview.
57. "Ute Tribal Chair Pleads Guilty, Resigns," *Cortez Journal*, March 23, 2004, 1.
58. "White Paper"; Mary Jane Yazzie to Harold Cuthair, May 31, 2004; Yazzie to Cuthair, July 19, 2004; WMUC.
59. Bradford interview.
60. Gary Shumway, interview with author, December 1, 2009.
61. Ibid.
62. Donna Singer, interview with author, March 7, 2010.
63. Ibid.
64. Eyetoo conversation.
65. Thell D. Black, interview with author and Winston Hurst, October 22, 2009.
66. James Slavens, conversation with author, October 15, 2009.
67. Ibid.
68. Shumway interview.
69. Lloyd Shumway, conversation with author, May 12, 2007; Carl L. Mahon, "Carl L. Mahon," *Blanding City Centennial Family Histories 1905–2005*, 2 (Blanding, UT: Shumway Family Publishing, 2005), 995.
70. "Scouts Erect Monument," *San Juan Record*, September 19, 1968, 15; "Boy Scouts Mark Posey Trail," *San Juan Record*, January 5, 1978, 2; Steve Lacy and Pearl Baker, *Posey: The Last Indian War* (Salt Lake City: Gibbs Smith, Publisher, 2007), 181–186.
71. Bradford interview.
72. Loretta Posey, conversation with author, March 18, 2010.
73. Buckley Jensen, "Fascinating Life of Chief Posey," *San Juan Record*, September 23, 2009, 5.
74. LaVerne Tate, "Billy Mike and His Courting Flute," *Blue Mountain Shadows* 7 (Winter 1990): 42–43; "White Mesa Man Will Perform Solo in Olympic Opening Ceremony," *San Juan Record*, February 6, 2002, 1.
75. Terri Winder, "Shirley Ketchum Denetsosie," *Blue Mountain Shadows* 23 (Winter 2003): 47–48.
76. Carol Edison, "Portraits of Tradition: A Tribute to White Mesa Folk Artists," *Blue Mountain Shadows* 23 (Winter 2003): 9–15, 56–57; Missy Votel, "The Willows of White Mesa," *Cross Currents*, July 16, 1999, 9–11.
77. Stewart Hatch, interview with author, August 5, 2009.
78. Young, *The Ute Indians*, 270.
79. Jack Cantsee Sr., interview with author, September 24, 2009.
80. Eyetoo conversation.

EPILOGUE

1. "The Old Settler," *San Juan Record*, March 30, 1952, 3.

Bibliography

Manuscripts

Amoss, Harold Lindsay, Jr. "Ute Mountain Utes." Doctoral dissertation, University of California — Northern Section, 1951.

Baker, Steven G., Jeffrey S. Dean, and Richard H. Towner. "Final Report for the Old Wood Calibration Project, Western Colorado." Montrose, CO: Centuries Research, May 1, 2008.

Bean, Jordan. "Jordan Bean." Unpublished account in possession of author, May 14, 1941.

Billings, Alfred N. "Memorandum Account Book and Diary of Alfred N. Billings, 1855." L. Tom Perry Special Collections, Harold B. Lee Library, Brigham Young University, Provo, UT.

Black, Edwin Z. "Monthly Time Book, 1933–1935." Department of the Interior, U.S. Indian Service. In possession of Ardelle Ostergaard Family, Blanding, UT.

Brugge, David M. "Navajo Use and Occupation of Lands North of the San Juan River in Present-day Utah." Unpublished manuscript. In author's possession.

Bureau of Land Management. Comb Wash Files. Field Office, Monticello, UT.

Childs, T. S. "A Statement and Appeal for the Southern Utes." n.d., n.p. On file in Special Collections, J. Willard Marriott Library, University of Utah, Salt Lake City.

Christensen, Christian Lingo. "Diary of Christian Lingo Christensen." L. Tom Perry Special Collections, Harold B. Lee Library, Brigham Young University, Provo, UT.

Church of Jesus Christ of Latter-day Saints. "Ute Mountain Ute Censuses, 1915–1931." On file in Family History Center, Blanding, UT.

Cloud-Smith, Sunshine, Mary Inez Rivera, and Everett Burch. "The Southern Ute Beliefs about the Ancient Anasazi." On file, BLM — Anasazi Heritage Center, Dolores, CO.

Correll, J. Lee. J. Lee Correll Collection, Tribal Archives, Navajo Nation, Window Rock, AZ.

Crosby, H. J. Letter from War Department with enclosures from Colonel C. H. Smith, September 29, 1881, MS 109. Special Collections, J. Willard Marriott Library, University of Utah, Salt Lake City.

Dalley, Julius S. "Mancos Jim Mesa — San Juan County."

Utah Writers' Project, August 11, 1942. Utah State Historical Society Library, Salt Lake City.

Daniels, Helen Sloan. "The Ute Indians of Southwestern Colorado." 1941. Cortez, CO, Public Library.

Douglass, William B. "Field Notes of the Survey of the Reservations Embracing the Natural Bridges National Monument, Cigarette Cave and the Snow Flat Cave," Oct. 3, 1908. Copy in Grand Gulch–Wetherill Collection, Edge of the Cedars Museum, Blanding, UT.

Dutchie, Edward, Jr. "Ute Winter and Summer Ranges." March 1986. Paper used with permission, in possession of author.

Dutchie, Patty. "The Seasons of the Year." Ute Mountain Ute Archives, American West Center, University of Utah, Salt Lake City.

Emmitt. "Creation." In "Ute Legends," Northern Ute Archives, American West Center, University of Utah, Salt Lake City.

Gorman, Howard. "The Growing Peyote Cult and the Use of Peyote on the Navajo Indian Reservation." 1938, Gladwell Richardson Collection, Special Collections, Cline Library, Northern Arizona University, Flagstaff.

Goss, James A. "Culture-Historical Inference from Utaztekan Linguistic Evidence." Paper presented at Plenary Symposium on Utaztekan Prehistory of the Society for American Archaeology and the Great Basin Anthropological Conference, May 1966.

Hafen, Leroy R. "Historical Summary of the Ute Indians and the San Juan Mining Region." n.d. Utah State Historical Society Library, Salt Lake City.

Hanson, William F. "The Lure of Tam-man Nacup: Springtime Festival of the Utes." Master's thesis, 1937. Special Collections, Harold B. Lee Library, Brigham Young University.

Hayden, Ferdinand V., Hayden Collection, Special Collections, American Heritage Center, University of Wyoming, Laramie, WY.

Hewitt, E. L. "Field Notes, 1906–09." Photocopy. Edge of the Cedars Museum, Blanding, UT.

Hunter, Lyman P. "San Juan Remembered." L. Tom Perry Special Collections, Harold B. Lee Library, Brigham Young University, Provo, UT.

Hurst, Winston B. "The Blanding Navajos: A Case Study of Off-Reservation Navajo Migration and

Settlement." Master's thesis, Eastern New Mexico University, Roswell, 1981.

Jackson, William H. "Diary—June 22, 1875 thru October 6, 1875." Microfilm. Colorado Historical Society, Denver.

Johnson, Greg. "Echoes in the Canyons: 'Superstition' and Sense in Ute Conceptions of Anasazi Things." Draft, April 14, 1994, on file in the Bureau of Land Management—Anasazi Heritage Center, Dolores, CO.

Jones, Kumen. Manuscript. Utah State Historical Society Library, Salt Lake City.

Jorgensen, Joseph Gilbert. "Functions of Ute Folklore." Unpublished master's thesis, University of Utah, 1960.

Jorgensen, Joseph Gilbert. "The Ethnohistory and Acculturation of the Northern Ute." Doctoral dissertation, Indiana University, 1964.

Kane, Francis F. "Diary of Francis F. Kane—Ute Removal, 1891." *Indian Rights Association Papers, 1868–1968*. Microfilm reel 8. Indian Rights Association, Philadelphia.

Kelly, Charles. "Functions of Ute Folklore." Master's thesis, University of Utah, 1960.

———. "Interview Notes with Hoskaninni Begay." Charles Kelly Papers. Special Collections, J. Willard Marriott Library, University of Utah, Salt Lake City.

———. "Notes." Charles Kelly Papers. Special Collections, J. Willard Marriott Library, University of Utah, Salt Lake City.

Knight, Carla. "The Utes and Their Environment." 1986. Unpublished paper, used with permission.

Leiby, Austin Nelson. "Borderland Pathfinder: The 1765 Diaries of Juan Maria Antonio de Rivera." Doctoral dissertation, Northern Arizona University, 1984.

Lyman, Albert R. *Among the Indians*, unpublished manuscript in possession of author, 1962.

———. "History of Blanding, 1905–1955." L. Tom Perry Special Collections, Harold B. Lee Library, Brigham Young University, Provo, UT.

———. "History of San Juan County, 1879–1917." L. Tom Perry Special Collections, Harold B. Lee Library, Brigham Young University, Provo, UT.

———. Journal, 1907. Special Collections, Harold B. Lee Library, Brigham Young University, Provo, UT.

———. "Willard Butt—100 Percent Man." L. Tom Perry Special Collections, Harold B. Lee Library, Brigham Young University, Provo, UT.

Lyman, Platte D. "Diary of Platte D. Lyman." L. Tom Perry Special Collections, Harold B. Lee Library, Brigham Young University, Provo, UT.

Macy, Patrick M. "The NAU Report on Native American Students in San Juan School District: A Ten Year Study, 1980–1990." San Juan School District, Blanding, UT, 1993.

Mancos, Town of. "Mancos Minutes, La Plata County, Colorado." Special Collections, J. Willard Marriott Library, University of Utah, Salt Lake City.

McLaughlin, James. James McLaughlin Papers, microfilm 8. Denver Public Library.

Muhlestein, Daniel K. "The Rise and Fall of the Cattle Companies in San Juan, 1880–1900." Utah State Historical Society Library, Salt Lake City.

Nielson, Beatrice P. "Settling of San Juan County." Special Collections, J. Willard Marriott Library, University of Utah, Salt Lake City.

Pace, William B. "Diary of William B. Pace during the Elk Mountain Mission, 1855–1856." Pace file, Utah State Historical Society Library, Salt Lake City.

Palmer, John Franklin. "Mormon Settlements in the San Juan Basin of Colorado and New Mexico." Master's thesis, Brigham Young University, 1967.

Palmer, William R. "Experiences in Gathering Indian Folklore," November 3, 1945. This and the following Palmer manuscripts can be found in the William R. Palmer Collection, Special Collections, Gerald R. Sherratt Library, Southern Utah University, Cedar City.

———. Field Notes. William R. Palmer Collection.

———. "Indian Life and Lore," William R. Palmer Collection.

———. "Indian Memorial Service for President Anthony W. Ivins." William R. Palmer Collection.

———. "Indians—Paiutes—Natural Science." Notes, n.d. William R. Palmer Collection.

———. "The Paiute Indian." January 1954 William R. Palmer Collection.

———. "San Juan Indians." William R. Palmer Collection.

———. "San Juan Trip, August 21–26, 1935." William R. Palmer Collection.

Pettit, Ethan. "Ethan Pettit Diary, August 6–September 12, 1855." Pettit file, Utah State Historical Society Library, Salt Lake City.

Pyle, Frank. "The Uprising of Polk and Posey in 1915." William Evans Collection, Special Collections, Harold B. Lee Library, Brigham Young University, Provo, UT.

Pyle, Warren. "The Story of the Beaver Creek Incident." Unpublished manuscript, Cortez Public Library, Cortez, CO.

Reagan, Albert B. "Mother Nature." Albert B. Reagan Collection, L. Tom Perry Special Collections, Harold B. Lee Library, Brigham Young University, Provo, UT.

Reynolds, Mary Stephanie. "Dance Brings about Everything: Dance Power in the Ideologies of Northern Utes of Uintah and Ouray Reservation and Predominantly Mormon Anglos of an Adjacent Uintah Basin Community." Doctoral dissertation, University of California, Irvine, 1990.

Richardson, Gladwell. Gladwell Richardson Collection, Special Collections, Cline Library, Northern Arizona University, Flagstaff, AZ.

Rogers, John D. "Piute Posey and the Last Indian Uprising." In Lloyd L. Young File, Utah State Historical Society Library, Salt Lake City.

San Juan Stake. History. Unpublished manuscript collection, Historical Archives, Church of Jesus Christ of Latter-day Saints, Salt Lake City.

Shelley, Fern Oliver. "The Life Story of William Edward Oliver, 1858–1935." In possession of James W. Oliver Family, Mapleton, UT.

Shields, Carolyn M. "A Study of the Educational Perceptions and Attitudes of Four Stakeholder Groups in the San Juan School District in 1998." Blanding: San Juan School District, 1999.

Silliman, Bert. "The Orejas del Oso Trail or Bears Ears Trail." Silliman Collection, Utah State Historical Society Library, Salt Lake City.

Silvey, Frank. "Historical Records Survey." September 10, 1936. This and the other Silvey manuscripts listed below can be found in the Silvey file, Utah State Historical Society Library, Salt Lake City.

———. History and Settlement of Northern San Juan County. n.p., n.d. On file at the Utah State Historical Society Library, Salt Lake City.

———. "Information on Indians," September 26, 1936. Silvey File.

———. "Pioneer Personal History Questionnaire," September 10, 1936. Silvey File.

———. "Indians in San Juan," June 10, 1940. Silvey File.

Sinajini v. Board of Education. Case materials. Dinébe'iiná Náhiilna Be Agha'diit'ahii Office, Mexican Hat, UT.

Sniffen, M. K. "The Meaning of the Ute 'War.'" Special Collections, J. Willard Marriott Library, University of Utah, Salt Lake City.

Southern Ute Files. American West Center, University of Utah, Salt Lake City.

Todd, Sam. "A Pioneer Experience." Utah State Historical Society Library, Salt Lake City.

Tyler, S. Lyman. "Before Escalante: An Early History of the Yuta Indians and Area North of New Mexico...." Doctoral dissertation, University of Utah, 1951.

Ute Mountain Ute Archives. American West Center, University of Utah, Salt Lake City.

Welsh, Herbert. "Address to General Audience, February 25, 1890." Special Collections, J. Willard Marriott Library, University of Utah, Salt Lake City.

———. "The Case of the Southern Utes." Harpers Weekly, April 2, 1892. On file in Special Collections, J. Willard Marriott Library, University of Utah, Salt Lake City.

———. Welsh to the Public, open letter, April 22, 1892, n.p.

White Mesa Branch of the Church of Jesus Christ of Latter-day Saints. Annual Reports. LDS Church History Building, Salt Lake City.

———. White Mesa Facilities File. Facilities Management Group of the Church of Jesus Christ of Latter-day Saints, Blanding, UT.

White Mesa Ute Council. Files. Blanding, UT.

White Mesa Ute Oral History Project. American West Center, University of Utah, Salt Lake City.

Young, William R. "The 1923 Indian Uprising in San Juan County, UT." In Lloyd L. Young file, Utah State Historical Society Library, Salt Lake City.

INTERVIEWS

Acton, Zelma. Interview with Deborah Fellbaum and Shirley E. Stephenson, July 11, 1972, and July 21, 1974, respectively, O.H. 1196a and b. Southeastern Utah Oral History Project, Utah State Historical Society and California State University, Fullerton.

———. Interview with Floyd O'Neil and Gregory C. Thompson, July 2, 1980, O.H. 774. White Mesa Ute Oral History Project, American West Center, University of Utah, Salt Lake City.

———. Interview with Robert S. McPherson, May 14, 2007.

Begay, Florence. Interview with Nelson Begay and Robert S. McPherson, April 29, 1988.

Begay, Nelson. Interview with Robert S. McPherson, March 1, 1987.

Benally, Slim. Interview with Baxter Benally and Robert S. McPherson, July 8, 1988.

Bigman, Tully. Interview with Baxter Benally and Robert S. McPherson, April 15, 1993.

Black, Allan. Interview with Gary Shumway, May 30, 1978, O.H. 1638. Southeastern Utah Oral History Project, Utah State Historical Society and California State University, Fullerton.

Black, Clessa. Conversation with Robert S. McPherson, February 15, 2010.

Black, Thell D. Interview with Winston Hurst and Robert S. McPherson, October 22, 2009.

Blueyes, Charlie. Interview with Baxter Benally and Robert S. McPherson, August 28, 1988.

Blueyes, Mary. Interview with Baxter Benally and Robert S. McPherson, July 25, 1988.

Bradford, Cleal. Conversation with Robert S. McPherson, March 11, 2010.

———. Interview with Robert S. McPherson, February 24 and March 10, 2009.

Brimhall, Dean. Interview with Charles Peterson, May 1, 1970. Utah State Historical Society Library, Salt Lake City.

Burke, Charles. Interview with Floyd O'Neil and Gregory C. Thompson, September 13, 1968, O.H. no. 374. Doris Duke Oral History Project, American West Center, University of Utah, Salt Lake City.

Burr, Eliza. Statement, November 30, 1948. In possession of author.

Butt, Uriah. Interview with Ruth Meo, May 29, 1978, O.H. no. 1628. Southeastern Utah Oral History Project, Utah State Historical Society and California State University, Fullerton.

Cantsee, Anderson. Interview with Aubrey Williams, January 28, 1961. Doris Duke #739, Doris Duke Indian Oral History Project, Special Collections, J. Willard Marriott Library, University of Utah, Salt Lake City.

Cantsee, Annie. Interview with Robert S. McPherson, August 4, 2009.

Cantsee, Chester. Interview with Floyd O'Neil and Gregory C. Thompson, March 22, 1980. White Mesa Ute Oral History Project, American West Center, University of Utah, Salt Lake City.

———. Interview with Aldean Ketchum and Robert S. McPherson, September 6, 1994.

Cantsee, Jack, Sr. Interview with Robert S. McPherson, September 24, 2009.

———. Conversation with Robert S. McPherson, January 26, 2010.

Cesspooch, Larry. Conversation with Robert S. McPherson, July 15, 2009.

Denver, Elmer, Louise Cuch, and Hazel Wardle. Interview with Susan Denver, n.d., in folder "Ute Legend Materials," American West Center, University of Utah, Salt Lake City.

Doris Duke Indian Oral History Project. Special Collections, J. Willard Marriott Library, University of Utah, Salt Lake City.

Duncan, Clifford. Conversation with Robert S. McPherson, September 11 and 18, 2009.

———. Interview with Floyd O'Neil and Gregory C. Thompson, November 14, 1983, Ute Indian Interview no. 853. American West Center, University of Utah, Salt Lake City.

Dutchie, Edward Sr., and Patty (Mills) Dutchie. Interview with Robert S. McPherson, May 7, 1996; May 13, 1996; and May 21, 1996.

Dutchie, Harry. Interview with Floyd O'Neil and Gregory C. Thompson, May 30, 1986, O.H. 789. White Mesa Ute Oral History Project, American West Center, University of Utah, Salt Lake City.

———. Interview with Gary Shumway, July 15, 1968, Duke no. 517. Doris Duke Oral History Project, Special Collections, J. Willard Marriott Library, University of Utah, Salt Lake City.

Dutchie, Patty Mills. Interview with Gregory C. Thompson and Floyd O'Neil, August 13, 1980. O.H. 779. White Mesa Ute Oral History Project, American West Center, University of Utah, Salt Lake City.

Eyetoo, Adoline. Interview with Robert S. McPherson, July 25, 2009.

———. Conversations with Robert S. McPherson, December 9, 2008.

Eyetoo, Rachel. Interview with Gerald Scheib and Gary Shumway, July 12, 1971. O.H. 777b. Southeastern Utah Oral History Project, Utah State Historical Society and California State University, Fullerton.

Eyetoo, Stella. Conversations with Robert S. McPherson, May 4, 2001; December 9, 2008; and March 17, 2010.

———. Interview with Aldean Ketchum and Robert S. McPherson, December 21, 1994; November 16, 2005; and July 11, 2009.

———. Interview with Floyd O'Neil and Gregory C. Thompson, July 1, 1980. O.H. 780. White Mesa Ute

Oral History Project, American West Center, University of Utah, Salt Lake City.

Graymountain, Gilmore. Interview with Marilyn Holiday and Robert S. McPherson, April 7, 1992.

Groves, Bertha. Interview with Ginger Bigsby and Barbara Beasley, April 18, 1991. Southern Ute Oral Histories, Center of Southwest Studies, Fort Lewis College, Durango, CO.

Hammond, Lucille. Interview with Sam Goodman and Robert S. McPherson, October 18, 1985.

Hatch, Ira. Interview with Robert S. McPherson, May 30, 1991.

Hatch, Stewart. Interview with Robert S. McPherson, August 5, 2009.

Howard, Maimi. Interview with Baxter Benally and Robert S. McPherson, July 19, 1988.

Hunt, Leann. Conversation with Robert S. McPherson, October 15, 2008.

Hunt, Ray. Interview with Robert S. McPherson, January 21, 1991.

Hunter, Lyman. Interview with Michael T. Hurst, February 21, 1973. CRC-J5. Posey War Oral History Project, Charles Redd Center for Western Studies, Harold B. Lee Library, Brigham Young University, Provo, UT.

Hurst, George. Interview with Michael T. Hurst, February 24, 1973. CRC-J7. Posey War Oral History Project, Charles Redd Center for Western Studies, Harold B. Lee Library, Brigham Young University, Provo, UT.

Hurst, Parley Oscar. Interview with Sandy McFadden and Gary Shumway, July 17, 1971. O.H. 697. Southeastern Utah Oral History Project, Utah State Historical Society and California State University, Fullerton.

Hurst, Phillip. Interview with Michael T. Hurst, September 2, 1972. CRC-J9. Charles Redd Center for Western Studies, Harold B. Lee Library, Brigham Young University, Provo, UT.

Hurst, Winston. Conversation with Robert S. McPherson, September 9, 1992; October 14, 2008.

Irwin, Don. Conversation with Robert S. McPherson, October 15, 2008.

Jacket, Lizzie. Interview with Robert S. McPherson, May 30, 1991.

Jones, Alma Uriah. Interview with Gary Shumway, August 4, 1981. CRC-K157. LDS Polygamy Oral History Project, Charles Redd Center for Western Studies, Harold B. Lee Library, Brigham Young University, Provo, UT.

Ketchum, Aldean. Interview with Robert S. McPherson, July 30, 2009.

———. Conversation with Robert S. McPherson, March 17, 2010.

Knight, Terry. Interview with Mary Jane Yazzie and Robert S. McPherson, December 19, 1994.

Lehi, Bonnie Mike. Interview with Robert S. McPherson, July 20, 2009.

Lovell, Steven. Conversation with Robert S. McPherson, February 15, 2010.

Manygoats, Joe. Interview with Marilyn Holiday and Robert S. McPherson, December 18, 1991.

Manygoats, Sally. Interview with Marilyn Holiday and Robert S. McPherson, April 8, 1992.

May, Corina. Conversation with Robert S. McPherson, March 18, 2010.

McCrum, Madeline Noland. Interview with Robert S. McPherson, June 24, 1993.

Mike, Billy. Interview with Aldean Ketchum and Robert S. McPherson, October 13, 1993.

———. Interview with Floyd O'Neil and Gregory C. Thompson, May 22, 1980, O.H. 789. White Mesa Ute Oral History Project, American West Center, University of Utah, Salt Lake City.

———. Interview with Gregory C. Thompson and James Schultz, May 22, 1980. White Mesa Ute History Project, American West Center, University of Utah, Salt Lake City.

Mike, Jim. Interview with Gary Shumway and Anna Marie Nat, June 20, 1968. Duke no. 550. Doris Duke Oral History Project, Special Collections, J. Willard Marriott Library, University of Utah, Salt Lake City.

Mike, Lola. Interview with Aldean Ketchum and Robert S. McPherson, November 16, 2005.

———. Conversation with Robert S. McPherson, March 17, 2010.

Nez, Martha. Interview with Baxter Benally and Robert S. McPherson, August 10, 1988.

Nielson, Lloyd. Interview with Gary Shumway and Kim Stewart, July 14, 1971. N.n. Southeastern Utah Oral History Project, Utah State Historical Society and California State University, Fullerton.

Noland, Lolla Kutch. Interview by grandchild (family member). n.d. In possession of Madeline Noland McCrum.

Oliver, Harvey. Interview with Baxter Benally and Robert S. McPherson, March 6, 1991.

Ostergaard, Ardelle. Conversation with Robert S. McPherson, February 5, 2009.

Perkins, Clarence. Interview with Mary Risher, June 29, 1971, O.H. 790. Southeastern Utah Oral History Project, Utah State Historical Society and California State University, Fullerton.

Perkins, John. Interview with Charles S. Peterson, n.d. Utah State Historical Society Library, Salt Lake City.

Posey, Loretta. Conversation with Robert S. McPherson, March 18, 2010.

Redd, Amasa Jay. Interview with Charles S. Peterson, July 27, 1973. Charles Redd Center for Western Studies, Harold B. Lee Library, Brigham Young University, Provo, UT.

Redd, James Monroe, Jr. Interview with Michael T. Hurst, February 15, 1973. CRC-J4. Charles Redd Center for Western Studies, Brigham Young University, Provo, UT.

Redd, Leland W. Interview with Louise Lynn, July 12, 1972, O.H. 10946. Southeastern Utah Oral History Project, Utah State Historical Society and University of California, Fullerton.

Rogers, John D. Interview with Michael T. Hurst, April 29, 1972. CRC-J6. Posey War Oral History Project, Charles Redd Center for Western Studies, Harold B. Lee Library, Brigham Young University, Provo, UT.

Sakizzie, Ella. Interview with Baxter Benally and Robert S. McPherson, May 14, 1991.

Sandberg, Nick. Conversation with Robert S. McPherson, April 11, 2008.

Shumway, Gary. Interview with Robert S. McPherson, December 1, 2009.

Shumway, Lloyd. Conversation with Robert S. McPherson, May 12, 2007.

Simpson, Fern. Interview with Deborah Fellbaum, July 12, 1972, O.H. 69-7B. Southeastern Utah Oral History Project, Utah State Historical Society and California State University, Fullerton.

Singer, Donna. Interview with Robert S. McPherson, March 7, 2010.

Slavens, James. Conversation with Robert S. McPherson, September 7 and October 15, 2009.

Stevens, Brigham. Interview with Mary Risher, July 18, 1971, O.H. 1096. Southeastern Utah Oral History Project, Utah State Historical Society and California State University, Fullerton.

Tibbitts, Kent. Conversation with Robert S. McPherson, February 15, 2010.

Titus, L. B. Interview with Sandra Caruthers, March 24, 1967. N.n. Doris Duke Oral History Project, Special Collections, J. Willard Marriott Library, University of Utah, Salt Lake City.

Whitmer, Alan. Interview with Robert S. McPherson, September 12, 2001.

Yazzie, Fred. Interview with Louanna Adakai and Robert S. McPherson, November 1, 1985.

———. Interview with Marilyn Holiday and Robert S. McPherson, November 5, 1987.

GOVERNMENT DOCUMENTS

Adjutant General's Office. "Letters Received, 1871–1915." RG 94. National Archives, Washington, DC.

Beckwith, E. G. "Report of Exploration of a Route for the Pacific Railroad near the 38th and 39th Parallels of Latitude." 1855. U.S. Congress, H. Doc. 129. National Archives, Washington, DC.

U.S. Bureau of Indian Affairs. "Letters Received, 1881–1939." RG 75. National Archives, Washington, DC.

———. "Superintendents' Annual Narrative and Statistical Reports from Field Jurisdictions of the BIA, 1907–1938." Microfilm 1011, roll 29. RG 75. National Archives, Washington, DC.

Fort Lewis. "Fort Lewis — Calendar of Letters Received, 1880." Special Collections, Center of Southwest Studies, Fort Lewis, Durango, CO.

Fort Lewis. "Outgoing Correspondence, 1883–1885."

Special Collections, Center of Southwest Studies, Fort Lewis, Durango, CO.

——. "Post Returns, October 1878 to August 1891." *Returns from U.S. Military Posts from 1800 to 1916.* Microfilm 624. National Archives, Washington, DC.

Hayden, Ferdinand V. *Ninth Annual Report of the United States Geological and Geographical Survey of Territories Embracing Colorado and Parts of Adjacent Territories: Being a Report of Progress of the Exploration for the Year 1875.* Washington, DC: Government Printing Office, 1877.

Kappler, Charles. *Indian Affairs—Laws and Treaties.* Washington, DC: Government Printing Office, 1913.

Macomb, John and John S. Newberry. *Report of the Exploring Expedition from Santa Fe, New Mexico, to the Junction of the Grand and Green Rivers of the Great Colorado of the West in 1859.* Washington, D.C.: Government Printing Office, 1876.

Powell, John W., and G. W. Ingalls. "Utes, Paiutes, Gosiute, and Shoshonean Indians—Special Report." February 23, 1874. *Report of the Secretary of the Interior,* 43d Cong., 1st sess., H.R. Exec. Doc. 157. National Archives, Washington, DC.

Pope, John. "Report of General John Pope." *Report of the Secretary of War.* 45th Cong., 3d sess. Washington, DC: Government Printing Office, 1878.

——. "The Utes." September 22, 1881. *Report of the Secretary of War,* I. Washington, DC: Government Printing Office, 1881.

Report of the Commission to Negotiate with the Ute Tribe of Indians. Washington, DC: Government Printing Office, 1873.

Smith, Joseph O. "Report of Agent for Southern Ute Agency." August 25, 1902, Reports of Agents and Others in Charge of Indians. U.S. Congress, House of Representatives, 57th Congress, 2nd Sess., (Washington, DC: Government Printing Office, 1902).

U.S. Army Commander, Department of New Mexico, 1857–1866. Records of the War Department. RG 98. National Archives, Washington, DC.

U.S. Army Commands, Department of Colorado. "Black Mountain Expedition." 1908. Records of the War Department. RG 98. National Archives, Washington, DC.

U.S. Bureau of Indian Affairs. "Consolidated Ute Indian Service Files, 1879–1952." RG 75. National Archives and Records Service Rocky Mountain Region, Federal Records Center, Denver.

——. *Report of the Commissioner of Indian Affairs.* Washington, DC: Government Printing Office, 1857–1899.

U.S. Congress. "Agreement with the Weeminuchi Band Ute Indians, Colorado." 62nd Cong., 3rd sess., S. Rep. 1133, 1913.

——. "Hearings before a Subcommittee of the Committee on Indian Affairs, May 13, 1931." 70th Cong., 2nd sess., S. Res. 79.

——. "Negotiations with Ute Indians." *Report of the Secretary of the Interior.* 42d Cong., 3d sess., H. Exec. Doc. 90, 1873.

——. "Report of the Governor of Utah." *Report of the Secretary of the Interior.* 51st Cong., 2d sess., H. Exec. Doc. 1, 1890.

——. "Report of Colonel L. P. Bradley to Secretary of War." *Report of the Secretary of the Interior.* 48th Cong., 2nd sess., Doc. 1, pt. 1, 1884.

——. *Report of the Secretary of War.* 36th Cong., 1st sess., S. Exec. Doc. 2. Washington, DC: Government Printing Office, 1859.

——. *Report of the Secretary of War.* 44th Cong., 2d sess., H. Exec. Doc. 1, pt. 2. Washington, DC: Government Printing Office, 1876.

——. *Report of the Secretary of the Interior.* 39th Cong., 2nd sess., H. Exec. Doc. 1. Washington, DC: Government Printing Office, 1866.

——. "Reservation of Certain Land in Utah as a School for Ute Indians." *Report of the Secretary of the Interior.* 68th Cong., 1st sess., S. Rep. 668, May 31, 1924.

——. "Southern Ute Agency Report." *Report of the Secretary of the Interior.* H.R. Exec. Doc. 1, pt. 5, Washington, DC: Government Printing Office, 1884–1887.

——. "Ute Indian Commission." *Letter from the Secretary of the Interior.* 50th Cong., 2d sess. S. Exec. Doc. 67, January 11, 1889. Washington, DC: Government Printing Office, 1889.

——. "Ute Indians in Colorado." *Letter from the Secretary of the Interior.* 46th Cong., 2d sess., S. Exec. Doc. 31. Washington, DC: Government Printing Office, 1879.

U.S. Department of the Interior. "Report of Agent for Southern Ute Agency." *Annual Reports of Department of the Interior Fiscal Years, 1901–1906.* Washington, DC: Government Printing Office.

——. "Report of Ute Commission." January 20, 1880. *Report of the Secretary of the Interior, Indian Affairs.* Washington, DC: Government Printing Office, 1880.

U.S. Office of Indian Affairs, Colorado Superintendency. "Letters Received, 1857–1907." RG 75. National Archives, Washington, DC.

U.S. Office of Indian Affairs, New Mexico Superintendency. "Letters Received, 1857–1889." RG 75. National Archives, Washington, DC.

Utah, State of. "Territorial Executive Papers, 1850–1896." Utah State Archives, Salt Lake City.

Books and Articles

Aberle, David F., and Omer C. Stewart. *Navaho and Ute Peyotism: A Chronological and Distributional Study.* University of Colorado Studies in Anthropology 6. Boulder: University of Colorado Press, 1957.

Aberle, David F. *The Peyote Religion among the Navajo.* Chicago: University of Chicago Press, 1966.

Adams, Jones. "In the Stronghold of the Piutes." *Overland Monthly* 22 (December 1893): 583–593.

American Heritage Dictionary. 2d ed. Boston: Houghton Mifflin Company, 1985.

Arny, W. F. M. *Indian Agent in New Mexico: The Journal of Special Agent W. F. M. Arny in 1870.* Ed. Lawrence R. Murphy. Santa Fe: Stagecoach Press, 1967.

Athern, Robert G., ed. "Major Hough's March into Southern Ute Country, 1879." *Colorado Magazine* 25, no. 3 (May 1948): 97–109.

Bailey, Lynn R. *Indian Slave Trade in the Southwest.* Los Angeles: Westernlore Press, 1966.

———. *The Long Walk: A History of the Navajo Wars, 1846–68.* Pasadena, CA: Westernlore Publications, 1978.

Baker, Steve G. "Historic Ute Archaeology: Interpreting the Last Hour Wickiup." *Southern Lore* 69, no. 4 (Winter 2003): 1–34.

———. "Trails, Trade, and West-Central Colorado's Gateway Tradition: Ethnohistorical Observations." *Southwestern Lore* 74, no. 1 (Spring 2008): 1–41.

Bannon, John Francis. *The Spanish Borderlands Frontier, 1513–1821.* Albuquerque: University of New Mexico Press, [1963] 1974.

Barber, Bernard. "A Socio-Cultural Interpretation of the Peyote Cult." *American Anthropologist* 43, no. 4 (Oct.–Dec. 1941): 673–675.

Barnes, F. A. "A Journey to the Rio del Tizon." *Canyon Legacy: A Journal of the Dan O'Laurie Museum* 9 (Spring 1991): 16–22.

———. "Update—Rivera's 1765 Expedition." *Canyon Legacy: A Journal of the Dan O'Laurie Museum* 10 (Summer 1991): 31–32.

Basso, Keith H. *Wisdom Sits in Places: Landscape and Language among the Western Apache.* Albuquerque: University of New Mexico Press, 1996.

Bayles, Jami. "The Blanding Ute Dormitory." *Blue Mountain Shadows* 9 (Winter 1991): 75–79.

Bean, Jordan. "Jordan Bean's Story and the Castle Valley Indian Fight." *Colorado Magazine* 20 (1943): 17–25.

Beeson, Maureen. "Electricity Comes to White Mesa." *Blue Mountain Shadows* 8 (Summer 1991): 45–46.

Bender, Norman J. "The Battle of Tierra Amarilla." *New Mexico Historical Review* 63, no. 3 (July 1988): 241–256.

Biggs, J. T. "Our Valley." Mesa, AZ: self-published, 1977.

Blackhawk, Ned. *Violence over the Land: Indians and Empires in the Early American West.* Cambridge, MA: Harvard University Press, 2006.

Boyd, James P. *Recent Indian Wars Under the Lead of Sitting Bull and Other Chiefs, with a Full Account of the Messiah Craze and Ghost Dances.* New York: Publishers Union, 1891.

Brewerton, George Douglas. "A Ride with Kit Carson through the Great American Desert and the Rocky Mountains." *Harpers New Monthly Magazine* 8 (April 1854): 306–334.

Bronson, Stanley W. "The Saviors of Avikan" (song). Self-published, 1987.

———. *The Ute Spiritual Cross of the San Juan Mission.* Self-published, 1999.

Brugge, David M. *Navajos in the Catholic Church Records of New Mexico, 1694–1875.* Research Report 1. Window Rock, AZ: Navajo Tribe, 1968.

Bunte, Pamela A., and Robert J. Franklin. *From the Sands to the Mountains: Change and Persistence in a Southern Paiute Community.* Lincoln: University of Nebraska Press, 1987.

Callaway, Donald G., Joel C. Janetski, and Omer C. Stewart. "Ute." In *Handbook of North American Indians*, vol. 11: *Great Basin.* Washington, DC: Smithsonian Institution, 1986, 336–367.

Cannon, John Q. "When the Utes Invaded Utah." *Improvement Era* 32, no. 1 (November 1928): 41–46.

Carrier, Jim. *West of the Divide: Voices from a Ranch and a Reservation.* Golden, CO: Fulcrum Publishing, 1992.

Carroll, Alex K., M. Nieves Zedeño, and Richard W. Stoffle. "Landscapes of the Ghost Dance: A Cartography of Numic Ritual." *Journal of Archaeological Method and Theory* 11, no. 2 (June 2004): 127–155.

Chamberlain, Ralph V. "Some Plant Names of the Ute Indians," *American Anthropologist* 2 (Jan.–Mar. 1909): 27–37.

Chapoose, Connor, and Y. T. Witherspoon (ed.). *Conversations with Connor Chapoose: A Leader of the Ute Tribe of the Uintah and Ouray Reservation.* Anthropological Papers 47. Eugene: Department of Anthropology and Oregon State Museum of Anthropology, 1993.

Chavez, Fray Angelico, and Ted J. Warner, ed. *The Dominguez-Escalante Journal: Their Expedition through Colorado, Utah, and New Mexico in 1776.* Provo, UT: Brigham Young University Press, 1976.

Christensen, Christian Lingo. "An Indian War Averted." *Improvement Era* 31, no. 9 (July 1928): 776–780.

Church, Minette C., Steven G. Baker, Bonnie J. Clark, Richard F. Carrillo, Jonathon C. Horn, Carl D. Spath, David R. Guilfoyle, and E. Steve Cassells. *Colorado History: A Context for Historical Archaeology.* Denver: Colorado Council of Professional Archaeologists, 2007.

Clark, Ruth S. "The Founding of Dolores." *Colorado Magazine* 5 (Fall 1927): 60–63.

Cloud, Ralph. "The Ute Creation Story." In *Ute Traditional Narratives*, ed. Talmy Givón, Ignacio, CO: Ute Press, 1985.

Coates, Lawrence G. "The Mormons and the Ghost Dance." *Dialogue: A Journal of Mormon Thought* 18, no. 4 (Winter 1985): 89–111.

Conetah, Fred A. *A History of the Northern Ute People.*

ed. Kathryn L. McKay and Floyd A. O'Neill. Salt Lake City: Uintay-Ouray Tribe/University of Utah press, 1982.

Correll, J. Lee. *Through White Men's Eyes: A Contribution to Navajo History*, I–VI. Window Rock, AZ: Navajo Heritage Center, 1979.

Cox, C. N. "Late Indian Troubles in the San Juan Country." *Colorado Magazine* 17, no. 6 (June 1940): 30–34.

Crampton, C. Gregory. "Utah's Spanish Trail." *Utah Historical Quarterly* 47 (Fall 1979): 361–382.

Crampton, C. Gregory and Stephen K. Madsen. *In Search of the Spanish Trail: Santa Fe to Los Angeles, 1829–1848*. Salt Lake City: Gibbs Smith, 1994.

Cutter, Donald G. "Prelude to a Pageant in the Wilderness." *Western Historical Quarterly* 8 (January 1977): 4–14.

Daniels, Helen Sloan. *The Pioneers of San Juan Country*, I–III. Durango, CO: Sarah Platt Decker Chapter, 1952.

Deets, Lee Emerson. "Paradox Valley — An Historical Interpretation of Its Structure and Changes." *Colorado Magazine* 11, no. 5 (September 1934): 186–198.

Delaney, Robert W. *Blue Coats, Red Skins, and Black Gowns: 100 Years of Fort Lewis*. Durango, CO: Durango Herald, 1977.

———. *The Ute Mountain Utes*. Albuquerque: University of New Mexico Press, 1989.

Deyhle, Donna. "Pushouts and Pullouts: Navajo and Ute School Leavers." *Journal of Navajo Education* 4, no. 2 (Winter 1989): 36–51.

Dobyns, Henry F., and Robert C. Euler. *The Ghost Dance of 1889 Among the Pai Indians of Northwestern Arizona*. Tucson: Prescott College Press, 1967.

Dunmire, William W., and Gail D. Tierney. *Wild Plants of the Pueblo Province: Exploring Ancient and Enduring Uses*. Santa Fe: Museum of New Mexico Press, 1995.

Dyk, Walter. *A Navaho Autobiography*. New York: Viking Fund, 1947.

Edison, Carol. "Portraits of Tradition: A Tribute to White Mesa Folk Artists." *Blue Mountain Shadows* 23 (Winter 2003): 9–15, 56–57.

Emmitt, Robert. *The Last War Trail: The Utes and the Settlement of Colorado*. Norman: University of Oklahoma Press, 1954.

Euler, Robert C. "Southern Paiute Archaeology." *American Antiquities* 29 (January 1964): 379–381.

Evans, Will, with Robert S. McPherson and Susan Woods, eds. *Along Navajo Trails: Recollections of a Trader*. Logan: Utah State University Press, 2005.

Fiske, Richard E., and H. Blaine Phillips II. *A Nineteenth Century Ute Burial from Northeast Utah*. Cultural Resource Series 16. Salt Lake City: Bureau of Land Management, 1984.

Forrest, Earle R. *With a Camera in Old Navaholand*. Norman: University of Oklahoma Press, 1970.

Fowler, Don D., and Catherine Fowler. *Anthropology of the Numa: John Wesley Powell's Manuscripts on the Numic People of Western North America, 1868–1880*. Smithsonian Contributions to Anthropology 14. Washington, DC: Smithsonian Institution, 1971.

———. "The Southern Paiute: AD 1400–1776." *The Protohistoric Period in the North American Southwest, AD 1350–1700*, ed. D. R. Wilcox and W. B. Masse, 129–162. Anthropological Research Papers 24. Tempe: Arizona State University, 1981.

Frazer, Robert W. *Forts of the West: Military Forts and Presidios and Posts Commonly Called Forts West of the Mississippi River to 1898*. Norman: University of Oklahoma Press, 1972.

Freeman, Dan A. *Four Years with the Utes: The Letters of Dan A. Freeman*. Waco, TX: W. M. Morrison Company, 1962.

Freeman, Ira S. *A History of Montezuma County*. Boulder, CO: Johnson Publishing, 1958.

Frémont, John C. *Memoirs of My Life*. Chicago: Clarke and Company, 1887.

Givón, Talmy. *Ute Traditional Narratives*. Ignacio, CO: Ute Press, 1985.

Goss, James A. "Traditional Cosmology, Ecology, and Language of the Ute Indians." In *Ute Indian Arts and Culture: From Prehistory to the New Millennium*, ed. William Wroth, 27–52. Colorado Springs: Colorado Springs Fine Art Center, 2000.

Hadley, Linda. *Hózhóóji Hane'* (Blessingway). Rough Rock, AZ: Rough Rock Demonstration School, 1986.

Hafen, Leroy R., and Ann W. Hafen. *The Old Spanish Trail: Santa Fe to Los Angeles*. Glendale, CA: Arthur H. Clark Company, 1954.

Hassell, Hank. *Rainbow Bridge: An Illustrated History*. Logan: Utah State University Press, 1999.

Haviland, William A. *Anthropology*. 9th ed. New York: Harcourt College Publishers, 2000.

Hawley, Florence, J. Jones, L. Jones, Morton Sloane, Beatrice Garner, Ernest Hill, William W. Wood, Jr., and Jacob Fried. "Culture Process and Change in Ute Adaptation — Part I." *El Palacio* 57, no. 10 (October 1950): 311–331.

Hawley, Florence, J. Jones, L. Jones, Morton Sloane, Beatrice Garner, Ernest Hill, William W. Wood, Jr., and Jacob Fried. "Culture Process and Change in Ute Adaptation — Part II." *El Palacio* 57, no. 11 (November 1950): 345–361.

Hill, Joseph J. "Spanish and Mexican Exploration and Trade Northwest from New Mexico into the Great Basin, 1765–1853." *Utah Historical Quarterly* 3 (January 1930): 2–23.

Hill, W. W. "The Navaho Indians and the Ghost Dance of 1890." *American Anthropologist* 46, no. 4 (Oct.–Dec. 1944): 523–527.

———. "Navaho Trading and Trading Ritual: A Study of Cultural Dynamics." *Southwestern Journal of Anthropology* 4 (Fall 1948): 371–396.

Hittman, Michael. "The 1870 Ghost Dance at Walker River Reservation: A Reconstruction." *Ethnohistory* 3 (Summer 1973): 247–278.

Holiday, John and Robert S. McPherson. *A Navajo Legacy: The Life and Teachings of John Holiday.* Norman: University of Oklahoma Press, 2005.

———. *Wovoka and the Ghost Dance.* Lincoln: University of Nebraska Press, [1990] 1997.

Hultkrantz, Åke. "Mythology and Religious Concepts," *Handbook of North American Indians*, vol. 11: *Great Basin.* Washington, DC: Smithsonian Institution, 1986, 630–640.

Hurlbut, P. K. "Where the Canyon Narrowed," in *Four Corners Geological Society, Canyon Lands Country,* ed. James E. Fassett, 55–57. Eighth Field Conference, September 22–25, 1975.

Iverson, Peter. *Diné: A History of the Navajos.* Albuquerque: University of New Mexico Press, 2002.

Jackson, William H. *William H. Jackson: Frontier Photographer Diaries, 1866–1874.* Glendale, CA: Arthur H. Clark Company, 1959.

———. *Time Exposure: The Autobiography of William Henry Jackson.* New York: G. P. Putnam and Sons, 1940.

Jackson, William H., and Howard R. Driggs. *The Pioneer Photographer.* New York: World Book Company, 1929.

Jacobs, G. Clell. "The Phantom Pathfinder: Juan Maria Antonio de Rivera and his Expedition." *Utah Historical Quarterly* 60 (Summer 1992): 201–223.

Jacobs, Wilbur R. "The Indian and the Frontier in American History: A Need for Revision." *Western Historical Quarterly* 4, no. 1 (January 1973): 43–54.

Jefferson, James, Robert W. Delaney, and Gregory C. Thompson. *The Southern Utes: A Tribal History.* Ignacio, CO: Southern Ute Tribe, 1972.

Jenson, Andrew. "The Elk Mountain Mission." *Utah Genealogical and Historical Magazine* 4 (1913): 189.

Jett, Stephen C. "The Great Race to Discover Rainbow Natural Bridge in 1909. *Kiva* 58 (1992): 3–65.

Johnson, Broderick H., ed. *Navajo Stories of the Long Walk Period.* Tsaile, AZ: Navajo Community College Press, 1973.

Jones, J. A. "A Reinterpretation of the Ute-Southern Paiute Classification." *Anthropological Quarterly* 27, no. 2 (April 1954): 53–58.

Jones, Sondra. "'Redeeming' the Indian: The Enslavement of Indian Children in New Mexico and Utah." *Utah Historical Quarterly* 67, no. 3 (Summer 1999): 220–241.

———. "The Trial of Don Pedro León." *Utah Historical Quarterly* 65, no. 2 (Spring 1997): 165–186.

Jorgensen, Joseph Gilbert. *The Sun Dance Religion: Power to the Powerless.* Chicago: University of Chicago Press, 1972.

———. "Ghost Dance, Bear Dance, and Sun Dance." *Handbook of North American Indians*, vol. 11: *Great Basin*, 660–672. Washington, DC: Smithsonian Institution, 1986.

Kelly, Charles. "Chief Hoskaninni." *Utah Historical Quarterly* 21, no. 3 (Summer 1953): 219–226.

Kelly, Isabel T., and Catherine S. Fowler. "Southern Paiute." In *Handbook of North American Indians*, vol. 11: *Great Basin*, 368–397. Washington. DC: Smithsonian Institution, 1986.

Kelly, Lawrence C. *Navajo Roundup: Selected Correspondence of Kit Carson's Expedition against the Navajo, 1863–1865.* Boulder, CO: Pruett Publishing, 1970.

Kluckhohn, Clyde. *Navaho Witchcraft.* Boston: Beacon Press, 1970.

Knack, Martha C. *Boundaries Between: The Southern Paiutes, 1775–1995.* Lincoln: University of Nebraska Press, 2001.

Knipmeyer, James H. "The Old Trappers Trail through Eastern Utah." *Canyon Legacy: A Journal of the Dan O'Laurie Museum* 9 (Spring 1991): 10–15.

Krech, Shepard, III. *The Ecological Indian: Myth and History.* New York: W. W. Norton and Company, 1999.

———. *Indian, Animals, and the Fur Trade: a Critique of Keepers of the Game.* Athens: University of Georgia Press, 1981.

Lacy, Steve, and Pearl Baker. *Posey: The Last Indian War.* Salt Lake City: Gibbs Smith, 2007.

Laird, Carobeth. *The Chemehuevis.* Banning, CA: Malaki Museum Press, 1976.

———. *Mirror and Pattern: George Laird's World of Chemehuevi Mythology.* Banning, CA: Malaki Museum Press, 1984.

Lamb, Sidney M. "Linguistic Prehistory of the Great Basin." *International Journal of American Linguistics* 24, no. 2 (1958): 95–100.

Laubin, Reginald, and Gladys Laubin. *The Indian Tipi: Its History, Construction and Use.* New York: Ballantine, 1957.

Lefler, Ellen. "Memories of the Ute Roundup." *Blue Mountain Shadows* 4 (Spring 1989): 28.

———. "Sheriff Newman and the Posey War." *Blue Mountain Shadows* 4 (Spring 1989): 24–27.

Leupp, Francis E. *The Latest Phase of the Southern Ute Question: A Report.* Philadelphia: Indian Rights Association, 1895.

Linton, Ralph. *Acculturation in Seven American Indian Tribes.* New York: D. Appleton-Century Company, 1940.

Locke, Raymond F. *The Book of the Navajo.* Los Angeles: Mankind Publishing Co., 1976.

Lopez, Russell, and Merry Palmer, with Ute Mountain Ute Tribe. "Legend of Sleeping Ute Mountain." Blanding: Utah State Office of Education and San Juan School District Media Center, 2006.

Lowie, Robert H. "Shoshonean Tales." *Journal of American Folklore* 37, no. 143 (Jan.–June 1924): 1–242.

Lyman, Albert R. "San Juan and its Piutes." *San Juan Record*, ongoing serial in 1950s and 1960s.

———. *The Edge of the Cedars: The Story of Walter C. Lyman and the San Juan Mission.* New York: Carlton Press, 1966.

———. *Indians and Outlaws: Settling of the San Juan Frontier.* Salt Lake City: Publishers Press, 1980.

———. *The Outlaw of Navaho Mountain.* Salt Lake City: Albert R. Lyman Trust, 1986.

———. "A Relic of Gadianton: Old Posey as I Knew Him." *Improvement Era* 26, no. 9 (July 1923): 791–801.

Madsen, Steven K. "A Letter Concerning the Location of the Ute Crossing of the Colorado River." *Spanish Traces* 6 no. 2 (Spring 2000): 33.

———. *Exploring Desert Stone: John N. Macomb's Expedition to the Canyonlands of the Colorado.* Logan: Utah State University Press, 2010.

———. "The Spanish Trail through Canyon Country." *Canyon Legacy: A Journal of the Dan O' Laurie Museum* 9 (Spring 1991): 23–29.

———. *The Spanish Trail: A Compilation of Spanish Trail Diaries and Maps.* N.p.: self-published, 1992.

Mahon, Carl L. "Carl L. Mahon." *Blanding City Centennial Family Histories, 1905–2005.* Blanding, UT: Shumway Family Publishing, 2005.

Manners, Robert A. *Paiute Indians,* vol. 1: *Southern Paiute and Chemehuevi.* New York: Garland Publishing, 1974.

Manypenny, George W. *Our Indian Wards.* New York: Da Capo Press, 1972.

Marsh, Charles S. *The Utes of Colorado: People of the Shining Mountains.* Boulder, CO: Pruett Publishing, 1982.

Martin, Calvin. *Keepers of the Game: Indian-Animal Relationships and the Fur Trade.* Berkeley: University of California Press, 1978.

Martorano, Marilyn A. "Culturally Peeled Trees and Ute Indians in Colorado." In *Archaeology of the Eastern Ute: A Symposium,* ed. Paul R. Nickens. CCPA Occasional Papers 1. [Denver]: Colorado Council of Professional Archaeologists, 1988.

———. "So Hungry They Ate the Bark off a Tree." *Canyon Legacy: A Journal of the Dan O' Laurie Museum* 1, no. 1 (Spring 1989): 9–12.

Matthews, Washington. "The Origin of the Utes." *American Antiquarian* 7 (September 1885): 271–274.

McCabe, Henry. *Cowboys, Indians, and Homesteaders.* N.p.: self-published, 1975.

McNeil, Lynda D. "Climbing Bear, Spirit Helper: Companion Petroglyphs at Shalabolino (Siberia) and Shavano Valley (Colorado, USA)." http://spot.colorado.edu/~lmcneil/ClimbingBear.pdf.

———. "Recurrence of Bear Restoration Symbolism: Minusinsk Basin Evenki and Basin-Plateau Ute." *Journal of Cognition and Culture* 8 (2008): 71–98.

———. "Ute Indian Bear Dance: Related Myths and Bear Glyphs." http://spot.colorado.edu/~lmcneil/UteBearDance.

McNitt, Frank. *Navajo Wars, Military Campaigns, Slave Raids, and Reprisals.* Albuquerque: University of New Mexico Press, 1990.

———. *Richard Wetherill, Anasazi: Pioneer Explorer of Southwestern Ruins.* Albuquerque: University of New Mexico Press, 1966.

McPherson, Robert S. *Comb Ridge and Its People: The Ethnohistory of a Rock.* Logan: Utah State University Press, 2009.

———. *A History of San Juan County: In the Palm of Time.* Salt Lake City: Utah State Historical Society, 1995.

———, ed. *The Journey of Navajo Oshley.* Logan: Utah State University Press, 2000.

———. "Much Ado about Nothing: The San Juan River Gold Rush, 1892–1893." *Utah Historical Quarterly* 67, no. 1 (Winter 1999): 68–87.

———. *Navajo Land, Navajo Culture: The Utah Experience in the Twentieth Century.* Norman: University of Oklahoma Press, 2001.

———. "Navajos, Mormons, and Henry L. Mitchell." *Utah Historical Quarterly* 55, no. 1 (Winter 1987): 50–65.

———. *The Northern Navajo Frontier, 1860–1900: Expansion Through Adversity.* Logan: Utah State University Press, 1988, 2001.

———. "Soldiering in a Corner, Living on the Fringe: Military Operations in Southeastern Utah, 1880–1890." *Utah Historical Quarterly* 77, no. 2 (Spring 2009): 126–150.

McPherson, Robert S., and Winston Hurst. "The Fight at Soldier Crossing, 1884: Military Considerations in Canyon Country." *Utah Historical Quarterly* 70, no. 3 (Summer 2002): 258–281.

Miller, David E. *Hole in the Rock: An Epic in the Colonization of the Great American West.* Salt Lake City: University of Utah Press, 1959.

Mooney, James. *The Ghost-Dance Religion and the Sioux Outbreak of 1890.* Chicago: University of Chicago Press, [1896] 1972.

Nickens, Paul R. "An Overview of Ethnographical and Archaeological Data for Ute Burial Practices." In *A Nineteenth Century Ute Burial from Northeast Utah,* ed. Richard E. Fike and H. Blaine Phillips II, 93–119. Cultural Resource Series 16. Salt Lake City: Bureau of Land Management, 1984.

Opler, Marvin Kaufmann. "The Character and History of the Southern Ute Peyote Rite." *American Anthropologist* 42, no. 3 (July–Sept. 1940): 463–478.

———. "The Southern Ute of Colorado." In *Acculturation in Seven American Indian Tribes,* ed. Ralph Linton, 119–207. New York: D. Appleton-Century Company, 1940.

O'Rourke, Paul M. *Frontier in Transition: A History of Southwestern Colorado.* Cultural Resource Series 10. Denver: Bureau of Land Management, 1980.

Osburn, Katherine M. B. *Southern Ute Women: Autonomy and Assimilation on the Reservation, 1887–1934.* Albuquerque: University of New Mexico Press, 1998.

Painter, Charles C. "Removal of the Southern Utes." *Lend a Hand* 5, no. 4 (April 1890): 258–269.

Palmer, Edward. "Notes on the Utah Utes by Edward Palmer, 1866–1877." In *Anthropological Paper no. 17*, edited by R. F. Heizer, 3–11. Salt Lake City: University of Utah, 1954.

Palmer, William R. "An Indian Legend." Palmer Collection, Special Collections, Gerald R. Sherratt Library, Southern Utah University. n.d.

———. "Indian Names in Utah Geography." *Utah Historical Quarterly* 1, no. 1 (Jan. 1928): 5–26.

———. The Pahute Fire Legend." *Utah Historical Quarterly* 6, no. 2 (April 1933): 62–64.

———. "The Religion of the Piutes," *The Improvement Era* 39, no. 9 (Sept. 1936): 534–537, 575–576.

———. "Utah Indians Past and Present: An Etymological and Historical Study of Tribes and Tribal Names from Original Sources." *Utah Historical Quarterly* 1, no. 1 (April 1928): 35–51.

———. *Why the North Star Stands Still and Other Indian Legends*. Springdale, UT: Zion Natural History Association, 1946.

Parkhill, Forbes. *The Last of the Indian Wars*. New York: Crowell-Collier Press, 1961.

Patterson, Carol. "Shavano Valley Rock Art Site Protection and Interpretive Project." Montrose, CO: Alpine Archaeological Consultants, 2005.

Pendergast, David M., and Clement W. Meighan. "Folk Traditions as Historical Fact: A Paiute Example." *Journal of American Folklore* 72, no. 284 (Apr.–June 1959): 128–133.

Perkins, Cornelia A., Marian Nielson, and Lenora Jones. *Saga of San Juan*. Salt Lake City: Mercury Publishing, 1968.

Petersen, Kenneth Lee. "Tabehuache and Elk Mountain Utes: A Historical Test of an Ecological Model." *Southwestern Lore* 43, no. 4 (December 1977): 5–21.

Peterson, John Alton. *Utah's Black Hawk War*. Salt Lake City: University of Utah Press, 1998.

Poll, Richard D., Thomas G. Alexander, Eugene Campbell, David E. Miller. *Utah's History*. Provo, UT: Brigham Young University Press, 1978.

Pyne, Stephen. *Fire in America: A Cultural History of Wildland and Rural Fire*. Princeton, NJ: Princeton University Press, 1982.

Quintana, Frances Leon. *Ordeal of Change: The Southern Utes and Their Neighbors*. Walnut Creek: Altamira Press, 2004.

Redd, Amasa Jay, ed. *Lemuel Hardison Redd, Jr., 1856–1923: Pioneer-Leader-Builder*. Salt Lake City: published privately, 1967.

Reed, Alan D. "Ute Cultural Chronology." In *An Archaeology of the Eastern Ute: A Symposium*, ed. Paul R. Nickens, 79–101. CCPA Occasional Papers 1. Denver: Colorado Council of Professional Archaeologists.

Reed, Verner Z. "The Southern Ute Indians." *Californian* 4 (Sept. 1893): 408–505.

———. *The Southern Ute Indians of Early Colorado*. Dillon, CO: Vistabooks, 1991.

Rickner, Thomas. *The History of the Pioneers of the Mancos Valley*. Mancos, CO: self-published, 1910.

Roberts, Ryan, and Jennifer Hurst. "Indian Education." *Blue Mountain Shadows* 9 (Winter 1991): 69–74.

Rockwell, Wilson. *The Utes: A Forgotten People*. Denver: Sage Books, 1956.

Rogers, A. M. "A True Narrative of an Indian Fight." *Echo of the Cliff Dwellers*. La Sal National Forest: U.S. Department of Agriculture, 1912.

Salmon, Rusty, and Robert S. McPherson. "Cowboys, Indians, and Conflict: The Pinhook Draw–Little Castle Valley Fight, 1881." *Utah Historical Quarterly* 69, no. 1 (Winter 2001): 4–28.

Sapir, Edward, ed. *Navaho Texts*. Iowa City: University of Iowa, 1942.

Scher, Zeke. "Jim Mike: The Man Who Discovered Rainbow Bridge" and "Synopsis of Events Leading Up to Jim Mike Plaque Ceremony of September 30, 1997." *Blue Mountain Shadows* 19 (Fall 1997): 17–23.

Scott, Hugh Lenox. *Some Memories of a Soldier*. New York: Century Company, 1928.

———. "Persons in the Foreground" (profile). *Current Opinion* (May 1915): 323–324.

Searcy, Helen M. "Col. Dave Day." *The Pioneers of San Juan Country*, I. Durango, CO: Sarah Platt Decker Chapter, 1942.

Secoy, Frank Raymond. *Changing Military Patterns on the Great Plains: 17th Century through Early 19th Century*. American Ethnological Society Monograph 21. Seattle: University of Washington Press, [1953] 1971.

Shumway, Gary, Jay Jones, Kay Jones, and Merle McDonald. *Cowboys and Indians: Interviews and Recollections of Marion Ashton and Alma Uriah Jones*. Flower Mound, TX: Shumway Publishing, 2009.

Shumway, Helen. "Elementary Memories." *Blue Mountain Shadows* 4 (Spring 1989): 29–31.

Silbernagel, Robert. *Troubled Trails: The Meeker Affair and the Expulsion of the Utes from Colorado*. Salt Lake City: University of Utah Press, 2011.

Simmons, Virginia McConnell. *The Ute Indians of Utah, Colorado, and New Mexico*. Boulder, CO: University Press of Colorado, 2000.

Smith, Anne M. *Ethnography of the Northern Utes*. Papers in Anthropology 17. Albuquerque: University of New Mexico Press, 1974.

———. *Ute Tales*. Salt Lake City: University of Utah Press, 1992.

Smith, Duane A. *Sacred Trust: The Birth and Development of Fort Lewis College*. Niwot: University Press of Colorado, 1991.

———. *A Time for Peace: Fort Lewis, Colorado, 1878–1891*. Boulder, CO: University Press of Colorado, 2006.

Smith, P. David. *Ouray, Chief of the Utes*. Ouray, CO: Wayfinder Press, 1986.

Snow, William J. "Utah Indians and the Spanish Slave

Trade." *Utah Historical Quarterly* 2, no. 3 (July 1929): 66–90.

Sonne, Conway B. *World of Wakara.* San Antonio, TX: Naylor Company, 1962.

Sprague, Marshall. *Massacre: The Tragedy at White River.* Lincoln: University of Nebraska Press, 1957.

Stacher, S. F. "The Indians at the Ute Mountain Reservation, 1906–9." *Colorado Magazine* 26, no. 1 (January 1949): 52–61.

———. "Memories of Chief Ignacio and Old Navaho Springs Sub-Agency." *Colorado Magazine* 17, no. 6 (June 1940): 212–221.

Steward, Julian H. *Basin-Plateau Aboriginal Sociopolitical Groups.* Bureau of American Ethnology Bulletin 120. Washington, DC: Smithsonian Institution, 1938.

———. *Ute Indians: Aboriginal and Historical Groups of the Ute Indians of Utah*, I. New York: Garland Publishing, 1974.

Stewart, Omer C. *Culture Element Distributions*, vol. 18: *Ute-Southern Paiute.* Anthropological Records 6, no. 4. Berkeley: University of California Press, 1942.

———. *Peyote Religion: A History.* Norman: University of Oklahoma Press, 1987.

———. *Ute Peyotism: A Study of a Cultural Complex.* University of Colorado Studies in Anthropology 1. Boulder: University of Colorado Press, 1948.

Stoffle, Richard W., Lawrence Loendorf, Diane Austin, and Angelita Bulletts. "Ghost Dancing the Grand Canyon: Southern Paiute Rock Art, Ceremony, and Cultural Landscapes." *Current Anthropology* 41 (2000): 11–38.

Stubbs, Brian D. *Uto-Aztecan: A Comparative Vocabulary.* Blanding, UT: self-published, 2008.

Tanner, Faun McConkie. *The Far Country: Moab and La Sal.* Salt Lake City: Olympus Publishing, 1976.

Tate, LaVerne. "Billy Mike and His Courting Flute." *Blue Mountain Shadows* 7 (Winter 1990): 42–43.

Thomas, Alfred Barnaby (trans. and ed.). *Forgotten Frontiers: A Study of the Spanish Indian Policy of Don Juan Bautista de Anza, Governor of New Mexico, 1777–1787.* Norman: University of Oklahoma Press, 1932.

Thompson, Gerald. *The Army and the Navajo: The Bosque Redondo Reservation Experiment, 1863–1868.* Tucson: University of Arizona Press, 1982.

Thompson, Gregory Coyne. *Southern Ute Lands, 1848–1899: The Creation of a Reservation.* Occasional Papers of the Center of Southwest Studies 1. Durango, CO: Fort Lewis College, 1972.

———. "The Unwanted Indians: The Southern Utes in Southeastern Utah." *Utah Historical Quarterly* 49, no. 2 (Spring 1981): 189–203.

Thornton, Russell. "Demographic Antecedents of a Revitalization Movement: Population Change, Population Size, and the 1890 Ghost Dance." *American Sociological Review* 46, no.1 (February 1981): 88–96

Train, Percy, James R. Heinrichs, and W. Andrew Archer. *Paiute Indians*, vol. 4 of *Medicinal Uses of Plants by Indian Tribes of Nevada.* New York: Garland Publishing, 1974.

Tyler, S. Lyman. "The Yuta Indians before 1680." *Western Humanities Review* 8 (Spring 1951): 153–163.

———. "The Spaniard and the Ute." *Utah Historical Quarterly* 22, no. 4 (October 1954): 343–361.

Uintah-Ouray Ute Tribe. *A Brief History of the Ute People.* Salt Lake City: Uintah-Ouray Tribe and the University of Utah Press, 1977.

———. *Stories of Our Ancestors: A Collection of Northern Ute Indian Tales.* Salt Lake City: University of Utah Press, 1974.

———. *"The Ute People."* Salt Lake City: University of Utah Printing Service, 1977.

University of Utah's American West Center and Utah Division of Indian Affairs. *Utah Indian Curriculum Guide.* Salt Lake City: University of Utah Print and Mail Services, 2009.

Ute Mountain Ute Tribe. "Early Days of the Ute Mountain Utes." Salt Lake City: Ute Mountain Ute Tribe and the University of Utah Press, 1985.

———. *Ute Mountain Ute Government.* Salt Lake City: Ute Mountain Ute Tribe and the University of Utah Press, 1986.

———. *Ute Mountain Utes: A History Text.* Salt Lake City: Ute Mountain Ute Tribe and the University of Utah Press, 1985.

———. *Ute Mountain Ute Stories, Games, and Noise Makers.* Salt Lake City: Ute Mountain Ute Tribe and the University of Utah Press, 1986.

Vale, Thomas R., ed. *Fire, Native Peoples, and the Natural Landscape.* Washington, DC: Island Press, 2002.

Van Cott, John W. *Utah Place Names*, Salt Lake City: University of Utah Press, 1990.

Vander, Judith. "The Shoshone Ghost Dance and Numic Myth: Common Heritage, Common Themes." *Journal of California and Great Basin Anthropology* 17, no. 2 (1995): 174–190.

Walker, Don. D. "The Carlisles: Cattle Barons of the Upper Basin." *Utah Historical Quarterly* 32, no. 3 (Summer 1964): 268–284.

———. "Cowboys, Indians, and Cavalry." *Utah Historical Quarterly* 34, no. 3 (Summer 1966): 254–262.

Walker, J. G., and O. L. Shepherd. *The Navajo Reconnaissance: A Military Exploration of the Navajo Country in 1859*, ed. Lynn R. Bailey. Los Angeles: Westernlore Press, 1964.

Weber, David J. *The American Frontier, 1821–1846: The American Southwest under Mexico.* Albuquerque: University of New Mexico Press, 1982.

———. *The Spanish Frontier in North America.* New Haven, CT: Yale University Press, 1982.

———. *The Taos Trappers: The Fur Trade in the Far Southwest.* Norman: University of Oklahoma Press, 1968.

Weber, Steven A., and P. David Seaman. *Havasupai Habitat: A. F. Whiting's Ethnography of a Traditional Indian Culture.* Tucson: University of Arizona Press, 1985.

Wetherill, Louisa Wade, and Harvey Leake. *Wolfkiller: Wisdom from a Nineteenth-Century Navajo Shepherd.* Salt Lake City: Gibbs Smith Publisher, 2007.

Wheat, Margaret M. *Survival Arts of the Primitive Paiutes.* Reno: University of Nevada Press, 1967.

Whiting, Beatrice Blyth. *Paiute Sorcery.* Publications in Anthropology 15. New York: Viking Fund, 1950.

Winder, Terri. "Shirley Ketchum Denetsosie." *Blue Mountain Shadows* 23 (Winter 2003): 47–48.

Wood, Nancy. *When Buffalo Free the Mountains: The Survival of America's Ute Indians.* Garden City, NY: Doubleday and Company, 1980.

Wroth, William. "Ute Civilization in Prehistory and the Spanish Colonial Period." In *Ute Indian Arts and Culture: From Prehistory to the New Millennium,* ed. William Wroth, 53–72. Colorado Springs: Colorado Fine Arts Center, 2000.

Yazzie, Mary Jane. "Life Traditions of the Utes of Avikan." *Blue Mountain Shadows* 7 (Winter 1990): 27–28.

Young, Richard K. *The Ute Indians of Colorado in the Twentieth Century.* Norman: University of Oklahoma Press, 1997.

NEWSPAPERS

Bayfield (CO) Blade, 1917

Blue Mountain (UT) Panorama, 1994–2006

Cortez (CO) Herald, 1916–1927

Cortez (CO) Journal, 2004

Cortez (CO) Journal-Herald, 1929

Cortez (CO) Sentinel, 1929–1932

Creede (CO) Candle, 1892

Cross Currents (Durango, CO), 1999

Denver Post, 1915–1918

Denver Republican, 1881–1884

Denver Times, 1915

Denver Tribune, 1881

Deseret Evening News (Salt Lake City), 1914

Deseret News (Salt Lake City), 1855–1997

Dolores (CO) News, 1880–1884

Dolores (CO) Star, 1908

Dove Creek (CO) Press and *San Juan Record* (Monticello, UT), 1952

Durango (CO) Herald, 1889

Durango (CO) Democrat, 1894–1918

Grand Valley (UT) Times, 1916

High Country News (Paonia, CO), 1995

Ignacio (CO) Chieftain, 1917–1923

Mancos (CO) Times, 1894–1904

Mancos (CO) Times Tribune, 1918–1919

Montezuma (CO) Journal, 1899–1915

Montezuma Valley (CO) Journal, 1987

Rocky Mountain News (Denver), 1875–1915

San Juan Blade (Monticello, UT), 1917

San Juan Record (Monticello, UT), 1931–2010

Salt Lake City Weekly, 2003

Salt Lake Evening Telegram, 1915

Salt Lake Herald, 1888

Salt Lake Herald Republican, 1915

Salt Lake Telegram, 1921

Salt Lake Tribune, 1890–2000

The (Ogden, UT) Standard, 1895

Times-Independent (Moab, UT), 1919–1933

Weekly Ignacio (CO) Chieftain, 1913

Weenuche Smoke Signals (Towaoc, CO), 1996

Whispering Sage (Blanding, UT), 1981

Index